I0818495

Hans Haacke
Retrospective

Edited by
Ingrid Pfeiffer and Luisa Ziaja

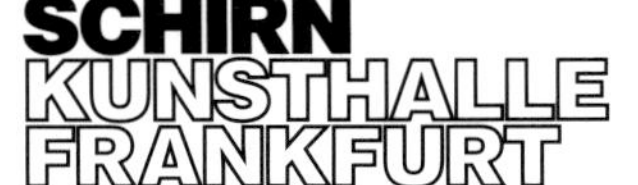

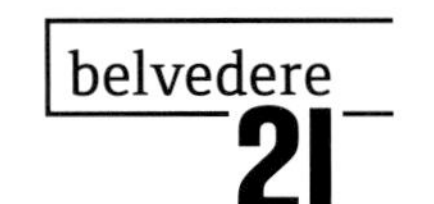

HIRMER

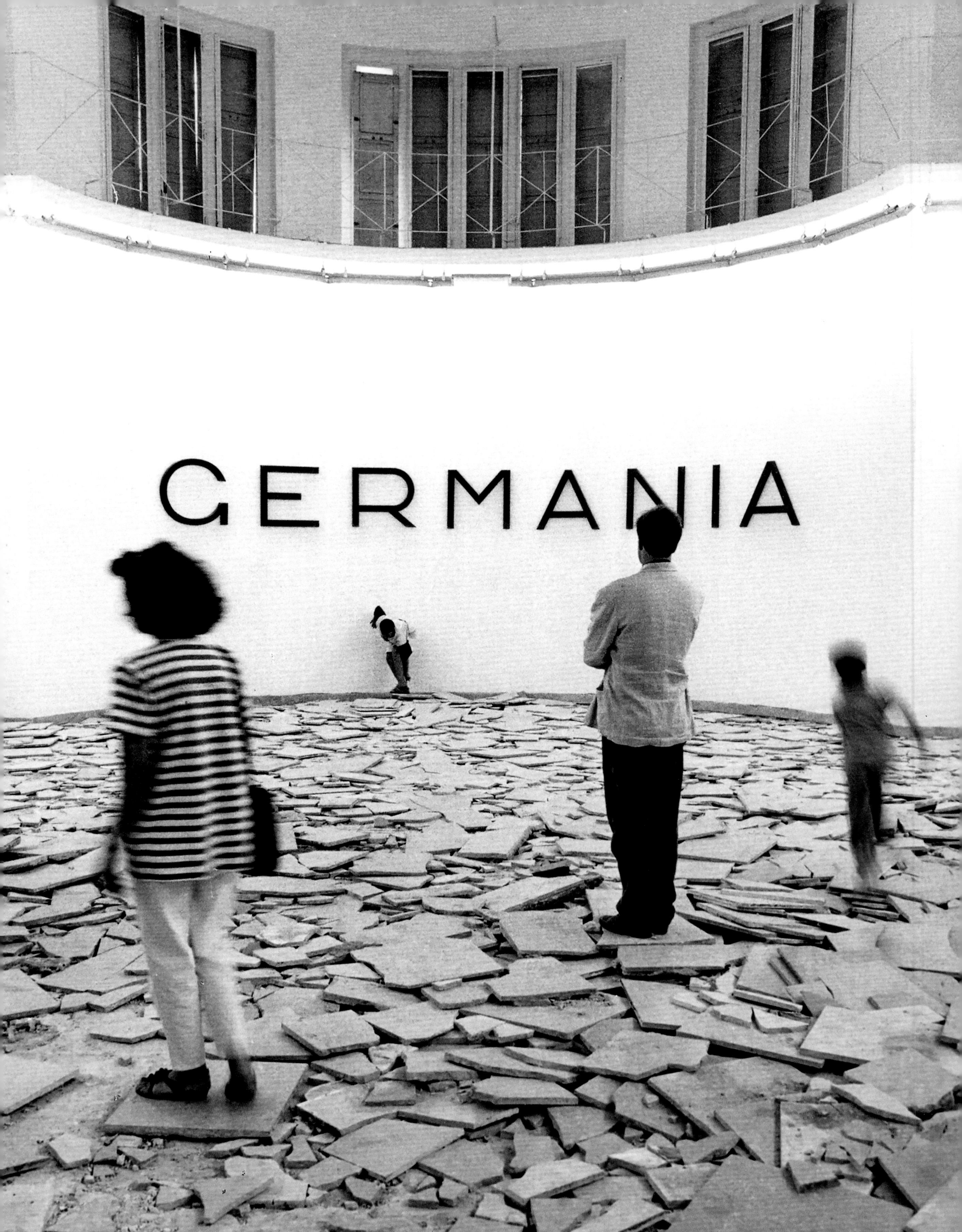
GERMANIA

Contents

Previous page: *GERMANIA*, 1993

Funded by the German Federal
Cultural Foundation

KULTURSTIFTUNG
DES
BUNDES

Funded by the Federal Government
Comissioner for Culture and the Media

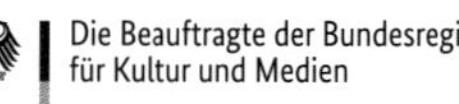

Additional support

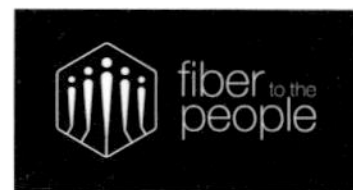

Mann Stiftung

Opening Remarks from the German Federal Cultural Foundation

A few years ago, Hans Haacke was ranked the most influential artist internationally by the German art magazine *Monopol* for his »political vigilance, direct contributions to debates, incorruptibility, and sharp institutional criticism.« Numerous contemporary artists continue to draw on his work, and he has decisively shaped and influenced what we understand as »political art« today. Nevertheless, according to the art sociologist Walter Grasskamp, only his name and a few spectacular works are known at best, but hardly the relationships between them, nor the complex development behind them.

From the early 1960s onward, Haacke pursued a very broad approach: on the one hand, he picked up on tendencies from ZERO and Minimal Art, but he also worked in the fields of ecology and the natural sciences, Conceptual Art, Land Art, Institutional Critique, public art, poster art, and many others. In a 1971 interview with Jeanne Siegel, the artist himself describes the world as »one supersystem with a myriad of subsystems, each one more or less affected by all the others.« In this sense, it was Jack Burnham's systems theory that offered Haacke the terminology for the kind of thinking that he still implements in his art to this day. In various work phases, he linked physical, biological, and social systems, visualized them through installations, and presented structures or cycles on the most diverse levels. In the process, Haacke's work is consistently political in its stringency. He was repeatedly excluded from exhibitions as a result of his directness, and he has consistently stood up for his convictions, including the defense of democratic principles in particular. His at times forthright yet factual commentary on the practices of certain companies, politicians, and personalities has occasionally been interpreted as bordering on activism. However, Haacke's own statements on this have been rather skeptical and have always emphasized that he is first and foremost an artist.

In this major exhibition project, the Schirn Kunsthalle Frankfurt will now newly present and reexamine this impressive spectrum of Haacke's work and reception. With around seventy works from 1959 to the present—spanning paintings, photographs, installations, actions, posters, and a film—the exhibition explores the question of how Hans Haacke was able to become such an influential figure in contemporary art, and what political art can still mean and achieve today in an international context.

The German Federal Cultural Foundation congratulates Hans Haacke on this special exhibition, which offers fresh insights into his many years of significant work, and would like to thank his gallery, the Paula Cooper Gallery in New York, the Schirn Kunsthalle Frankfurt, its director Dr. Sebastian Baden, and its curator Dr. Ingrid Pfeiffer, as well as the Belvedere 21, Vienna as the second station of the exhibition, its general director Stella Rollig, and its chief curator Luisa Ziaja. We hope all exhibition visitors will have some vivifying experiences, along with the openness to be inspired and unsettled by the works of the always contemporary Hans Haacke.

Katarzyna Wielga-Skolimowska
Executive Board / Artistic Director

Kirsten Haß
Executive Board / Administrative Director

Colophon

This catalogue is published in conjunction with the exhibition

Hans Haacke: Retrospective

Schirn Kunsthalle Frankfurt
November 8, 2024 – February 9, 2025

Belvedere 21, Vienna
February 28 – June 9, 2025

Catalogue

Editors
Ingrid Pfeiffer, Luisa Ziaja

Editing
Ingrid Pfeiffer, Luisa Ziaja, Theresa Dann-Freyenschlag, Cornelia Eisendle

Publication Managers
Natalie Storelli, Schirn
Eva Lahnsteiner, Belvedere

Project Management, Hirmer Publishers
Jutta Allekotte, Katja Durchholz

Copyediting
Dawn Michelle d'Atri

Translation
Good & Cheap Art Translators
(German–English, English–German)

Graphic Design
Andreas Wesle, Vienna

Production
Katja Durchholz, Hirmer Publishers

Image Processing
Pixelstorm, Vienna

Paper
GardaPat 13 Kiara, 125 g/m^2

Typeface
Plain Medium

Printing
optimal media GmbH, Röbel/Müritz

Printed in Germany

ISBN
978-3-7774-4422-2 (German edition)
978-3-7774-4423-9 (English edition)

Hirmer Publishers
Managing Director: Kerstin Ludolph
Bayerstraße 57–59
80335 Munich
Germany

www.hirmerpublishers.com
www.hirmerpublishers.co.uk

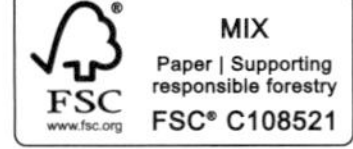

Bibliographic information published by the Deutsche Nationalbibliothek.
The Deutsche Nationalbibliothek lists this publication in the Deutsche Nationalbibliografie; detailed bibliographic data is available online at http://dnb.de.

All work texts with the abbreviation TDF by Theresa Dann-Freyenschlag

Exhibition, Schirn Kunsthalle Frankfurt

Director
Sebastian Baden

Deputy Director and Head of Exhibitions
Esther Schlicht

Curator
Ingrid Pfeiffer

Curatorial Assistant
Cornelia Eisendle

Technical Services
Christian Teltz, Oliver Taschke, Stefan Schell

Registrars
Caroline Käding, Elke Walter, Fanny Bengsch

Head of Installation Team
Andreas Gundermann

Conservators
Vera Gunder, Stefanie Gundermann, Susanne Silbernagel

Exhibtion Architecture
Karsten Weber, Düsseldorf

Exhibition Design
Studio Heyhey, John Russo

Press
Johanna Pulz, Julia Bastian, Maya Röttger, Thea Stroh

Schirn Magazine
Julia Schaake

Marketing
Luise Bachmann, Heike Stumpf, Doroteya Shmileva

Engagement
Hannah Doll, Corinna Fröhling

Education
Laura Heeg, Simone Boscheinen, Lisa Reinhard, René Sander, Sarah Schweizer, Samanea Karrfalt

Events and Visitor Management
Selma Wels, Vivien Shahzad, Constanze Götz

Administration
Boris Deckelmann, Tanja Mayer, Kristian Strauß

Curatorial Consultant to the Management
Luise Leyer

Assistants to the Director
Samira Koch, Katharina Schuchmann

Head of Cleaning Services
Rosaria La Tona

Reception
Christiane Kalla, Nazareth Zeggay

FRIENDS OF THE SCHIRN KUNSTHALLE E. V.

Executive Board

Antje Conzelmann (Chairperson)
Sebastian Baden
Jan Bauer
Sylvia von Metzler

Board of Trustees

Schirn Contemporaries

Jan Bauer and Lena Wallenhorst
Jochen and Anja Baumann
Olaf Gerber and Nicole Emmerling de Oliveira
Markus Hammer and Birgit Heller
Philip Holzer
Björn Robens
Reiner Sachs and Brigitta Bailly
Julia Schönbohm and Ralf Böckle
Hartmut and Petra Schröter
Sascha and Sevilay Wilhelm

Corporate Members

DEGELER GmbH & Co KG
Deutsche Bank AG
Deutsche Beteiligungs AG
Deutsche Börse Group
DWS Investment Group
Europäische Zentralbank
Fraport AG
Gemeinnützige Hertie-Stiftung
Grisebach GmbH
Haus & Grund Frankfurt am Main e. V.
Landwirtschaftliche Rentenbank
Morgan Stanley Europe SE
Nomura Financial Products Europe GmbH
ODDO BHF SE
UBS Europe SE
Verianos SE
White & Case LLP

Management

Tamara Fürstin von Clary
Tereza Šípková

PARTNERS

Corporate Partners of the Schirn Kunsthalle Frankfurt

Allianz Global Investors
Bank Julius Bär
Bank of America
BARCLAYS
Bloomberg L.P.
HEUSSEN Rechtsanwaltsgesellschaft mbH
Le Méridien Frankfurt
PPI AG
PwC

Cultural Partner

hr2-kultur

Exhibition, Belvedere, Vienna

General and Artistic Director
Stella Rollig

CFO
Wolfgang Bergmann

Curator
Luisa Ziaja

Assistant Curator
Theresa Dann-Freyenschlag

Exhibition and Collection Management
Stephan Pumberger, Monica Strinu

Exhibition Production
Eszter Vályi, Monica Strinu

Exhibition Architecture
studio-itzo, Vienna

Chief Curator
Luisa Ziaja

Art Mediation
Michaela Höß

Communication and Marketing
Lisa Stadler

Visitor Services
Margarete Stechl

Research Center
Christian Huemer

Conservation
Stefanie Jahn

Belvedere
Prinz Eugen-Strasse 27
1030 Vienna
Austria
www.belvedere.at/en

Following page: View of the installation *DER BEVÖLKERUNG (TO THE POPULATION)* in the northern atrium of the Reichstag building in Berlin, 2008

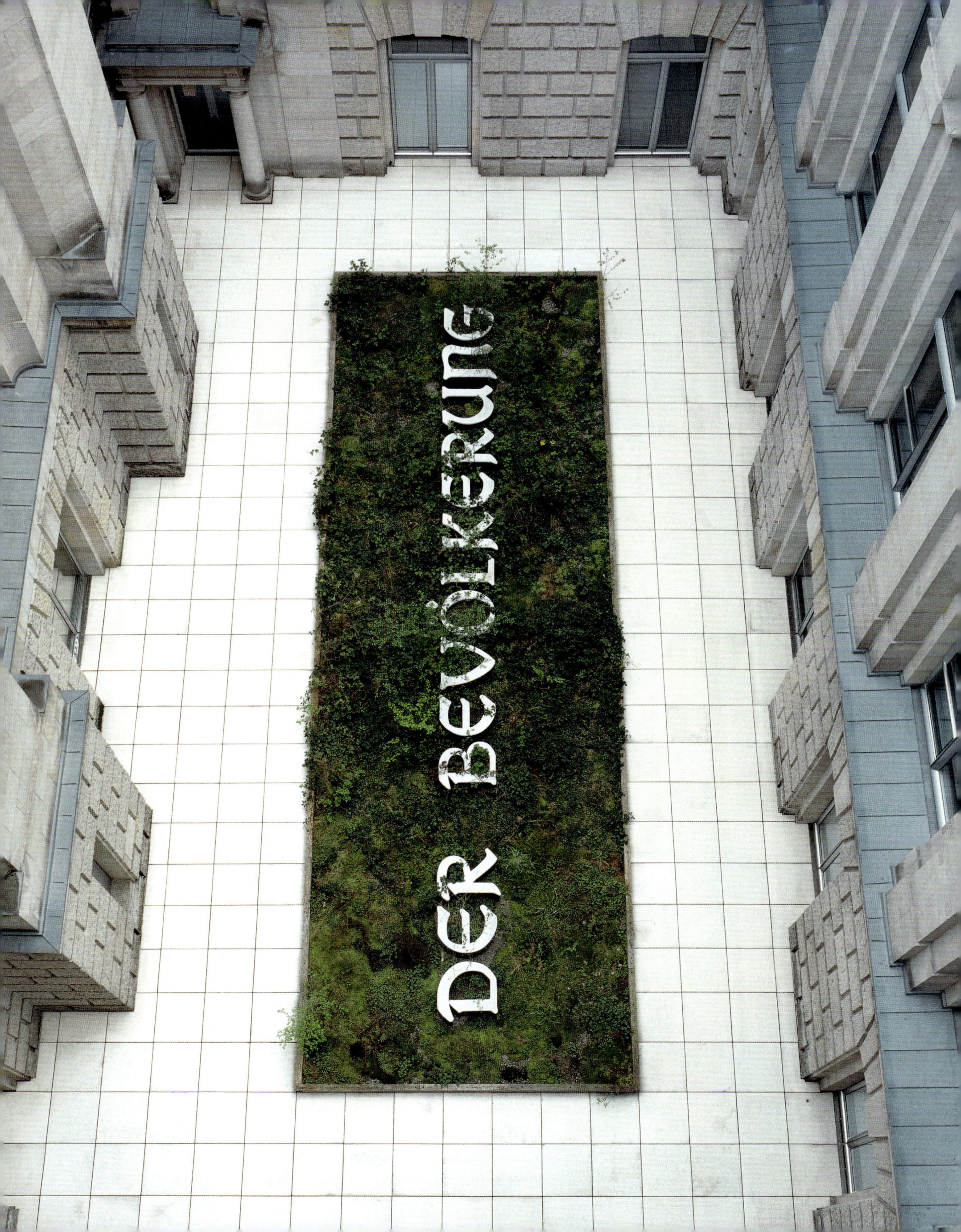
DER BEVÖLKERUNG

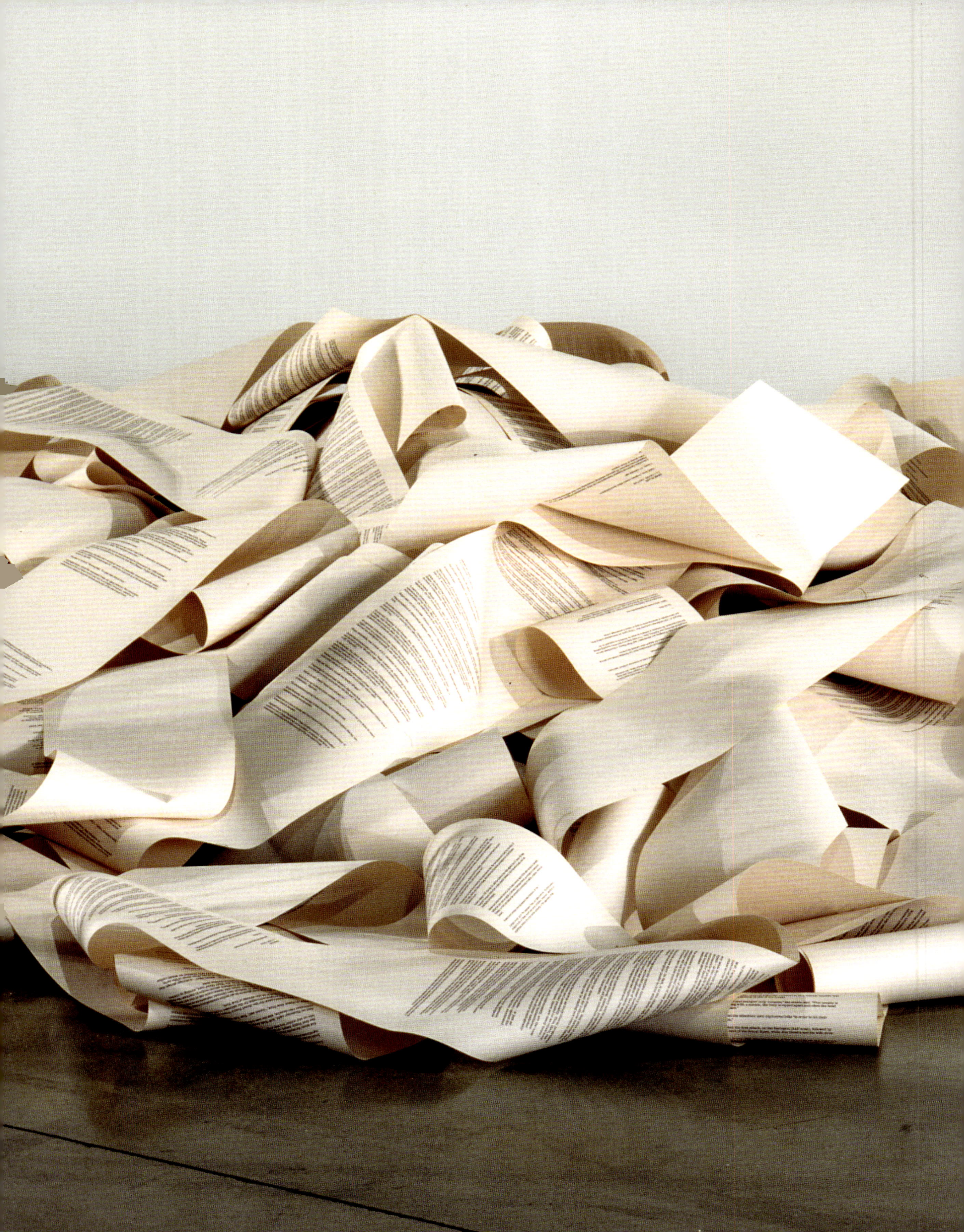

Foreword

Hans Haacke, born 1936 in Cologne, is a legend of political Conceptual Art. After studying at the Staatliche Werkakademie (State Art Academy) in Kassel (1956–60) and spending time abroad in Paris, Philadelphia, and New York, Haacke moved to New York permanently in 1965, where he still lives and works to this day. There, he spent thirty-five years teaching as a professor at the renowned Cooper Union for the Advancement of Science and Art. As a founding figure of artistic Institutional Critique, the German-American artist exposed the complex relationships between art and society, and has had a lasting influence on subsequent generations of artists. Since the early 1970s, Haacke has focused on sociopolitical structures and subjected them to sharp, often ruthless analyses. To this end, he draws on sociological methods of observation and investigation, researching backgrounds, data, and facts in order to reveal power relations within the art world and beyond. Since the 1980s, he has thematized the connections between biographies and company histories in relation to historical political disputes; conflicts of interest between public institutions, private individuals, and politicians and businesspeople; and, last but not least, antidemocratic tendencies. For Haacke, the occasionally controversial discussions surrounding his work, which have led to him being excluded from several exhibitions, are an integral part of his artistic practice.

The last European retrospective of Hans Haacke's work was almost twenty years ago in Hamburg and Berlin. And prior to that, the only monographic exhibition of the artist was shown in Austria in 2001. With this cooperation between the Schirn Kunsthalle Frankfurt and the Belvedere, Vienna, we are now presenting Hans Haacke's equally diverse and highly topical work once again—and from today's perspective—in a comprehensive solo exhibition. The democratic potential of this oeuvre is especially relevant now, at a time when democracies around the world are increasingly being challenged by the authoritarian demands of right-wing autocrats. Haacke's critical practice deserves to be conveyed and made accessible to a broad international audience, also because the artist is always concerned with involving viewers and encouraging them to take a stand and to promote awareness of diversity and

Previous page: *News*, 1969 (detail)

freedom of expression. With this exhibition, we are presenting an artist whose work shaped political Conceptual Art in the second half of the twentieth century and became a role model for many current tendencies in contemporary art. The exhibitions in Frankfurt and Vienna comprise around seventy exhibits from the late 1950s to current artistic production, including iconic early works from the 1960s, important real-time systems, works that require the public's participation, and expansive (historical) political installations.

Our sincere and heartfelt thanks go first and foremost to Hans Haacke, who supervised the exhibition and accompanying catalogue with extraordinary dedication. We also extend thanks to Anthony Allen, Jake Ewert, and their team from Paula Cooper Gallery, New York, which has long represented the artist and has supported us in many ways on the current project, including with numerous loans.

Furthermore, a number of important collections and museums have made significant loans to this ambitious project, for which we are very grateful: Art Gallery of Ontario, Toronto; Collection FRAC Bourgogne, Dijon; Generali Foundation Collection – permanent loan to the Museum der Moderne, Salzburg; Hamburger Bahnhof – Nationalgalerie der Gegenwart, Berlin; LACMA, Los Angeles; Museum Abteiberg, Mönchengladbach; Museum Ludwig, Cologne; MACBA, Barcelona; Paula Cooper Gallery, New York; Sfeir-Semler Gallery, Beirut/Hamburg; H.E. Sheikh Jassim bin Abdulaziz Al-Thani and H.E. Sheikha Al-Mayassa bint Hamad bin Khalifa Al-Thani; Collection Lila and Gilbert Silverman, Detroit; Tate London; Werkstatt DER BEVÖLKERUNG with Oliver Schwarz, Berlin; Whitney Museum of American Art, New York. Thanks also go to all private lenders who prefer not to be named.

It would never have been possible to realize such an ambitious project without the generous and constant backing of our partners and supporters. The Schirn Kunsthalle Frankfurt thanks first and foremost the German Federal Cultural Foundation, especially Katarzyna Wielga-Skolimowska, artistic director, and Dr. Marie Haff, head of general project funding, for their willingness to support a project that goes beyond the more narrow context of art to explore volatile issues within society. Further, thanks are extended to fiber to the people GmbH and its executive director Hans-Peter Heidler. Once again, the Mann Foundation has kindly supported the exhibition publication, for which I warmly thank Mr. and Mrs. Mann. Our sincere thanks are also due to the City of Frankfurt am Main for sponsoring our work and for its ongoing support of the Schirn Kunsthalle Frankfurt. On behalf of all decision-makers, we extend thanks to Mayor Mike Josef and to Ina Hartwig, head of the cultural department.

Our special thanks go to the curators of the exhibition, Ingrid Pfeiffer in Frankfurt and Luisa Ziaja in Vienna, who conceived this exhibition project and then pursued it with the utmost commitment over many years in collaboration with Hans Haacke and his gallery, moving it forward on all levels and impressively realizing it. Alongside them, the curatorial assistants Cornelia Eisendle and Theresa Dann-Freyenschlag have worked with great dedication on the realization of the exhibition and this publication. We would also like to thank all the authors of the present bilingual volume: Sabeth Buchmann, Hubertus Butin, Theresa Dann-Freyenschlag, Cornelia Eisendle, Stephan Geene, Vanessa Joan Müller, Ingrid Pfeiffer, Ursula Ströbele, Luisa Ziaja, and the interview partners Paul Maenz and Gerd de Vries. Andreas Wesle was responsible for the adept design of the exhibition catalogue. We wish to thank Annette Siegel and Dawn Michelle d'Atri for the copyediting and Good & Cheap Art Translators for the translations. Moreover, we thank the publication managers of the Schirn and the Belvedere, Natalie Storelli and Eva Lahnsteiner, for their characteristically professional production of this bilingual publication. At Hirmer Verlag, our particular thanks go to Kerstin Ludolph and Jutta Allekotte. Our gratitude is likewise extended to Karsten Weber in Düsseldorf and to Martina Schiller and Rainer Stadlbauer from studio itzo in Vienna for the careful and extraordinarily successful exhibition architectures in the respective venues.

We are sincerely grateful to the staff of both museums, who met the challenges of this cooperation with outstanding commitment and made this extremely enriching collaboration possible. On the Schirn side, we would especially like to thank the following colleagues: Esther Schlicht (deputy director and head of exhibitions), Caroline Käding (head of organization), Christian Teltz (head of technical resources), Johanna Pulz (head of PR), Luise Bachmann (head of marketing), Hannah Doll and Corinna Fröhling (engagement), Laura Heeg (head of education), Selma Wels (head of events and visitor management), and Boris Deckelmann (head of administration and accounting).

On the Belvedere side, we would particularly like to thank our colleagues Kerstin Krenn and Katalin Várdai (art mediation), Monica Strinu and Eszter Valyi (exhibition management), Johannes Stacher (technical support), Matthias Müller (conservator), Andreas Obernosterer-Rupprecht (cultural property protection), Irene Jäger (PR), and Lisa Martha Janka (digital communication).

Sebastian Baden
Director Schirn Kunsthalle Frankfurt

Stella Rollig
General Director Belvedere, Vienna

Photographic Notes, documenta 2, 1959

In 1959, Hans Haacke was a twenty-three-year-old student trainee helping out with the exhibition setup and supervision at documenta 2 in Kassel. The quintennial had been founded four years earlier by the painter and academy professor Arnold Bode in order to reconnect with international modernist currents after the civilizational rupture of National Socialism. Haacke's snapshots capture the tense and often telling interactions between the viewers and the artworks in the exhibition space with an analytical gaze: two self-assured fraternity members turn their backs on an abstract work by Wassily Kandinsky; a young woman with a baby carriage explores the exhibition space; cleaning staff walk past canvases stacked against the walls.

While researching the documenta archive in 1981, Walter Grasskamp discovered an unlabeled print with a motif that clearly stood out from other photographs of the large-scale exhibition. He published this photograph in the magazine *Kunstforum International* and gave Hans Haacke a freshly printed copy. A few days later, Haacke revealed himself to be the creator of the photograph, which he had hardly intended as an artwork twenty-two years earlier. It wasn't until 2001 that Hans Haacke compiled a selection of twenty-six prints from a larger convolut for the photographic series *Photographic Notes, documenta 2*. In retrospect, these early photographs already contain approaches that anticipate central elements of his oeuvre: the sociological method of observation; the critical interrogation of political, social, and cultural systems; and the disclosure of power relations.

TDF

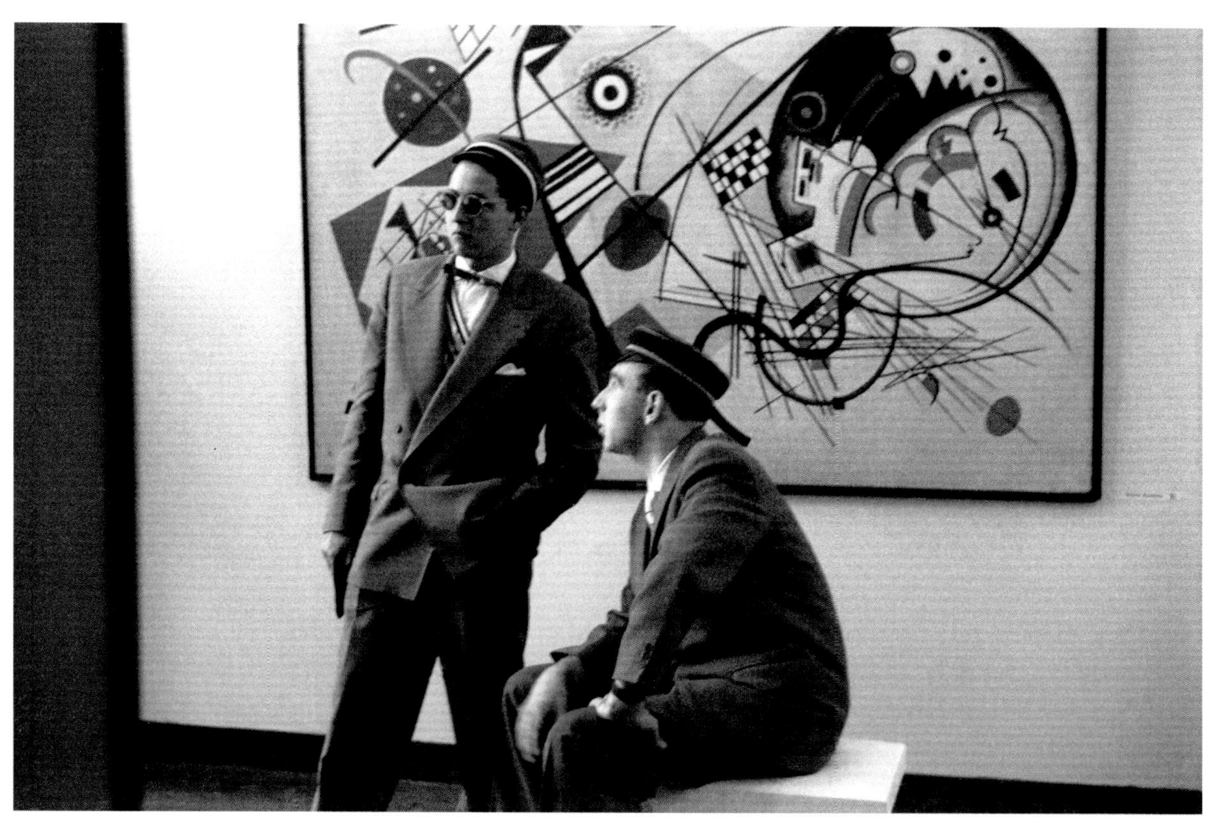

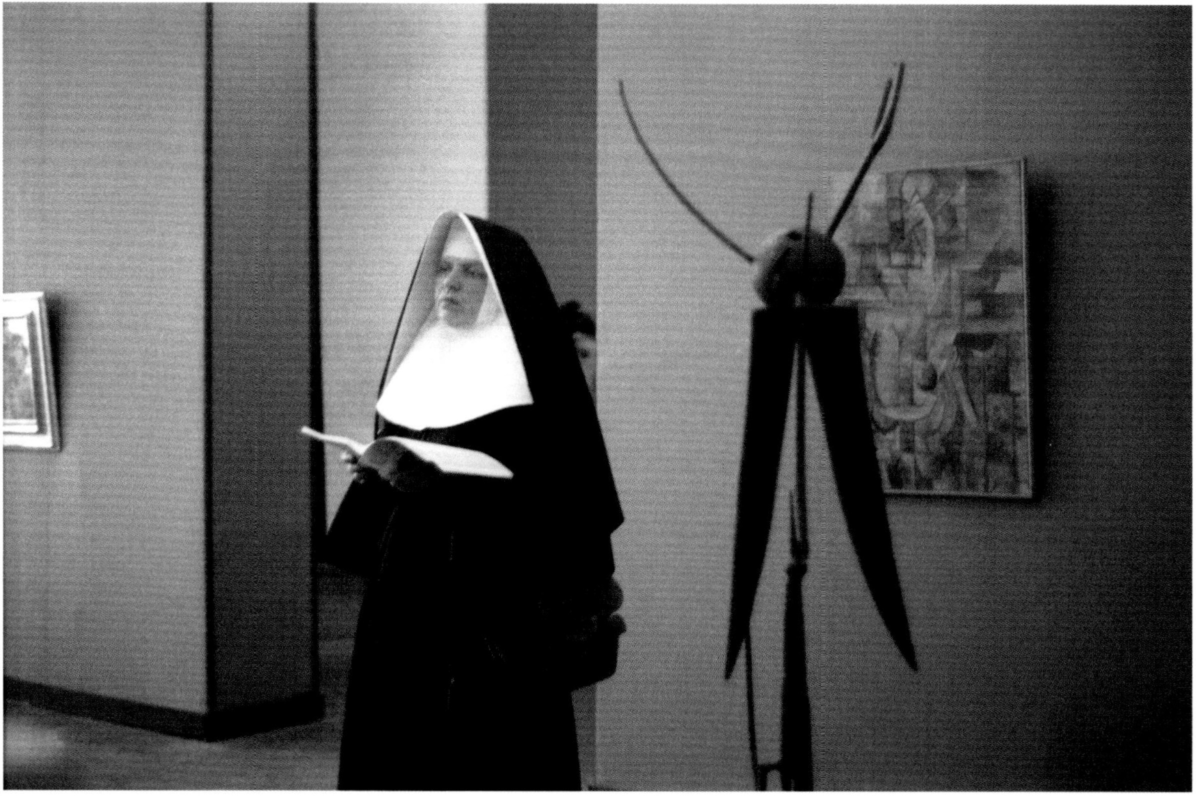

Photographic Notes, documenta 2, 1959

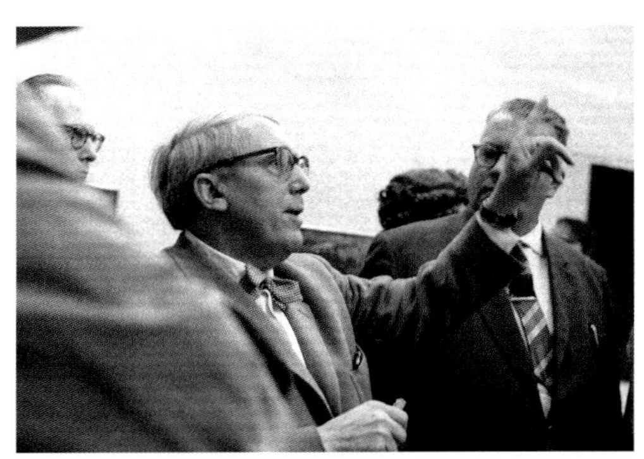
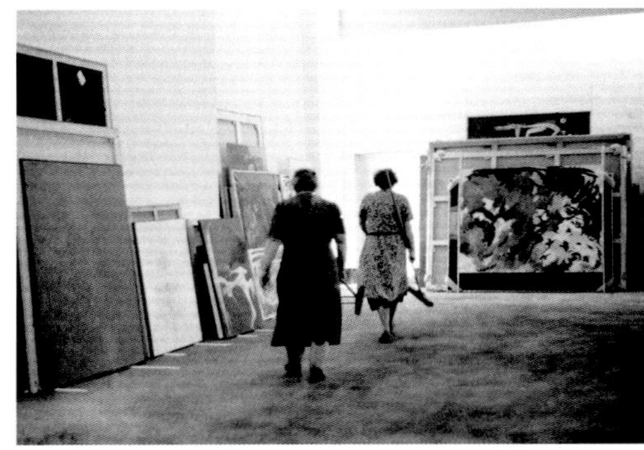
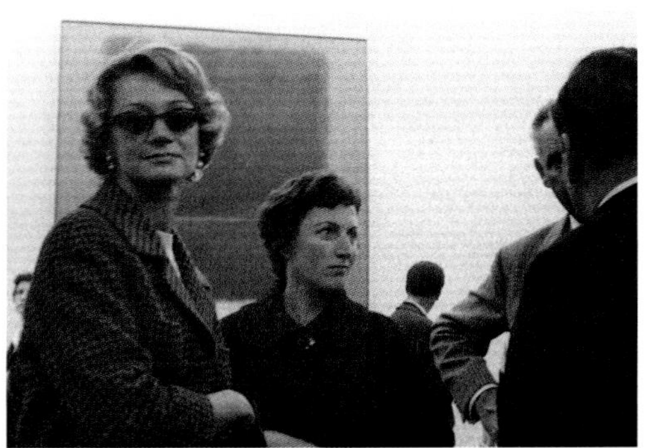
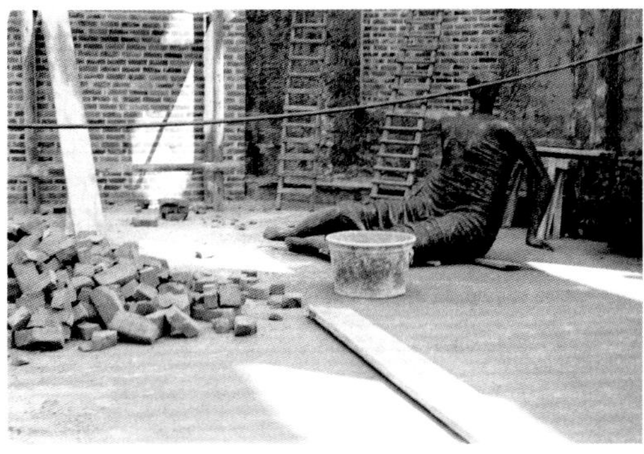
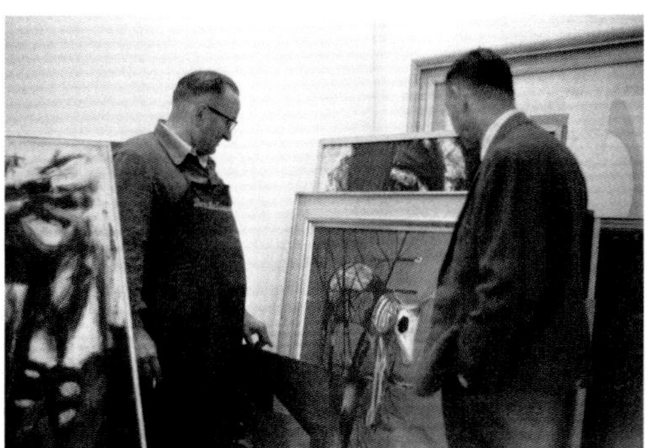
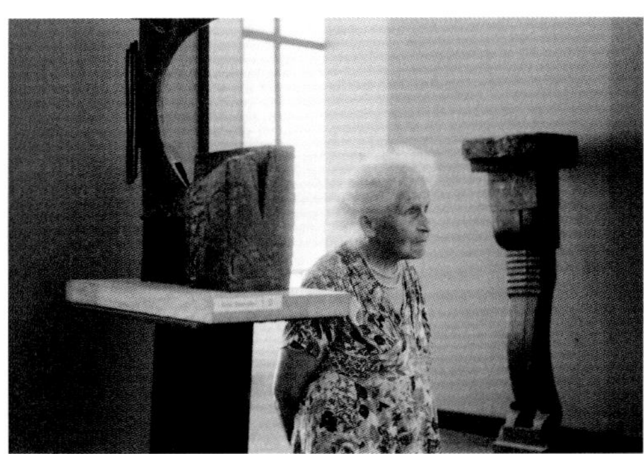

Photographic Notes, documenta 2, 1959

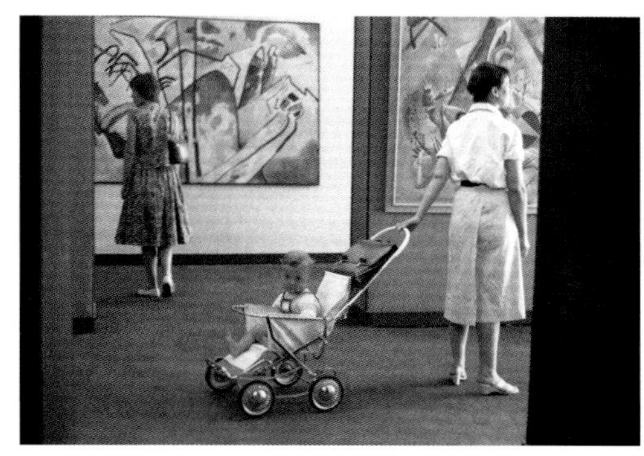
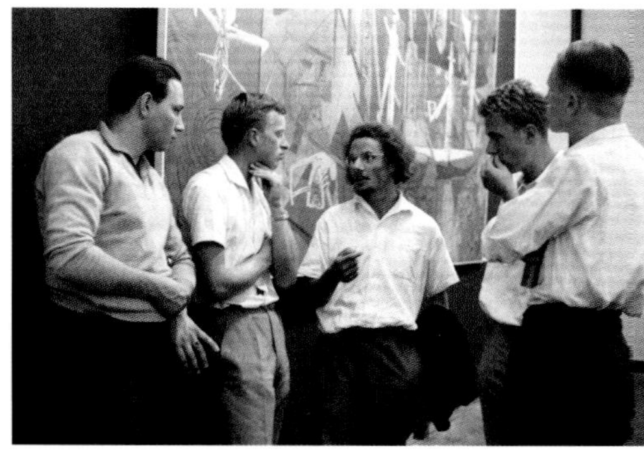
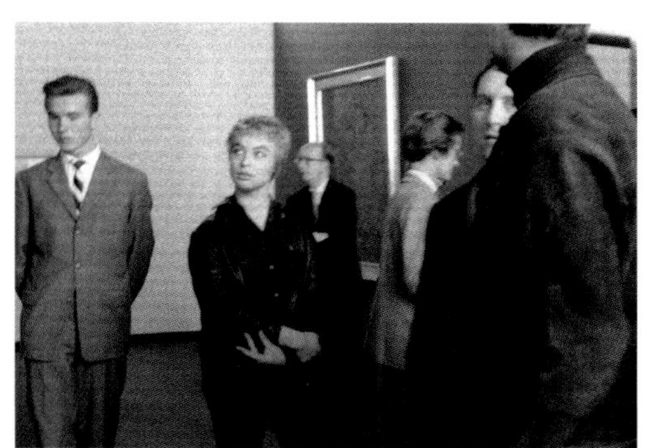
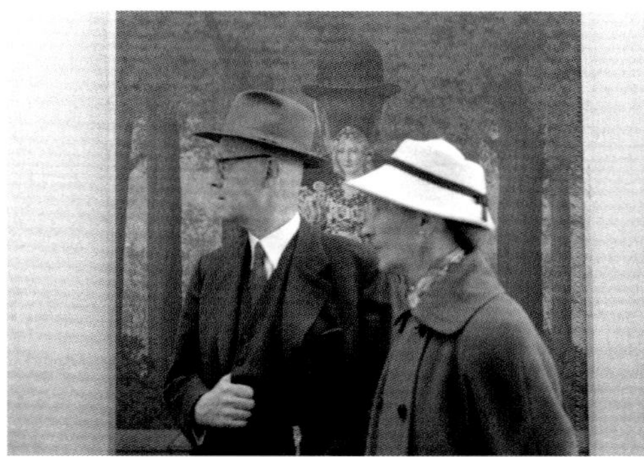
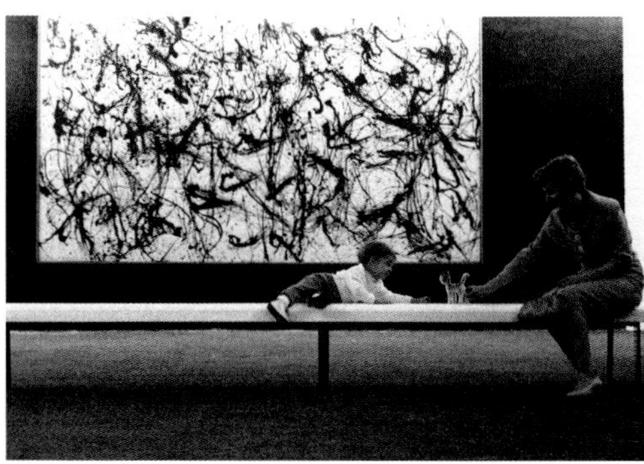
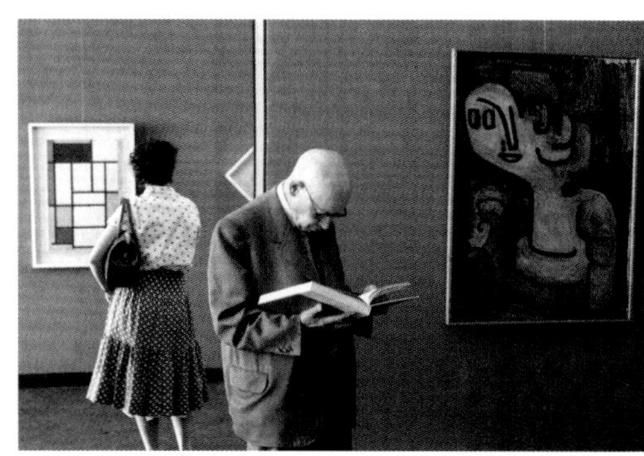

Photographic Notes, documenta 2, 1959

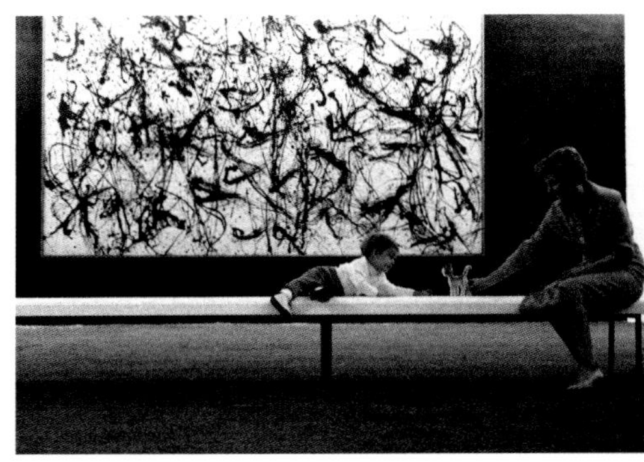

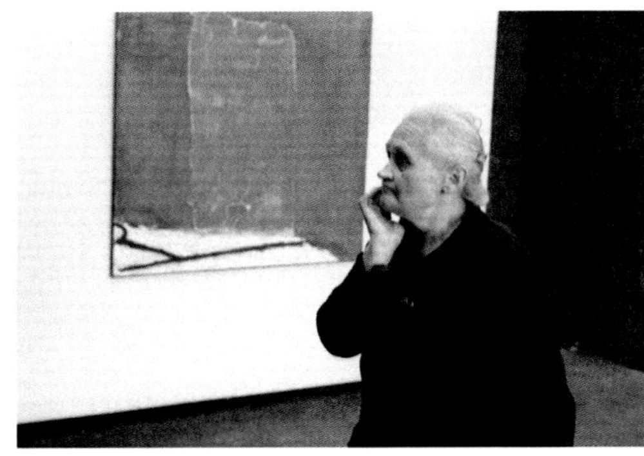

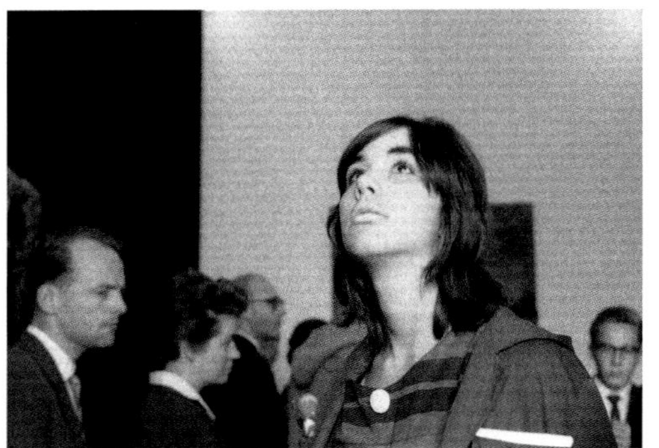

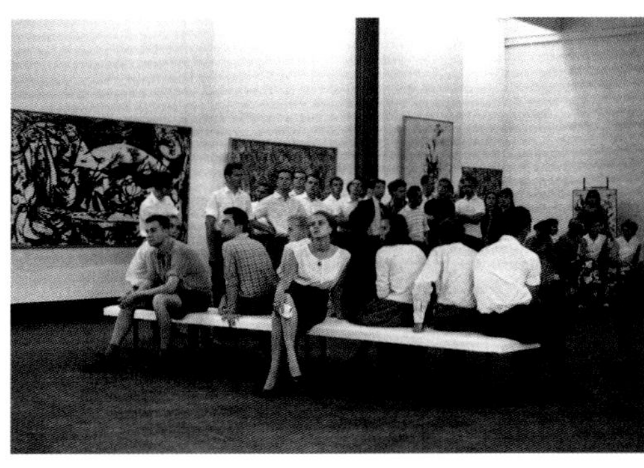

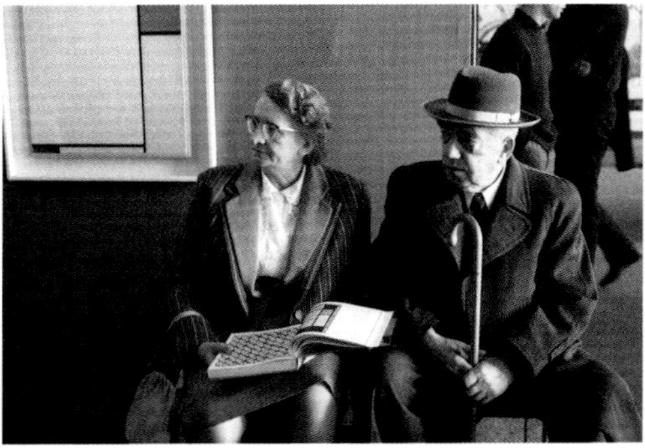

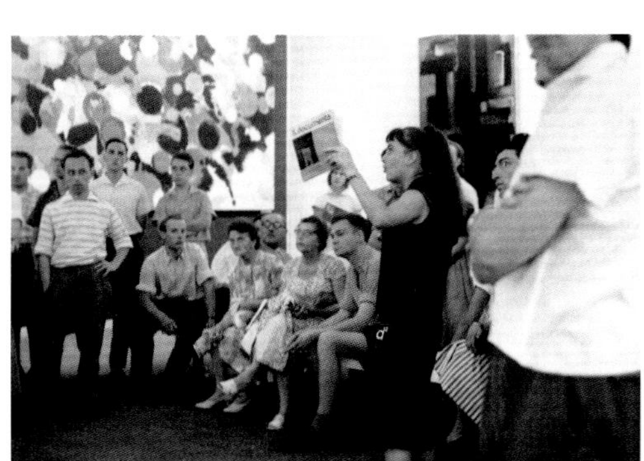

Photographic Notes, documenta 2, 1959

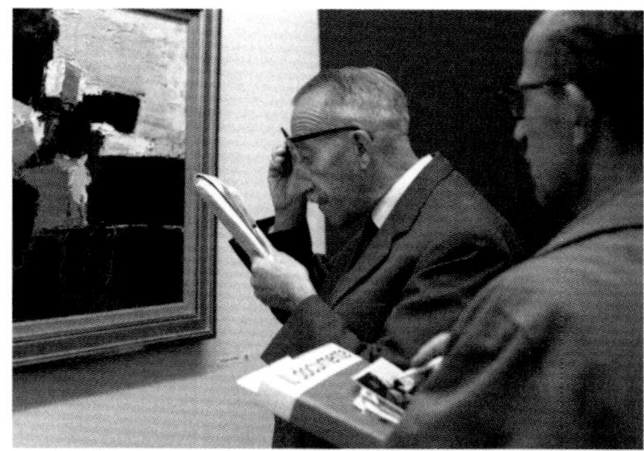
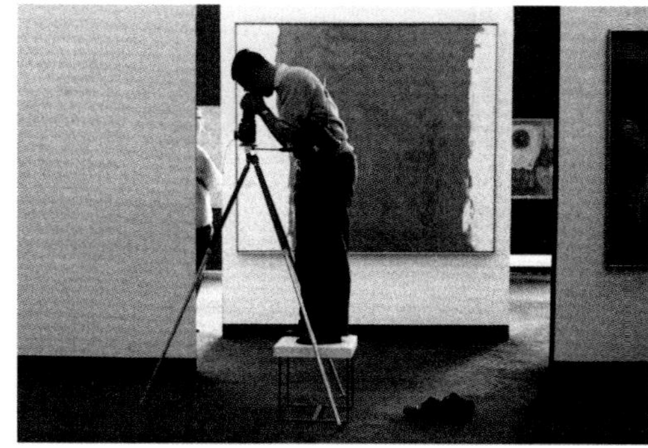
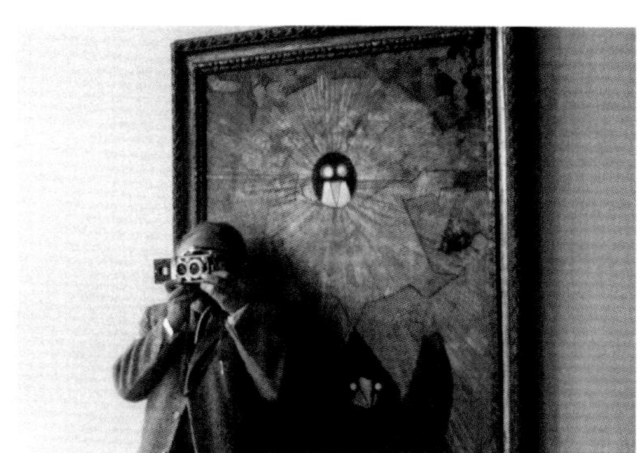
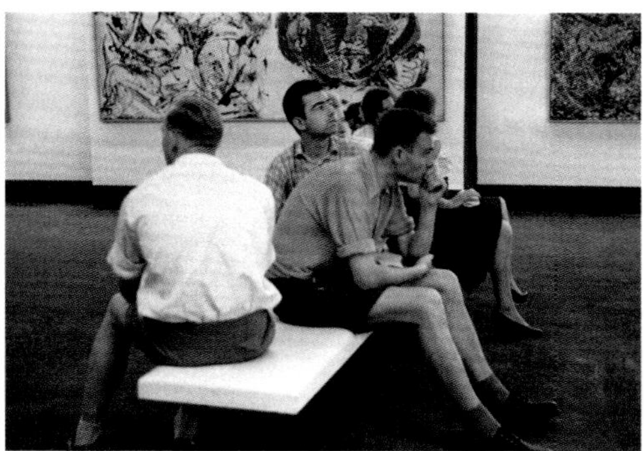
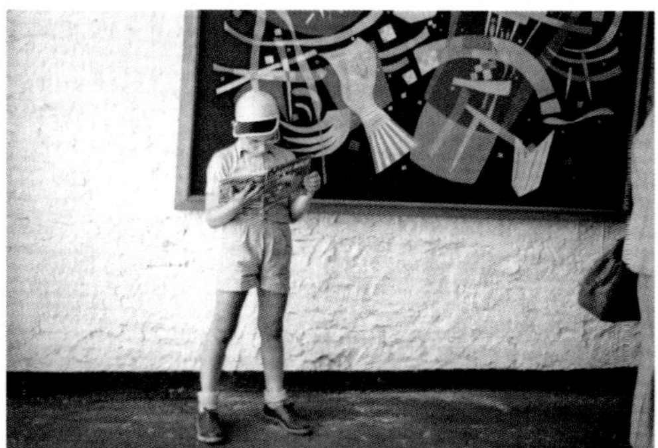
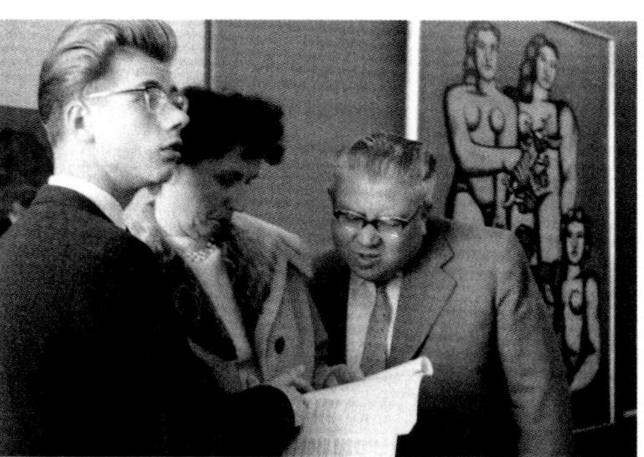

Photographic Notes, documenta 2, 1959

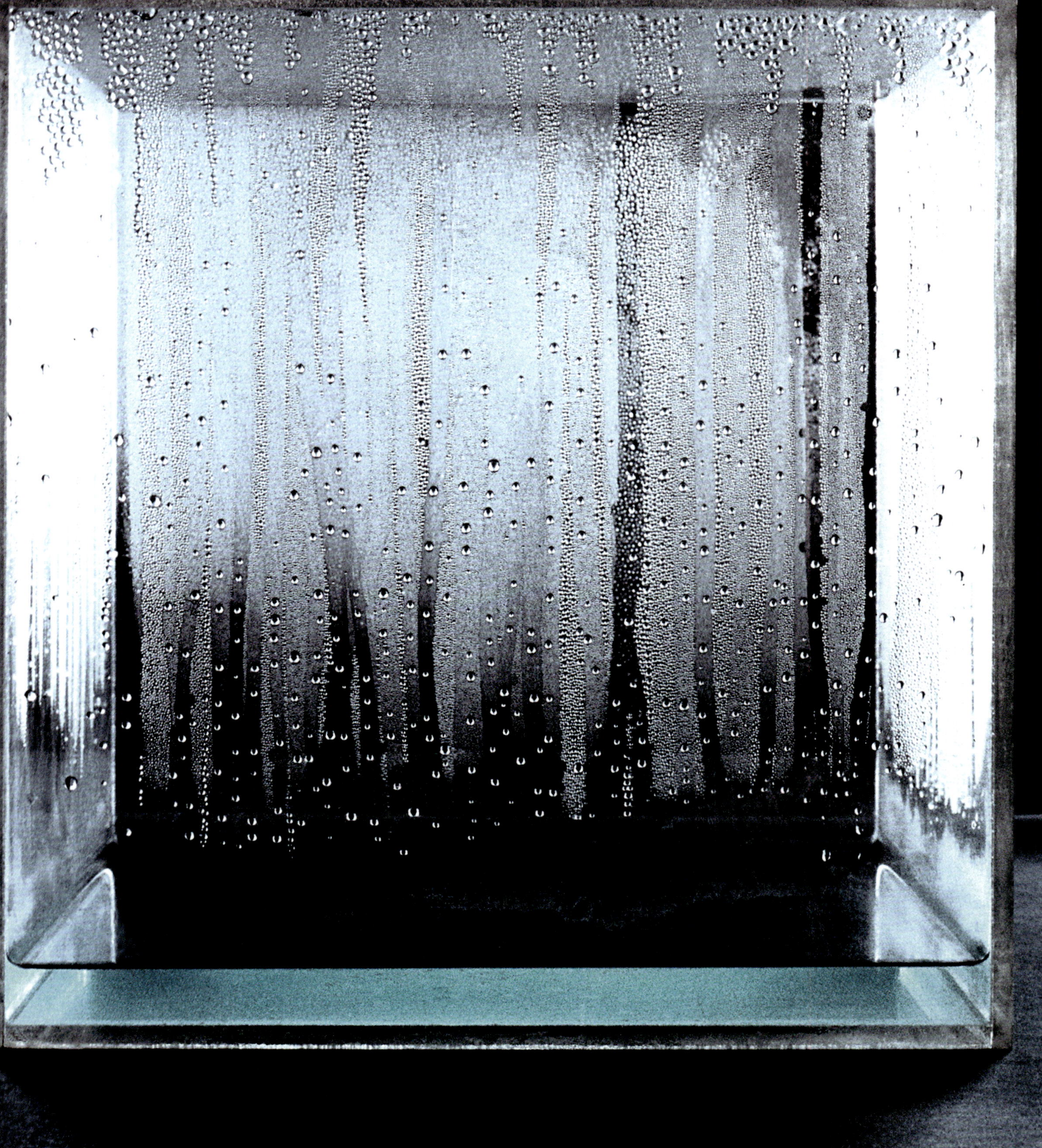

Real-Time, Natural, and Other Systems: On Hans Haacke's Early Work

Ingrid Pfeiffer

1
See Hans Haacke's invitation card for the exhibition *Wind und Wasser* at Galerie Schmela, Düsseldorf, 1965, n.p.

2
See Jack W. Burnham, »Hans Haacke: Wind and Water Sculpture,« *Tri-Quarterly Supplement* 1 (Spring 1967), n.p., and Walter Grasskamp, Molly Nesbit, and Jon Bird, eds., *Hans Haacke* (London and New York: Phaidon Press, 2004), p. 100.

3
Benjamin H. D. Buchloh is one of those who only saw Haacke's early work as a precursor to his »real« political works. See Benjamin H. D. Buchloh, »The Entwinement of Myth and Enlightenment,« in *Hans Haacke: Obra Social*, exh. cat. Fundacio Antoni Tapies, Barcelona (Barcelona: Fundació Antoni Tàpies, 1995), pp. 45–61.

. . . make something which experiences, reacts to its environment, changes, is Nonstable . . .
. . . make something indeterminate, which always looks different, the shape of which cannot be predicted precisely . . .
. . . make something which cannot »perform« without the assistance of its environment . . .
. . . make something which reacts to light and temperature changes, is subject to air currents and depends, in its functioning, on the forces of gravity . . .
. . . make something which the »spectator« handles, with which he plays and thus animates . . .
. . . make something which lives in time and makes the »spectator« experience time . . .
. . . articulate something Natural . . .
— Hans Haacke, Cologne, January 1965

This passage by Haacke was first published in German on the occasion of his exhibition *Wind und Wasser* at Galerie Schmela in Düsseldorf in 1965,[1] then in a slightly modified form in several publications on the artist's early work, some of which are in English,[2] so it is clear that he continued to see it as valid.

Like hardly any other contemporary artist, Hans Haacke has written texts on his own works since the early 1960s that explain the creation of the works and his inner motivations in clear and comprehensible language. Yet this formulation is different: the artist suggests more than he explains, allowing space for associations. The whole text entails implicit instructions, though its arrangement gives it the character of a poem. At the same time, it contains key terms related to Haacke's conception of art, which will be discussed in the following.

Although created as early as 1963 and 1964–65, works like the *Condensation Cube* (figs. 1 and 6) and his *Blue Sail* (figs. p. 51) regularly feature in many of Haacke's solo and group exhibitions. Although it was primarily the sociological, political works like *MoMA Poll* from 1970 (fig. p. 107) and *Shapolsky et al.* from 1971 (fig. pp. 111–14, 119) that were seen as characteristic of Haacke in the past,[3] his physical, biological, and

Fig. 1: Hans Haacke, *Large Condensation Cube*, 1963–67

ecological works from the 1960s have also been gaining increasing prominence in recent years, contributing to a deeper understanding of his oeuvre as a whole.[4]

Hans Haacke's artistic development progressed rapidly—from his studies at the Werkakademie (State Art Academy) in Kassel and his work at documenta II in 1959, to scholarships in Paris (1959–60) and the United States (1961–63), his return to Germany (1963–65), and his final move to New York in 1965. The artist was involved in many currents and developments of the European and American avant-gardes early on, and likewise in a series of groundbreaking exhibitions, such as Harald Szeemann's *When Attitudes Become Form* in 1969 at the Kunstmuseum Bern or *Information* in 1970 at The Museum of Modern Art (MoMA) in New York.[5] Haacke also exhibited in Frankfurt am Main early on, for instance in 1967 in the exhibition *Serielle Formationen* curated by Peter Roehr and Paul Maenz. This exhibition was the first thematic presentation on minimalist tendencies in Germany[6] and it juxtaposed forty-eight German and international artists.[7]

The manifold relationships between Haacke's work and that of other artists, groups, and movements of the 1960s would offer enough material for a comprehensive study that has yet to be undertaken.[8] This early phase was characterized by enormous productivity and networking. An examination of the works shows how little Haacke's practice could be pinned down to a single style, specific group, or material from the outset.[9] His thinking was more systematic and fundamental. It was clear from the very beginning that he was searching for a different kind of content, which later led to the sociopolitical works mentioned above.

Early Painting

His paintings from 1960 (figs. pp. 34–35) were covered in uniform structures and broke with the gestural works of his teacher Fritz Winter in Kassel and the Tachist tendencies he got acquainted with in Paris. In *Ce n'est pas la voie lactée (This Is Not the Milky Way)* (fig. p. 35), the artist worked with a dense field of closely spaced blue dots to make the surface vibrate optically.[10] Due to their differing densities, one can observe darker and lighter areas, creating a kind of blue space that counteracts the grid of paint dots.

The work's title entails a deliberate rejection of any romantic interpretation that would assume the blue surface is supposed to trigger associations of the sky and outer space in the viewer. Although Haacke repeatedly emphasized the »objective« clarity of his approach, of his simple grids and structures, one cannot help but think of Yves Klein's radical actions in the Paris art scene of the 1950s; his symbolic signing of the blue sky in Nice, his leap into the void, the staging of white rooms, and his use of the elements air, water, and earth[11] were all formative for Haacke, as Edward Fry emphasized in Haacke's first monograph in 1972.[12] In 1960, Haacke made a series of

4
This was first thematized in two exhibitions curated by Ursula Ströbele: *Hans Haacke*, Zentralinstitut für Kunstgeschichte, Munich, 2019–20, and *Hans Haacke: Art Nature Politics*, Museum Abteiberg, Mönchengladbach, 2020.

5
See the bibliography in the present volume, pp. 260–61.

6
Renate Wiehager, ed., *Serielle Formationen: 1967/2017; Re-Inszenierung der ersten deutschen Ausstellung internationaler minimalistischer Tendenzen*, exh. cat. Daimler Contemporary, Berlin (Cologne: Snoeck, 2017), p. 9.

7
Haacke participated with a work titled *Formation* from 1963 (ink on paper, 76 × 53 cm), which has not yet been relocated. Paul Maenz and Peter Roehr, eds., *Serielle Formationen*, exh. cat. Studio Galerie, Frankfurt am Main (Frankfurt am Main: Stiftung Studentenhaus, 1967), n.p.

8
The most comprehensive study to date is Ursula Ströbele, *Hans Haacke und Pierre Huyghe: Non-Human Living Sculptures seit den 1960er-Jahren*, vol. 5 of *Schriftenreihe des Studienzentrums zur Moderne* (Berlin and Boston: De Gruyter, 2024).

9
»I don't consider myself a naturalist, nor for that matter a conceptualist or a kineticist . . .«; Jeanne Siegel, »An Interview with Hans Haacke,« *Arts Magazine* 45, no. 7 (May 1971), quoted in *Working Conditions: The Writings of Hans Haacke*, ed. Alexander Alberro (Cambridge, MA: The MIT Press, 2016), p. 33.

10
Hans Haacke, »Untitled Talk at Annual Meeting of Intersocietal Color Council, New York, April 1968,« in *Working Conditions*, p. 17.

11
See Olivier Berggruen, Max Hollein, and Ingrid Pfeiffer, eds., *Yves Klein*, exh. cat. Schirn Kunsthalle Frankfurt and Museo Guggenheim Bilbao (Ostfildern-Ruit: Hatje Cantz, 2004).

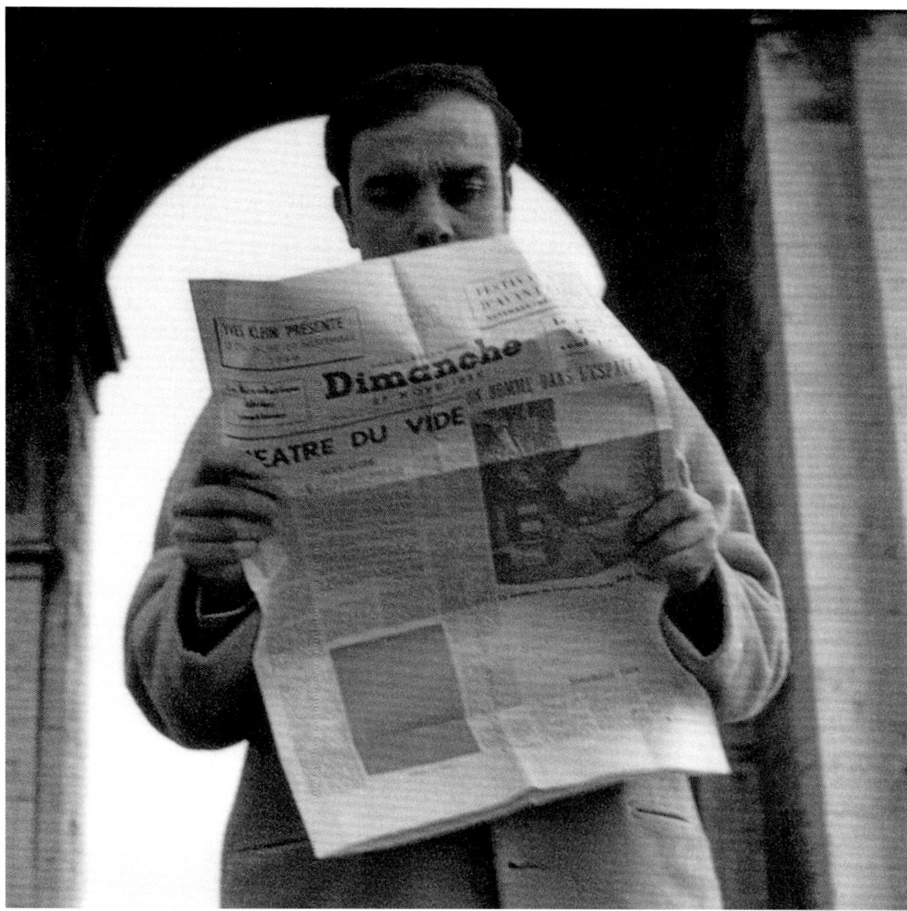

Fig. 2: Photograph of Yves Klein's performance *Dimanche 27 novembre, le journal d'un seul jour* at the Festival d'Art d'Avant-Garde Paris, November 27, 1960, Yves Klein Archive, Paris, photo: Hans Haacke

photographs of Yves Klein's action with the fake newspaper *Dimanche* on the Place de Varsovie in Paris (fig. 2).[13] Even after his death in 1962, Klein continued to appear regularly in the publications of the Düsseldorf-based ZERO group and exerted an enormous posthumous influence on the artists associated with the circle.[14]

Haacke later described his encounter with Klein as impressive but also distant,[15] and as a member of a younger generation he came to reject Klein's mysticism. Elsewhere, he mentions the Parisian group GRAV (Groupe de recherche d'art visuel)[16] and the Greek sculptor Takis as important for his own development.[17] The latter had already used magnetic fields and electrical energy, as Haacke would do later on in works like *High Voltage Discharge Traveling* from 1968.

Haacke and ZERO

Haacke connected ZERO with his own interest in new materials and techniques as well as his focus on sensory effects. In 1959, the artist saw Otto Piene's works for the first time at the Vertiko Gallery in Bonn,[18] wrote to him a year later,[19] and eventually visited him in his Düsseldorf studio. He found Piene's experiments with light and shadow »sensational.«[20] Their initial meeting developed into a lively correspondence and respectful friend-

12
Edward Fry, »Introduction,« in Edward Fry, *Hans Haacke: Werkmonographie* (Cologne: DuMont Schauberg, 1972), quoted in *October Files: Hans Haacke*, ed. Rachel Churner (Cambridge, MA: The MIT Press, 2015), p. 26.

13
Five of these photographs are in the Yves Klein archive in Paris, https://www.yvesklein.com/fr/ressources?sh=Dimanche.

14
The Japanese Gutai group had already used water and earth as art materials in the 1950s and Haacke got to know its members at several ZERO exhibitions. Fry, *Hans Haacke: Werkmonographie*, p. 12. Jack Burnham also mentions Haacke's great fascination with Japanese haiku poems in Burnham, »Hans Haacke: Wind and Water Sculpture,« pp. 6–7.

15
Hans Haacke, »On Yves Klein: 20 years later, 1982,« in *Working Conditions*, pp. 104–08.

16
One GRAV motto was »No more mystifications«; quoted from Gabriele Hoffmann, *Hans Haacke: Art Into Society – Society Into Art* (Kromsdorf: VDG Weimar, 2011), p. 20.

17
Alberro, *Working Conditions*, p. 105.

18
Hans Haacke in conversation with Christiane Hoffmans, in *Piene im Gespräch*, ed. Jürgen Wilhelm in collaboration with the ZERO Foundation (Munich: Hirmer, 2015), p. 45.

19
Hans Haacke to Otto Piene, Kassel, May 20, 1960, Archive of the ZERO Foundation, Düsseldorf, NL Piene, inv. mkp.ZERO. 2.I.1067_1.

20
Haacke in conversation with Hoffmans, in Wilhelm, *Piene im Gespräch*, p. 45.

ship. The older Piene readily accepted Haacke into the ZERO circle and introduced him not only to the most important galleries in Germany, such as Alfred Schmela in Düsseldorf, but also to the Howard Wise Gallery in New York. Both artists went back and forth between Germany and the US during the 1960s and both later taught at American institutions for extended periods—Piene at MIT in Cambridge, Massachusetts, and Haacke at the Cooper Union School of Art in New York City.

Between 1962 and 1965, Haacke exhibited a total of ten times with the—changing and heterogeneous—ZERO network (figs. 3 and 4), not just in Germany, but also in the Netherlands, Italy, England, and the United States.[21] Many of these exhibitions did not explicitly refer to the term »ZERO« in their titles, while some were in cooperation with similar movements in other countries such as the Dutch NUL movement (fig. 4) and touched on other areas and themes such as Op Art, Kinetic Art, Land Art, and Fluxus. As a »large reservoir of ideas,«[22] the loose association with ZERO was an ideal environment for Haacke, who continued making major leaps as he worked on his own development and pursued his individual path in a productive exchange with the movement, but also in conflict with it.

Haacke's focus on grid structures and optical effects in his early paintings continued into his mirror foil reliefs from 1961 onward, which now dispensed with literary titles in favor of factual numbers and letters (figs. p. 37).[23] In 1962, Haacke described his intentions for them as follows: »There is neither a correct nor an incorrect point of view from which to look at them. Their environments—including the spectator—form an integral part of them. . . . They are not fixed; their appearances are infinite.«[24]

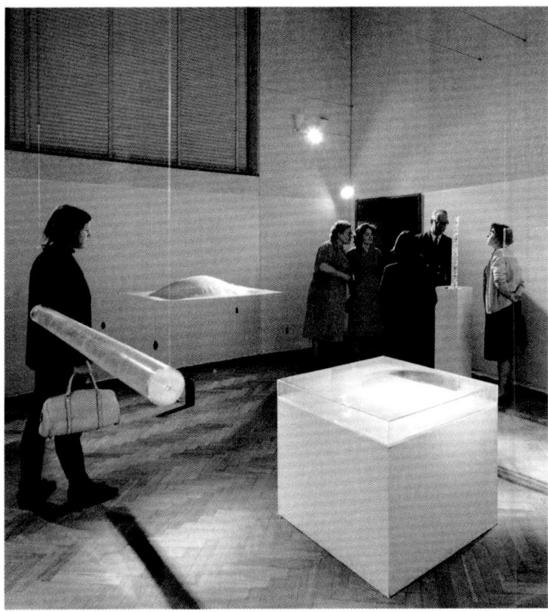

Fig. 3: Installation view, Stedelijk Museum Amsterdam, works by Hans Haacke, 1965, courtesy 0-INSTITUTE

From Object to Process

Real interaction with the public was already desired in the mirror reliefs and was subsequently expanded, for example in his *Rain Tower*, the first »usable« three-dimensional work from 1962 (fig. 5). Here, Haacke worked with water for the first time, which would drip through the evenly spaced openings in the various levels of the transparent tower like a kind of »hourglass.«[25] When the audience rotated the object, the process would start anew, like a seemingly simple science experiment. By this point, Haacke had already started using easily available transparent plexiglass elements, and in the following years it remained his preferred material for making visible natural or physical processes and universal relationships: »These geometric shapes,« said Haacke, »possess an extremely pristine clarity and absoluteness . . . The organic happening of the inside and the geometrically shaped container enhance each other.«[26]

The most famous example, which remains especially fascinating to this day, is his aforementioned *Condensation Cube* from 1963 to 1967 (figs. 1 and 6), which is an acrylic glass cube enclosing a small amount of water. Depending on the

21
See the bibliography in the present volume, pp. 260–61.

22
Dirk Pörschmann and Margriet Schavemaker, »Rendezvous mit einer vergessenen Avantgarde,« in *ZERO*, ed. Dirk Pörschmann and Margriet Schavemaker, exh. cat. Martin-Gropius-Bau, Berlin, and Stedelijk Museum Amsterdam (Cologne: König, 2015), p. 18.

23
This group of works is close to Heinz Mack's works like the *Lamellen-Relief* from 1959; on this, see Romina Dümler, »Von Möwen und anderer Natur: Die gemeinsame ZERO-Präsentation von Hans Haacke, Heinz Mack, Otto Piene und Günter Uecker,« in *Opening the Archive: The ABCs of ZERO* (Berlin: Hatje Cantz, 2024), p. 258.

24
Quoted from *Hans Haacke: For Real; Works 1959–2006*, exh. cat. Deichtorhallen, Hamburg, and Akademie der Künste, Berlin (Düsseldorf: Richter, 2006), p. 82.

25
Edward Fry, »Introduction,« in *Hans Haacke: Werkmonographie*, quoted in *October Files*, p. 27.

26
Interview with Jack Burnham (1967), in *October Files*, p. 22.

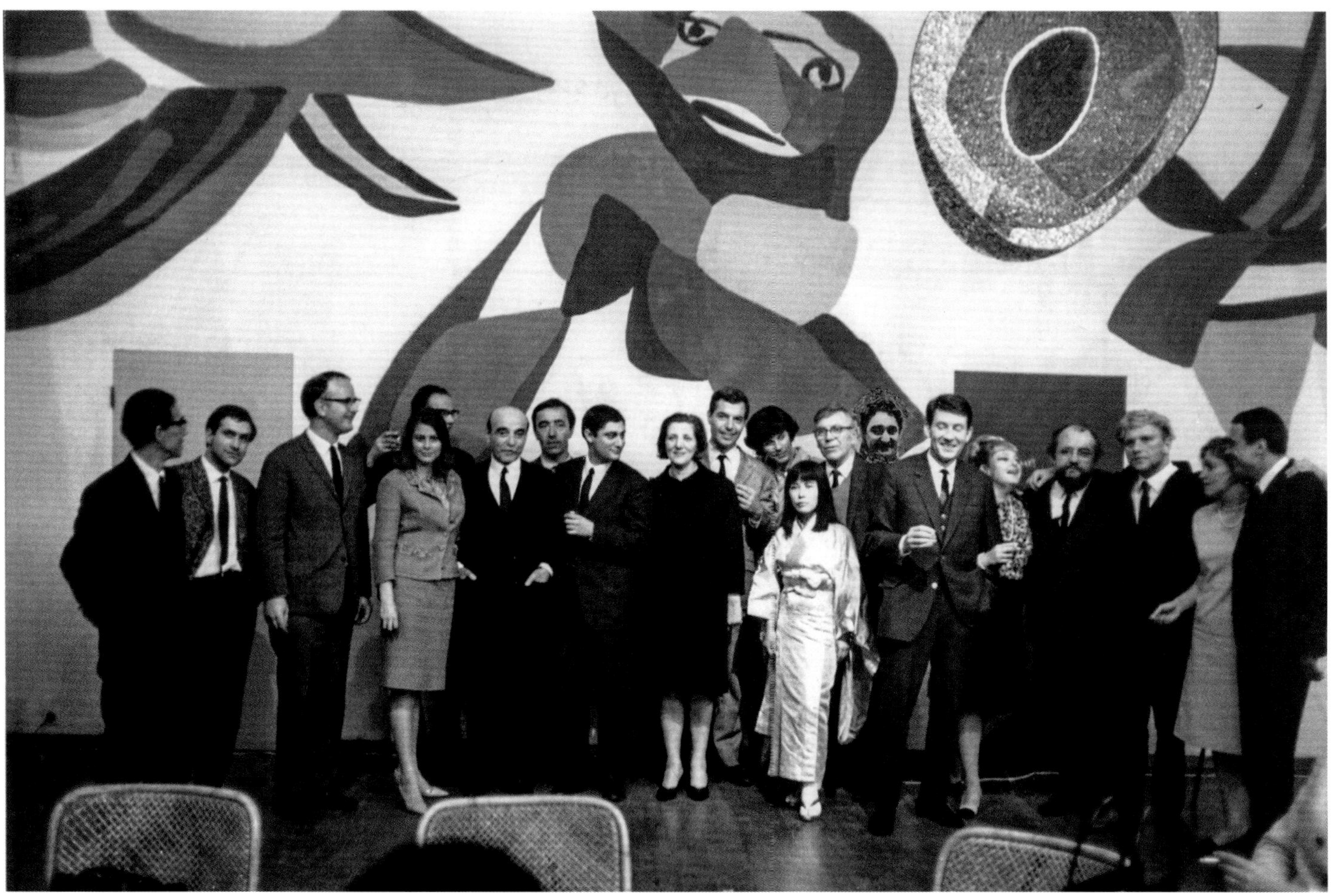

Fig. 4: *NUL 1965*, exhibition at the Stedelijk Museum Amsterdam, 1965, from left to right: Jiro Yoshihara, Hans Haacke, Henk Peeters, Rotraut Klein, Jan J. Schoonhoven, Lucio Fontana, Pol Bury, Gianni Colombo, Teresita Fontana, Edy de Wilde, Nono Reinhold-de Wilde, Yayoi Kusama, George Rickey, Jesús Rafael Soto, Otto Piene, Nanda Vigo, Alfred Schmela, Heinz Mack, Emile Soestbergen, Günther Uecker, courtesy 0-INSTITUTE

external conditions, light and room climate, people and their body heat, the water evaporates and condenses on the inner walls until the drops become so large that gravity draws them downward and the process begins anew. It is an experiment for those who are familiar with the water cycle, states of matter, and simple physical laws; but also a drama of drops and patterns, of time and chance, since the forms of condensed water are never the same, leaving space for one's own associations and individual experiences. »There was this fantastic cycle of evaporation, condensation, then the droplets falling. That is a process evolving all by itself. This was the first time I had something that was literally responding to its environment,« Haacke later said.[27]

The *Condensation Cube* would become a signature work for Haacke and already hinted at what would later become characteristic of his oeuvre: the preference for objective facts, for the simplest material and the clearest form, as well as the transition from »object« (or sculpture) to »process.« Haacke also called the cubes »weather boxes« and later even compared the meteorological climate with the political »climate.«[28]

The inclusion of both the viewer and the spatial or museum environment has already been implemented here, which has led some critics to identify the work as an early example of Institutional Critique.[29]

27
Interview with Jeanne Siegel (1971), in *Working Conditions*, p. 36.

28
John Tyson, »The Artist as ›Weatherman‹: Hans Haacke's Critical Meteorology,« in *Nervous Systems: Art, Systems, and Politics since the 1960s*, ed. Johanna Gosse and Timothy Stott (Durham, NC: Duke University Press, 2022), pp. 55–77.

29
Ibid., p. 56.

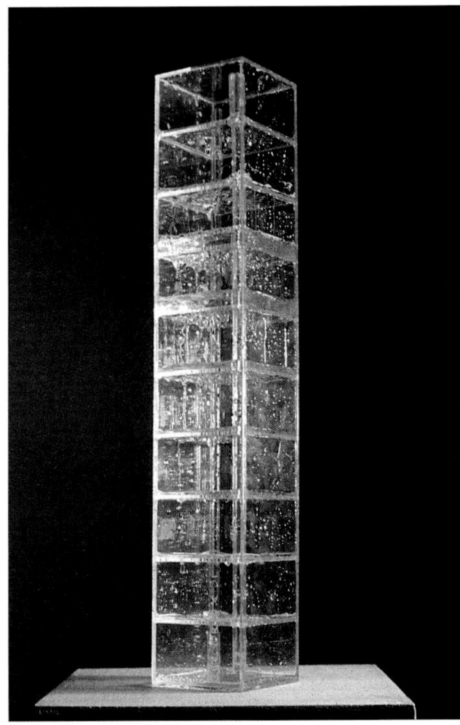

Fig. 5: Hans Haacke, *Rain Tower*, 1962, acrylic glass and destilled water, 83.2 × 10.2 × 10.2 cm, courtesy the artist and Paula Cooper Gallery, New York

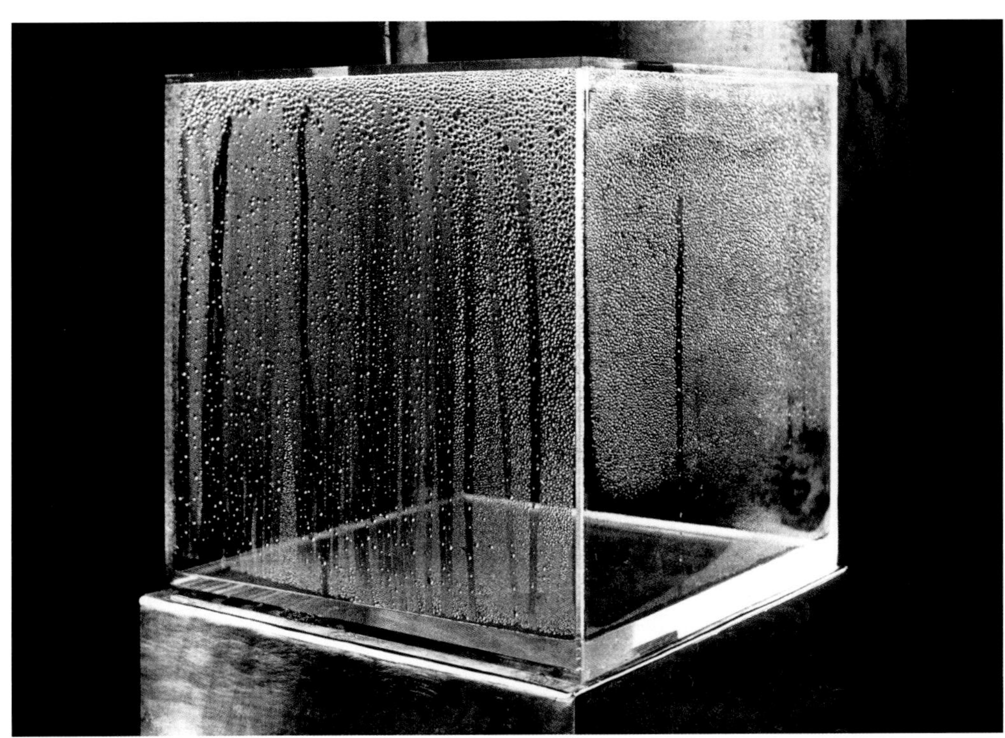

Fig. 6: Hans Haacke, *Small Condensation Cube*, 1963–65, acrylic glass, destilled water, 30.5 × 30.5 × 30.5 cm, courtesy the artist and Paula Cooper Gallery, New York

In a group of works from 1966–67, which includes *Ice Stick* (fig. p. 44), *Floating Ice Ring* (fig. p. 45), and *Ice Table*, Haacke continued working with the physical states of water. In these works, however, the moisture is on the outside and the cold is on the inside, so that over time a white layer of ice forms on the cold elements. »The condensation,« says Haacke, »as much as the formation of ice, figuratively speaking, is related to growth.«[30] It was thus a natural step for him to make biological growth processes experienceable in exhibition spaces via works such as *Grass Grows* (fig. p. 73) or *Directed Growth* (fig. p. 71). According to Edward Fry, Haacke sought to »eliminate arbitrary boundaries within our culture between art, science, and society.«[31]

Haacke showed most of the process-based »experimental setups« in museum interiors and demonstrated the water cycle, evaporation, condensation, crystallization, liquefaction, and air movements, such as the floating of objects. From 1967 on, he extended these locations into outdoor spaces and »performed« on the roof of his studio.

There were natural processes as well as processes controlled by him with water vapor (fig. 7), poured water (fig. pp. 60–61), or melting snow (fig. 8), which Haacke documented in photographs. The ideas of »time« and »articulating something Natural« mentioned above remained significant for many of these works.

His projects with different liquids, in tubes and other containers (fig. p. 41), again demonstrated physical processes, for example when two differently colored, but actually immiscible types of liquid formed colored ornaments and

30
Interview with Jeanne Siegel, 1971, in *Working Conditions*, p. 37.

31
Fry, »Introduction,« in *Hans Haacke: Werkmonographie*, quoted in *October Files*, p. 40.

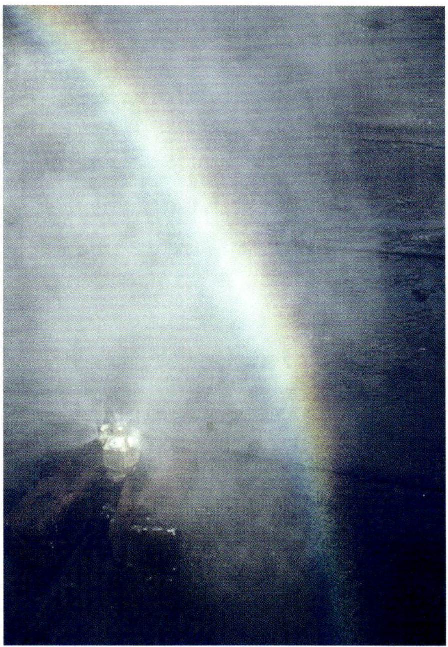

Fig. 7: Hans Haacke, *Water in Wind*, summer 1968, documenation of the action, on the rooftop of the artist's studio at 95 East Houston Street, New York, courtesy the artist and Paula Cooper Gallery, New York

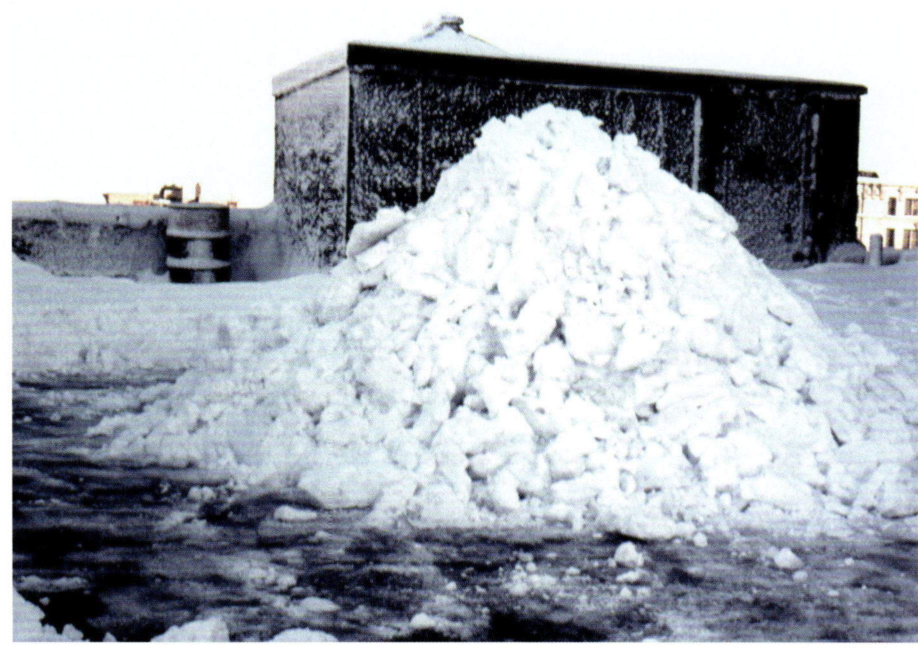

Fig. 8: Hans Haacke, *Snow Pile: Melting and Evaporating*, February 10, 11, 12, 1969, documentation of the action on the rooftop of the artist's studio at 95 East Houston Street, New York, courtesy the artist and Paula Cooper Gallery, New York

patterns if their vessel was shaken or turned. In these and many other works, Haacke presented structural parallels to natural phenomena.[32]

Interaction and the activation of the viewer had been decisive for the ZERO actions,[33] and, as previously mentioned, Haacke also encouraged visitors to perform, to do something, to act, and to use their bodies interactively early on in various works. However, he went even further, since »static objects,« according to Haacke, stood »in essential contrast to the actual processual character of the world that we can experience . . . They not only suggest an immutability that is incompatible with the real course of things, but also promote an intellectually and politically devastating status quo thinking.«[34]

Actions with Animals and Ecology

In 1966, the year that also saw the dissolution of the ZERO group, Haacke planned a joint »Seagull Island« together with Heinz Mack, Otto Piene, and Günter Uecker as part of the *ZERO op zee* exhibition on the pier at the lido in Scheveningen, Netherlands. As Haacke's sketches of the ultimately unrealized project show (fig. 9), the lured seagulls were to form a »seagull sculpture.« He also drew a »flock of seagulls« and wrote: »It is important to find out what seagulls like to eat. A small boat with this favorite food would have to be anchored on the open sea and attract the seagulls. The result would be a constantly changing flying sculpture.«[35]

32
»Haacke's photo archive contains a large number of nature photographs with abstract patterns and ornaments, including cloud images, formations of trees, spider webs with dew . . .«; Ströbele, *Hans Haacke und Pierre Huyghe*, p. 197.

33
Pörschmann and Schavemaker, »Rendezvous mit einer vergessenen Avantgarde,« p. 14.

34
Hans Haacke in conversation with Karin Thomas, Galerie Maenz, September 4, 1971, in Karin Thomas, *Kunst – Praxis heute: Eine Dokumentation der aktuellen Ästhetik* (Cologne: DuMont Schauberg, 1972), p. 101.

35
Letter from Haacke to the International Gallery Orez, February 28, 1966, cited in Dümler, »Of Seagulls and Other Nature,« p. 260.

Otto Piene's and Günter Uecker's oeuvres also include works with seagulls, and they continued developing the ideas behind the unrealized work in Scheveningen on their own: Piene in 1968 with *The Birds Sculpture* for the Boston Harbor Project on the occasion of the 200th anniversary of the Boston Harbor.[36] Uecker later worked on the seagull theme in two films from 1970: *Floating Afloat* and *Seagull Sculpture in Motion*.[37]

In 1969, Haacke created his »Seagull Sculpture« with the action *Live Airborne System* on Coney Island in New York: Haacke only selected one dynamic photograph as part of the work; it shows the flocks of seagulls aggressively competing to devour some bread which the artist used as bait (fig. pp. 68–69). It is hardly a harmonious or idyllic image representing the supposed opposite of human society.

Flocks of seagulls eating dead fish were then given a completely new interpretation in his 1972 Krefeld triptych (fig. pp. 84–85), when Haacke made the extreme pollution of the Rhine the subject of a clearly indicting, political-ecological work for the first time.[38] As early as 1970, the artist had created a *Monument to Beach Pollution* (fig. pp. 78–79) from garbage he collected on a beach in Carboneras, Spain. Its hill-like shape recalls *Grass Grows*, and the piece is considered one of the earliest works of ecological art.[39]

Haacke's action *Chickens Hatching* (figs. 10, 11, and pp. 66, 67) in Ontario from 1969 is also more disturbing than delightful. Haacke directly presented birth and growth processes in the exhibition space in »real time« by letting chicks be incubated and hatch. As is often the case, he used a stringent and orderly »minimalist« box structure—the teeming, disorderly biology is squeezed into a narrow, man-made scheme.[40]

Haacke transformed the largely positive feelings that animals trigger into a terrifying experience in the art context: even the few surviving photographs of the action give the feeling of the objectification of living beings and the exploitation of animals. Presumably, our views today are different to those of 1969 (when live animals were still allowed in museums).

Piene had described the goals of ZERO as such: »One of our most important intentions was the reharmonization of man and nature . . . [the artist] uses new technical means as well as the forces of nature.«[41] The younger Haacke no longer seemed to share this optimistic view. More analytical than his ZERO colleagues, he discovered early on his rather abstract interest in larger systems, which he sought to make visible. His desire to bring about real social change, to critique and directly intervene, increasingly set him apart from his contemporaries.

Real-Time Systems

»Sometime in '65 or '66, I was introduced to the concept of systems,« Haacke noted in a much-cited interview from 1971 done in the run-up to his canceled solo show at the Guggenheim Museum.[42] He had already met the sculptor and systems

36
This project was not realized either. For more details, see ibid.

37
Ibid., p. 261.

38
See Ursula Ströbele's essay in the present volume, pp. 80–89.

39
Grasskamp et al., *Hans Haacke*, pp. 42–43.

40
Ursula Ströbele refers to this group of works as »Non-Human Living Sculptures«; see Ströbele, *Hans Haacke und Pierre Huyghe*, pp. 135–39.

41
Quoted from Pörschmann and Schavemaker, *ZERO*, p. 244.

42
Interview with Jeanne Siegel, 1971, in *Working Conditions*, p. 34.

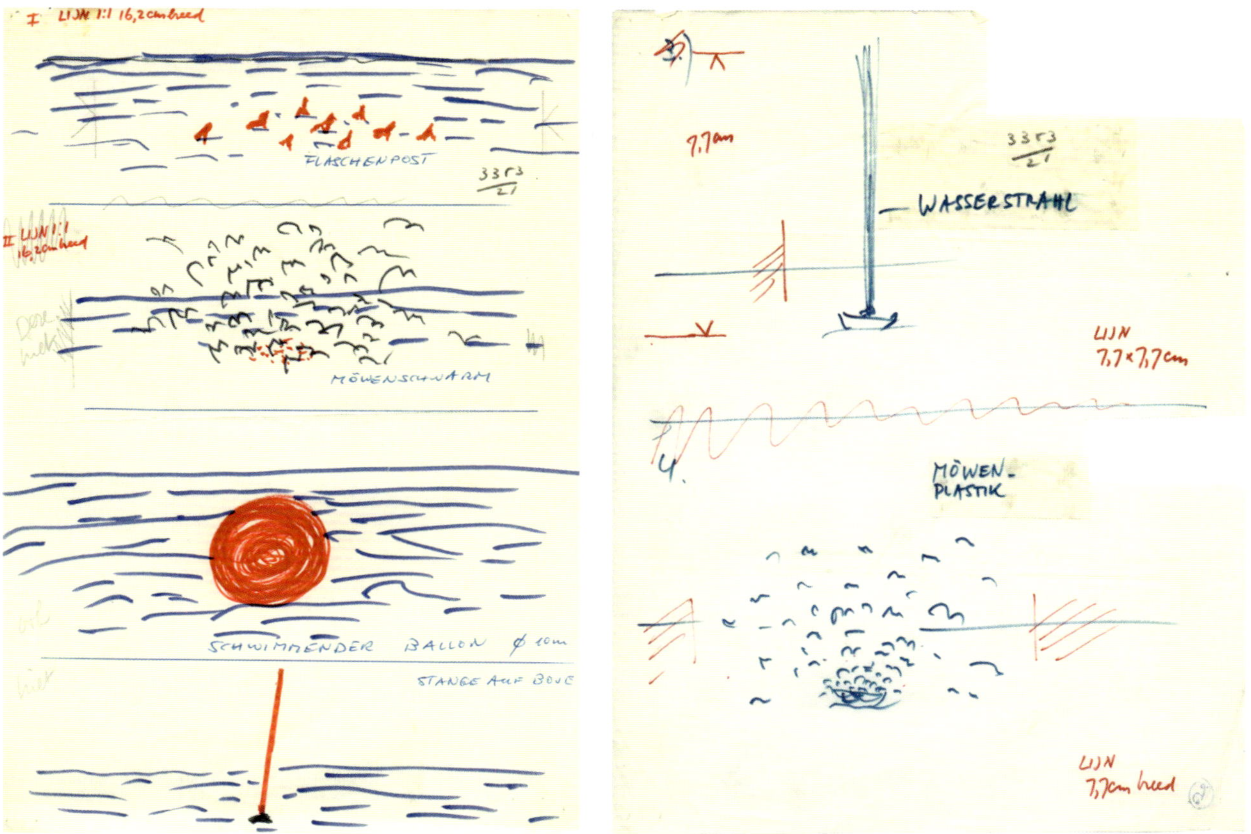

Fig. 9: Hans Haacke, *Mövenplastik*, prososal drawings for *ZERO on Sea*, 1965, Collection Anthing Vogel / Haags Gemeentearchief The Hague, courtesy 0-INSTITUTE

theorist Jack Burnham in Philadelphia in 1962, but it wasn't until around 1965 that Haacke found a vocabulary suitable to his own artistic practice in Burnham's formulations. One of Burnham's major texts, titled »Systems Esthetics,« was published in the magazine *Artforum* in 1968. There, he highlighted Haacke as a pioneering artist in the new field of »post-formalist« art.[43] Haacke understood »system« to mean the interaction of elements in a whole, whereby a transfer of matter/energy and/or information takes place.[44]

Haacke's works, like the *Condensation Cube* and his actions with animals, function as »real time« processes that also continue in the viewer's absence. Burnham remained the most important theorist for Haacke's work until around 1970. Like many other artists of the 1960s, the concept of »expanded sculpture« became decisive for him, though few others went as far as he did in terms of using the new possibilities in such a broad and consistent way, both materially and theoretically.

Likewise, the biologist Ludwig von Bertalanffy published his *General System Theory* in 1968, which further influenced and confirmed Haacke's view of structural analogies.[45] With the eminently important creation of parallels between physical, biological, and social systems, Haacke found an adequate theoretical framework for his works that were otherwise phenomenologically disparate. Despite his use of different materials and techniques, spanning photographs, objects, actions, and installations, the structural parallels or analogies formed a common thread running throughout Haacke's works, which only

43
Jack Burnham, »Systems Esthetics,« *Artforum* 7, no. 1 (September 1968), https://www.artforum.com/features/systems-esthetics-201372/.

44
Haacke in conversation with Thomas, in Thomas, *Kunst – Praxis heute*, p. 102.

45
See, among others, Alexander Alberro, »Hans Haacke and the Rules of the Game,« in Alberro, *Working Conditions*, pp. 24–26.

seem superficially heterogeneous. The fact that »everything is connected to everything else,« as Haacke emphasized,[46] becomes increasingly obvious when viewed as a whole.

Constructed from plastic tubes, the work *Circulation* from 1969 (figs. pp. 57–59) resembles an organism spreading out on the floor, with water being pumped through its »veins.«[47] His project *Ant Co-op* from the same year, which Haacke documented with a close-up photograph (fig. p. 63), was both a biological and a social system: the regularity of the tunnels dug by the ants reveals their own order and architecture typical of their species.[48] In many of his works, Haacke visually and comparatively presented the most diverse »orders«—physical, biological, and later also social.

For the aforementioned exhibition at the Guggenheim Museum in 1971, an experiment was planned with a tamed black mynah bird, a kind of starling, which Haacke wanted to train to say the short phrase »all systems go,« though this only worked to a limited extent. The bird was called Norbert, after Norbert Wiener, the inventor of cybernetics and forefather of the computer system.[49] The naming of the bird also reveals Haacke's subtle sense of humor and his reflexive questioning of his own position, despite the seriousness of his work. As with many other works and actions, only one photograph of the bird in the cage has survived (fig. pp. 64–65).

Photography played an important role in Haacke's work from the very beginning, as he used it to document many of his actions, such as those with animals (*Live Airborne System*, *Ant Co-op*, figs. pp. 63, 68–69), but also the actions with water in outdoor spaces (fig. pp. 248–49). The remaining photographs are expressive and far more than snapshots, since they show his analytical and »composing« gaze as well as his focus on the essential—much like Haacke's first photo series at documenta II in 1959, which shows visitors and their behavior in the exhibition spaces.[50]

Although Haacke worked in a process-oriented way very early on, there is only one film that describes his work from this period[51]—a WDR feature from 1969 which is a mixture of documentary and artist film (figs. pp. 75–77).[52] This rare document shows details of many works from the 1960s and the artist in action.[53] Quick edits between shots emphasize the aforementioned parallels between plastic tubes, droplets, flocks of seagulls, and ant trails. The film also shows a baby, Haacke's first son, whose birth certificate from 1969 the artist transformed into an allusive social system (fig. 12).

At the time, it was customary in the United States to record a fingerprint of the mother and prints of the child's feet for identification purposes. On top of the official's writing, Haacke placed a stamp that read »Collaboration Linda & Hans Haacke« and thus declared the »result,« that is, their child, to be a joint work of art, a unique event in the context of Conceptual Art. In addition, the name »Carl Samuel Selavy« refers to Marcel Duchamp, whom Haacke was strongly influenced by at the time.[54] In later works such as *Broken R.M. ...* (fig. p. 174) and *Nothing to Declare* (fig. p. 175), Haacke continued this productive engagement with the French artist.[55]

46
Here, Haacke is quoting Lenin via a report by Saatchi & Saatchi PLC; »Interview mit Hans Haacke,« *Texte zur Kunst* 80 (December 2010), quoted from Alberro, *Working Conditions*, p. 245.

47
Ströbele, *Hans Haacke und Pierre Huyghe*, p. 160.

48
Fry, »Introduction,« in *Hans Haacke: Werkmonographie*, quoted in *October Files*, p. 34.

49
See Norbert Wiener, *Cybernetics or Control and Communication in the Animal and the Machine* (Cambridge, MA: The MIT Press, 1948).

50
See *Photographic Notes, documenta 2*, 1959, in the present volume, p. 14.

51
An early film that has not yet been mentioned in written sources on Haacke is located in the archive of the 0-Institute in Voorschoten, Netherlands. Titled *Water and Air*, the 1965 film (15 min.) is about the artist in his Cologne studio and was directed by Gerd Winkler, Hessischer Rundfunk.

52
Hans Haacke: Selbstporträt eines deutschen Künstlers in New York, WDR, 1969, 23 min.; see also Ströbele, *Hans Haacke und Pierre Huyghe*, pp. 190–95.

53
See Ursula Ströbele, »Fundstück aus dem WDR Archiv, Köln: Selbstporträt eines deutschen Künstlers in New York,« *Kunstchronik* 73, no. 7, special issue *Kunst Natur Politik – Jetzt!* (2020), pp. 388–96.

54
»I thought of signing the rain, the sea, the fog, and so on like Duchamp signed his bottle rack . . . ,« Haacke said in an interview with Jack Burnham in 1967; quoted from *October Files*, p. 23.

55
Haacke writes about the differences between Duchamp's ready-mades and his own conception in »Provisional Remarks« (1971), in Alberro, *Working Conditions*, p. 49.

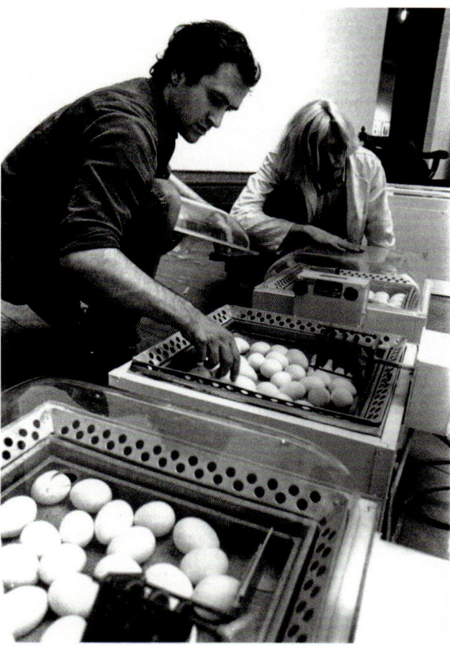

Fig. 10: *Mr. Hans Haacke installing Chickens Hatching*, September 26, 1969, for the exhibition *New Alchemy: Elements, Systems, Forces*, Art Gallery of Ontario, 1969

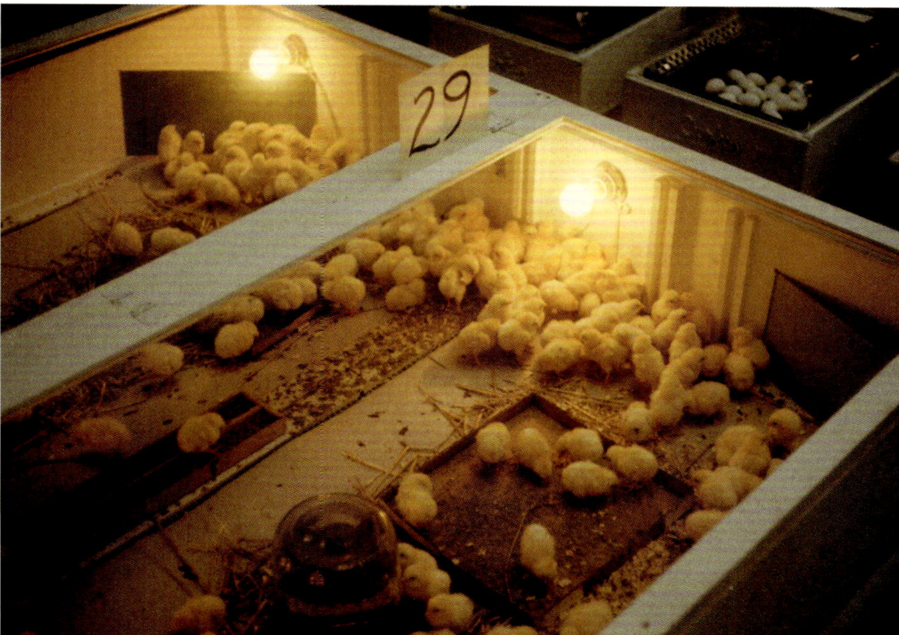

Fig. 11: Hans Haacke, *Chickens Hatching*, 1969 (detail), at the exhibition *New Alchemy: Elements, Systems, Forces*, Art Gallery of Ontario, 1969

The transitions between physical, biological, and socio-political works in Haacke's oeuvre remained fluid: for the 1971 Guggenheim exhibition, Haacke had planned a water system to be constructed for the building in addition to the by now famous work ***Shapolsky et al.*** (figs. pp. 111–14, 119), as well as the piece *Directed Growth* (fig. p. 71), for which he had already started growing the beans before the exhibition was canceled. Haacke had implemented similar basic ideas in *Bowery Seeds* from 1970 (fig. p. 72): the seeds growing freely on the roof of his studio in New York evoke the much later bed in the Bundestag's inner courtyard for *DER BEVÖLKERUNG* from 2000, which also grew without further intervention (figs. pp. 226–27).

Everything Is Political

»I believe that a rational, almost positivistic approach . . . can be pushed to a point where it blossoms into something very poetic, weightless, and irrational,« Haacke said in 1967.[56] He thus reflected on the ambivalences of his conceptions. Despite the objectivity and sobriety he strove for, Haacke worked with metaphors and comparisons from nature that linked different systems. For example, he compared the movement of natural materials like air and water with the human respiratory rhythm[57] or with natural »time patterns« that underlie all natural structures and which humans perceive as harmonious—in contrast to artificial ones or those created by machines.[58]

56
Interview with Jack Burnham, in *October Files*, p. 22.

57
Ibid. p. 19.

58
Ibid.

Without »mystifying« anything himself, as Haacke described it, his works from the 1960s leave plenty of room for free interpretation and association. They remain impressive to this day, although we now perceive them differently than when they were made—that is, when the materials and actions used were still new and revolutionary in themselves. Thus, many of Haacke's early works with natural phenomena like wind, water, ice, animals, and plants seem timeless and universal at first glance, but also less »critical« than his later works.

But Haacke vehemently resisted this distinction: »I am uneasy about the common way of singling out so-called committed art . . . The qualification ›committed‹ or ›political‹ suggests the existence of a ›non-committed‹ art, or worse yet that there is a ›normal art‹ alongside the ›committed‹ one. All public articulations, including artistic ones, have potential social consequences . . . .«[59] Elsewhere he wrote: »Physical and biological systems are per se political.«[60]

It is to Haacke's credit that he broke with ideas of »style« and other formal and material boundaries in art production so consistently so early on. Even his early work demonstrates his ability to transcend all kinds of boundaries with ease, and to constantly reinvent himself. Despite many parallels to other artists and movements of the 1960s, Haacke's early artistic activity clearly points to a different future, one that is based on a belief in processes of change. The urge to change and move,[61] with all conceivable artistic means, is what distinguishes him, and it is an attitude he maintained into his late career.

59
Stefan Römer, »Zur Soziologie der künstlerischen Strategie: Ein Interview mit Hans Haacke,« *Texte zur Kunst* 2, no. 8 (December 1992), p. 52.

60
Quoted from Tyson, »The Artist as ›Weatherman‹: Hans Haacke's Critical Meteorology,« p. 55.

61
»My belief in the pervasive pattern of change developed through my observation of all that was going on around and within me,« Haacke wrote in 1968; Hans Haacke, »Untitled Talk at Annual Meeting of Intersocietal Color Council, New York, April 1968,« in *Working Conditions*, p. 16.

UNIVERSITY HOSPITAL
New York University Medical Center

HAACKE BABY BOY
188530 8E
H.LEHFELDT

NEWBORN IDENTIFICATION

Haacke Linda	188515	
MOTHER'S NAME	MOTHER'S UNIT NO.	RELIGION
CARL SAMUEL SELAVY		
INFANT'S NAME	INFANT'S UNIT NO.	

1/13/69	3:14	☐ AM ☑ PM
DATE OF BIRTH	TIME OF BIRTH	

W	Boy	5 9½	19"
COLOR	SEX	WEIGHT	LENGTH

IDENT-A-BAND NO. 5099

SEX AND IDENTIFICATION CHECKED BY:

1.PHYSICIAN ________ M.D.

2.DELIVERY ROOM B Frankel R.N.

3.NURSERY D Chernook R.N.

I hereby acknowledge that I have checked the ident-a-band parts sealed on the baby and on me and found that they were identically numbered and contained the correct identifying information and that I am taking my baby home.

COLLABORATION LINDA & HANS HAACKE

Date 1/22/69

B. Arlotta R.N.

WITNESS HOSPITAL REPRESENTATIVE PARENT Linda Haacke

BABY'S LEFT FOOT PRINT	MOTHER'S RIGHT INDEX FINGER	BABY'S RIGHT FOOT PRINT
	PRINTS TAKEN BY NAME B. Frankel	

NEWBORN IDENTIFICATION

Fig. 12: Hans Haacke, *Newborn Identification (Collaboration Linda & Hans Haacke)*, 1969

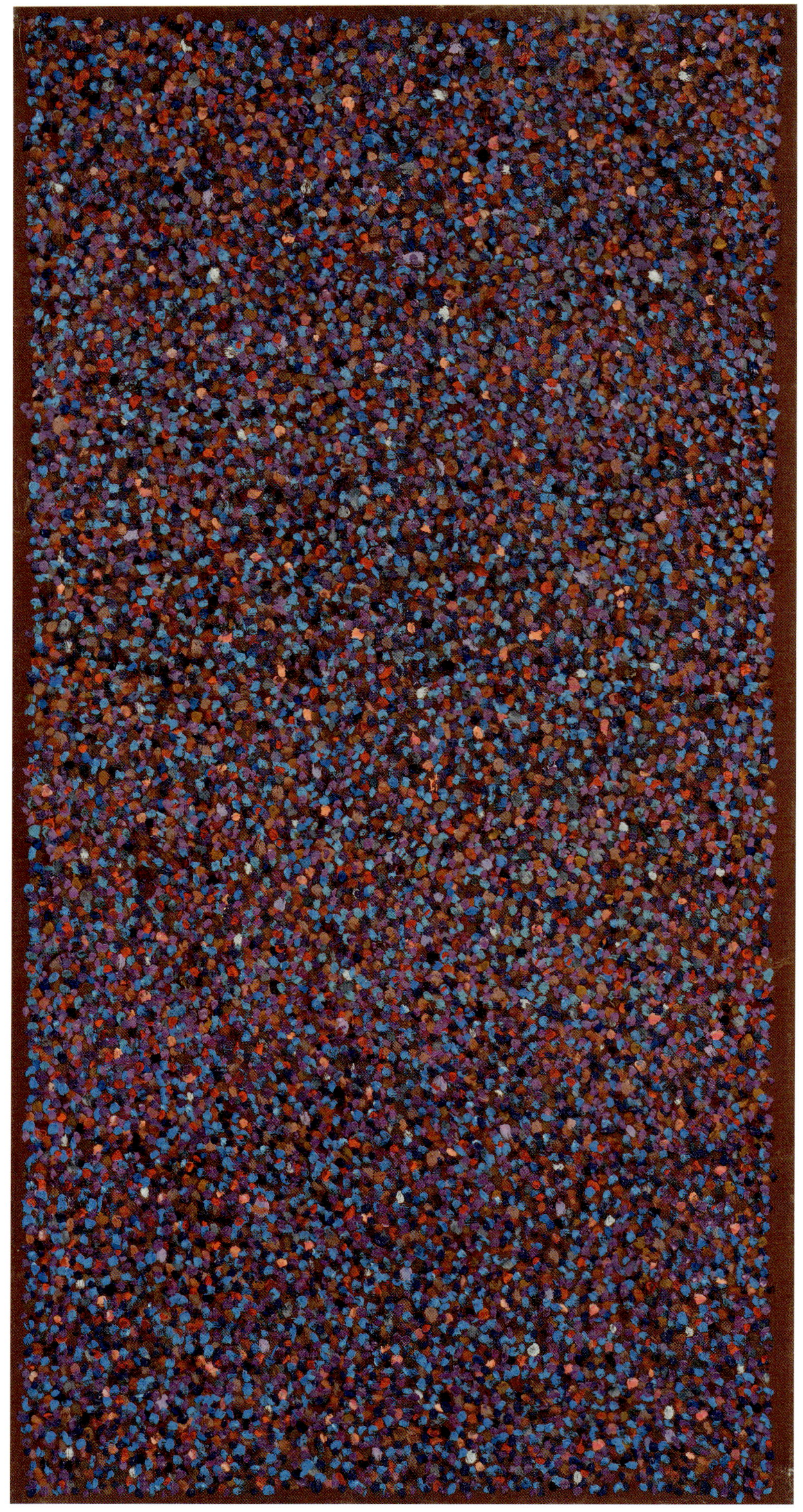

Untitled, 1960

Ce n'est pas la voie lactée (This Is Not the Milky Way), 1960

Mirror objects, 1961

Observing my mirror objects made of polished stainless steel, I note: There is neither a correct nor an incorrect point of view from which to look at them. Their environments—including the spectator—form an integral part of them. The environment is constantly participating in their creation. They are not fixed; their appearances are infinite.

They are exceeding their material boundaries and are limited, respectively, by the boundaries of sight in the space in which they happen to be, the workshop, the exhibition room, and the stars. They show different kinds of spaces inseparably linked together.

I define as volume the space they occupy materially, that is, as air-displacing objects that offer resistance. It is static, measurable, limited. I define as vibration the space that seems to move toward the spectator, away from him, and parallel to the horizon, when nearly homogeneous elements are seen, arranged in a nearly regular pattern, and when the distance between the elements is too wide to see them simultaneously with precision. This dynamic space is non-material. It is moving within immeasurable limits and can be perceived only optically.

These qualities are the same for both reflected and materially existing elements. Reflection is creating unreal space, changing or static depending on the immobility or mobility of the surroundings, which are reduced to their visual qualities. Although it can be perceived only optically, it can be measured. It is non-material, limited respectively by the boundaries of sight and created exclusively by light rays. The incessant communication—to see and be seen—of the mirror-objects with the world and the spectator, their insoluble connection of real and unreal, static and dynamic, material and non-material space, their indetermination, all fascinate me.

Hans Haacke, Philadelphia, January 7, 1962

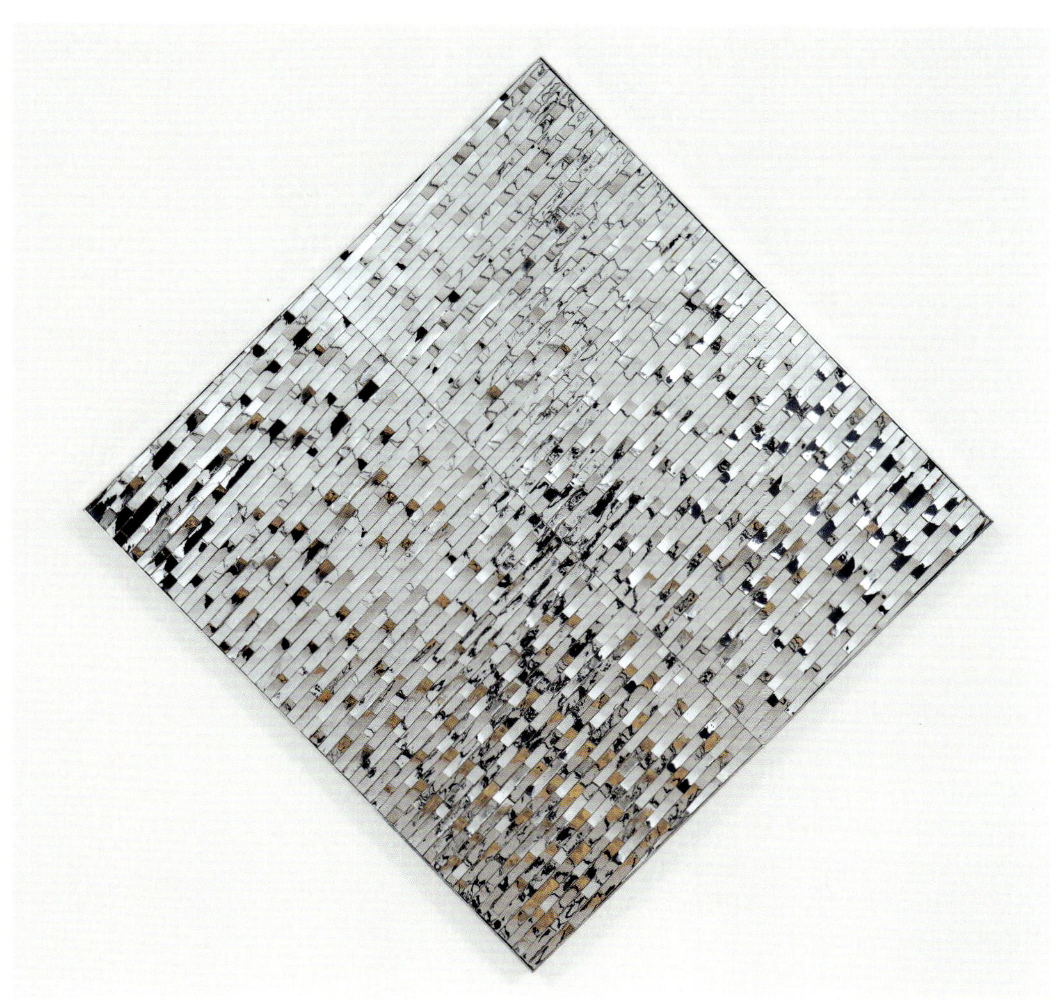

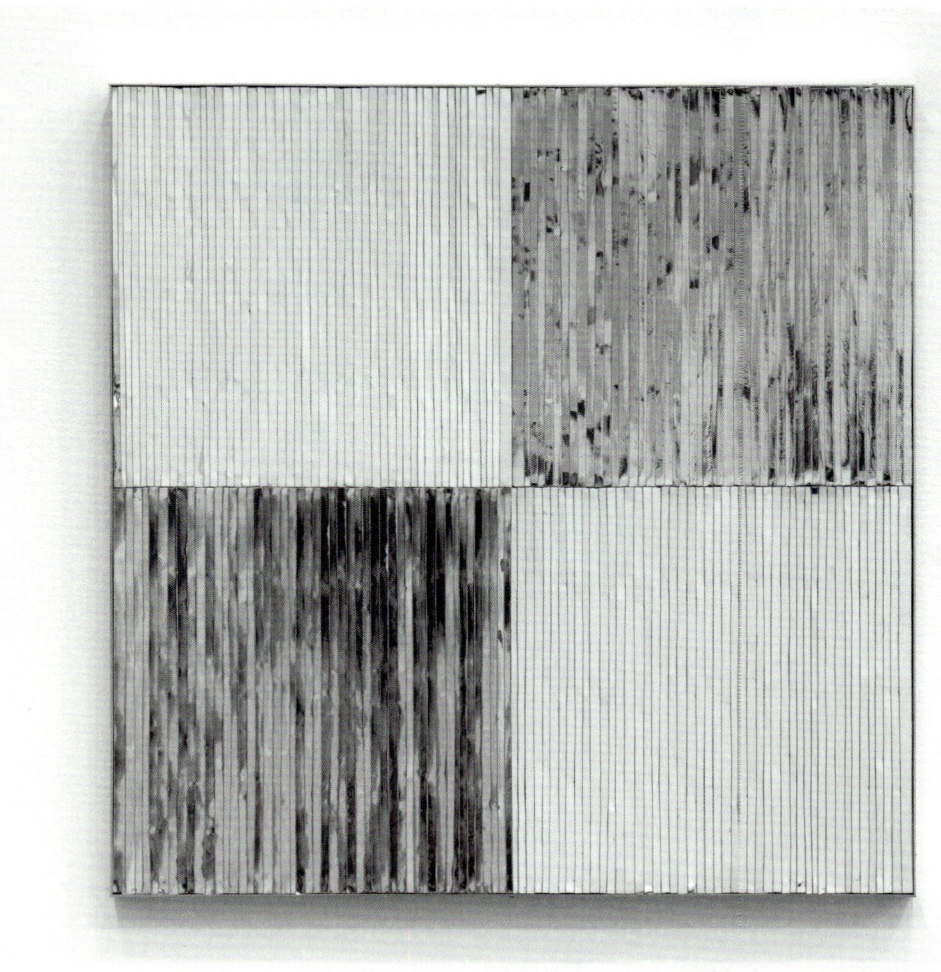

B7-61, 1961
A7-61, 1961

Large Condensation Cube, 1963–67

I have partially filled plexiglass containers of a simple stereometric form with water and have sealed them. The intrusion of light warms the inside of the boxes. Since the inside temperature is always higher than the surrounding temperature, the water enclosed condenses: a delicate veil of drops begins to develop on the inside walls. At first, they are so small that one can distinguish individual drops only at a very close distance. The drops grow—hour by hour—small ones combining with larger ones. The speed of growth depends on the intensity and the angle of the intruding light. After a day, a dense cover of clearly defined drops has developed, and they all reflect light. As the condensation continues, some drops reach such a size that their weight overcomes the forces of adhesion and they run down the walls, leaving a trace.

This trace starts to grow together again. Weeks after, manifold traces, running side by side, have developed. The size of the drop varies according to its age. The process of condensation does not end. The box has a constantly but slowly changing appearance, which never repeats itself. The conditions are comparable to a living organism that reacts in a flexible manner to its surroundings. The image of condensation cannot be precisely predicted. It changes freely, bound only by statistical limits. I like this freedom.

Hans Haacke, New York, October 1965

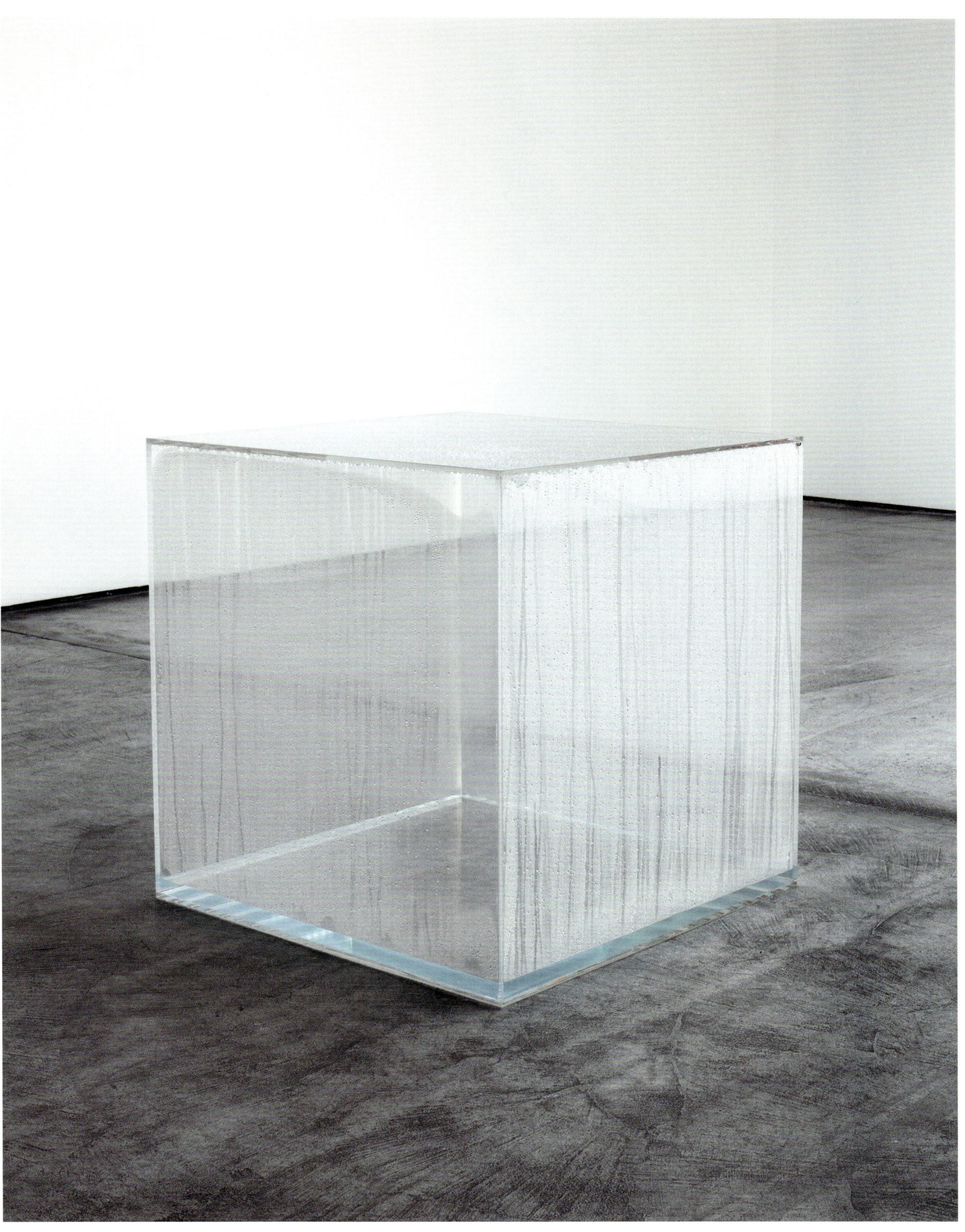

Large Condensation Cube, 1963–67

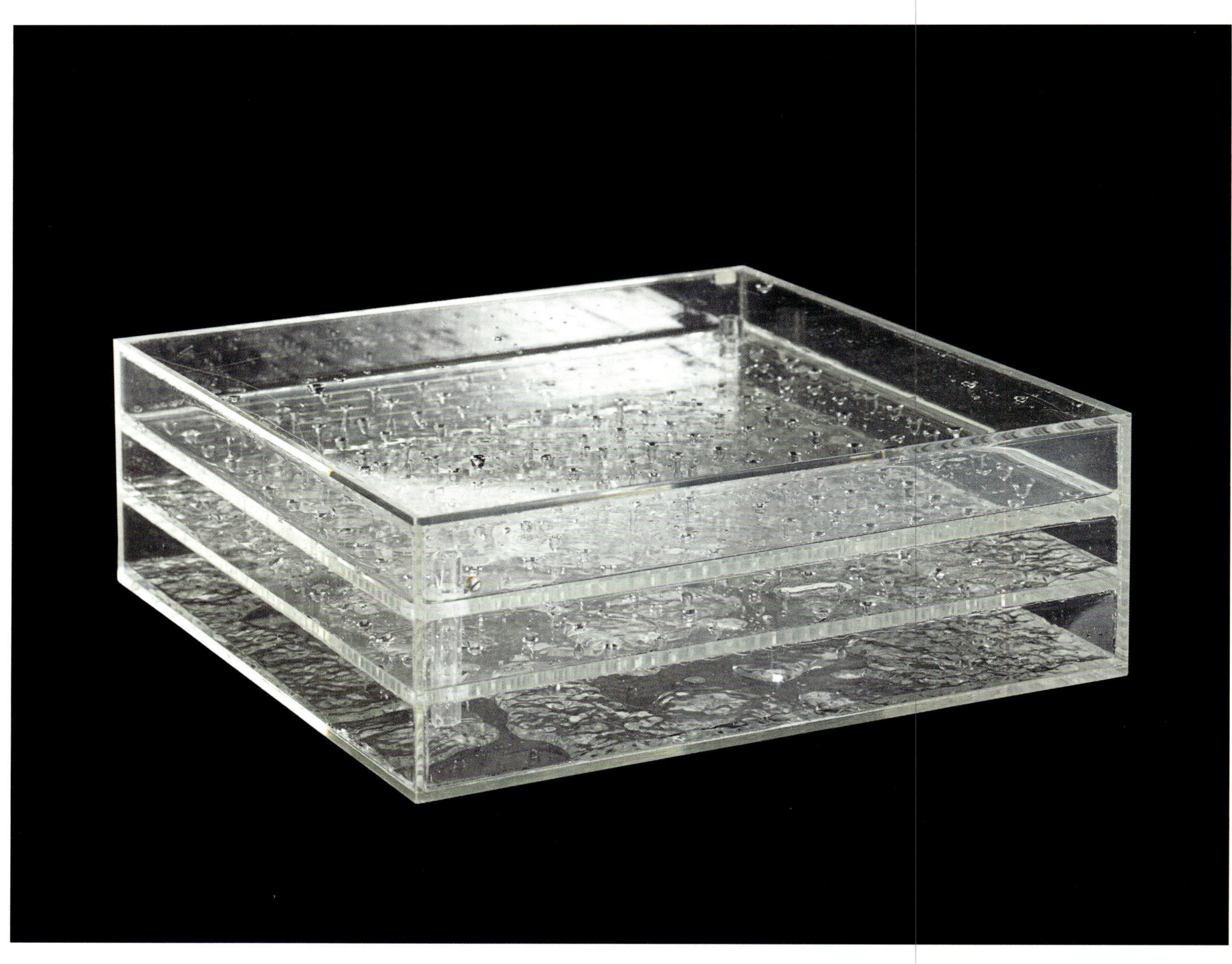

Double Decker Rain, 1963

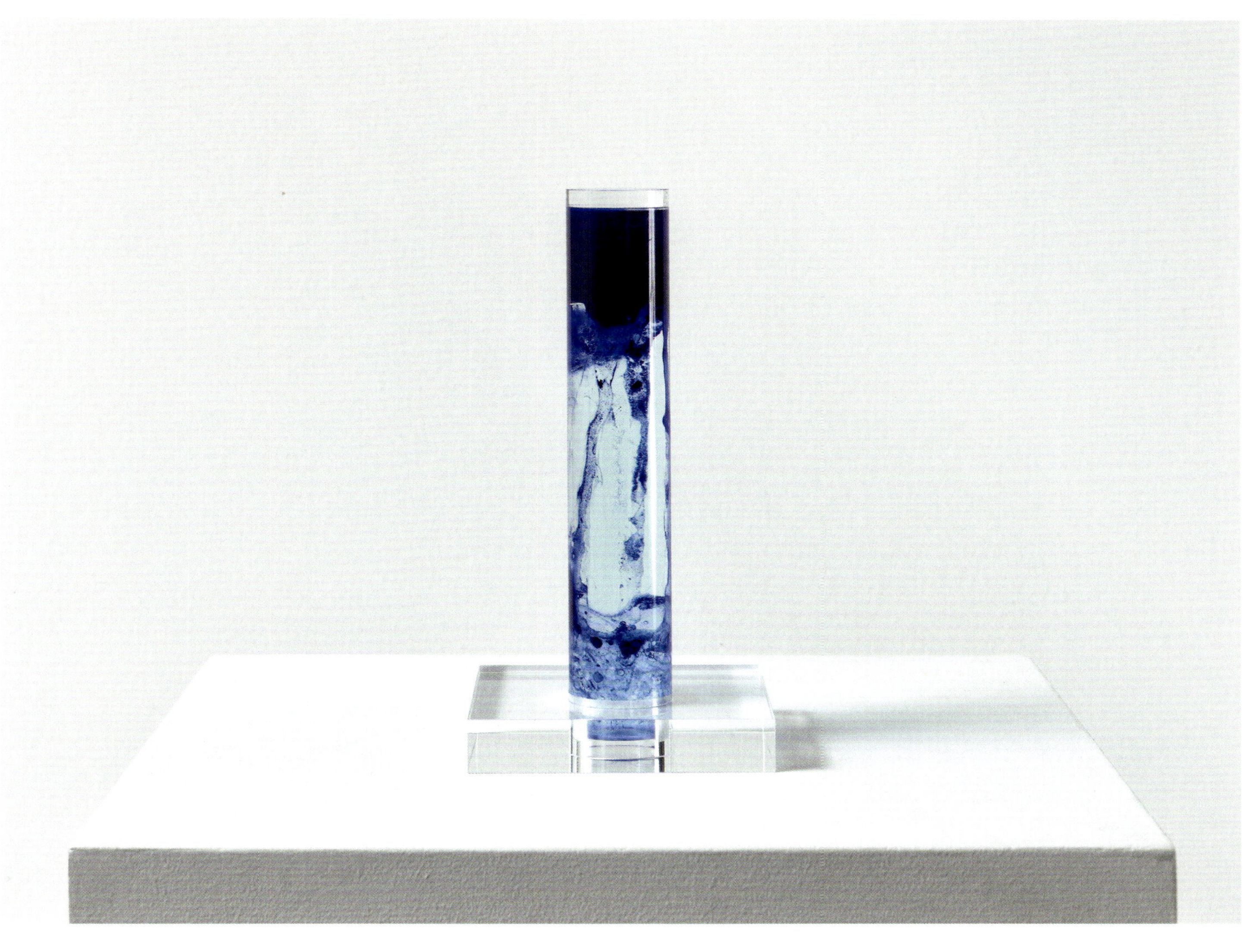

Column with Two Immiscible Liquids, 1965

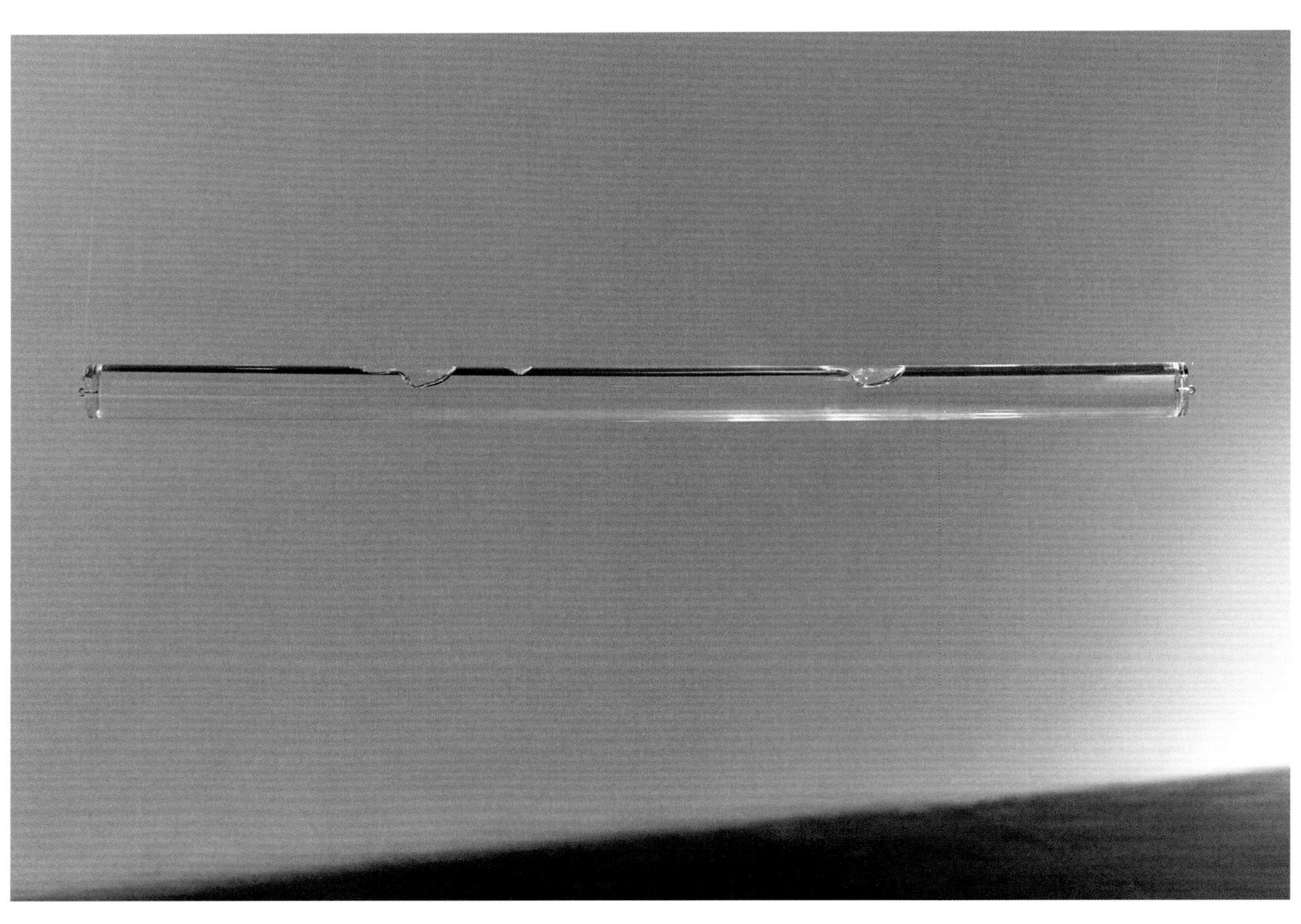

Large Water Level, 1964–65

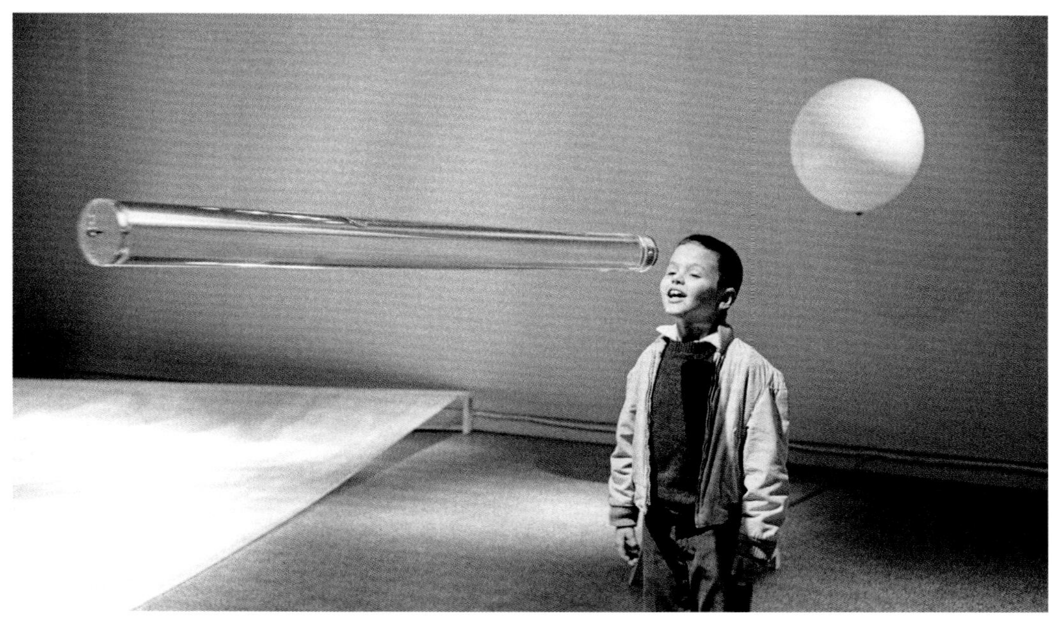

Large Water Level, 1964–65
Installation view, MIT Cambridge, Massachusetts, 1967

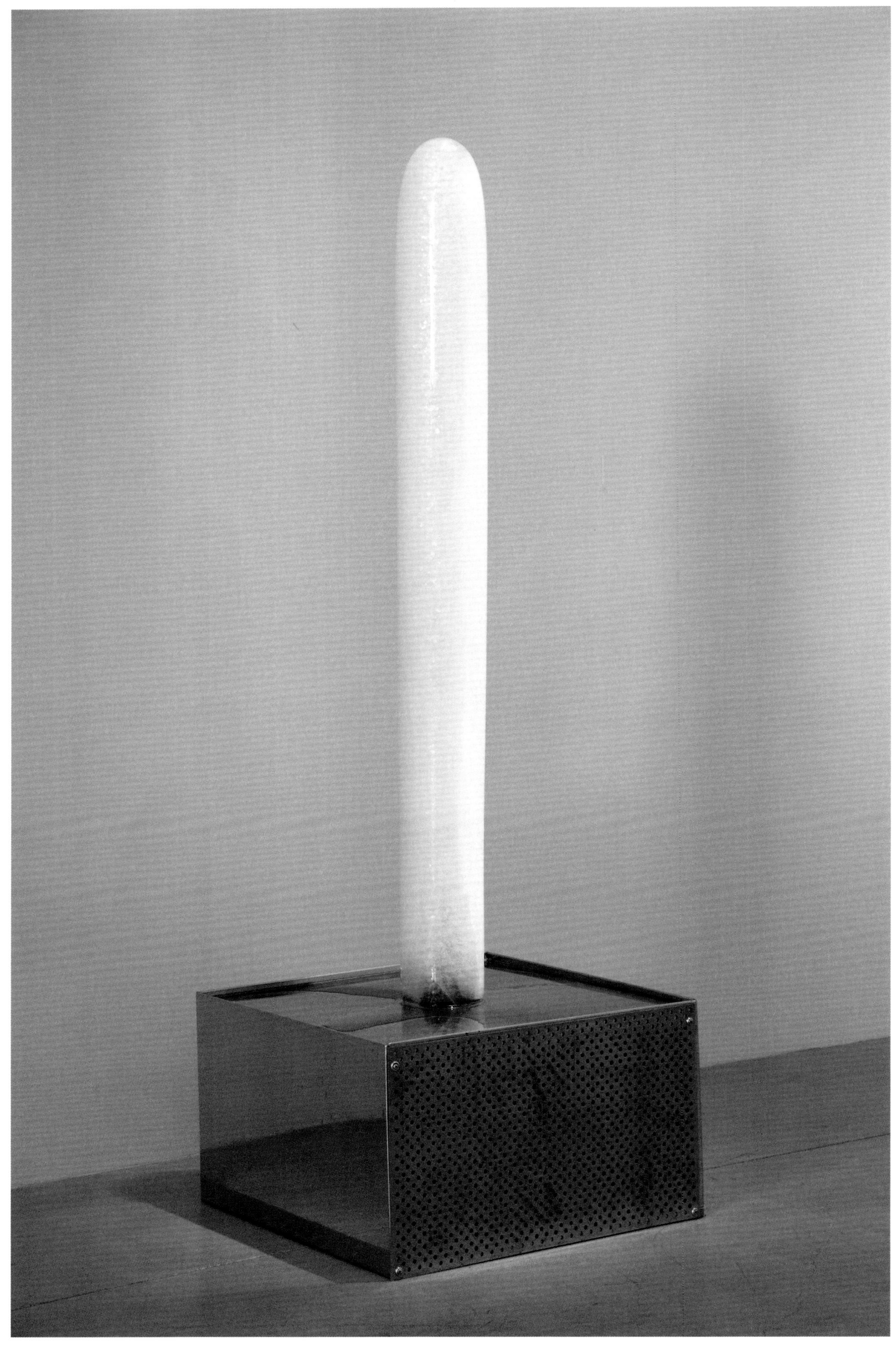

Ice Stick, 1966

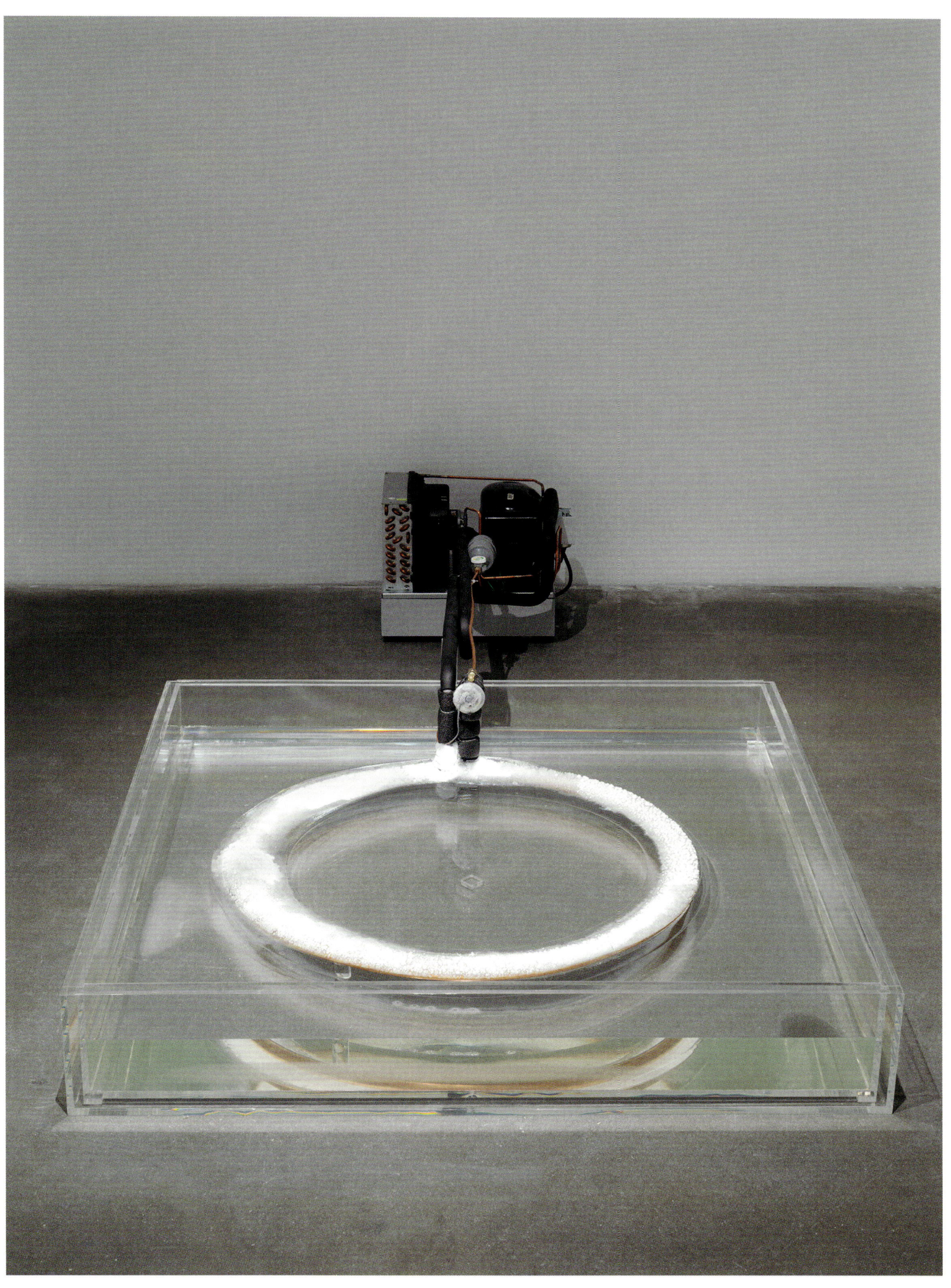

Floating Ice Ring, 1970

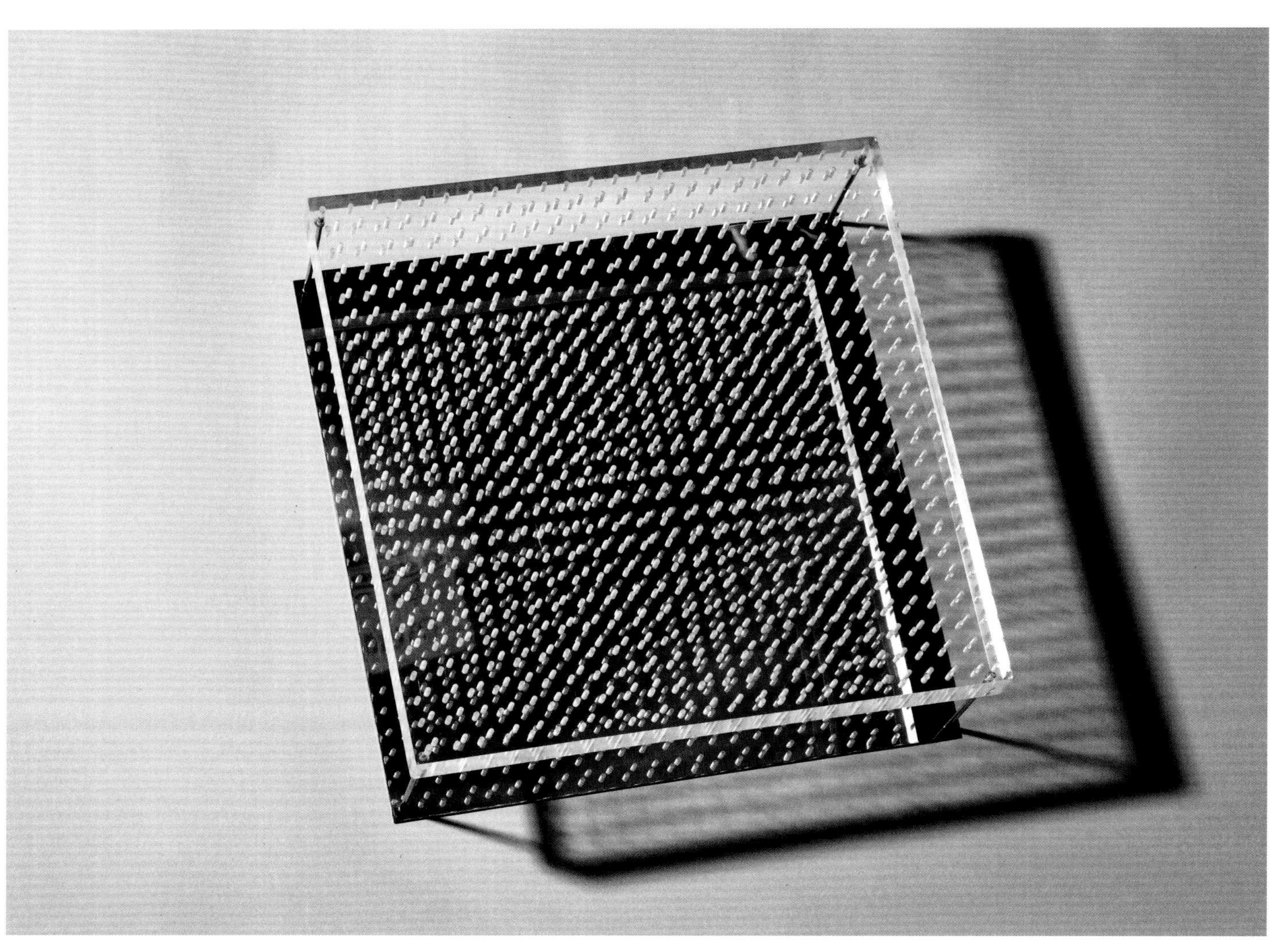

Les Couloirs de Marienbad (The Corridors of Marienbad), 1962

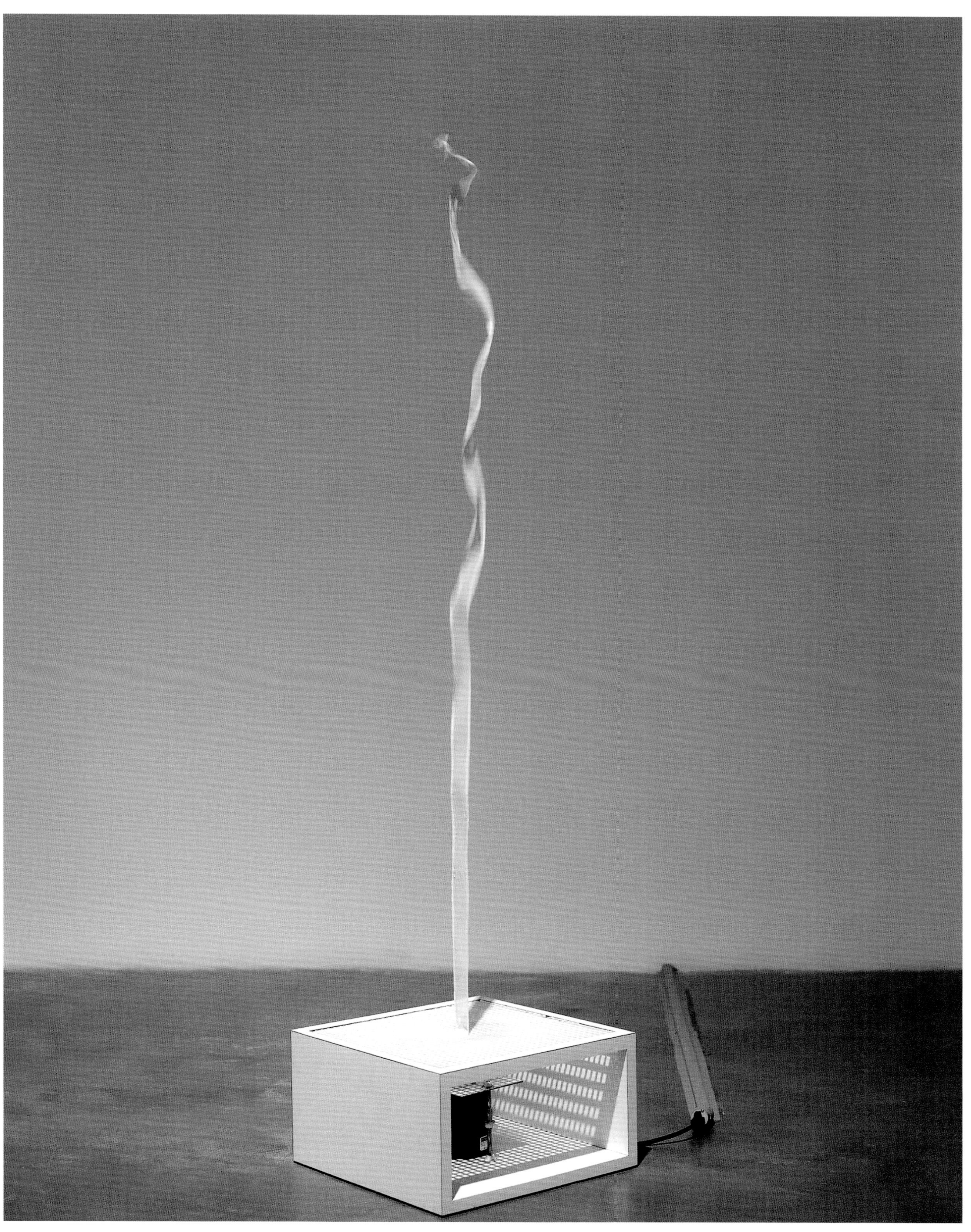

White Waving Line, 1967

Sphere in Oblique Air Jet, 1964

In talking about nature, we most often think only in terms of trees, the blue sky, etc., and not of the underlying forces and patterns of organization. Neither do we immediately realize that these same conditions are the basis of all technological achievements. An airplane is subject to the same aerodynamic laws as the seagull. We seem to be so accustomed to looking at the gestalt of natural phenomena and interpreting it in a heartwarming, romantic manner that we neglect to perceive the physical laws forming the gestalt.

Hans Haacke, 1964, updated in 2011

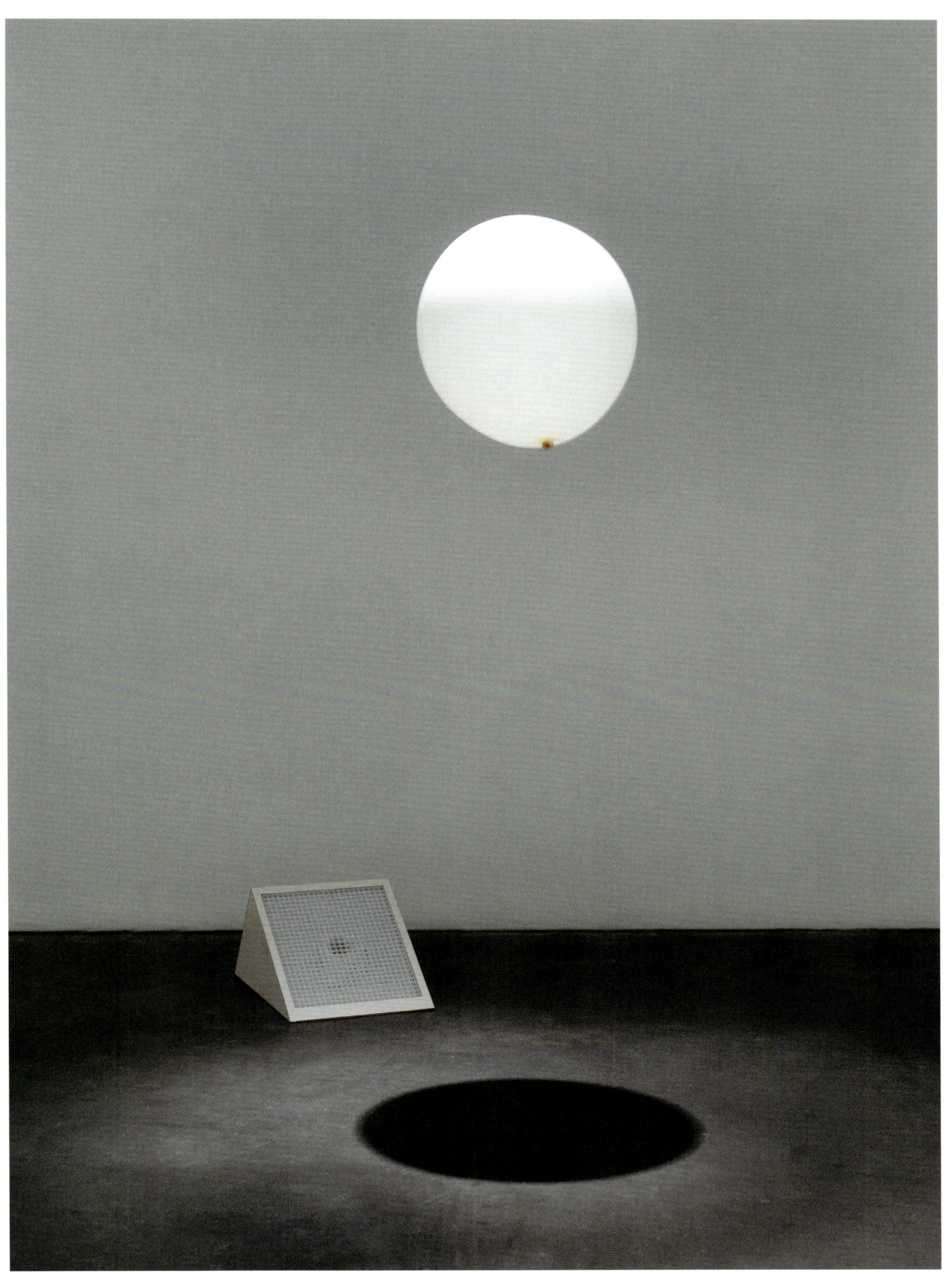

Sphere in Oblique Air Jet, 1964/2011

Blue Sail, 1964–65

If wind blows into a light piece of material, it flutters like a flag or swells like a sail, depending on the way in which it is suspended. The direction of the stream of air and its intensity also determine its movements. None of these movements are without an echo from the others. A common pulse goes through the membrane. The swelling on one side makes the other side recede; tensions arise and decrease. The sensitive fabric reacts to the slightest changes in air conditions. A gentle draft makes it swing lightly; a strong air current allows it to swell almost to the bursting point or pulls so that it furiously twists itself about. Since many factors are involved, no movement can be predicted precisely.

The wind-driven fabric behaves like a living organism, all parts of which constantly influence each other. The unfolding of the organism in a harmonious manner depends on the intuitiveness and skill of the »wind player.« Their means to reach the essential character of the material are manipulations of the wind sources and the shape and method of suspending the fabric. Their materials are wind and flexible fabric; their tools are the laws of nature. The sensitivity of the wind player determines whether the fabric is given life and breathes.

Hans Haacke, Cologne, August 1965

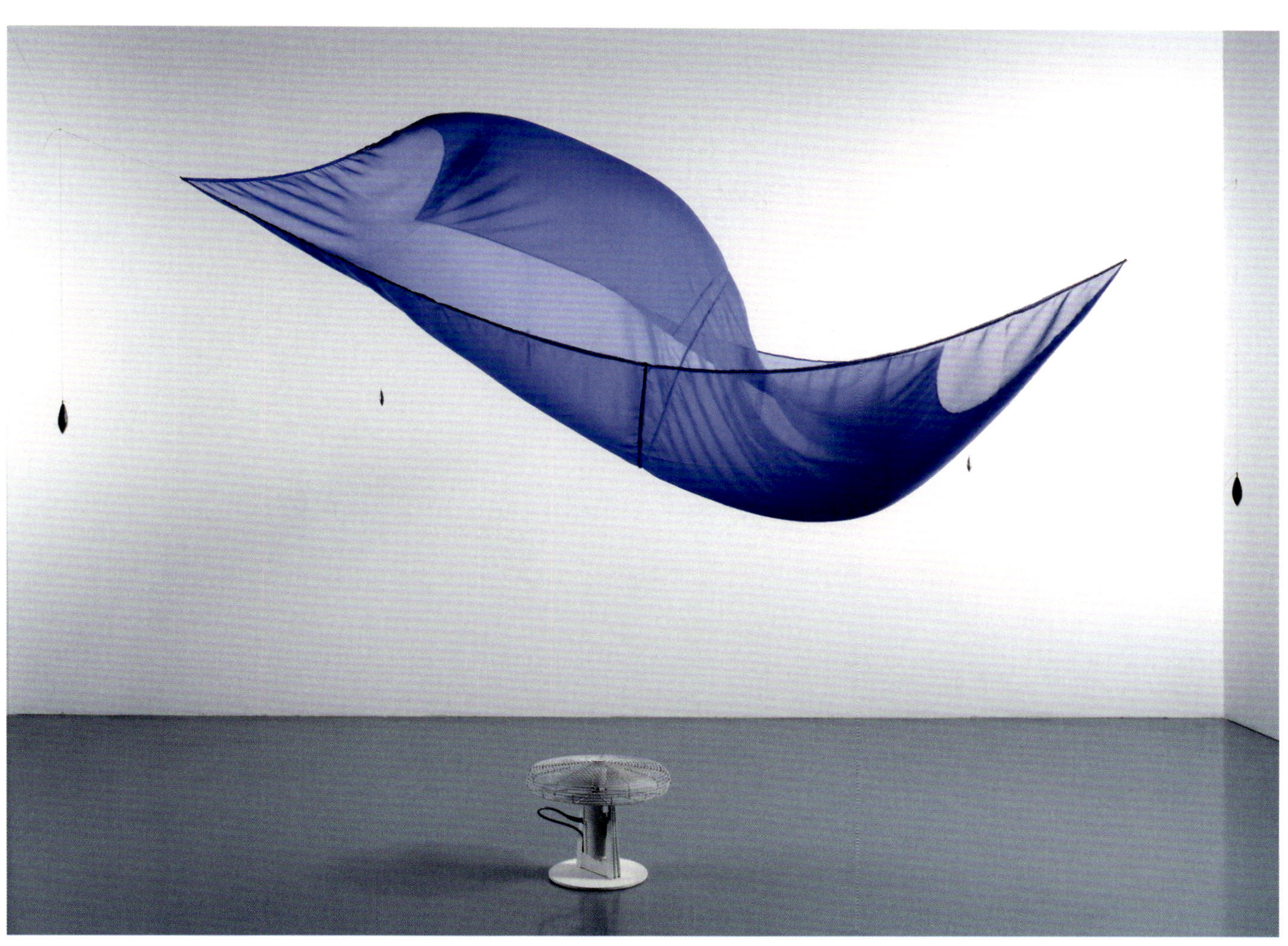

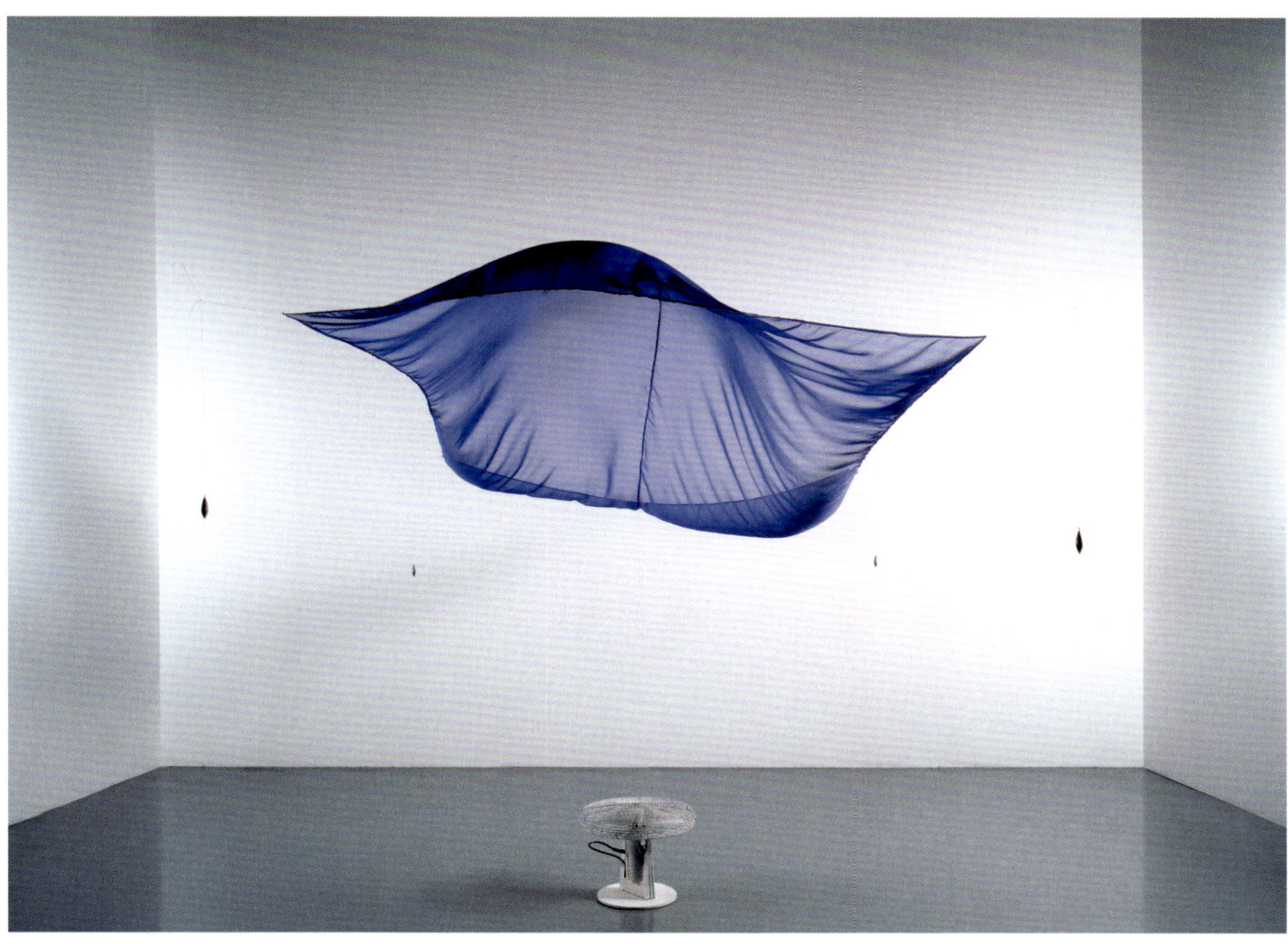

Blue Sail, 1964–65

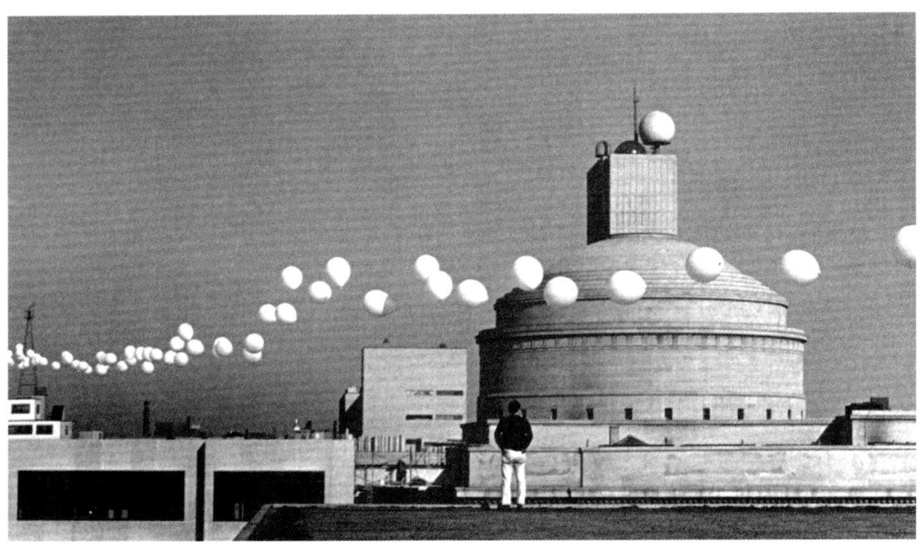

Performance of *Sky Line* in 1967 at MIT, Cambridge, Massachusetts

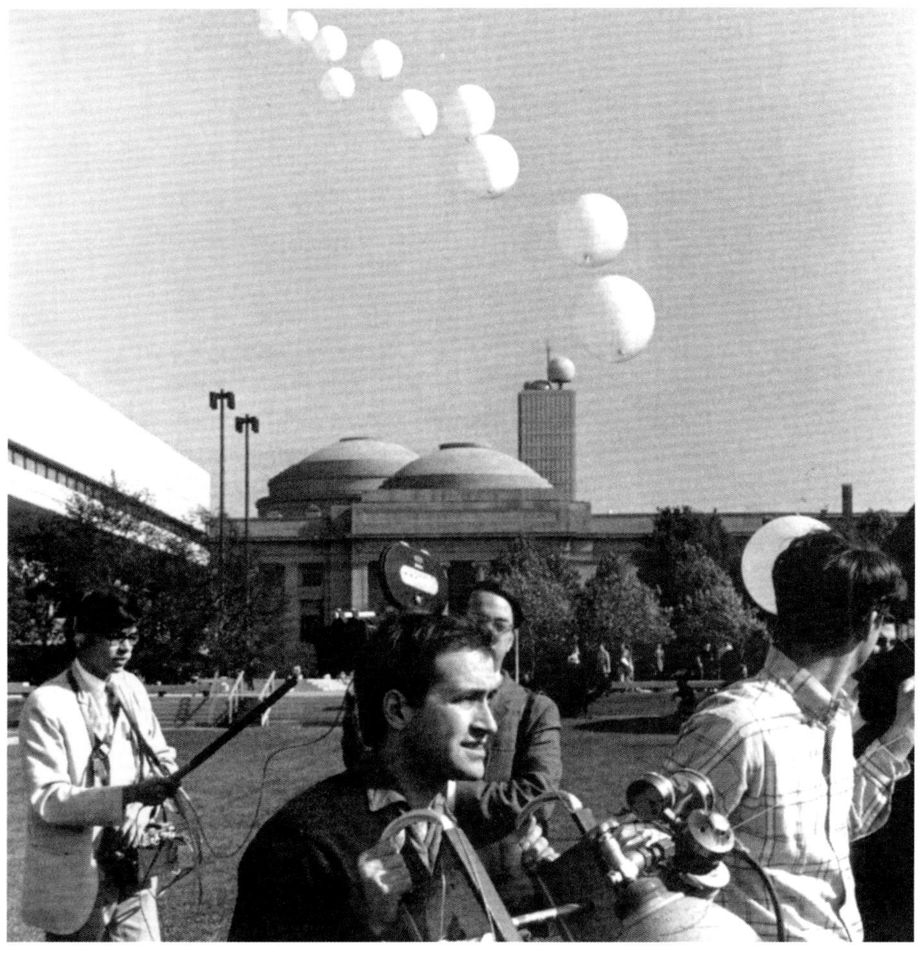

Hans Haacke performing *Sky Line* with students 1967 at MIT, Cambridge, Massachusetts

Following pages: Performance of *Sky Line* in the exhibition *Kinetic Environment 1 and 2* in Central Park, New York, 1967

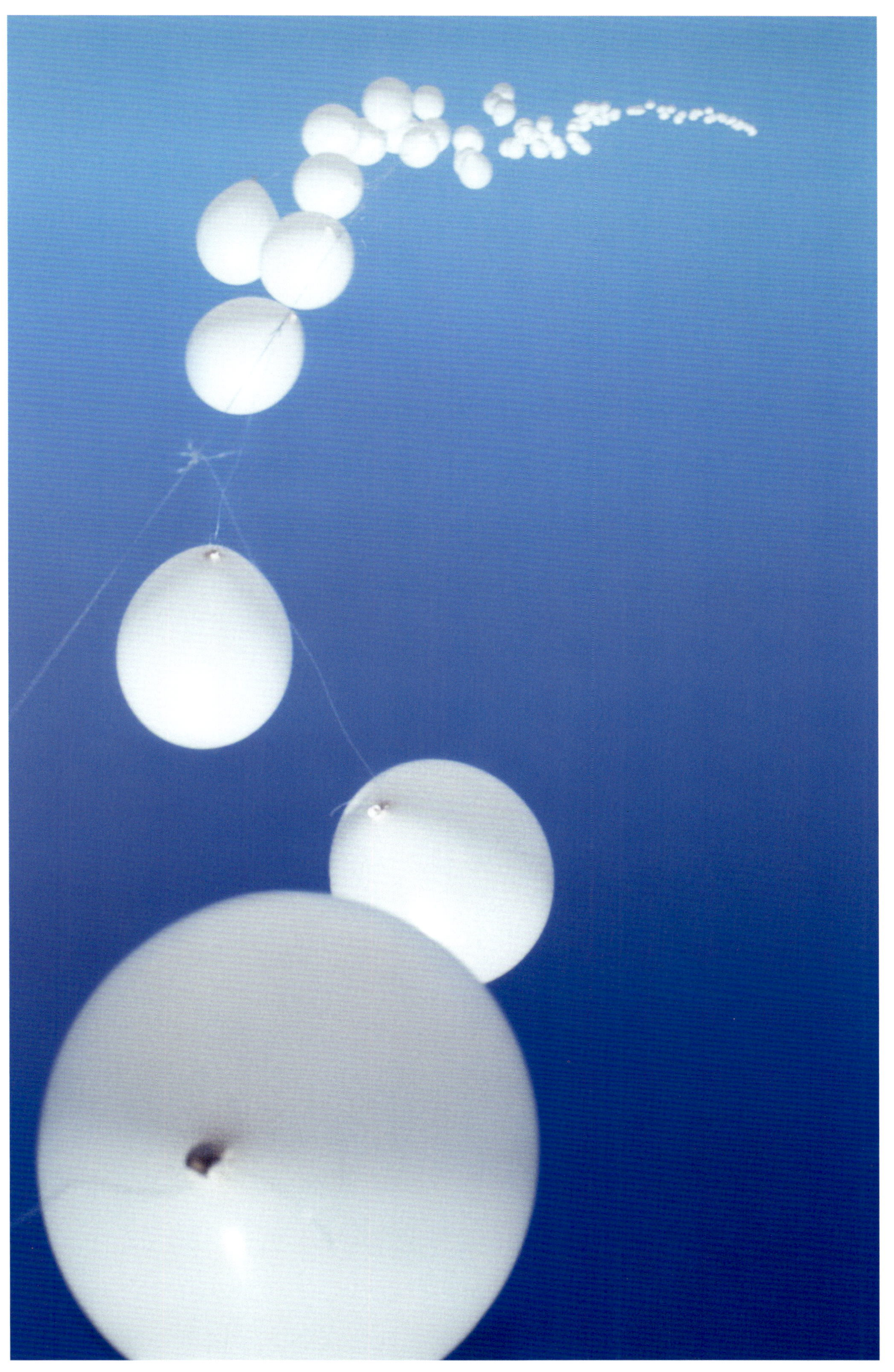

Sky Line, 1967

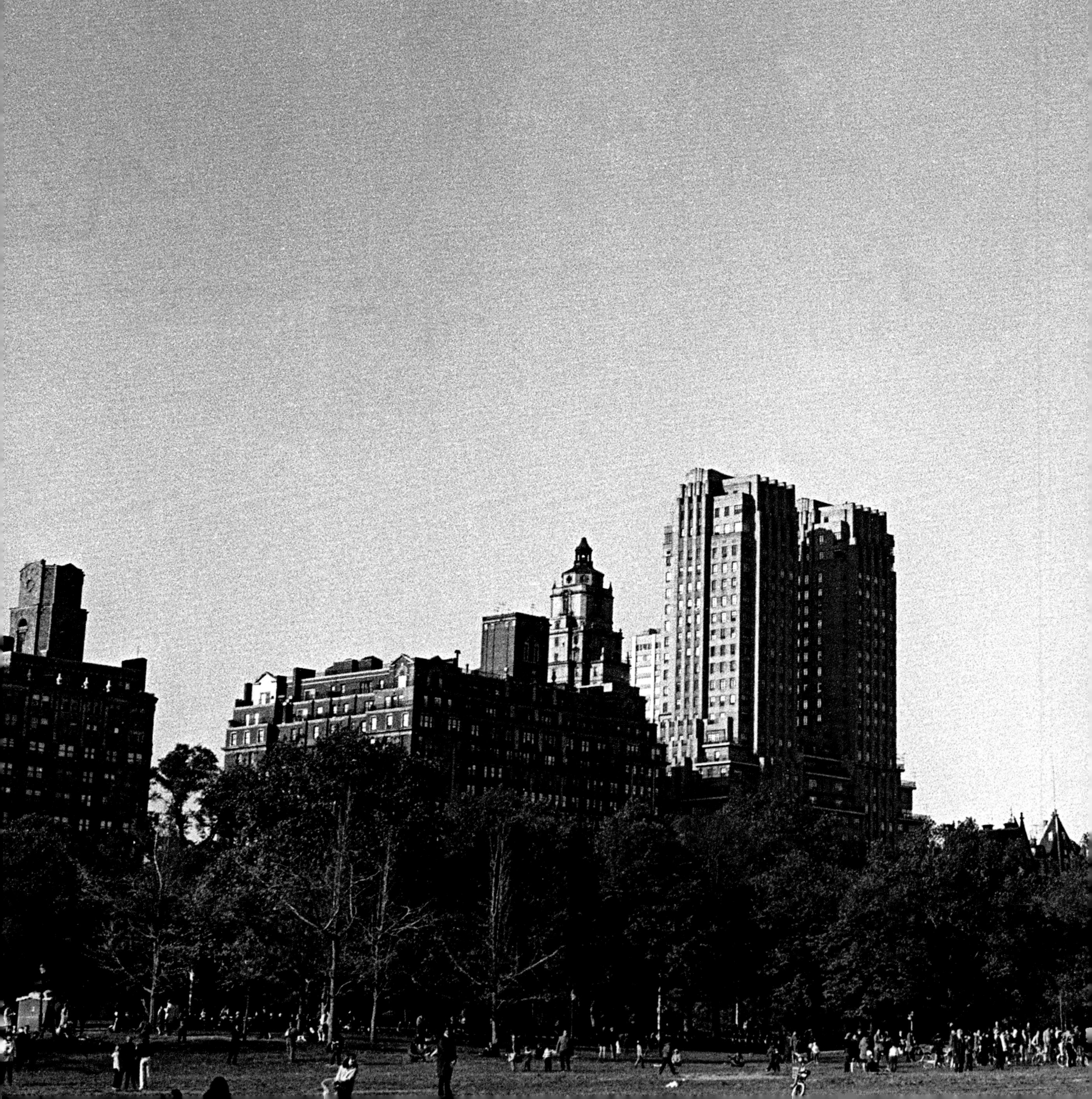

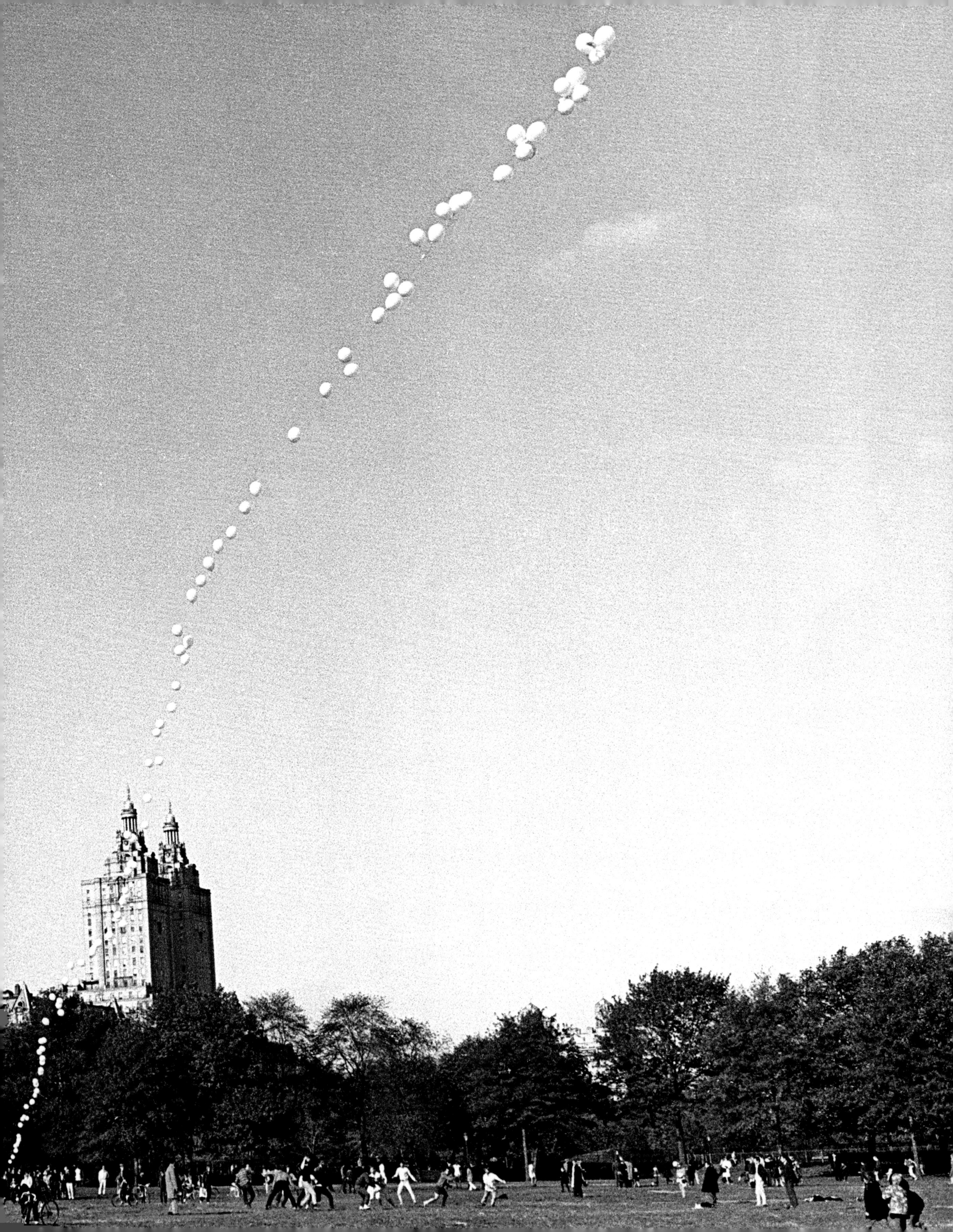

Circulation, 1969

For *Circulation*, I was concerned with having a shape that didn't impose itself as something important. The shape is primarily determined by technical factors: the material comes in plates or rods or tubes—in other words, in a form that mass production and versatility of commercial uses impose. The overriding requirement, however, is that I allow the process to have its way. I have to provide an appropriate container for the water, for example, or create a condition in which what I am aiming for can function best. Consequently, my decisions are not stylistic (inert, hard edge, soft edge, antiform, etc.), but primarily functional. I am not aiming for a particular look, so visual terms do not apply.

Naturally, everyone has preferences that determine what they choose to do and how this will ultimately appear. For instance, I don't like heavy-looking things, so I gravitated toward comparatively immaterial things, visually. That eventually led me to abandon the visual artist's aim of organizing perceptual patterns. If a system can be seen, I don't object to it and I take care of its looks—much the way a mathematician does with an equation. A very important difference between the work of minimal sculptors and my work is that they were interested in inertness, whereas I was concerned with change.

From the beginning, the concept of change has been the ideological basis of my work. All the way down, there's absolutely nothing static . . . nothing that does not change or instigate real change. Most minimal work disregards change. Things claim to be inert, static, immovably beyond time. But the status quo is an illusion, a dangerous illusion politically.

Hans Haacke, 1969

Following page: *Circulation*, 1969 (detail)

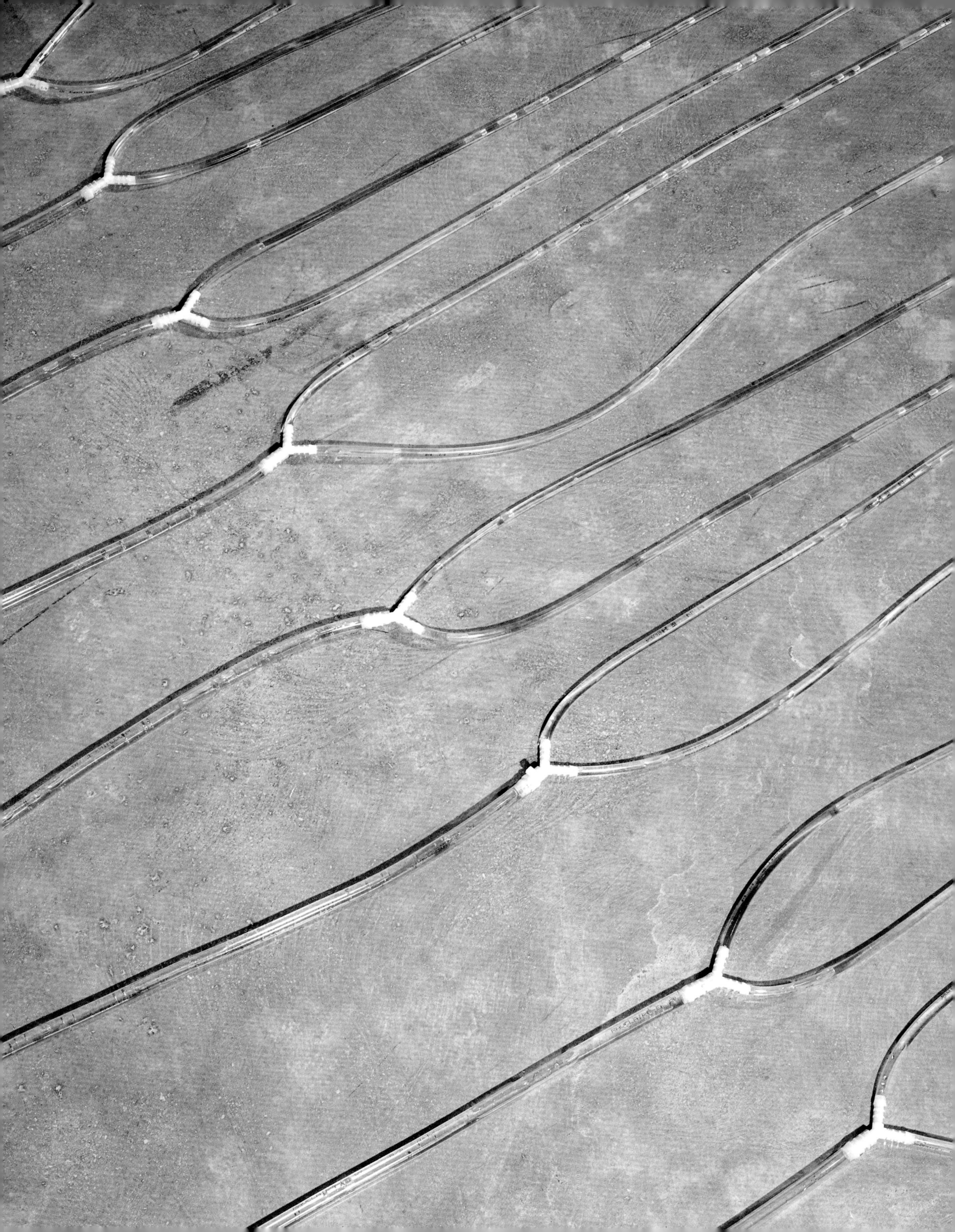

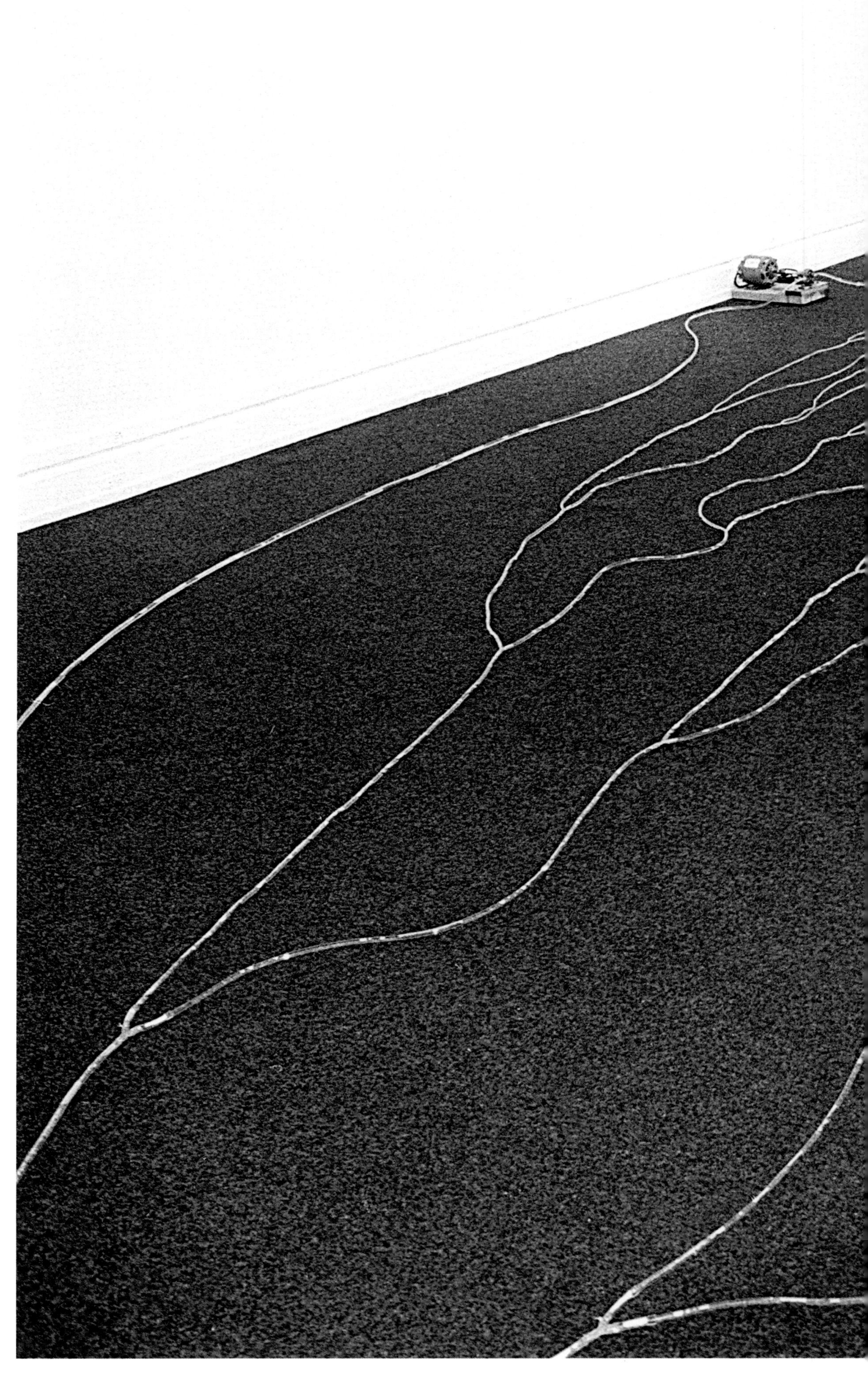

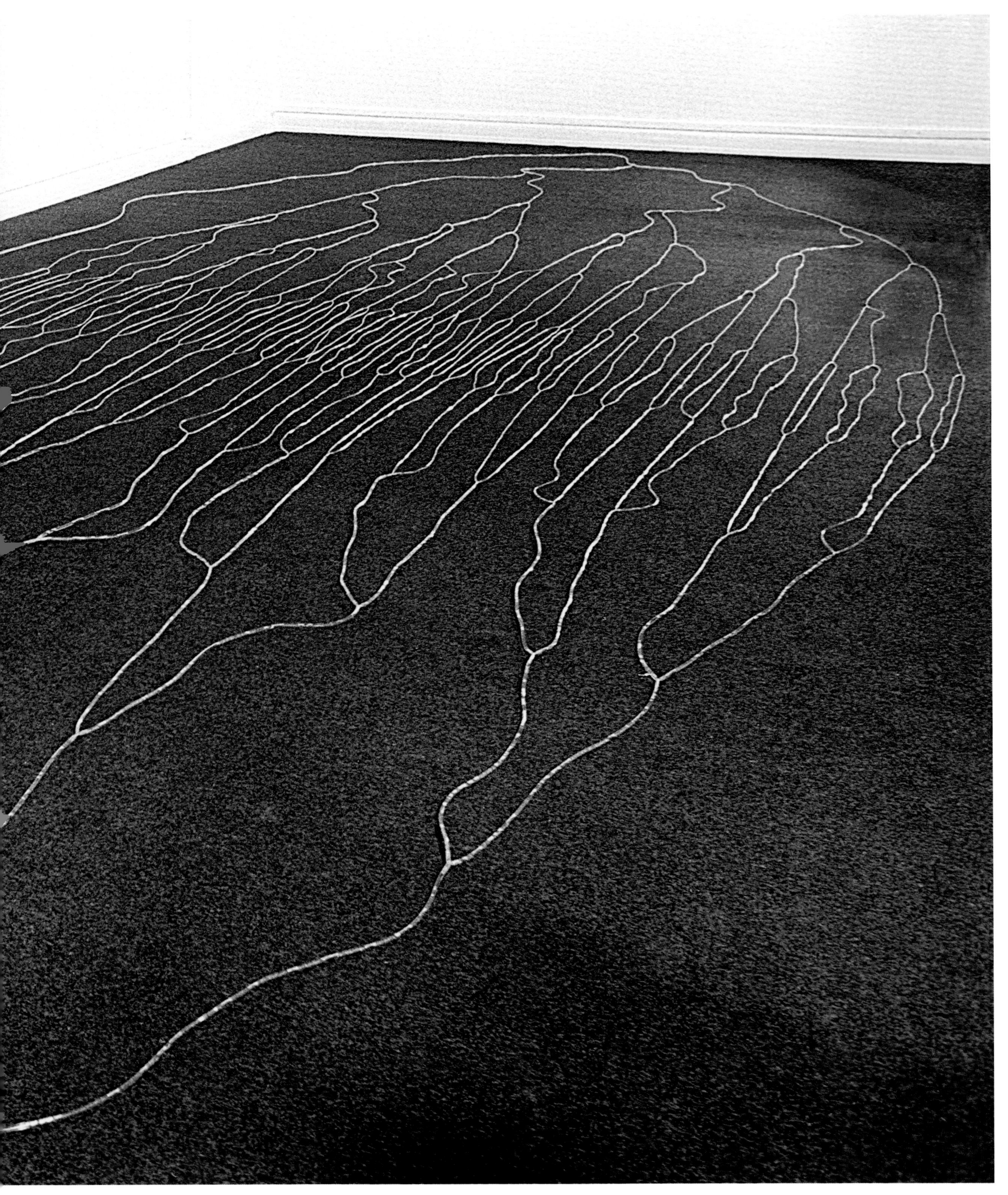

Circulation, 1969

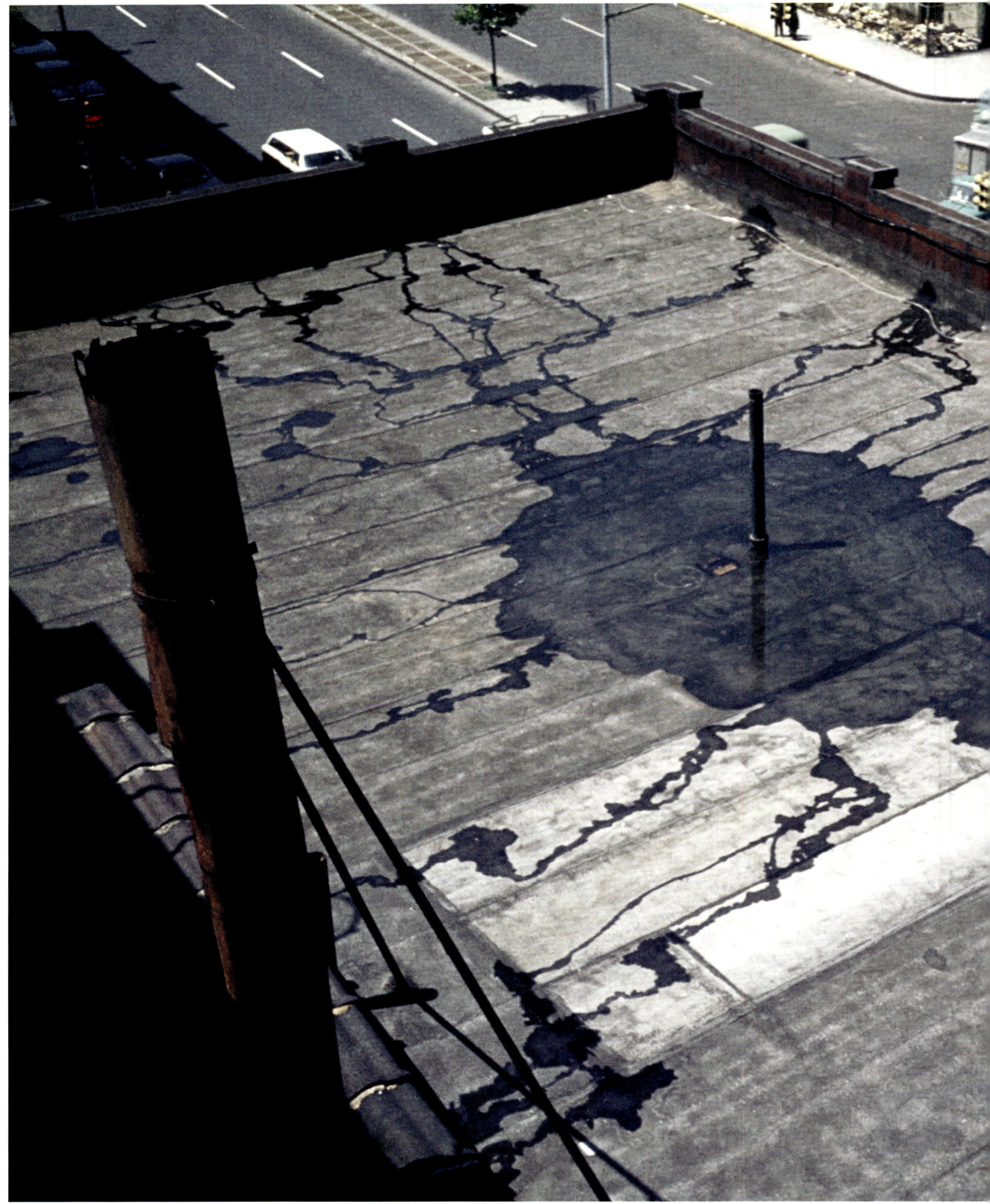

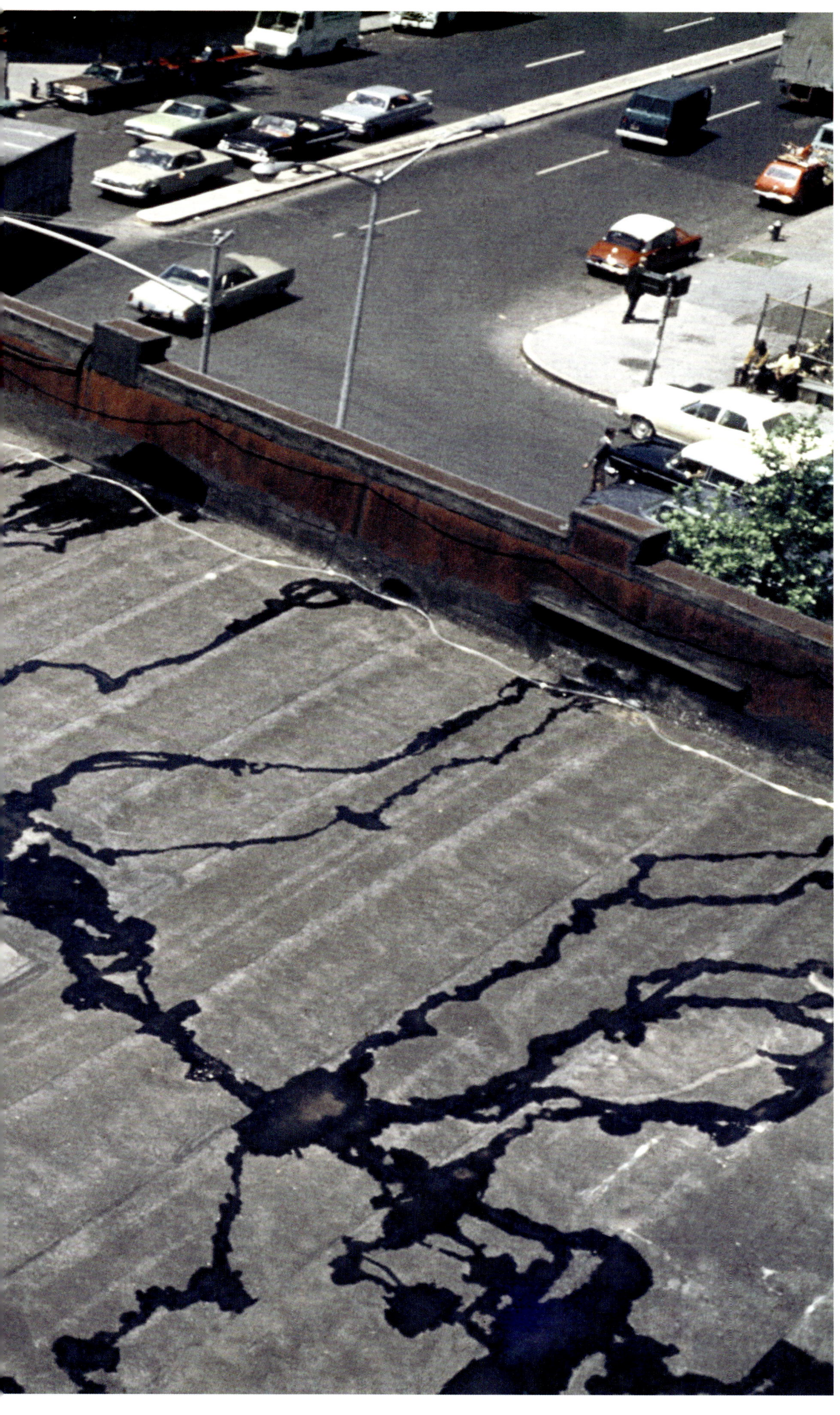

Cycle, 1969

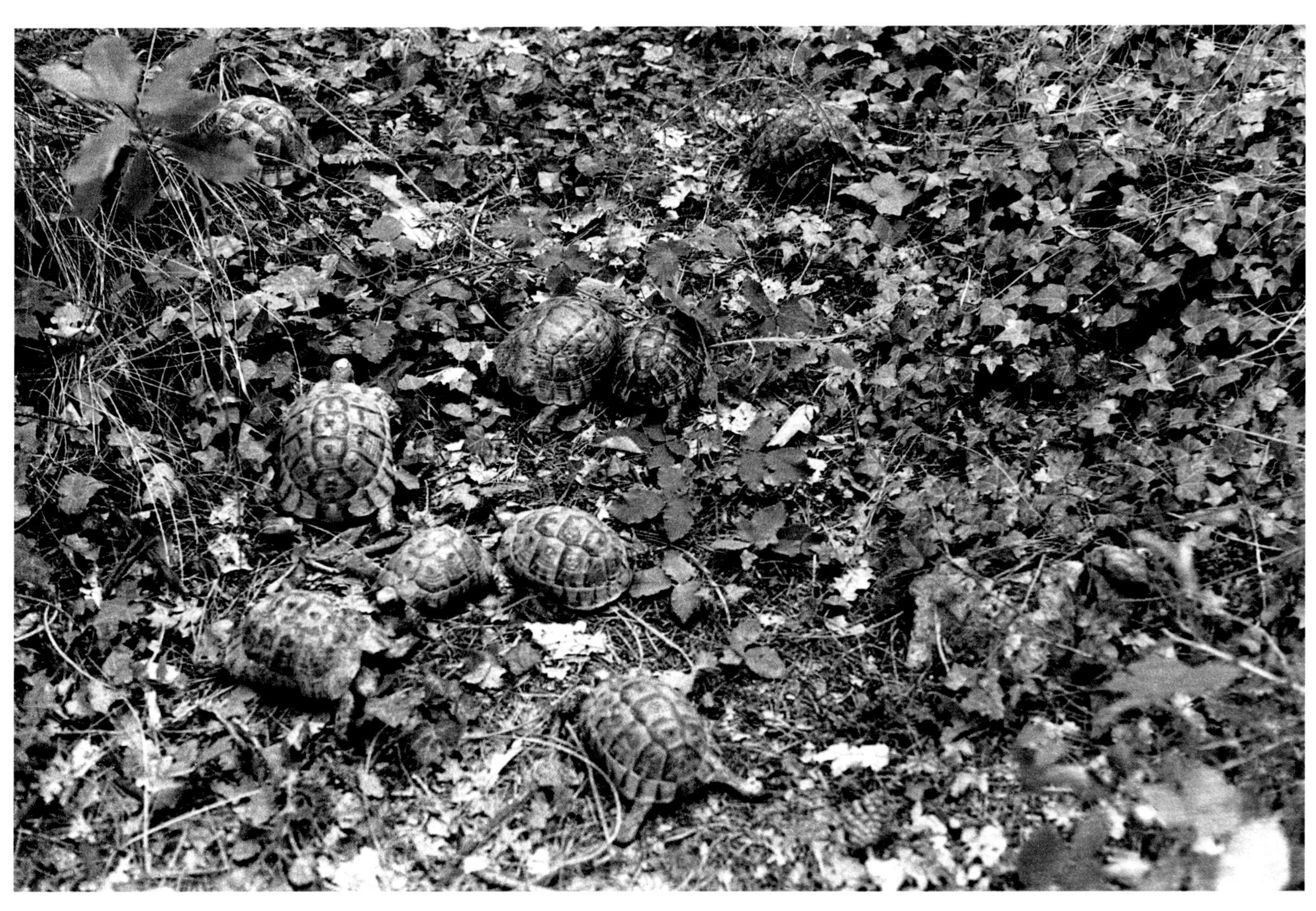

Ten Turtles Set Free, 1970

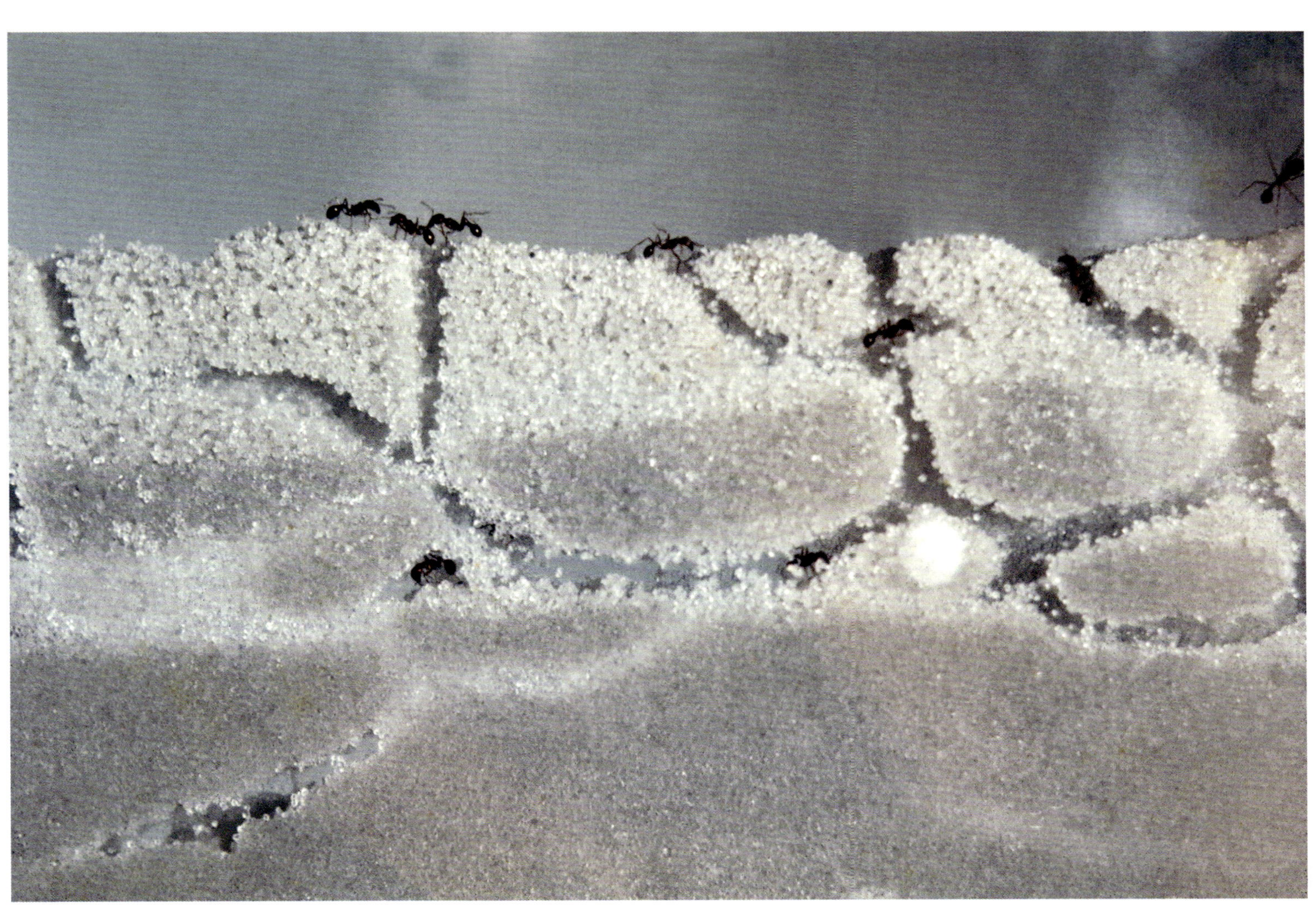

Ant Co-op, 1969
Following pages: *Norbert: All Systems Go*, 1970–71

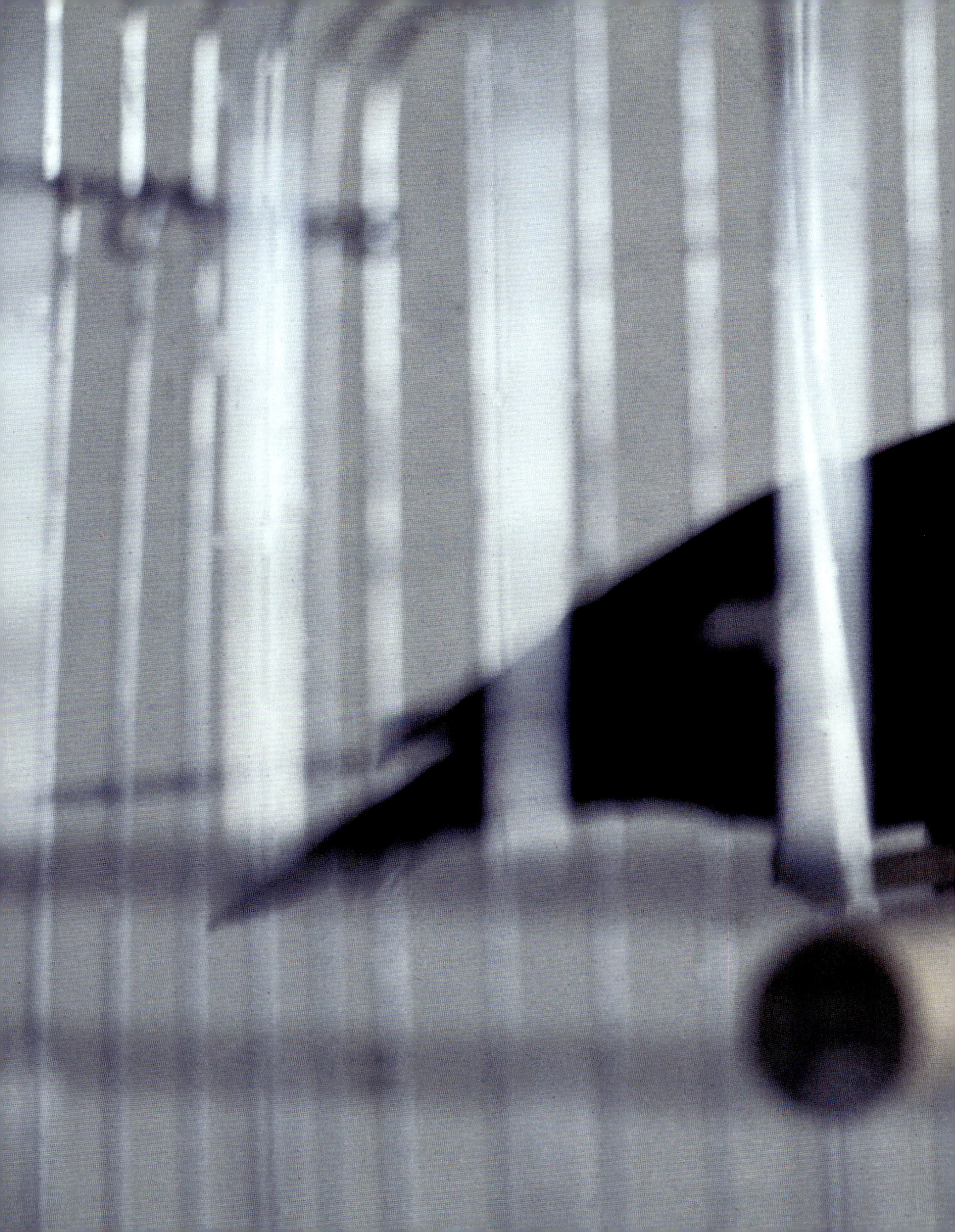

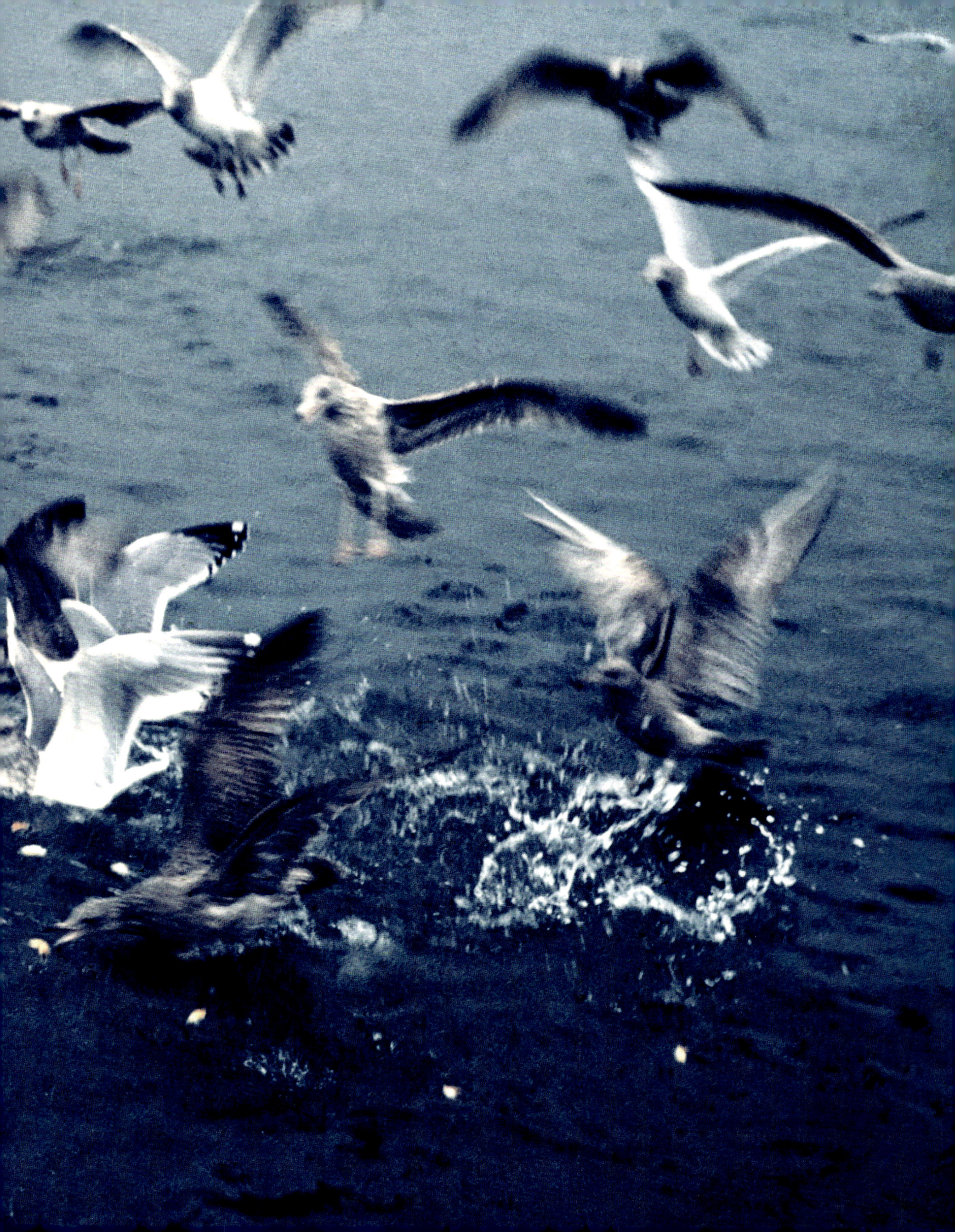

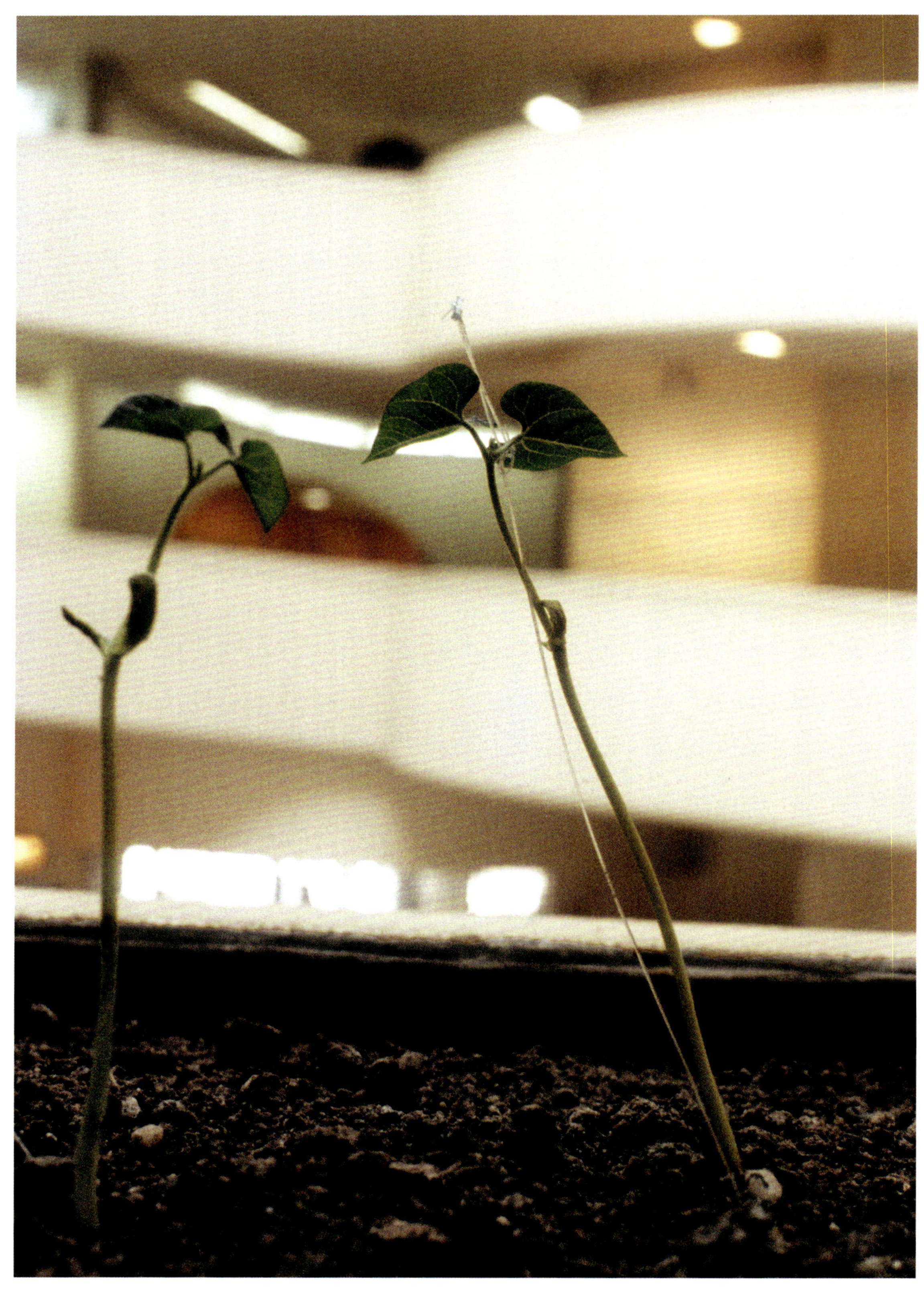

Guggenheim Beans, 1971
beans growing on the first ramp of the Solomon R. Guggenheim Museum, New York, prior to the cancellation of the exhibition, 1971

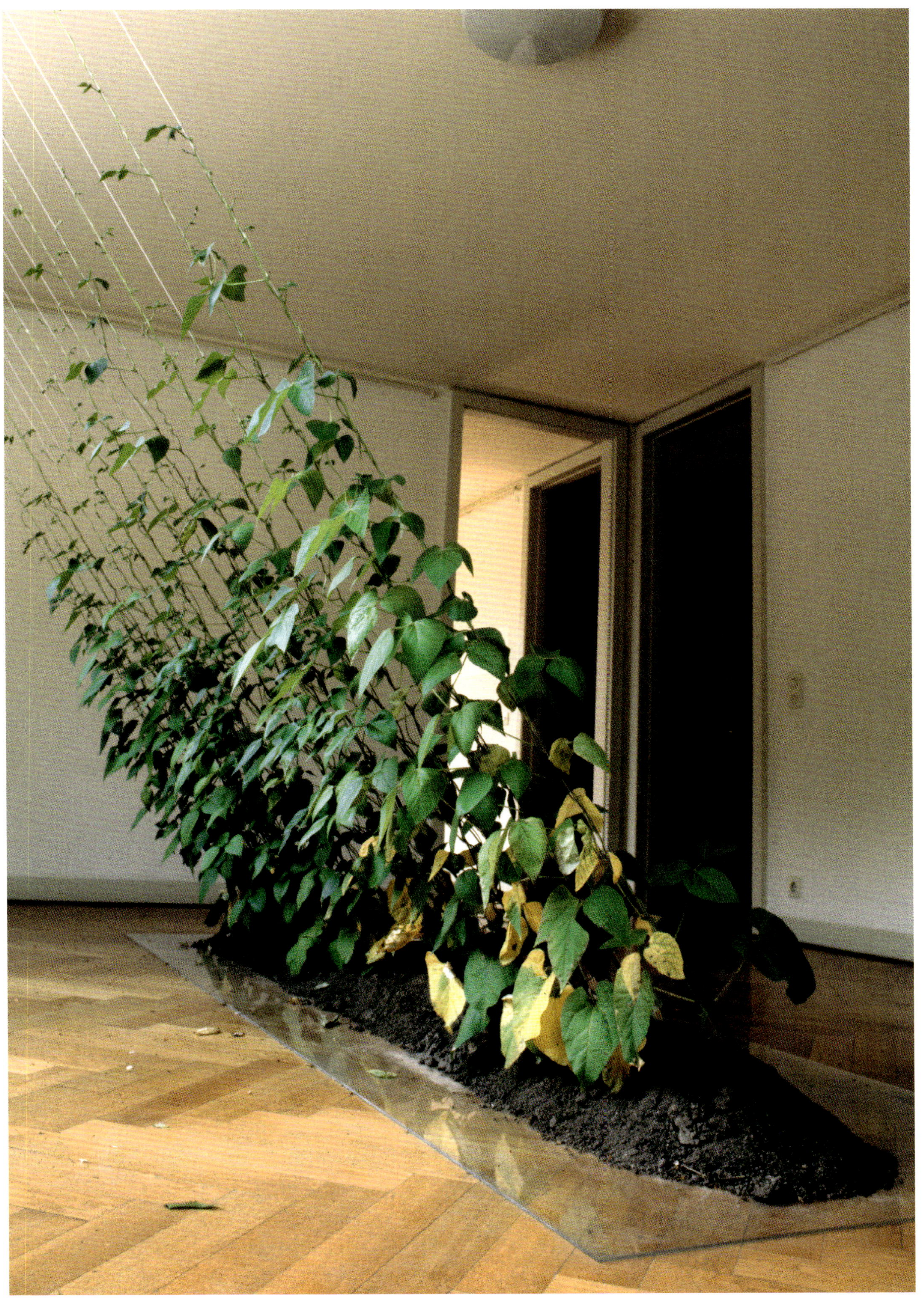

Directed Growth, 1970–72

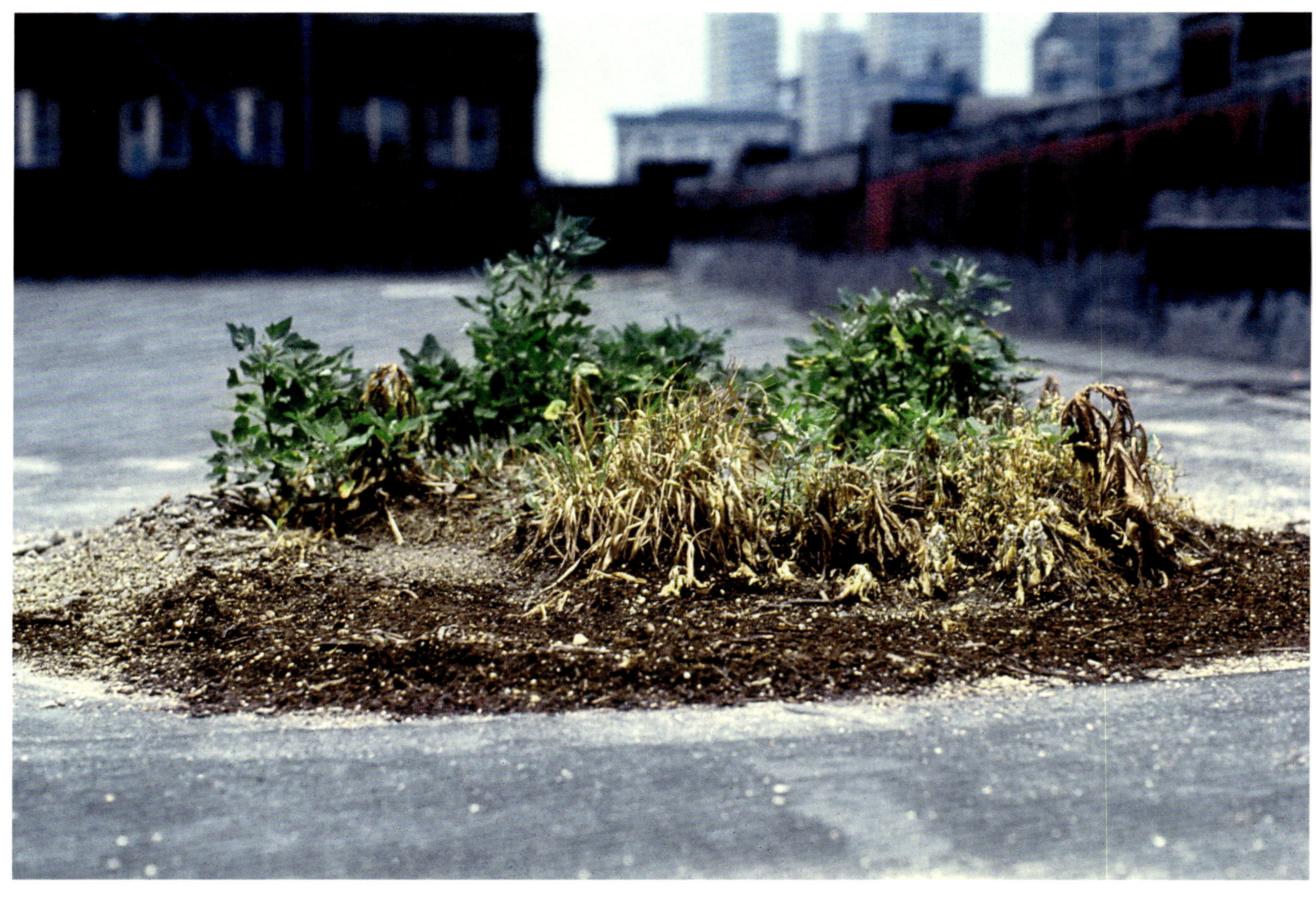

Bowery Seeds, 1970

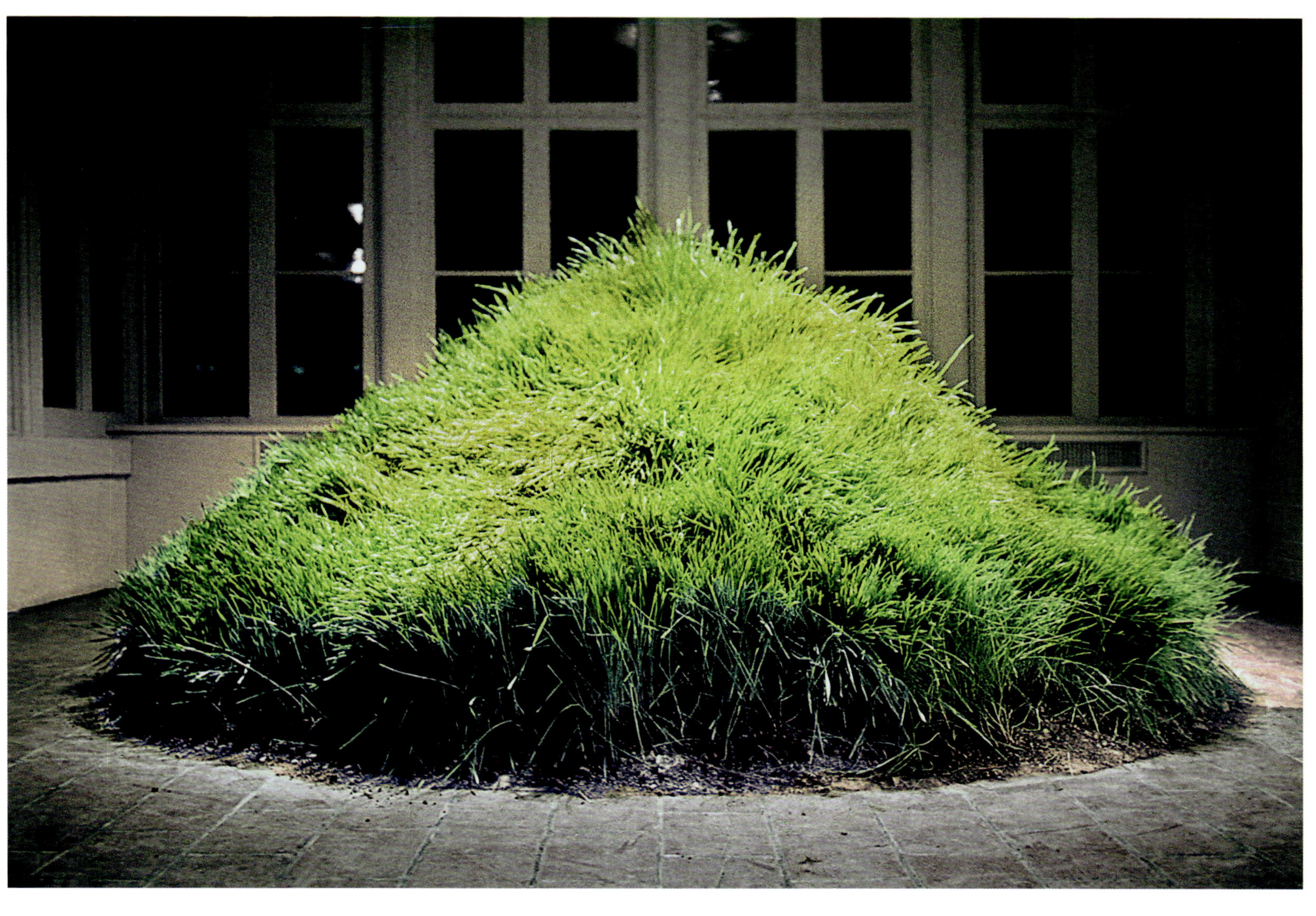

Grass Grows, 1969

Hans Haacke: Self-Portrait of a German Artist in New York, 1969

The artist film *Hans Haacke: Self-Portrait of a German Artist in New York* combines a rapid succession of shots of water droplets, mist, ice, and snow—details from his works of the time—with images of his son, born in the same year, people dancing on Coney Island, and the subway network. Woven into this is the genesis of Haacke's *Live Airborne System*. We observe the artist buying bread in a supermarket, taking it to the beach on Coney Island, and feeding the seagulls drawn to him with breadcrumbs.

Despite their diversity, the images merge to form an abstract narrative, reflecting the idea of systemic equations between nature, culture, and technology. Everything is connected, interacts with each other, and illustrates Haacke's development from static objects to a living, real-time system that reacts to its surroundings and constantly changes. In the absence of any comprehensive explanation, the film still conveys Haacke's artistic adaptation of approaches from systems theory and cybernetics that defined his early work and led to his expanded concept of sculpture.

As Haacke himself put it: »A ›sculpture‹ that physically reacts to its environment is no longer to be regarded as an object. The range of outside factors affecting it, as well as its own radius of action, reach beyond the space it materially occupies. It thus merges with the environment in a relationship that is better understood as a ›system‹ of interdependent processes.« The film portrait was shot by Eila Hershon and Roberto Guerra, and first broadcast on Westdeutscher Rundfunk (WDR) on November 14, 1969.

TDF

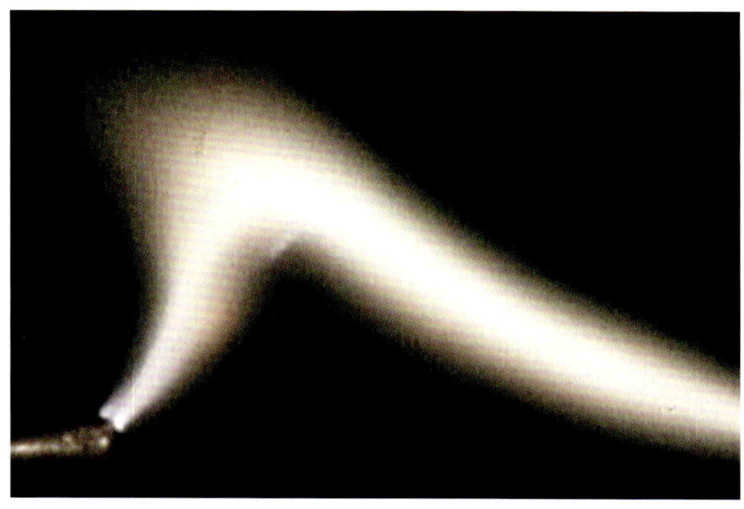
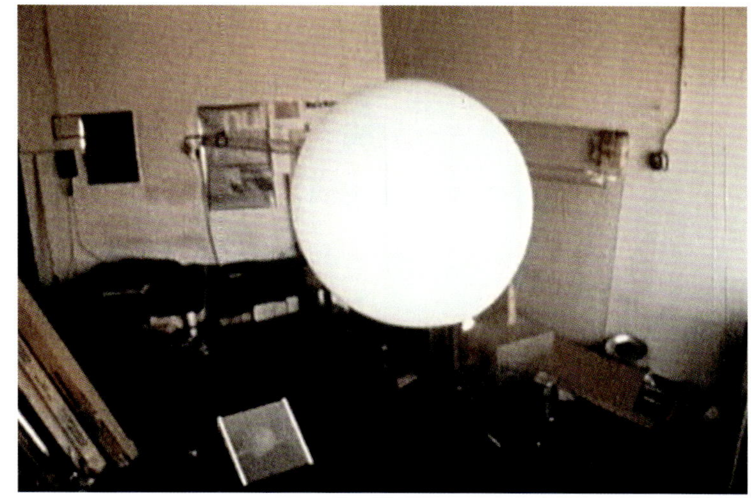
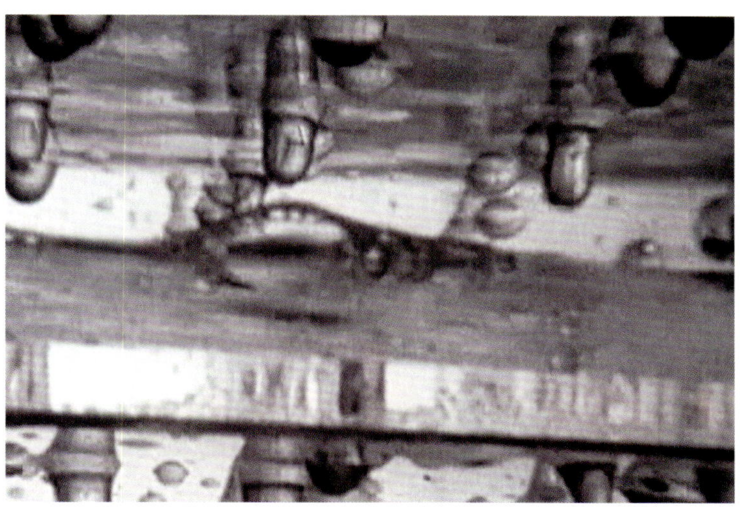
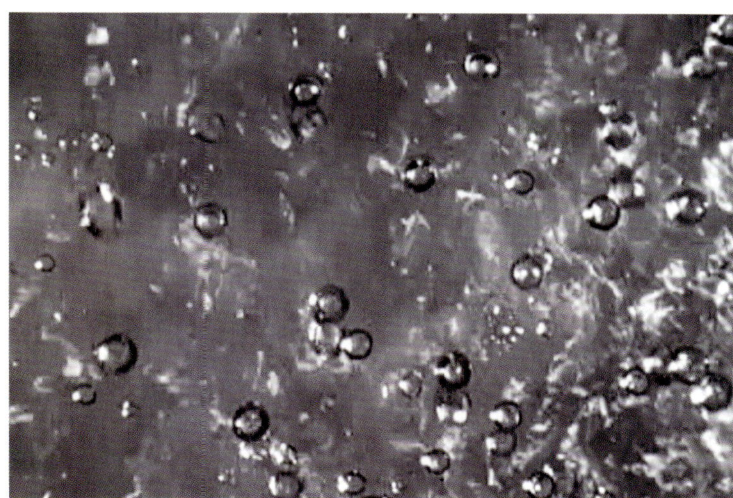
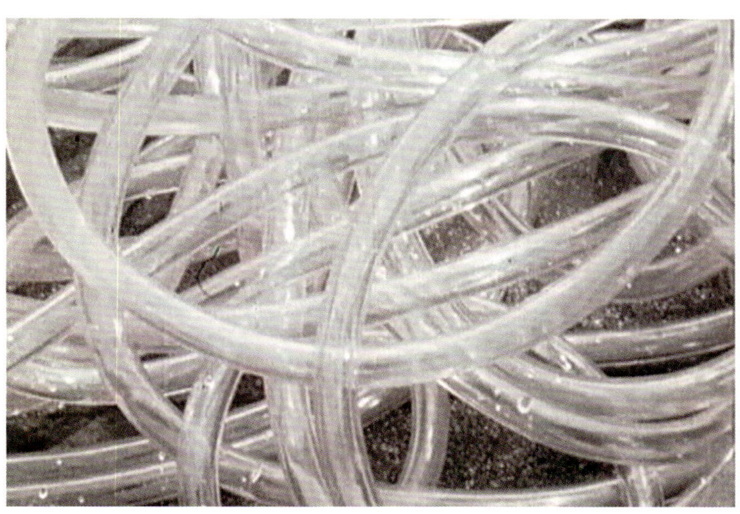
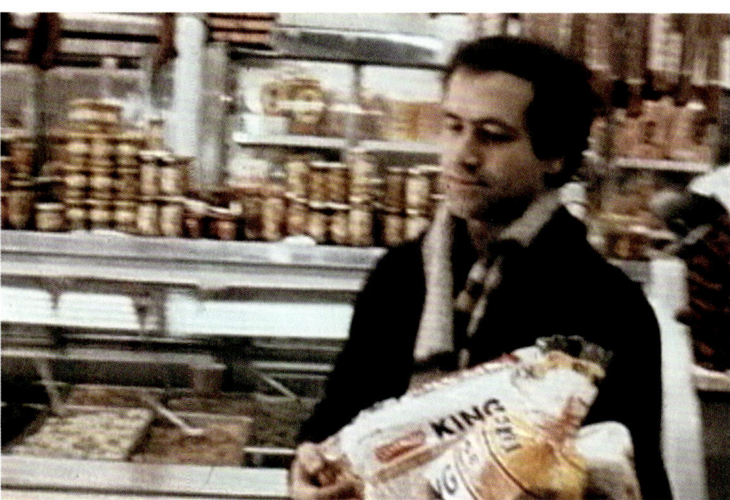

Hans Haacke: Self-Portrait of a German Artist in New York, 1969

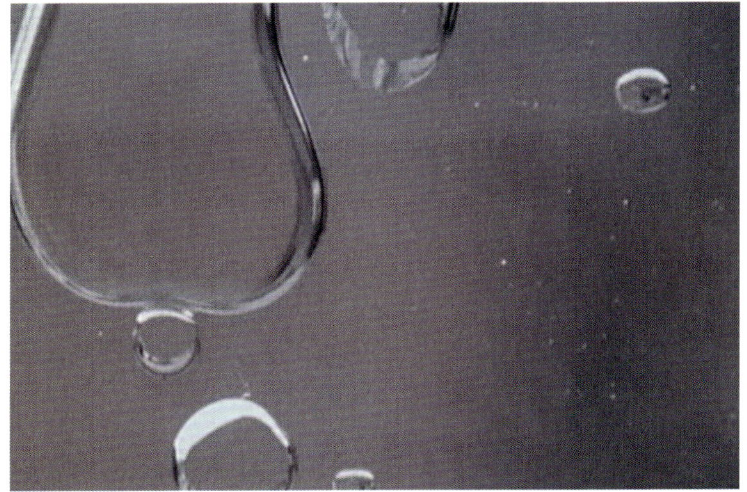

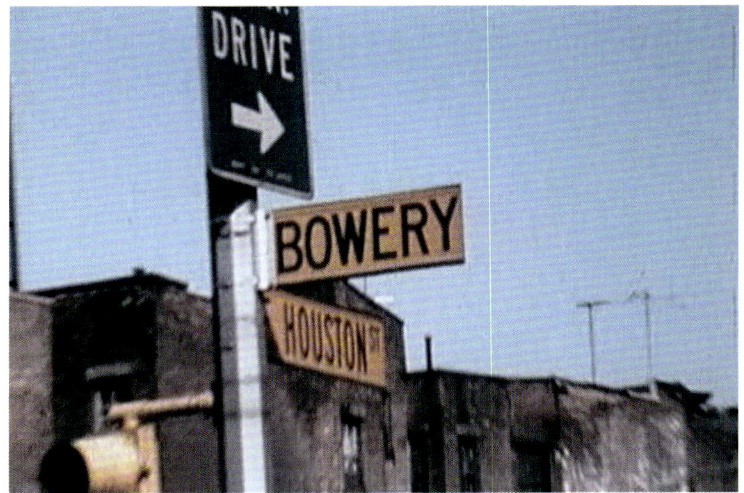

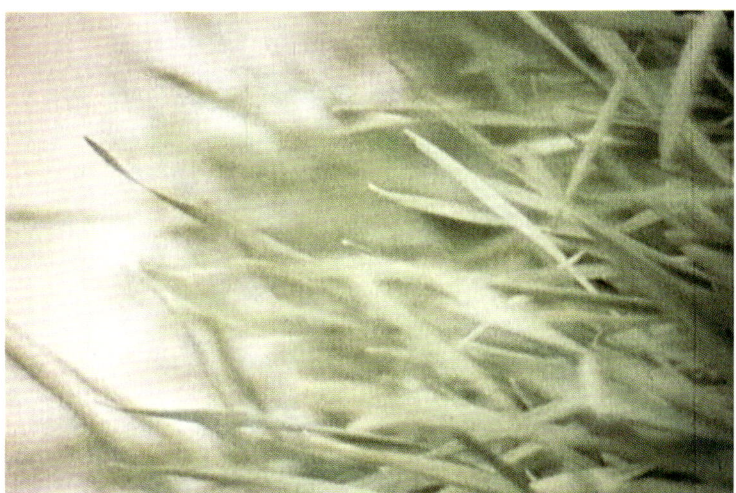

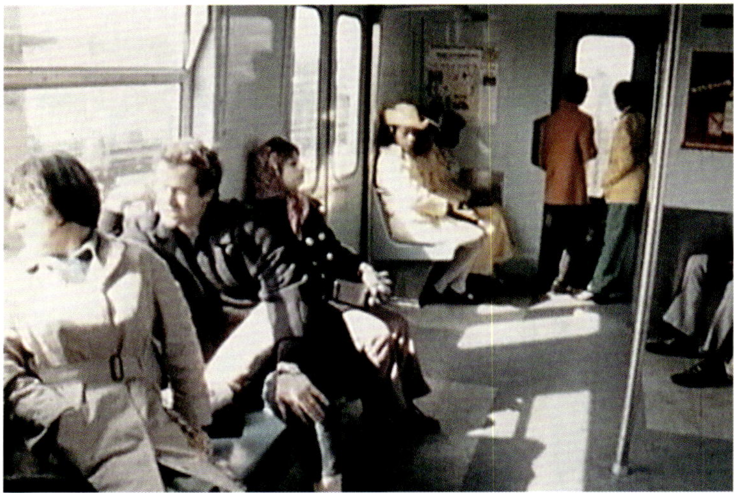

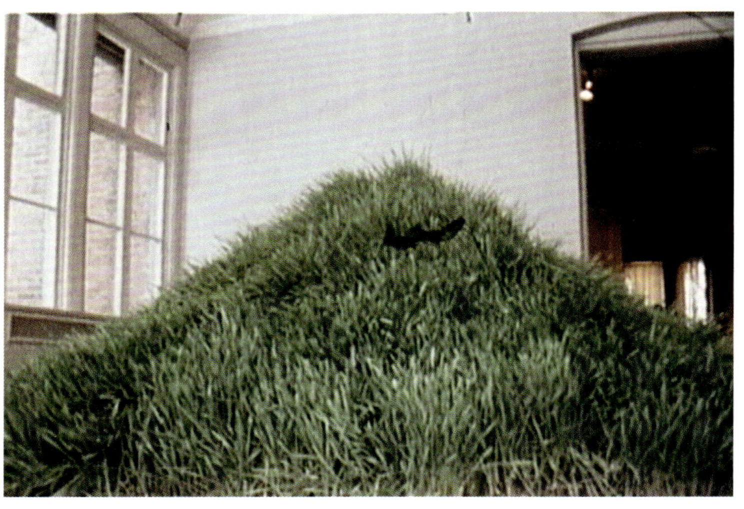

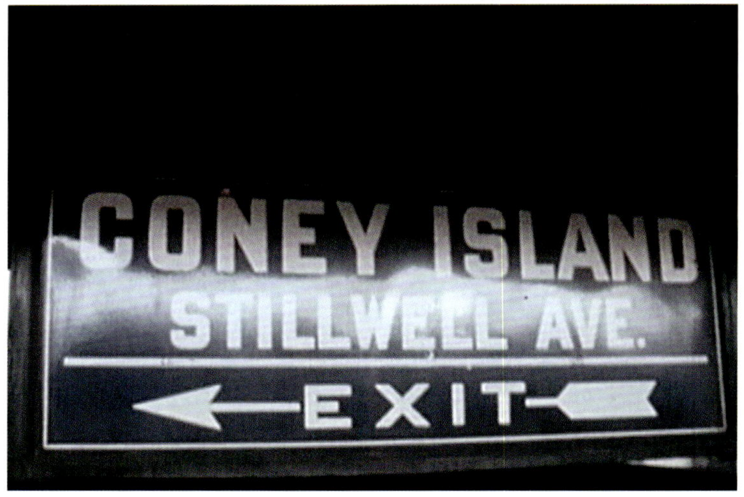

Hans Haacke: Self-Portrait of a German Artist in New York, 1969

Bitte zu einem anderen
Fernsehkanal umschalten,
10 mal tief durchatmen,
dann zurückschalten!

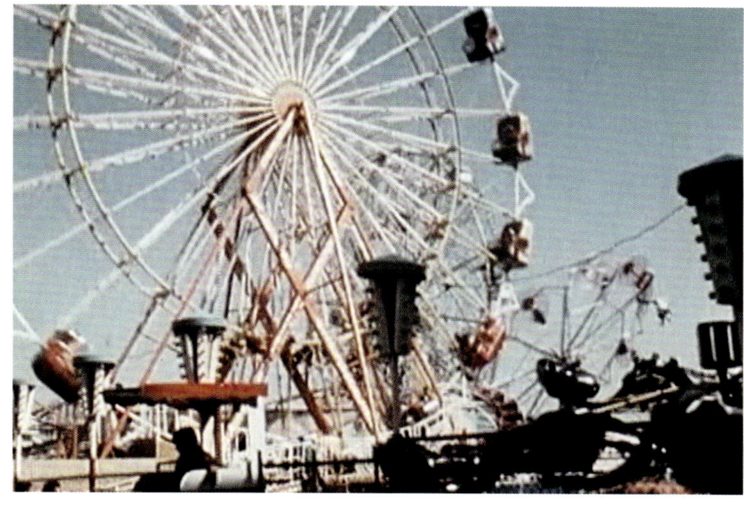

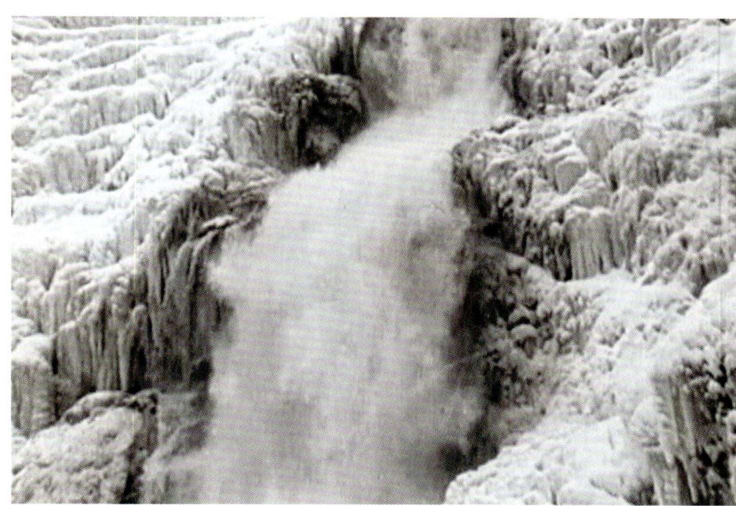

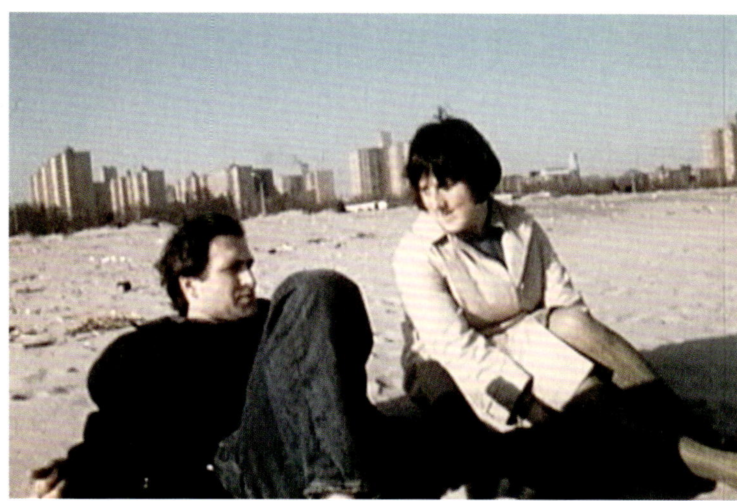

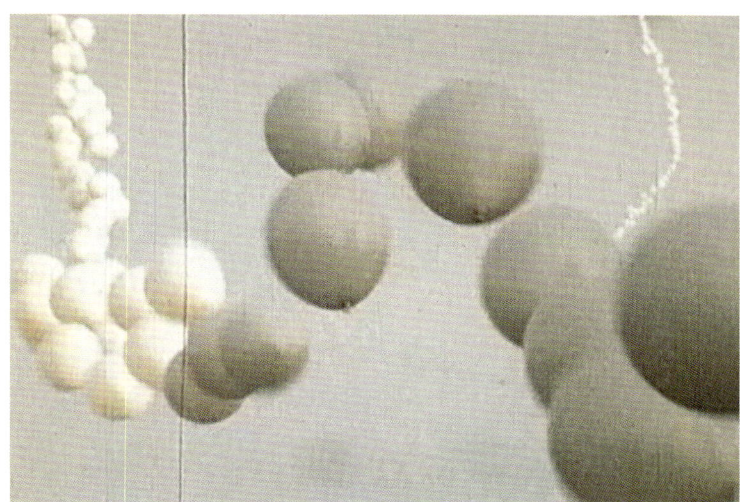

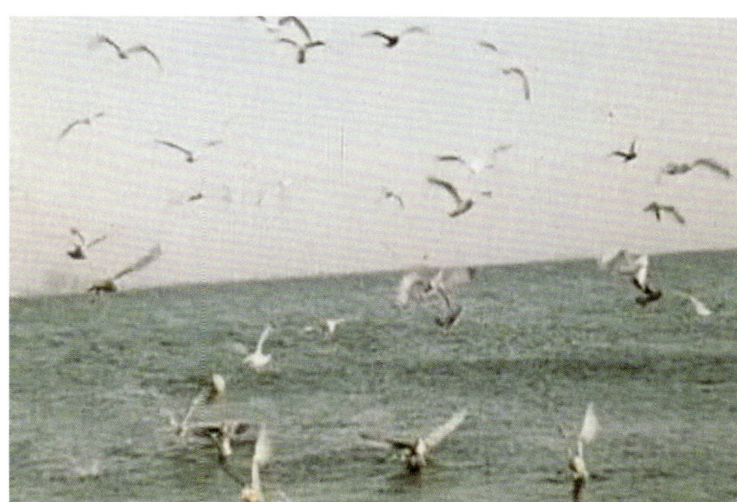

Hans Haacke: Self-Portrait of a German Artist in New York, 1969
Following pages: *Monument to Beach Pollution*, 1970

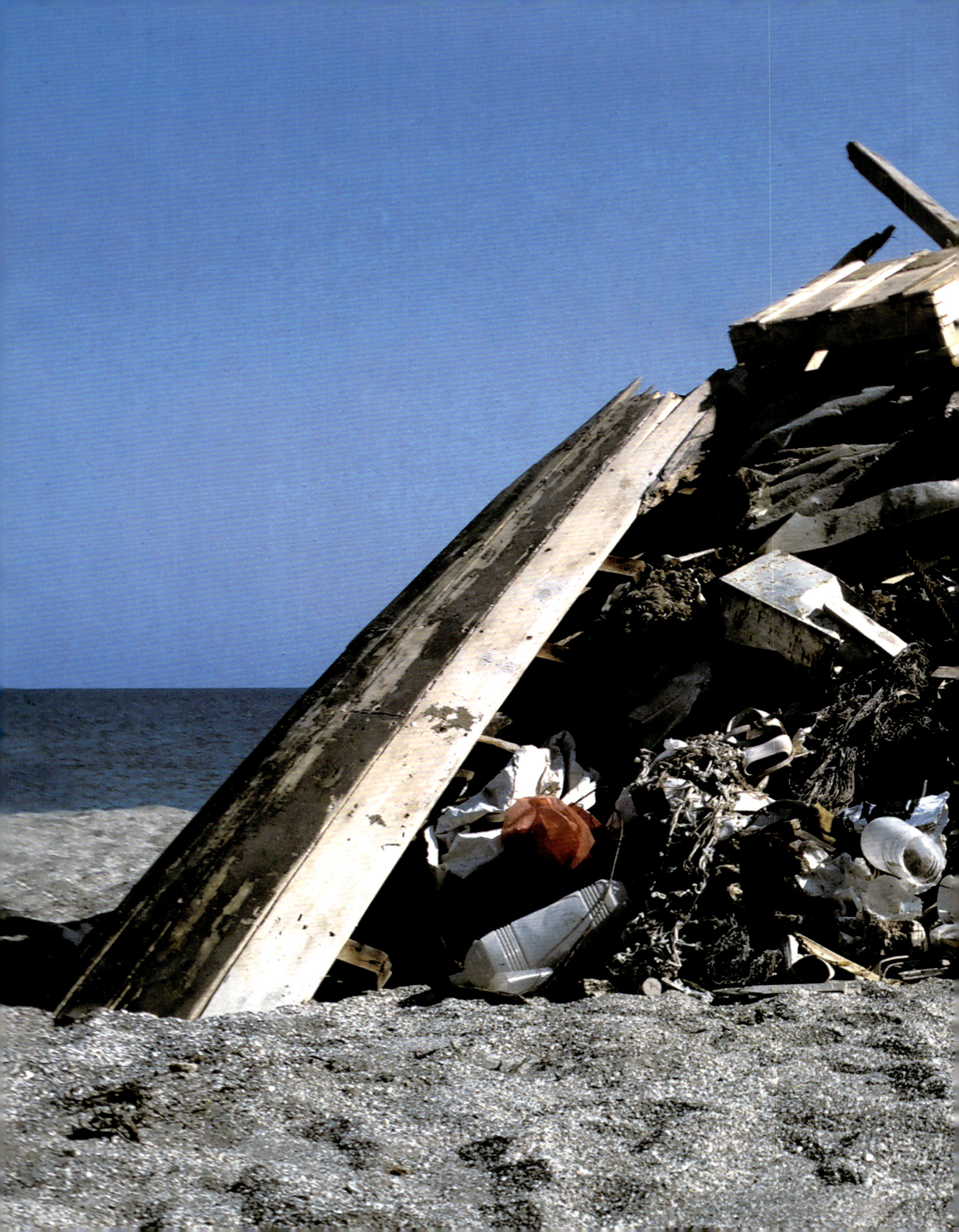

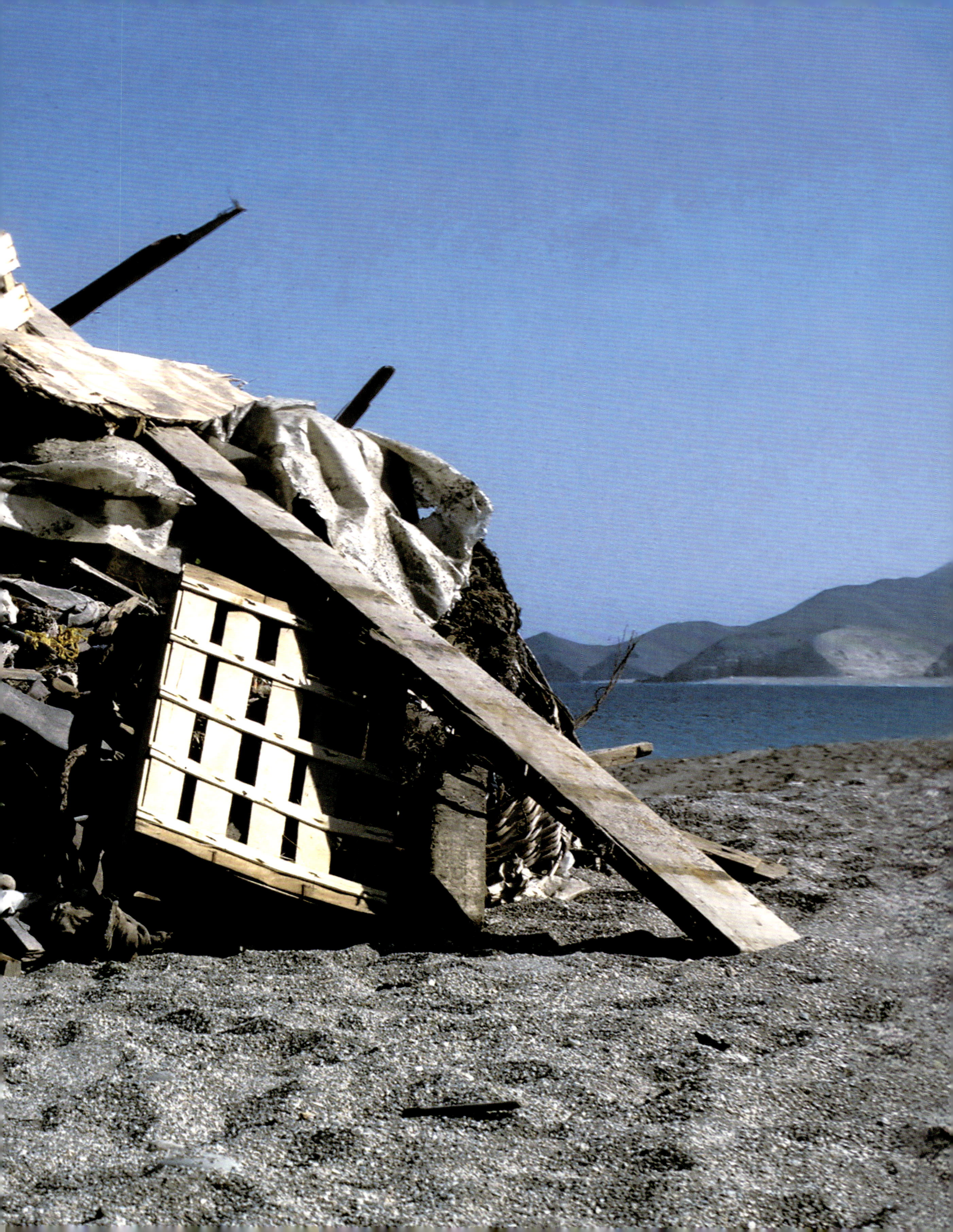

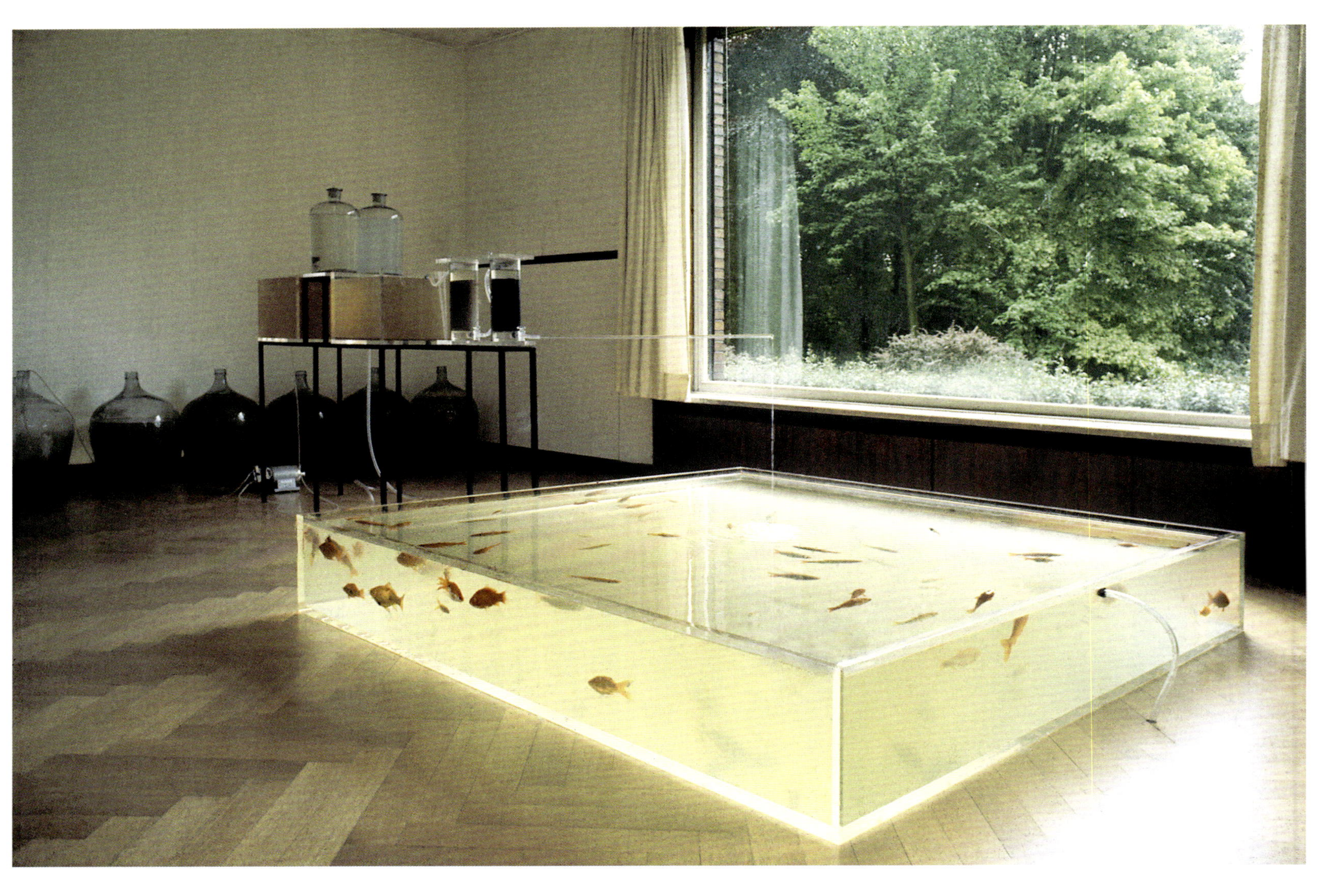

Fig. 1: Hans Haacke, *Rhine Water Purification Plant*, 1972

Water as a Sculptural and Political Material: Hans Haacke in Krefeld

Ursula Ströbele

»They are things that are only themselves. But they have a second layer.«[1] This seemingly curt sentence is how Paul Wember, director of the Kunstmuseen Krefeld at the time, described the site-specific works that Hans Haacke conceived for his solo exhibition there in 1972. The artist sought to overturn the arbitrary distinctions between art, science, and society, and thus to free art from its mythical function.[2] Haacke's *Demonstrationen der physikalischen Welt: Biologische und gesellschaftliche Systeme* (Demonstrations of the Physical World: Biological and Social Systems), as the exhibition was called, were part of a series of exhibitions that Wember had initiated on the subject of art and nature.[3] Thanks to Wember's commitment and prudent foresight, the museum in Krefeld developed into an important center for contemporary European art under his direction from 1947 to 1975.

Haacke's first major solo exhibition at an art institution in Germany marked a turning point in his work in systems aesthetics. Together with Jack Burnham—sculptor, art theorist, and companion—Haacke expanded the understanding of sculpture into »sculpture as a real-time system.«[4] In contrast to traditional object-based aesthetics, the focus here was on sculptural networks informed by American systems theory and cybernetics, which consisted of interacting elements, some of which were living coactors like plants and animals, that (only) unfolded their experimental openness before the eyes of the audience. Since then, Haacke's artistic approach has been characterized by his interest in what are known as biological, physical, and social systems. He thematized their reciprocal interactions in his own iconography of the political and ecological, which he presented as unified in the aforementioned show.

At the time, Krefeld was an industrial center on the left bank of the Rhine and had the reputation of being the biggest »Rhine polluter.« A wide variety of usage interests were at odds here: the Rhine served as an important transport route in terms of infrastructure, a reservoir for drinking and cooling water, a recreational area, a nature reserve, and a receptacle for wastewater. By considering the related sociological, economic, ecological, and political aspects, the artist thus developed occasionally provocative works on the theme of water as a system reflecting society as a whole.

1
Paul Wember, ed., *Hans Haacke: Demonstrationen der physikalischen Welt; Biologische und gesellschaftliche Systeme*, exh. cat. Kaiser-Wilhelm-Museum, Haus Lange, Krefeld (Krefeld: Haus Lange, 1972), n.p.

2
Ibid.

3
The program had previously included exhibitions by Haus-Rucker-Co (1971), Dieter Roth (1971), Menashe Kadishman (1972), and Peter Hutchinson (1972), as well as the exhibition *Ikebana Aktion* (1972).

4
See Jack Burnham, »Systems Aesthetics (Artforum 7. 1. 1968),« in Jack Burnham, *Dissolve into Comprehension: Writings and Interviews, 1964–2004*, ed. Melissa Ragain (Cambridge, MA: The MIT Press, 2015), pp. 115–25.

His water works exhibited in Krefeld included physical systems, for example in *Large Condensation Cube* (1963–67, fig. p. 39), *Circulation* (1969, fig. pp. 58–59), and *Floating Ice Ring* (1970, fig. p. 45). The latter work consists of a cooling coil in a tub of water. The cooling freezes the water into ice; and due to its lower weight, the ice rises upward with the metal ring while simultaneously absorbing humidity from the surroundings. Such physical processes like temperature change, air flow, evaporation, and condensation are what Haacke sought to make visible in his partly participatory, sculptural, real-time systems.

With his well-known *Rhine Water Purification Plant* (fig. 1)—a biological system—the artist demonstrated the intimate entanglement of art, nature, and politics. It is a miniature purification plant that filtered and cleaned industrially polluted Rhine water from the Ruhr area, then »channeled it into a basin where goldfish demonstrate a sense of well-being.«[5] Haacke had taken his cue from the real local water treatment plant on site shortly before putting his version into operation. Carboy bottles of Rhine water from Krefeld-Uerdingen that were continuously refilled lined the wall.[6] They served as storage tanks for the water to be purified, which was routed into a reaction tank via a pump. Chlorine bleach, caustic soda, and ferrous sulfate were then added before the water flowed into another settling tank. The last station consisted of two cylindrical gravel and activated carbon filters. The purified water then flowed into the goldfish tank, after which it was channeled back into the groundwater or into the garden via a hose in the ground. Haacke himself described his work as beautiful with a sensual aura.[7]

In a photograph of the exhibition situation, there is an exceptionally stark contrast between the purist modern architecture of Haus Lange in Krefeld, a former villa, which Ludwig Mies van der Rohe designed for a silk manufacturer, with strip parquet flooring and a large window front facing the garden, and the minimalist, technical aesthetics of the treatment plant with its dirty Rhine water. The view of the surrounding park is theatrically framed by curtains on both sides, so that nature appears as if on a stage. An article in the *Rheinische Post* newspaper from May 19, 1972, even spoke of a »nature demonstration« instead of a (nature) representation—in reference to the scenario that played out before the visitors' eyes for the duration of the show.[8] The effect of the physical and biological laws presented was to be intensified via the confrontation with an unusual venue, namely, the museum. Here, art served to problematize a specific situation, to which Haacke drew public attention by presenting the relevant facts and simultaneously offering a sculptural model for a solution. The alienation caused by the shift in location was addressed numerous times in the reception at the time, in the sense that Haacke's real-time systems lost their neutrality as fragments of reality when situated in the new context of the museum. Paul Wember repeatedly emphasized the simplicity of the experimental setup and materials in the works presented: »It is nothing more

5
»Die Kunst und das Abwässer-Problem: Hans Haacke stellt im Museum Lange Umweltobjekte aus,« *Rheinische Post*, May 19, 1972, cited in Wember, *Hans Haacke: Demonstrationen der physikalischen Welt*, n.p.

6
Stefan Schröder in conversation with the author on December 4, 2017 (author's archive). He recalls how, as a nine-year-old, he fetched water from the Rhine with his father for Haacke's work.

7
Hans Haacke, in Margaret Sheffield, »Hans Haacke: Interview with Margaret Sheffield,« *Studio International* (March–April 1976), pp. 117–23, esp. p. 117.

8
»Die Kunst und das Abwässer-Problem: Hans Haacke stellt im Museum Lange Umweltobjekte aus,« *Rheinische Post*, May 19, 1972, cited in Wember, *Hans Haacke: Demonstrationen der physikalischen Welt*, n.p.

9
Ibid.

10
Hans Haacke, quoted by Edward Fry in *Hans Haacke: Werkmonographie* (Cologne: DuMont Schauberg, 1972), p. 47.

than the facts that are being shown. . . . Haacke, and we as organizers, would actually like to present everything to you with this neutrality.«[9] That such a statement may not have been entirely true, or even possibly the result of strategic institutional considerations, can be seen in the works themselves and is evidenced by something the artist had said two years prior: »Not only can you demonstrate the modes of operation of politics and nature; you can also influence them.«[10]

A photograph documents the presentation of wastewater samples from the municipal dischargers and those of the paint factory Farbenfabrik Bayer AG Uerdingen on a shelf (fig. 2). During the project, Haacke had two of the water samples tested

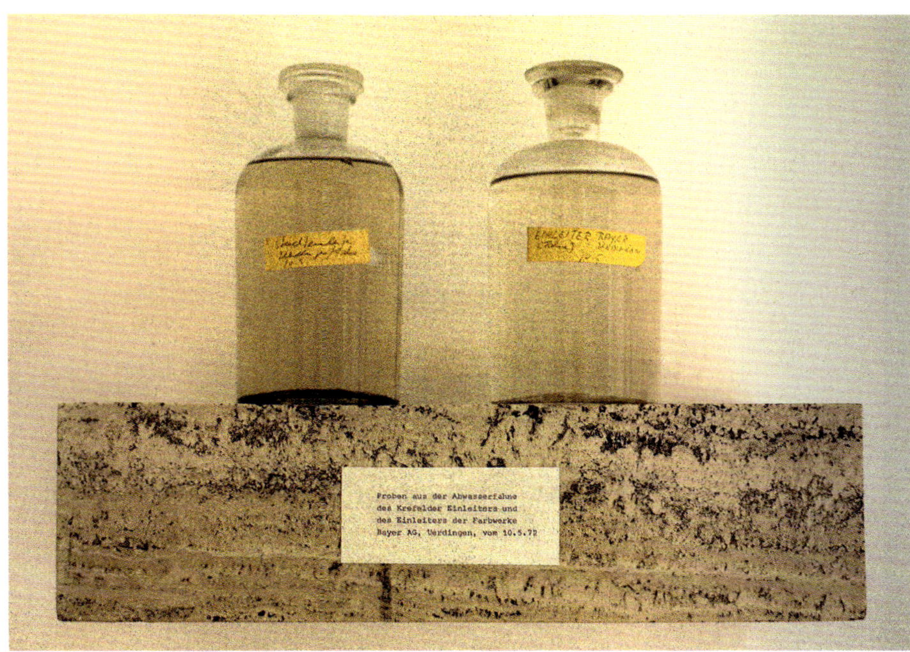

Fig. 2: Hans Haacke, *2 Water Samples from the Plume of Wastewater from the City of Krefeld's Outlet and Effluence (Near the Company Farbwerke Bayer AG, Uerdingen)*, 1972

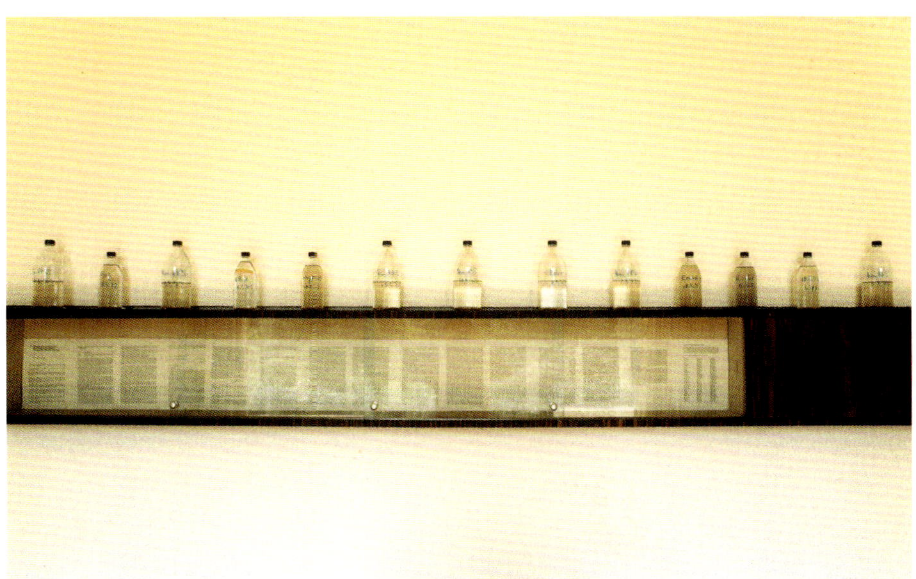

Fig. 3: Hans Haacke, *13 Water Samples from the Rhine and Tributary Rivers in North Rhine Westphalia*, 1972

42 Millionen cbm ungeklärtes Abwasser
sind 1971 von der Stadt Krefeld
in den Rhein eingeleitet worden.

Unterhalb der Einleitungsstelle ist das Rheinwasser
polysaprob - übermässig verunreinigt.

Für 20 Millionen cbm industrielles
und 9 Millionen cbm häusliches Abwasser
wurden Kanalgebühren erhoben.

Die Gebühren betragen pro cbm -,21 DM
ab 20.000 cbm -,17 DM
ab 500.000 cbm -,12 DM
pro qm Regenabflussfläche -,21 DM

Wie stark und mit welchen Schmutzstoffen das Abwasser
verunreinigt ist, hat auf die Höhe der Kanalgebühren
keinen Einfluss.

So werden in den Kanalgebühren nicht berücksichtigt:

die entsprechend unterschiedliche Höhe zukünftiger
Klärkosten,
die relative Größe der verursachten Umweltschäden,
die relative Belastung des öffentlichen Haushalts für
die Sanierung.

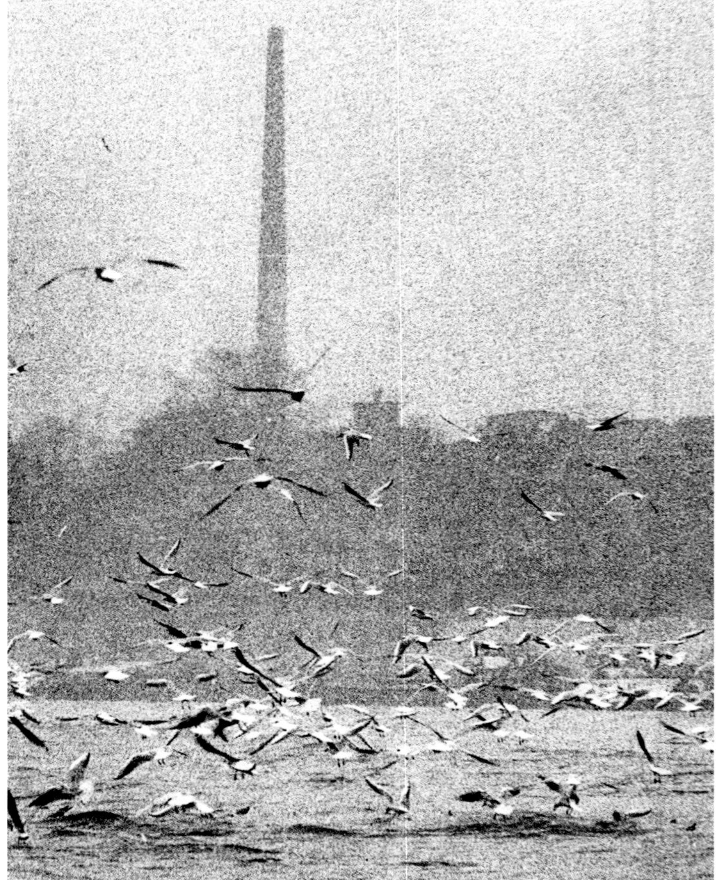

Fig. 4: Hans Haacke, *Krefeld Sewage Triptych*, 1972

11 Fry, *Hans Haacke: Werkmonographie*.

14.600 t absetzbare Stoffe und 7.300 t gelöste Stoffe
sind 1971 von der Stadt Krefeld
in den Rhein eingeleitet worden.

Anteil am Krefelder Abwasser haben, ungefähr:

215.000 Einwohner	9.000.000 cbm
TAG Schroers & Co.	2.900.000 cbm
Maizena GmbH	2.000.000 cbm
Vereinigte Seidenwebereien	1.800.000 cbm
Holtz & Willemsen GmbH	1.500.000 cbm
Deutsche Edelstahlwerke AG.	1.400.000 cbm
Färberei-Ges. Flores & Co.	1.000.000 cbm
Guano-Werke AG.	500.000 cbm
Städt. Badeanstalten	500.000 cbm
Chem. Fabrik Stockhausen & Cie.	400.000 cbm
Krefelder Milchhof GmbH	400.000 cbm
Voss-Biermann & C.L. Senger KG.	330.000 cbm
Städt. Krankenanstalten	300.000 cbm
Städt. Tierpark	300.000 cbm
Kaufhof AG. Krefeld	250.000 cbm
Therachemie GmbH	250.000 cbm
Molenaar, Lawaczeck & Co.	210.000 cbm
Brauerei Rhenania	200.000 cbm
Brauerei Tivoli GmbH	200.000 cbm
UNIFRANK Lebensmittelwerke GmbH	200.000 cbm
Städt. Schlachthof	100.000 cbm

Die Farbenfabriken Bayer AG., Uerdingen unmittelbar in den Rhein eingeleitet. 164.250.000 cbm

by the municipal chemical testing center. The findings and accompanying letter were reproduced in the publication for the exhibition. According to the report, similar chemical substances were detected in the Rhine water from the Krefeld municipal discharger and the Bayer Uerdingen main discharger: ammonia, nitrites, and chloride. This proportion of nitrogenous organic substances was the result of industrial wastewater and the salt mines on the Upper Rhine. Furthermore, this water had »unfavorable bacteriological findings« with a large number of germs, including coli bacteria. In another work, Haacke presented thirteen water samples from the Rhine and tributary rivers in North Rhine-Westphalia from the period May 9–11, 1972, with corresponding laboratory findings (fig. 3).

Another central work, perhaps the key work in the exhibition, is the *Rhine Krefeld Sewage Triptych* (fig. 4). In the central image, one can see a chimney rising into the sky on the horizon behind a gray veil of haze, flanked by the silhouettes of accompanying buildings, and the shape of a bank sloping down to the water is discernible to the front. The foreground is dominated by a flock of flying seagulls, the scenery bathed in diffuse light. Only the flanking panels provide information about the central subject: the left panel contains volume data and a scale of fees for wastewater disposal, while the right panel provides information about settleable and dissolved substances in Krefeld's wastewater and the main dischargers into the municipal sewer network. It shows that private households were financially disadvantaged in terms of wastewater charges as compared to the main industrial dischargers, even though the latter were responsible for the majority of hazardous substances in the wastewater, for environmental damage, and for the cost of decontamination.

The central field of the picture shows the discharge point of the Bayer paint factories at kilometer 765.7 in the Uerdingen district of Krefeld on January 21, 1972, where seagulls were snapping up dying fish from the Rhine. This had been a familiar image ever since the 1969 scandal of the mass fish deaths caused by endosulfan, an insecticide detected in the river. Here, the seagull combines ambivalent connotations: its cries may evoke holidays at the North Sea, walks along the dikes, and crab sandwiches snatched from children's hands; at the same time, it is also a synanthropic species, a scavenger, and a sign of changing environmental conditions, as in Haacke's triptych.

In the Krefeld exhibition, the photograph in the central panel has a dual function: Haacke chose a different perspective of the same motif for the poster, and he also used a mirrored version of it for the cover of the book *Hans Haacke: Werkmonographie* edited by Edward Fry and published in the same year.[11] The coarse black-and-white grain underscores the motif's initially enigmatic character, which echoes the aesthetics of press images of the smog in the Ruhr area at the time and only becomes recognizable through the accompanying

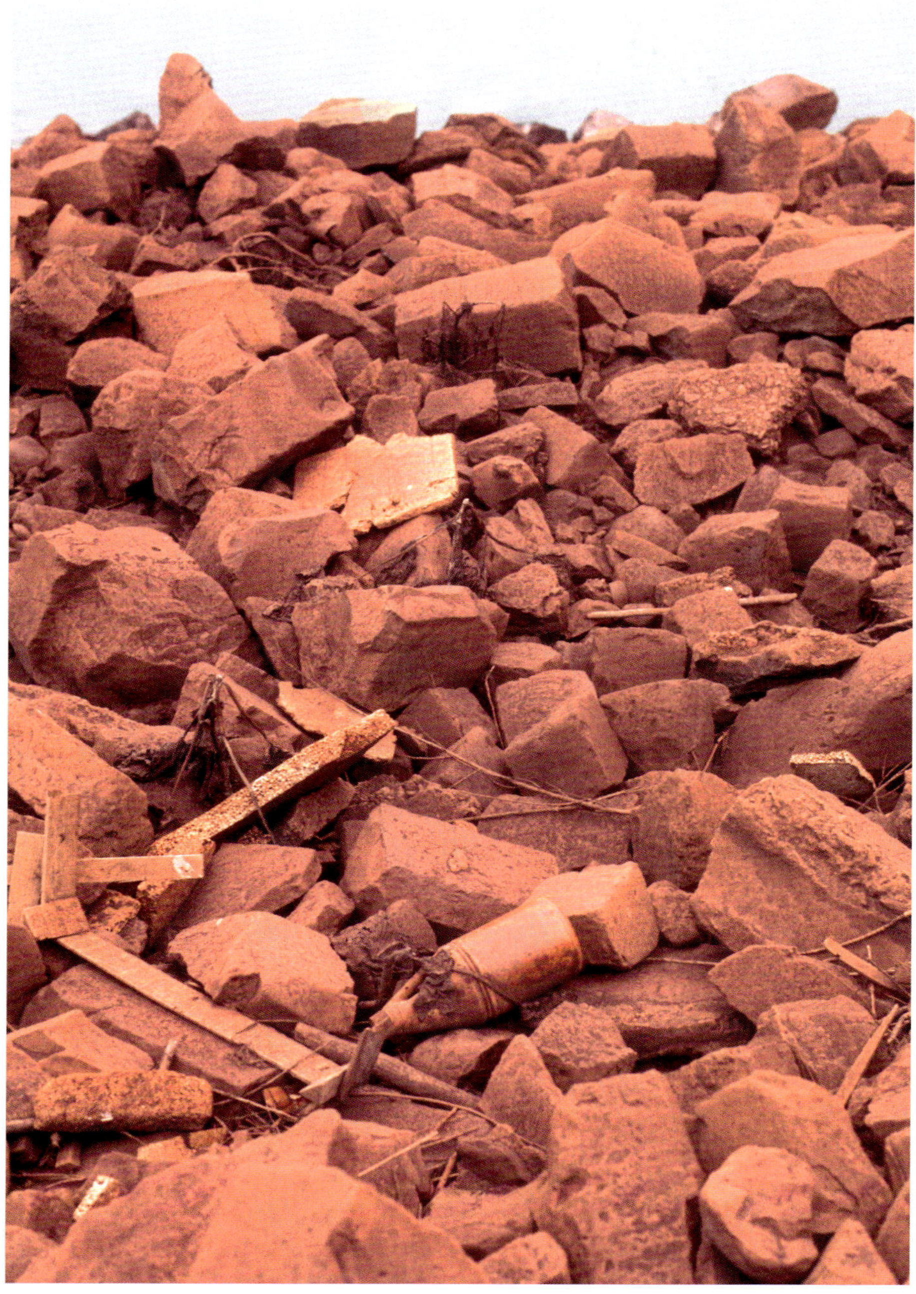

Fig. 5: Hans Haacke, *Rhine Riverbank Near a Loading Facility Operated by Farbenfabrik Bayer AG*, Uerdingen, 1972

text. How things actually looked there is pictured in a close-up photograph, also on display, which shows stones covered in a layer of red dust (iron oxide) and accompanied by flotsam-like civilizational waste (fig. 5). The title here is similarly prosaic: *Rhine Riverbank Near a Loading Facility Operated by Farbenfabrik Bayer AG.* Other color slides from the artist's archive also capture the scenery in Uerdingen from different perspectives: ships anchoring or sailing, machines at the industrial production and loading site, the pollution of the shore—an interest that Haacke also addressed in his *Monument to Beach Pollution* (fig. pp. 78–79)—and circling seagulls following the ships.

A few years earlier, Rachel Carson had published her famous book *Silent Spring* (1962); the first Earth Day was held in 1970 worldwide, for which Robert Rauschenberg designed a

12
See Robert Rauschenberg Foundation, »Earth Day,« https://www.rauschenbergfoundation.org/art/art-context/earth-day.

13
See Deutscher Bundestag, »Materialienband zum Umweltprogramm der Bundesregierung,« December 23, 1971, p. 228, http://dipbt.bundestag.de/doc/btd/06/027/0602710zu.pdf.

14
Hans Haacke, in a letter to Paul Wember, July 31, 1972, Archiv Kaiser-Wilhelm-Museum, Krefeld.

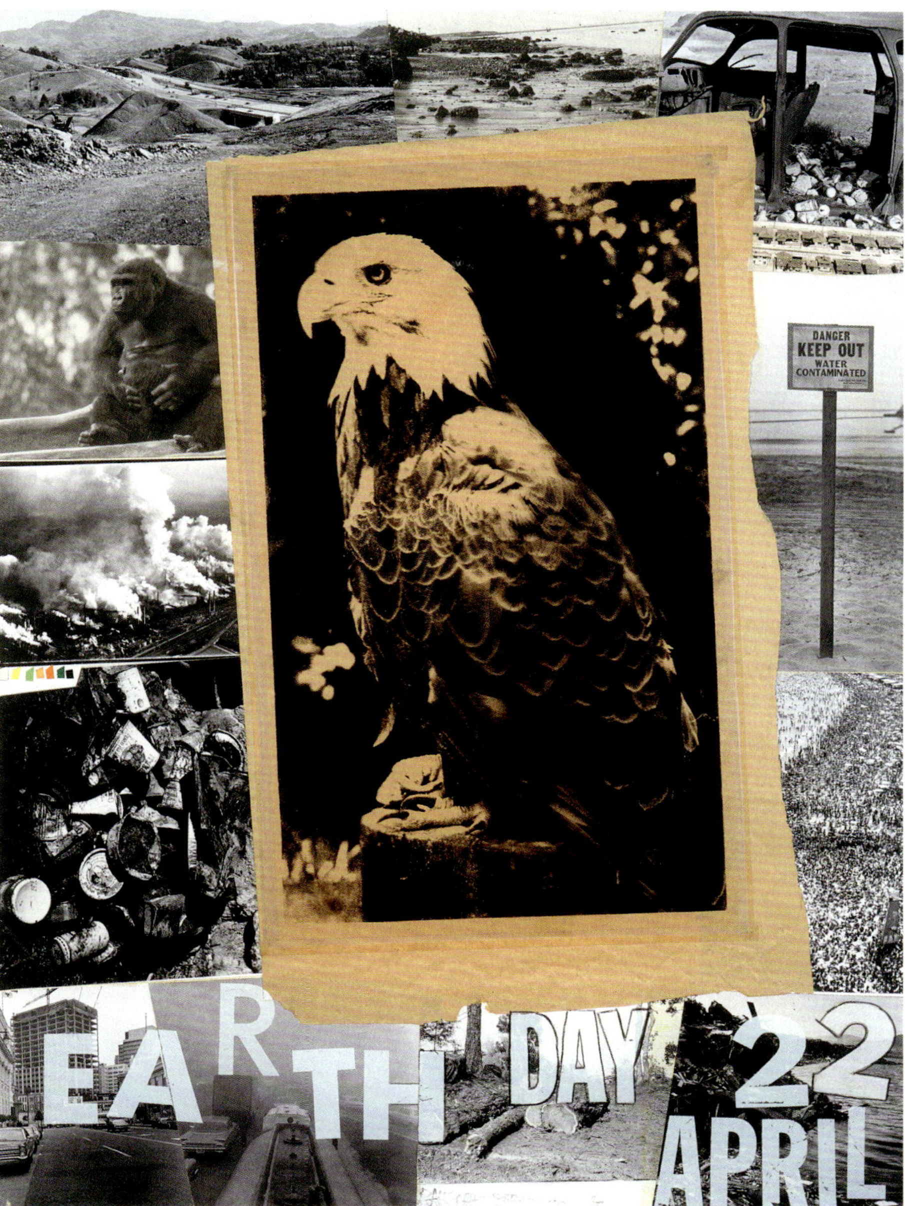

Fig. 6: Robert Rauschenberg, *Earth Day 22 April Poster*, 1970, photographs, photo acetate, and kraft paper on illustration board, 101.6 × 75.9 cm, Robert Rauschenberg Foundation

poster (fig. 6);[12] the year of the exhibition, 1972, saw the publication of the Club of Rome's study *The Limits to Growth*; and shortly afterward the (first) oil crisis would hit. In 1971, the West German government adopted an environmental program aimed at improving water quality in Germany, which resulted in more water treatment plants being built in the following years.[13] The themes of Haacke's exhibition were thus closely linked to the sociopolitical debates of the time. He explicitly thanked the museum's management for their support of his critical project in a letter: ». . . I never had the feeling with you that I should modify my plans for reasons of realpolitik, finance, or artistic ideology. This was such a fortunate situation that it must be explicitly noted.«[14]

His *Krefeld Sewage Triptych* is an industrially induced, environmentally and politically charged development of *Live Airborne System* (fig. pp. 68–69), a work that the artist had planned in 1965 on the occasion of a ZERO Festival in Scheveningen in the Netherlands and finally realized on November 30, 1968, on Coney Island in New York.[15] Haacke threw breadcrumbs into the ocean to attract seagulls. He thought of the flight formation, mass, and varying spatial expansion of the flock of birds as »seagull sculpture,« thus underscoring his expanded, temporally focused understanding of sculpture based on systems aesthetics.

Other works documenting the pollution of the Rhine complemented the Krefeld show, including a table hung on the wall created by the State Institute for Hydrology (newly founded in 1969) on wastewater dischargers in North Rhine-Westphalia (1972) with information on the number of inhabitants in municipalities ranging from Bonn and Bad Godesberg to Kleve and the factories located there, as well as the type, quantity, and treatment of the wastewater. Haacke also presented quotes from the Committee for Youth, Family and Health of the German Bundestag from 1971, as well as paragraphs 22 and 38 from the Federal Water Act of July 27, 1957 (BGBl. I, p. 1110), which had been passed to protect water bodies and regulate the criminal prosecution of water pollution. In the early 1970s, many wastewater treatment plants were outdated, and their performance no longer matched the increased wastewater load or its concentration of pollutants. Haacke also integrated a visitor survey—part of a so-called social system—into his show, and its results were included in the publication. One question was related to nature conservation, explicitly in terms of the costs for the population which had been publicly discussed.

Haacke's interweaving of art, nature, and politics culminates in his microclimatic, meteorological works: in the museum garden, he installed *Transplanted Moss Supported in an Artificial Climate* (fig. 7), thus continuing the water cycle within the framework of the exhibition. The water (indirectly) filtered by the *Rhine Water Purification Plant* and channeled into the groundwater fed a well drilled especially for the exhibition. This groundwater was sprayed via a pump into the branches of a weeping willow, trickled back onto the ground like rain, and created a moist climate under the tree, which benefited a moss culture that had settled there. Looking back, Haacke addresses the double meaning of »climate« with a nod to humanity's socioecological responsibility: »There was the meteorological aspect, which kept us from taking our coats off, and there was the social dimension, which nagged us to take a position as citizens.«[16] He repeatedly referred to the use of meteorological terms in political debates, whether it was »thaw weather« as a metaphor for a policy of détente or a »low in the relationship between two countries.«[17] Haacke's artificial climate under the weeping willow is thus also an institution-critical »demonstration« of creating his own independent climate through art or in the field of art, much like his artistic, environmental, and political engagement with the pollution of the Rhine and the use of water as a sculptural and political material.[18]

15
In 1965, Hans Haacke, Heinz Mack, Otto Piene, and Günther Uecker conceived an outdoor sculptural ensemble for the exhibition *Zero on Sea* on a pier in Scheveningen, Netherlands. It consisted of barrels with oil fires on rafts, buoys as mobile sculptures, messages in bottles with ZERO letters, silver skin on the water, smoke objects, and a floating feeding station for seagulls. See also Ursula Ströbele, »Fundstück aus dem WDR Archiv, Köln: Selbstporträt eines deutschen Künstlers in New York,« *Kunstchronik* 73, no. 7 (2020), *Kunst Natur Politik – Jetzt!*, pp. 388–96.

16
Hans Haacke, cited in Cecilia Alemani, »Interview with Hans Haacke,« in *Working Conditions: The Writings of Hans Haacke*, ed. Alexander Alberro (Cambridge, MA: The MIT Press, 2016), pp. 237–42, esp. p. 242.

17
Hans Haacke, »Provisorische Bemerkungen,« in Fry, *Hans Haacke: Werkmonographie*, p. 63.

18
On the connection between Haacke's water-related works (e.g., *Condensation Cube*) and his institution-critical approach, see also John A. Tyson, »The Artist as ›Weatherman‹: Hans Haacke's Critical Meteorology,« in *Nervous Systems: Art, Systems, and Politics since the 1960s*, ed. Johanna Gosse and Timothy Stott (Durham, NC: Duke University Press, 2022), pp. 55–77.

This text has been adapted from the habilitation thesis: Ursula Ströbele, *Hans Haacke und Pierre Huyghe: Non-Human Living Sculptures seit den 1960er-Jahren* (Berlin and Boston: De Gruyter, 2024), https://www.degruyter.com/document/doi/10.1515/9783111027159/html.

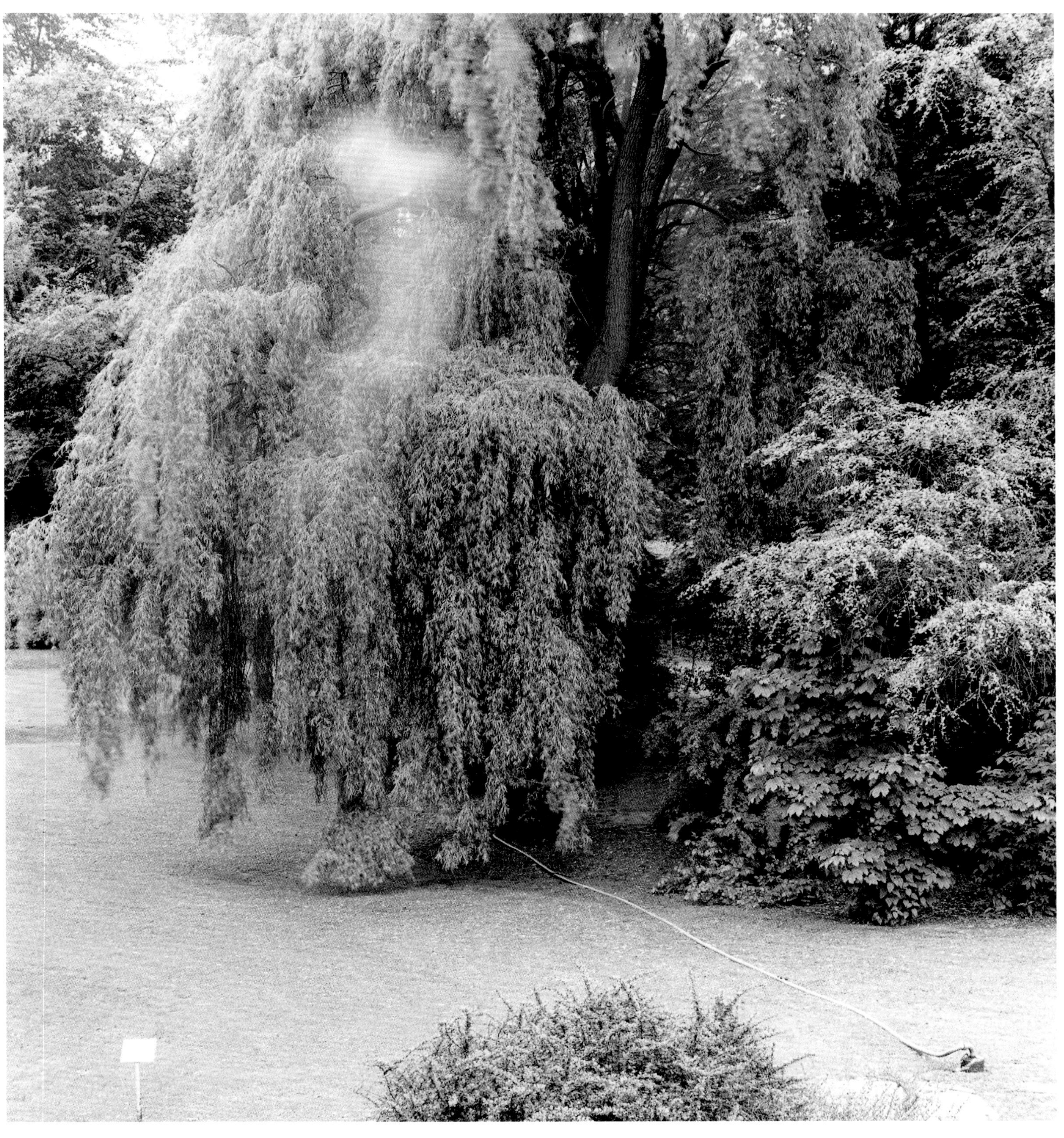

Fig. 7: Hans Haacke, *Transplanted Moss Supported in an Artificial Climate*, 1972, Museum Haus Lange, Krefeld

Photoelectric Viewer-Controlled Coordinate System, 1968

Hans Haacke first installed the work in 1968 at the Howard Wise Gallery in New York. It consists of a darkened room with fourteen photoelectric sensors installed at waist height, infrared projectors, and twenty-eight light bulbs fixed at head height. The intervals between the individual elements are the width of one body. The grid-like network of infrared beams activates when people enter the room, and the bulbs switch on depending on their position.

Viewers become agents and enter into a kind of »symbiotic relationship« with their environment. When visitors perform an action like stepping forward, gesticulating, or dancing, one light bulb goes out and the next light bulb in the sequence switches on. The viewer's body thus becomes an integral part of the artwork. Their movements are echoed and amplified by the lights as well as the shadows cast on the wall. When another person enters the room, the process is set in motion once again and a non-verbal inter-action begins.

TDF

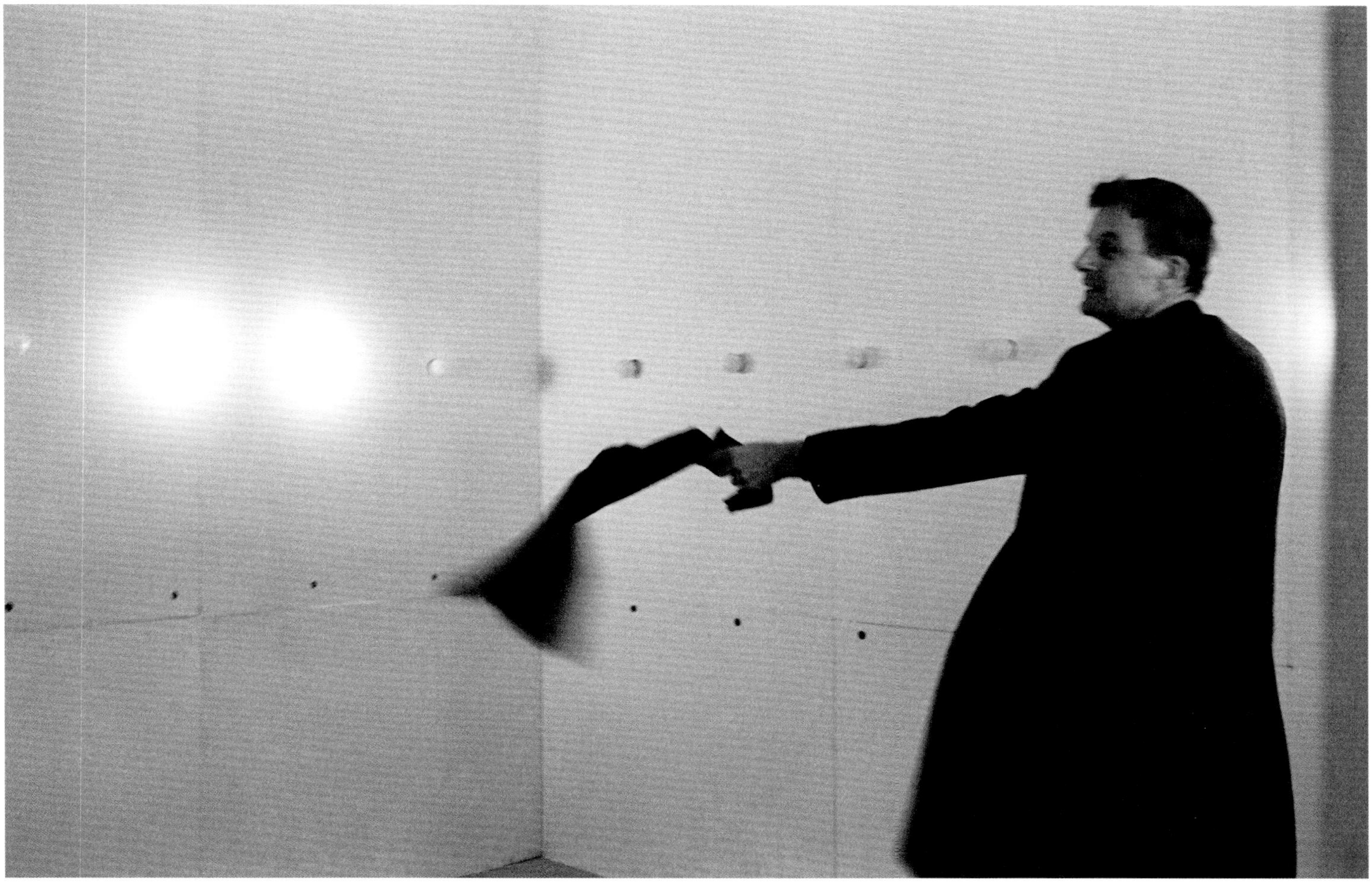

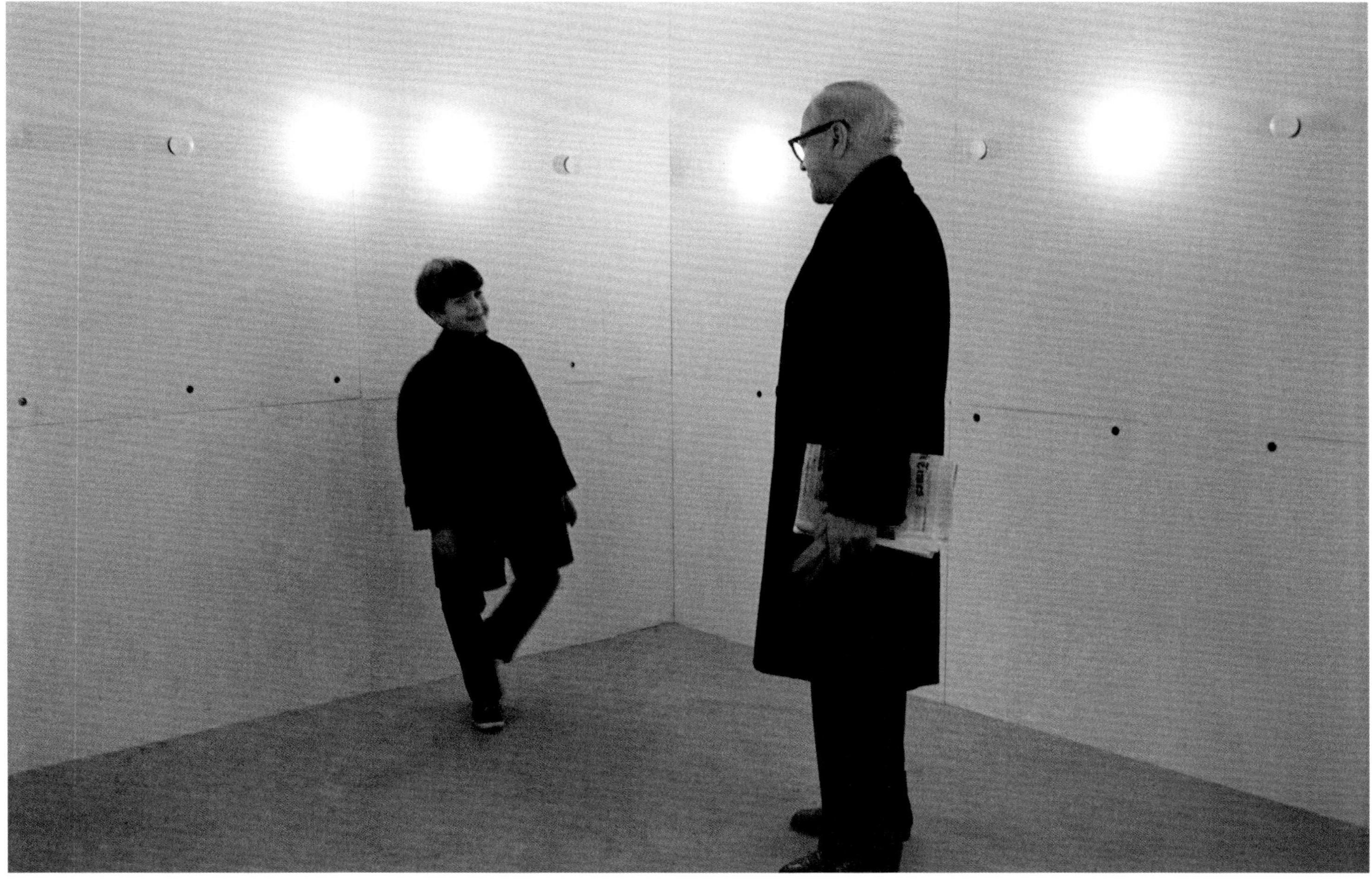

Photoelectric Viewer-Controlled Coordinate System, 1968

News, 1969

During *Prospect 69* in Düsseldorf, a teletype machine installed at the Kunsthalle printed out messages transmitted by the dpa (Deutsche Presse-Agentur) news wire service. On the day after the transmission, the paper printouts were displayed for further reading, and, eventually, on the third day, these rolls were labeled, dated, and stored in transparent tubular containers. During the time of the exhibition, the West German federal elections were held. *Prospect 69* was organized with the stated goal of providing a preview of the exhibition programs for the following year of an internationally selected group of galleries. These galleries cofinanced the exhibition.

Two months later, on the occasion of a one-person exhibition at Howard Wise Gallery in New York (1969), a teletype machine in the gallery printed the UPI (United Press International) news service. In this installation, as in the previous one, the printed paper rolls were displayed after the day of transmission and then stored in twenty-six plastic containers. For an installation at the Jewish Museum, as part of the exhibition *Software* (1970), five teletype machines simultaneously recorded the wire services of ANSA (Italian), dpa (German), the New York Times News Service, Reuters, and UPI. The printouts accumulated on the floor and were not posted or preserved beyond the time of the exhibition. This was also the way *News* was presented in the exhibition *Directions 3: Eight Artists* at the Milwaukee Art Center (1971). In Milwaukee, the wire services recorded were those of the *Los Angeles Times, The Washington Post, The New York Times*, and UPI. For this presentation, the wire services recorded are those of selected media from Frankfurt and Vienna.

Hans Haacke, written in 1969, updated in 2024

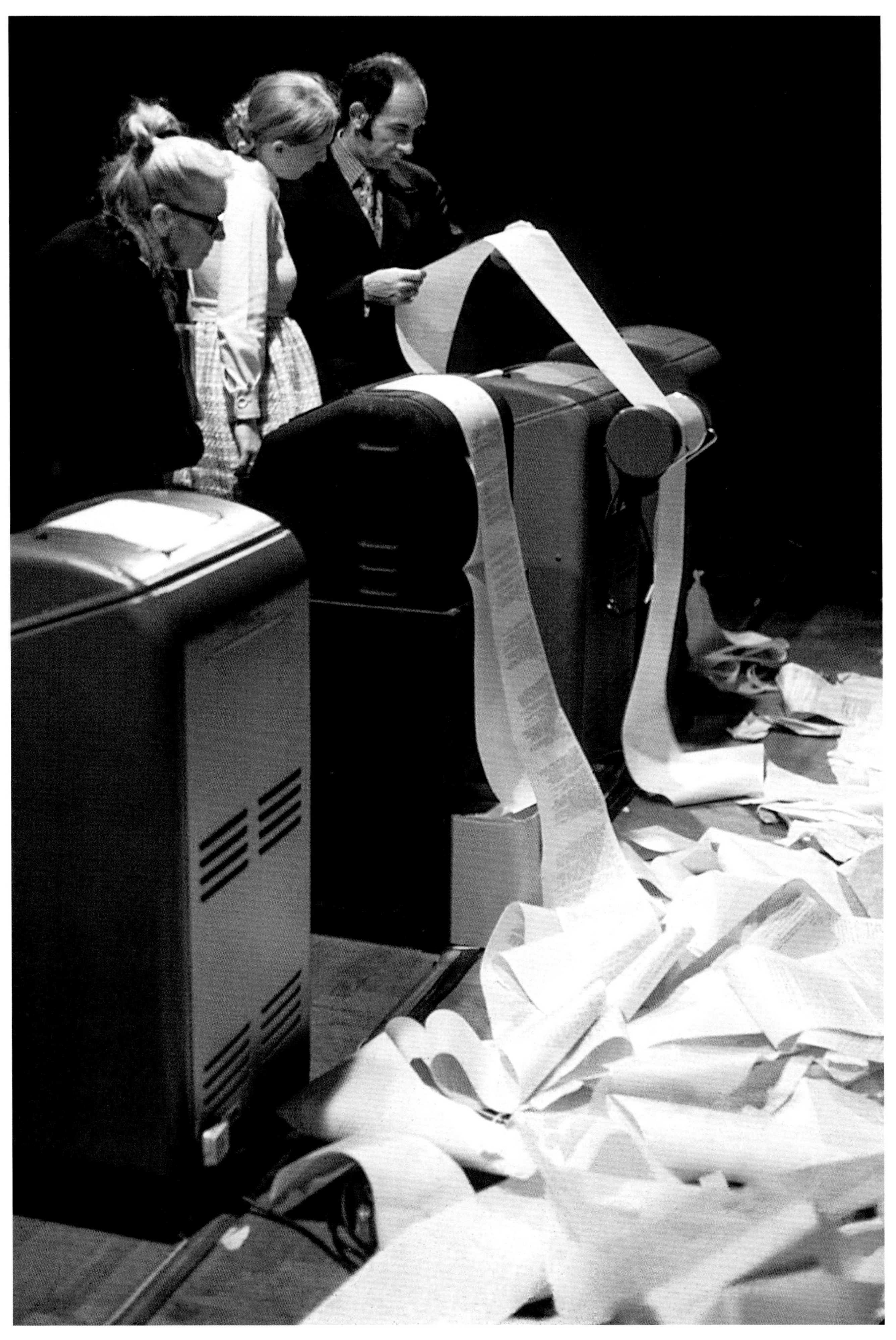

News, 1969
Installation view, Jewish Museum, New York, 1970
Following pages: Installation view, Paula Cooper Gallery, New York, 2005

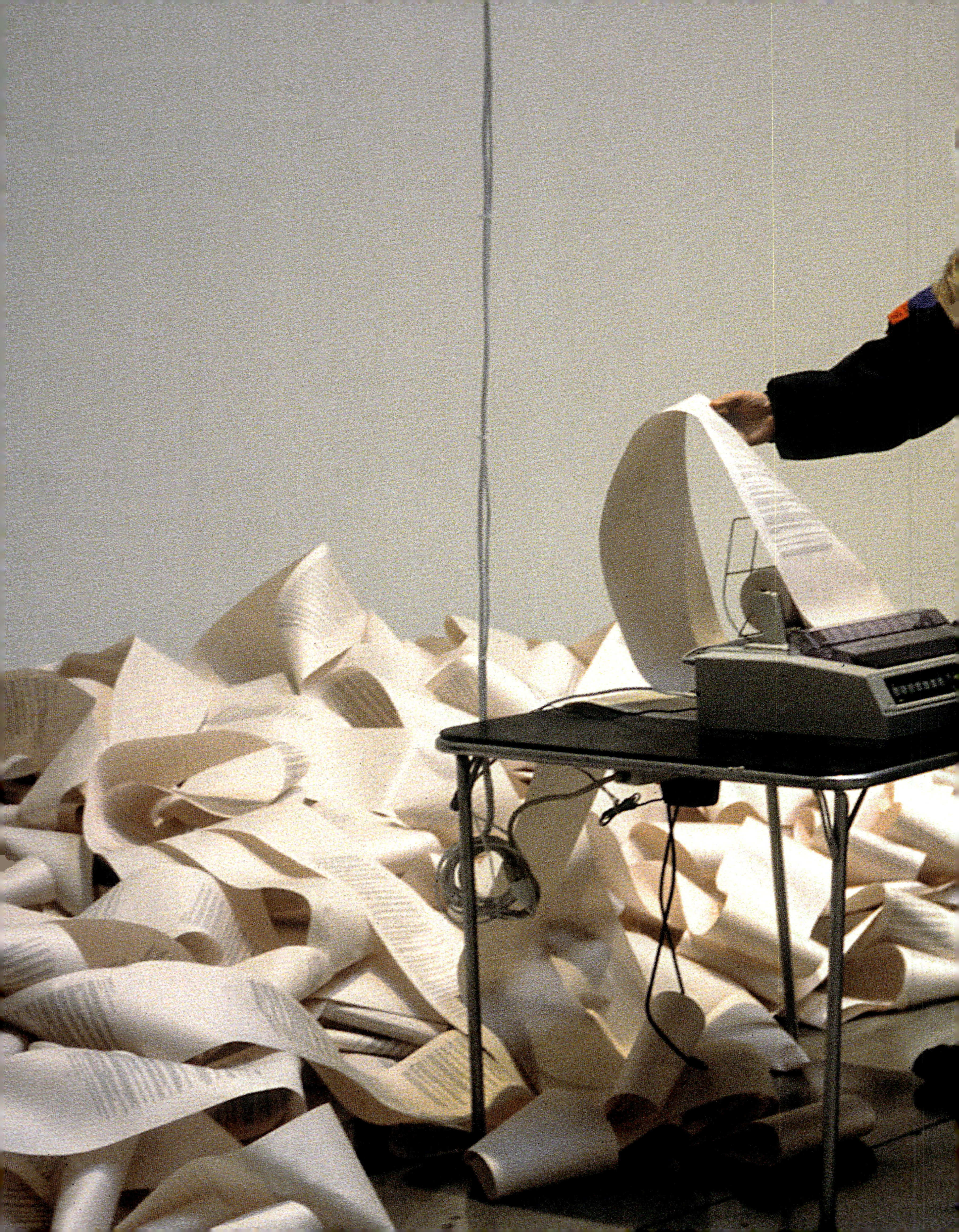

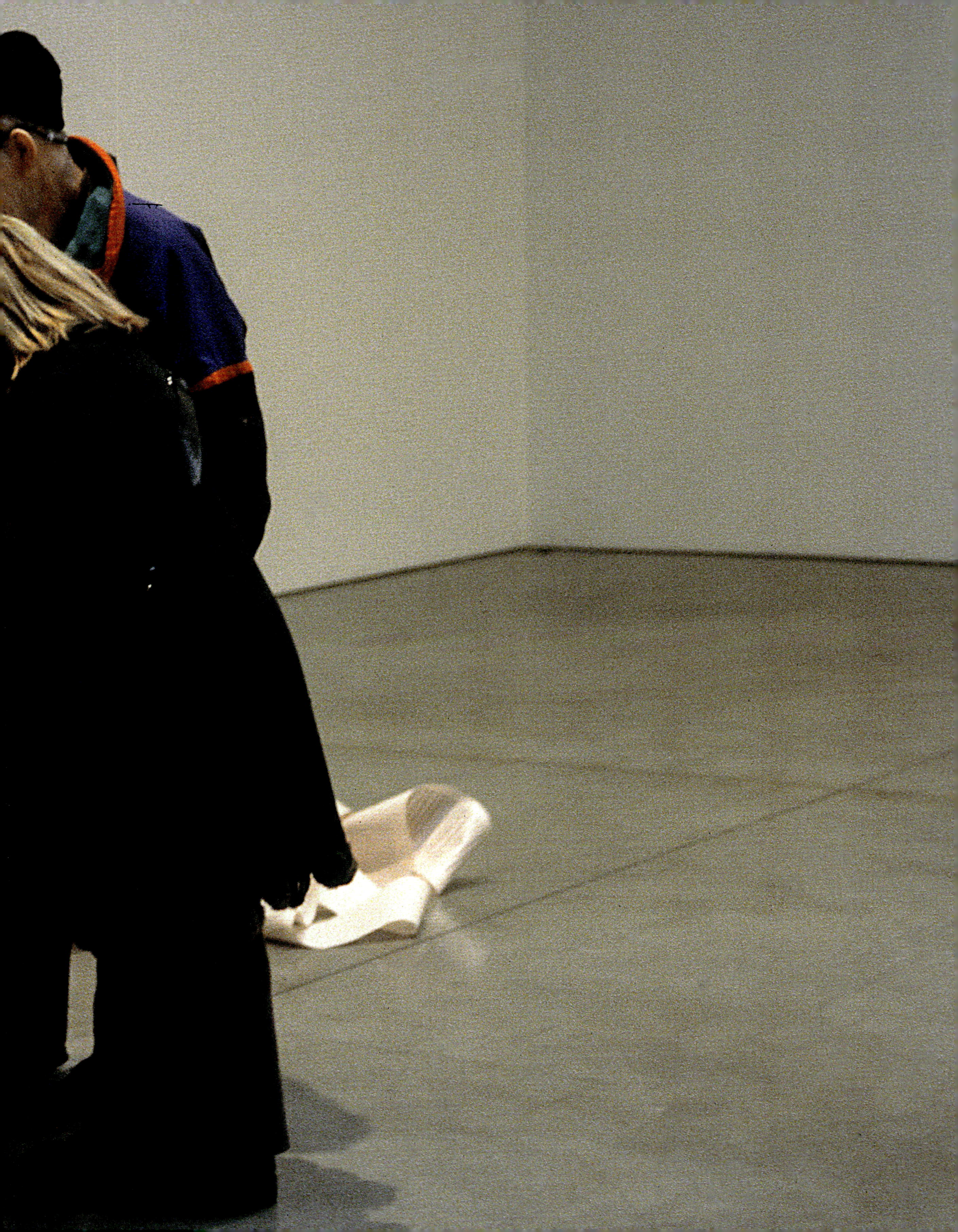

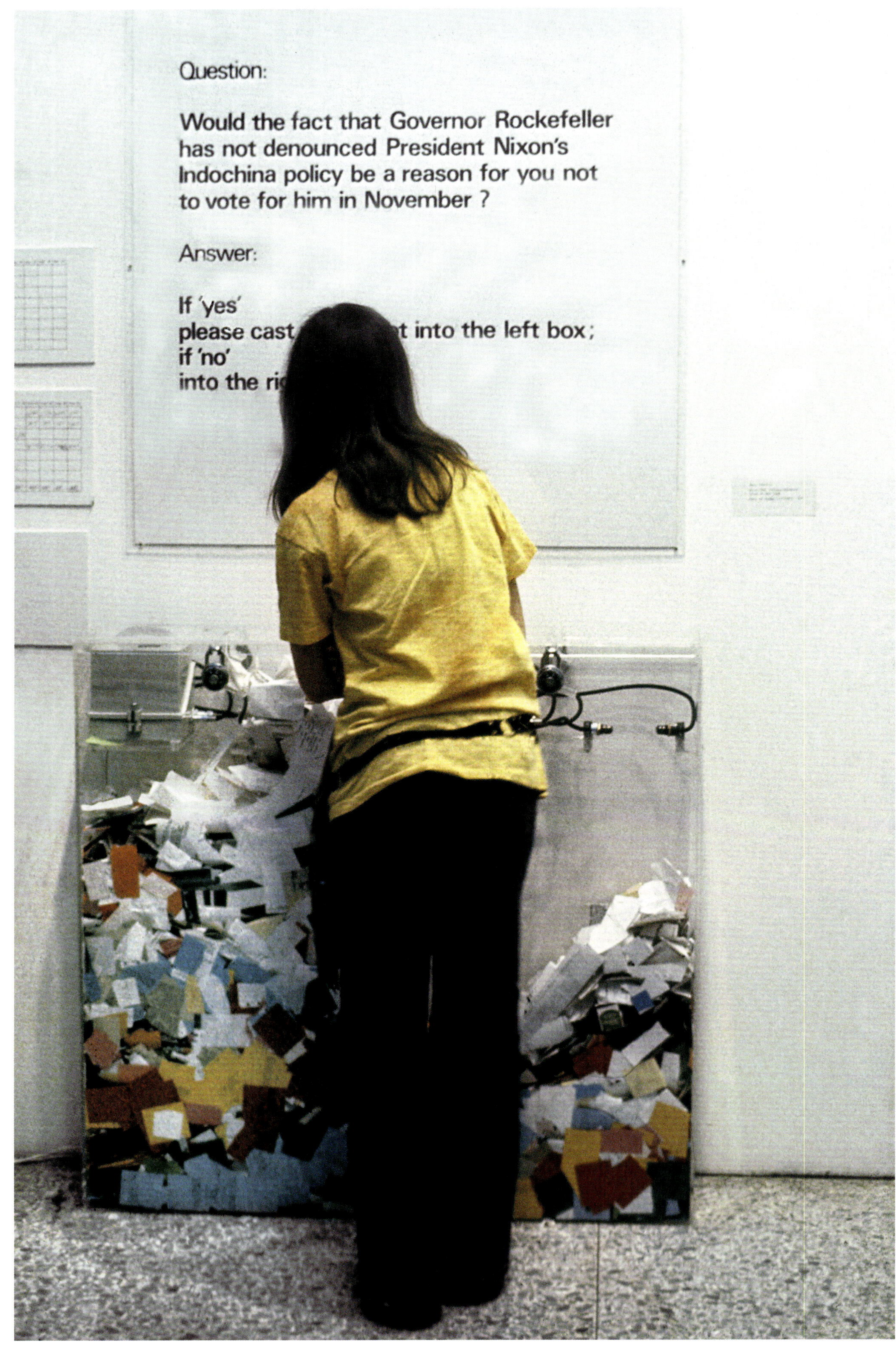

Fig. 1: Hans Haacke, *MoMA Poll*, 1970

Hans Haacke and Conceptual Art

Hubertus Butin

In 1971, Hans Haacke stated in an interview: »I don't consider myself a naturalist, nor for that matter a conceptualist or a kineticist, an earth artist, elementalist, minimalist, a marriage broker for art and technology, or the proud carrier of any other button that has been offered over the years.«[1] And once again in 2019 he emphasized: »I am wary of labels, no matter which ones.«[2] Understandably, artists find it restrictive when others try to pin them down or reduce them to a certain style or movement. Although Hans Haacke is widely considered the most important representative of a decidedly political strand of Conceptual Art[3] and exhibited alongside numerous Conceptual Artists at Galerie Paul Maenz in Cologne during the 1970s and 1980s, he clearly doesn't appreciate being described as such. But even if one abstains from applying the usual art-historical categories and labels, it still makes sense to reflect on his work in the context of Conceptual Art and ask which art-theoretical principles from those years around 1970 played an important role for him—especially since those years laid the foundation for much of his art in the following decades.

Art historians such as Benjamin H. D. Buchloh and Gregor Stemmrich have pointed out that international Conceptual Art is hardly a clearly defined movement.[4] Likewise, their colleague Alexander Alberro has emphasized that Conceptualism emerged as »a contested field of multiple and opposing practices.«[5] Nevertheless, one can generally note, even at the risk of too great a generalization, that the Conceptual Art of the 1960s and 1970s vehemently questioned the conventions of painting and sculpture, along with all their frames and plinths, via its fundamental rejection of the auratic object. Galleries and museums thus found themselves exhibiting texts, tables, scores, telegrams, index cards, files, videos, maps, schematic drawings, and documentary photographs instead (fig. 2). The artists no longer wanted to be seen as the genius creators of autonomous forms, but rather sought to avoid any trace of subjectivity and to recede into the background of their works. In terms of reception, these works could no longer be read from a formalistic perspective that was entirely beholden to the viewer's perception in keeping with the ideal of the modernist artwork prescribed by the influential American critic Clement Greenberg. Instead, the artists were primarily concerned with

1
Hans Haacke, in Jeanne Siegel, »An Interview with Hans Haacke,« *Arts Magazine* 45, no. 7 (May 1971), p. 18.

2
Hans Haacke, in »Hans Haacke in Conversation with Gary Carrion-Murayari and Massimiliano Gioni,« in *Hans Haacke: All Connected*, ed. Massimiliano Gioni and Gary Carrion-Murayari, exh. cat. New Museum, New York (London and New York: Phaidon, 2019), p. 228.

3
See Barbara Straka, »Das Zeitlose des Gegenwärtigen und die Gegenwärtigkeit des Zeitlosen,« in *Hans Haacke: Nach allen Regeln der Kunst*, exh. cat. Neue Gesellschaft für bildende Kunst, Berlin, and Kunsthalle Bern (Berlin: NGBK, 1984), p. 113.

4
Benjamin H. D. Buchloh, »From the Aesthetic of Administration to Institutional Critique (Some Aspects of Conceptual Art 1962–1969),« in *l'art conceptuel, une perspective*, exh. cat. Musée d'Art Moderne de la Ville de Paris (Paris: Musée d'Art Moderne, 1989), p. 41; Gregor Stemmrich, in »Gregor Stemmrich,« interview by Stefan Römer, Berlin, July 17, 2004, in *Conceptual Paradise*, http://conceptual-paradise.zkm.de/interview-stemmrich/.

5
Alexander Alberro, »Reconsidering Conceptual Art, 1966–1977,« in *Conceptual Art: A Critical Anthology*, ed. Alexander Alberro and Blake Stimson (Cambridge, MA, and London: The MIT Press, 1999), p. XVII.

the concept in the sense of an idea that took precedence over material production and aesthetic form. Sol LeWitt, one of the most important American Conceptual Artists, programmatically stated in his 1967 »Paragraphs on Conceptual Art« that »in conceptual art the idea or concept is the most important aspect of the work. When an artist uses a conceptual form of art, it means that all of the planning and decisions are made beforehand and the execution is a perfunctory affair. . . . Conceptual art is made to engage the mind of the viewer rather

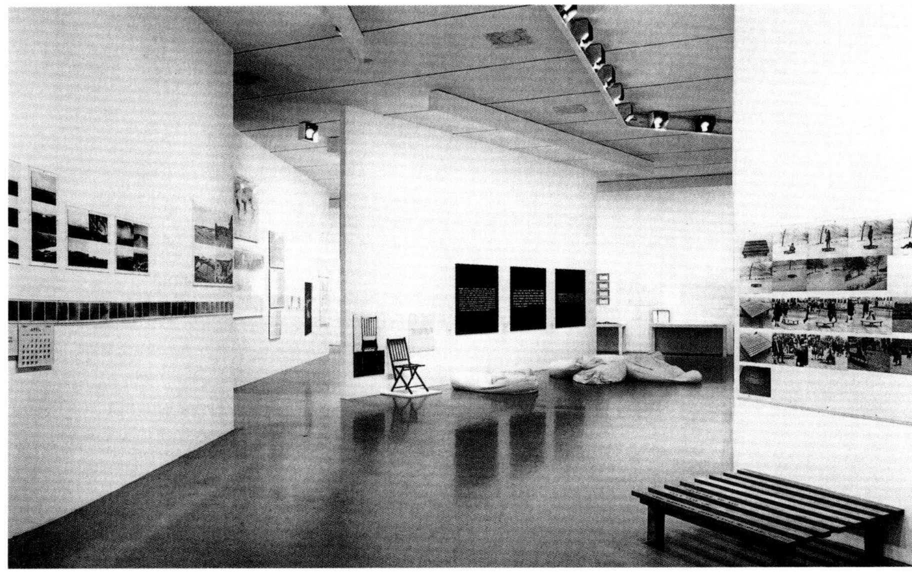

Fig. 2: Installation view of the exhibition *Information*, The Museum of Modern Art, New York, July 2 to September 20, 1970

than his eye or emotions.«[6] Sol LeWitt thus redefined not only the preconditions of artistic production, but also those of reception.

In the following, two of Hans Haacke's works will be discussed against the backdrop of five selected thematic categories within Conceptual Art which form a family of terms: participation, verbalization, documentation, seriality, and Institutional Critique.[7] Based on these categories, it can be seen to what extent Hans Haacke's works from around 1970 have »an unmistakable and prominent position in the context of conceptual art.«[8]

Participation

In 1969, Hans Haacke started shifting his focus from biological and physical systems to social ones, which he analyzed and visualized in order to spark sociopolitical debates in the art context. In his site-specific installation *MoMA Poll* (fig. 1), presented as part of the 1970 group exhibition *Information* at The Museum of Modern Art (MoMA) in New York, the artist surveyed visitors about their political convictions.[9] He set up two transparent plexiglass boxes—one labeled »Yes,« the other »No«—equipped with electronic counters (fig. p. 107). Those

6
Sol LeWitt, »Paragraphs on Conceptual Art,« *Artforum* 10 (Summer 1967), pp. 80 and 83.

7
Peter Osborne set up a comparable, though not identical, typological scheme for Conceptual Art in Peter Osborne, *Conceptual Art* (London and New York: Phaidon, 2002), p. 19.

8
Walter Grasskamp, »No-Man's Land,« in *Hans Haacke: Bodenlos*, ed. Klaus Bussmann and Florian Matzner, exh. cat. Venice Biennale, German Pavilion (Ostfildern: Edition Cantz, 1993), p. 45.

9
Hans Haacke, »Poll of MOMA Visitors,« in *Information*, ed. Kynaston L. McShine, exh. cat. The Museum of Modern Art, New York (New York: MoMA, 1970), p. 57.

10
Haacke, »Hans Haacke in Conversation with Gary Carrion-Murayari and Massimiliano Gioni,« p. 102.

11
Jon Hendricks and Jean Toche, eds., *GAAG: The Guerilla Art Action Group, 1969–1976; A Selection* (New York: Temporary Services, 1978), n.p.

taking part in the poll were asked to answer the following question by putting a ballot in the corresponding box: »Would the fact that Governor Rockefeller has not denounced President Nixon's Indochina Policy be a reason for you not voting for him in November?«[10] At the time, the Republican Nelson Rockefeller was in the running to be reelected as the Governor of the State of New York. Just two months before the museum exhibition opened, US President Richard Nixon had ordered the bombing and military occupation of Cambodia. Haacke's public survey was not only politically controversial, but also explosive in terms of cultural politics, since Nelson Rockefeller was a member of MoMA's Board of Trustees at the time and his brother David was the chairman. Already in 1969, the artists of the Guerrilla Art Action Group had vocally demanded, in a performance, the Rockefellers' resignation from all museum positions (fig. 3).[11] One of the family's companies manufactured weapons for the Vietnam War, and their civic engagement also served as a fig leaf for their dubious economic interests. More than two thirds of the participants in Haacke's public poll voted against Nelson Rockefeller as a possible governor.

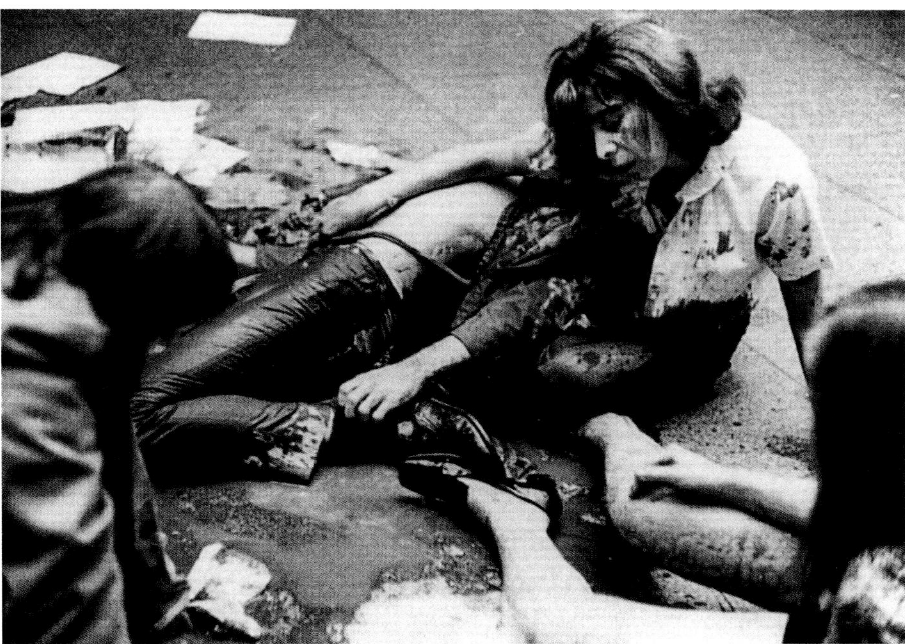

Fig. 3: Photograph of the performance *Blood Bath* by the Guerilla Art Action Group, demanding the resignation of the Rockefellers from the board of The Museum of Modern Art, New York, action in the museum's lobby, November 18, 1969

Participation in the sense of actively involving the audience in artistic projects was a widespread strategy around 1970 and could be found in the work of several Conceptual artists, but also in Happenings, the Fluxus movement, and Viennese Actionism. Likewise, Hans Haacke's *MoMA Poll* was not intended for passive or contemplative reception. Instead, the visitors actively contributed to the realization of the artistic work in a processual way. Through their necessary participation, the project no longer appeared as a hermetic autonomous work, but as an open structure which implied an expansion of

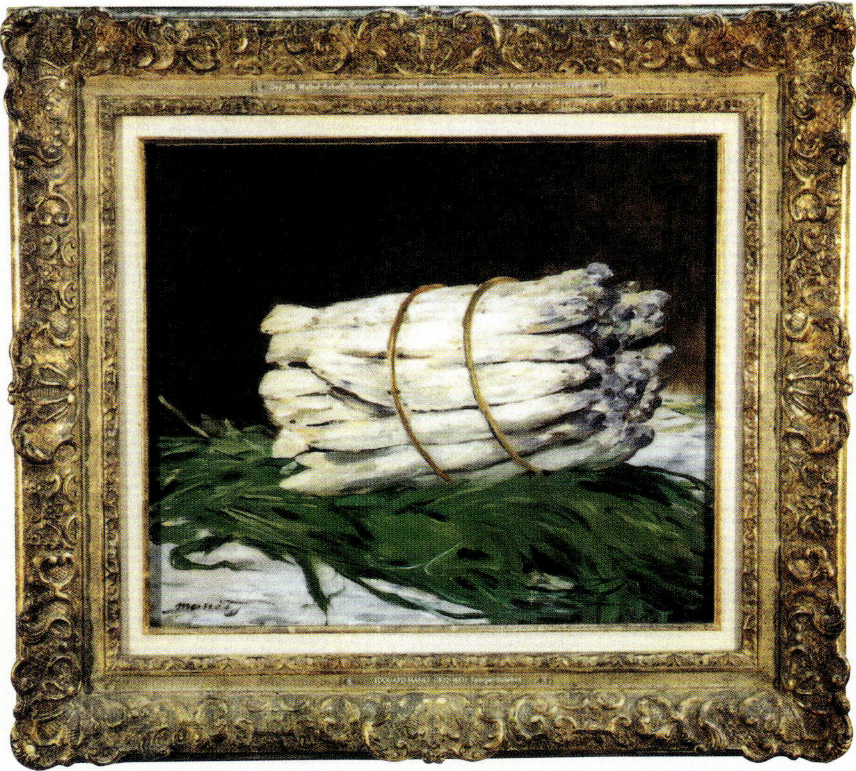

Fig. 4: Édouard Manet, *La botte d'asperges (Bunch of Asparagus)*, 1880, oil on canvas, 46 × 55 cm, color reproduction for *Manet-PROJEKT '74*, 83 × 94 cm

12
Hans Haacke, quoted in Stefan Römer, »Zur Soziologie der künstlerischen Strategie« (interview), *Texte zur Kunst* 2, no. 8 (December 1992), p. 59.

13
Henry Flynt, »Concept Art,« in *An Anthology of Chance Operations*, ed. La Monte Young and Jackson Mac Low, 2nd ed. (New York: H. Friedrich, 1970), n.p.

the concept of art. More concretely, the piece confronted the museum as an institution, and the public as a social group, with the political climate as though in a mirror image or a »statistical self-portrait,«[12] and this made the political climate the object of reflection.

Verbalization, Documentation, and Seriality

In 1974, Hans Haacke realized one of his most important works, *Manet-PROJEKT '74* (figs. pp. 123–33), which can be used to illustrate several conceptual categories that are especially relevant to this work and to Conceptual Art in general. The term likely made its first appearance in a 1961 essay by the American artist Henry Flynt, which was published two years later under the title »Concept Art.« The text contains the following definition: »›Concept art‹ is first of all an art of which the material is *concepts*, as the material of e.g. music is sound. Since *concepts* are closely bound up with language, concept art is a kind of art of which the material is language.«[13] Even if this focus on linguistic signs is too one-sided, since Conceptual Art does not necessarily have to work with language, probably language was the most frequently used medium in the movement alongside photography. Haacke does not use language as a universal system of syntactically and semantically defined signs in a literary or poetic way; rather, it appears as a vehicle of factual information based on research, which the artist uses to

14
Benjamin H. D. Buchloh, »Hans Haacke: Memory and Instrumental Reason,« *Art in America* (February 1988), p. 159, note 13 (emphasis in the original).

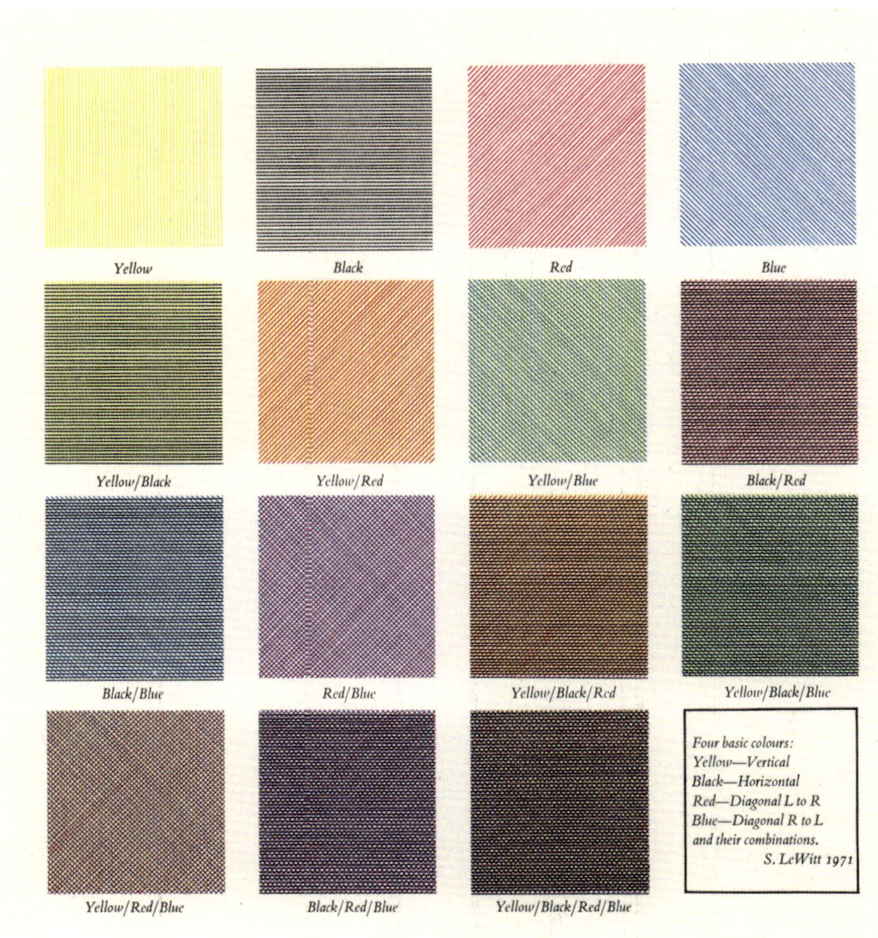

Fig. 5: Sol LeWitt, *Four basic kinds of lines & colour*, artist's book, concept and table of contents on the third page, London and New York, 1971, 20.3 × 25.4 cm, private collection

pursue an enlightening impetus, albeit with restraint. In 1971, he explained his approach with the following words: »I do not want to practice agitation which appeals or accuses. . . . *Facts* are probably stronger and often less comfortable than even the best intended opinions.«[14]

Manet-PROJEKT '74 was created on the occasion of the group exhibition *PROJEKT '74* in Cologne, which was dedicated to recent aspects of European and American art. It was held at the municipal Kunsthalle and the Wallraf Richartz Museum, among other venues. The artist suggested presenting Édouard Manet's 1880 still life *Bunch of Asparagus* (fig. 4) from the museum's collection together with the results of research into the painting's provenance. In the planned installation, ten black-and-white text and photo panels were to be displayed alongside the original oil painting. Each of the individual panels (screen prints and glued-on photographs) featured the biographical details and portraits of the following people or institutions: the painter Édouard Manet, the six previous owners of his still life, and Hermann Josef Abs as the initiator of the Cologne museum's acquisition of the painting in 1968, as well as the patrons on the Wallraf Richartz Museum's Board of Trustees and the companies that made it financially possible to purchase the painting from the Swiss art market. Prominent

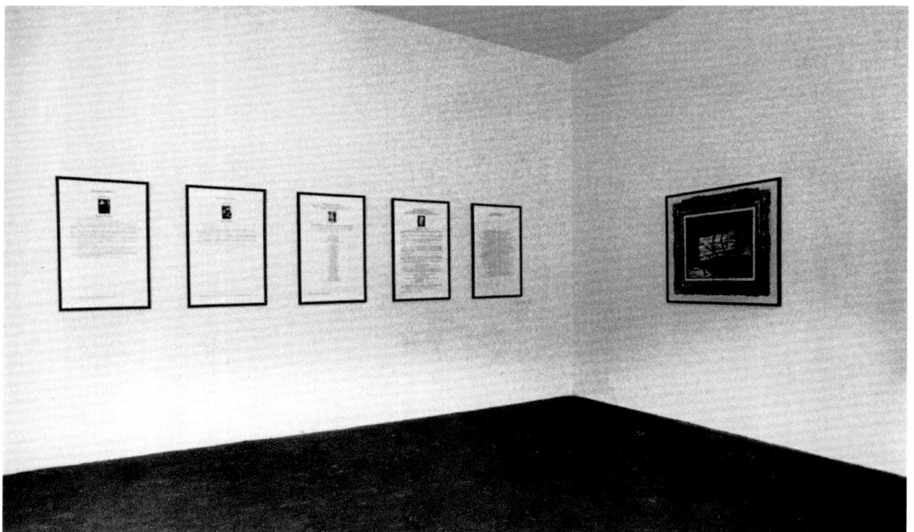

Fig. 6: *Hans Haacke: Manet-PROJEKT '74*, exhibition view, Galerie Paul Maenz, Cologne, 1974

previous owners of the work included the Parisian collector Charles Ephrussi, the Berlin art dealer Paul Cassirer, and the Impressionist painter Max Liebermann.

Language is the primary medium of this conceptual work. The rhetorical style of the biographies is pointedly factual and avoids any subjective statements—in other words, they contain no personal commentary. It also means that there is no reference to Hans Haacke as the author of the texts, which seem like encyclopedia entries and suggest neutrality, even though the information was compiled by the artist.

The portraits of all the people involved, the short biographies, and some of the known sale prices clearly illustrate the origin and history of the still life in the form of a sober documentary register. The practice of simply presenting real circumstances as facts is frequently found in Conceptual Art, for example in photographic form in the works of Bernd and Hilla Becher, Christian Boltanski, Hans-Peter Feldmann, and Ed Ruscha. In addition to Hans Haacke, the artists Douglas Huebler, On Kawara, Joseph Kosuth, and Martha Rosler should be mentioned for conceptual works in textual, that is, written form.

In addition to these artistic practices of verbalization and documentation, seriality is another trait of Haacke's *Manet-PROJEKT '74*. Working in series is one of the most fundamental strategies of Conceptual Art, but also of Minimal Art and Pop Art. Seriality as a concept is always based on the principle of repeating the same or at least similar things. The American Conceptual Artist Mel Bochner formulated the foundational sentence in 1967: »Serial order is a method, not a style.«[15] Thus, for Bochner, the application of serial principles is not a stylistic phenomenon that corresponds to a specific aesthetic, but the manifestation of a specific artistic approach. In contrast to an intuitive or even expressive practice, Bochner advocates a systematic method that is conceptually defined. In his ten panels, Haacke likewise follows a strict concept of repetition

15
Mel Bochner, »The Serial Attitude,« *Artforum International* 4 (December 1967), p. 28.

16
Sol LeWitt, »Serial Project #1, 1966,« *Aspen Magazine* 5–6 (1967), n.p. (this issue edited by Brian O'Doherty).

17
Buchloh, »From the Aesthetic of Administration to Institutional Critique,« p. 41.

18
Pierre Bourdieu, in Pierre Bourdieu and Hans Haacke, *Free Exchange* (Cambridge: Polity Press, 1995), p. 1.

through a uniform aesthetic in terms of their size, font, graphic design, and serial hanging. This standardization makes the installation look almost scientific.

Another artist who also explored the possibilities of serial work intensively is the aforementioned Sol LeWitt, who introduced the term »Conceptual Art« into art discourse in 1967 and is considered the most important American representative of a largely minimalist tendency in the movement (fig. 5). As early as 1966, he had declared: »The serial artist does not attempt to produce a beautiful or mysterious object but functions merely as a clerk cataloging the results of his premise.«[16] The art historian Benjamin H. D. Buchloh thus aptly described this artistic practice as an »aesthetic of administration.«[17]

Institutional Critique

Hans Haacke's *Manet-PROJEKT '74* is a paradigmatic example of the tendency within Conceptual Art known as Institutional Critique. Such a sociocritical or explicitly socially oriented approach can also be found in Haacke's fellow artists Michael Asher, Marcel Broodthaers, and Daniel Buren. The fundamental aim is to analyze and raise awareness of the social, economic, and institutional conditions under which art is produced, exhibited, sold, and received. Attention is thus directed away from the purely sensory perception of an art object and toward reflection on the operational aspects of the art system and the interpretive authority they confer. As the French sociologist Pierre Bourdieu emphasizes, Hans Haacke has »a truly remarkable ›eye‹ for seeing the particular forms of domination that are exerted on the art world.«[18] Haacke has consistently criticized institutions, especially in terms of the economic conditions of art. In many of his works, he has used documentary and informative methods to make it clear that there is no such thing as an autonomous or pure art insulated from economic realities. An artistic work is not only an aesthetic and symbolic cultural artifact; it is always also a commodity and thus subjected to the profanities of money and market activities. Works of art are situated in a system of entanglements and dependencies that is strongly influenced by economic factors.

The second to last of the ten panels in *Manet-PROJEKT '74* shows this especially clearly: the print contains biographical data on Hermann Josef Abs (fig. p. 132), who, as Chairman of the Board of Trustees and the Friends of the Wallraf Richartz Museum, was instrumental in the acquisition of the Manet painting in 1968. Abs was a member of the executive and supervisory boards of Deutsche Bank, both in the Federal Republic of Germany and during the Third Reich. As one of the most powerful bankers and a key figure in the German economy, he had a lasting influence on the fortunes of both systems. During the National Socialist era, he held key positions in over fifty companies as well as in banking and business organizations. He thus played an important role in the political, financial, and economic stabilization of the Nazi regime. Horst Keller, the director of the Wallraf Richartz Museum, categorically rejected the presentation of Haacke's work, as he did not want the web of entanglements between art and capital to be revealed in his museum. In June 1974, he wrote to the artist in feigned naivety about Hermann Josef Abs: »A museum knows nothing about economic power . . . .«[19] Although what he probably should have written is: »The museum doesn't want to know anything about the somewhat dubious historical power of its patron.« One can assume that what the director wanted most was to prevent the banker's Nazi history from being publicly remembered. Critical examination of the National Socialist pasts of leading figures in West Germany was still taboo in conservative circles at the time. By his own account, Horst Keller feared the indignation of his culturally and politically powerful patron,[20] even though Hans Haacke's *Manet-PROJEKT '74* did not express any explicit criticism, but simply listed facts that were intended to speak for themselves. Nevertheless, Keller prevented the installation from being exhibited in preemptory deference to Hermann Josef Abs. The artist was disinvited and thus subjected to institutional censorship.[21] During the exhibition, however, he was still able to present his work in the Cologne gallery of Paul Maenz and Gerd de Vries, where a color reproduction was shown next to the panels instead of Manet's original oil painting (fig. 6).

Hans Haacke's oeuvre has consistently offered critical reflection on the political, economic, and institutional frameworks of art. In the 1960s and 1970s, he helped initiate a historical paradigm shift within Conceptual Art in terms of artistic methods and content. He significantly transformed the self-image of artists, the role of the viewer, and the appearance of art. In his installation *MoMA Poll*, he worked with the principle of participation, among other things. His *Manet-PROJEKT '74* is based on the categories of verbalization, documentation, seriality, and Institutional Critique. Even if subsequent generations eventually came to question or even negate these Conceptual Art principles in theory and practice, their art-historical significance and influence have been greater and more far-reaching than it may sometimes seem in our fast-paced art world. The work of many artists since the 1980s would have been inconceivable without an engagement with Conceptual Art. The 2011 exhibition *With Reference to Hans Haacke* at the Hamburger Bahnhof museum in Berlin (fig. 7) presented works by almost one hundred younger colleagues who all drew on Hans Haacke's artistic practice.[22] This impressively demonstrates the ongoing relevance of his works and the history of Conceptual Art, even if his entire oeuvre cannot be reduced to this category.

19
Horst Keller, letter to Hans Haacke from June 4, 1974, reprinted on Hans Haacke's poster *Zur Zensur meiner Arbeit für PROJEKT '74 durch das Wallraf-Richartz-Museum* (On the Censorship of My Work on PROJEKT '74 by the Wallraf Richartz Museum), published by Galerie Paul Maenz, Cologne, 1974. The letter is quoted in Buchloh, »Hans Haacke: Memory and Instrumental Reason,« p. 99.

20
Horst Keller, in Hans Haacke, »Manet-PROJEKT '74,« in *Hans Haacke: Nach allen Regeln der Kunst*, p. 12.

21
Hans Haacke, »Manet-PROJEKT '74,« in *Deutschlandbilder: Kunst aus einem geteilten Land*, ed. Eckhart Gillen, exh. cat. Martin-Gropius-Bau, Berlin (Cologne: Dumont, 1997), pp. 350–55.

22
Hans Dickel and Oliver Schwarz, eds., *With Reference to Hans Haacke*, exh. cat. Hamburger Bahnhof, Berlin (Cologne: Verlag der Buchhandlung Walther König, 2011).

with references by
Vito Acconci
Dennis Adams
Doug Ashford
Alice Aycock
Fritz Balthaus
Michel Blazy
Monica Bonvicini
Tania Bruguera
Matthew Buckingham
Daniele Buetti
Daniel Buren
Victor Burgin
Ernst Burkel
Lutz Dammbeck
Dellbrügge & de Moll
Georg Diez/
Christopher Roth
Mark Dion
Maria Eichhorn
Olafur Eliasson
Harun Farocki
Hans Peter Feldmann
Rainer Ganahl
Jochen Gerz
Liam Gillick
Rodney Graham
Paul Graham
Renée Green
Ingo Günther
Jens Haaning
Helen Mayer &
Newton Harrison
Mona Hatoum
Thomas Hirschhorn
Jenny Holzer
Sabine Hornig
Fabrice Hybert
Leiko Ikemura
Alfredo Jaar
Emily Jacir
Christian Jankowski
Joan Jonas
Mary Kelly
Vitaly Komar
Joseph Kosuth
Susanne Kriemann
Philipp Lachenmann
Louise Lawler
Sharon Lockhart
Heinz Mack
Teresa Margolles
John Menick
Olaf Metzel
John Miller
Naeem Mohaiemen
Jonathan Monk
François Morellet
Christian Philipp Müller
Matt Mullican
Antonio Muntadas
Warren Neidich
Shirin Neshat
Carsten Nicolai
Olaf Nicolai
Marcel Odenbach
Jorge Pardo
Pavel Pepperstein
Dieter Pfannenstiel
Otto Piene
Adrian Piper
Phillip Pocock
Walid Raad
David Reeb
Martha Rosler
Karin Sander
Thomas Scheibitz
Julia Scher
Cornelia Schleime
Oliver Schwarz
Andreas Siekmann
Santiago Sierra
Keith Sonnier
Klaus Staeck
Franz Stauffenberg
Tatiana Trouvé
Günther Uecker
Liselot van der Heijden
Katrin v. Maltzahn
Mark Wallinger
Peter Weibel
Lawrence Weiner
Krzysztof Wodiczko
Erwin Wurm
Heimo Zobernig

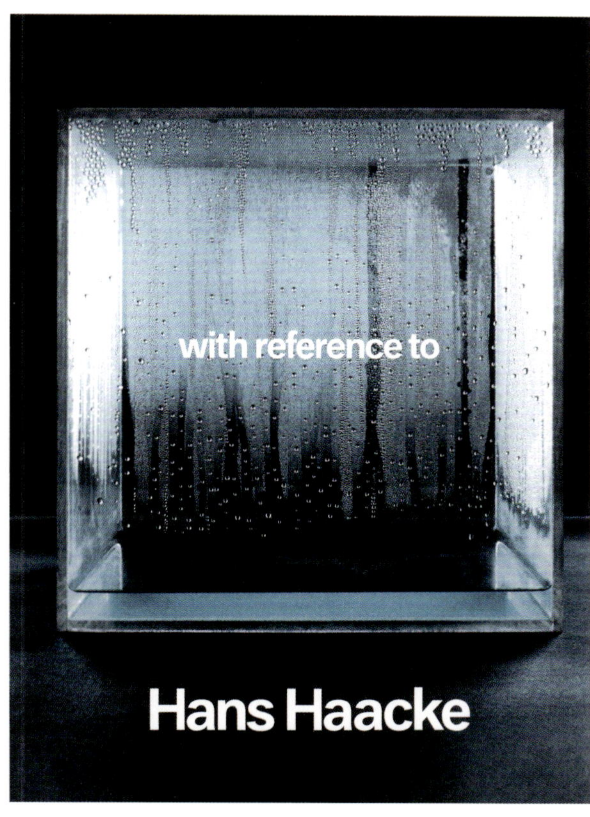

Fig. 7: Hans Dickel and Oliver Schwarz, editors, *With Reference to Hans Haacke*, exhibition catalogue Hamburger Bahnhof, Berlin, 2011, front and back cover

MoMA Poll, 1970

Visitors to the *Information* show at The Museum of Modern Art in 1970 were asked to respond on ballots to a question posted above two transparent boxes in the exhibition. Automatic counters recorded the ballots placed in the boxes. By the end of the exhibition, they had tallied 25,566 »Yes« votes (68.7 percent) and 11,563 »No« votes (31.3 percent). Of a total of 299,057 visitors, 37,129 (12.4 percent) had participated. The question referred to Nelson Rockefeller, the four-term Republican governor of the state of New York (1959–73), who was running for reelection in 1970. Two months before the opening of the exhibition, the United States bombed and invaded Cambodia, even though that country had declared itself neutral in the Vietnam conflict. In protest, large antiwar demonstrations were held throughout the United States. On the campus of Kent State University, four protesting students were shot dead by the Ohio National Guard. Many New York artists joined the Art Strike, an ad hoc group that called for the temporary closing of museums.

The Rockefeller family had played an important role in founding MoMA in 1929. Nelson Rockefeller was a member of MoMA's board of trustees from 1932 until his death in 1979. From 1939 to 1941, he was president, and from 1957 to 1958, chairman of the board. At the time of the *Information* show, Nelson's brother David Rockefeller served as chairman (1962–72 and 1987–93). Until his retirement in 1981, David was also chairman of Chase Manhattan Bank, one of the most powerful banks in the United States. Their sister-in-law, Mrs. John D. Rockefeller III, also held the chairmanship of MoMA (1985–87). David Rockefeller quotes the *MoMA Poll* question in his autobiography.

Hans Haacke, 2004

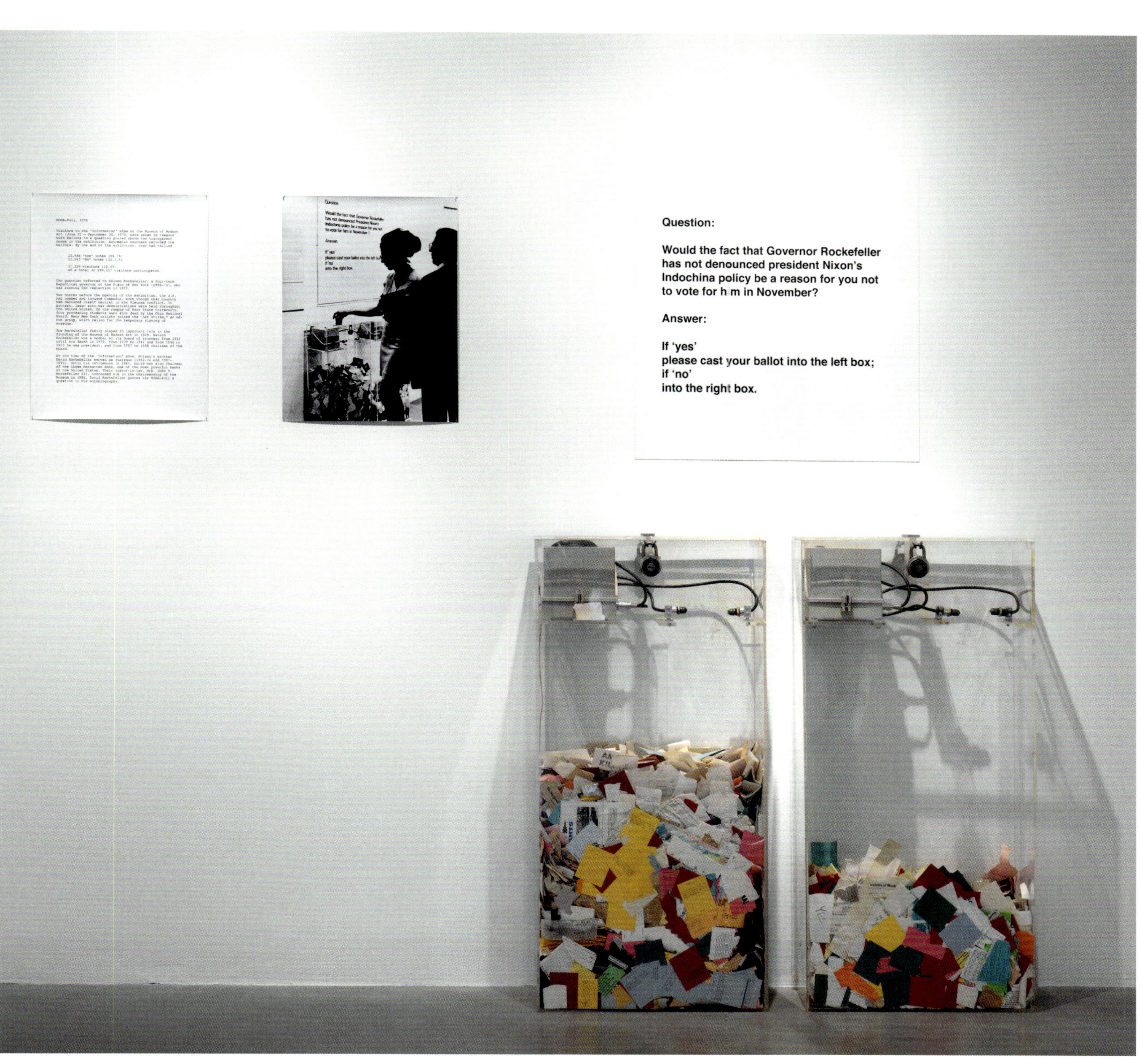

MoMA Poll, 1970

Gallery-Goers' Residence Profile, Parts 1 and 2, 1969–70

For *Gallery-Goers' Birthplace and Residence Profile, Part 1* (1969), I asked the people that came to my exhibition to mark with a blue pin on large maps where they were living. After the show, I traveled to all those spots on the Manhattan map that were marked by a blue pin and took a photograph of the building or approximate location. I came up with about 730 photographs for Manhattan (naturally, not every visitor participated in the game). The photographs were enlarged to five by eight inches. They were meant to be displayed on the wall of the Guggenheim Museum according to a geographical score. All those spots that were east of Fifth Avenue would go upward on the wall from a horizontal centerline; those west would go downward. The respective distance from Fifth Avenue determines the sequence of pictures east and west. The Fifth Avenue spine takes up approximately thirty-six yards of wall space.

Sometimes the photographs reach up to the ceiling, while on other occasions it becomes a very jagged distribution. The »composition« is determined by the information provided by gallery goers. No visual considerations play a role. Each vertical row of photographs represents a street. The street blocks in question are listed on typewritten cards positioned on the horizontal axis. All this sounds very innocent and apolitical. The information I collected, however, is sociologically quite revealing. The public of commercial art galleries, and probably that of museums, lives in easily identifiable and restricted areas.

The main concentrations are on the Upper West Side (Central Park and adjoining blocks, and West End Avenue with adjoining blocks); the Upper East Side, somewhat heavier in the Madison and Park Avenue areas; and below 23rd Street on the east and west sides, with clusters on the Lower East Side and in the loft district. The photographs give an idea of the economic and social fabric of the immediate neighbourhood of the gallery goers. The art scene is obviously dominated by the middle- and upper-income strata of society or their dropout children. I leave it up to the viewer as far as how to evaluate this situation. The viewer continues the work by drawing their own conclusions from the information presented.

Hans Haacke, 1970

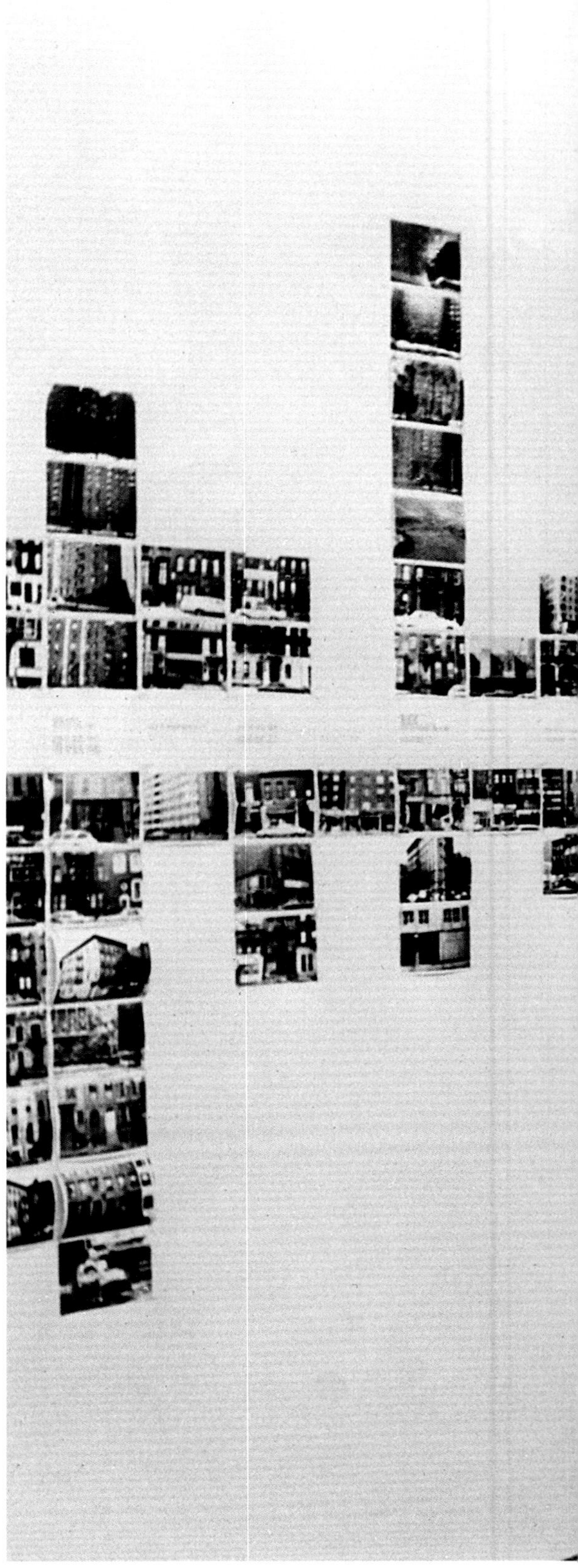

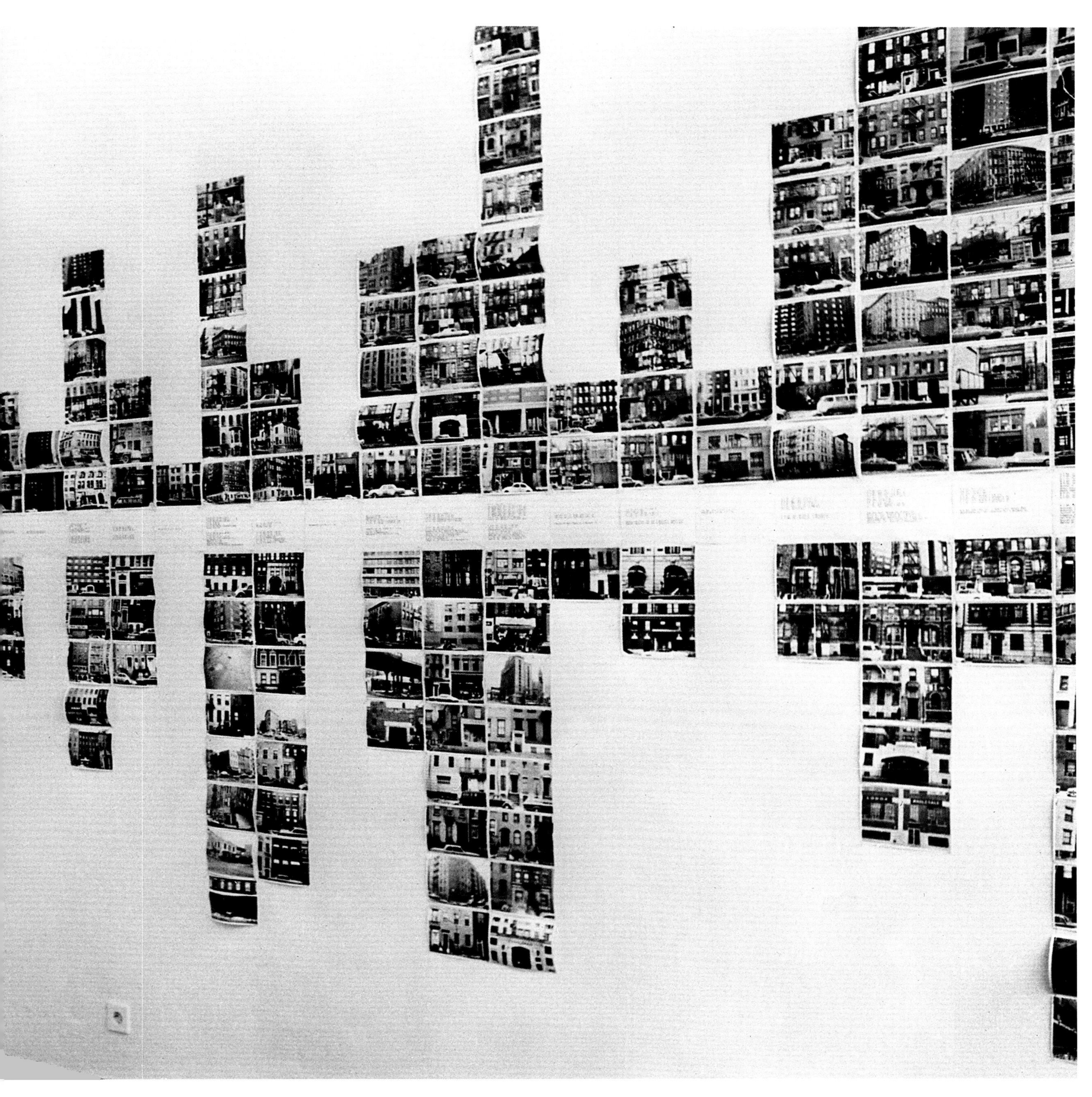

Gallery-Goers' Residence Profile, Parts 1 and 2, 1969–70 (detail)
Installation view Galerie Paul Maenz, Cologne, 1971

Shapolsky et al. Manhattan Real Estate Holdings, a Real-Time Social System, as of May 1, 1971

In 1971, the Shapolsky real estate group, headed by Harry Shapolsky and nominally owned by about seventy different corporations, frequently bought, sold, and mortgaged properties within the group. What amounted to self-dealing had tax advantages (mortgage payments are tax deductible) and obscured the actual ownership of the properties. The boards of these seventy odd corporations each included at least one member of the Shapolsky family or someone with close ties. The 142 known properties were located predominantly on the Lower East Side and in Harlem—both slum areas of New York City in 1971—where they constituted the largest concentration of real estate under the control of a single group. The information for the work was culled from public records at the New York County Clerk's Office.

Thomas Messer, then the director of the Solomon R. Guggenheim Museum, rejected this work and two others that had been made for a solo exhibition at the museum. He cancelled the exhibition six weeks before the opening when I refused to withdraw the disputed works. Messer called them »inappropriate« for exhibition at the museum and stated that he had to »fend off an alien substance that had entered the art museum organism.« Edward F. Fry, the curator of the exhibition, was fired when he defended the works. Artists held a protest demonstration in the museum. More than one hundred artists pledged not to exhibit at the Guggenheim »until the policy of art censorship and its advocates are changed.« Many commentators assumed that the trustees of the Guggenheim Museum had links to the Shapolsky real estate group. There is no evidence to support such suspicions.

Hans Haacke, 2006

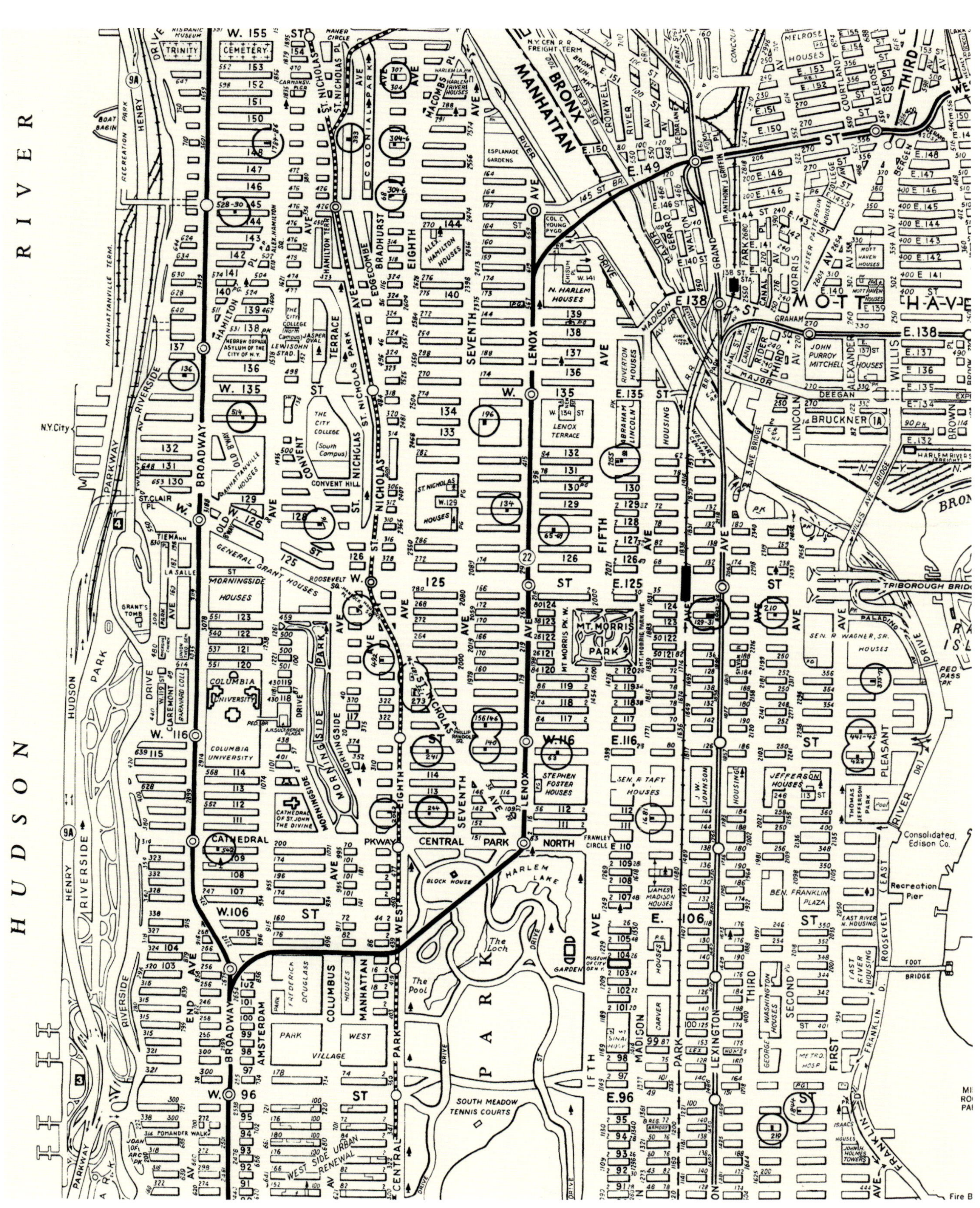

Shapolsky et al. Manhattan Real Estate Holdings, a Real-Time Social System, as of May 1, 1971

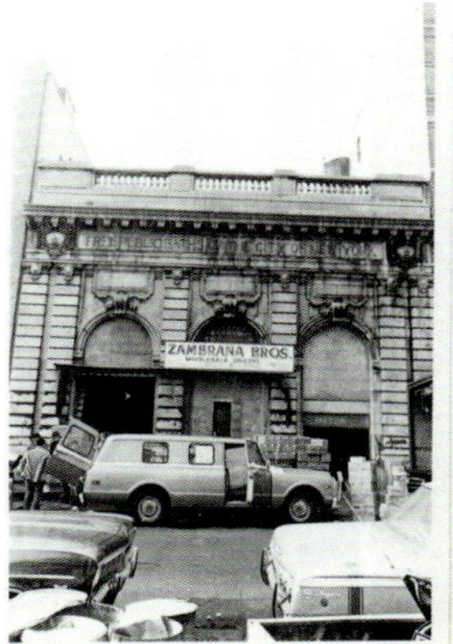

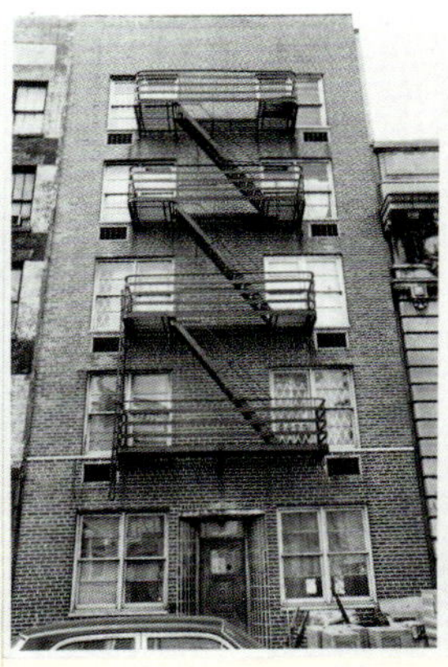

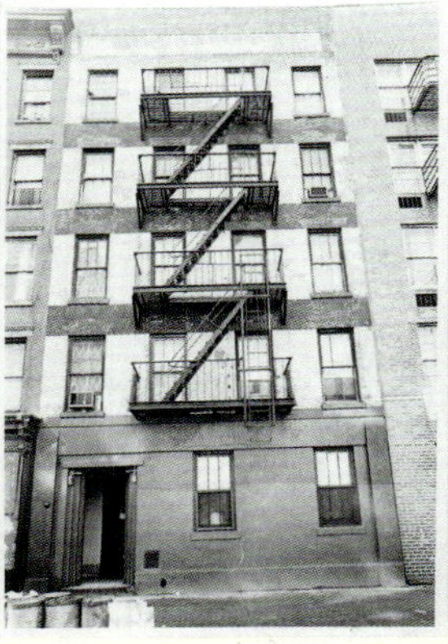

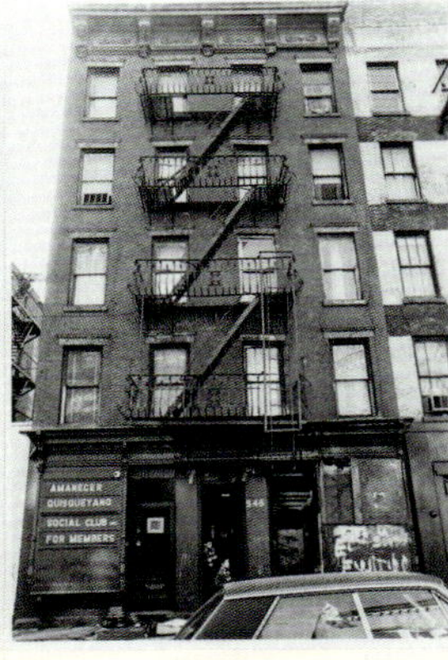

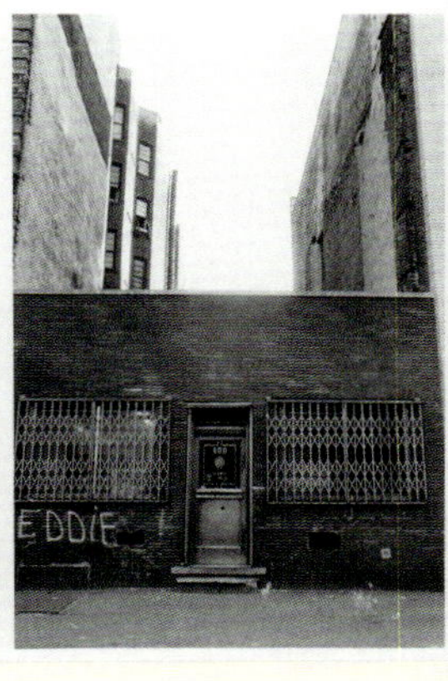

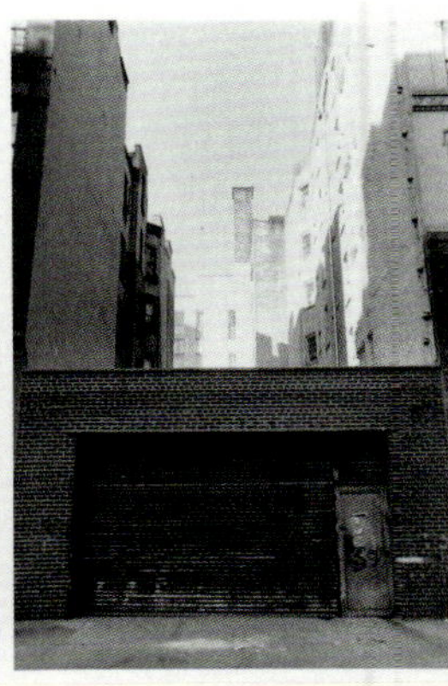

538-40 E 11 St.
Block 404 Lot 23
50 x 94' 2 story bldg.

Owned by One Fifty Four Realty Corp., 608 E 11 St. NYC
Contracts signed by Harry N. Gruber, Pres.('54/60/64)
George Greenberger, Vicepres.('61)
Harry J. Shapolsky, Sec.('51)
Principal Harry N. Gruber and Harry J. Shapolsky(according to Real Estate Directory of Manhattan)

Acquired at auction from City of New York, 4-20-1961, for $19 500.-

$15 000.- mortgage at 5 1/2 % interest, 4-17-1961, due 4-17-1976, held through assignment, 3-1-1966, by New York City Employees' Retirement System

Assessed land value $18 000.-, total $35 000.- (1971)

542 E 11 St.
Block 404 Lot 25
25 x 94' 5 story walk-up old law tenement

Owned by One Fifty Four Realty Corp., 608 E 11 St., NYC
Contracts signed by Harry N. Gruber, Pres.('54/60/64)
George Greenberger, Vicepres. ('61)
Harry J. Shapolsky, Secretary ('51)
Principal Harry J. Shapolsky(according to Real Estate Directory of Manhattan)

Acquired 10-28-1955 from Theobald et al

No mortgage(1972)

Assessed land value $9 000.- total $54[illegible] 000.-(1971)

544 E 11 St.
Block 404 Lot 26
25 x 94' 5 story walk-up converted dwelling

Owned by Ray Dome Realty Corp., 608 E 11 St., NYC
Contracts signed by Ernest Callipari, Pres.('69/70)
Principal Harry J. Shapolsky(according to Real Estate Directory of Manhattan)

Acquired 1-2-1969, from 544 E 11 St. Corp., 509 Madison Ave., Ruth Cohen, President

Due $25 447.67 of $35 256.44 purchase money mortgage, 4-9-1960, held through assignment, 5-7-1969, by 174 East 3rd St. Corp., 608 E 11 St. NYC, Harry J. Shapolsky and Catherine Greco principals according to Real Estate Directory of Manhattan

Assessed land value $9 000.- , total $70 000.- (1971)

546 E 11 St.
Block 404 Lot 27
25 x 94' 5 story walk-up old law tenement

Owned by One Fifty Four Realty Corp., 608 E 11 St. NYC
Contracts signed by Harry N. Gruber, Pres. ('54/60/64)
George Greenberger, Vicepres. ('61)
Harry J. Shapolsky, Secretary ('51)
Principal Harry J. Shapolsky(according to Real Estate Directory of Manhattan)

Acquired 4-28-1967 from Anthony Fazio, executor of will of Rosalia Fazio

No mortgage(1971)

Assessed land value $9 000.- total $22 000.- (1971)

608 E 11 St.
Block 393 Lot 11
25 x 94' 1 story store bldg.

Business office of Shapolsky related corporations
Owned by 194 Ave. A Realty Corp., 608 E 11 St., NYC
Contracts signed by Sam Shapolsky, President('58)
Harry J. Shapolsky, Pres.('60)
Alfred Fayer, Vicepres. ('58)
Principal Harry J. Shapolsky(according to Real Estate Directory of Manhattan)

Acquired 3-27-1963 from Surenko Realties Inc, 608 E 11 St., NYC, Harry J. Shapolsky, President(63)

No mortgage(1971)

Assessed land value $8 500.- , total $24 000.- (1971)

609 E 11 St.
Block 394 Lot 64
25 x 103' 1 story garage

Owned by 194 Ave. A Realty Corp., 608 E 11 St., NYC
Contracts signed by Sam Shapolsky, President ('58)
Harry J. Shapolsky, Pres.('60)
Alfred Fayer, Vicepres. ('58)
Principal Harry J. Shapolsky(according to Real Estate Directory of Manhattan)

Acquired 3-27-1963 from Surenko Realties Inc., 608 E E St., NYC, Harry J. Shapolsky, Pres. ('63)

No mortgage(1971)

Assessed land value $9 000.- , total $14 000.-(1971)

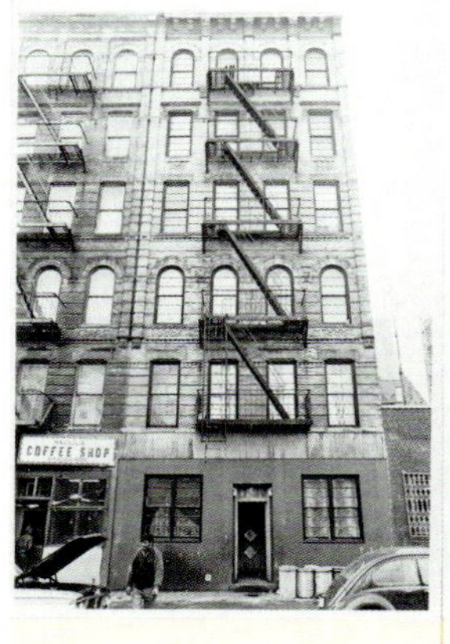

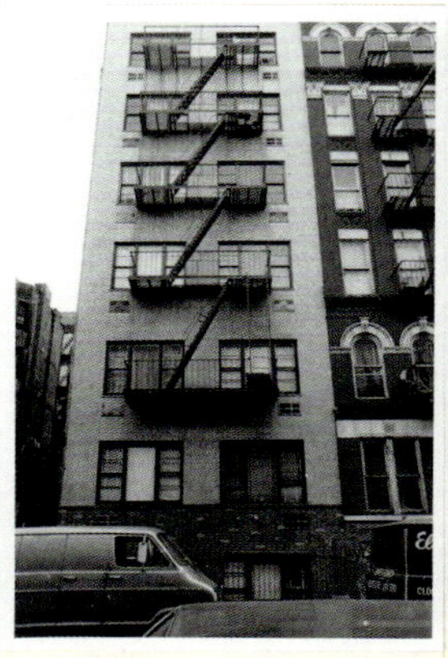

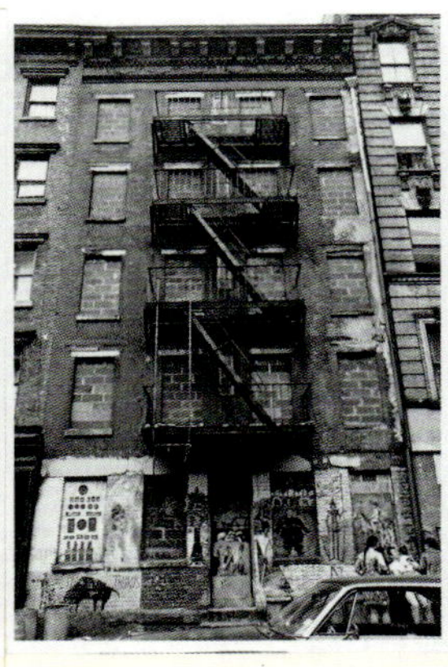

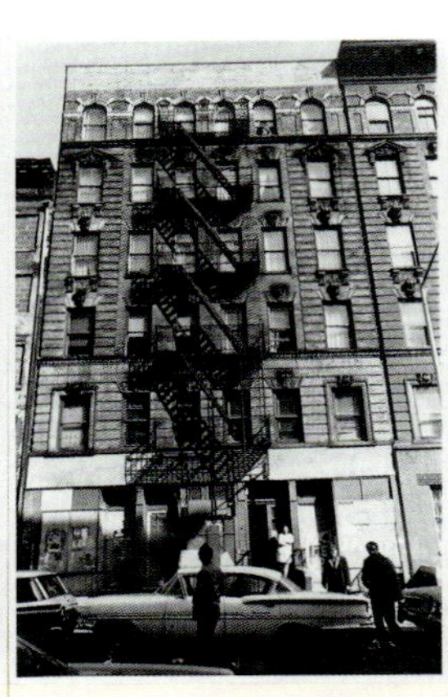

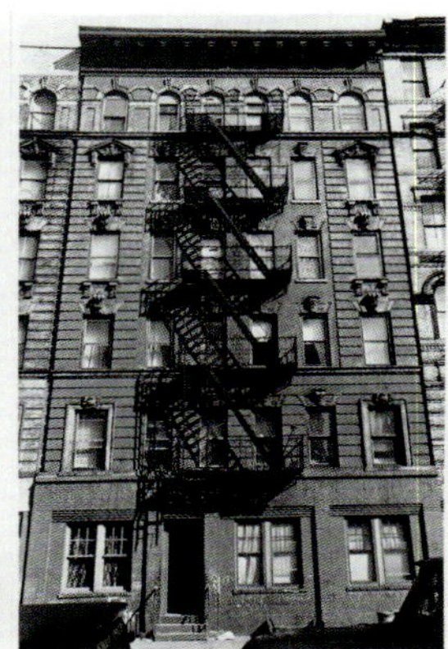

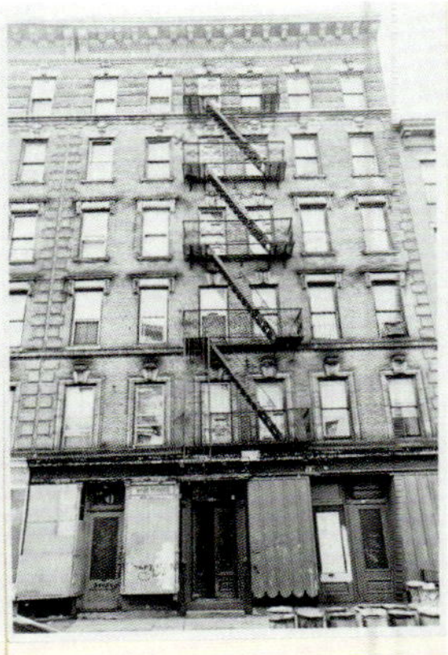

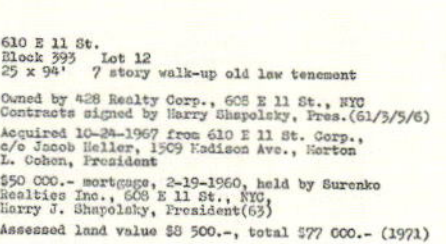

610 E 11 St.
Block 393 Lot 12
25 x 94' 7 story walk-up old law tenement

Owned by 428 Realty Corp., 608 E 11 St., NYC
Contracts signed by Harry Shapolsky, Pres.(61/3/5/6)

Acquired 10-24-1967 from 610 E 11 St. Corp., c/o Jacob Heller, 1509 Madison Ave., Morton L. Cohen, President

$50 000.- mortgage, 2-19-1960, held by Surenko Realties Inc., 608 E 11 St., NYC, Harry J. Shapolsky, President(63)

Assessed land value $8 500.-, total $77 000.- (1971)

624 E 11 St.
Block 393 Lot 19
25 x 94' 6 story elevator apt. bldg.

Owned by S & K Estates Inc., 608 E 11 St., NYC
Contracts signed by Harry J. Shapolsky, President('38)
Daniel Kirschenbaum, Pres.('67)
Donald Sherman, President('68/69)
Principal Harry J. Shapolsky(according to Real Estate Directory of Manhattan)

Acquired 4-26'71 at auction from Kingsboro Mortgage Corp.

No mortgage

Assessed land value $[illegible]500.- , total $35 000.- (1971)

625 E 11 St.
Block 394 Lot 56
25 x 103' 5 story walk-up old law tenement

Owned by East No. 1 Realty Corp., 608 E 11 St., NYC
Contracts signed by Pearl Shapolsky, President
Alfred Fayer, Vice President
George Greenberger, Vice President

Acquired 1-20-1972 from Shapol Realty Corp., 608 E 11, NYC
Contracts signed by Harry Shapolsky, Pres.(51/61/64/65/68/72)
Pearl Shapolsky, Pres.(66)
Abraham Haftel, Pres.(70)
Alfred Fayer, Vice President(61)

No mortgages(1972)

Assessed land value $9 000.- , total $10 000.- (1971)

627-29 E 11 St.
Block 394 Lot 55
37 x 103' 6 story walk-up new law apt. bldg.,stores

Owned by Shapol Realty Corp., 608 E 11 St., NYC
Contracts signed by Harry Shapolsky, Pres.(51.61/4/5/8)
Pearl Kleinberg(Shapolsky)Pres.(66)
Abraham Haftel, Pres.('70)
Principal Harry J. Shapolsky(according to Real Estate Directory of Manhattan)

Acquired 6-23-1964 through foreclosure from Malan Construction Corp. defendant

Assessed land value $13 000.- , total $55 000.- (1971)

631 E 11 St.
Block 394 Lot 53
37 x 103' 6 story walk-up new law apt. bldg. stores

Owned by Kirshop Realty Corp., 608 E 11 St., NYC, and 216 E 89 St., Brooklyn
Contracts signed by Sam Kirschenbaum, Pres.('56/59)
Daniel Kirschenbaum, Pres.('66/69)
Denise Kirschenbaum, Pres.('68)
Principal Sam Kirschenbaum and Harry J. Shapolsky (according to Real Estate Directory of Manhattan)

Acquired 2-18-1959 from Sany Realty Corp., 77-37 168th St., Flushing, L.I., Hyman Barr, Pres.

No mortgage(1971)

Assessed land value $13 500.-, total $52 000.- (1971)

504 E 12 St.
Block 405 Lot 10
37 x 103' 6 story walk-up new law apt.bldg. stores

Owned by Espearl Realty Corp., 608 E 11 St., NYC
Contracts signed by Harry J. Shapolsky, Secretary('65)
Principal Harry J. Shapolsky(according to Real Estate Directory of Manhattan)

Acquired 8-16-1961 from Nebrodi Realty Corp., 508 E 12 St. NYC, John Lo Presti, Treasurer

$50 000.- mortgage at 6% interest(also on 508 E 12 St.) 5-24-1965, held by Sarah Platnick and Jennie Gross, 2250-83 St., Brooklyn

Assessed land value $13 500.- , total $43 000.- (1971)

Shapolsky et al. Manhattan Real Estate Holdings, a Real-Time Social System, as of May 1, 1971

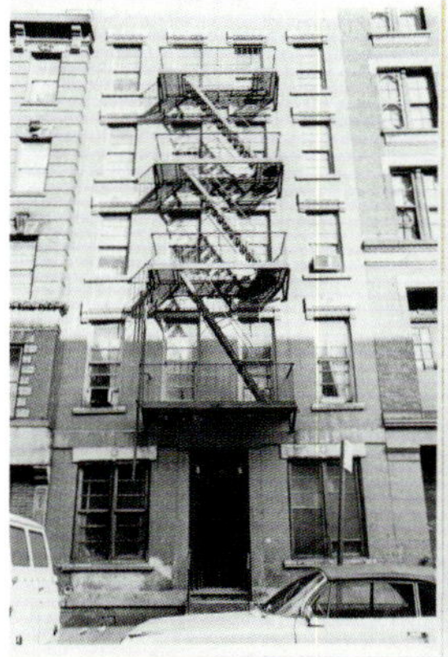

733 E 9 St.
Block 379 Lot 48
25 x 92' 5 story walk-up apt. bldg.

Owned by 232 Harper Estates Realty Inc., 608 E 11, NYC
Contracts signed by Pearl Kleinberg(Shapolsky), President ('57/62/3/4)
Harry J. Shapolsky, Secretary('62)

Acquired 12-11-1956 from Julia Bulowa, 45 W 54 St. NYC

No mortgage(1971)

Assessed land value $6 700.- total $52 000.- (1971)

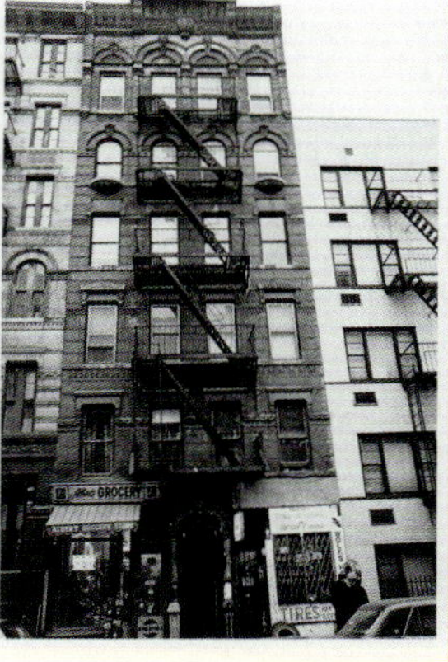

223 E 10 St.
Block 452 Lot 46
25 x 94' 6 story walk-up old law tenement

Owned by Shapol Realty Corp., 608 E 11 St., NYC
Contracts signed by Harry Shapolsky, Pres.(51/51/4/5/8)
Pearl Kleinberg(Shapolsky)Pres.(66)
Abraham Haftel, President(70)
Principal Harry J. Shapolsky(according to Real Estate Directory of Manhattan)

Acquired 2-3-1961 from East 10th Street Salvage Corp., 21 E 40 St., NYC, c/ David F. Foley

No mortgage(1971)

Assessed land value $10 500.- , total $25 000.- (1971)

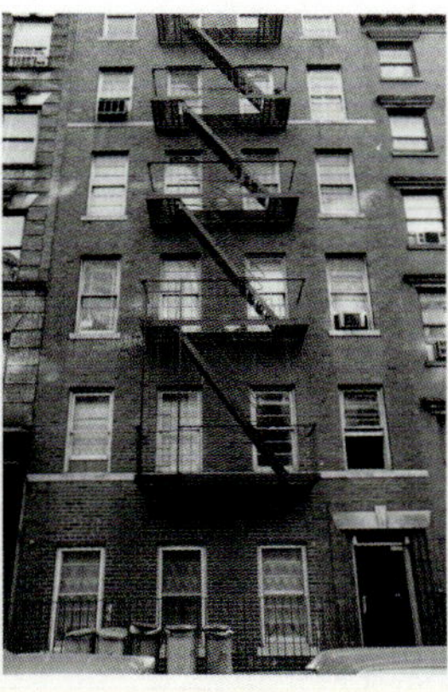

278 E 10 St.
Block 437 Lot 20
25 x 92' 6 story semi-fireproof elevator apt. bldg.

Owned by 278 Tenth Inc., 1503 Oriental Blvd., Brooklyn
Contracts signed by Abraham Haftel, President('56/57)

Acquired 8-26-1955 from Isidore Zwirn

$85 000.- extended and consolidated mortgage at 6% interest held through assignment, 5-15-1969, by S & K Estates Inc., 608 E 11 St., NYC (due $25 834.33),
contracts signed by Donald Sherman, President('68/69)
Daniel Kirschenbaum, President('67)
Harry J. Shapolsky, President('58)
Principal Harry J. Shapolsky(according to Real Estate Directory of Manhattan)

Assessed land value $8 500.- , total $130 000.- (1971)

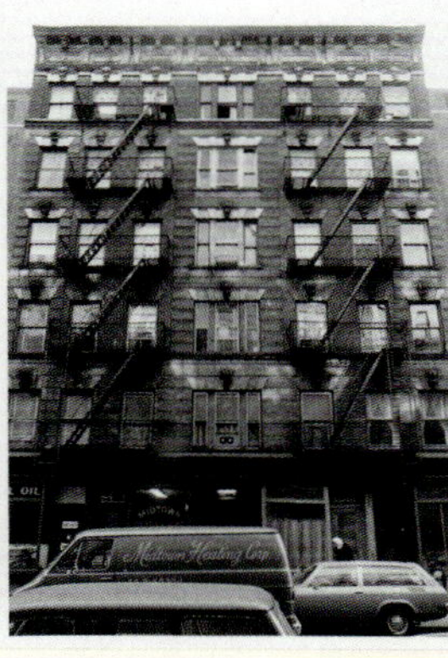

280-82 E 10 St.
Block 437 Lot 21
50 x 92' 6 story walk-up old law tenement

Owned by 177 Mulberry Realty Corp., 608 E 11 St., NYC
Contracts signed by Harry J. Shapolsky, President ('57)
Pearl Kleinberg(Shapolsky)Pres.('60)

Acquired 12-2-1958 from heirs of Herman Segal

No mortgage(1971)

Assessed land value $17 000.- total $65 000.- (1971)

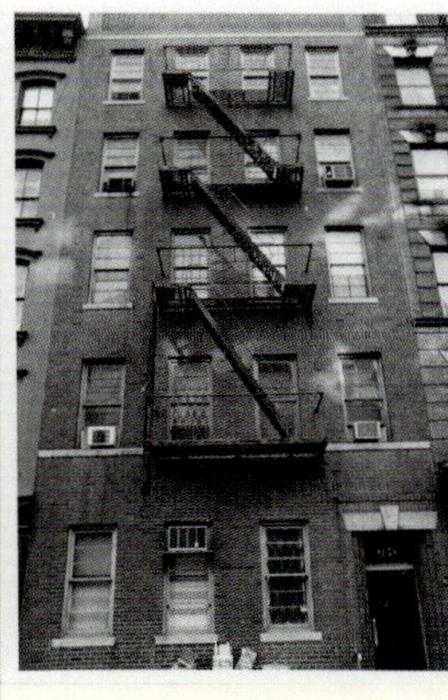

284 E 10 St.
Block 437 Lot 23
25 x 92' 5 story walk-up converted dwelling

Owned by Jath Realty Corp., 1503 Oriental Blvd, Brooklyn
Contracts signed by Fannie Haftel, President('52/63)
Principal Abraham Haftel(according to Real Estate Directory of Manhattan)

Acquired 8-25-1952 from 284 East 10th Street Realty Corp., 284 E 10 St., NYC

$48 000.- mortgage at 6% interest, 8-18-1953, due 11-18-1973, held by The Ministers and Missionaries Benefit Board of The American Baptist Convention, 475 Riverside Drive, NYC

Assessed land value $8 500, total $80 000.- (1971)

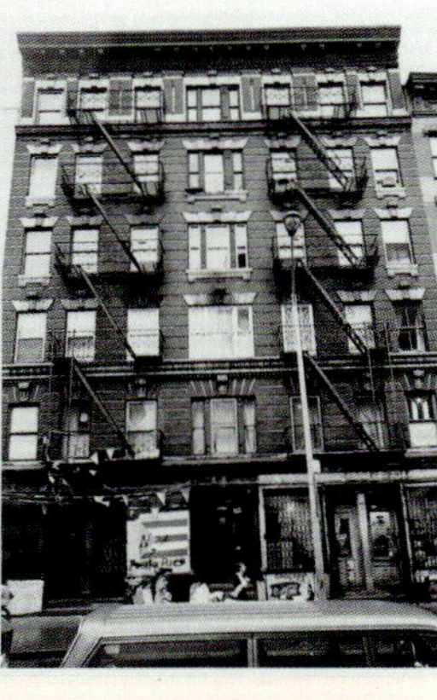

374-78 E 10 St.
Block 392 Lot 22
37 x 103' 6 story walk-up new law apt.bldg., stores

Owned by 419 Tenth Corp., 216 E 89 St., Brooklyn
Contracts signed by Sam Kirschenbaum, Pres.('52/7/9)
Rae Kirschenbaum, Pres.('59)
Harry J. Shapolsky, Secretary(57)

Acquired 9-9-1959 from 374 East 10th Street Corp., 32 Broadway, NYC, Joseph Berler, Secretary

No Mortgage(1971)

Assessed land value $13 500.-, total $52 000.- (1971)

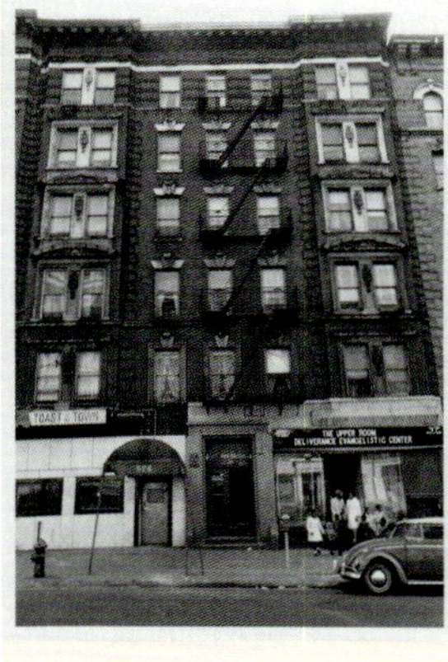

528-30 W 145 St.
Block 2076 Lot 51
50 x 99' 6 story walk-up new law apt.bldg.(built betw.'01-20)

Owned by Shapmor Realty Corp., 608 E 11 St., NYC
Principal Harry J. Shapolsky(according to Real Estate Directory of Manhattan)

Acquired 3-5-1964 from Palmo Realty Corp., 233 Broadway, NYC, James P. Pallaci, Vicepresident

No mortgage(1971)

Assessed land value $28 500.- , total $70 000.- (1971)

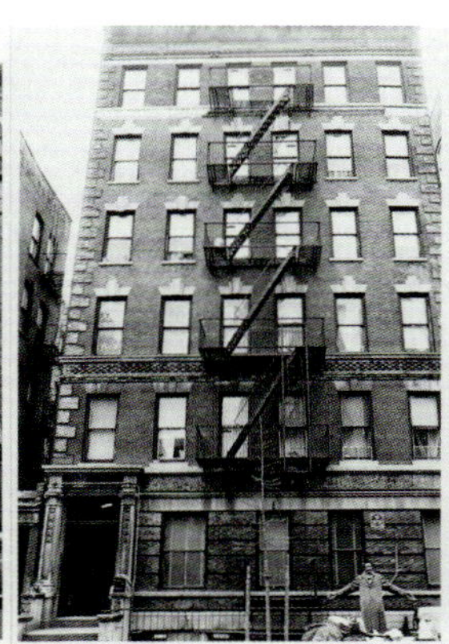

304 W 146 St.
Block 2045 Lot 18
6 story walk-up new law apt. bldg.(1901-20)

Owned by Lijuto Realty Corp., 608 E 11 St., NYC
Contracts signed by Clara Moskowitz, President('67/68)
Principal Harry J. Shapolsky(according to Real Estate Directory of Manhattan)

Acquired 7-6-1967 through foreclosure

$96 611.68 mortgage, 7-1-1968, at 6% interest, held by Pearl Shapolsky, 127 E 36 St., NYC (also on 306 W 146 St. and 68 Bradhurst Ave.); half of this mortgage assigned to 428 Realty Corp., 608 E 11 St., NYC, 5-5-1969, Harry J. Shapolsky, President('61/3/5/6)

Assessed land value $40 000.- , total $80 000.- (also 306 W 146 St.) (1971)

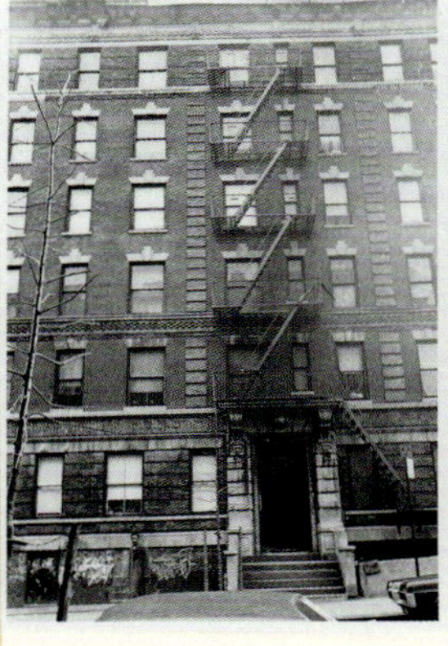

306 W 146 St.
Block 2045 Lot 16
6 story walk-up new law apt. bldg.(1901-20)

Owned by Lijuto Realty Corp., 608 E 11 St., NYC
Contracts signed by Clara Moskowitz, President('67/68)
Principal Harry J. Shapolsky(according to Real Estate Directory of Manhattan)

Acquired 7-6-1967 through foreclosure

$96 611.68 mortgage, 7-1-1968, at 6% interest, held by Pearl Shapolsky, 127 E 36 St., NYC (also on 304 W 146 St. and 68 Bradhurst Ave.); half of this mortgage assigned to 428 Realty Corp., 608 E 11 St., NYC, 5-5-1969, Harry J. Shapolsky, President('61/3/5/6)

Assessed land value $40 000.- , total $80 000.- (also 306 W 146 St.) (1971)

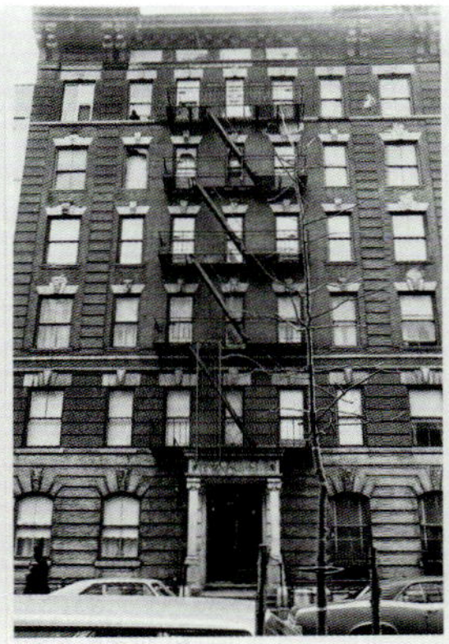

304-06 W 149 St.
Block 2045 Lot 79
50 x 99' 6 story new law walk-up apt. bldg.

Owned by 194 Ave. A Realty Corp., 608 E 11 St., NYC
Contracts signed by Harry J. Shapolsky, Pres. (1960)
Sam Shapolsky, President('58)
Alfred Fayer, Vicepresident('58)
Donald Sherman, Vicepresident('71)
Principal Harry J. Shapolsky(according to Real Estate Directory of Manhattan)

Acquired 12-27-1971 from Daniel Kirschenbaum, 216 E 89 St., Brooklyn

$38 000.- mortgage, 5-3-1955, at 5% interest, held through assignment, 4-30-1969, by Shalane Realty Estates, Inc., 608 E 11 St., NYC, Pearl Shapolsky, Pres., due $3 199.92

$10 000.- mortgage, 5-3-1955, at 5% interest, due 4-29-1961, held through assignment, 4-29-1964, by Shalane Realty Estates, Inc.

$20 000.- mortgage, 11-21-1963, at 2% interest, due 11-13-1973, held through assignment, 3-17-1964, by Shalane Realty Estates, Inc.

Assessed land value $15 000.-, total $57 000.- (1971)

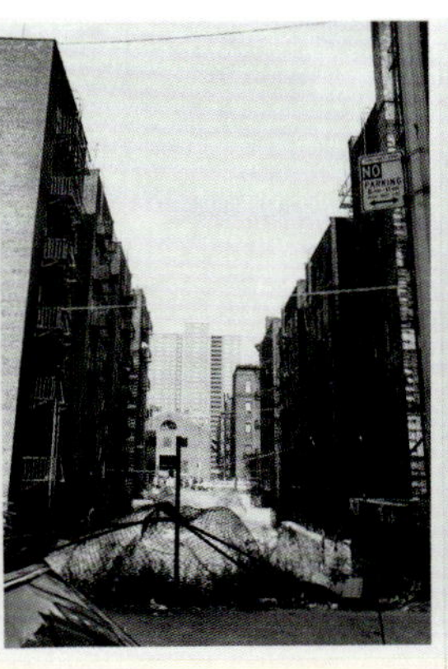

- W 152 St.
Block 2046 Lot 55
25 x 99' vacant

Owned by 174 E 3 St. Corp., 608 E 11 St., NYC
Contracts signed by Harry J. Shapolsky, Pres.('49/61)
Ernest Callipari, Pres.('48/49)
Anna Callipari, Pres.('50/59)
Catherine Greco, Pres.('61/64/66)
Harry J. Shapolsky, Sec.('49/51/61/66)
Principal Harry J. Shapolsky(according to Real Estate Directory of Manhattan)

Acquired 8-18-1961 at auction from City of New York

No mortgage(1971)

Assessed land value $4 000.- (1971)

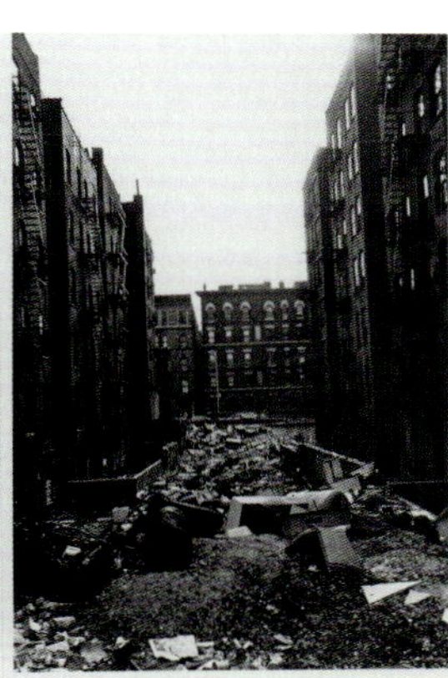

- W 153 St.
Block 2046 Lot 64
25 x 99' vacant

Owned by 174 E 3 St. Corp., 608 E 11 St., NYC
Contracts signed by Harry J. Shapolsky, Pres.('49/61)
Ernest Callipari, Pres.('48/49)
Anna Callipari, Pres. ('53/59)
Catherine Greco, Pres.('61/64/66)
Harry Shapolsky, Sec.('49/51/61/66)
Principal Harry J. Shapolsky(according to Real Estate Directory of Manhattan)

Acquired 8-18-1961 at auction from City of New York

No mortgage(1971)

Assessed land value $4 000.- (1971)

Shapolsky et al. Manhattan Real Estate Holdings, a Real-Time Social System, as of May 1, 1971

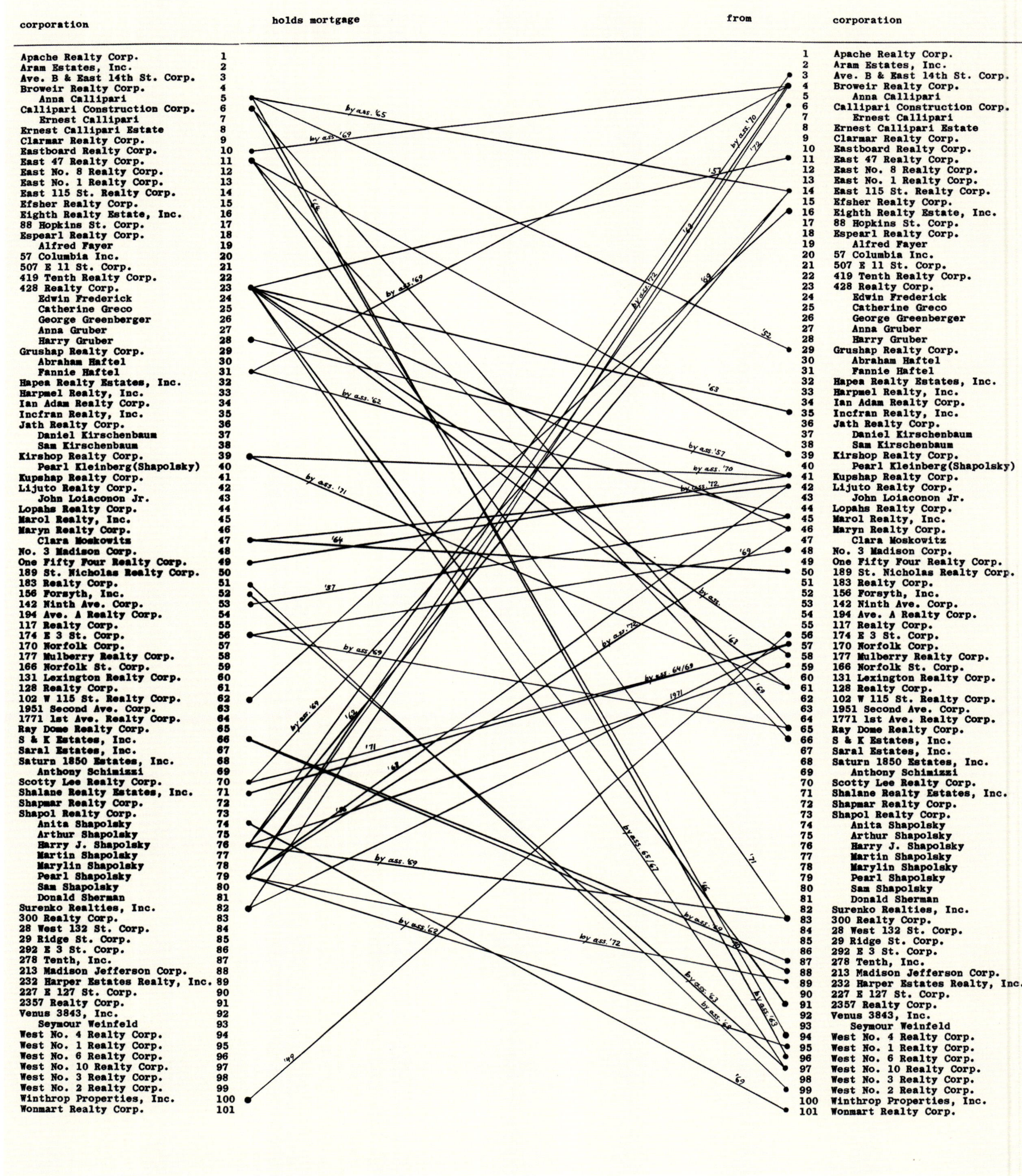

Shapolsky et al. Manhattan Real Estate Holdings, a Real-Time Social System, as of May 1, 1971

»Real Time« as Infrastructure: Two Works by Hans Haacke and Infrastructural Critique

Sabeth Buchmann and Stephan Geene

In 1974, Hans Haacke repeated and modified a gesture that had created an art-political scandal in 1971. For two of his works that were planned to be shown in a solo exhibition at the Guggenheim Museum in New York in 1971, the artist had researched an intricate network of real-estate deals and revealed the people behind the corporate constructs by name. When Haacke refused to withdraw *Shapolsky et al. Manhattan Real Estate Holdings, a Real-Time Social System, as of May 1, 1971* (figs. pp. 111–14, 119)—the title of one of the two works—Thomas Messer, director of the Guggenheim Museum at the time, subsequently canceled the entire exhibition in a blatant act of censorship, despite the solidarity of its curator, Edward F. Fry. Three years later, Haacke documented the almost century-long provenance history of Édouard Manet's 1880 painting *Bunch of Asparagus* in his subsequently famous work *Manet-PROJEKT '74* (figs. pp. 123–33), originally planned for the exhibition *PROJEKT '74* in Cologne. The painting had been donated to the Wallraf Richartz Museum by its association of patrons, chaired by the German manager Hermann Josef Abs, in memory of Konrad Adenauer, a CDU politician who became the first Chancellor of the (West German) Federal Republic of Germany and died in 1967. The information panels contain detailed personal and biographical as well as professional and economic facts about the previous owners, starting with the French Jewish collector, art historian, and banker Charles Ephrussi and ending with Abs. The corresponding panel for Abs lists his various functions as a member of the board of Deutsche Bank and as a member of the supervisory boards of numerous other companies, which testifies to the entanglements between business and politics (fig. p. 132). The work was also censored, this time by Horst Keller, then director of the Wallraf Richartz Museum, and the artist was excluded from the exhibition despite protests from some of his colleagues.

One can identify a distinct, clearly evaluative form of reception in censorship since the work's political content was obviously taken seriously. And, of course, the attempt to make reception impossible makes this not only an explicit theme, but also a part of the work itself—especially in the case of an artist who had already made the social conditions of the reception of art into its expanded participatory content in his *MoMA Poll*[1] (among others). To put it bluntly, the act of censorship reveals how artistic works are always also entangled in institutional, cultural, and political processes of meaning, how they can initiate and/or exacerbate them. In other words, Haacke's works integrated existing (power) structures into aesthetic perception, yet they also provoked reactions that exemplify the ways in which a work's reception can be constitutive of the work itself.

In our assessment, the repetition of Haacke's gestures does not primarily consist in the artist's strategic intention—indeed, who sets out to be excluded from an exhibition?—but rather in the way his works connected with the infrastructures of art reception that went beyond individual institutions, that is, with internal and external publics, museums and the market, society and politics. After all, it was thanks to an art dealer that Haacke's *Manet-PROJEKT '74* could still be realized despite institutional censorship. The work was shown shortly afterward at Galerie Paul Maenz in Cologne, where the original *Bunch of Asparagus* that the museum declined to lend was replaced by a photographic reproduction. This in turn led to a shift: an internal institutional (self-)reflection gave rise to a critique that addressed the ostensibly autonomous institution from an immanent outside, namely, from the art market. Accordingly, this raises questions about the positioning of critique in the system of art evaluation. What we mean here is the discourse-dependent relationship between aesthetic judgment and market value; and in this instance, there are indications of the market's significance for the formation of Western Institutional Critique in the 1970s, which tends to be neglected in the specialist literature. Marked by acts of institutional censorship, such boundaries of what can be said and seen[2] have significantly contributed to the status of Institutional Critique as an independent genre associated with political activism, which persists to this day.

Yet, the forms of intervention chosen by Haacke are hardly limited to the articulation of political criticism or even the journalistic uncovering of scandals. The materiality and staging of his installation-based works are in a strikingly charged relationship to their semantics. This manifests, among other things, in his eschewal of agitprop, of perpetrator-victim polarization, of legal findings or forensic evidence. In their place, one finds an emphatically sober, seemingly scientific listing of facts, structures, and actors in the art world; stylistically

1
In 1970, there was urging to remove Haacke's *MoMA Poll* from the *Information* exhibition at The Museum of Modern Art in New York by the Rockefeller brothers: Nelson Rockefeller, governor of the State of New York (whose policies were the subject of Haacke's work), and David Rockefeller, then chairman of the MoMA Boards. John Hightower, the MoMA director at the time, took a stand and the work was shown after all. Hightower was later dismissed in 1972 after only nineteen months in office.

2
Loosely based on Michel Foucault, *The Archaeology of Knowledge*, trans. A. M. Sheridan Smith (New York: Pantheon Books, 1972).

3
See Carol Armstrong, *Manet Manette* (New Haven, CT: Yale University Press, 2002), pp. 280–81.

4
Marina Vishmidt, »Between Not Everything and Not Nothing: Cuts Toward Infrastructural Critique,« in *Former West: Art and the Contemporary after 1989*, ed. Maria Hlavajova and Simon Sheikh (London and Cambridge, MA: The MIT Press, 2017), p. 265.

5
Keller Easterling, »Direct (Dispositional) Action,« in *Broken Relations: Infrastructure, Aesthetics, and Critique*, ed. Martin Beck, Beatrice von Bismarck, Sabeth Buchmann, and Ilse Lafer (Leipzig: Spector Books, 2022), p. 18.

speaking, *Shapolsky et al.* and *Manet-PROJEKT '74* continue the systemic thinking based on the exchange relationships between work, environment, and reception that already emerged in Haacke's *Condensation Cube* series (1963–67).

The exhibited reproduction of Manet's famous asparagus painting drew attention not only to the documented provenance history, but also to the question of why a harmless bunch of asparagus of all things should become such a politically charged object of speculation. Given the play that Manet was staging between materiality and subject, between modern economy (the fictitious equivalence of vegetables and painting) and modernist abstraction (think of René Magritte's *Ceci ne pas une pipe*), the still life seems like an anticipation of Haacke's institution-critical interweaving of the work and its historical provenance: the piece commissioned by Ephrussi, its first owner, exceeded his expectations, which prompted him to increase the previously agreed upon payment of 800 francs by another 200 francs. According to the American art historian Carol Armstrong, when Manet then painted a single asparagus spear and sent it to his patron on the grounds that it had been missing from the bundle, he insinuated that Ephrussi had thus received a piece of art equivalent to the purchase price of a foodstuff.[3] The way in which Manet negotiated the transaction between artist and collector in the ambivalence of painterly opacity and economic transparency testifies to an awareness of the interplay between pictorial-symbolic and material-real value production through the sheer application of certain quantities of paint. The combination of impasto painting technique and impressionistic brushwork lends the subject a self-sufficient object character—as if only a bundle of asparagus were needed to interrelate the mercantile infrastructures of art and consumer culture.

In the form that Haacke uses to link the documentation of the provenance of a self-reflexive work back to the circumstances of its production via its presentation on an easel, one could identify the kind of shift from institutional to infrastructural critique that the art and cultural critic Marina Vishmidt proposes in her 2017 essay »Between Not Everything and Not Nothing: Cuts Toward Infrastructural Critique«[4]—a shift that seeks to escape the reproductive, and therefore system-stabilizing, function of critique by extending it to relations of social (re)production. There, one also finds an echo of how the architectural theorist Keller Easterling suggests we grasp infrastructure, namely, in an attempt to »thicken an understanding of the interactive agency of things in a technical or cultural assemblage.« When she speaks of a »modelling thought from sociotechnical networks of humans and nonhumans,«[5] it is because the question of the possibilities for transformation within the dominant relations of (re)production always goes hand in hand with the question of the possibilities for a transformation of behavior. It is precisely herein that we believe a central aspect of Haacke's projects can be identified.

It is thus, perhaps, hardly a coincidence that the technologically reproduced canvas of Manet's painting stands out within the information-aesthetically designed documentation, while also becoming an indicator of interlocking (infra)-structures of institutional representation and political economy. Of course, Haacke's works are not exempt from this, for they too find their way into collections and museums, and are invested with value-securing significance through the form of their presentation and reception (of which this essay is but one example). There is a difference, however, in that Haacke's works imprint the immanence of aesthetic autonomy (»Art Remains Art«) with an infrastructural perspective that, in the case of *Manet-PROJEKT '74,* allows us to see a provenance history which testifies to denial and repression, private commercial transactions, and political instrumentalization. The panel on Hermann Josef Abs brings to a head the interplay of economic and patronage interests in the then relatively young West Germany by reflecting the deadly system of forced labor, war economics, and the Holocaust under the Third Reich. Abs, who had already held key positions at Deutsche Bank and IG Farben before 1945, represents the afterlife or even survival of this system and sought to whitewash his complicity with the help of his international network as a business consultant and arts patron. With *Manet-PROJEKT '74*, Haacke achieved nothing less than a visualization of West Germany's political (pre)history through an infrastructural mode of perception, which he was able to exemplify using a work of modern art whose donation was intended to ennoble the Adenauer era that, by 1974, had already passed.[6]

In our opinion, the fact that Haacke was declared the antipode of the art market by institutional representatives like Thomas Messer and Horst Keller, as well as by advocates of Institutional Critique and occasionally even by himself, seems to miss the most important part of this project: his witty quotation and modification of aesthetic museum conventions, such as text-image montage, framing, and hanging, integrated a critique of the suppression of complicit power and representation interests. Instead of attributing Haacke's works from the 1970s to an external or interventionist politicization of art, imported from the outside so to speak, what seems most significant to us is the way in which he addresses or activates infrastructural relationships and continuities in and between aesthetic modernism and so-called postmodernism. One of the reasons for this may lie in his system-based works of the early and mid-1960s. As already suggested with his *Condensation Cube,* these works were concerned with natural feedback processes in the exhibition space; here, one might also think of his *Rain Tower* (fig. p. 26) from 1962. The water in the plexiglass cubes condensed in different ways, depending on the sunlight and time of day. His so-called closed systems were thus already aimed at an infrastructural interaction with the surrounding space and climatic conditions, the function of which was to change the behavior of the objects.

6
Perhaps Haacke's reworking of the German Pavilion for the 1993 Venice Biennale (fig. p. 201) should also be read similarly. Although in this work he literally breaks the ground of the pavilion that was rebuilt under National Socialism, he does not nullify its authoritarian character, but rather deliberately intensifies it.

Following page: *Shapolsky et al. Manhattan Real Estate Holdings, a Real-Time Social System, as of May 1, 1971*

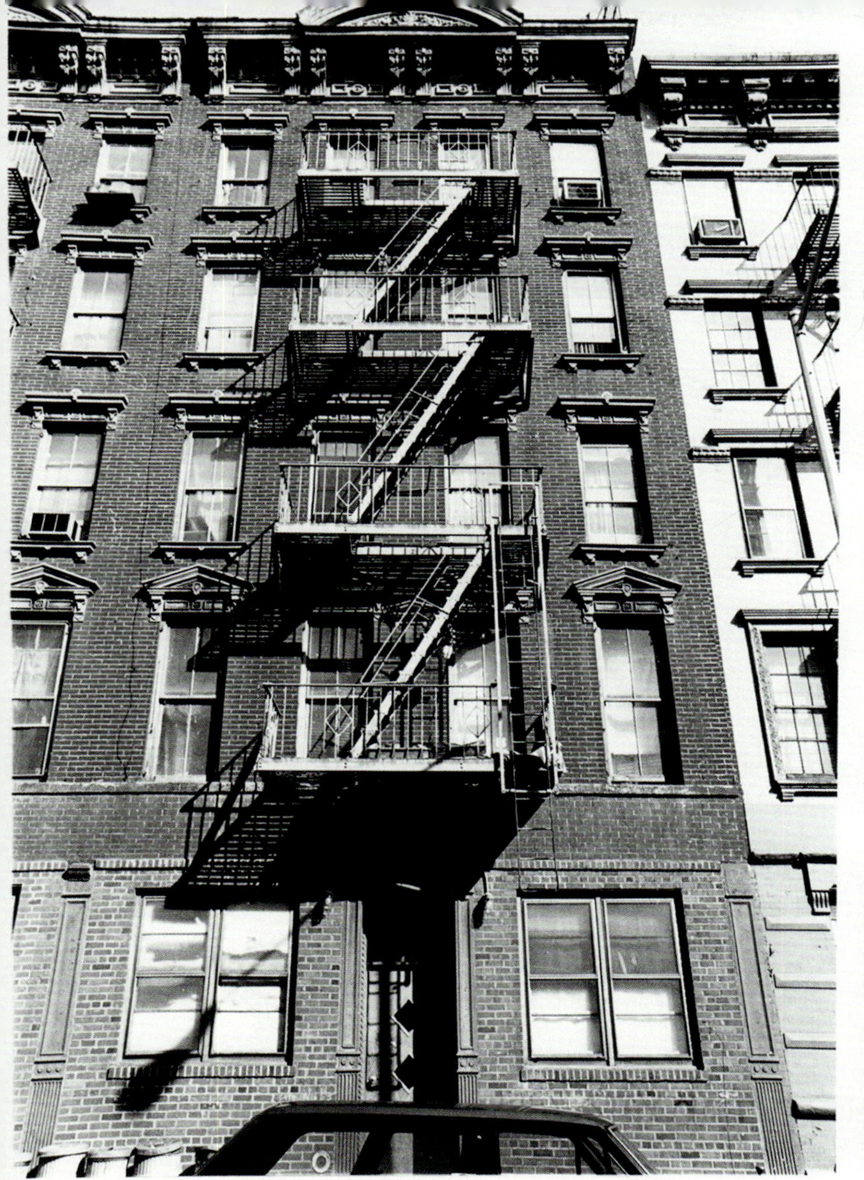

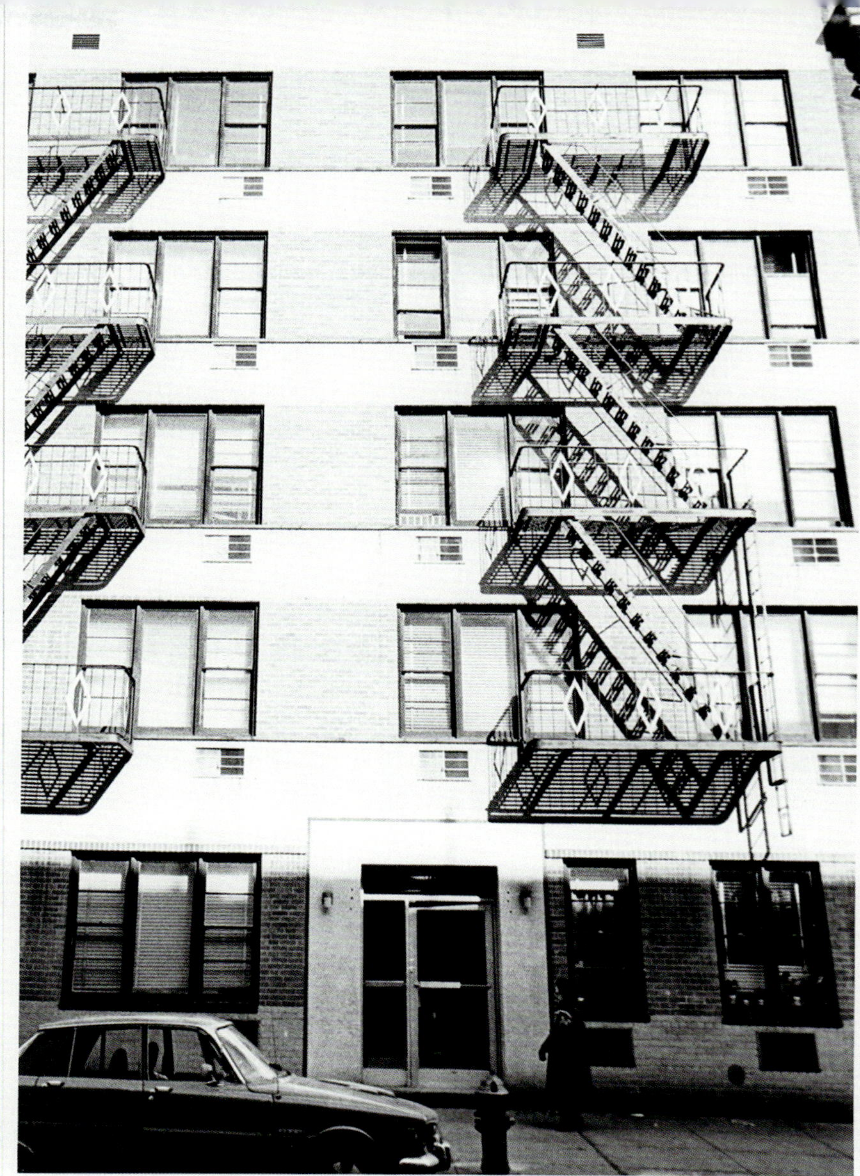

339 E 6 St.
Block 448 Lot 36
25 x 90' 5 story walk-up old law tenement

Owned by Kupshap Realty Corp., 608 E 11 St., NYC
Contracts signed by Harry M. Gruber, Pres.(57/9/62/4/8)
Harry J. Shapolsky, Pres.(59)
Harry J. Shapolsky, Sec. (48/59/61)
Principal Harry M. Gruber(according to Real Estate Directory of Manhattan)

Acquired 3-31-1948 from Mildred C. Zwinge

$70 000.- mortgage at 6% interest, 10-7-1959 (also on 337 E 6 St.), held through assignment for $33 263.48 by Kirshop Realty Corp., 608 E 11 St., NYC, 3-23-1970, contracts signed by Sam Kirschenbaum, Pres.(66/69)
Daniel Kirschenbaum, Pres.(66/69)
Denise Kirschenbaum, Pres.(68)
Principal occasionally Harry J. Shapolsky(according to Real Estate Directory of Manhattan)

Assessed land value $9 500.-, total $23 000.- (1971)

515-17 E 6 St.
Block 402 Lot 57
53 x 40' 5 story walk-up old law tenement

Owned by One Fifty Four Realty Corp., 608 E 11 St. NYC
Contracts Signed by Harry M. Gruber, President('60/64)
Harry J. Shapolsky, Secretary('51)
George Greenberger, Vicepresident ('61)
Principal Harry J. Shapolsky(according to Real Estate Directory of Manhattan)

Acquired 3-11-1964 from Kupshap Realty Corp.
608 E 11 St., NYC
Contracts signed by Harry M. Gruber, President('62/4/8)
Harry J. Shapolsky, President('59)
Harry J. Shapolsky, Secretary('61)

$165 000.- mortgage at 6% interest, 6-15-1964, due 6-15-1974, held by
The Ministers and Missionaries Benefit Board of The American Baptist Convention, 475 Riverside Drive, NYC

Assessed land value $19 000.- total $105 000.- (1971)

Haacke developed, as he himself has explained, his system-oriented approach to art through close communication with the US art and media theorist Jack Burnham. During a 1970 conversation with Jeanne Siegel, he even suggested »reserving the term *system* for sculptures in which a conversion of energy, matter, or information takes place, ones that are not contingent on perceptual interpretation.«[7] To the extent that this definition testifies to a cybernetic understanding of art production—which can also be seen in the time index of *Shapolsky et al. Manhattan Real Estate Holdings, a Real-Time Social System, as of May 1, 1971*—we once again encounter a scientific-analytical approach to the problem of how to aesthetically illustrate infrastructures that elude direct perception. In cybernetics or computing, »real time« would refer to the predefined time interval in which a system is able to respond (almost immediately), but for Burnham »real time« also implied a certain responsiveness to the world »external« to the art object, which was contrasted with and went beyond the »ideal time« of art reception. For example, when the water or information level within the system rises, water or information is reduced elsewhere in order to avoid flooding (in the literal and metaphorical sense).

With his cybernetic systems, Haacke installed precisely those a-subjective sensibilities and forms of behavior shared by human and nonhuman actors at which Easterling's conceptualization of infrastructure also aims. *Manet-PROJEKT '74* can thus be described as a cybernetic expansion of the »canvas« into the overlapping infrastructures of art and economy: infrastructures that consist of diachronic and synchronic networks of artists, collectors, gallerists, art critics, and visitors, as well as easels, canvases, paints, motifs, objects, frames, exhibition walls, lighting, opening hours, accessibility, property relations, real estate, urban environments, communication and information media, global transportation and trade routes, and so forth. Haacke integrates their interrelationships into the image of art, which otherwise remains to this day characterized by a claim to autonomy.

Following Brian Larkin's essay »Promising Forms: The Political Aesthetics of Infrastructure,« Haacke's chosen modes of representation, such as photo-text montages and diagrammatic display panels, reveal system-forming »semiotic and aesthetic vehicles« that, according to the US anthropologist, can appear both as networked infrastructures and as distinct objects.[8] Vishmidt also emphasizes that infrastructures can be representational as well as sites of »social abstraction,«[9] which are altogether constituted by concrete interdependencies: without a road there is no traffic, nor can one use the freeway without a gas supply.

7
Series of conversations with Jeanne Siegel from December 1970 to February 1971 (prior to the Guggenheim cancellation), published in May 1971 in *Arts Magazine*, cited in Edward Fry, *Hans Haacke: Werkmonographie* (Cologne: DuMont Schauberg, 1972).

8
Brian Larkin, »The Politics and Poetics of Infrastructure,« *Annual Review of Anthropology* 42 (2013), https://www.annualreviews.org/content/journals/10.1146/annurev-anthro-092412-155522.

9
»A literal reading of ›infrastructure‹ as bridges, tunnels, and sewers is thus ineradicably tied to its function as a locus of social abstraction. It's for this reason we could suggest, for example, that the dangerously frayed built environment of the United States offers one of the best views on the formerness of the ›West‹ as a progressive theodicy, leveled down by necrocapitalist extraction, while it still exerts a disproportionate capacity to project violence across the globe and on its residents. Broken infrastructure is loquacious.« Vishmidt, »Between Not Everything and Not Nothing,« p. 266.

10
Ibid., p. 265.

It seems that Haacke's thinking, trained in cybernetic systems theory, has always integrated the interactivity of (im)-materialities crucial for infrastructural critique; according to Vishmidt, infrastructural critique also entails the possibility of a (self-)interruption of institutionalized formats and routines—in other words, precisely what Haacke's works do in an entirely (inter)active sense. »Time is an infrastructure because it is a condition of possibility for conscious perception and action; infrastructure is made of time insofar as infrastructure is that which repeats. The repetition is normalized into everyday routine, and when it stops functioning, an aperture is cut into artifice—through which history and power relations can be seen.«[10]

Manet-PROJEKT '74, 1974

In 1974, to celebrate its 150th anniversary, the Wallraf Richartz Museum in Cologne organized the exhibition *PROJEKT '74*. The show was to present »aspects of international art at the beginning of the 1970s.« Invited to participate, Haacke submitted an outline for a new work: Manet's *Bunch of Asparagus* (1880), in the collection of the Wallraf Richartz Museum, is on a studio easel in an approximately 6 by 8 meters (20 by 26 feet) room of *PROJEKT '74*. Panels on the wall present the social and economic positions of the persons who have owned the painting, and the prices paid for it. The museum's curator of modern art responded that even though this was »one of the best projects submitted,« it could neither be realized in the exhibition nor presented in the catalogue.

The director of the museum, Dr. Keller, objected to the listing of Hermann Josef Abs's nineteen positions on boards of directors (Abs had been instrumental in acquiring the painting for the museum). Dr. Keller explained: ». . . a grateful museum and an appreciative city . . . must protect initiatives of such an extraordinary nature from any interpretation that might later throw even the slightest shadow on it . . .« And he remarked: »A museum knows nothing about economic power; however, it does, indeed, know something about spiritual power.« On the day of the museum's press opening, the excluded work went on exhibition at Galerie Paul Maenz in Cologne. Standing in for the original *Bunch of Asparagus* was a full-size color reproduction. Daniel Buren incorporated facsimiles of the censored panels into his work in the museum's anniversary show.

The General Director of Cologne Museums, Prof. von der Osten, had them pasted over with paper. Until his death in 1994, Hermann Josef Abs was barred from entering the United States because of his role at Deutsche Bank, during the Nazi period, in the »Aryanization« of Jewish property. Recently it has become known that Abs had been chairman of the board of directors of a firm making tools for Hitler's arms industry. The company used forced labor and prisoners of war under very harsh working conditions. 144 of those who did not perform to the company's expectations were sent to the Buchenwald concentration camp.

Hans Haacke, 1974

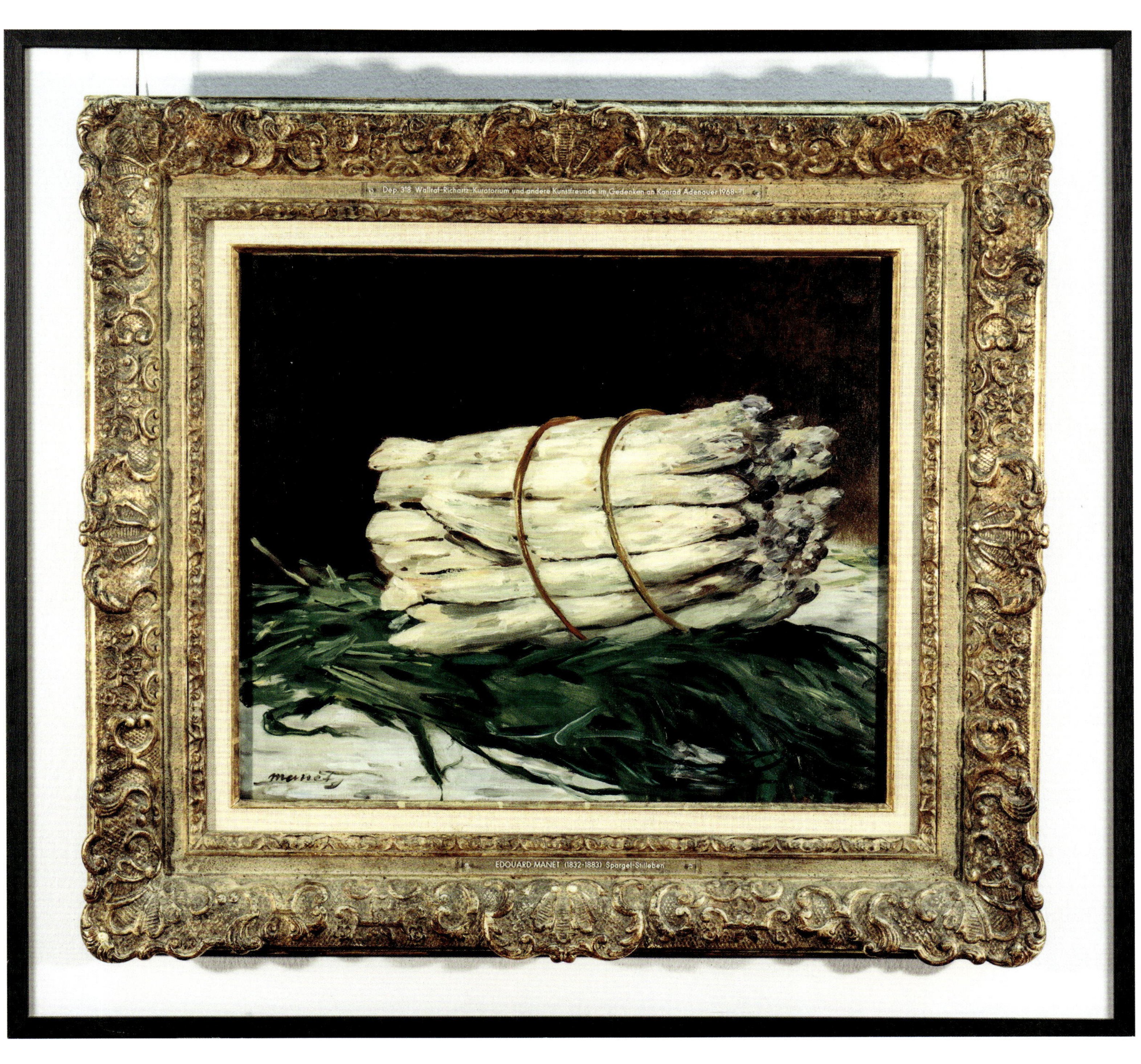

Manet-PROJEKT '74, 1974
Also pp. 124–33

Das Spargel-Stilleben

1880 für 800 Francs gekauft durch

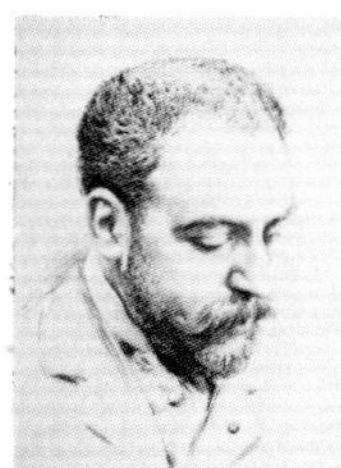

Charles Ephrussi

Geboren 1849 in Odessa, gestorben 1905 in Paris. – Entstammt jüdischer Bankiersfamilie mit Bankunternehmen in Odessa, Wien und Paris. Familiäre Beziehungen zur franz. Hochfinanz (Baron de Reinach, Baron de Rothschild).

Studiert in Odessa und Wien. – 1871 Übersiedlung nach Paris.

Eigene Bankgeschäfte. – Kunstschriftstellerische Arbeiten u. a. über Albrecht Dürer, Jacopo de Barbarij und Paul Baudry. 1875 Mitarbeit an der „Gazette des Beaux Arts", 1885 Mitinhaber, 1894 Herausgeber.

Mitglied zahlreicher kultureller Komitees und Salons der Pariser Gesellschaft. Organisiert mit Gustave Dreyfus, der Comtesse Greffulhes und der Prinzessin Mathilde Kunstausstellungen und Konzerte, u. a. von Werken Richard Wagners. – Zweites Vorbild für Marcel Prousts Swann.

Sammelt Kunst der Renaissance, des 18. Jahrhunderts, Albrecht Dürers, Ostasiatische Kunst und Werke zeitgenössischer Maler.

Zahlt Manet statt der vereinbarten 800 Francs für das „Spargel-Stilleben" insgesamt 1000 Francs. Aus Dankbarkeit schickt ihm Manet das Stilleben eines einzelnen Spargels (1880, Öl auf Leinwand, 16,5 x 21,5 cm, Paris Musée de l'Impressionisme) mit der Bemerkung: „Es fehlte noch in Ihrem Bündel".

Ritter (1882) und Offizier (1903) der Ehrenlegion.

Gravure von M. Patricot „Charles Ephrussi" aus „La Gazette des Beaux Arts", Paris 1905

Das Spargel-Stilleben

1880 gemalt von

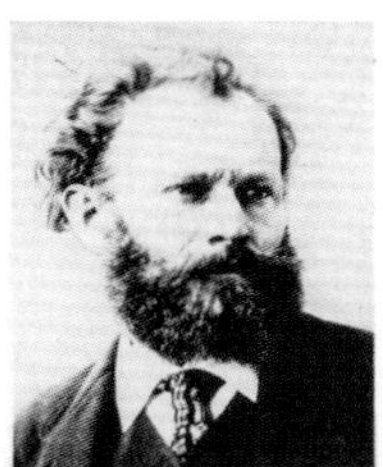

Edouard Manet

Lebt von 1832 bis 1883 in Paris. – Entstammt einer katholischen Familie des franz. Großbürgertums. Vater Auguste Manet Jurist, Personalchef im Justizministerium, später Richter (magistrat) am Cour d'appel de Paris (Berufungsgericht). Republikaner. Ritter der Ehrenlegion. – Großvater Clément Manet Bürgermeister von Gennevilliers an der Seine, vor Paris. Familie besitzt dort ein 54 Hektar großes Landgut. – Mutter Eugénie Désirée Fournier, Tochter eines franz. Diplomaten, der die Wahl Marschall Bernadottes zum schwedischen König betrieb. Karl XIV. von Schweden ihr Pate. – Ihr Bruder Clément Fournier Artillerieoberst. Demissioniert während der Revolution 1848. – Zwei Brüder Manets im Staatsdienst.

Manet besucht renommiertes Collège Rollin (Mitschüler Antonin Proust, späterer Politiker und Schriftsteller). Entgegen dem väterlichen Wunsch nach einem Jurastudium fährt er für kurze Zeit zur See. Fällt bei der Aufnahmeprüfung zur Seekadettenanstalt durch.

1850–56 Kunststudium im Privatatelier von Thomas Couture, einem erfolgreichen Salonmaler. Studienreisen nach Italien, Deutschland, Österreich, der Schweiz, Belgien, Holland, Spanien.

Finanziell unabhängig. Nicht auf den Verkauf seiner Bilder angewiesen. Wohnt in großen standesgemäß eingerichteten Häusern in Paris, mit Dienerschaft.

Stellt ab 1861 mit wechselndem Erfolg im Salon und in Kunsthandlungen aus. 1863 Beteiligung am „Salon des Réfusés" (Salon der Zurückgewiesenen). Bilder werden wegen Verstössen gegen die Konvention von der offiziellen Kritik bekämpft. Kritische Unterstützung durch Zola, Mallarmé, Rimbaud.

Heiratet 1863 nach dem Tod seines Vaters Suzanne Leenhoff, seine ehemalige Klavierlehrerin, die Tochter eines holländischen Musikers. Léon Edouard Koëlla, ihr 1852 geborener Sohn, ist ein illegitimes Kind Manets; wird von ihm adoptiert.

Stellt 1867 aus Protest gegen die konservative Jury 50 Bilder in einer für 18 000 Francs selbstfinanzierten Baracke auf einem Grundstück des Marquis de Pomereu in der Nähe der Weltausstellung in Paris aus. Anhänger unter jüngeren, besonders impressionistischen Künstlern.

Als Nationalgardist 1870 bei der Verteidigung von Paris im Deutsch-Französischen Krieg, Meldegänger im Regimentsstab. Während der Pariser Kommune bei seiner Familie in Südfrankreich. – Antiroyalist. Bewunderer des Republikaners Léon Gambetta, des späteren Ministerpräsidenten.

1871 umfangreiche Bilderkäufe durch den Kunsthändler Durand-Ruel, einem Freund impressionistischer Malerei. Findet Anerkennung in den für künstlerische Neuerungen aufgeschlossenen Kreisen der Pariser Gesellschaft. Zahlreiche Porträtaufträge. 1881 Gewinn der 2. Medaille des Salons. Auf Vorschlag Antonin Prousts Ernennung zum Ritter der Ehrenlegion.

Während seiner tödlichen Krankheit Behandlung durch früheren Leibarzt Napoleon III.

1883 Gedächtnisausstellung in der Ecole des Beaux-Arts Paris. Katalogvorwort von Emile Zola. Verkaufserlös zugunsten der Erben 116 637 Francs.

Photo : Durand-Ruel

Das Spargel-Stilleben

zwischen 1900 und 1902 gekauft durch

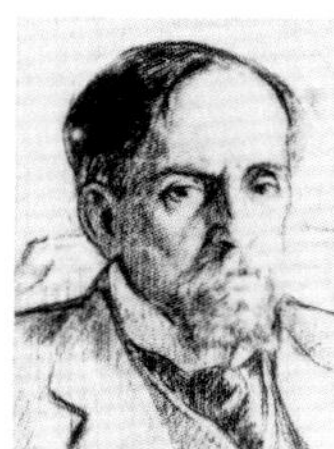

Alexandre Rosenberg

Geboren um 1850 in Preßburg (Bratislava), Slovakei. – Entstammt jüdischer Familie. Emigration nach Paris im Alter von 9 Jahren.

1870 Gründung einer Kunst- und Antiquitätenhandlung in Paris.

Heiratet 1878 Mathilde Jellineck aus Wien. Sie haben drei Söhne und eine Tochter.

Fortführung der Firma nach seinem Tode 1913 durch den 1881 in Paris geborenen Sohn Paul Rosenberg. Spezialisierung auf die Kunst des 19. und 20. Jahrhunderts. – Gegenwärtig Paul Rosenberg & Co. in New York, geführt durch den Enkel Alexandre Rosenberg.

Kohlezeichnung von Louis Charlot „Alexandre Rosenberg" (Ausschnitt), 1913.

Das Spargel-Stilleben
von unbekanntem Datum an im Besitz von oder in Kommission bei

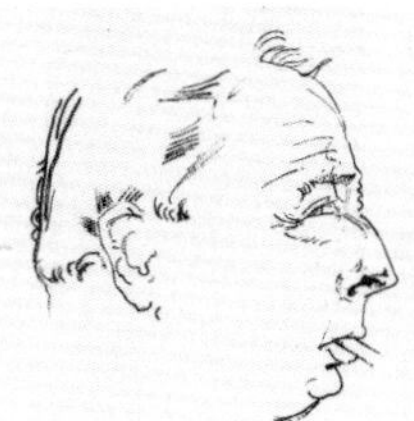

Paul Cassirer

Geboren 1871 in Görlitz, Selbstmord 1926 in Berlin. – Entstammt wohlhabender jüdischer Familie. Vater Louis Cassirer gründet mit 2 Söhnen die Firma Dr. Cassirer & Co., Kabelwerke in Berlin. – Bruder Prof. Richard Cassirer, Berliner Neurologe. – Vetter Prof. Ernst Cassirer bekannter Philosoph.

Kunstgeschichtsstudium in München. Mitredakteur des „Simplizissimus". Eigene literarische Arbeiten.

Gründet mit Vetter Bruno Cassirer 1898 in Berlin Verlags- und Kunsthandlung. 1901 Trennung. Weiterführung als Kunstsalon Paul Cassirer, Victoriastraße 35, in vornehmer Berliner Gegend.

Mit der Künstlervereinigung „Berliner Sezession" Kampf gegen offizielle Hofkunst. Trotz Unwillen des Kaisers Handel und publizistische Förderung des franz. Impressionismus. Enge Beziehungen zum Pariser Kunsthändler Durand-Ruel. Verhilft den Deutschen Malern Trübner, Liebermann, Corinth und Slevogt zum Erfolg.

1908 Gündung des Verlags Paul Cassirer für Kunstliteratur und Belletristik. Publikationen des literarischen Expressionismus. 1910 Gründung der Halbmonatsschrift „Pan" und „Pan"-Gesellschaft zur Förderung von Bühnenwerken, u. a. Wedekind.

Aus erster Ehe eine Tochter und ein Sohn (Selbstmord im 1. Weltkrieg). Heiratet 1910 in zweiter Ehe die Schauspielerin Tilla Durieux.

1914 Kriegsfreiwilliger. Erhält Eisernes Kreuz in Ypern. Wird Kriegsgegner.

Zeitweilig in Haft (beschuldigt, unrechtmäßig franz. Bilder verkauft zu haben). Flucht in die Schweiz und Aufenthalt in Bern und Zürich bis Kriegsende. Verhilft Harry Graf Keßler zu franz. Kontakten für Verhandlungen mit Frankreich im Auftrage Ludendorffs. Verlegt mit Max Rascher pazifistische Literatur.

Nach der Revolution 1918 in Berlin Eintritt in die USPD. Verlegt sozialistische Bücher, u. a. von Kautzky und Bernstein.

Grund für Selbstmord 1926 vermutlich Konflikt mit Tilla Durieux.

Weiterführung des Kunstsalons Paul Cassirer in Amsterdam, Zürich und London durch Dr. Walter Feilchenfeldt und Dr. Grete Ring, eine Nichte Max Liebermanns.

Lithographie von Max Oppenheimer, „Bildnis Paul Cassirer", um 1925.

Das Spargel-Stilleben

1907 für 24 300,– RM gekauft durch

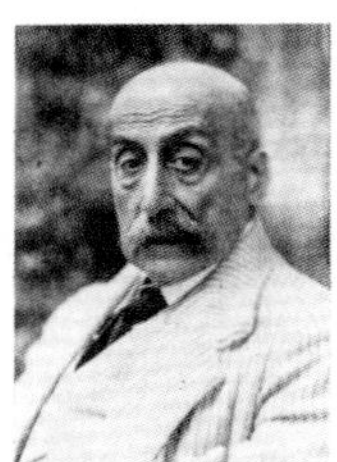

Max Liebermann

Maler, lebt von 1847 bis 1935 in Berlin. – Entstammt einer jüdischen Fabrikantenfamilie. Vater Louis Liebermann Textilindustrieller in Berlin. Besitzt ebenfalls Eisengießerei Wilhelmshütte in Sprottau, Schlesien. – Mutter Philipine Haller, Tochter eines Berliner Juweliers (Gründer der Firma Haller & Rathenau). – Bruder Prof. Felix Liebermann, bekannter Historiker. – Vetter Walther Rathenau, Industrieller (AEG), Reichsaußenminister (1922 ermordet).

Liebermann besucht renommiertes Friedrich-Werdersches Gymnasium in Berlin zusammen mit Söhnen Bismarcks. – Kunststudium im Privatatelier Steffeck, Berlin, und auf der Kunstakademie Weimar. Längere Arbeitsaufenthalte in Paris, Holland, München. – Freiwilliger Krankenpfleger im Deutsch-Französischen Krieg 1870/71.

Heiratet 1884 Martha Marckwald, zieht nach Berlin zurück. 1885 Geburt der Tochter Käthe Liebermann.

Erbt 1894 väterliches Palais am Pariser Platz 7 (Brandenburger Tor). Baut 1910 Sommersitz am Wannsee, Große Seestraße 27 (seit 1971 Clubhaus des Deutschen Unterwasserclubs e.V.). Finanziell unabhängig. Lebt nicht vom Verkauf seiner Werke.

1897 Gesamtausstellung in der Berliner Akademie der Künste. Große Goldene Medaille. Seine durch Realismus und franz. Impressionismus beeinflußten Bilder werden von Wilhelm II. empört abgelehnt. – Malt Genreszenen, Stadtlandschaften, Strand- und Gartenszenen, Gesellschaftsporträts, Künstler, Wissenschaftler, Politiker. – Ausstellung und Verkauf durch Kunstsalon Paul Cassirer in Berlin. Werke in öffentlichen Sammlungen u. a. Wallraf-Richartz-Museum Köln.

Professorentitel 1897. – Präsident der „Berliner Sezession" (Künstlervereinigung gegen Hofkunst) 1898–1911, Rücktritt wegen Opposition jüngerer Künstler. – 1898 Mitglied, 1912 im Senat, 1920 Präsident der Preußischen Akademie der Künste. Rücktritt 1933. – Ehrendoktor der Universität Berlin. Ehrenbürger der Stadt Berlin. Ritter der franz. Ehrenlegion. Orden von Oranje-Nassau. Ritter des Ordens Pour le mérite und andere Auszeichnungen.

Besitzt Werke von Cézanne, Daumier, Degas, Manet, Monet, Renoir. Deponiert seine Sammlung 1933 im Kunsthaus Zürich.

1933 von Nazis aus allen Ämtern entlassen. Ausstellungsverbot. Entfernung seiner Bilder aus öffentlichen Sammlungen.

Stirbt 1935 in Berlin. Frau Martha Liebermann begeht 1943 Selbstmord, um sich drohender Verhaftung zu entziehen.

Photo um 1930

Das Spargel-Stilleben

vererbt an

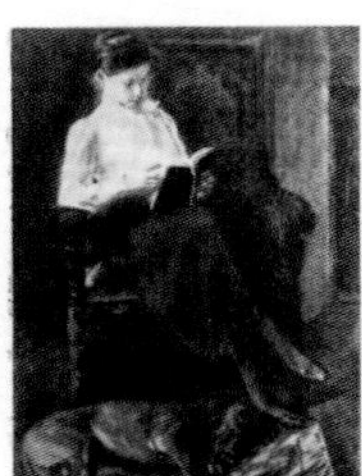

Käthe Riezler

Geboren 1885 in Berlin, gestorben 1951 in New York.

Tochter des Malers Max Liebermann und seiner Frau Martha Marckwald.

Heiratet 1915 in Berlin Dr. phil. Kurt Riezler. 1917 Geburt der Tochter Maria Riezler.

Dr. Kurt Riezler, geboren 1882 in München, Sohn eines Kaufmanns. Studium der Klassischen Antike an der Universität München. 1905 Dissertation: „Das zweite Buch der pseudoaristotelischen Ökonomie".

1906 Eintritt ins Auswärtige Amt in Berlin. Legationsrat, später Gesandter. Arbeitet im Stab des Reichskanzlers von Bethmann-Hollweg. 1919/20 Leiter des Büros des Reichspräsidenten Friedrich Ebert.

1913 unter dem Decknamen J. J. Ruedorffer Veröffentlichung der „Prolegomena zu einer Theorie der Politik", 1914 „Grundzüge der Weltpolitik in der Gegenwart". – Später Publikationen zur Geschichtsphilosophie, zur politischen Theorie und Ästhetik.

1927 Honorarprofessor, stellvertretender Geschäftsführer und Vorsitzender des Kuratoriums an der Goethe Universität in Frankfurt am Main.

1933 Entlassung durch Nazis.

Umzug der Familie nach Berlin in das Haus Max Liebermanns, Pariser Platz 7. – Erben 1935 seine Kunstsammlung, die Liebermann 1933 dem Kunsthaus Zürich in Obhut gegeben hatte.

1938 Emigration der Familie nach New York. Sammlung folgt dorthin.

1939 erhält Dr. Riezler eine Professur für Philosophie an der New School for Social Research in New York, einer von Emigranten gegründeten Universität. Gastprofessuren an der University of Chicago und der Columbia University in New York.

Käthe Riezler stirbt 1951. Dr. Riezler emeritiert 1952, stirbt in München 1956.

Pastell von Max Liebermann, „Die Tochter des Künstlers" 1901

Das Spargel-Stilleben

vererbt an

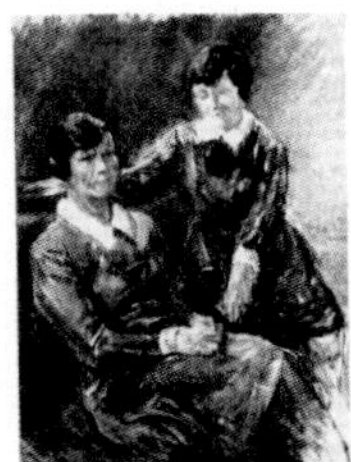

Maria White

Geboren 1917 in Berlin. – Tochter von Prof. Dr. Kurt Riezler und Käthe Liebermann.

Emigriert 1938 mit ihren Eltern nach New York.

Heiratet Howard Burton White.

Howard B. White, geboren 1912 in Montclair, N. J., studiert 1934–38 an der New School for Social Research in New York, wo Dr. Kurt Riezler lehrt. 1941 Rockefeller Stipendium. Promoviert 1943 an der New School zum Doctor of Science.

Unterrichtet an der Lehigh University und am Coe College. Gegenwärtig Professor im Graduate Department of Political and Social Science der New School for Social Research. Lehrt Political Philosophy.

Veröffentlichungen u. a. „Peace Among the Willows – The Political Philosophy of Francis Bacon", den Haag 1968. „Copp'd Hills Towards Heaven – Shakespeare and the Classical Polity," den Haag 1968.

Maria und Howard B. White leben in Northport, N. Y. Sie haben zwei Kinder.

Ölbild von Max Liebermann „Tochter und Enkelin des Künstlers" (Maria Riezler im Bild rechts), um 1930

Das Spargel-Stilleben
1968 über Frau Marianne Feilchenfeldt, Zürich
für 1 360 000,- DM erworben durch das

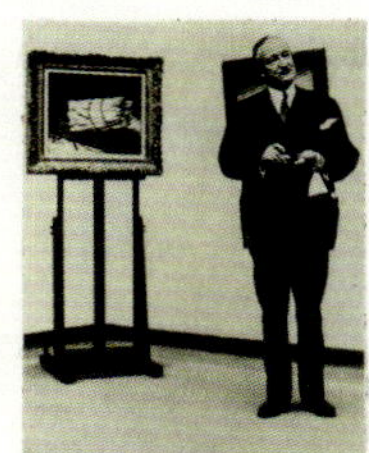

Wallraf-Richartz-Kuratorium und die Stadt Köln

Dem Wallraf-Richartz-Museum von Hermann J. Abs, dem Vorsitzenden des Kuratoriums, am 18. April 1968 im Andenken an Konrad Adenauer als Dauerleihgabe übergeben.

Das Wallraf-Richartz-Kuratorium und Förderer-Gesellschaft e. V.

Vorstand

Hermann J. Abs
Prof. Dr. Kurt Hansen
Dr. Dr. Günter Henle
Prof. Dr. Ernst Schneider
Prof. Dr. Otto H. Förster
Prof. Dr. Gert von der Osten (geschäftsführend)

Kuratorium

Prof. Dr. Viktor Achter
Dr. Max Adenauer
Fritz Berg
Dr. Walther Berndorff
Theo Burauen
Prof. Dr. Fritz Burgbacher
Dr. Fritz Butschkau
Dr. Felix Eckhardt
Frau Gisela Fitting
Prof. Dr. Kurt Forberg
Walter Franz
Dr. Hans Gerling
Dr. Herbert Girardet
Dr. Paul Gülker
Iwan D. Herstatt
Raymund Jörg
Eugen Gottlieb von Langen
Viktor Langen
Dr. Peter Ludwig
Prof. Dr. Heinz Mohnen
Cai Graf zu Rantzau
Karl Gustav Ratjen
Dr. Hans Reuter
Dr. Hans-Günther Sohl
Dr. Dr. Werner Schulz
Dr. Nikolaus Graf Strasoldo
Christoph Vowinckel
Otto Wolff von Amerongen

Hermann J. Abs bei der Übergabe des Bildes

Das Spargel-Stilleben erworben durch die Initiative des Vorsitzenden des Wallraf-Richartz-Kuratoriums

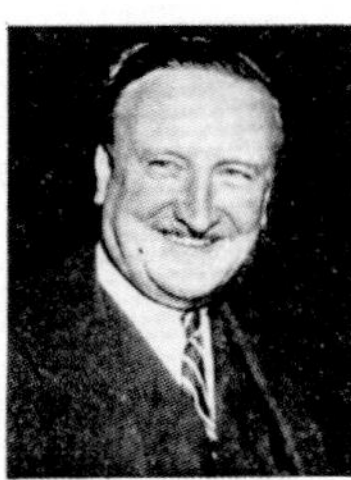

Hermann J. Abs

Geboren 1901 in Bonn. – Entstammt wohlhabender katholischer Familie. Vater Dr. Josef Abs, Rechtsanwalt und Justizrat, Mitinhaber der Hubertus Braunkohlen AG. Brüggen, Erft. Mutter Katharina Lückerath.

Abitur 1919 Realgymnasium Bonn. – Ein Sem. Jurastudium Universität Bonn. – Banklehre im Kölner Bankhaus Delbrück von der Heydt & Co. Erwirbt internationale Bankerfahrung in Amsterdam, London, Paris, USA.

Heiratet 1928 Inez Schnitzler. Ihr Vater mit Georg von Schnitzler vom Vorstand des IG. Farben-Konzerns verwandt. Tante verheiratet mit Baron Alfred Neven du Mont. Schwester verheiratet mit Georg Graf von der Goltz. – Geburt der Kinder Thomas und Marion Abs.

Mitglied der Zentrumspartei. – 1929 Prokura im Bankhaus Delbrück, Schickler & Co., Berlin. 1935-37 einer der 5 Teilhaber der Bank.

1937 im Vorstand und Aufsichtsrat der Deutschen Bank, Berlin. Leiter der Auslandsabteilung. – 1939 von Reichswirtschaftsminister Funk in den Beirat der Deutschen Reichsbank berufen. – Mitglied in Ausschüssen der Reichsbank, Reichsgruppe Industrie, Reichsgruppe Banken, Reichswirtschaftskammer und einem Arbeitskreis im Reichswirtschaftsministerium. – 1944 in über 50 Aufsichts- und Verwaltungsräten großer Unternehmen. Mitgliedschaft in Gesellschaften zur Wahrnehmung deutscher Wirtschaftsinteressen im Ausland.

1946 für 6 Wochen in britischer Haft. – Von der Alliierten Entnazifizierungsbehörde als entlastet (5) eingestuft.

1948 bei der Gründung der Kreditanstalt für Wiederaufbau. Maßgeblich an der Wirtschaftsplanung der Bundesregierung beteiligt. Wirtschaftsberater Konrad Adenauers. – Leiter der deutschen Delegation bei der Londoner Schuldenkonferenz 1951-53. Berater bei den Wiedergutmachungsverhandlungen mit Israel in Den Haag. 1954 Mitglied der CDU.

1952 im Aufsichtsrat der Süddeutschen Bank AG. – 1957-67 Vorstandssprecher der Deutschen Bank AG. Seit 1967 Vorsitzender des Aufsichtsrats.

Ehrenvorsitzender des Aufsichtsrats:
Deutsche Überseeische Bank, Hamburg – Pittler Maschinenfabrik AG, Langen (Hessen)
Vorsitzender des Aufsichtsrats:
Dahlbusch Verwaltungs-AG, Gelsenkirchen – Daimler Benz AG, Stuttgart-Untertürkheim – Deutsche Bank AG, Frankfurt – Deutsche Lufthansa AG, Köln – Philipp Holzmann AG, Frankfurt – Phoenix Gummiwerke AG, Hamburg-Harburg – RWE Elektrizitätswerk AG, Essen – Vereinigte Glanzstoff AG, Wuppertal-Elberfeld – Zellstoff-Fabrik Waldhof AG, Mannheim

Ehrenvorsitzender:
Salamander AG, Kornwestheim – Gebr. Stumm GmbH, Brambauer (Westf.) – Süddeutsche Zucker-AG, Mannheim
Stellvertr. Vors. des Aufsichtsrats:
Badische Anilin- und Sodafabrik AG, Ludwigshafen – Siemens AG, Berlin-München
Mitglied des Aufsichtsrats:
Metallgesellschaft AG, Frankfurt
Präsident des Verwaltungsrats:
Kreditanstalt für Wiederaufbau – Deutsche Bundesbahn

Großes Bundesverdienstkreuz mit Stern, Päpstl. Stern zum Komturkreuz, Großkreuz Isabella die Katholische von Spanien, Cruzeiro do Sul von Brasilien. – Ritter des Ordens vom Heiligen Grabe. – Dr. h.c. der Univ. Göttingen, Sofia, Tokio und der Wirtschaftshochschule Mannheim.

Lebt in Kronberg (Taunus) und auf dem Bentgerhof bei Remagen.

Photo aus Current Biography Yearbook 1970, New York

Das Spargel-Stilleben erworben mit Stiftungen von

Hermann J. Abs, Frankfurt
Viktor Achter, Mönchengladbach
Agrippina Rückversicherungs AG., Köln
Allianz Versicherung AG., Köln
Heinrich Auer Mühlenwerke, Köln
Bankhaus Heinz Ansmann, Köln
Bankhaus Delbrück von der Heydt & Co., Köln
Bankhaus Sal. Oppenheim jr. & Cie., Köln
Bankhaus C. G. Trinkaus, Düsseldorf
Dr. Walter Berndorff, Köln
Firma Felix Böttcher, Köln
Robert Bosch GmbH, Köln
Central Krankenversicherungs AG., Köln
Colonia Versicherungs-Gruppe, Köln
Commerzbank AG., Düsseldorf
Concordia Lebensversicherungs AG., Köln
Daimler Benz AG., Stuttgart-Untertürkheim
Demag AG., Duisburg
Deutsch-Atlantische Telegraphenges., Köln
Deutsche Bank AG., Frankfurt
Deutsche Centralbodenkredit AG., Köln
Deutsche Continental-Gas-Ges., Düsseldorf
Deutsche Krankenversicherungs AG., Köln
Deutsche Libby-Owens-Ges. AG., Gelsenkirchen
Deutsche Solvay-Werke GmbH, Solingen-Ohligs
Dortmunder Union-Brauerei, Dortmund
Dresdner Bank AG., Düsseldorf
Farbenfabriken Bayer AG., Leverkusen
Gisela Fitting, Köln
Autohaus Jacob Fleischhauer K. G., Köln
Glanzstoff AG., Wuppertal
Graf Rüdiger von der Goltz, Düsseldorf
Dr. Paul Gülker, Köln
Gottfried Hagen AG., Köln
Hein. Lehmann & Co. AG., Düsseldorf
Hilgers AG., Rheinbrohl
Hoesch AG., Dortmund
Helmut Horten GmbH, Düsseldorf
Hubertus Brauerei GmbH, Köln
Karstadt-Peters GmbH, Köln
Kaufhalle GmbH, Köln
Kaufhof AG, Köln
Kleinwanzlebener Saatzucht AG., Einbeck
Klöckner Werke AG., Duisburg
Kölnische Lebens- und Sachvers. AG., Köln
Viktor Langen, Düsseldorf-Meerbusch
Margarine Union AG., Hamburg
Mauser-Werke GmbH, Köln
Josef Mayr K. G., Hagen
Michel Brennstoffhandel GmbH, Düsseldorf
Gert von der Osten, Köln
Kurt Pauli, Lövenich
Pfeifer & Langen, Köln
Preussag AG., Hannover
William Prym Werke AG., Stolberg
Karl-Gustav Ratjen, Königstein (Taunus)
Dr. Hans Reuter, Duisburg
Rheinisch-Westf. Bodenkreditbank, Köln
Rhein.-Westf. Isolatorenwerke GmbH, Siegburg
Rhein.-Westf. Kalkwerke AG., Dornap
Sachtleben AG., Köln
Servais-Werke AG., Witterschlick
Siemag Siegener Maschinenbau GmbH, Dahlbruch
Dr. F. E. Shinnar, Tel-Ganim (Israel)
Sparkasse der Stadt Köln, Köln
Schlesische Feuervers.-Ges., Köln
Ewald Schneider, Köln
Schoellersche Kammgarnspinnerei AG., Eitorf
Stahlwerke Bochum AG., Bochum
Dr. Josef Steegmann, Köln-Zürich
Strabag Bau AG., Köln
Dr. Nikolaus Graf Strasoldo, Burg Gudenau
Cornelius Stüssgen AG., Köln
August Thyssen-Hütte AG., Düsseldorf
Union Rhein. Braunkohlen AG., Wesseling
Vereinigte Aluminium-Werke AG., Bonn
Vereinigte Glaswerke, Aachen
Volkshilfe Lebensversicherungs AG., Köln
Jos. Voss GmbH & Co. KG., Brühl
Walther & Cie. AG., Köln
Wessel-Werk GmbH, Bonn
Westdeutsche Bodenkreditanstalt, Köln
Westd. Landesbank Girozentrale, Düsseldorf
Westfalenbank AG., Bochum
Rud. Siedersleben'sche O. Wolff-Stiftg., Köln

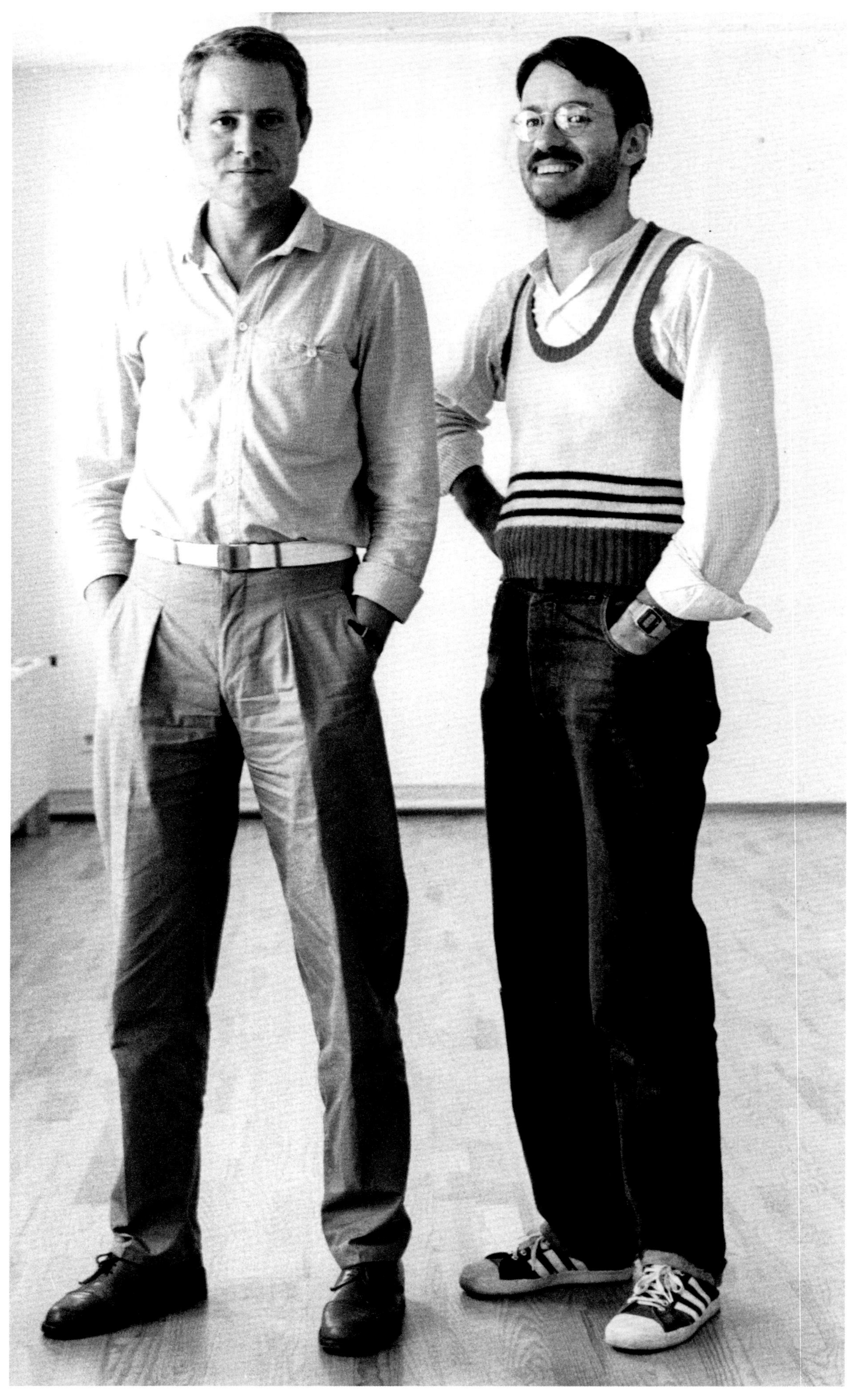

Fig. 1: Paul Maenz (left) and Gerd de Vries, 1979

Paul Maenz and Gerd de Vries in Conversation with Ingrid Pfeiffer and Luisa Ziaja

Berlin, March 27, 2024

IP Mr. Maenz, I'd like to start at the beginning. In your book *Art Is to Change*, you recount how you lived in New York City from 1965 to 1967, where you founded Kineticism Press in 1966—a publishing house that planned to specialize in books, exhibition catalogues, and multiples—together with the curator Willoughby Sharp. Hans Haacke had been living in New York permanently since the fall of 1965 and also knew Sharp well. I'm assuming you met each other through him. Or how did things come about?

PM In New York, I was working in a completely different field, namely, advertising, but of course I had brought my art interests from Germany with me. And the only gallery that was important for my generation of European art lovers was the Howard Wise Gallery. That's where you'd meet. Contemporary European art was hardly visible in the United States at the time. And it was at Howard Wise that I met Willoughby Sharp, whose wife was incidentally a dancer from Düsseldorf. Willoughby was familiar with ZERO and the new tendencies in Europe, and it was certainly through him that I met Hans Haacke. That was fifty or sixty years ago by now, so of course I don't recall all the details that easily. In any case, Willoughby was seen as a kind of »Rasputin of kinetic art« in New York since he had dedicated himself to kinetics—an art form that wasn't so current in the United States, in contrast to Europe. This led us to found Kineticism Press, with an office in the famous Pan Am building, of course: Willoughby liked to do things in a big way. But the activities of our little press didn't last long. Willoughby went on to found *Avalanche*, a wonderful, now legendary art magazine. Like Willoughby himself, it is no longer alive.

LZ In 1968, Kineticism Press published the catalogue for *Air Art*, a traveling exhibition that, as the title suggests, was dedicated to the artistic use of air and featured works by Hans Haacke, among others. Were you still involved in this project?

PM No, I was already back in Frankfurt am Main by then. The only project that Willoughby and I actually realized together was a Günther Uecker monograph, the first in English, along with a multiple: a wooden board with a thick nail that Uecker had hammered in at an angle and dipped in white paint of the kind used to mark road crossings, together with the Uecker monograph in the same format in a plexiglass box. We had planned to produce 2,000—like I said, Willoughby liked to do things in a big way. In the end, only a few hundred were made. But it was a really beautiful edition. Every now and then, individual copies still pop up at auction to this day.

IP I have another question that goes back to the beginnings. One thing that you and Hans Haacke have in common is that you both studied under former Bauhaus artists—you under Max Burchartz at the Folkwang School in Essen and Haacke under Fritz Winter at the Academy in Kassel. Did you ever discuss this influence?

PM Hardly. For me at least, Max Burchartz's teaching, but also the person himself, was a major turning point in general. Through him, it was the first time I got to see art from the inside, so to speak; before that it was more of an interested view from the outside. But I don't think I ever spoke about this »Bauhaus background« with Hans Haacke. What connected us and served as a kind of basis was more of an interest in the factual, in the structure or function of systems, in other words the tangible—as opposed to the romantic, like in the work of Yves Klein, to name just one of the beloved artists of the time.

LZ After your return to Frankfurt in 1967, you and Peter Roehr organized the exhibition *Serielle Formationen* in the Studio Gallery at Goethe University Frankfurt. Hans Haacke was one of forty-eight artists you showed, which was surely inspired by your New York experiences, right?

PM Yes, of course. Sol LeWitt, Carl Andre, Donald Judd, Agnes Martin, and Dan Flavin were also shown, some of them for the first time in Europe. The exhibition aimed to demonstrate the relationship between various serial formal approaches—but also the conceptual differences, despite the often similar appearances of »seriality,« which was an international phenomenon back then.

IP I noticed that the work Haacke showed was titled *Formation*, incidentally the only one with this title. Did Haacke inspire you to choose the exhibition title?

PM No, that was Peter Roehr. He came up with the title and more importantly was the initiator of *Serielle Formationen*. Ultimately, his entire oeuvre revolved around the theme of repetition, more exclusively and radically than almost anyone else.

IP How did you decide to open your gallery in Cologne in 1971 with an exhibition by Hans Haacke of all people, and not with the works of your close friend Peter Roehr?

PM Peter Roehr had already died in 1968, only twenty-four years old. Together with my friend Heimar Schröter, I inventoried his artistic estate in 1969 and prepared the works for an exhibition that then took place in 1971 at Museum Schloss Morsbroich in Leverkusen. Then came the move from

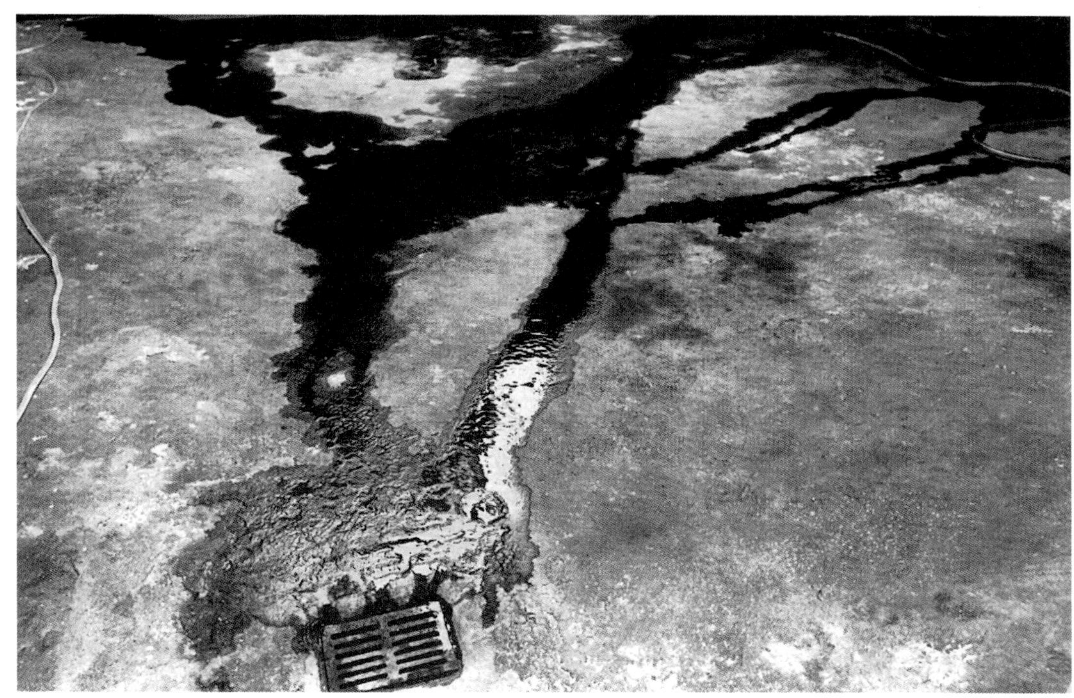

Fig. 2: Hans Haacke, *Trickle, Maenz Gallery*, 1971, installation, Galerie Paul Maenz, January–February 1971

Frankfurt to Cologne, together with Gerd de Vries. And there were good reasons for starting a new gallery in Cologne with Hans Haacke in 1971: Haacke was still a young artist relatively unknown here, but his New York address brought a certain international flair. After all, the goal was to create a broader context and not just stay stuck in a local one, like the situation in Frankfurt, for example. Whatever the case, the gallery's program quickly took off and for years it was a hotspot for Conceptual Art, so to speak—alongside Konrad Fischer's terrific Düsseldorf gallery. Some members of the group, as defined and launched by the »godfather« of Conceptual Art, Seth Siegelaub—such as Robert Barry, Lawrence Weiner, Joseph Kosuth, and Douglas Huebler—were just as much at home at Fischer's in Düsseldorf as they were here in Cologne. It goes without saying that such an »ambitious« situation wasn't without competitive pressures. Surviving commercially with not exactly commercial work like dry Conceptual Art was sometimes an art in itself. But back to Hans Haacke.

GdV I remember that Paul once told me about a very early agreement between himself and Hans Haacke: if Paul ever opened a gallery, the first show would be one by Hans Haacke. And that's how it turned out.

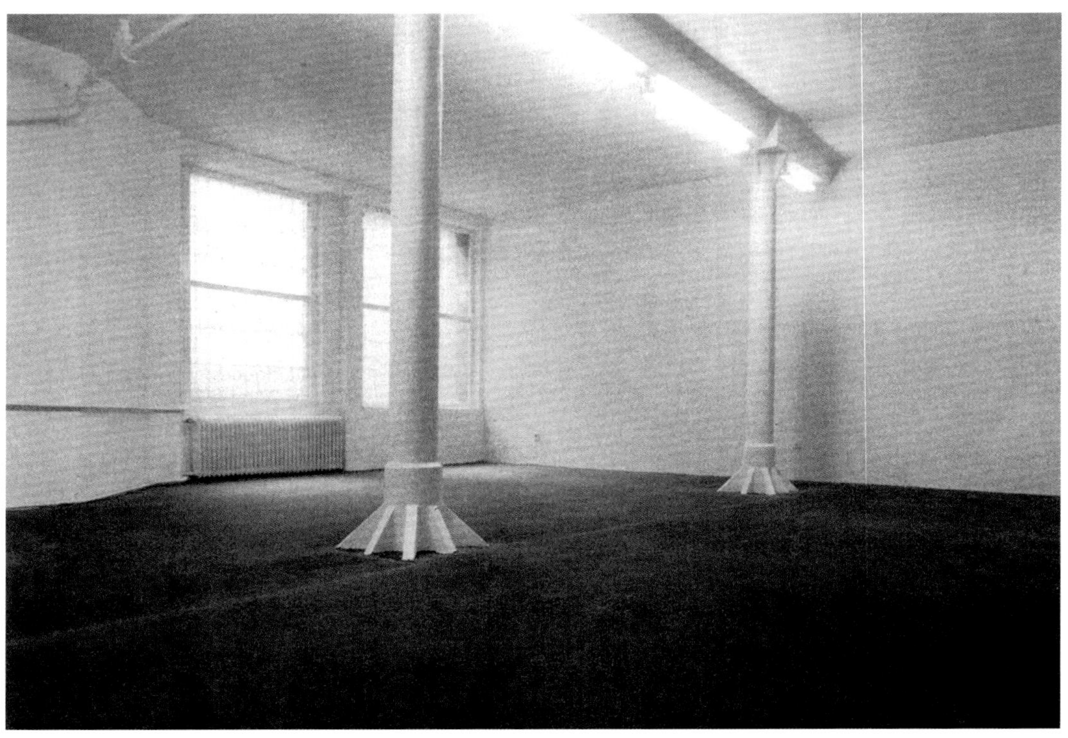

Fig. 3: Galerie Paul Maenz, Lindenstraße 32, Cologne, 1971

IP Among other things, you presented *Floating Ice Ring* (fig. p. 45) and *Trickle, Maenz Gallery* (fig. 2), works that focused on physical phenomena and systems. Did Haacke make the selection or were there already certain works that were important to you? How did they fit into your space on Lindenstraße 32 in Cologne (fig. 3)?

PM Like all the other artists, Hans decided on the selection himself, of course, and this first exhibition was very promising indeed. We managed to sell the spectacular *Floating Ice Ring* right off the bat to the collector and art dealer Reinhard Onnasch for 8,000 Deutschmarks—a lot of money at the time, especially for an artist who hardly had a market yet. Another work took place in the gallery's small inner courtyard: water dripped from a perforated hose lying on the floor and made its way according to the slope. A simple »physical system«—Haacke at his best.

LZ What were the reactions to works like that back then?

PM There were certainly interested visitors who asked follow-up questions, and we'd try to explain the »systemic dimension« of the individual works. But that was all more than manageable. The situation was completely different to today: it was already a success if an exhibition only had sixteen visitors. However, they were usually really interested and informed—more participants than audience.

GdV Really, you couldn't imagine it being any more »modest.« For example, we sent an excited letter via airmail to our artist Joseph Kosuth in New York saying that his exhibition had twenty-three visitors. Today that would be almost laughable. Times have changed rapidly over the years. Our last exhibition on Bismarckstraße in Cologne—Anselm Kiefer—had around 2,000 guests at the opening in 1989.

PM The first few years actually weren't always easy, but we inevitably overcame the hurdles quite well, not least because of our convictions. We were sure that what we were doing was right and important and had to be done. That's another reason why we documented the gallery's activities from the very beginning and regularly published illustrated annual reports (fig. 4). Gerd's contributions were especially crucial here—his tenacity and scholarly meticulousness. Much of it only proved its importance later on, for example as a reliable information source or valuable archival material.

LZ The list of artists you worked with early on is impressive indeed. How would you describe the concept or program behind the gallery?

PM There's a phrase by Seth Siegelaub that we kept quoting and also used as a postmark: »Art is to change what you expect from it.« A kind of guideline that also meant we sometimes had to throw certainties overboard and maintain a fundamental openness.

GdV Unlike other gallery concepts, our program wasn't hermetic or aimed at imposing a certain canon at any cost. Rather, we always tried to open up the program, and in the first year, for example, we also showed Italian artists associated with Arte Povera alongside American Conceptual Art. This principle continued throughout the gallery's twenty-year history. In any case, what always remained central was following the development of art and the artists, even if it went against our financial interests, which it often did.

LZ After his first solo exhibition, Hans Haacke had three more at the gallery by 1981 (1973, 1974, 1981) and also participated in two group exhibitions in 1974 and 1983 that we'll discuss later. The second exhibition took place in 1973 in your Brussels branch on Avenue Louise, which was only in operation until April 1974. Do you still remember the works that Haacke showed back then? And how did the Brussels gallery come about in the first place?

PM There were people in Belgium and the Netherlands that were interested right from the start, very committed collectors who could make quick decisions in the lower five-figure range, but rarely went beyond that. My perhaps somewhat naïve response to that was to open an additional gallery in Brussels: two floors with a small floor plan in a shopping arcade on the elegant Avenue Louise, the gallery space downstairs, upstairs a sofa that became a bed in the evening, and a sink with cold water . . .

GdV In the 1973 exhibition, Hans Haacke presented the installation *News* (fig. p. 93). It consisted of a telex machine that continuously printed out the latest news, which was then preserved in plexiglass cylinders.

PM We made wonderful exhibitions with beautiful, successful invitations (fig. 5). But from the first day to the last, we didn't manage to sell a thing, absolutely nothing—with one exception, a work by Piero Manzoni that went to the museum in Krefeld. As a result, we closed the branch rather quickly: »War's nicht Offenbarung, dann war's halt Erfahrung« (If it wasn't a revelation, then at least it was an experience), as Hildegard Knef might have said. By the way, there was also a gas explosion in the shopping arcade shortly afterward, so it was ultimately a blessing in disguise.

IP After these more »conventional« exhibitions, so to speak, there was the unintentionally spectacular show with *Manet-PROJEKT '74* in 1974 (figs. pp. 102, 123–33). From July 4 to 31, for just about three weeks, you exhibited the second work that led a museum to cancel Haacke at short notice. How did you find out about it? How much time did you have to react or decide whether to present the work in the gallery?

PM I no longer remember whether it was Hans's idea or our own, but I do know that, given the power dynamics of the Rhineland art scene at the time, no one would have willingly agreed to get involved with a coup like that. Incidentally, it was very similar to the later *Der Pralinenmeister (The Chocolate Master*, figs. pp. 150–63), Haacke's critical work about the all-powerful Rhineland entrepreneur and collector Peter Ludwig. We'll certainly come back to this later.

LZ Not only did the exhibition include Haacke's planned presentation—of course, with Édouard Manet's *Bunch of Asparagus* as a reproduction—you also published the correspondence between Haacke and the relevant officials in the invitation and as a poster. An unambiguous statement that made the work even more explosive . . .

PM Absolutely. It was also about Hermann Josef Abs, an influential figure in the world of finance who was active as a patron of the arts and had made the purchase of Manet's painting possible.

GdV His involvement in the financial aspects of the Nazi regime's machinery of power was common knowledge. By the way, he also walked into the gallery unannounced one day, a completely inconspicuous man, and said, »You probably weren't expecting this.« We really weren't, but we also weren't particularly impressed by the unexpected visit.

IP Do you think the decision not to show Haacke's work was an act of preemptive obedience on the part of the museum director, or that Abs possibly hadn't objected to the presentation at all?

PM Conceivably, but we don't know.

PAUL MAENZ
JAHRESBERICHT 1973
KÖLN & BRÜSSEL

ASKEVOLD PENONE
ATKINSON PILKINGTON
BALDWIN POIRIER
BARRY RAMSDEN
BURGIN ROEHR
BURN RUSHTON
FELDMANN SALVO
HAACKE WERY
KAWARA
KOSUTH ART &
MANZONI LANGUAGE

Fig. 4: *Paul Maenz. Jahresbericht 1973. Köln & Brüssel (Paul Maenz. Annual Report 1973. Cologne & Brussels)*, 1973

GdV It was Hans's idea to make the correspondence public; we certainly didn't give him any ideas on that point. He was an authority for whom it was always important to make political dimensions visible, often with an »enlightening impetus.«

PM What's really admirable is Haacke's consistency in staying true to his principles over so many years and decades. Think, for example, of what was known as the »Siegelaub contract,« which regulates every purchase and documents it for all time, including the financial aspects. Appropriate and precise as it was, it definitely made some sales difficult, if not impossible.

IP Did the fact that Haacke was uninvited by the director of the Wallraf Richartz Museum cause much of a scandal in the Cologne art scene?

PM Interestingly, it wasn't discussed that intensively. Which one could read as a sign of tolerance, though it was basically more about apathy. In the end, people were just trying to mind their own business. There wasn't the differentiated art world of today.

IP It happened again in 1981, but that was probably less well known: Hans Haacke had critically portrayed Peter Ludwig in his *Der Pralinenmeister (The Chocolate Master),* and the work was not presented in the major exhibition *Westkunst* at the Cologne trade fair—and once again you showed it in your gallery. Given the situation in Cologne, with the new building for the Museum Ludwig and all, that must have been pretty controversial, right?

PM Yes, of course it was. The criticism of Peter Ludwig made people prick up their ears. We weren't that interested in provocation and scandals, but rather in making this very special work by Hans Haacke visible, as well as the artist himself.

LZ Much like *Manet-PROJEKT '74*, it also involved printed matter—an exhibition catalogue that recorded and published the contents of the work beyond the exhibition. Was that an important aspect, especially in light of Peter Ludwig's great influence? And who came up with the idea?

PM That was probably our idea. We were always conscious of the importance of recording, of documenting, also for the sake of »art history.« And someone like Peter Ludwig, the »chocolate master,« was ultimately a European figure of the highest order. Barely half a century has passed since then, and it's already becoming clear how helpful it is to have very simple but original sources available. Incidentally, it is hardly a coincidence that the American Getty Foundation tried to acquire our archive shortly after the gallery closed, just as ZADIK (Central Archive of the International Art Trade) in Cologne did later on.

LZ The last show to include Hans Haacke was *Master Works of Conceptual Art* in 1983, the first presentation in the new space at Bismarckstraße 50 and in a way a tribute to the original idea of the gallery. Possibly also a conclusion? You worked with many of the artists represented here, like Hanne Darboven, for example, until the gallery ceased operations in 1990. Why didn't the collaboration with Haacke continue?

GdV The reasons were varied and also very practical. Ultimately, Haacke's works and projects had developed far beyond the gallery

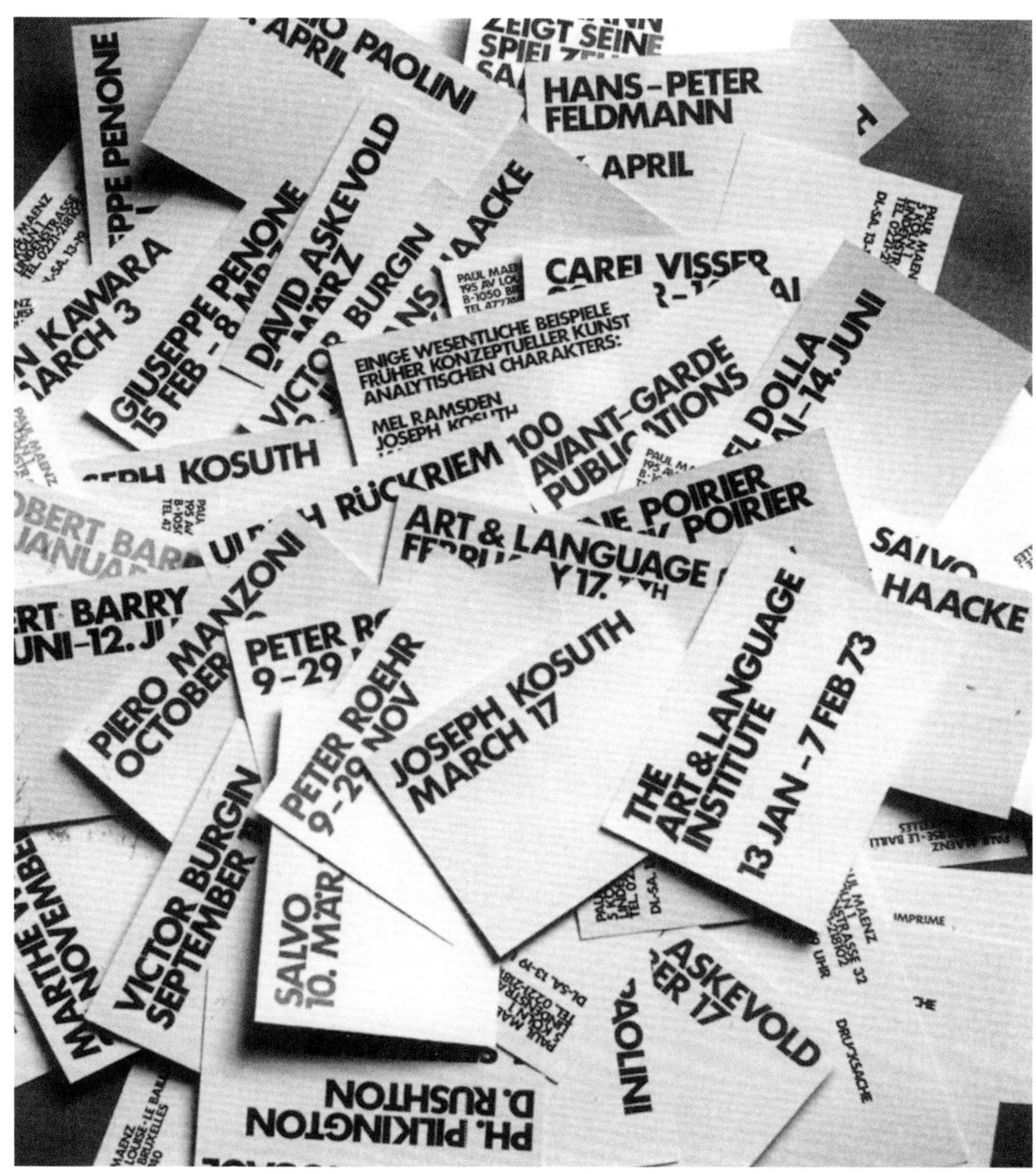

Fig. 5: Invitation cards from Galerie Paul Maenz, 1970s

format by then—they were larger, more extensive, and at home in completely different contexts.

PM That's true. Though it wasn't just that we would've struggled to realize a Haacke exhibition at the scale he was working in by then. We probably also found it more necessary, more natural, to take care of new artists, and at the same time we were also dealing with the »artistic upheavals« of that era, the turbulent 1980s—like I said, »Art is to change . . . .«
But despite all that, the gallery's »conceptual backbone« remained intact until the end, in 1990, which the exhibition you've just mentioned, *Master Works of Conceptual Art* from 1983, hopefully made clear. It included artists ranging from Daniel Buren and Joseph Kosuth to Niele Toroni, Art & Language, Lawrence Weiner, and also Hans Haacke with his installation *News*.

The Right to Life, 1979

The Allied Chemical Corporation, like American Cyanamid, has required the sterilization of female employees of child-bearing age if they wanted to continue in certain jobs. Two women have undergone the operation.

Other large chemical companies have also practiced »protective discrimination,« usually restricted to moving women of child-bearing age into lower paid jobs within the company, where they are not exposed to toxic substances. Reported among these companies are Dow Chemical, Monsanto, DuPont, General Motors, Bunker Hill Smelting, St. Joseph Zinc, Eastman Kodak, and Firestone Tire and Rubber.

In 1980, several women affected by American Cyanamid's »fetal protection policy« sued the company. After three and a half years of pretrial proceedings, the case was settled for $200,000, plus costs and attorney's fees. In another lawsuit against American Cyanamid, the U.S. Court of Appeals for the District of Columbia, in an opinion authored by Judge Robert Bork (appointed by President Reagan), ruled on the Occupational Safety and Health Act. This law stipulates that an employer must provide a safe workplace.

American Cyanamid is a diversified multinational corporation with headquarters in Wayne, New Jersey. Among the company's better known perfumes are Temps, Niki de Saint Phalle, Pierre Cardin, and Geoffrey Beene; it also makes Old Spice aftershave for men.

Hans Haacke, 1986

AMERICAN CYANAMID

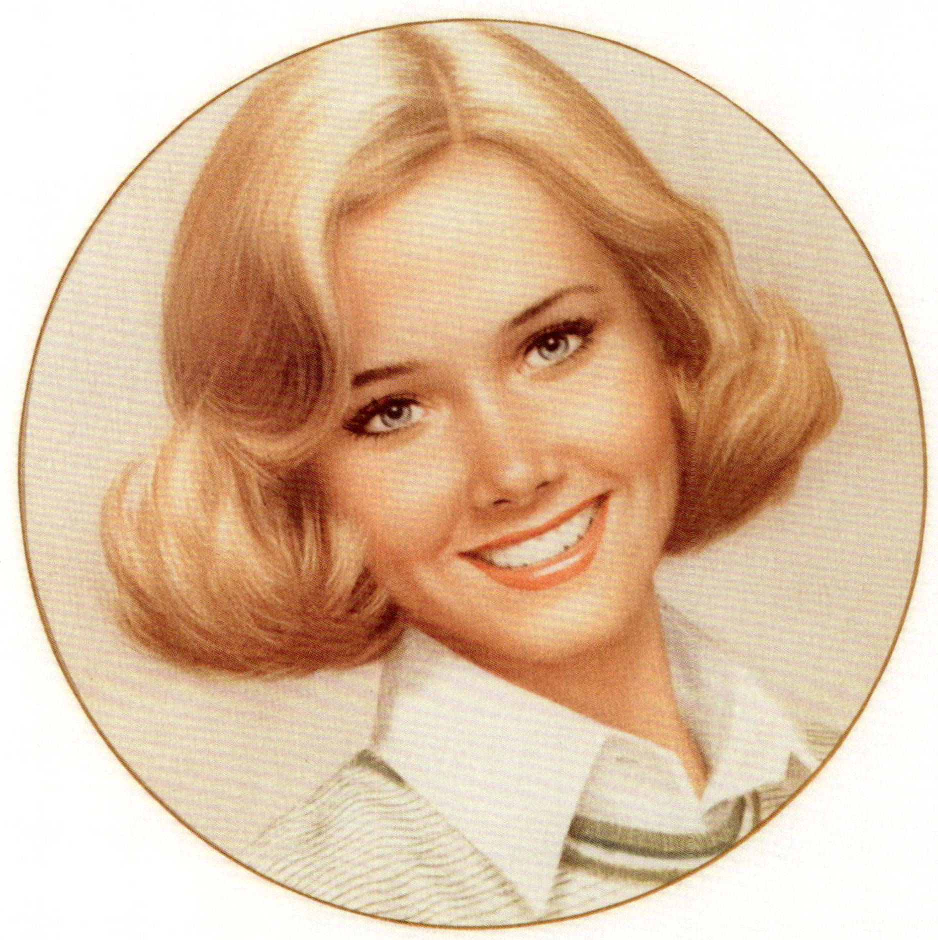

AMERICAN CYANAMID is the parent of BRECK® Inc., maker of the shampoo which keeps the Breck Girl's hair clean, shining and beautiful.

AMERICAN CYANAMID does more for women. It knows: "We really don't run a health spa."

And therefore those of its female employees of child-bearing age who are exposed to toxic substances are now given a choice.

They can be reassigned to a possibly lower paying job within the company. They can leave if there is no opening. Or they can have themselves sterilized and stay in their old job.

Four West Virginia women chose sterilization.

AMERICAN CYANAMID...

Where Women have a Choice

Portrait of BRECK Girl by James Donnelly. Text © by Hans Haacke. 1979

The Right to Life, 1979

Thank You, Paine Webber, 1979

After thirty years, *Thank You, Paine Webber* gained an unfortunate new topicality. While much had changed, we were rudely reminded that much is still the way it was then. The exploitation of people's misery— in this particular case, for PR purposes, but indicative of corporate attitudes and behavior more generally—continues unabated. The use of a photo of an unemployed worker from Detroit during the Great Depression on the cover of a powerful brokerage firm's 1977 annual report is a telling sign of how ingrained this »culture« really is—not to speak of the consequences of investment strategies that led to that depression and more recent economic disasters. The lead essay in the 1977 annual report had the promising title »Where Do Jobs Come From? A Concise Report on Unemployment and Wall Street's Role in Preventing It.« A year later, the annual report offered another enlightening piece: »Do You Sincerely Want to Be Poor? Paine Webber's Centennial Essay on the Future of American Capitalism.«

At the opening of the new millennium, Donald B. Marron, the smiling young man on the left in the group photo of the Paine Webber 1977 annual report, led the merger of his brokerage firm with UBS, the giant Swiss bank and wealth manager. During his twenty years as CEO of Paine Webber, Marron amassed a substantial corporate art collection. The Museum of Modern Art in New York opened its new building in 2005 with an exhibition of this collection under the UBS logo. It so happened that Marron—now CEO of the private equity firm Lightyear Capital—had been the president of the museum's board of trustees for many years and, in 2005, was its vice president.

Another link to the art world: UBS has been the main sponsor of the Art Basel fairs in Basel, Miami Beach, and Hong Kong. UBS, like its American brethren, invested massively in the subprime mortgage casino and was bailed out by Swiss taxpayers. On top of that, the US government accused UBS of knowingly assisting wealthy US taxpayers in tax avoidance. The bank was pressured to reveal the names of thousands of the beneficiaries of its assistance. Today, these accretions are part of our reading of these two panels from 1979.

Hans Haacke, 1986, updated in 2019

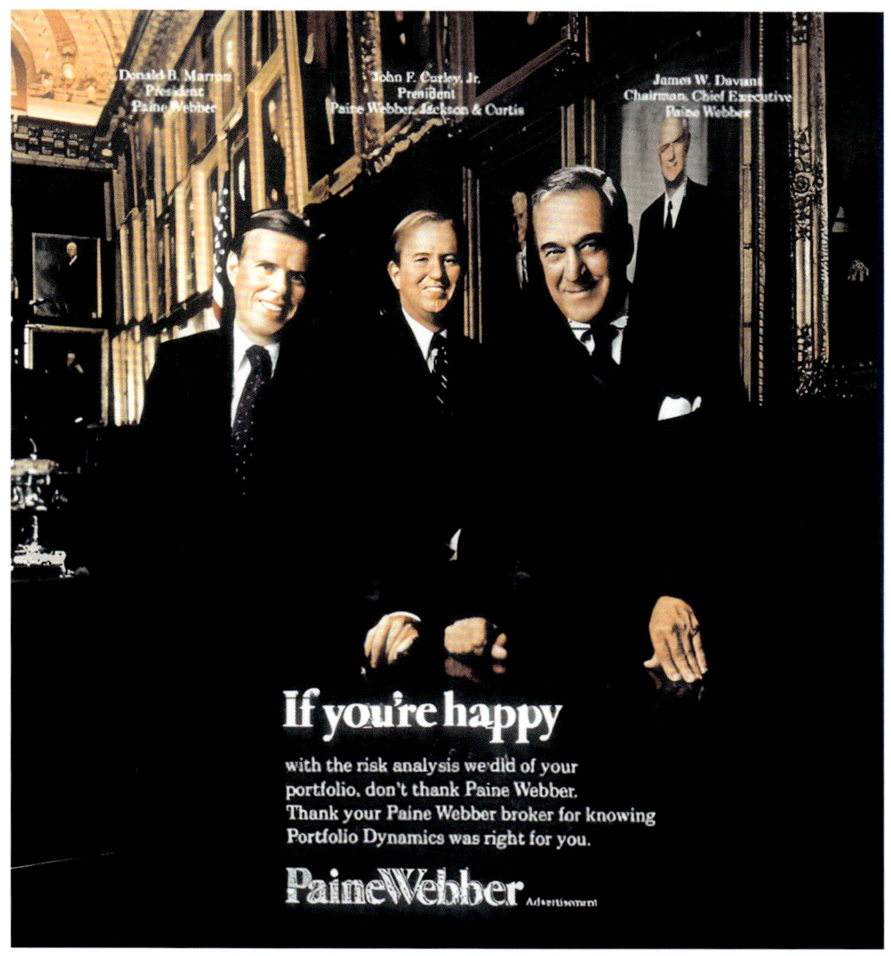

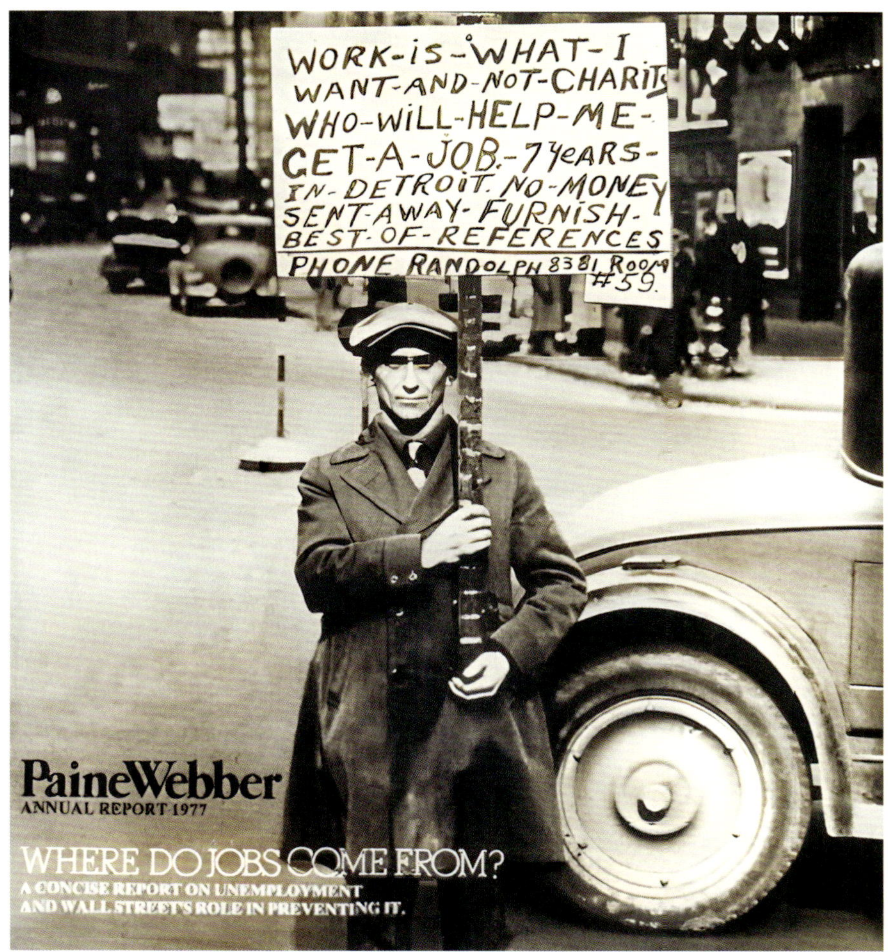

Thank You, Paine Webber, 1979

Der Pralinenmeister (The Chocolate Master), 1981

The German chocolate manufacturer and art collector Peter Ludwig once said: »The market for Pop Art has been determined by the activities of Mr. and Mrs. Ludwig.« Through donations of artworks, promised gifts, and loans, he also tried to determine the programming and professional appointments in public museums. His contract with the City of Cologne provided: »Appointments for the position of director as well as the professional staff of the Museum Ludwig are made in consultation with Mr. and Mrs. Ludwig or the surviving spouse. Prof. Dr. Ludwig and his wife are fully apprised of the museum's ongoing work (e.g. exhibitions, acquisitions, publications).« The construction of the museum, a condition for Ludwig's contributions, cost the city DM 273 million.

Busts of the collector and his wife, sculpted by Arno Breker, were unveiled at the museum's opening in 1986. Yearly maintenance was estimated at DM 40 million. In 1983, Peter Ludwig sold 144 illuminated manuscripts to the Getty Museum (since 1977 the City of Cologne had paid two curators for research on the manuscripts and the publication of a four-volume catalogue). A Ludwig Foundation for Art was endowed with DM 30 million from the sale. It invested its capital in Ludwig's ailing chocolate enterprise.

Nevertheless, licensing agreements and factories eventually had to be sold or closed. After the Getty sale, the collector was charged with nonpayment of DM 1.5 million in property taxes. Shortly before his death in 1996, Peter Ludwig asked the 1,400 unionized workers in his German factories to agree to an increase of their work week by two hours, the reduction of vacation days by three, and the elimination of overtime pay—all without wage adjustments. If his demands were not accepted, Ludwig threatened to move his production to Poland and Turkey. Two years after his death, his widow, Irene Ludwig, sold the company. She passed away in 2010.

Hans Haacke, 2006, updated in 2019

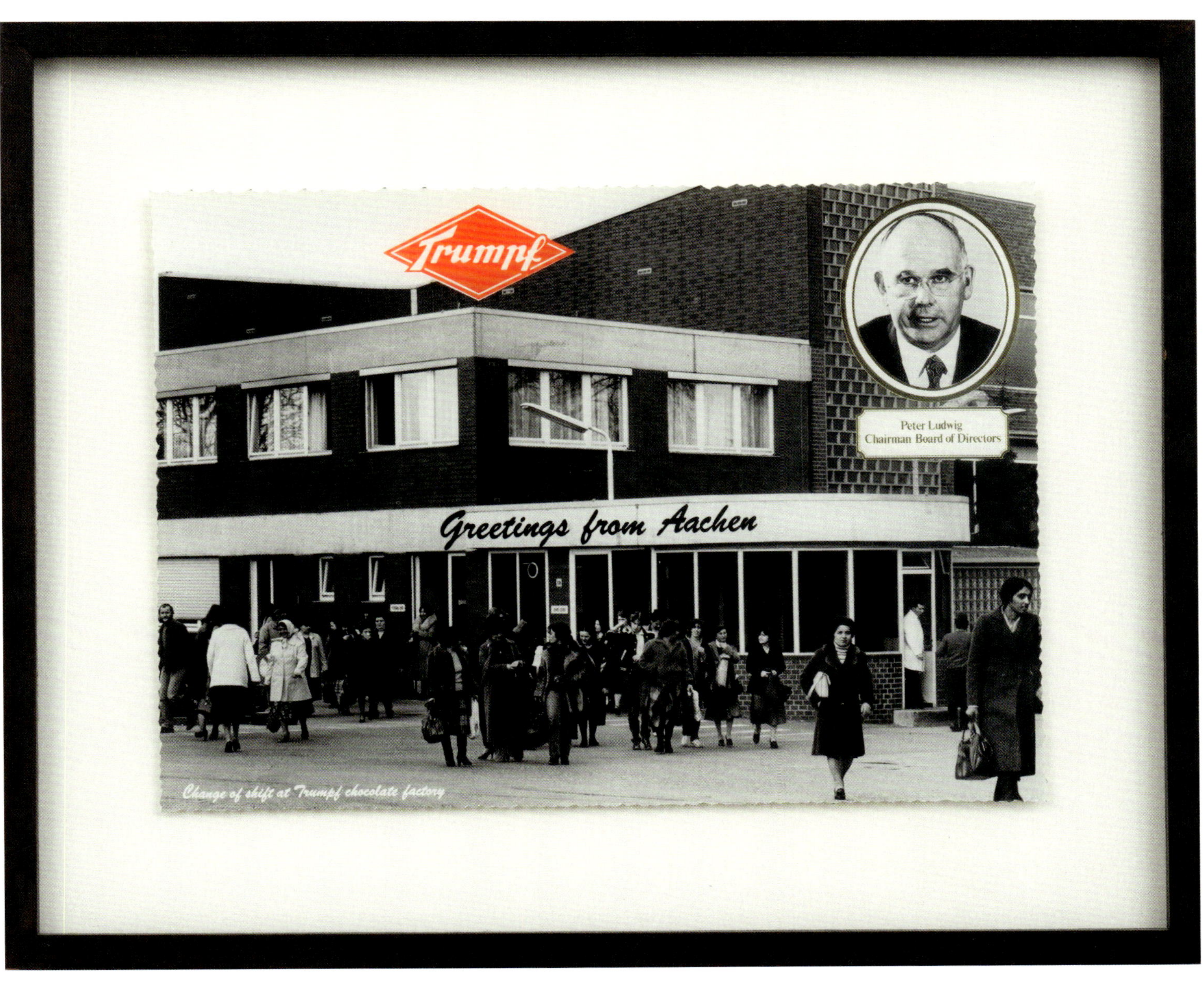

Greetings from Aachen, 1981
Following pages: *Der Pralinenmeister (The Chocolate Master)*, 1981

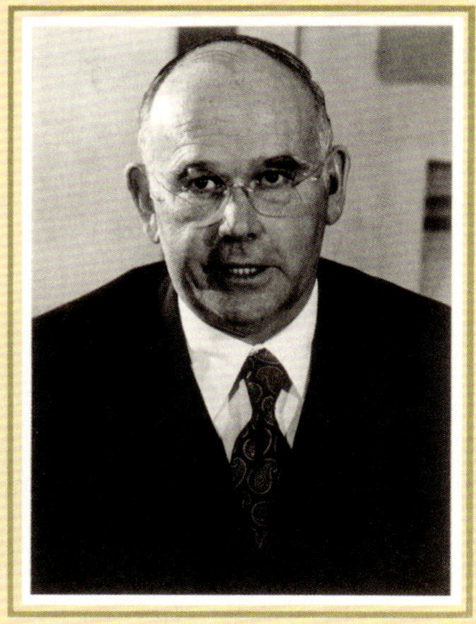

Prof. Dr. Dr. h. c. Peter Ludwig
Aufsichtsratsvorsitzender der
Leonard Monheim AG.

Kunstbesitz in Dauerleihgaben ist vermögensteuerfrei

Peter Ludwig wurde 1925 in Koblenz als Sohn des Industriellen Fritz Ludwig (Kalkwerke Ludwig) und Frau Helene Ludwig, geb. Klöckner, geboren.

Nach dem Wehrdienst (1943–45) studierte er Jura und Kunstgeschichte; Promotion 1950 über *»Das Menschenbild Picassos als Ausdruck eines generationsmäßig bedingten Lebensgefühls«*. Die Dissertation stützt sich auf Bezüge zwischen zeitgenössischer Literatur und dem Werk Picassos. Historische Ereignisse werden kaum berücksichtigt.

1951 heiratete Peter Ludwig Irene Monheim, eine Mitstudentin, und trat in die *Leonard Monheim KG.*, Aachen, seines Schwiegervaters ein. 1952 wurde er geschäftsführender Gesellschafter, 1969 Vorsitzender der Geschäftsleitung und 1978 Vorsitzender des Aufsichtsrats der *Leonard Monheim AG.*, Aachen.

Peter Ludwig ist Aufsichtsratsmitglied der *Agrippina Versicherungs-Gesellschaft* und der *Waggonfabrik Uerdingen*; er ist Vorsitzender des Bezirksbeirates der *Deutschen Bank AG*, Köln-Aachen-Siegen.

Seit Anfang der 50er Jahre sammeln Peter und Irene Ludwig Kunst, zunächst alte Kunst. Seit 1966 konzentrieren sie sich auf moderne Kunst: Pop Art, Photorealismus, Pattern Painting, Kunst aus der DDR und die *»neuen Wilden«*. Seit 1972 hält Peter Ludwig als Honorarprofessor der Kölner Universität kunsthistorische Seminare im *Museum Ludwig* ab.

Dauerleihgaben moderner Kunst befinden sich im *Museum Ludwig*, Köln, der *Neuen Galerie-Sammlung Ludwig* und dem *Suermondt-Ludwig-Museum* in Aachen, den *Nationalgalerien* in West- und Ostberlin, dem *Kunstmuseum Basel*, dem *Centre Pompidou* Paris, und den Landesmuseen in Saarbrücken und Mainz. Im Kölner *Schnütgen-Museum*, im Aachener *Couven-Museum* und im bayrischen *Nationalmuseum* befinden sich mittelalterliche Werke. Das Kölner *Rautenstrauch-Joest-Museum* beherbergt Objekte aus dem präkolumbianischen Amerika, aus Afrika und Ozeanien.

Das Kölner *Wallraf-Richartz-Museum* erhielt 1976 als Schenkung eine Pop Art-Sammlung (jetzt *Museum Ludwig*), das *Suermondt-Museum* in Aachen 1977 mittelalterliche Kunst (jetzt *Suermondt-Ludwig-Museum*). Dem *Antikenmuseum Basel* (jetzt *Antikenmuseum Basel und Museum Ludwig*) wurde 1981 eine Kollektion griechisch-römischer Kunst geschenkt, die Dauerleihgaben aus Kassel, Aachen und Würzburg einschließt. In eine *Österreichische Stiftung Ludwig für Kunst und Wissenschaft* wurde 1981 eine Sammlung moderner Kunst eingebracht.

Peter Ludwig sitzt in der Ankaufskommission der *Landesgalerie Düsseldorf*, im International Council des *Museum of Modern Art*, New York, und im Advisory Council des *Museum of Contemporary Art*, Los Angeles.

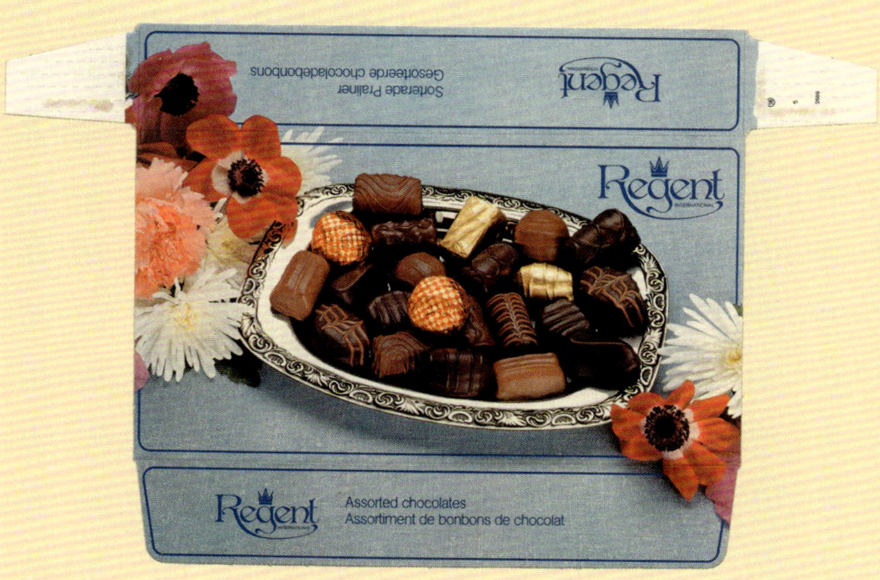

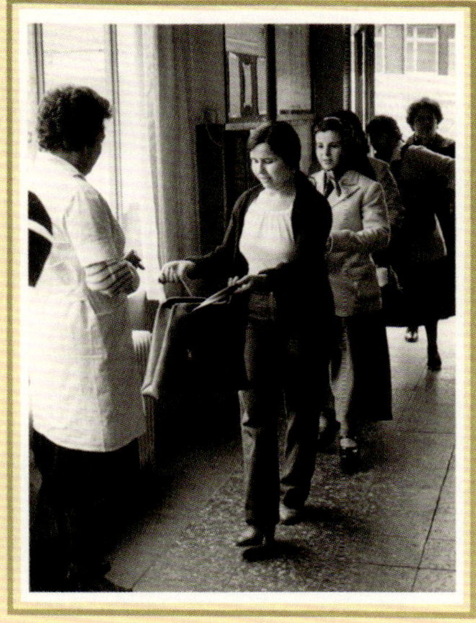

Arbeiterinnen in einem Werk
der Leonard Monheim AG.

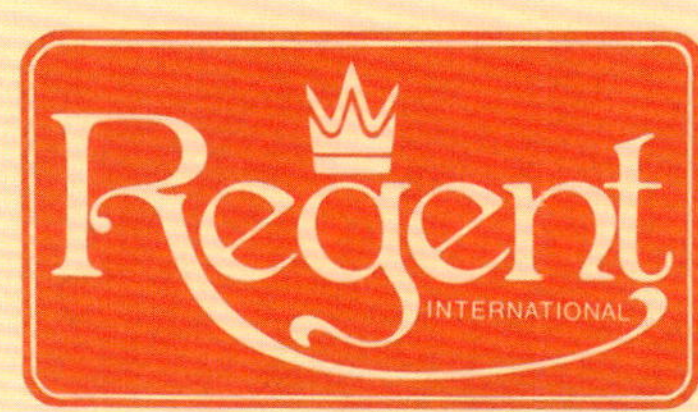

Die Monheim-Gruppe vertreibt Tafelschokolade und Pralinen der Marke Regent zu Niedrigpreisen vor allem über Aldi und Automaten.

Die Fertigung erfolgt in Aachen, wo das Unternehmen mit rund 2500 Arbeitern und Angestellten in 2 Werken die größten Produktionsstätten und seine Hauptverwaltung betreibt. Die Zahl der Arbeiter im Werk Saarlouis beträgt ca. 1300, in Quickborn ca. 400 und in West-Berlin ca. 800.

Insgesamt hat Monheim in Deutschland 1981 wie vor 10 Jahren rund 7000 Beschäftigte – bei verdreifachtem Umsatz. Davon sind 5000 Frauen. Die Zahl der gewerblich Beschäftigten beträgt 5400. Darunter sind zwei Drittel ungelernte Arbeitskräfte. Zusätzlich werden ca. 900 meist ungelernte Saisonarbeiter eingestellt.

Der von der Gewerkschaft Nahrung-Genuß-Gaststätten ausgehandelte Tariflohn bewegt sich zwischen DM 6,02 (Tarifgruppe E – Fließbandarbeit unter 18 Jahre) und DM 12,30 (Tarifgruppe S – qualifizierte Facharbeiter). Das niedrigste Gehalt, gemäß Tarifvertrag, beträgt DM 1097,–, das der höchsten Gehaltsstufe mindestens DM 3214,–.

Die überwiegende Mehrzahl der 2500 ausländischen Arbeitskräfte sind Frauen. Sie stammen vornehmlich aus der Türkei und Jugoslawien. Aber auch Gastarbeiterinnen aus Marokko, Tunesien, Spanien und Griechenland sind angeworben worden (»Kopfpreis« 1973: DM 1000,–). Ausländische Arbeiterinnen kommen auch täglich aus dem belgischen und holländischen Grenzgebiet.

Das Unternehmen unterhält in Aachen auf seinem umzäunten Betriebsgelände und an anderen Orten Wohnheime, in denen Gastarbeiterinnen zu dritt oder viert in einem Zimmer untergebracht sind (der Bau von Unterkünften für ausländische Arbeitskräfte wird von der Bundesanstalt für Arbeit subventioniert). Die Monatsmiete wird vom Lohn einbehalten.

Besuche werden von der Betriebsleitung kontrolliert und zum Teil abgewiesen. Das bischöfliche Presseamt und der Caritasverband in Aachen beurteilten die Wohnverhältnisse folgendermaßen: *»Da die meisten dieser Frauen und Mädchen lediglich am Arbeitsplatz und innerhalb der Wohnheime menschliche Kontakte knüpfen können, leben sie praktisch in einem Getto.«*

Da Monheim keine Kindertagesstätte habe, müßten Gastarbeiterinnen, die ein Kind bekommen, das Heim verlassen oder für ihr Kind eine für sie kaum erschwingliche Familienpflegestelle suchen, oder aber sie müßten das Kind zur Adoption anbieten.

»Es dürfte für eine große Firma, bei der so viele Mädchen und Frauen beschäftigt sind, ohne weiteres möglich sein, eine Kindertagesstätte zu errichten.«

Die Personalabteilung antwortete darauf, Monheim sei *»eine Schokoladenfabrik und kein Kindergarten«*. Für eine Kindertagesstätte könne kein Personal beschafft werden. Die Firma sei kein Sozialamt.

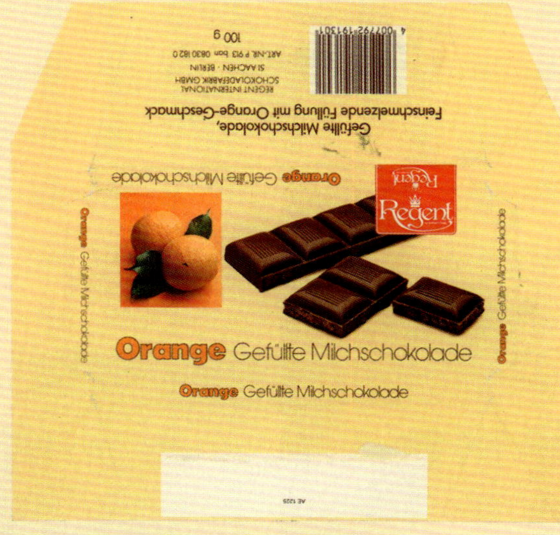

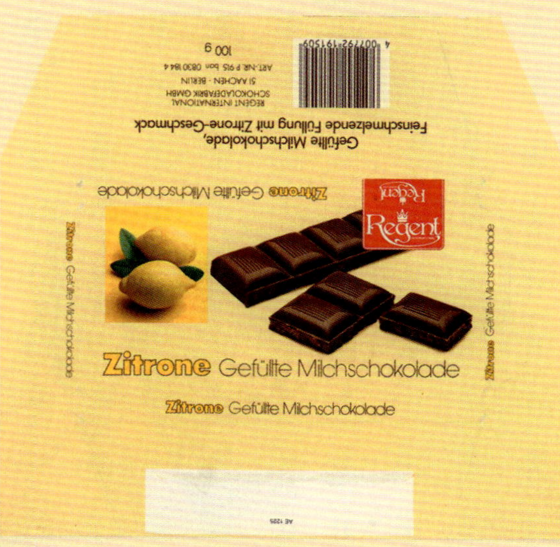

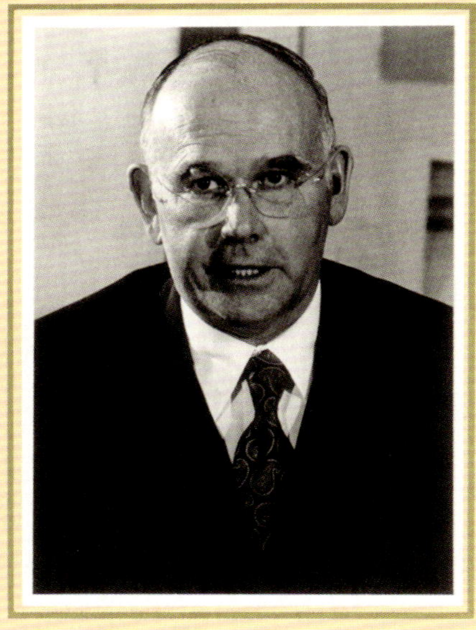

Prof. Dr. Dr. h. c. Peter Ludwig
Aufsichtsratsvorsitzender der
Leonard Monheim AG.

»Wir arbeiten nicht mit Drohungen« Peter Ludwig

Peter und Irene Ludwig übergaben dem Kölner Wallraf-Richartz-Museum 1968 als Dauerleihgabe eine Sammlung moderner Kunst, in der vornehmlich Werke der Pop Art vertreten waren.

1976 ist diese Sammlung der Stadt Köln mit der Auflage geschenkt worden, daß die Stadt Köln ein Museum für die Kunst des 20. Jahrhunderts errichtet, das den Namen *Museum Ludwig* erhält:

»Die Eheleute Ludwig bzw. der Überlebende von ihnen sind berechtigt, von diesem Vertrag zurückzutreten und die Herausgabe aller laut Vertrag geschenkten Kunstgegenstände zu verlangen, wenn die Gesamtfertigstellung und Eröffnung des Museums Ludwig nicht bis zum 9. Juli 1985 gewährleistet ist.« Der 9. Juli 1985 ist der 60. Geburtstag von Peter Ludwig.

Mit dem Museumsbau ist zwischen Dom und Rhein begonnen worden. Die Bauleitung veranschlagte die Kosten 1980 auf DM 219 Millionen. Die mit dem Bau notwendige Neugestaltung der Umgebung erhöht die Kosten insgesamt voraussichtlich auf weit über DM 300 Millionen. Die Unterhalts- und Personalkosten des Museums werden auf rund DM 10 Millionen geschätzt.

Unabhängig vom Bauvorhaben waren unverzüglich alle Werke ab 1900 – einschließlich sämtlicher Schenkungen Kölner Sammler – aus dem Wallraf-Richartz-Museum auszugliedern und organisatorisch in das neugegründete *Museum Ludwig* aufzunehmen, das vorläufig in den Räumen des Wallraf-Richartz-Museums untergebracht ist. Ebenfalls sollen alle Neuerwerbungen zeitgenössischer Kunst dem *Museum Ludwig* zugefügt werden.

Im Schenkungsvertrag wurde ferner vereinbart: *»Die Berufung dieses Direktors (des Museums Ludwig) sowie der wissenschaftlichen Mitarbeiter des Museums Ludwig erfolgt nach Anhörung der Eheleute Ludwig bzw. des überlebenden Ehegatten. Herr Professor Dr. Ludwig und seine Ehefrau werden über die laufende Arbeit dieses Museums (z. B. Ausstellungswesen, Ankäufe, Publikationen) voll informiert.«*

Mit den Eheleuten Ludwig ist zweimal jährlich eine *»Grundsatzbesprechung«* zu führen, in der *»über die Arbeit des Museums Ludwig umfassend und detailliert gesprochen wird«.*

Zum Wert der Schenkung erklärte Peter Ludwig: *»Daß die Sammlung heute 45 Millionen wert ist, ist vor allem dem Umstand zu danken, daß sie jahrelang in einem so prominenten Haus wie dem Wallraf-Richartz-Museum gezeigt wurde. Ich habe für die Bilder und Objekte zusammen nicht mehr als 5 Millionen ausgegeben.«*

Die Stadt Köln machte Peter Ludwig zum Ehrenbürger.

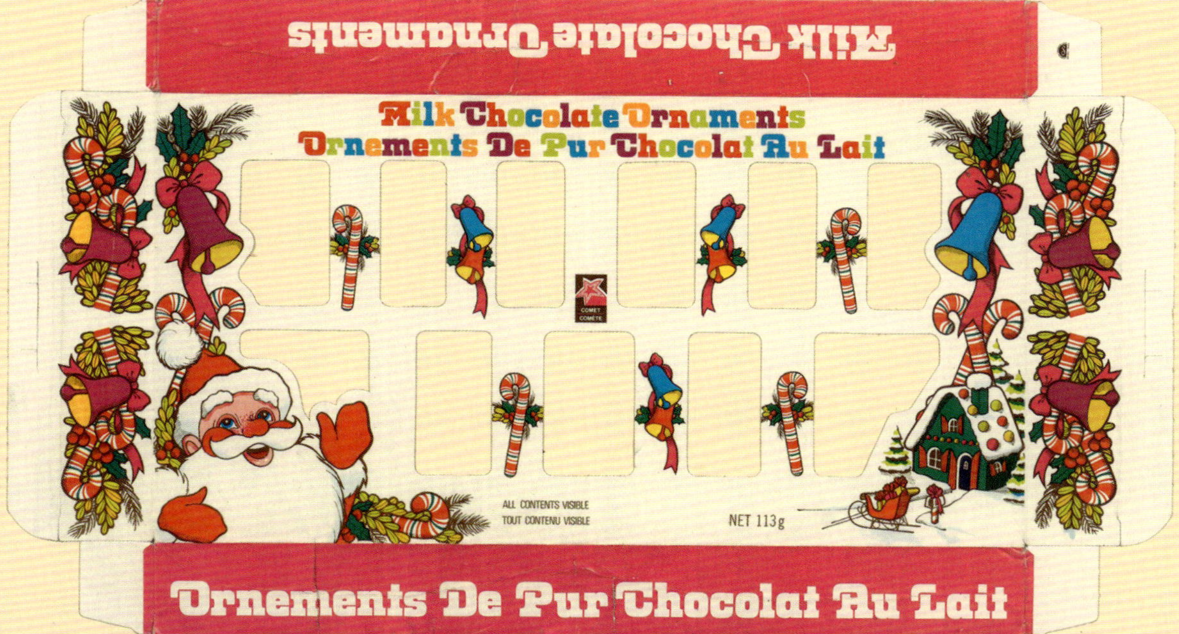

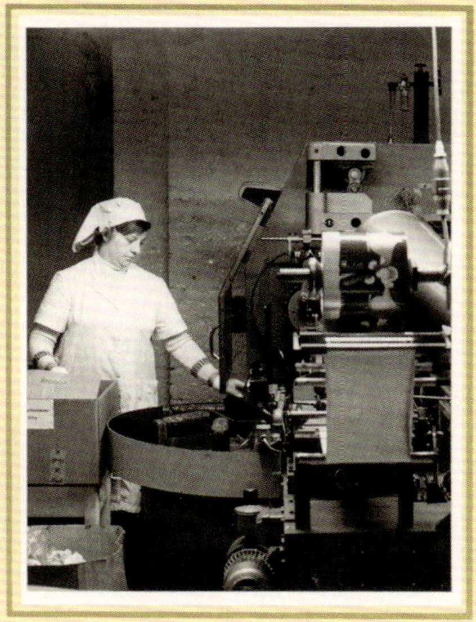

Arbeiterin in einem Werk der Leonard Monheim AG.

COMET CONFECTIONARY LTD

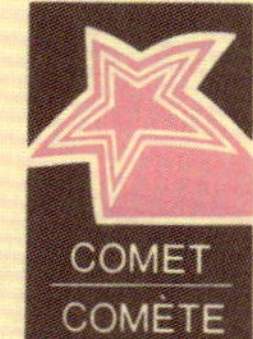

LA CONFISERIE COMÈTE LTÉE

Die Monheim-Gruppe erwarb 1959 in St. Hyacinthe bei Montreal die Schokoladefabrik der *Kambly Company*. Zunächst unter dem Namen *Regent Chocolate Ltd.* produzierte die kanadische Tochtergesellschaft Tafelschokolade und Saisonartikel. Nach Erweiterungen in den Jahren 1968 und 1970 nahm das Werk ein Gelände von 9000 qm ein.

1974 traten nach dem Verzehr von *Regent*-Schokoladenhasen, Christbaumkugeln und den für *Wookworth* in Toronto hergestellten Milchschokolade *Crunch Brake-ups* Salmonellenvergiftungen auf. Die Gesundheitsbehörden Kanadas und der Vereinigten Staaten untersagten darauf den weiteren Verkauf von *Regent*-Erzeugnissen. Die bereits ausgelieferte Ware mußte zurückgerufen werden. Das Werk wurde zur Entseuchung geschlossen.

Unter einem neuen Namen, *Comet Confectionary Ltd./Confiserie Comète Ltée.*, wurde der Betrieb nach einem halben Jahr mit einer Kapitaleinlage von DM 5,3 Millionen wieder aufgenommen. Günstige Darlehen der Quebec Industrial Development Corp. und des Department of Regional Economic Expansion – zum Teil zinslos – in Höhe von can. $ 4,25 Millionen sowie stille Reserven der Tochtergesellschaft förderten die Wiedereröffnung.

Die Arbeitnehmer, in der Mehrzahl Frauen und ungelernt, deren Stundenlohn 1973 nur wenig über dem gesetzlich vorgeschriebenen Mindestlohn von can. $ 1,85 lag, gründeten 1974 während der Stillegung des Betriebes eine Gewerkschaft, den *Syndicat des Salariés de la Confiserie Comète St-Hyacinthe (C.S.N.)*.

Vor dem Abschluß des 3. Tarifvertrages von 1979 wurde *Comet* bestreikt. Gemäß diesem auf zwei Jahre befristeten Vertrag betrugen der Mindestlohn can. $ 5,16 und der Höchstlohn $ 7,15. Saisonbedingt schwankt die Zahl der Arbeiter und Angestellten zwischen 200 und 500.

Comet vertreibt ihre Erzeugnisse unter den Marken *Comet, van Houten* und den Hausnamen zahlreicher Firmen in Kanada und den Vereinigten Staaten für die sie anonym produziert (u. a. *Dalt, Orion, Sarah Lee*). Über die Hälfte der Fertigung, vor allem Saisonartikel, wird seit Jahren in die Vereinigten Staaten exportiert.

Comet besorgt auch den Vertrieb von Erzeugnissen der Marke *van Houten*, die in Europa hergestellt worden sind, für den kanadischen Markt.

Die Monheim-Geschäftsführung beurteilt das Ergebnis von *Comet* anhaltend positiv. Im Geschäftsjahr 1979/80 steigerte sich der Umsatz um 31,7 % auf can. $ 35 Millionen. Der Gewinn stieg um 40,9 % auf $ 0,8 Millionen. Er wurde nicht ausgeschüttet, sondern in den Betrieb investiert.

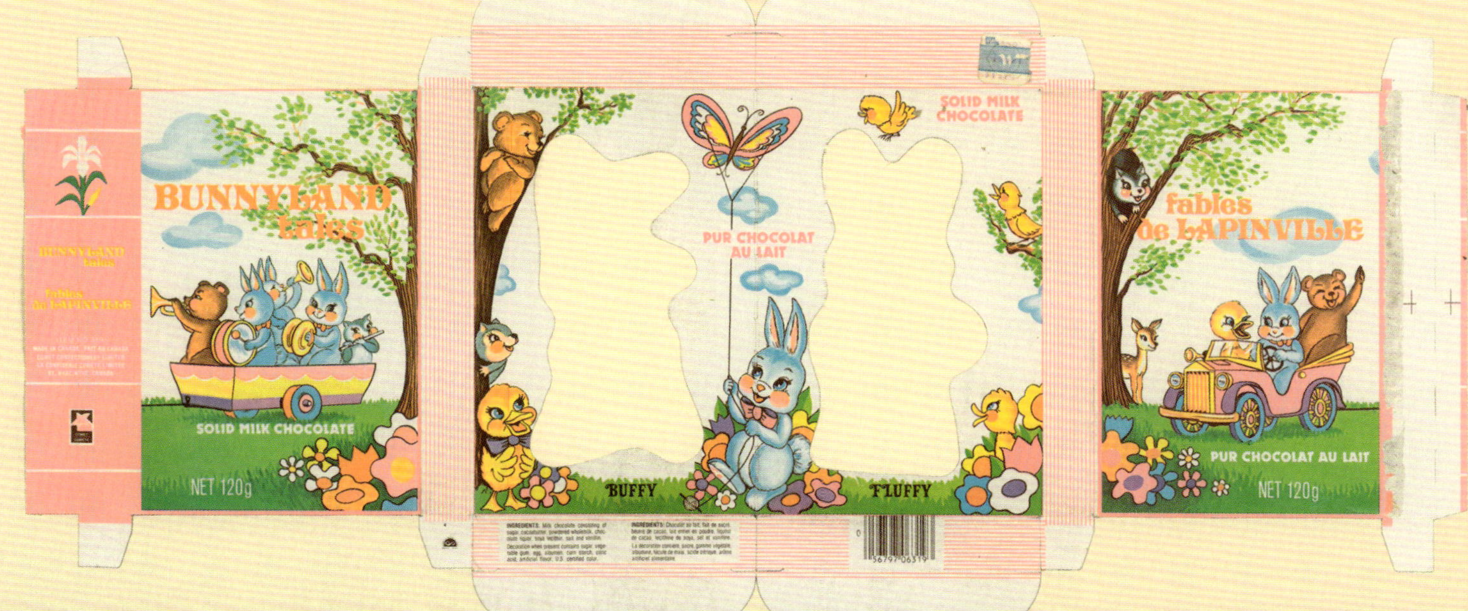

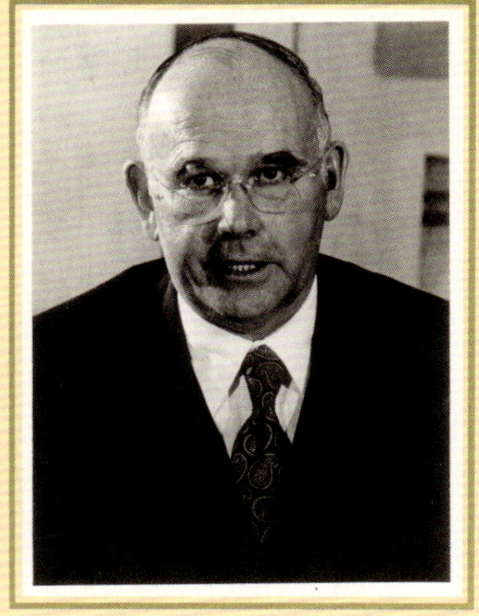

Prof. Dr. Dr. h. c. Peter Ludwig
Aufsichtsratsvorsitzender der
Leonard Monheim AG.

Bei Stiftungen entfallen für Ehegatten bis zu 35 Prozent Erbschaftsteuer

Die *Neue Galerie-Sammlung Ludwig* der Stadt Aachen präsentiert gewöhnlich – oft in programmatischen Ausstellungen – die Neuerwerbungen von Peter Ludwig. Sie ist auch der Ausgangspunkt für Wanderausstellungen und Dauerleihgaben an andere Museen. Ihr Direktor arbeitet eng mit dem Sammler zusammen.

1977 gingen 22 Werke von Aachen als Dauerleihgabe in die *Nationalgalerie* in Ostberlin. Neuerworbene Malerei aus der DDR wurde daraufhin in Aachen gezeigt.

In Aachen wurde 1978 auch eine Ausstellung für das *Museum für moderne Kunst* in Teheran zusammengestellt (bis zum Sturz des Schahs leitete das Museum ein Stiefbruder der Kaiserin). Das *Centre Pompidou* in Paris und andere europäische Institute erhielten ebenfalls namhafte Dauerleihgaben aus Aachen.

Seit 1976 plant die Stadt Aachen deshalb, durch einen Museumsneubau Peter Ludwig dazu zu bewegen, seine Sammlung in Aachen zu belassen. An der Monheim-Allee soll ab 1982 für DM 40 Millionen ein Neubau erstehen. Die Vollendung ist für 1985 zum 60. Geburtstag des Sammlers vorgesehen. Eine Zusage, seine Sammlung in Aachen zu lassen, hat er nicht gegeben.

Als die Stadt 1976 ihre niedrige Gewerbesteuer anhob, drohte Peter Ludwig (CDU): *»Mit der Verdummbeutelung muß ein Ende sein ... Mit Steuererhöhungen will ich aber kein Museum!«*

1979 vergab er den bedeutendsten Teil der Aachener Sammlung als Dauerleihgabe an das neugegründete *Museum moderner Kunst* in Wien. Dr. Dieter Ronte, der in Köln den Bau des *Museums Ludwig* überwachte, wurde zum Direktor des Wiener Museums ernannt.

1981 wurde eine Auswahl von 161 Werken im Nennwert von öS 150 Millionen (ca. DM 10 Mio.) in eine neugegründete *Österreichische Stiftung Ludwig für Kunst und Wissenschaft* eingebracht. Die Republik Österreich verpflichtete sich, öS 150 Millionen für Ankäufe, Ausstellungen und andere Stiftungszwecke beizusteuern.

Im Stiftungsrat sitzen Peter und Irene Ludwig mit 2 von ihnen benannten Personen. Österreich stellt seinerseits 4 Mitglieder. Der Vorsitz wechselt in jährlichem Turnus zwischen Peter Ludwig und einem Vertreter Österreichs. Den Eheleuten Ludwig steht für 10 Jahre ein Vetorecht über die Disposition (Ausstellung, Leihgaben etc.) der von ihnen gestifteten Werke zu.

Frau Irene Ludwig wurde in Wien zum Professor ernannt. Peter Ludwig erhielt die Ehrenbürgerschaft.

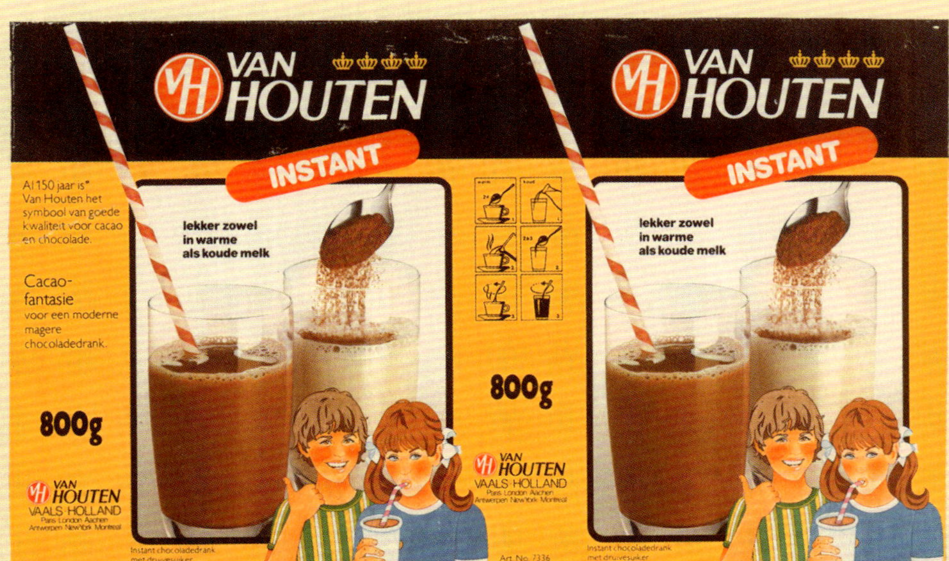

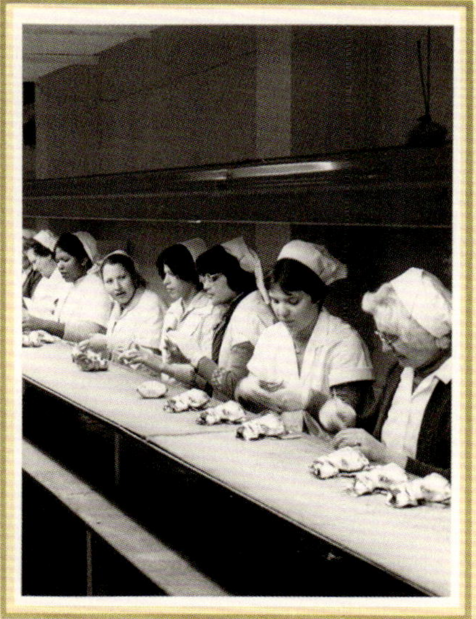

Arbeiterinnen in einem Werk
der Leonard Monheim AG.

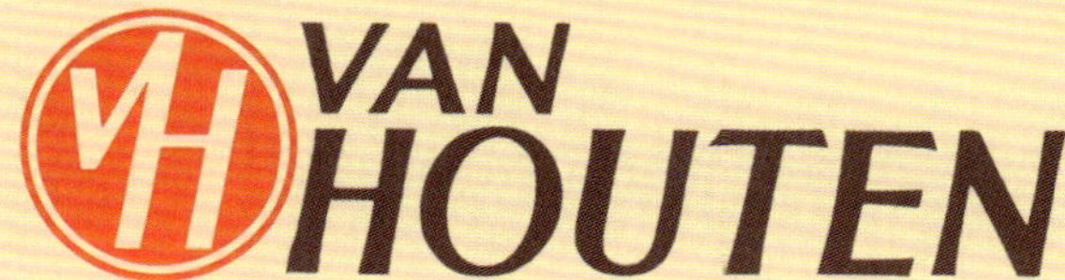

Die Monheim-Gruppe erwarb 1971 von der amerikanischen Peter & Paul, Inc. weltweit die Produktions-, Marken- und Vertriebsrechte für *van Houten*-Erzeugnisse.

Seither betreuen die *van Houten*-Tochtergesellschaften der Monheim Gruppe ihr gesamtes Gruppenexportgeschäft über eigene Vertriebsorganisationen in Deutschland, Frankreich (1979/80 Umsatz FF 122,7 Millionen), Großbritannien, Kanada, den Niederlanden und den Vereinigten Staaten.

Darüber hinaus sind Ostasien und die DDR bedeutende Handelspartner. Eine Expansion des Marktes in die Sowjetunion und andere Ostblockländer ist geplant. Kooperationsverhandlungen sind 1980 auch mit österreichischen Unternehmen aufgenommen worden, die den Markt des Alpenlandes für Monheim-Erzeugnisse erschließen sollen.

Rund 34 % (DM 403 Millionen) des Konzernumsatzes wurden im Geschäftsjahr 1979/80 außerhalb der Bundesrepublik erzielt.

Neben dem Markenartikelgeschäft betreibt *van Houten* auch die Herstellung von Industrieprodukten wie Kakaobutter, Kakaopulver, Kuverture, Kakaomassen und Rohkakao.

Insgesamt investierte Monheim von 1971 bis 1975 allein in West-Berlin für die *van Houten*-Produktion von Kakaopulver und Kakaobutter DM 60 Millionen. Diese Sachanlagen wurden wesentlich durch die Vergünstigungen des Berlinförderungsgesetzes getragen (Sonderabschreibungen, Investitionszuschüsse und andere Steuererleichterungen).

Die Monheim-Gruppe schloß 1973 mit *AGROS*, dem staatlichen Außenhandelsunternehmen von Polen, einen Kooperationsvertrag. Daraufhin wurde 1975 in der *Schokoladenfabrik Wawel* in Krakau mit der Lizenzproduktion von *van Houten* Tafelschokolade begonnen. Ein Teil der Erzeugnisse ist für den Export bestimmt.

Mit den staatlichen Außenhandelsfirmen der DDR wurden 1974 ebenfalls Gestattungsverträge zur Herstellung instantisierter Kakaogetränke der Marke *van Houten* unterzeichnet.

Die Schulen der DDR werden seither mit dem Kakaotrunk *Trinkfix* beliefert. Monheim-Produkte sind sonst nur in Intershops und Delikatläden erhältlich. Ein Teil der Produktion wird exportiert, auch in die Bundesrepublik. Für die Fertigung in Polen und der DDR stellt die Monheim-Gruppe nicht nur technisches Wissen bereit, sondern liefert auch hochspezialisierte Anlagen.

An Orten, in denen Erzeugnisse der Monheim-Gruppe gefertigt, vertrieben oder Geschäftsbeziehungen angeknüpft werden sollen, sind häufig Leihgaben aus dem Kunstbesitz des Aufsichtsratsvorsitzenden Peter Ludwig anzutreffen (*Nationalgalerie* in Ost-Berlin, Polen, Schweiz, Frankreich, Österreich, Saarbrücken, Aachen, geplant in der UdSSR).

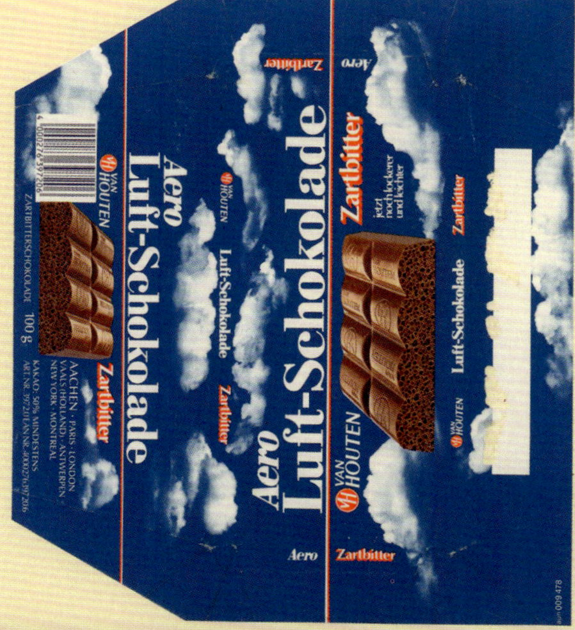

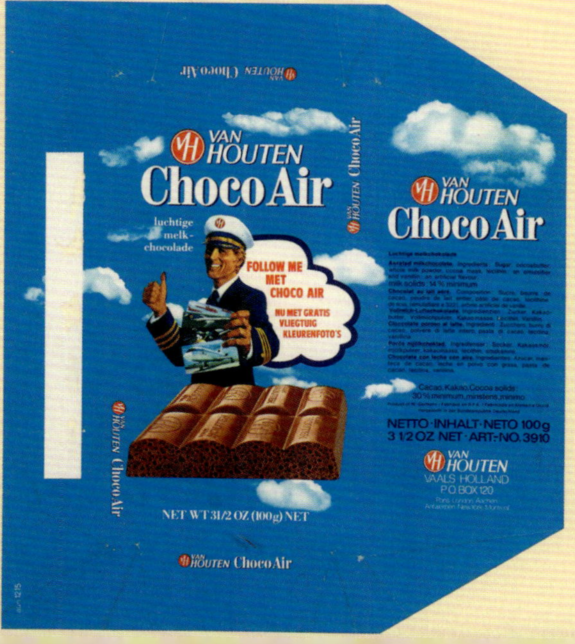

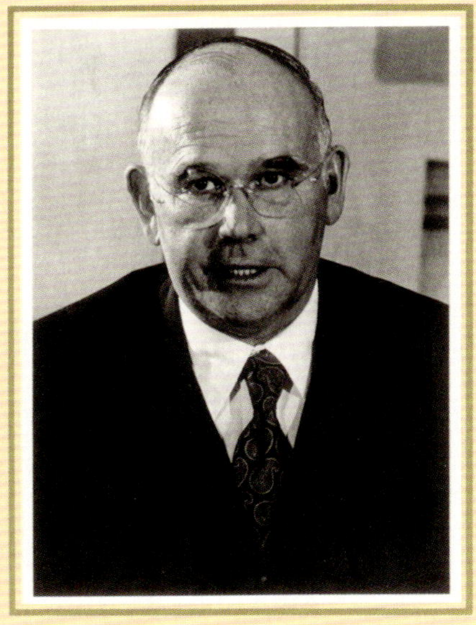

Prof. Dr. Dr. h. c. Peter Ludwig
Aufsichtsratsvorsitzender der
Leonard Monheim AG.

Stiftungen sind jährlich zu 10 Prozent des Einkommens steuerabzugsfähig

Peter Ludwig unterbreitete dem Bund, dem Land Nordrhein-Westfalen und der Stadt Köln im Sommer 1980 einen gemeinsam erarbeiteten Entwurf einer *Urkunde über die Errichtung der Stiftung Ludwig zur Förderung der bildenden Kunst und verwandter Gebiete* mit dem Sitz in Köln nebst einer Satzung. Das Dokument ist das Ergebnis fast einjähriger Gespräche zwischen den drei öffentlichen Partnern der projektierten Stiftung und Peter Ludwig.

Die Stiftungspläne blieben der Öffentlichkeit verborgen, bis der *Kölner Stadt-Anzeiger* sie dank einer Indiskretion am 6. September publizierte.

Dem Stiftungsentwurf zufolge beabsichtigen die Eheleute Irene und Peter Ludwig, Kunstwerke in die Stiftung einzubringen, die in einer Anlage aufgeführt sein sollen. Über den Inhalt der Anlage ist öffentlich nichts bekannt.

Soweit das Stiftungsgut ausgeliehen ist, würde die Stiftung in die Rechte und Pflichten der Stifter als Verleiher eintreten. Irene und Peter Ludwig beabsichtigen, auch ihren künftigen Kunsterwerb der Stiftung zuzuwenden.

Der Umfang und der Wert des Stiftungsgutes ist bis zur Offenlegung einer Liste nicht einzuschätzen. Es wird spekuliert, es handele sich um die mittelalterlichen Werke, die sich als Dauerleihgabe im Kölner *Schnütgen-Museum* befinden (Schätzwert DM 100 Mio), um präkolumbianische, afrikanische und ozeanische Kunst, die im *Rautenstrauch-Joest-Museum* in Köln aufbewahrt werden, und um Werke moderner Kunst, die an zahlreiche europäische Museen ausgeliehen sind.

Für 10 Jahre wird den Eheleuten Ludwig ein Einspruchsrecht zugebilligt »*in Fragen der Disposition über den vom Ehepaar Ludwig eingebrachten Kunstbesitz*«.

Dauerleihgaben in Museen ersparen dem Leihgeber die Kosten der sachgerechten Lagerung, Pflege, konservatorischen Betreuung und Sicherung seines Kunstbesitzes. Die wissenschaftliche Erschließung der Werke sowie ihre Ausstellung und Publikation in Katalogen und Besprechungen erhöhen ihren Wert.

Solange Kunstbesitz öffentlich zugänglich gemacht wird, ist er von der Vermögensteuer (jährlich 0,5 % ihres Wertes) befreit.

Eine Stiftung kann jährlich zu 10 % des insgesamt zu versteuernden Jahreseinkommens abzugsfähig sein. Es ist manchmal möglich, diese Vergünstigungen auf mehrere Jahre zu verteilen.

Kunstbesitz ist erbschaftsteuerpflichtig. Für den überlebenden Ehegatten entfällt bei einer Stiftung von über DM 100 Millionen eine Steuerschuld von 35 % des Wertes: DM 35 Millionen.

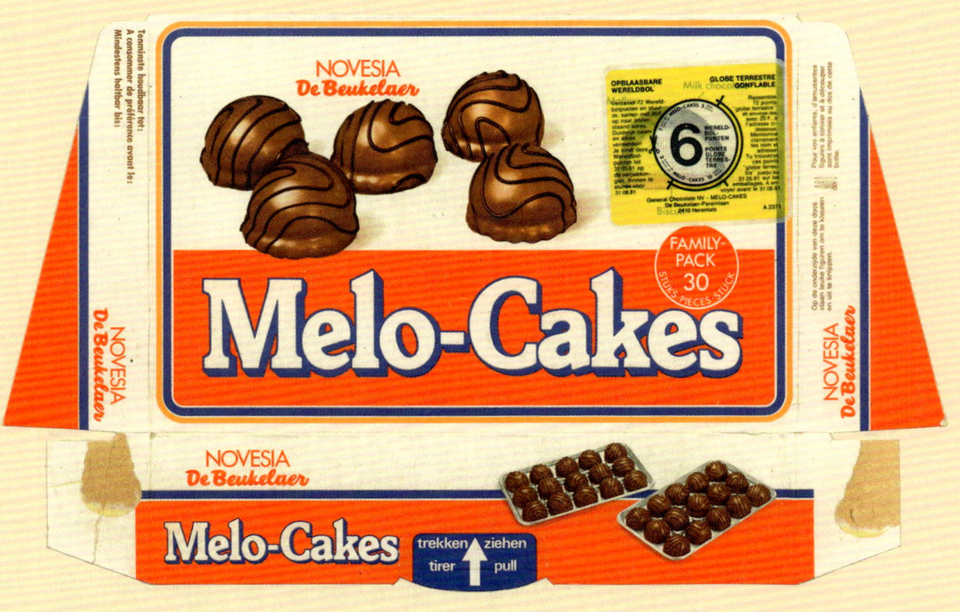

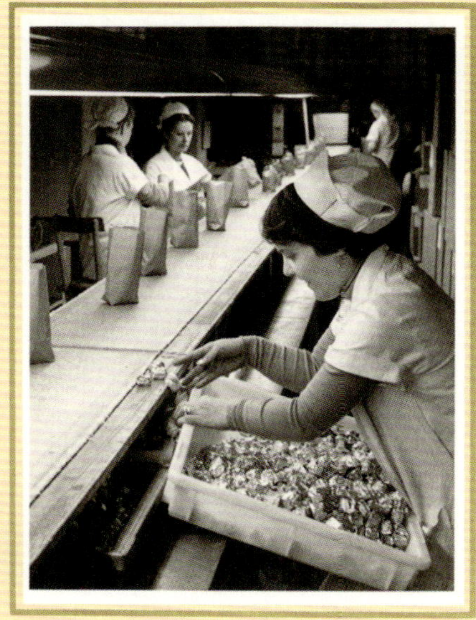

Arbeiterinnen in einem Werk der Leonard Monheim AG.

NOVESIA De Beukelaer

Die Monheim-Gruppe übernahm 1978 von der *General Buiscuit Co.* 75 % der Anteile der belgischen *General Chocolate N.V./S.A.* für einen Gesamtpreis von bfrs. 350 Millionen. Die restlichen Anteile verblieben im Besitz der deutschen *P. F. Feldhaus-Novesia* in Neuß.

General Chocolate stellt in Herentals (Belgien) und in Neuß Schokoladenerzeugnisse her, die unter der Marke *Novesia/De Beukelaar* vornehmlich in den Benelux-Ländern, der Bundesrepublik und Frankreich vertrieben werden. Zur Zeit der Übernahme beschäftigten die beiden Produktionsstätten jeweils 500 Arbeiter und Angestellte. Das Umsatzvolumen betrug rund DM 200 Millionen.

Im Anschluß an den Erwerb der Aktienmehrheit durch die Monheim-Gruppe beschloß das Ministerium für flämische Regionalwirtschaft bei einer Darlehensaufnahme von bfrs. 478 Millionen (knapp DM 32 Millionen) eine direkte Unterstützung in Form von Zinszuschüssen und Kapitalprämien von bfrs. 68 Millionen für die Modernisierung und Rationalisierung der Betriebsanlagen in Herentals zu gewähren.

Außerdem stellte die halbstaatliche Gesellschaft für Kreditgewährung an die Industrie ein vom Staat garantiertes Darlehen von bfrs. 288 Millionen bereit. Das belgische Tochterunternehmen sollte auch für drei Jahre in den Genuß gewisser Steuererleichterungen kommen.

Die Monheim-Gruppe beabsichtigte, aus eigenen Mittel bfrs. 310 Millionen zu investieren.

1979 wurde die Beteiligung der Monheim-Gruppe an *General Chocolate* auf 100 % aufgestockt. Damit gelangten auch die deutschen Beteiligungsgesellschaften *Novesia-Schokolade GmbH* und *Meurisse Schokolade GmbH* in Neuß völlig in den Monheim-Einflußbereich.

Die Konzernleitung beschloß 1980, die *Novesia*-Betriebsstätten in Neuß (Umsatz im Geschäftsjahr 1979/80 rund DM 80 Millionen) stillzulegen und ihre Produktion der *Goldnußtafeln* und *Goldnuß Pärchen* in anderen Monheim-Werken rationeller fortzusetzen. 350 Arbeitnehmer sind davon betroffen.

Im belgischen Herentals werden unter anderem die *Melo Cakes, Leo, Ascot, Big Nuts, BibiP* und *Alu*, vornehmlich gefüllte Schokolade oder mit Schokolade überzogene Waffeln, hergestellt. Der Vertrieb von *Alu* und *Leo* geschieht vor allem durch Automaten.

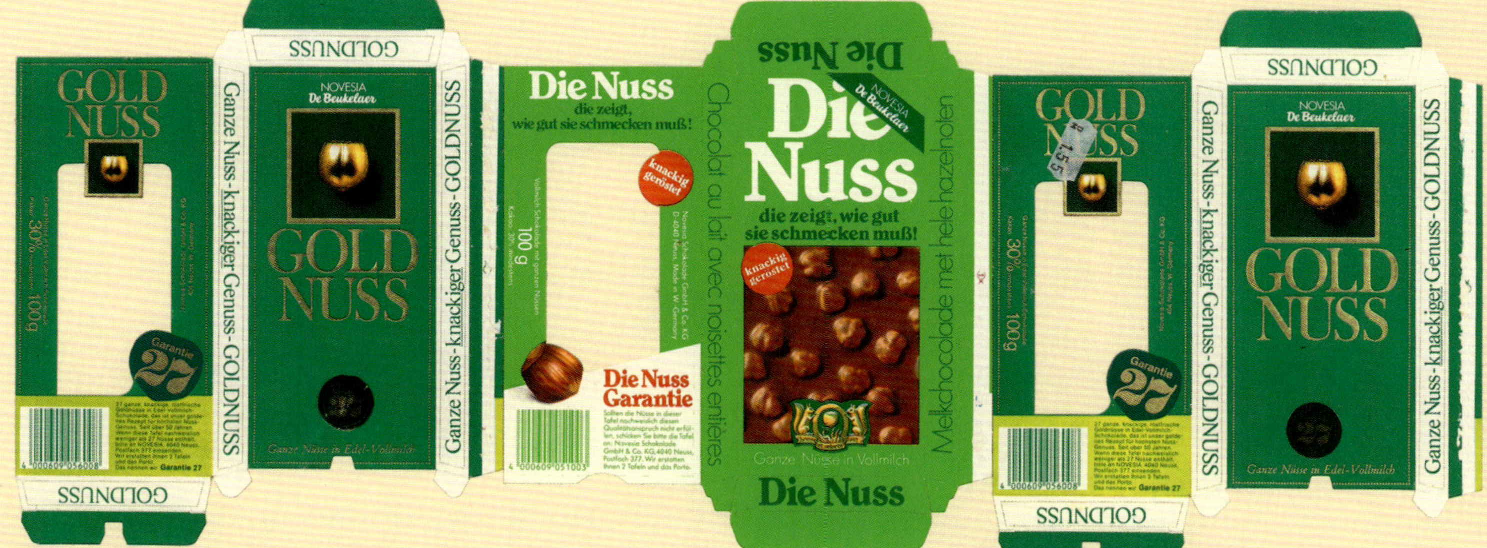

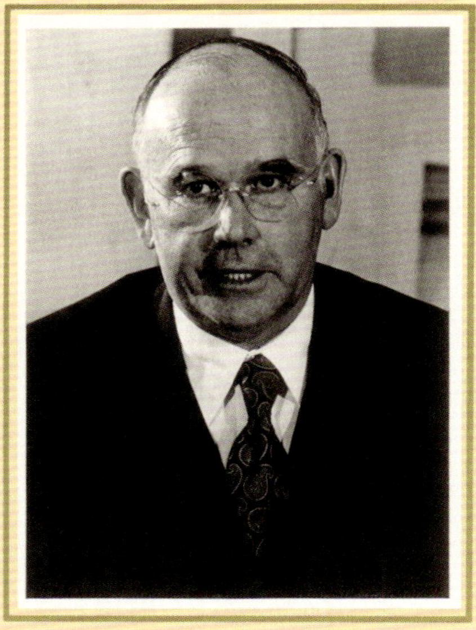

Prof. Dr. Dr. h. c. Peter Ludwig
Aufsichtsratsvorsitzender der
Leonard Monheim AG.

Wehe der (Kunstmarkt-) Koje, an der er vorbeigegangen ist

Peter Ludwig über sich selber

In der Satzung der von Peter und Irene Ludwig vorgeschlagenen und zusammen mit dem Bund, dem Land Nordrhein-Westfalen und der Stadt Köln geplanten *Stiftung Ludwig* heißt es:

»Für Stiftungszwecke betreibt die Stiftung das Museum Ludwig in Köln, das sie verwaltet und erhält.«

»Der Stiftungsrat entscheidet besonders über die Berufung und Abberufung des ... Direktors des Museums Ludwig.«

Im Falle der Stiftungsauflösung *»fallen das Grundstück des Stiftungsmuseums und die Gegenstände, die ihren gewöhnlichen Standpunkt in Köln haben, der Stadt Köln ohne Gegenleistung zu«*.

Daraus folgt, daß die Stadt Köln sich – für die Dauer der Stiftung – ihrer Verfügungsgewalt über ihre Sammlung der Kunst des 20. Jahrhunderts entledigt. Betroffen wären nicht nur die Pop Art Sammlung, welche die Eheleute Ludwig 1976 geschenkt hatten, sondern auch die dem *Wallraf-Richartz-Museum* von Kölner Sammlern geschenkten Werke, die in das *Museum Ludwig* integriert worden sind, sowie die Eigenerwerbungen des Museums.

Der Neubau des *Museums Ludwig* (Baukosten DM 219 Millionen) soll anscheinend ebenfalls der *Stiftung Ludwig* übereignet und möglicherweise seine Unterhalts- und Personalkosten von ihr übernommenwerden.

In der Satzung ist ferner für die Stiftung *»von der Stadt Köln zur Verfügung gestellten Beamtenplanstellen der Stadt«* die Rede.

Die öffentlichen Stiftungspartner sprechen von jährlichen Beitragszahlungen – auch der Stadt Köln –, die zumindest am Anfang mehrere Millionen DM betragen sollen (der Ankaufsetat der 8 Kölner Museen beläuft sich auf DM 1,1 Mio.).

Die Vertreter der Stadt Köln gehören zu den entschiedensten öffentlichen Verfechtern der *Stiftung Ludwig*. Pressekommentaren zufolge befürchten sie, die Eheleute Ludwig zögen ihre umfangreichen Leihgaben – entgegen einem ausdrücklichen früheren Versprechen – ab, wenn die von ihnen projektierte *Stiftung Ludwig* nicht zustande kommt. Peter Ludwig hatte einmal angedeutet: *»Es gibt vielleicht noch andere Regierungen, mit denen man auch sprechen kann und auch spricht.«*

Köln erhofft sich aber auch, daß durch ihre Beteiligung in der Stiftung ein Teil der erheblichen Bau- und Folgekosten des neuen *Museums Ludwig* von Bund und Land mitgetragen werden.

Der Generaldirektor der Kölner Museun, Hugo Borger, spricht auch von einer wünschenswerten künstlerischen *»Oberzentrumsfunktion«* der Stadt. Einhellig sagen die städtischen Vertreter: *»Ohne Ludwig geht hier nichts mehr.«*

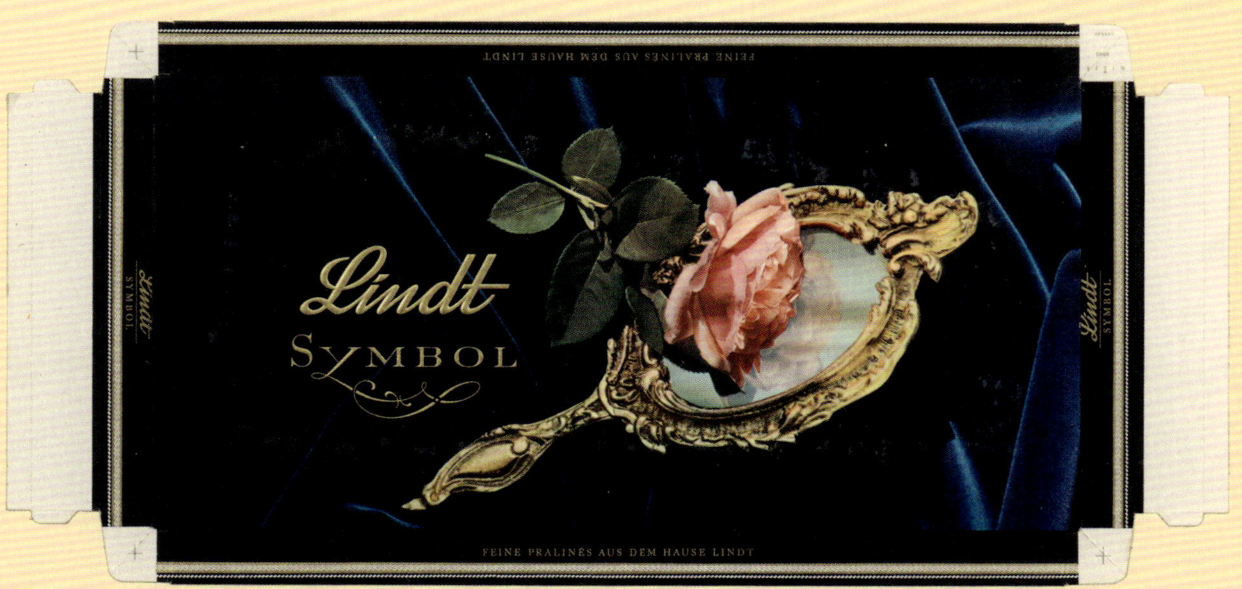

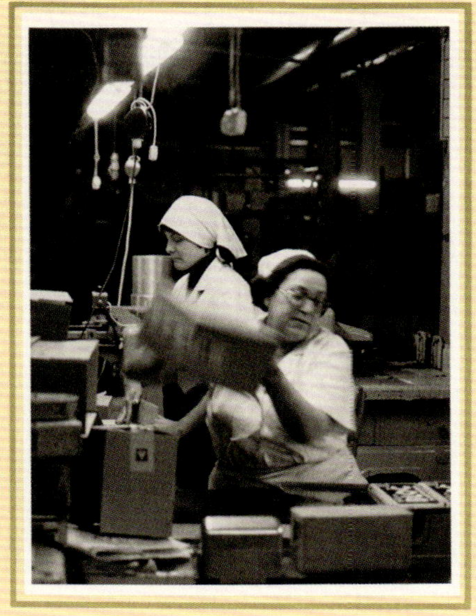

Arbeiterin in einem Werk
der Leonard Monheim AG.

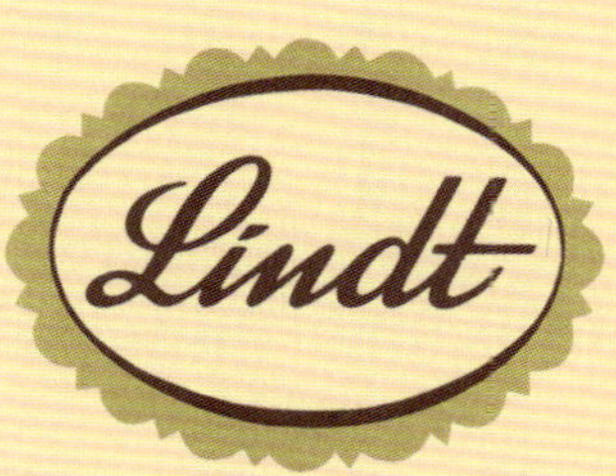

Die Zusammenarbeit der Monheim-Gruppe mit der schweizerischen *Lindt & Sprüngli* geht in die Zeit vor dem 2. Weltkrieg zurück. Monheim hält gegenwärtig jeweils 80 % der Anteile von *Lindt & Sprüngli GmbH, Aachen*, und *Lindt & Sprüngli BV. Niederlande*. Die Restanteile verbleiben beim Stammhaus, der *Lindt & Sprüngli AG., Kilchberg/Schweiz*.

In Lizenz werden von Monheim *Lindt*-Erzeugnisse, Pralinen, Tafelschokolade und Saisonartikel, für den deutschen und niederländischen Markt produziert (geschätzter Umsatz 1979/80 sfrs. 195 Millionen — ein Drittel des *Lindt*-Weltumsatzes).

Die Monheim-Gruppe hatte auch mit der englischen *John Mackintosh and Sons Ltd.* und der amerikanischen *Peter & Paul, Inc.* Lizenzproduktions- und Vertriebsabkommen.

Erzeugnisse der Marke *Lindt* werden vornehmlich in einem Werk in der Aachener Innenstadt hergestellt, wo sich auch die Monheim-Verwaltungszentrale befindet.

Einem Aachener Gerücht zufolge beabsichtigte Monheim 1977 die Verlagerung eines Teiles seiner Produktion in ein Zweigwerk bei Saarlouis. Damit wären 1000—1800 Arbeitsplätze in Aachen verlorengegangen.

Die Konzernleitung erklärte dagegen zur gleichen Zeit, sie bemühe sich vielmehr darum, die Fertigung nach Aachen-Süsterfeld zu verlegen und die dort existierende Betriebsstätte zu erweitern:

»Dazu bedarf es beträchtlicher Mittel. Eine Konzentration der Aachener Betriebsstätten in Süsterfeld müßten vom Land und von der Stadt bezuschußt werden.«

Die Stadt Aachen entschloß sich im selben Jahr, das 20 000 qm große Areal in der Innenstadt zum Sanierungsgebiet zu erklären und für den Bau von Einfamilienhäusern mit Gärten zu erwerben.

Für die Aufgabe des Werkes im Stadtzentrum und als Erstattung der mit der Verlagerung anfallenden Kosten wird Monheim aus öffentlichen Mitteln eine Entschädigung von DM 45,7 Millionen gezahlt. 75 % der Summe werden vom Land Nordrhein-Westfalen getragen.

Monheim beabsichtigte, einen Teil seines für 1980 vorgesehenen Investitionsvolumens von DM 60 Millionen für den Bau des neuen Werkes und eines Verwaltungsgebäudes zu verwenden. Durch höhere Automatisation soll die Fertigung kostensparend rationalisiert werden. Der Bau in Aachen-Süsterfeld wird voraussichtlich bis Ende 1982 vollendet sein.

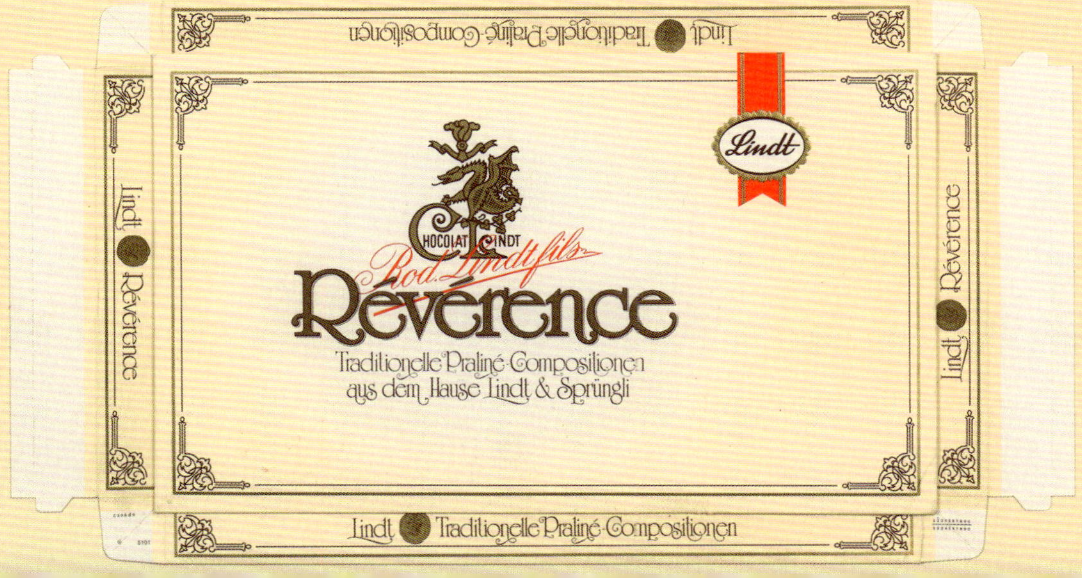

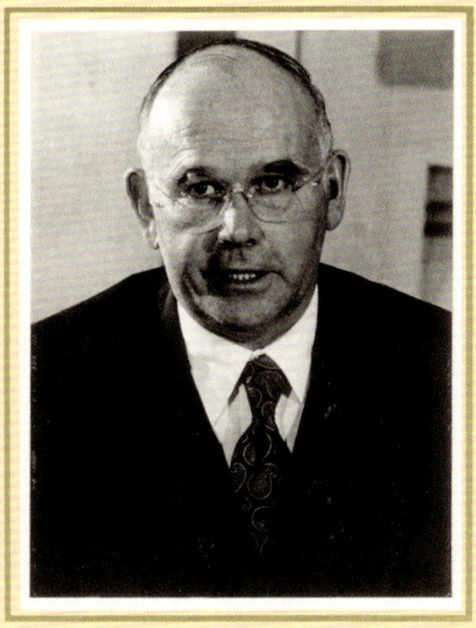

Prof. Dr. Dr. h. c. Peter Ludwig
Aufsichtsratsvorsitzender der
Leonard Monheim AG.

Auch Mäzene haben ihren Preis

Peter Ludwig

Die Satzung der von Peter und Irene Ludwig vorgeschlagenen und zusammen mit dem Bund, dem Land Nordrhein-Westfalen und der Stadt Köln geplanten *Stiftung Ludwig* nennt als Aufgaben der Stiftung:

1. *Pflege, Betreuung und Verwaltung des Kunstbesitzes der Stiftung.*
2. *Erweiterung des Kunstbesitzes und Sicherung wertvollen deutschen Kunstgutes im Sinne von Absatz 1 gegen Abwanderung ins Ausland.*
3. *Wissenschaftliche Erschließung des Kunstbesitzes der Stiftung.*
4. *Konzeption und Durchführung von Kunstausstellungen.*
5. *Förderung von regionalen, überregionalen und internationalen Maßnahmen im Bereich der bildenden Kunst einschließlich verwandter Gebiete.*

Im Stiftungsrat sitzen Peter und Irene Ludwig, zwei von ihnen benannte Personen sowie jeweils vier vom Bund, vom Land und der Stadt Köln benannte Mitglieder. *Der Vorsitzende ist Peter Ludwig.* Der Stiftungsrat faßt seine Beschlüsse mit einfacher Mehrheit, bei Stimmengleichheit entscheidet der Vorsitzende.

Für 10 Jahre steht Peter und Irene Ludwig »ein Einspruchsrecht gegen Beschlüsse des Stiftungsrates zu, soweit diese Fragen der Dispositionen über den vom Ehepaar Ludwig eingebrachten Kunstbesitz betreffen«.

Kritiker der *Stiftung Ludwig* weisen auf die kunstpolitische Macht hin, die dem Privatmann Peter Ludwig durch die tonangebende Position in einer öffentlich finanzierten Stiftung zufallen würde. Der Sammler sagt selber: *»In solchen Gremien muß ja ein Konsensus herbeigeführt werden. Da traue ich mir allerdings zu, daß mein Fach- und Sachverstand ein Gewicht haben.«*

Man befürchtet, daß die numerische Überlegenheit der öffentlichen Vertreter im Stiftungsrat wegen ihrer widersprüchlichen Interessen und der großen Abhängigkeit der Stadt Köln von Peter Ludwig wenig Gewicht habe. Das Vetorecht des Sammlerehepaars und die doppelte Stimme des Vorsitzenden bei Stimmengleichheit bekräftige seine dominierende Stellung.

Seinen Einfluß auf den Kunstmarkt beurteilt der Sammler so: *»Der Markt für Pop Art ist entscheidend durch die Aktivitäten des Ehepaars Ludwig geprägt worden.«*

Die Kombination der Finanzkraft der Stiftung mit seiner eigenen gäbe Peter Ludwig im Ausstellungswesen, bei kunstpolitischen Entscheidungen und auf dem Kunstmarkt eine Machtfülle, mit der er das Kunstgeschehen international noch mehr als bisher entscheidend in seinem Sinne steuern könnte.

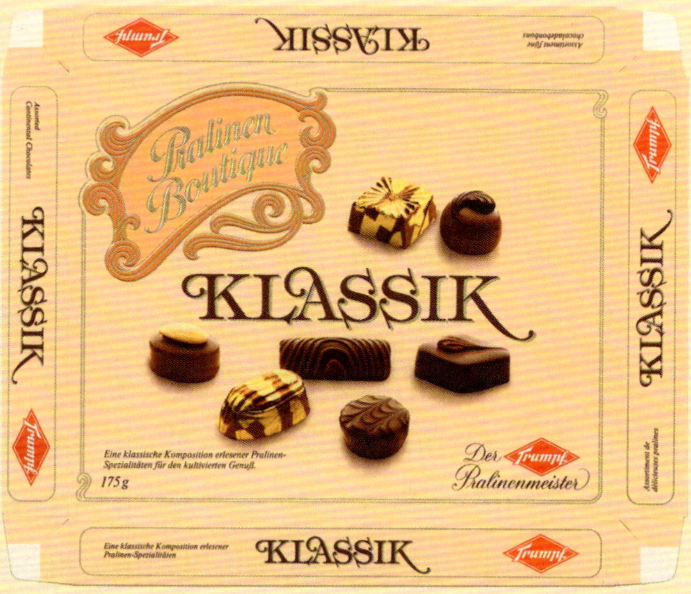

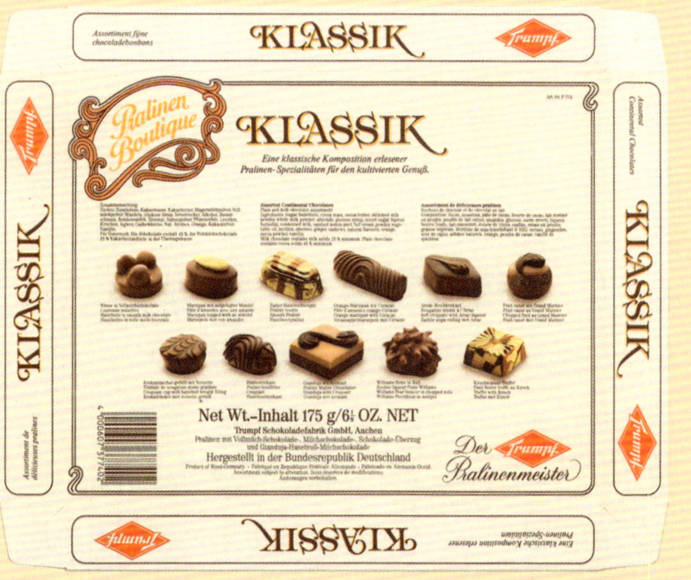

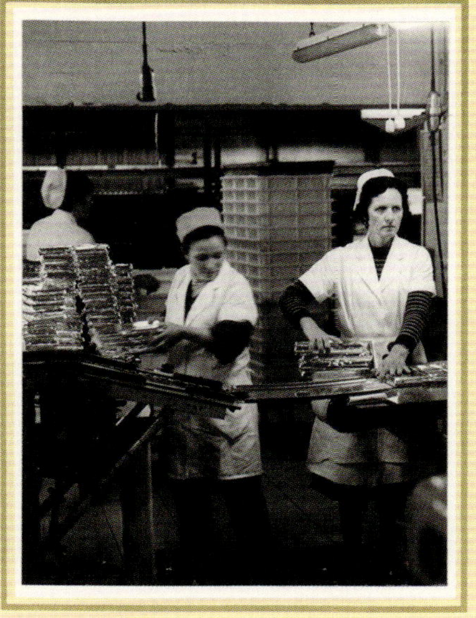

Arbeiterinnen in einem Werk der Leonard Monheim AG.

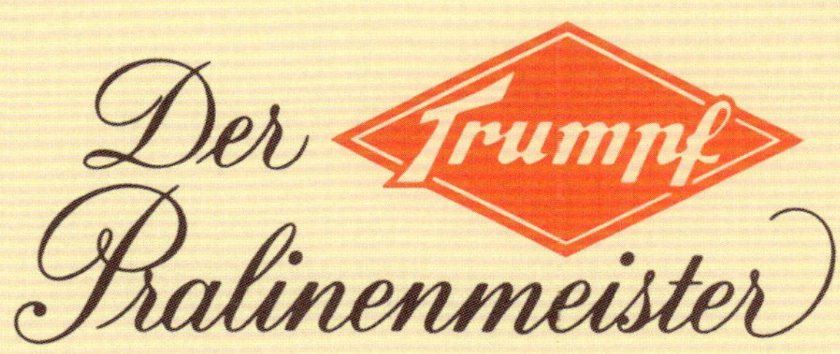

Die Monheim-Gruppe vertreibt unter ihrer Hausmarke *Trumpf* Tafelschokolage, *Schogetten*, Pralinen, Kakao, Saisonartikel und Kaubonbons. Die Fertigung erfolgt durch Tochtergesellschaften in Aachen, Quickborn bei Hamburg, Saarlouis und der seit 1979 unter neuem Namen selbständig operierenden *Trumpf-Schokolade- und Kakaofabrik Berlin GmbH*.

Die in der Vergangenheit völlig zu Monheim gehörende Berliner Gesellschaft ist 1979 zu 51 % an die neugegründete selbständige *Trumpf Berlin GmbH* veräußert worden, die ihrerseits den Kauf durch Ausgabe atypischer stiller Beteiligungen an Private finanzierte. Auf diese Weise sind Monheim 1979 rund DM 100 Millionen zugeflossen, die das Unternehmen *»steuerneutral«* (Ludwig) verwandte.

Dazu boten sich Investitionen an (in Berlin für 1980 DM 25 Millionen geplant) sowie die Anlage in steuerbegünstigten Berlindarlehen (12 % des Darlehens bis zu 50 % der Jahressteuerschuld abzugsfähig). Außerdem wurden Rücklagen gebildet und Abschreibungen auf Rohkakaobestände und -Kontrakte getätigt.

Das Werk in Berlin-Neukölln ist 1953 gegründet und Anfang der 70er Jahre erheblich vergrößert und modernisiert worden. Dabei kamen Monheim die Vergünstigungen der Berlinförderung zugute: die 75%ige Sonderabschreibung von Sachanlagen im 1. Jahr (in der BRD 2—3 %), öffentliche Investitionszuschüsse von 10 % oder mehr der Anlagekosten, beim Warenverkauf in die Bundesrepublik eine Umsatzsteuerpräferenz von 4,5—6,2 % und andere Steuererleichterungen.

In der DDR werden *Trumpf*-Markenartikel aufgrund von Gestattungsverträgen aus dem Jahre 1974 hergestellt. Die Erzeugnisse sind fast ausschließlich in Intershops und Delikatläden erhältlich und werden zum Teil auch exportiert.

Monheim übernimmt und vertreibt die Erzeugnisse der *Trumpf Berlin GmbH* (u. a. *Schogetten*). Außer von Kaufhäusern werden *Trumpf*-Waren in sehr großen Posten von Aldi abgenommen.

Bekannte Namen auf dem Markt sind außer den 1966 eingeführten *Schogetten* unter Pralinen *Edle Tropfen in Nuß, Gute Geister in Nuß, Frische Fruchtschlückchen, Marzipanstars, Wappenklasse, Tradition* und *Klassik*.

Auf dem deutschen Markt hat Monheim mit allen Marken insgesamt bei Tafelschokolade einen Anteil von 18 %, bei Pralinen von 25 % und bei Saisonartikeln ebenfalls 25 %. Der ausgewiesene Kakaogehalt der Produkte bewegt sich zwischen 25 % und 54 %.

Von der Welternte an Kakaobohnen verarbeitet Monheim 5 % (70 000 Tonnen) bei einer Jahresproduktion von 100 000 Tonnen (1980). Im Geschäftsjahr 1978/79 lagerte das Unternehmen Rohstoffe im Werte von DM 246,6 Millionen.

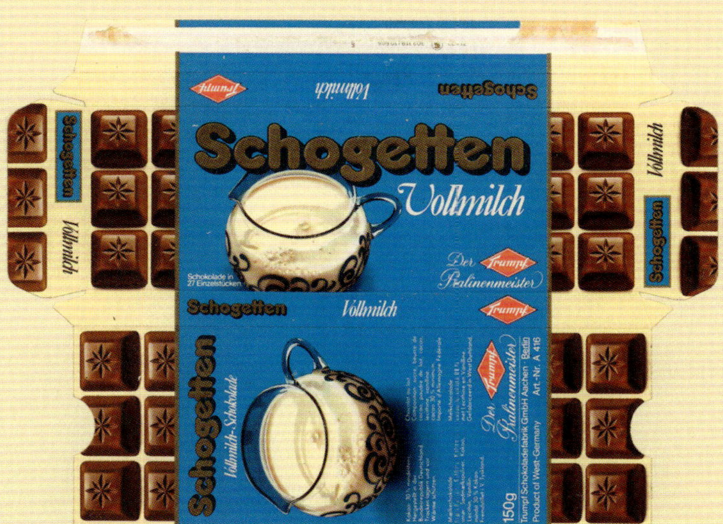

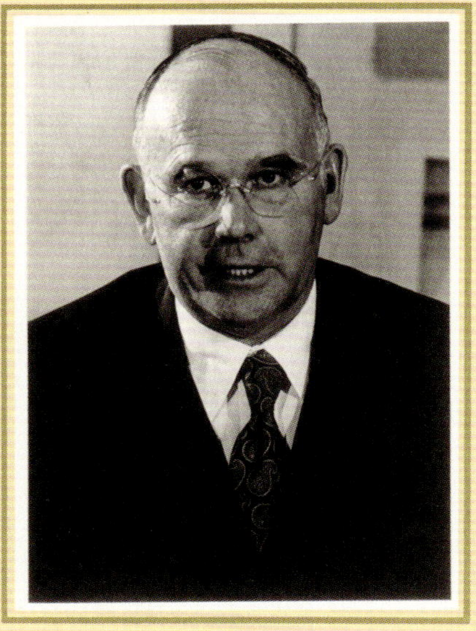

Prof. Dr. Dr. h. c. Peter Ludwig
Aufsichtsratsvorsitzender der
Leonard Monheim AG.

Nichts liegt uns ferner als kulturpolitische Macht

Peter Ludwig

Die Satzung der von Peter und Irene Ludwig vorgeschlagenen und zusammen mit dem Bund, dem Land Nordrhein-Westfalen und der Stadt Köln geplanten *Stiftung Ludwig* sieht eine finanzielle Beteiligung der drei öffentlichen Partner am Stiftungsvermögen vor. Über ihre Höhe gibt sie keine Auskunft.

Der Kölner Kulturdezernent Peter Nestler sagte dazu im März 1981: *»Nach dem augenblicklichen Stand wird die Stiftung jährlich ein Finanzvolumen von 14 Millionen haben.«* Dagegen nannte ein Vertreter der Landesregierung als *»Denkzahl«* einen Betrag von 2,7 Millionen, der von jedem der öffentlichen Stiftungspartner im ersten Jahr entrichtet werden solle.

Das Land Nordrhein-Westfalen hat 1981 seine traditionellen Zuschüsse von DM 3 Millionen an die kommunalen Ausstellungsinstitute um ein Drittel gekürzt. Infolgedessen können Ausstellungen nicht mehr wie geplant durchgeführt werden, und Kataloge können nicht erscheinen. Auch der Ankaufsetat der Landesgalerie Düsseldorf von DM 3 Millionen wurde trotz steigender Kunstpreise um eine Million beschnitten.

Die Leiter der betroffenen Institute hegen den Verdacht, die einschneidenden Kürzungen seien auf die 1982 zu erwartenden Zahlungen an die *Stiftung Ludwig* zurückzuführen. 15 kommunale Museumsdirektoren (Köln und Aachen ausgenommen) wandten sich deshalb in einem Protestschreiben *»mit großer Entschiedenheit ... gegen eine von Bund und Land subventionierte Macht- und Finanzkonzentration«* in Köln. Sie fürchten, *»die auf lokalen Initiativen gründende Vielgestaltigkeit der Museumslandschaft«* würde *»durch die Stiftung Ludwig schwerstens bedroht«*.

Die Beteiligung des Bundes erregt verfassungsmäßige Bedenken. Demnach beeinträchtige sie die Kulturhoheit der Länder und gäbe dem Bund ein kulturpolitisches Instrument, das ihm die Verfassung nicht zubilligt. Bayern denkt an eine Verfassungsklage.

Dagegen schlug Baden-Württemberg die Gründung einer verfassungsmäßig unbedenklichen *»Kulturstiftung der deutschen Bundesländer«* vor. Diese *»Einkaufsgenossenschaft der Bundesländer«* solle die Abwanderung wertvoller Werke der deutschen Kunst- und Kulturgeschichte in Fällen verhindern, in denen ein Ankauf die finanziellen Kräfte eines einzelnen Museums übersteigt.

Die Abwanderung von Werken ins Ausland zu verhüten, ist aber auch eine der wesentlichen Aufgaben, denen die *Stiftung Ludwig* dienen soll. Es ist ebenfalls eines der Ziele der bisher nicht funktionsfähigen Nationalstiftung.

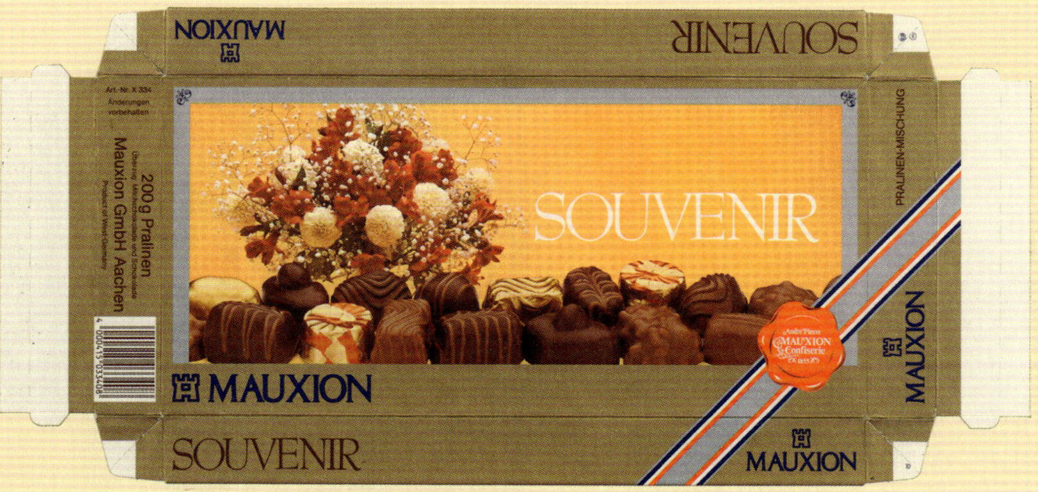

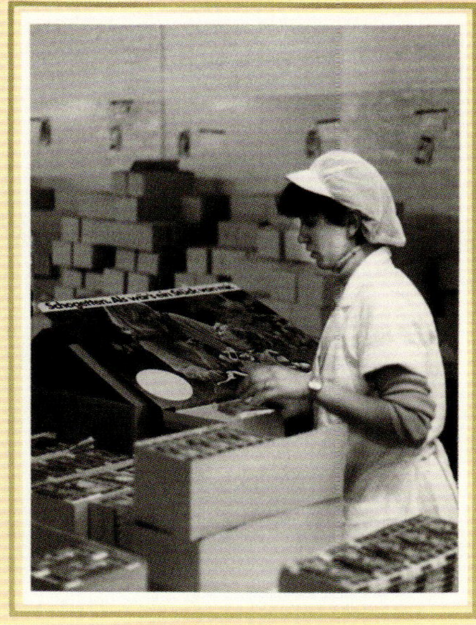

Arbeiterin in einem Werk
der Leonard Monheim AG.

MAUXION

Die Monheim-Gruppe übernahm 1959 die *Schokoladenfabrik Mauxion KG* und stellt seither unter der Marke *Mauxion* Pralinen und Saisonartikel her. Nach dem 2. Weltkrieg entwickelte sich das Unternehmen folgendermaßen:

1951 Einrichtung eines Zweigwerkes in Quickborn bei Hamburg.

1952 Peter Ludwig geschäftsführender Gesellschafter. Eröffnung eines Werkes in Berlin-Neukölln (1979 Umwandlung in selbständige *Trumpf Berlin GmbH* mit 49 % Monheim Anteil).

1959 Erwerb einer Schokoladenfabrik in St. Hyacinthe bei Montreal (operiert seit 1974 unter dem Namen *Comet Confectionary Ltd.*).

1960 Angliederung der *A. Poser Schokoladenfabrik GmbH* in Saarlouis.

1969 Peter Ludwig Vorsitzender der Geschäftsleitung.

1971 Alleinproduktions- und Markenrechte für *van Houten*-Produkte. Übernahme der weltweiten *van Houten*-Vertriebsorganisation.

1974 Lizenzproduktion in der DDR und Polen.

1979 Übernahme aller Anteile der belgischen *General Chocolate NV/SA* mit Werken in Herentals (Belgien) und Neuß.

1980 Beteiligung an der neuerrichteten Kakao-Handelsgesellschaft *Eurobras BV.*, Amsterdam. Kooperationsverhandlungen mit dem österreichischen *Konsum* und dem Lebensmittelkonzern *Julius Meindl AG*, Wien. Erschließung des österreichischen Marktes geplant, möglicherweise gemeinsamer Export in Ostblockländer.

Die Obergesellschaft *Leonard Monheim KG*, Aachen, wurde 1978 in eine Aktiengesellschaft umgewandelt.

Die ehemaligen Komplementäre Prof. Peter Ludwig, Dieter Monheim und Dr. Bernd Monheim aus der 3. Monheim–Generation halten *»deutlich mehr als 50 %«* des Grundkapitals von DM 41,5 Millionen. Die Aktien lauten auf den Namen und können nur mit Zustimmung der Gesellschaft übertragen werden. Sie verbleiben völlig in Familienbesitz.

Aufsichtsratsvorsitzender der *Leonard Monheim AG* ist Prof. Peter Ludwig.

Die Monheim-Gruppe umfaßt 24 inländische und 16 ausländische Beteiligungsgesellschaften. Im Geschäftsjahr 1979/80 betrug der Umsatz weltweit DM 1,358 Milliarden (rund 34 % außerhalb der Bundesrepublik).

Die inländischen Gewinne wurden mit insgesamt DM 19,4 Millionen besteuert. Wenn keine Nachzahlungen zu leisten waren, kann die Gewinnhöhe auf rund DM 34 Millionen geschätzt werden.

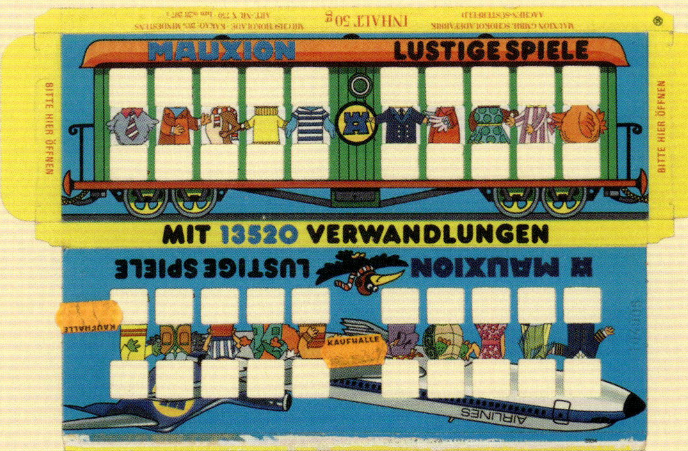

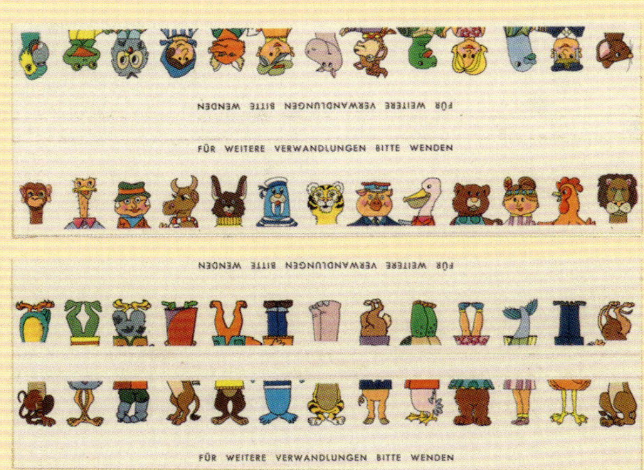

Oil Painting: Homage to Marcel Broodthaers, 1982

A week before the opening of documenta 7, in June 1982, President Reagan attended a NATO summit conference in Bonn, Germany, and delivered a speech to the Bundestag, the Parliament of the Federal Republic of Germany, to gain support for the stationing of cruise and Pershing II missiles in West Germany. His visit was met with a huge demonstration against nuclear arms, the largest demonstration in Germany since World War II. Hans Haacke took the photograph of that rally.

Two days after the rally in Bonn, a record-breaking anti-nuclear march, attended by over 500,000 people, wound through the streets of New York to Central Park. As a result of a lessening of tensions between the Soviet Union and the United States, a treaty was signed in 1987 eliminating all intermediate-range nuclear missiles that the two powers had stationed on European soil.

Hans Haacke, 2006

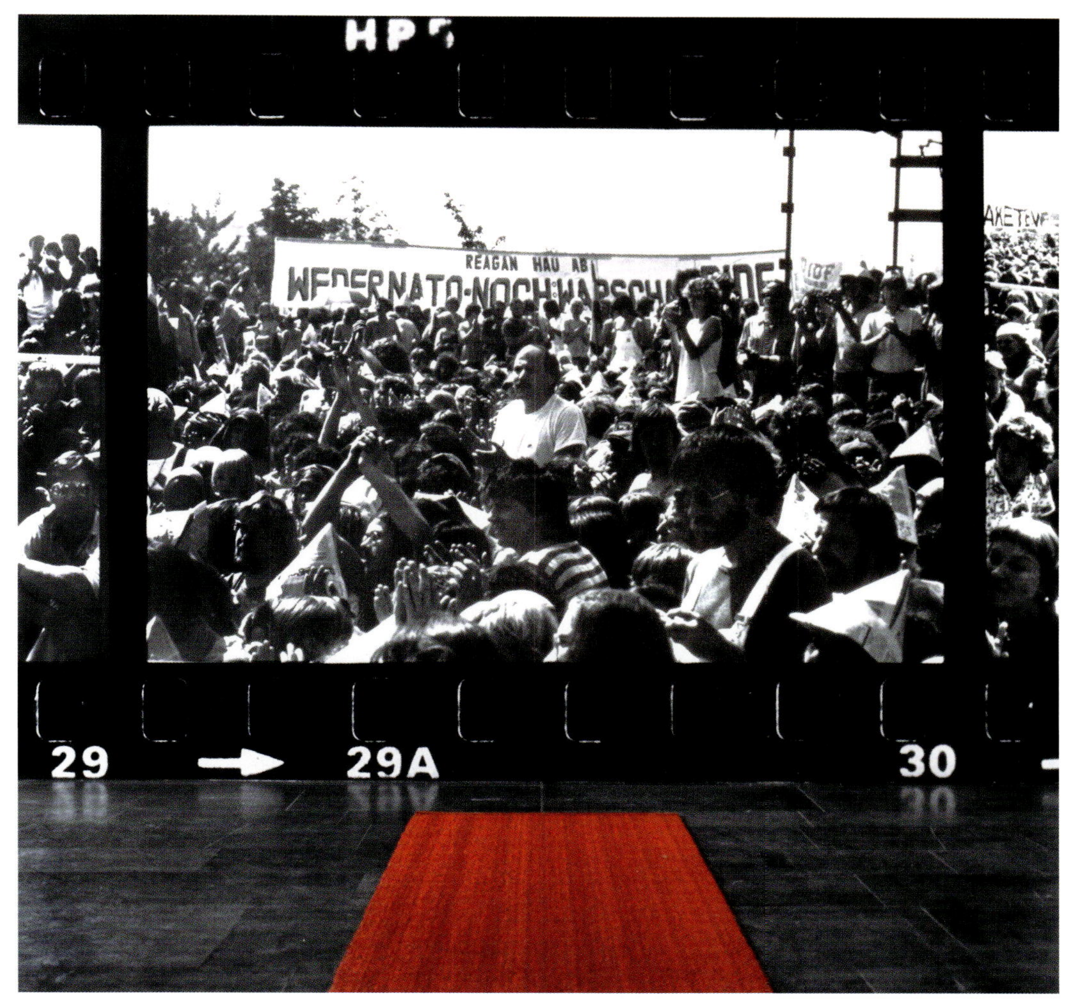

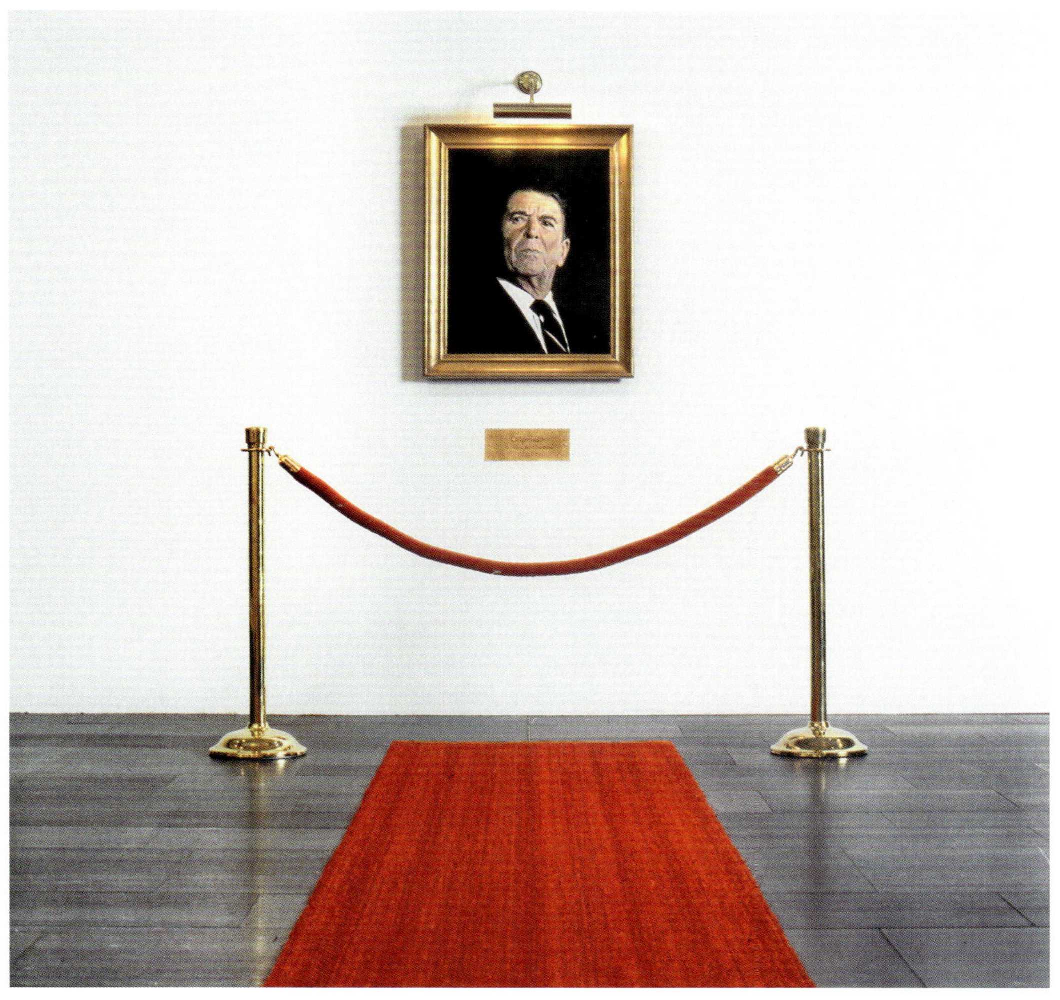

Oil Painting: Homage to Marcel Broodthaers, 1982
Also pp. 166–67 (detail)

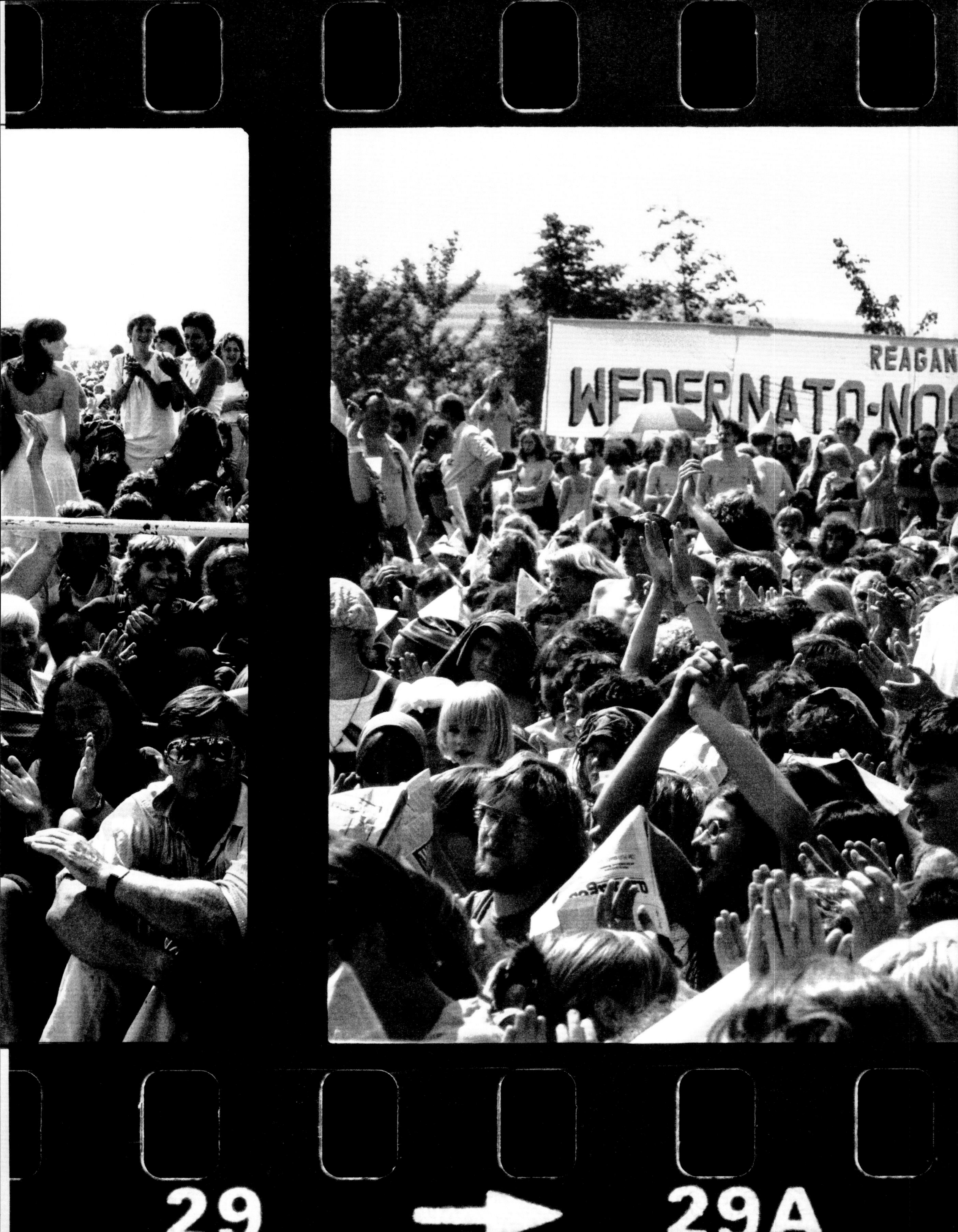

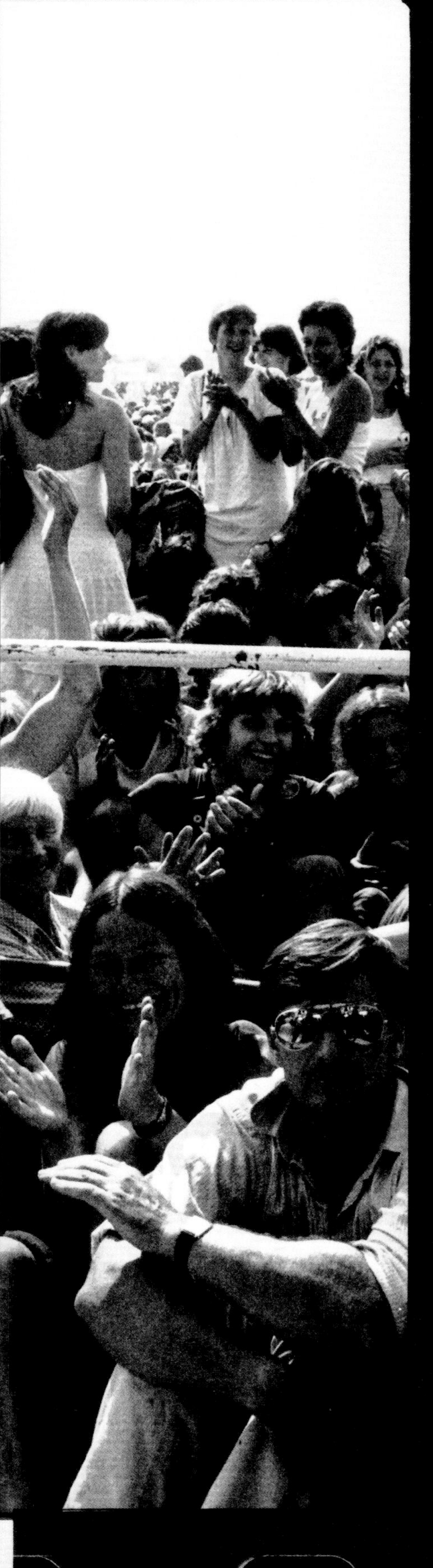
REAGAN
WEDERNATO-NO
29
29A

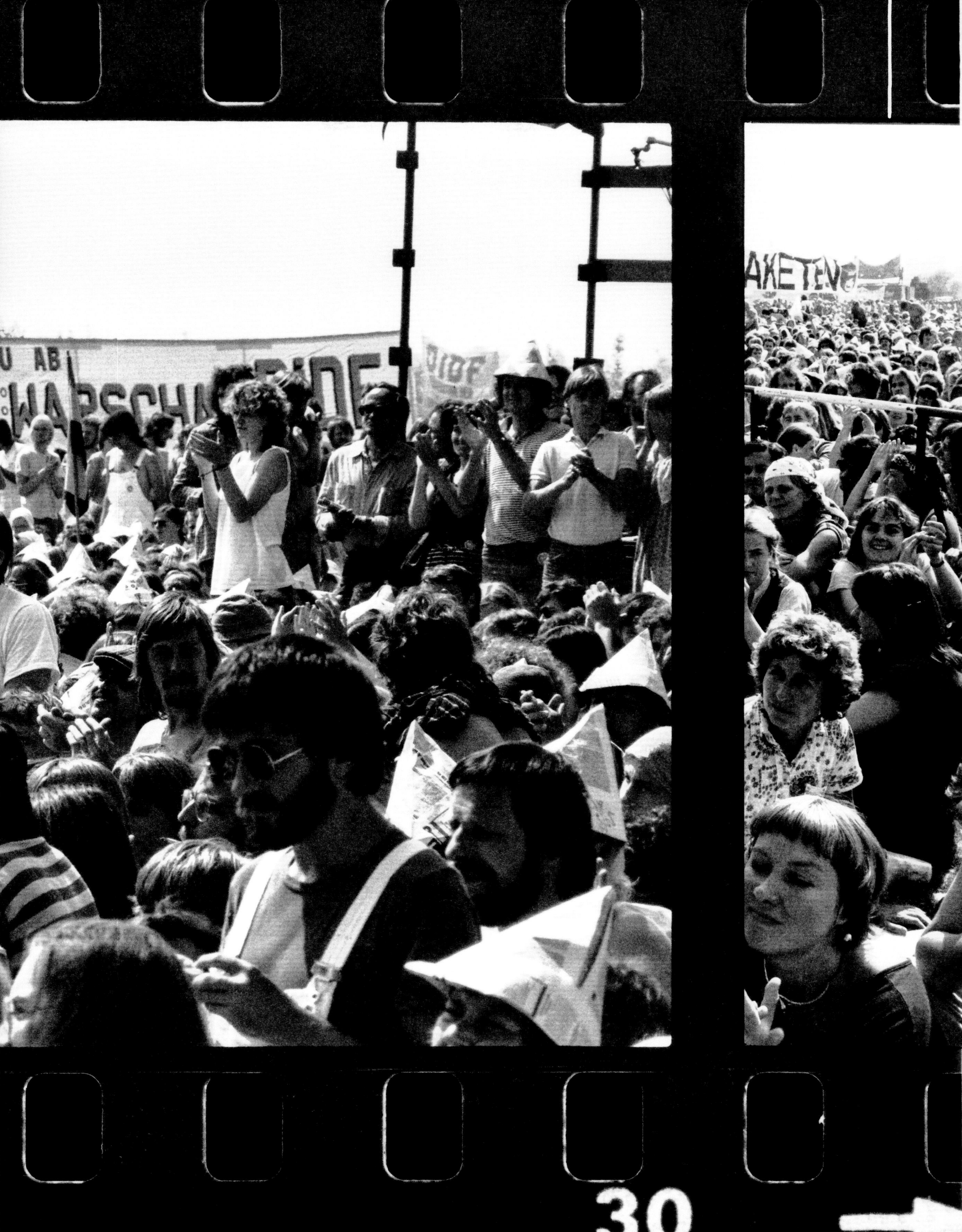
U AB
WARSCHA
AKETEN
30

Taking Stock (unfinished), 1983–84

The sculpture of *Pandora* (1890) in the Tate Gallery collection is by Harry Bates. »MS« and »CS« on the broken plates are the initials of the brothers Maurice and Charles Saatchi. In 1982, when Charles Saatchi was an influential member of the Patrons of New Art of the Tate Gallery, the Tate gave Julian Schnabel a solo exhibition; nine of the eleven paintings displayed belonged to Saatchi. Charles Saatchi was also on the board of London's Whitechapel Gallery. After *Taking Stock (unfinished)* was exhibited at the Tate, he resigned from the Patrons of New Art and the Whitechapel Gallery board.

Saatchi had begun collecting art in the early 1970s. From Photo-Realism and pattern painting, his interests shifted to Minimalism, Neo-Expressionism, and Neo-Geo works. During the 1990s, he focused on Young British Art (YBA), and he began to champion painting the following decade. Throughout these years, he sold works from his collection and was a partner in art investment companies, some of them registered in tax havens. *Sensation* (1997), an exhibition of YBA works from his collection at the Royal Academy of Arts in London and the Brooklyn Museum, was sponsored by Christie's, the auction house through which he usually sells works from his holdings.

Charles Saatchi's art purchases were initially financed through Saatchi & Saatchi Company, the advertising agency he and his brother started in 1970 and built into the largest holding company of ad agencies in the world. By 1994, shareholders had ousted both brothers from their positions on the board of the company. Two years later, they opened M&C Saatchi in London. Saatchi & Saatchi ran Margaret Thatcher's election campaigns in 1979, 1983, and 1987. They were awarded the British Airways account as well as accounts of other state-owned entities. Maurice Saatchi credited the Tories: »We owe them everything.«

He became a life peer in 1996. In 2003, Michael Howard appointed him co-chairman of the Conservative Party. During Howard's candidacy for the Tory leadership, he held a news conference at the museum that Charles Saatchi had opened in 2003 at County Hall, on the banks of the Thames. The museum closed that location after three years amid controversy. Lord Saatchi resigned from the party chairmanship in 2005. He caused an uproar when he submitted a bill of £1.5 million for M&C Saatchi's work on the Tory election campaign of that year.

Hans Haacke, 2006

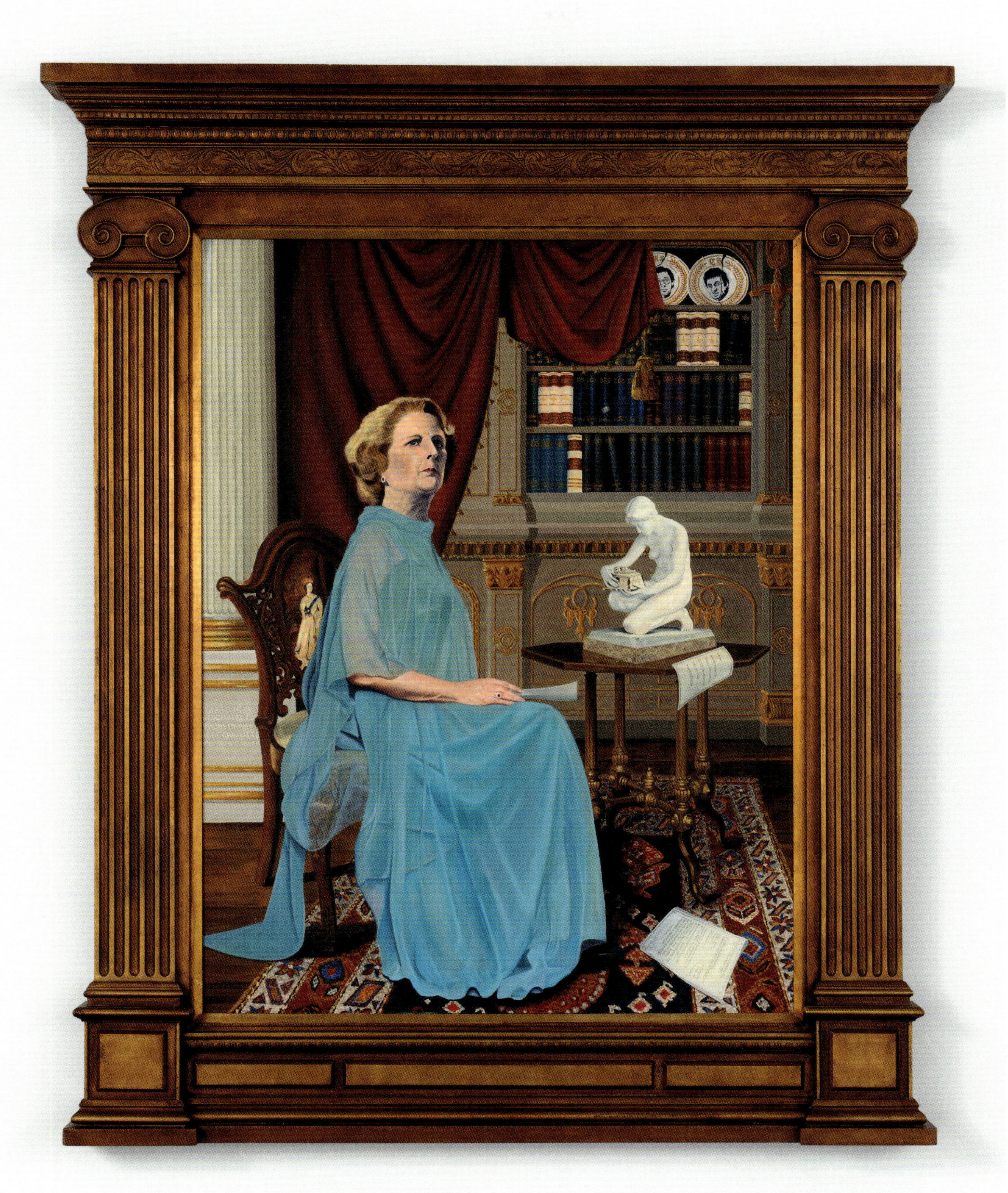

Taking Stock (unfinished), 1983–84

Buhrlesque, 1985

Until 1999, Oerlikon-Bührle was the largest arms manufacturer in Switzerland. A diversified holding, it also produced machine tools, aircraft, automotive parts, welding equipment, and textiles, as well as shoes and accessories, and was active in real estate and hotel operations. Dr. Dietrich Bührle, for decades the chairman and CEO of the company, was said to be the richest man in Switzerland. Until they took it public in 1973, he and his sister were the company's sole owners.

They retained a majority of the shares. In the 1930s, Dietrich Bührle's father built the company, a family business, into a major weapons manufacturer. During World War II, Oerlikon supplied cannons and ammunition to the Axis powers Germany, Italy, and Romania, worth 543.4 million Swiss francs. In 1970, Dietrich Bührle received an eight-month suspended sentence for illegal arms sales to numerous countries. In spite of a UN arms embargo against South Africa, Oerlikon continued to deliver and grant licenses for the production of military equipment to the apartheid regime: guns and ammunition for ground combat, weaponry for helicopters and naval vessels, anti-aircraft guns, and military aircraft. Bührle was awarded the highest decoration of South Africa in 1978. Swiss authorities maintained friendly contacts with the apartheid regime. In 1984, a delegation of the South African army, in full battle gear, marched in a popular two-day march organized annually by the Swiss Non-commissioned Officers Association. *PARATUS*, the periodical of the South African Defence Force, celebrated this event as a successful goodwill operation.

In 1977, Oerlikon-Bührle took over Bally, a Swiss manufacturer of shoes and accessories with a world reputation for elegance. It sold its Bally shares, in 1999, to Texas Pacific Group in the United States and its military production facilities to Rheinmetall in Germany. Dietrich Bührle, like his father, Emil Bührle, who had studied art history and was an art collector, collects art and is a prominent donor to the Zurich Kunsthaus. In 1990, the National Gallery in Washington, DC, exhibited the Bührle collection under the title *The Passionate Eye*.

Hans Haacke

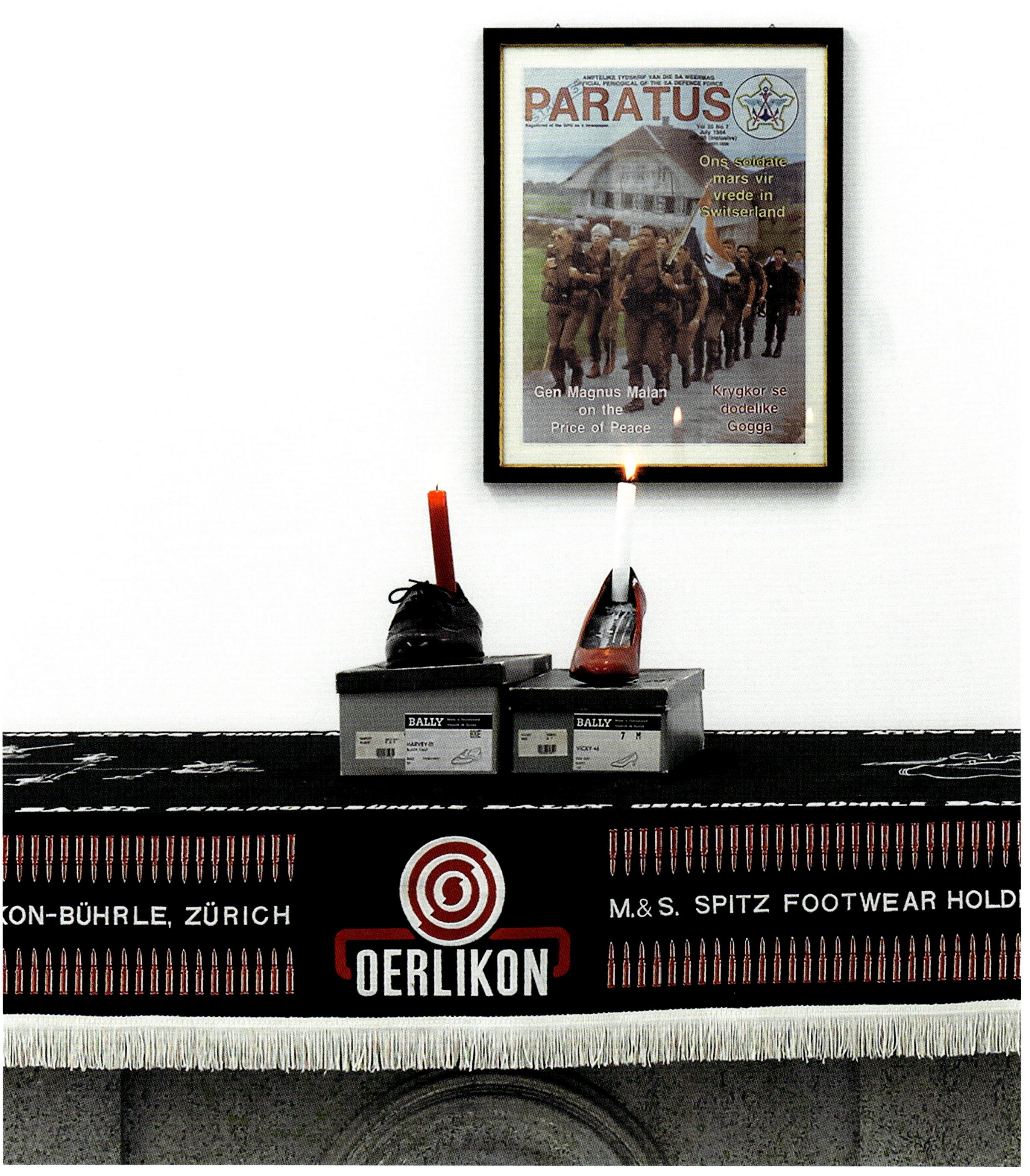

Buhrlesque, 1985 (detail)

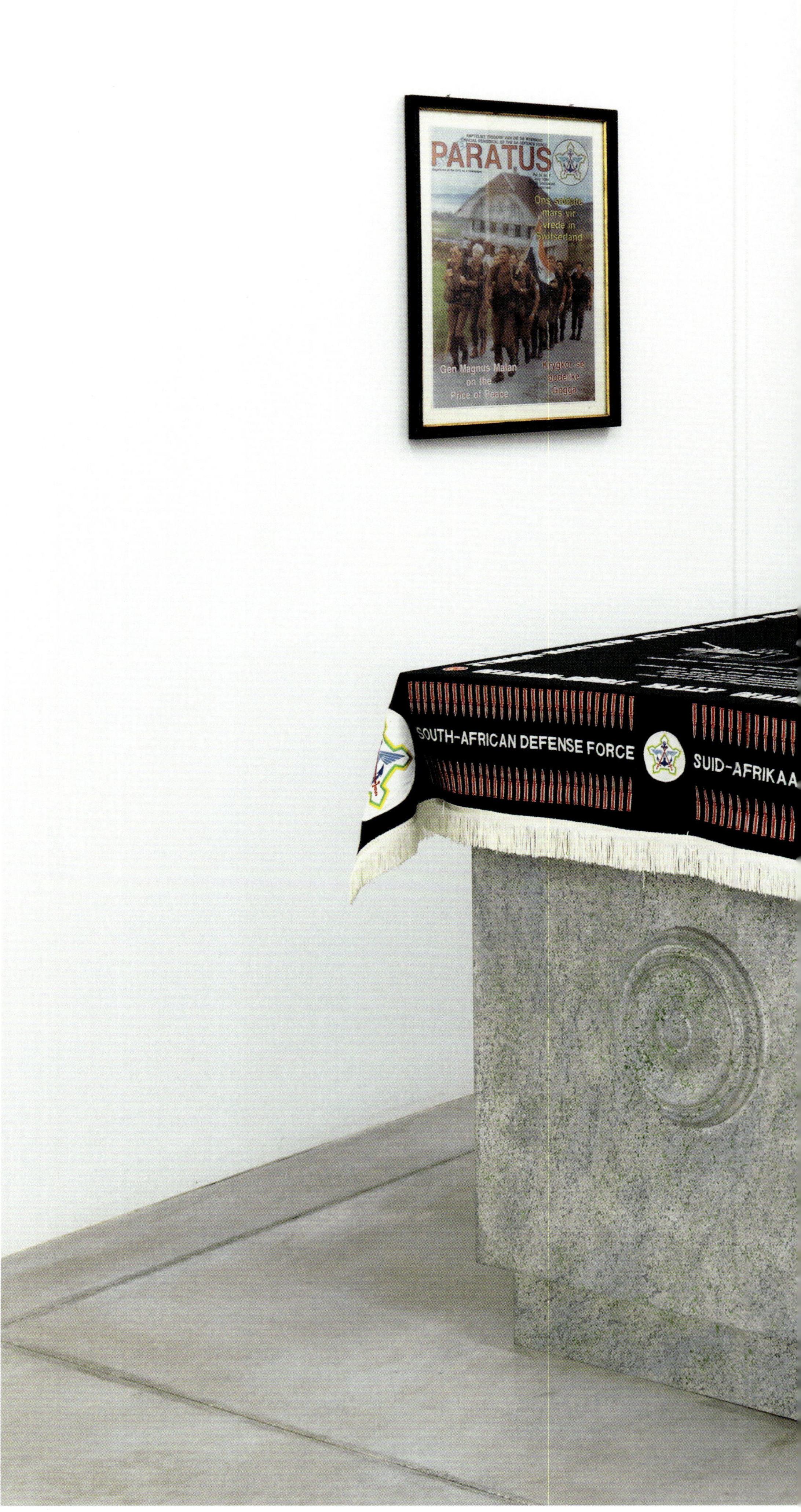
PARATUS
Ons soldate mars vir vrede in Switserland
Gen Magnus Malan on the Price of Peace
Krygkor se dodelike Gogga
SOUTH-AFRICAN DEFENSE FORCE

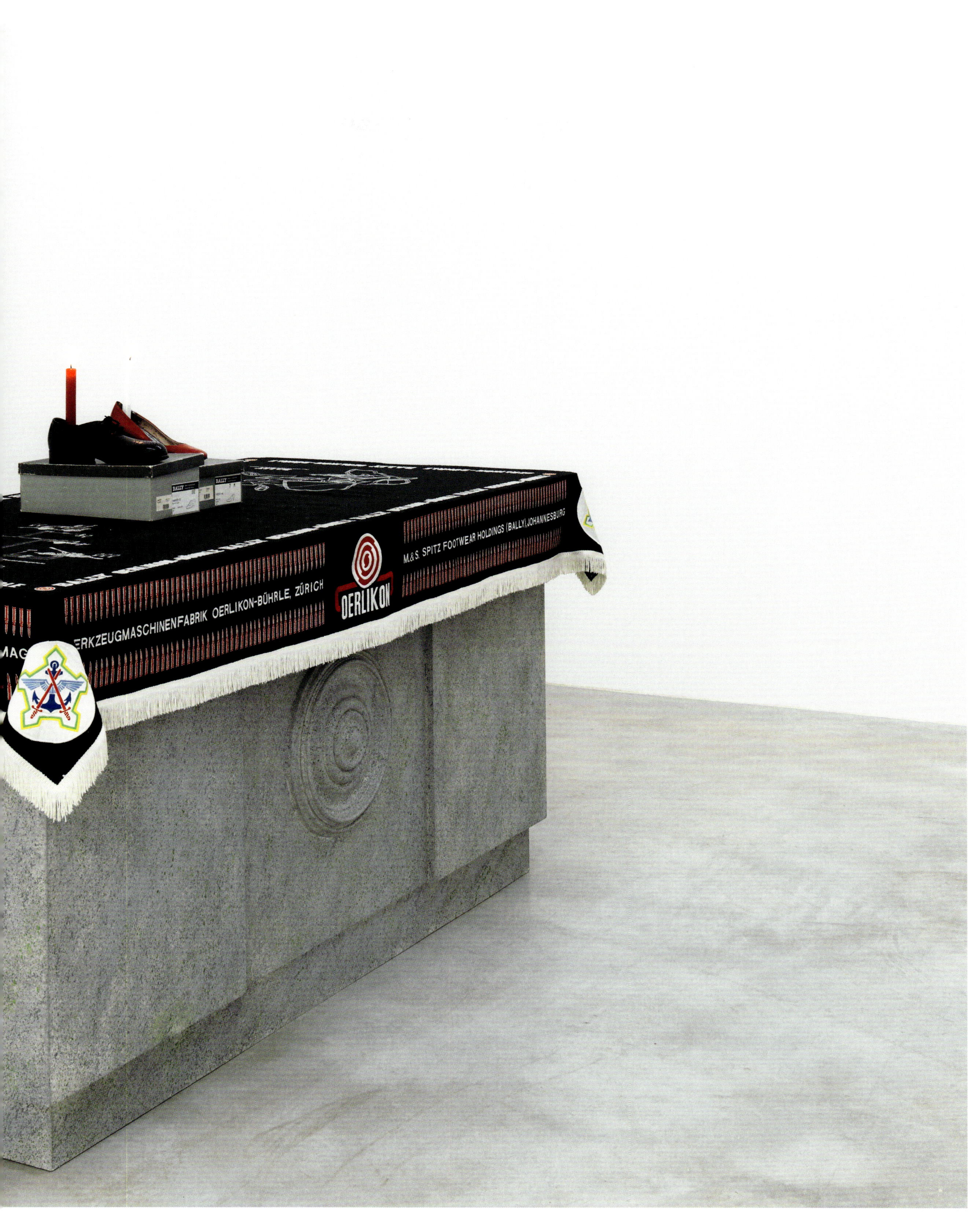

Buhrlesque, 1985

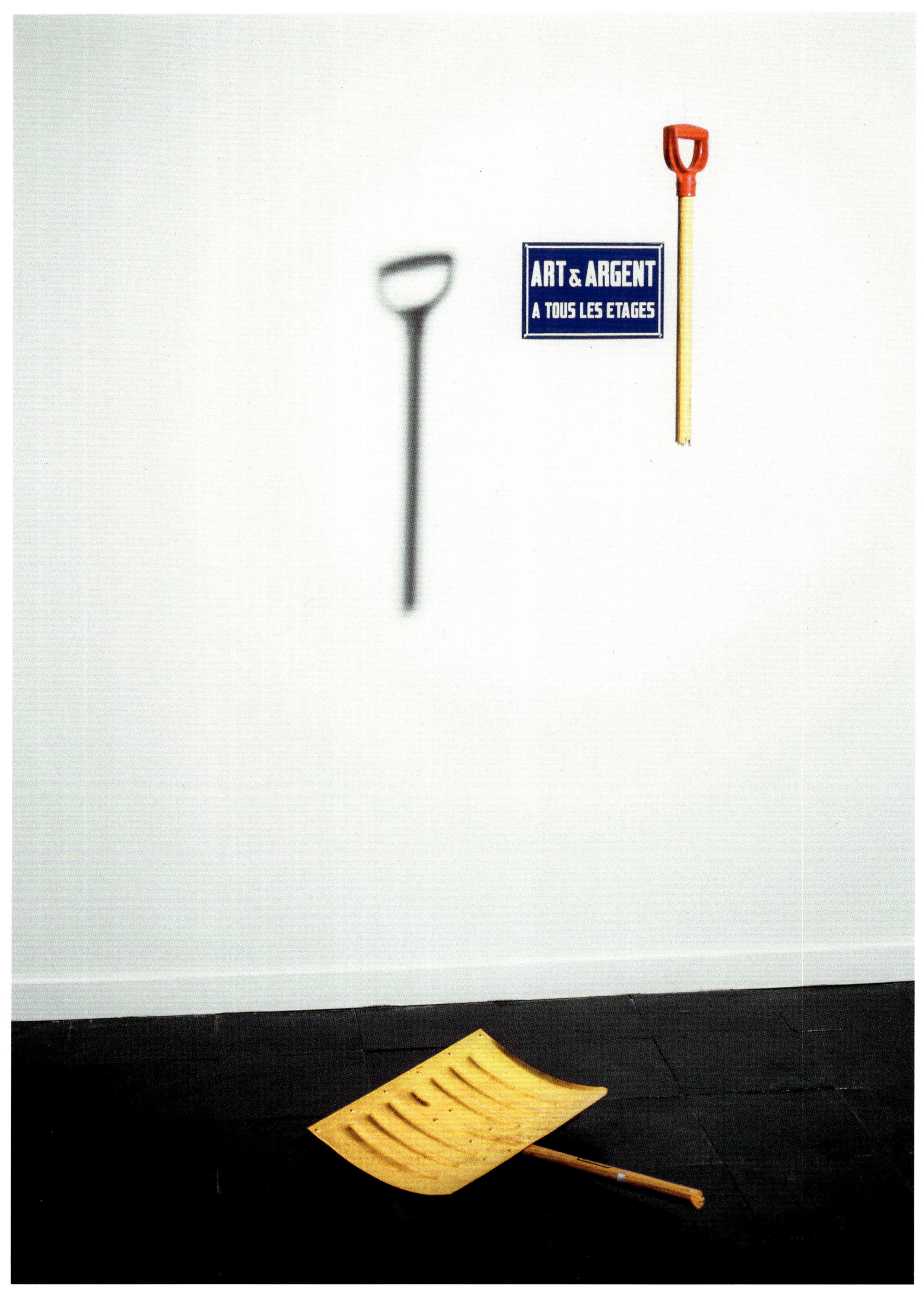

Broken R.M. …, 1986

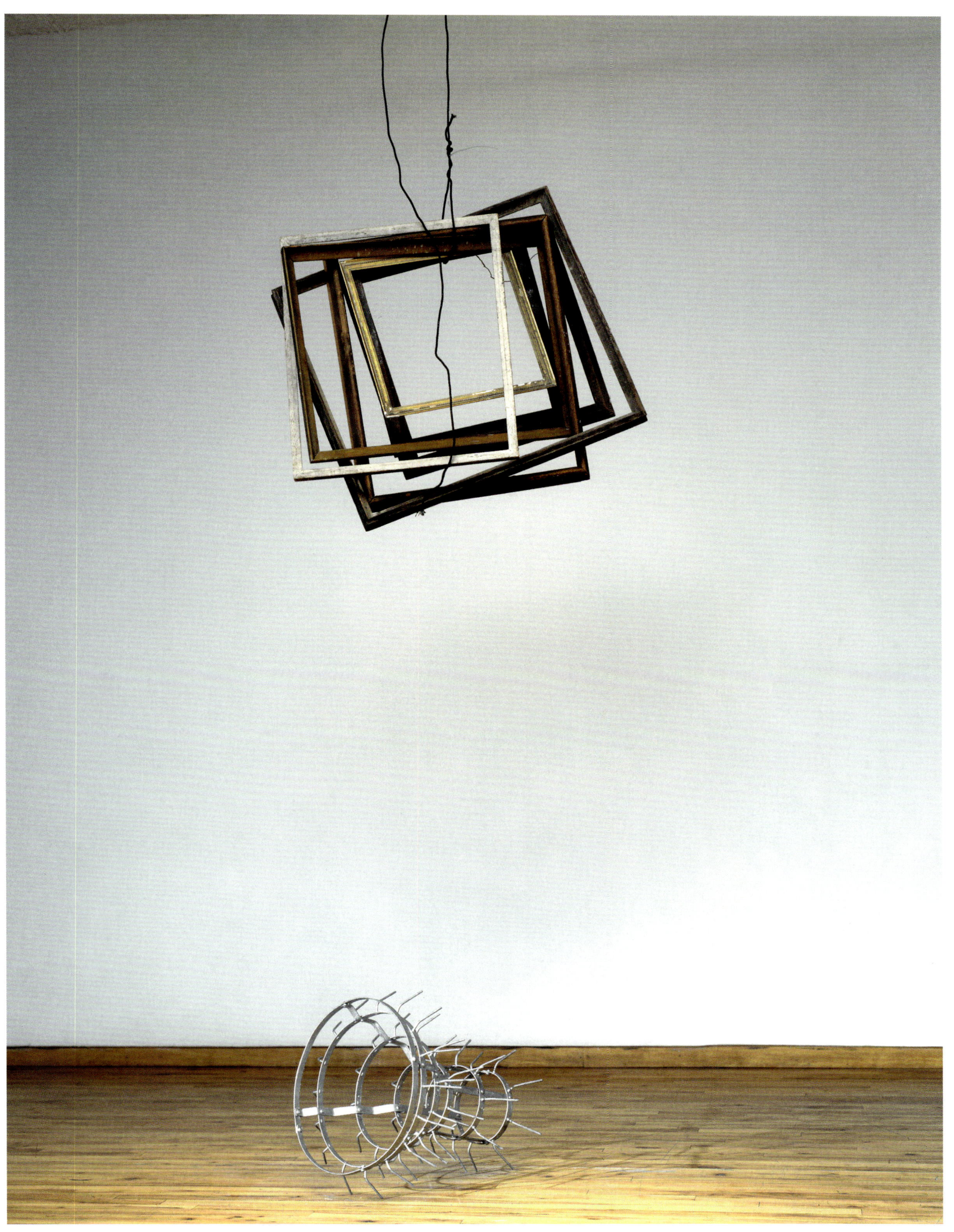

Nothing to Declare, 1992

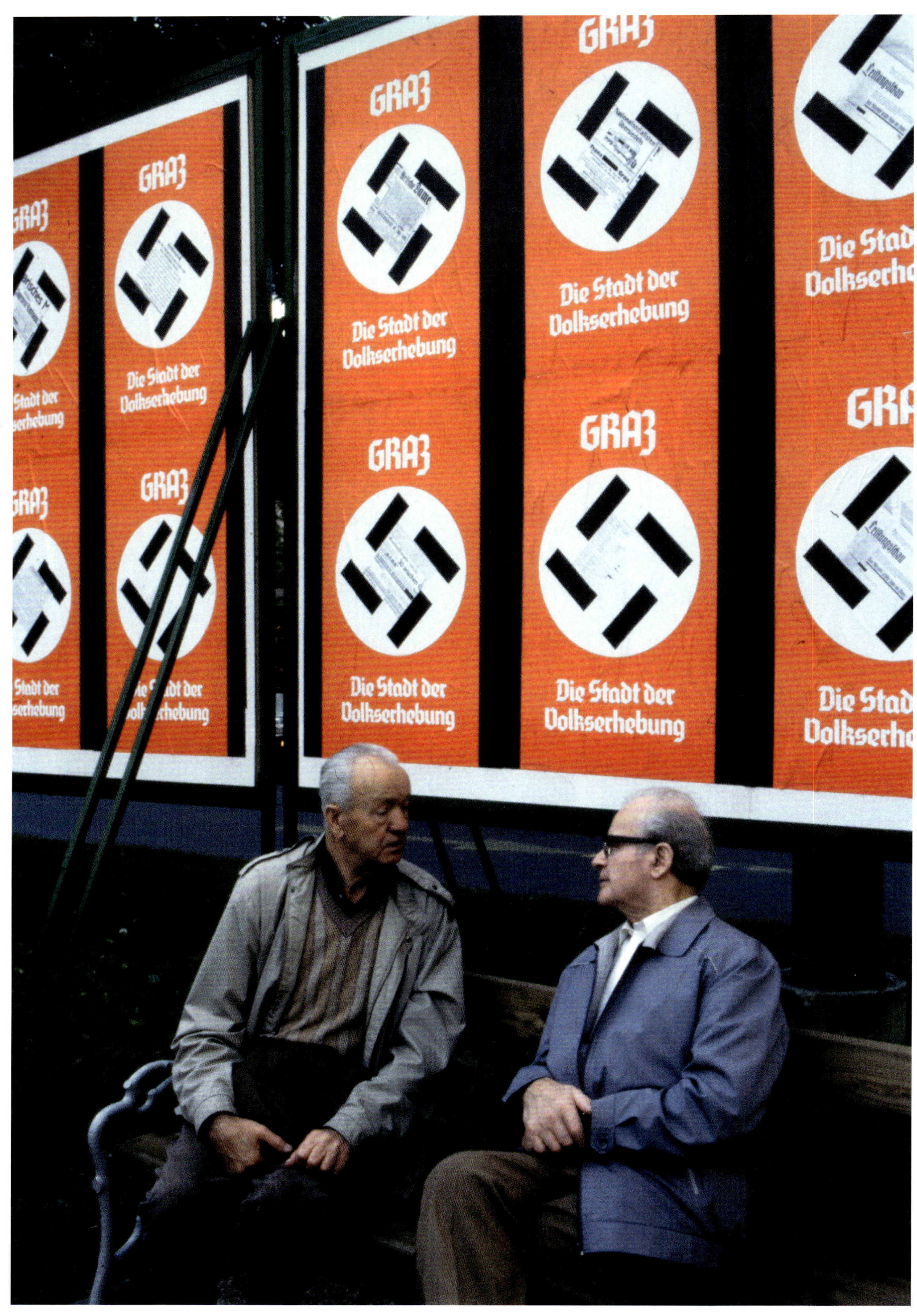

Fig. 1: Hans Haacke, *Und Ihr habt doch gesiegt (And You Were Victorious After All)*, 1988, in the framework of *Points of Reference 38/88*, steirischer herbst, Graz 1988, archive steirischer herbst

The Presence of the Past: Hans Haacke's »Acts of Counter-Memory« in Post-Nazism

Luisa Ziaja

Haacke's reconstructions of cultural memory are neither nostalgic nor conciliatory; rather, they alert us to current facts.
— Benjamin H. D. Buchloh[1]

In 1969, as part of *Prospect 69*,[2] Hans Haacke installed a telex machine in the Städtische Kunsthalle Düsseldorf that printed out all the news communicated by the German Press Agency (dpa) each day, thus transferring it into the exhibition space (fig. 2). The next day, the rolls of paper were hung on the wall for further reading, and on the day after they were dated and stored in plexiglass containers. Haacke tersely titled his work *Nachrichten*. Two months later, he showed the installation under the English title *News* at the Howard Wise Gallery in New York, where he sourced his newsfeed from the agency UPI – United Press International. As part of Jack Burnham's influential show *Software* at the Jewish Museum in New York the following year, Haacke then used five teleprinters to simultaneously broadcast news from American, Italian, and German agencies, with the printouts forming ever-growing piles of paper that were not archived (fig. p. 10). With *News*, Hans Haacke made social realities, political events, economic developments, and everything else reported as news the subject of his work for the first time. The artist defined the origin of the information according to the respective place and time of the presentation. Generally speaking, the specific initial conditions of each exhibition—its place and time—became decisive factors in the development of his work from then on.

The late 1960s in the United States and Europe were marked by sociopolitical upheaval and revolts related to civil rights movements against racial discrimination, student protests against reactionary right-wing concepts of teaching and living, and demonstrations against the Vietnam War. As early as 1963, Haacke had been deeply impressed by the rally of the civil rights activist Martin Luther King Jr. in Washington, DC; after King's assassination in April 1968, the artist felt a growing urgency for his work to have a more resolute relationship to society:

1
Benjamin H. D. Buchloh, »Hans Haacke: Memory and Instrumental Reason,« *Art in America* 76 (February 1988), pp. 96–109 and 157–59, esp. p. 98.

2
Prospect 69, Kunsthalle Düsseldorf, September 18 to October 12, 1969. Initiated by the art critic Hans Strelow and the gallerist Konrad Fischer, exhibitions in the *Prospect* series took place five times from 1968 to 1976.

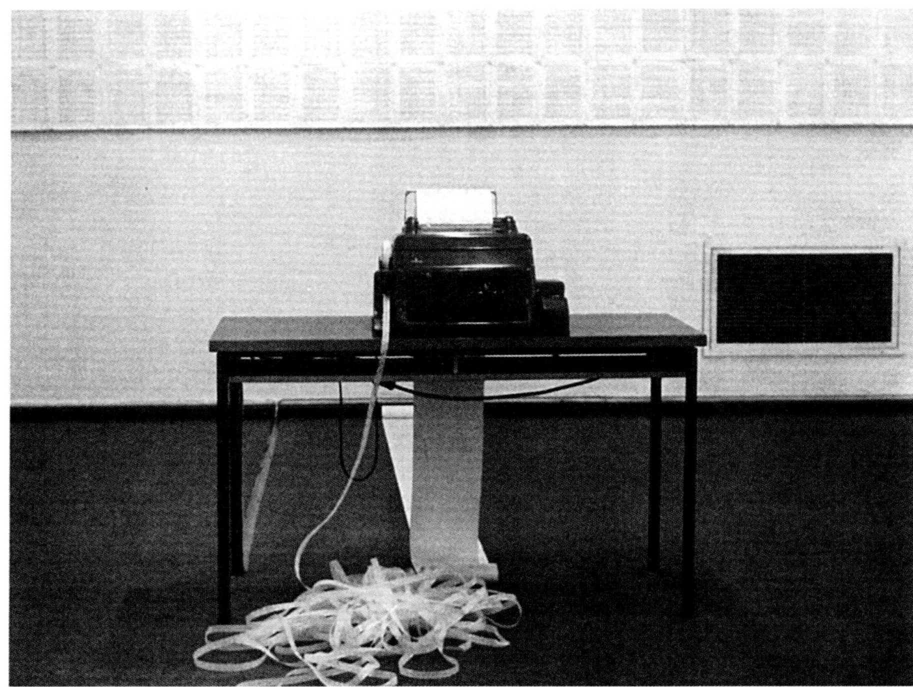

Fig. 2: Hans Haacke, *News*, 1969, in the exhibition *Prospect 69*, Kunsthalle Düsseldorf, September–October 1969, courtesy the artist and Paula Cooper Gallery, New York

»I realized that my work did not address the fraught social and political world in which we lived. It was an incident that made me understand that, in addition to what I had called physical and biological systems, there are also social systems and that art is an integral part of the universe of social systems.«[3]

This pivotal expansion of his idea of art happened against the backdrop of a general politicization of the art field and, more specifically, Haacke's involvement in the anti-war movement and as a co-initiator of the Art Workers' Coalition, which formed in 1969. As an association of various protagonists in the art world, the Art Workers' Coalition called for a comprehensive democratization of museums through reforms related to the right of artists to have a say; the presence of marginalized, female, and non-white positions; fair economic conditions; programmatic political participation; and the inclusion of the public. During the few years of its activity, the group became an essential platform for the intersections of art and activism in New York.[4]

Hans Haacke also attributes his fundamentally power-critical attitude to his upbringing in Germany on the heels of National Socialism. Born in 1936, he experienced the Nazi era and World War II in a family that was critical of the regime and did not stay silent after 1945. His awareness of recent German history and the crimes of the National Socialists was to have a lasting impact on Haacke's view of the world and his present:

»At some point, my parents told me the truth. It wasn't until the 1950s that I understood the whole disaster. I became aware of this dark chapter in German and European history under Hitler, and I started looking at the world through this lens.«[5]

3
Quoted from »Hans Haacke in Conversation with Gary Carrion-Murayari and Massimiliano Gioni,« in *Hans Haacke: All Connected*, ed. Gary Carrion-Murayari and Massimiliano Gioni, exh. cat. New Museum, New York (London: Phaidon, 2019), pp. 218–32, esp. p. 222.

4
See Lucy Lippard, »The Art Workers' Coalition: Not a History,« *Studio International* 180, no. 927 (November 1970), pp. 171–74. For a profound analysis of Haacke's role and its impact on his work, see Julia Bryan-Wilson, »Hans Haacke's Paperwork,« in *Art Workers: Radical Practice in the Vietnam War Era* (Berkeley, Los Angeles, and London: University of California Press, 2009), pp. 173–213.

5
Quoted from »Hans Haacke: Der Nonkonformist; Ein Gespräch von Heinz-Norbert Jocks,« *Kunstforum International* 266, *Die Kunst des Gehens* (March–April 2020), pp. 202–21, esp. p. 212.

6
See Margaret Ann Ewing's dissertation »A Politics of Action: Hans Haacke in Germany, 1972–2006« (University of Illinois at Urbana-Champaign, 2015).

7
Buchloh, »Hans Haacke: Memory and Instrumental Reason,« pp. 98 and 101–02.

8
For a comprehensive overview of Germany's politics of memory after 1945, see Torben Fischer and Matthias N. Lorenz, eds., *Lexikon der »Vergangenheits-bewältigung« in Deutschland: Debatten- und Diskursgeschichte des Nationalsozialismus nach 1945* (Bielefeld: Transcript, 2015), esp. Chapter II.C »Ungebrochene Karrieren,« pp. 98–100.

One constant running through the artist's entire oeuvre is his engagement with this history, with continuities after 1945 and with repercussions up to the current political reality.[6] Particularly in the context of a retrospective presented in Germany and Austria, it seems appropriate to retrace Hans Haacke's strategies of a critical »counter-memory,« to anchor them in a time- and site-specific context, and to update them in perspective.

As Benjamin H. D. Buchloh elaborates in his 1988 analysis »Hans Haacke: Memory and Instrumental Reason,« from which the quote at the beginning of this article stems, the artist's historical-political works—Buchloh speaks of »reconstructions of cultural memory«—are neither about nostalgia nor reconciliation, but rather about raising awareness of historical facts and current contexts. In the post-Nazi afterwar societies of the 1970s and 1980s, this fact-oriented, specific remembrance work, which names perpetrators and deeds and points to potential and actual continuities, was met with incomprehension, resistance, censorship, and destruction—as will be shown in the following. According to Buchloh, people instead preferred to mourn the barbarism of the Nazi past via ambiguous, poetic-meditative, conciliatory-sublime approaches like those of Joseph Beuys or Anselm Kiefer. By contrast, Haacke's artistic means are conditioned by the political and cultural circumstances in which he inscribes his work. His practice of collecting and presenting knowledge functions as a kind of ideology critique that challenges the validity of hegemonic aesthetic concepts and their modes of representation. This anti-aesthetic impulse, the factographic dimension of Haacke's work, uses new techniques to develop another form of historical knowledge that addresses different social groups and different modes of experience.[7]

In the installation *News*, everyday reality and politics break into the supposedly neutral white cube of the exhibition space. In the late 1960s, West Germany went through profound social upheaval. Following a period of authoritarian conservative restoration during the Adenauer era, the first generation born after the war demanded that the Nazi past be addressed, and there was a call for more civil rights, a greater say at universities, as well as the overcoming of authoritarianism and moral concepts that were perceived as outdated. For example, the student movement's slogan »Unter den Talaren Muff von 1000 Jahren« (Under the gowns, the stench of a thousand years) was a play on the Nazis' proclamation of a »Thousand-Year Reich.« It aimed to highlight the insufficient denazification of public institutions after 1945, where many collaborators were able to continue their careers without interruption.[8]

During the runtime of *Prospect 69* in the fall of that year, the news was dominated by coverage of the Bundestag elections, which were to take place at the end of September. The leading candidates of the two major parties were Kurt-Georg Kiesinger (CDU) and Willy Brandt (SPD), who had respectively headed a grand coalition as Chancellor and Foreign

Minister since 1966. The contrasting biographies of the two party leaders demonstrate the contradictory nature of the coalition and, ultimately, of German society. Brandt was a resistance fighter in exile in Oslo from 1933, who returned to Germany in 1945 as a correspondent for Scandinavian newspapers at the Nuremberg Trials. Kiesinger had been a member of the National Socialist German Workers' Party (NSDAP) from 1933 and made his career as a lawyer in the Foreign Office from 1940 on, ultimately becoming deputy head of the radio policy department and a liaison for the Reich Ministry for Public Enlightenment and Propaganda. His Nazi past only became known to the general public when the journalist Beate Klarsfeld slapped him in the face and called him a Nazi during the 1968 CDU party conference in Berlin.[9] This scandal probably wasn't decisive for the election, but for the first time in the Federal Republic's twenty-year history, a social-liberal coalition of the SPD and FDP emerged from the election with a narrow majority. Willy Brandt became the first Social Democratic Chancellor and summed up his policies under the motto »Mehr Demokratie wagen« (We want to dare more democracy).[10]

9
Ibid., Chapter IV A3 »Kiesinger-Ohrfeige,« pp. 195–96.

10
The first Brandt cabinet introduced numerous reforms in social, educational, and legal policy and implemented a new *Ostpolitik*. See Peter Borowsky, »Sozialalliberale Koalition und innere Reformen,« in *Informationen zur politischen Bildung*, ed. Federal Agency for Civic Education, vol. 258: *Zeiten des Wandels: Germany 1961–1974* (Bonn: Bundeszentrale für Politische Bildung, 2002), https://www.bpb.de/shop/zeitschriften/izpb/zeiten-des-wandels-258/.

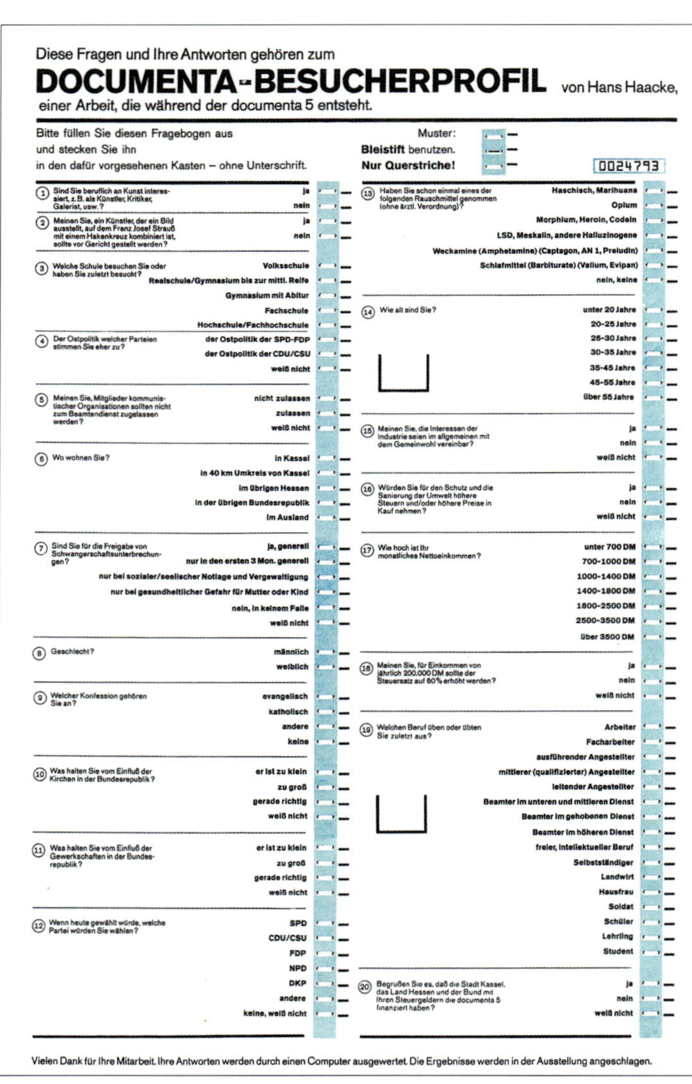

Diese Fragen und Ihre Antworten gehören zum

DOCUMENTA-BESUCHERPROFIL von Hans Haacke,

einer Arbeit, die während der documenta 5 entsteht.

Bitte füllen Sie diesen Fragebogen aus
und stecken Sie ihn
in den dafür vorgesehenen Kasten – ohne Unterschrift.

Muster:
Bleistift benutzen.
Nur Querstriche!

0024793

(1) Sind Sie beruflich an Kunst interessiert, z.B. als Künstler, Kritiker, Galerist, usw.?
ja / nein

(2) Meinen Sie, ein Künstler, der ein Bild ausstellt, auf dem Franz Josef Strauß mit einem Hakenkreuz kombiniert ist, sollte vor Gericht gestellt werden?
ja / nein

(3) Welche Schule besuchen Sie oder haben Sie zuletzt besucht?
Volksschule / Realschule/Gymnasium bis zur mittl. Reife / Gymnasium mit Abitur / Fachschule / Hochschule/Fachhochschule

(4) Der Ostpolitik welcher Parteien stimmen Sie eher zu?
der Ostpolitik der SPD-FDP / der Ostpolitik der CDU/CSU / weiß nicht

(5) Meinen Sie, Mitglieder kommunistischer Organisationen sollten nicht zum Beamtendienst zugelassen werden?
nicht zulassen / zulassen / weiß nicht

(6) Wo wohnen Sie?
in Kassel / in 40 km Umkreis von Kassel / im übrigen Hessen / in der übrigen Bundesrepublik / im Ausland

(7) Sind Sie für die Freigabe von Schwangerschaftsunterbrechungen?
ja, generell / nur in den ersten 3 Mon. generell / nur bei sozialer/seelischer Notlage und Vergewaltigung / nur bei gesundheitlicher Gefahr für Mutter oder Kind / nein, in keinem Falle / weiß nicht

(8) Geschlecht?
männlich / weiblich

(9) Welcher Konfession gehören Sie an?
evangelisch / katholisch / andere / keine

(10) Was halten Sie vom Einfluß der Kirchen in der Bundesrepublik?
er ist zu klein / zu groß / gerade richtig / weiß nicht

(11) Was halten Sie vom Einfluß der Gewerkschaften in der Bundesrepublik?
er ist zu klein / zu groß / gerade richtig / weiß nicht

(12) Wenn heute gewählt würde, welche Partei würden Sie wählen?
SPD / CDU/CSU / FDP / NPD / DKP / andere / keine, weiß nicht

(13) Haben Sie schon einmal eines der folgenden Rauschmittel genommen (ohne ärztl. Verordnung)?
Haschisch, Marihuana / Opium / Morphium, Heroin, Codein / LSD, Meskalin, andere Halluzinogene / Weckamine (Amphetamine) (Captagon, AN 1, Preludin) / Schlafmittel (Barbiturate) (Valium, Evipan) / nein, keine

(14) Wie alt sind Sie?
unter 20 Jahre / 20-25 Jahre / 25-30 Jahre / 30-35 Jahre / 35-45 Jahre / 45-55 Jahre / über 55 Jahre

(15) Meinen Sie, die Interessen der Industrie seien im allgemeinen mit dem Gemeinwohl vereinbar?
ja / nein / weiß nicht

(16) Würden Sie für den Schutz und die Sanierung der Umwelt höhere Steuern und/oder höhere Preise in Kauf nehmen?
ja / nein / weiß nicht

(17) Wie hoch ist Ihr monatliches Nettoeinkommen?
unter 700 DM / 700-1000 DM / 1000-1400 DM / 1400-1800 DM / 1800-2500 DM / 2500-3500 DM / über 3500 DM

(18) Meinen Sie, für Einkommen von jährlich 200.000 DM sollte der Steuersatz auf 60 % erhöht werden?
ja / nein / weiß nicht

(19) Welchen Beruf üben oder übten Sie zuletzt aus?
Arbeiter / Facharbeiter / ausführender Angestellter / mittlerer (qualifizierter) Angestellter / leitender Angestellter / Beamter im unteren und mittleren Dienst / Beamter im gehobenen Dienst / Beamter im höheren Dienst / freier, intellektueller Beruf / Selbstständiger / Landwirt / Hausfrau / Soldat / Schüler / Lehrling / Student

(20) Begrüßen Sie es, daß die Stadt Kassel, das Land Hessen und der Bund mit ihren Steuergeldern die documenta 5 finanziert haben?
ja / nein / weiß nicht

Vielen Dank für Ihre Mitarbeit. Ihre Antworten werden durch einen Computer ausgewertet. Die Ergebnisse werden in der Ausstellung angeschlagen.

Fig. 3: Hans Haacke, *Documenta Visitors' Profile, 1972*, questionnaire, 29.7 × 21 cm, documenta 5, Kassel, 1972

11
See »Kämpfe ums Kanzleramt: Franz Josef Strauß,« *Monitor*, WDR, September 22, 1969, https://www.youtube.com/watch?v=3sW2y-Hizjc, as well as »Die wollen Franz Josef, und die haben ihn,« *Der Spiegel* 46, *Strauß und die CSU: Barzels Schatten*, November 5, 1972, https://www.spiegel.de/spiegel/print/index-1972-46.html.

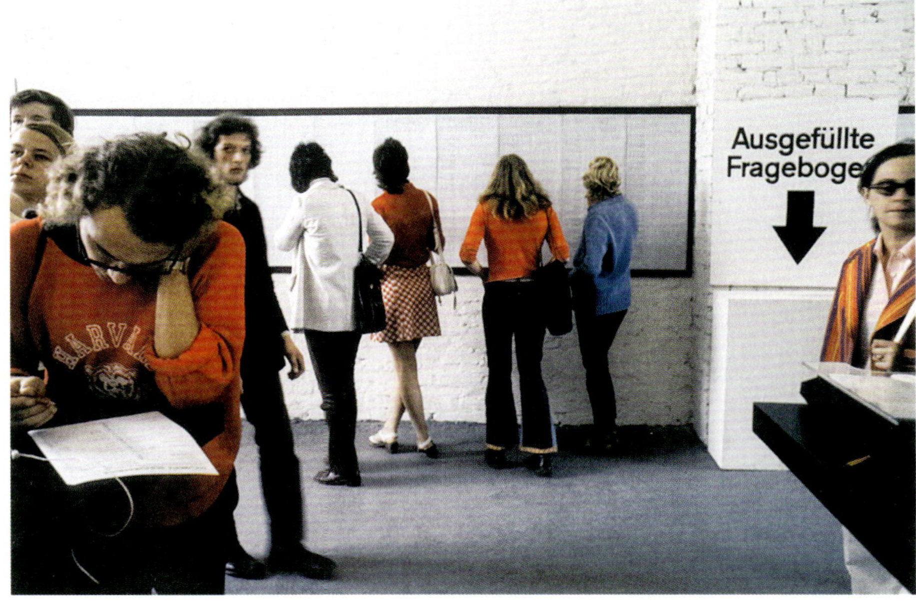

Fig. 4: Hans Haacke, *Documenta Visitors' Profile*, 1972, installation view at documenta 5, Kassel, 1972

Only three years later, a vote of no confidence against Brandt led to the dissolution of the Bundestag and the holding of new elections. This in turn formed the backdrop for a work by Hans Haacke that not only used a confrontation with political realities to alienate viewers from the imaginative refuge supposedly afforded by art—it actively involved them. For Harald Szeemann's legendary documenta 5 in Kassel (1972), Haacke realized the *Documenta-Besucherprofil (Documenta Visitors' Profile)*, a »questionnaire with ten demographic questions and ten about opinions on current sociopolitical problems« (fig. 3). The multiple-choice questionnaire was offered in German, English, and French, and it was to be filled out by the visitors and then deposited in a box provided for this purpose. The evaluation was performed by means of electronic data processing in the regional computer center; the results were continuously displayed in the form of statistics in the same room at documenta (fig. 4). Opinion questions—such as »The Ostpolitik of which party do you prefer?«; »Are you for the legalization of abortion?«; and »Would you be willing to pay higher taxes and/or prices for the rehabilitation of the environment?«—reflected the Brandt administration's reform policies, some of which were highly controversial. Another question is especially interesting in our context: »Do you think an artist who exhibits a painting depicting Franz Josef Strauß with a swastika should be prosecuted?« Here, Hans Haacke makes a thoroughly polemical reference to an intensive discussion on the relationship between the CSU chairman Franz Josef Strauß and the Nazi dictatorship. A former member of the National Socialist Motor Corps (NSKK), Strauß with his unabashed right-wing rhetoric became one of the most controversial and polarizing politicians of the postwar period.[11]

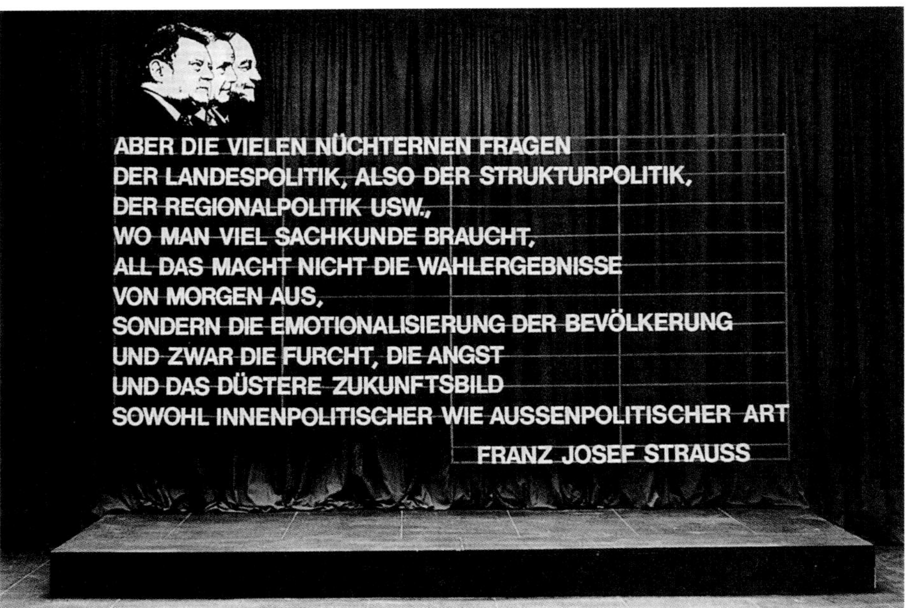

Fig. 5: *Aus Liebe zu Deutschland (Out of Love for Germany)*, 1976, installation view at the Frankfurter Kunstverein, Frankfurt am Main, 1976

Haacke took a concrete look at this with his installation *Aus Liebe zu Deutschland (For the Love of Germany)* as part of his solo exhibition at the Frankfurter Kunstverein in 1976 (fig. 5):[12] referring to the CDU/CSU's election slogan in the title, he quoted Strauß's infamous Sonthofen speech, in which his demagogic undermining of democracy became recognizable. Haacke combined the unmasking quote in large letters with the profiles of Franz Josef Strauß, Alfred Dregger (party chairman in Hesse), and Hans Karl Filbinger (Minister President of Baden-Württemberg), who represented the radical far-right wing of the CDU/CSU. The latter was forced to resign in the summer of 1978 due to a controversy surrounding his active participation in the unjust system of the Nazi jurisdiction, which became known as the »Filbinger Affair.« In the eyes of an increasingly sensitized public, Filbinger embodied »an almost ideal type of a conservative-authoritarian habitus that promised success in dictatorship and democracy alike, which was also characterized by ›pathologically good conscience‹ . . . and a ›pathologically bad memory‹.«[13]

But back to Haacke's 1972 *Documenta Visitors' Profile*: over the course of three months, 41,810 people took part in the survey, which amounted to 19.8 percent of all visitors.[14] As Rosalyn Deutsche elaborated, Hans Haacke's aim in his surveys of exhibition visitors—the most famous of which is probably *MoMA Poll* from 1970 (fig. p. 107)—was nothing less than to form »the art audience into a democratic public, one that thinks and acts politically . . .« His »experience of German Fascism—the economic and political opponent of democratic relations and freedoms . . . led him to keep his ear to the ground in order to detect the presence or approach of anti-democratic tendencies within democracies.«[15] Knowing his audience and addressing them directly were central to creating a self-image

12
See *Aus Liebe zu Deutschland*, in *Hans Haacke: Unfinished Business*, ed. Brian Wallis, exh. cat. New Museum, New York (Cambridge, MA, and New York: The MIT Press, 1986), pp. 174–75.

13
Fischer and Lorenz, *Lexikon der »Vergangenheitsbewältigung« in Deutschland*, Chapter IV B4 »Filbinger Affair,« pp. 219–22, esp. p. 221.

14
See Hans Haacke, »Memories and Thoughts about My Art World Visitors Polls of Many Decades,« in *Hans Haacke: Swiss Institute Visitors Poll*, ed. Simon Castets and Alison Coplan, exh. cat. Swiss Institute, New York (New York: Swiss Institute, 2022), pp. 10–16, esp. p. 13.

15
Rosalyn Deutsche, »The Art of Not Being Governed Quite So Much,« in *Hans Haacke: for real – Works, 1959–2006*, ed. Matthias Flügge and Robert Fleck, exh. cat. Akademie der Künste, Berlin, and Deichtorhallen, Hamburg (Düsseldorf: Richter, 2006), pp. 62–79, esp. pp. 63–64.

16
Ibid., p. 71.

17
See Rosalyn Deutsche, »Property Values: Hans Haacke, Real Estate, and the Museum,« in Wallis, *Hans Haacke: Unfinished Business*, pp. 20–37, esp. p. 26.

18
See Franziska Leuthäußer, »Café Deutschland: Im Gespräch mit der ersten Kunstszene der BRD: Hans Haacke,« Städel Museum website, May 25, 2016, https://cafedeutschland.staedelmuseum.de/gespraeche/hans-haacke.

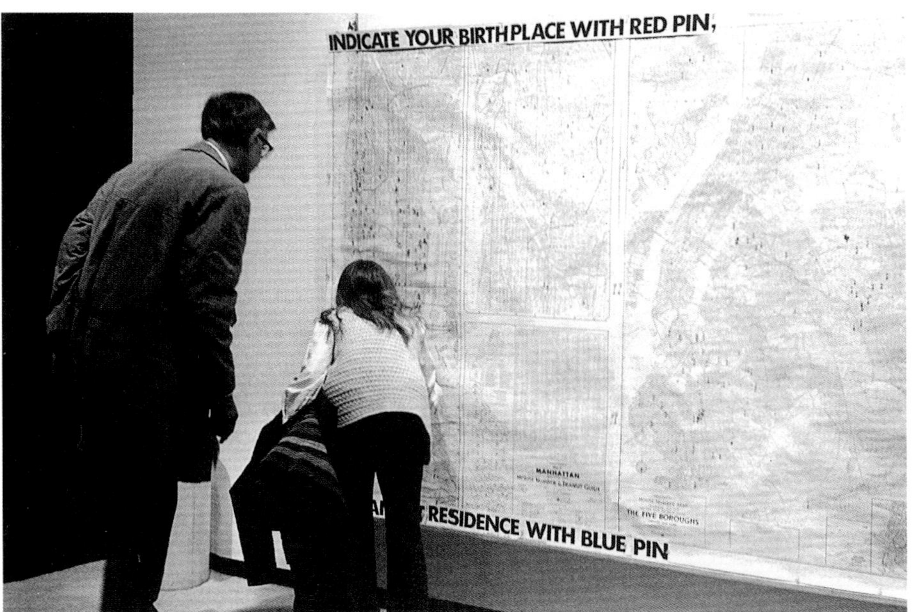

Fig. 6: Hans Haacke, *Gallery-Goers' Birthplace and Residence Profile, Part 1*, 1969, printed city map on cork board, red and blue pins, 163.2 × 223.5 × 5.1 cm, installation view at Howard Wise Gallery, New York, 1969

of the art public and thereby creating »awareness among the art public about itself.«[16]

Haacke's first work of this kind was made at the Howard Wise Gallery in New York in 1969, the same year as *News*. In *Gallery-Goers' Birthplace and Residence Profile, Part 1*, he asked visitors to mark their places of birth and residence on maps with red and blue pins (fig. 6). The visual evaluation took place in the second part of the work, in which Haacke photographed all the residential addresses in Manhattan and arranged the resulting 737 images according to their geographical position in relation to 5th Avenue as a horizontal axis. The information provided by the gallery goers determined the form of the installation and also revealed the economic and social contexts in which they predominantly lived, their social status, and their class position (fig. pp. 108–09). The space of art, whether gallery or museum, was functionally shifted from being a place of passive contemplation to a place of actively questioning the audience, which was in turn encouraged to question the art world's many unspoken principles, such as neutrality and autonomy.[17]

Hans Haacke had in fact been interested in exhibition visitors from an early age. As a student at the Staatliche Werkakademie (State Art Academy) in Kassel, he worked as a set-up assistant and as a guard at documenta 2 in the summer of 1959 and photographed his everyday observations in the exhibition and behind the scenes. Haacke shot around 300 photographs of the exhibition, that he later described as a key experience, but primarily of its visitors and the different ways in which they approached the artworks on display.[18] He captured curious and inquisitive, sometimes doubtful and perplexed gazes consulting the exhibition catalogue, a panorama of postwar German society encountering artworks that had been ostracized during the Nazi era. Haacke, who was still studying painting at the time, didn't think of these photographs as artworks when they were taken. More than twenty years later, in 1981, Walter Grasskamp published a volume of the magazine *Kunstforum* entitled *Mythos Documenta: Ein Bilderbuch zur Kunstgeschichte* (Documenta Myth: A Picture Book on Art History), which was dedicated to the first six editions of the mega exhibition. In the chapter »documenta 2,« he reproduced an anonymous photograph (fig. p. 15) that had caught his eye among hundreds of other photos in the archive for its seeming clairvoyance, and commented on it as follows:

»Two students in front of Kandinsky's *Continuous Stroke* (1929). No photograph shows as clearly as this one the kind of country that documenta was invented in. Should we admire these thoughtful corps students for their open-mindedness in subjecting themselves to modern art here, or is it merely bewilderment that they cleverly conceal behind the mask of critical appreciation? Do they also realize that there's something wrong with this scene or do they blame the picture they are looking at? . . . Photography is the art destined to depict the historically notorious nonsimultaneity of the simultaneous, and this unknown photographer at the Documenta II has achieved a small, appropriate masterpiece. It is 1959, only fourteen years since the war also brought death to those officers who, as corps students, had given fascism a foothold at the universities. . . . The documenta has an international reputation, but it is a ›rest‹ German event, as shown by the two students here in full formal garb. Four years earlier, in 1955, the supporting association for the newly founded documenta was called ›Abendländische Kunst des 20. Jahrhunderts e. V.‹ (Western Art of the 20th Century) which amounted to luring customers under false pretenses, including these two.«[19]

Shortly after publication, Hans Haacke revealed himself to be the unknown photographer who had succeeded in creating this »masterpiece« of visual sensitivity for the contradictions of post-Nazi Germany in the 1950s.[20] It wasn't until 2001 that he compiled a set of twenty-six photographs from the entire pool into the work *Photographic Notes, documenta 2*, which was subsequently shown in numerous exhibitions, including at documenta 14 in Kassel and Athens in 2017. With *Visitors' Profile*, Haacke thus returned to the 1972 documenta as an artist and questioned the audience that he had so keenly observed as a student.

Two years later, Hans Haacke conceived the installation *Manet-PROJEKT '74* (figs. pp. 123–33) as an explicit act of critical counter-memory, focusing on the uninterrupted career of a Nazi functionary up to the present day.[21] On the occasion of the 150th anniversary of the Wallraf Richartz Museum in Cologne, he was invited to contribute to the large-scale exhibition *PROJEKT '74 / Kunst bleibt Kunst* (PROJEKT '74 / Art Remains Art). Here, Haacke took his inspiration from a museum brochure praising the recent donation of Édouard Manet's *Bunch of Asparagus* (1880) by the museum's association of patrons to

19
Walter Grasskamp, »Zwei Studenten,« *Kunstforum International* 49, *Mythos Documenta: Ein Bilderbuch zur Kunstgeschichte* (1982), pp. 49–80.

20
See Walter Grasskamp, »Bilder einer Ausstellung,« in *Hans Haacke: Fotonotizen Documenta 2, 1959* (Berlin and Munich: Deutscher Kunstverlag, 2012), pp. 5–21.

21
Also see the contributions on this work by Hubertus Butin and by Sabeth Buchmann and Stephan Geene in this volume, pp. 97–105 and 115–21.

commemorate the first Chancellor of West Germany, Konrad Adenauer.[22] The main protagonist in this acquisition was the chairman of the board of trustees, the influential banker Hermann Josef Abs, a figure who had played a variety of roles during the Nazi era and in postwar Germany. From 1938, Abs was a member of the board of Deutsche Bank, which was entrusted with the forced »Aryanization« of Jewish banks and companies, and he was also involved in the Nazi war economy based on forced labor in industry and concentration camp subcamps.[23] Only briefly imprisoned after the war, Abs was later classified as an »exonerated« person (*Entlastete*) in the denazification process and resumed holding executive positions from 1948 on, for example at Deutsche Bank after 1952. He became Adenauer's advisor on financial policy, conducted negotiations abroad, and held mandates on up to thirty supervisory boards, making him a central figure in the West German economy until the 1970s.[24] Through a court case that Abs successfully brought against the East Berlin historian Eberhard Czichon to prevent the distribution of the latter's 1970 study *Der Bankier und die Macht: Hermann Josef Abs in der deutschen Politik* (The Banker and Power: Hermann Josef Abs in German Politics),[25] his complicity with the Nazi regime and his postwar career became the subject of public discussion.[26]

For Hans Haacke, the »sinister role« Abs played triggered an interest in the biographies of the various owners of the Manet painting. Accordingly, his concept was to present the painting on an easel and have it accompanied by ten panels that provide information »on the social and economic status of the people . . . who owned the still life over the years and what prices were paid for the painting.«[27] According to Haacke:

»Except for Manet and Abs, who had solicited donations from German corporations to acquire *Bunch of Asparagus* for the museum, everyone featured with biographies in my extended provenance were Jewish. Thus the innocent-looking still life had accumulated a heavy crust of history.«[28]

Even though the information Haacke collected was easily accessible public knowledge, it famously proved so explosive that his work was once again censored by a museum—that is, after the cancellation of the exhibition at the Guggenheim Museum in 1971. Benjamin Buchloh analyzes the work *Manet-PROJEKT '74* as a decisive development in Haacke's oeuvre, »which integrated factographic inquiry, mnemonic recuperation, and a politically radicalized form of site specificity.« The piece follows Walter Benjamin's famous dictum from his »Theses on the Philosophy of History« that every document of culture is simultaneously a document of barbarism. »Situated along this boundary, the work is precariously balanced between its reconstruction of history and its resistance to spectacularizing memory and thereby subjecting the victims of history to another ritual of exposure and violence.«[29] By tracing the genealogy of ownership on the basis of objective data, Haacke makes visible the history and relevance of Jewish collectors from the late nineteenth century onward, but also the

22
See Yve-Alain Bois, Douglas Crimp, and Rosalind Krauss, »A Conversation with Hans Haacke,« *October* 30 (Fall 1984), pp. 23–48, esp. p. 36.

23
See Harold James, *Die Deutsche Bank und die «Arisierung»* (Munich: Beck, 2001).

24
See Alexander Nützenadel, »Abs, Hermann Josef,« *NDB-online*, July 1, 2023, https://www.deutsche-biographie.de/118500260.html#dbocontent.

25
Eberhard Czichon, *Der Bankier und die Macht: Hermann Josef Abs in der deutschen Politik* (Cologne: Pahl-Rugenstein, 1970).

26
See Nützenadel, »Abs, Hermann Josef.«

27
Julia Friedrich, »Hans Haacke: Manet-PROJEKT '74,« Museum Ludwig, online database, https://museum-ludwig.kulturelles-erbe-koeln.de/documents/obj/05118105.

28
Adam Szymczyk, »The Indelible Presence of the Gurlitt Estate: Adam Szymczyk in conversation with Alexander Alberro, Maria Eichhorn, and Hans Haacke,« in *South as a State of Mind*, Issue #9 [documenta 14 #1], ed. Quinn Latimer and Adam Szymczyk, https://www.documenta14.de/de/south/.

29
Benjamin H. D. Buchloh, »Hans Haacke: The Entwinement of Myth and Enlightenment,« in *Hans Haacke: Obra Social*, exh. cat. Museu Tápies, Barcelona (Barcelona: Fundacio Antoni Tápies, 1995), pp. 45–60, esp. pp. 51–53.

existential, irreversible rupture that the Nazi policies of persecution and extermination meant for them. At the same time, the mere factual enumeration of biographical data in the case of the perpetrator is so revealing that the barbaric side of culture comes to light. With his research into changes of ownership, Haacke also anticipated the systematic provenance research that only kicked off in the late 1990s after the declaration of the Washington Principles,[30] investigating the history of cultural assets seized through Nazi persecution with a view to their restitution.[31]

The historical-political arena of public space as a special form of site- and context-specific work initially concerned Hans Haacke in 1988: steirischer herbst, an interdisciplinary cultural festival founded in Graz in 1968, addressed the »Anschluss« or annexation of Austria to the German Reich fifty years earlier under the title *Guilt and Innocence in Art*. The exhibition *Bezugspunkte 38/88* (Points of Reference 38/88) aimed to challenge the invited international artists »to confront history, politics, and society, and thus regain intellectual territory which has been surrendered to everyday indifference in a tactical retreat, a retreat that has been continual, unconscious, and manipulated,« according to the curator Werner Fenz. »The choice of places, which were points of reference for the Nazi regime—and are in some cases now marked as such, but in others only now being brought back to memory—represents the historical dimension. . . . The creative use made of these places constitutes the artistic contribution.«[32] During his research, Haacke came across photographs of a ceremony held in the city center on July 25, 1938, to award Graz the honorary title »Stadt der Volkserhebung« (City of the People's Uprising) (fig. 7). Under the motto »Und Ihr habt doch gesiegt« (And You Were Victorious After All), the city, which had long been considered a stronghold of early »illegal« National

30
Washington Conference Principles on Nazi-Confiscated Art, released in connection with The Washington Conference on Holocaust-Era Assets, Washington, DC, December 3, 1998, https://www.state.gov/washington-conference-principles-on-nazi-confiscated-art/.

31
See Constantin Goschler and Jürgen Lillteicher, eds., *»Arisierung« und Restitution: Die Rückerstattung jüdischen Eigentums in Deutschland und Österreich nach 1945 und 1989* (Göttingen: Wallstein, 2002).

32
Werner Fenz, »Ausstellungsprotokolle. Protokoll 1: Das Konzept,« in *Bezugspunkte 38/88*, ed. steirischer herbst (Graz: steirischer herbst, 1988), pp. 169–71, esp. p. 169, published in English as: Werner Fenz and Maria-Regina Kecht, »Protocols of the Exhibition ›Points of Reference 38/88‹,« *October* 48 (Spring 1989), pp. 71–74.

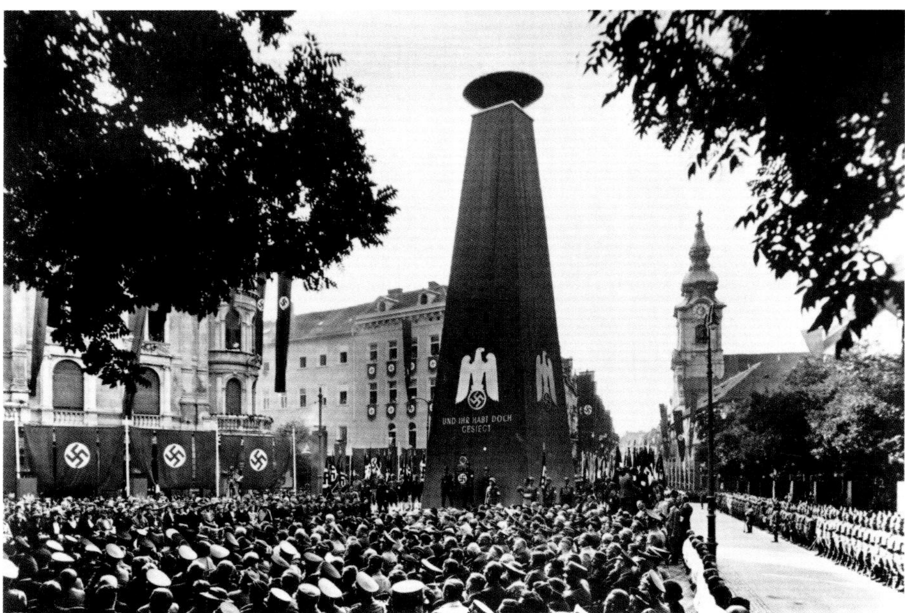

Fig. 7: *Rally »Graz, City of National Uprising« in Remembrance of the 4th Anniversary of the July Putsch 1938*, covered Mariensäule, Am Eisernen Tor / Herrengasse, Graz, 1938, Universalmuseum Joanneum Graz / Multimedia Collections

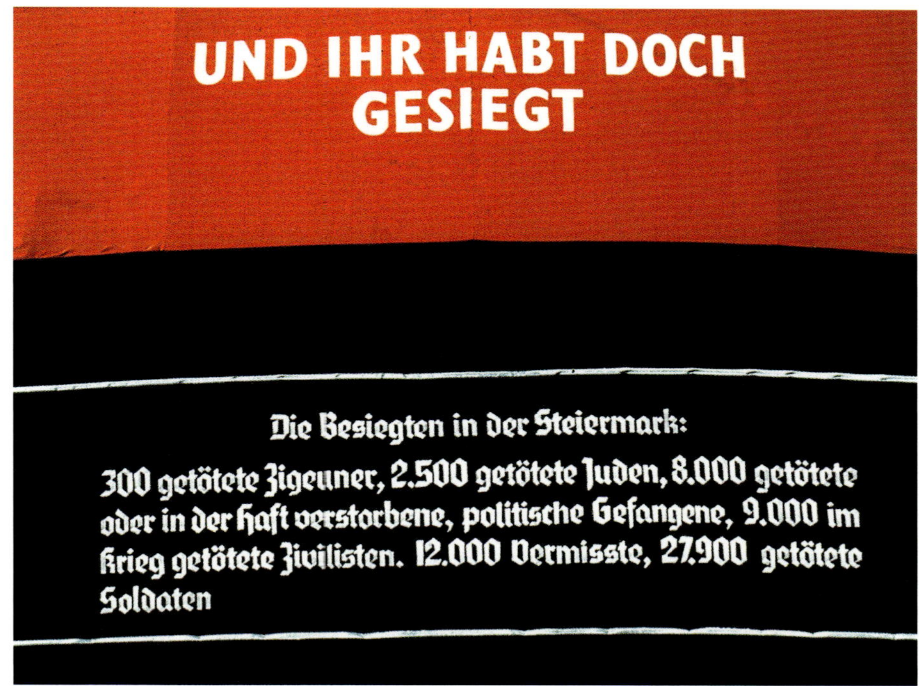

Fig. 8: Hans Haacke, *Und Ihr habt doch gesiegt (And You Were Victorious After All)*, 1988 (detail), Generali Foundation Collection

Socialists, and where the swastika flag was hoisted on the town hall even before the »Anschluss«, commemorated the »heroes« of the failed July Putsch in 1934 and the suppressed Munich Putsch of 1923.[33] For the ceremony, the city's baroque Mariensäule (Marian column) was crowned with a fire bowl and clad with red fabric in the form of a monumental obelisk, which bore the Nazi emblem of the Reichsadler (imperial eagle) and swastika as well as the dedication »Und Ihr habt doch gesiegt.« At *Bezugspunkte 38/88*, Hans Haacke reconstructed the column's appearance from July 1938, but added a list of the victims of the Nazi regime at the foot of the obelisk under the inscription »Die Besiegten in der Steiermark« (The Vanquished of Styria) (fig. 8). Not far from it, he placed a billboard with sixteen large-format red posters featuring a swastika and the inscription »Graz – Stadt der Volkserhebung.« In the middle of the swastikas were collages of Graz classified ads and newspaper reports from 1938, which testify to the population's anti-Semitism and the local drive to »Aryanize«: »business takeovers,« people looking for an »Aryan« partner, the burning of the synagogue, lists of confiscated Jewish property (fig. 1).[34] Immediately after the »Anschluss,« there were so-called »wild Aryanizations« throughout Austria in March and April 1938—pogrom-like lootings of Jewish property involving brutal violence and destruction by members of the Schutzstaffel (SS), Sturmabteilung (SA), and Gestapo, but also by greedy ordinary citizens. The Nazi authorities quickly put a stop to these uncontrolled and unregulated activities, only to then carry out the expropriations on an unprecedented scale using illegitimate, quasi-legalized anti-Jewish policies.[35]

33
See Wolfram Dornik, »Von der ›deutschesten Stadt der Monarchie‹ zur ›Stadt der Volkserhebung‹: Politische Strukturen in Graz 1918–1938; Zwischen Brüchen und Kontinuitäten,« in *Graz 1918–38: Historisches Jahrbuch der Stadt Graz*, vol. 48 (Graz: Leykam, 2018), pp. 19–74.

34
See Hans Haacke, *Und Ihr habt doch gesiegt*, 1988, in *Mia san mia: Hans Haacke*, ed. Sabine Breitwieser, exh. cat. Generali Foundation, Vienna (Dresden: Philo Fine Arts, 2001), pp. 126–47.

35
See Goschler and Lillteicher, *»Arisierung« und Restitution*.

In the accompanying catalogue, Hans Haacke commented on the project as follows: »›And you were victorious after all,‹ the Nazis proclaimed, full of pride, on the red fabric with their eagle and the swastika, which decorated the *Mariensäule* in Graz on July 25, 1938. They were referring to themselves. Fifty years later, I hope we can make sure that their cheering will turn out to have been premature.«[36] With the accurate reconstruction of the National Socialist victory monument, which dominated the square and was visible from afar, Haacke made this repressed history and the complicity in it tangible in the present. His dedication serves as a targeted intervention that transforms the message of the Nazi monument into a haunting memorial for the victims of National Socialism. In addition to directly addressing »you,« it simultaneously reminds us of the perpetrators. The collaged posters show how pervasive these crimes were throughout society on the everyday level.

Right from the start, the installation provoked the most violent reactions. There were already incidents during construction, and after the opening it triggered outraged debates on site and in the media on a daily basis. The posters were repeatedly torn down, then replaced. Despite a night-time security service, an arson attack was carried out on the obelisk on November 2, 1988, one week before the exhibition ended, severely damaging the work and the Madonna figure beneath it (fig. p. 195). Haacke had obviously struck a nerve in Austria's historical and political consciousness. The public debate about Austria's complicity in the National Socialist past had only just gotten underway with the »Year of Remembrance« in 1988. The Republic of Austria, since its reestablishment in April 1945, had used the so-called victim theory to define itself as the first victim of the Nazi regime and successfully renounced any guilt. But only two years earlier, in 1986, the scandal known as the Waldheim affair surrounding the wartime past of presidential candidate Kurt Waldheim had started to make this claim look increasingly flawed and ultimately untenable. Waldheim, former Secretary-General of the United Nations, had concealed his membership in the SA cavalry regiment and his war service in the Balkans. When confronted with the suspicion that he had participated in war crimes as a Wehrmacht officer, he simply remarked: »During the war, I did nothing different from hundreds of thousands of other Austrians, namely, fulfilling my duty as a soldier.« His statement suddenly revealed the contradictions of Austrian historical policy along with its central element, the victim thesis, and subsequently triggered a fundamental shift in the way the Nazi past was dealt with.[37]

Haacke's installation reflects the virulence and controversial nature of the Austrian discourse on remembrance with its twofold transformation of a Nazi victory monument: into both a memorial for the victims and a monument of shame. After the arson attack, civil society initiatives were formed, demonstrations and public discussions took place. In a statement on Haacke's billboard, steirischer herbst commemorated the

36
steirischer herbst, *Bezugspunkte 38/88*, p. 55, published in English as: Hans Haacke, »Und ihr habt doch gesiegt, 1988,« *October* 48 (Spring 1989), pp. 79–87.

37
See Heidemarie Uhl, »Das ›erste Opfer‹: Der österreichische Opfermythos und seine Transformationen in der Zweiten Republik,« *Österreichische Zeitschrift für Politikwissenschaft (ÖZP)* 1 (2001), pp. 19–34.

38
See Heidemarie Uhl, »Schichtungen des österreichischen Gedächtnisses: Der Ort der neuen Denkmalkultur im Geschichtsbewusstsein der Zweiten Republik,« in Breitwieser, *Mia san mia: Hans Haacke*, pp. 51–81.

39
Petra Kipphoff, »Bodenlos in den Gärten der Kunst,« *Die Zeit*, June 18, 1993, p. 53. Cited from Florian Matzner, »Hans Haacke – ein Künstler im Öffentlichen Dienst,« *kritische berichte: Zeitschrift für Kunst- und Kulturwissenschaften* 22, no. 3 (1994), pp. 22–29, esp. p. 22.

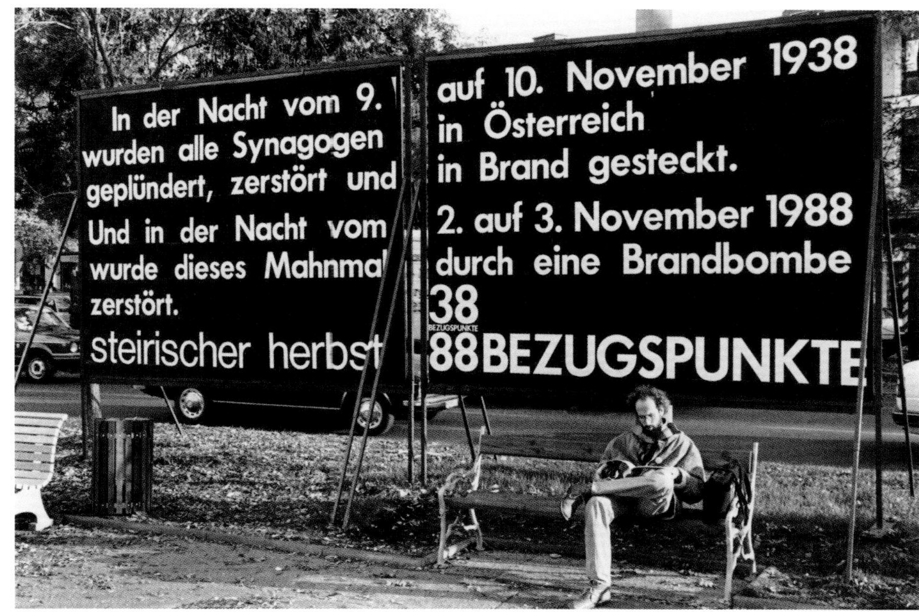

Fig. 9: Billboard with statement by steirischer herbst after the arson attack, archive steirischer herbst

November pogroms of 1938 and the destruction of the memorial in 1988 (fig. 9). The perpetrators, a well-known »old Nazi« and two unemployed neo-Nazis, were charged with »reengagement in the National Socialist sense« and sentenced to prison. The disturbing power of Hans Haacke's temporary countermonument intervened in Austria's crumbling self-image based on denial and repression, thus making a significant contribution toward establishing a new culture of remembrance.[38]

The Austrian historical-political context was to occupy Haacke in two further projects. In 1996, he was invited to submit a design for the memorial for victims of National Socialism at the Feliferhof military firing range in Graz, which remained unrealized (figs. pp. 205–07). In 2001, Haacke developed the installation *Mia san mia* for his solo exhibition at the Generali Foundation in Vienna, which offered a revealing caricature of contemporary right-wing populist aesthetics that traced their ideological origins back to the Nazi era. The work was developed against the backdrop of a coalition, denounced throughout Europe, between the Austrian People's Party (ÖVP) and the Freedom Party of Austria (FPÖ) (fig. 10).

A German feuilleton described the *GERMANIA* installation at the 1993 Venice Biennale as an »artistic act of cool, brutal enlightenment, for which there is nothing comparable in Haacke's work or at the Biennale.«[39] The setting was the German Pavilion shortly after German reunification. Hans Haacke had been invited to represent Germany in Venice, alongside the Korean artist Nam June Paik, who was teaching in Düsseldorf at the time. His chosen point of departure was the pavilion's inscription »GERMANIA,« with all its layers of meaning, and the building itself, which had been given its current appearance by the National Socialists in 1938. At the same time, it was also

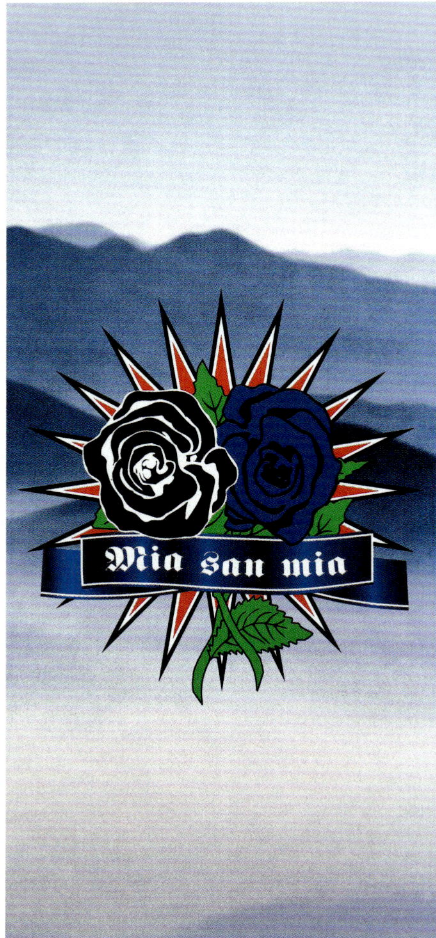

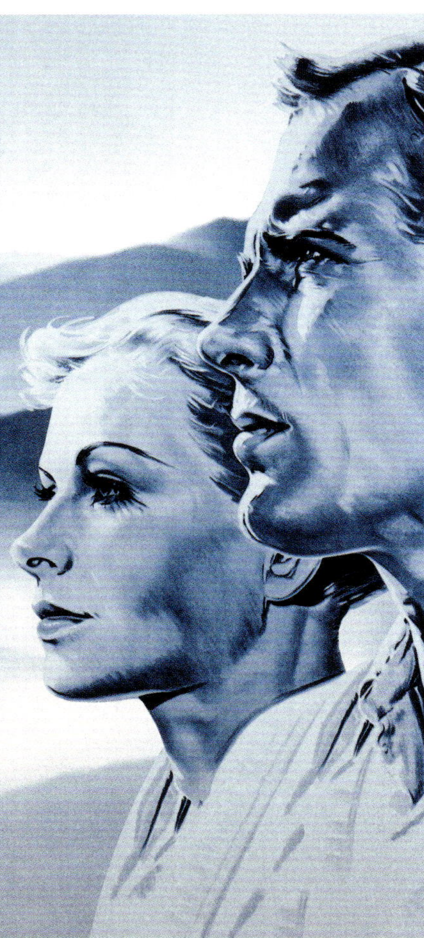

Fig. 10: Hans Haacke, *Mia san mia (We Are Who We Are)*, 2001 (detail), courtesy Generali Foundation

important to reflect on the political situation in newly reunified Germany at the time, which was and remains characterized by the resurgence of nationalism, right-wing radicalism, and racism. Haacke described it as a »battlefield.«[40] Above the door, where a Reichsadler with a swastika was once displayed during the Nazi era, he hung an oversized 1 Deutsche Mark coin from 1990, the year the two Germanys reunified. In the entrance area, Haacke installed a red wall that blocked the view into the room and displayed a photograph of Adolf Hitler's visit to the 1934 Biennale, accompanied by the Duce (fig. 11). Behind it, a scene of destruction: the Chiampo Mandorlato floor slabs laid in 1938 have been torn up and the marble debris scattered wildly throughout the space. The facade lettering »GERMANIA« was repeated on the wall of the apse, this time in steel referring to Adolf Hitler's megalomanic plans for a new Berlin. The reception of Haacke's sensational installation was ambivalent, although he was ultimately awarded the Golden Lion for the best pavilion together with Paik:

»The difference between the reactions of the German audience and the foreign visitors could not have been more drastic. Many Germans were cautiously waiting and didn't know how to deal with it. The German ambassador in Rome,

40
»Die Symbolik des Ortes: Ein Gespräch mit Hans Haacke« (Venice, June 12, 1993), *Neue bildende Kunst* 3, no. 4 (1993), p. 22.

41
Quoted from »Hans Haacke: Der Nonkonformist,« *Kunstforum International*, pp. 202–21.

42
Hans Haacke, »Gondola! Gondola!,« in *Hans Haacke: Bodenlos*, ed. Klaus Bußmann and Florian Matzner, exh. cat. German Pavilion at the Venice Biennale (Stuttgart: Edition Cantz, 1993), pp. 7–17.

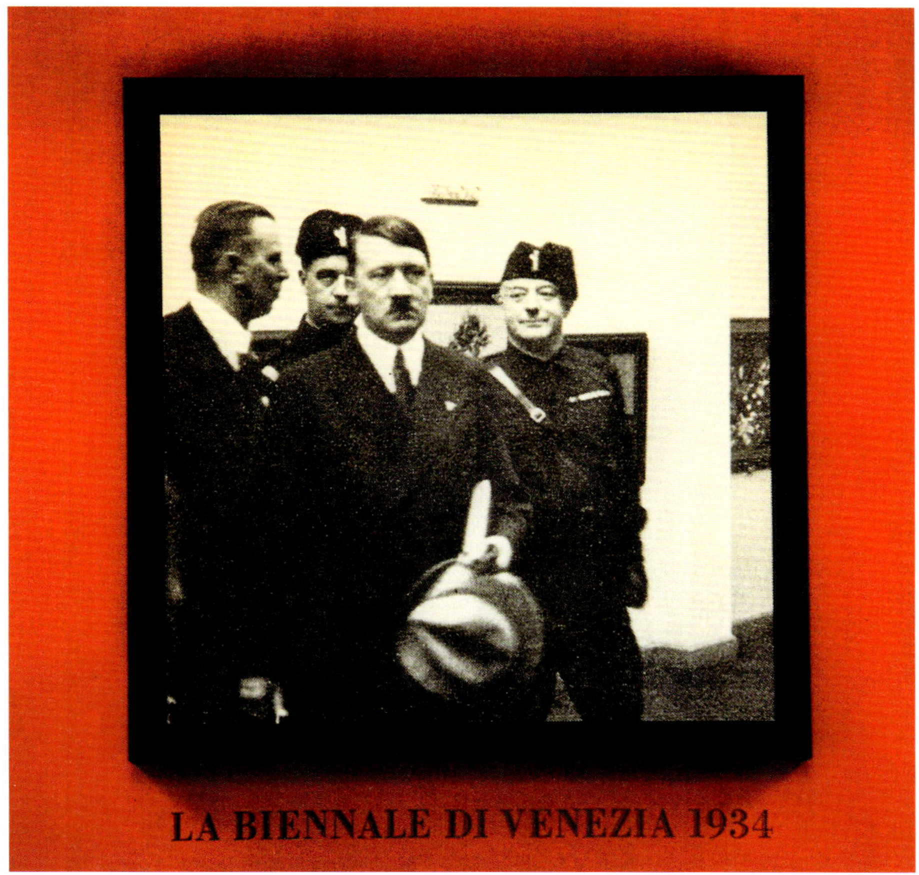

Fig. 11: Hans Haacke, *GERMANIA*, 1993 (detail), courtesy the artist and Paula Cooper Gallery, New York

who came to the opening, remained very taciturn. He didn't want to talk to me. By contrast, many foreign visitors were emotionally engaged. Every now and then I saw people picking up broken pieces from the floor and smashing them more, as if they wanted to settle some outstanding score in their own family.«[41]

Haacke conceived his act of destruction in response to the results of his research into Hitler's visit to the fascist Biennale in 1934 and the National Socialists' subsequent representational policies in Venice. Once again, it is the visible and invisible continuities, the forgotten and suppressed connections between art, politics, and economics, that preoccupy him, which he then presented in the form of a satire with journalistic undertones under the title »Gondola! Gondola!« in the exhibition catalogue.[42] Here, the sculptor and painter Arno Breker plays a central role, and his 1939 sculpture *Die Bereitschaft* (Readiness) featured prominently in the German Pavilion of 1940—a year after Hitler's invasion of Poland and the outbreak of World War II (fig. 12). As the most important sculptor of the Nazi regime, Breker had shaped its aesthetics of steeled heroic figures ready to sacrifice their lives. During the denazification after 1945, he was only classified as a follower (*Mitläufer*), even though he was named on the Nazis' list of important artists, the so-called *Gottbegnadeten* or artists blessed by God. All the

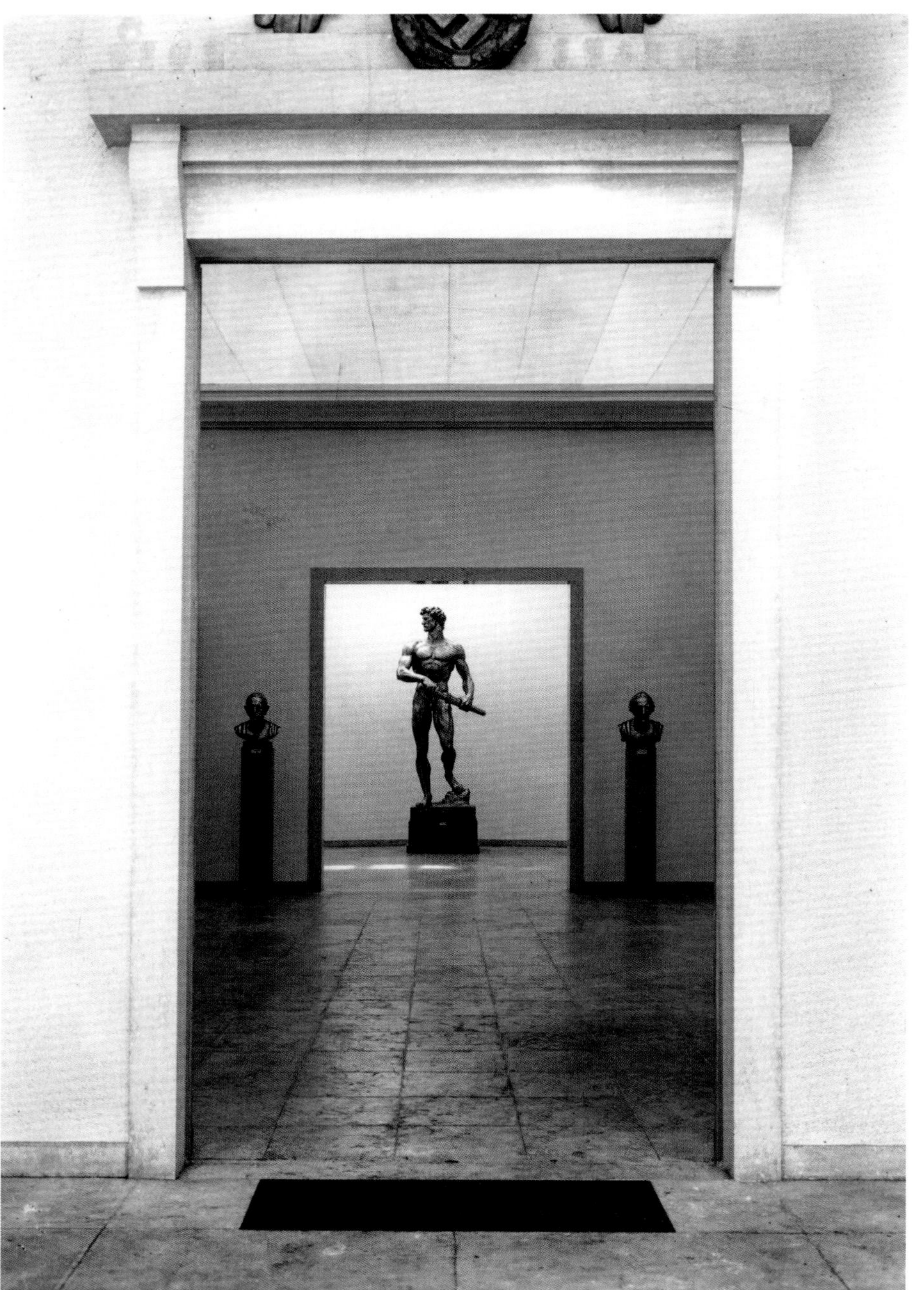

Fig. 12: Arno Breker, *Readiness*, 1939, view from the entrance of the German Pavilion, 22nd Venice Biennale, 1940

same, Breker continued to receive public, but most of all private, commissions after the war by figures such as Hermann Josef Abs and Peter Ludwig, both of whom Haacke famously portrayed in other major works.

In his insistence on foregrounding power relations, continuities and complicities, historical facts and their effects on the constitution of the present, Haacke anticipated recent revisions of art and art history in the postwar period, such as those undertaken by two exhibitions at the Deutsches Historisches Museum in 2021. The first, *Documenta: Politics and Art*, thus revealed, among other things, the involvement of documenta's founding staff in the Nazi regime, especially that of Werner Haftmann, a key figure in the first three editions and founding director of the Neue Nationalgalerie in West Berlin, who had been a member of the SA and NSDAP and was wanted as a war criminal for torturing Italian partisans.[43] Meanwhile, the parallel exhibition *»Divinely Gifted«: National Socialism's Favoured Artists in the Federal Republic* examined the biographies, works, and reception of the *Gottbegnadeten* who, after 1945, were still able to continue building on the careers they had begun under National Socialism. Raphael Gross, president of the Deutsches Historisches Museum Foundation, stated the key finding as: »Like almost all other areas of German and Austrian society, there wasn't any zero hour in art after Nazi rule ended.«[44]

Hans Haacke's long-standing examination of historical politics in the post-Nazi era extends from 1959 to recent history—think of *DER BEVÖLKERUNG (TO THE POPULATION)* (2000) or *We (All) Are the People* (2017). By reflecting specific social and political contexts and refusing any conciliatory, quasi »redemptive« gestures, it traces the fault lines and contradictions within the very presence of that, namely, our past.[45]

43
Raphael Gross et al., eds., *documenta: Politics and Art*, exh. cat. Deutsches Historisches Museum, Berlin (Munich, London, and New York: Prestel, 2021).

44
Raphael Gross, »Vorwort,« in *Die Liste der »Gottbegnadeten«: Künstler des Nationalsozialismus in der Bundesrepublik*, ed. Wolfgang Brauneis and Raphael Gross, exh. cat. Deutsches Historisches Museum, Berlin (Munich, London, and New York: Prestel, 2021), p. 11.

45
See Luisa Ziaja, »Geschichte – Erinnerung – Kunst: Zum Potenzial eines schwierigen Verhältnisses,« in *Recollecting: Raub und Restitution*, ed. Alexandra Reininghaus (Vienna: Passagen Verlag, 2009), pp. 23–28.

Und Ihr habt doch gesiegt
(And You Were Victorious After All), 1988

Since 1968, the annual »steirische herbst« festival is held in Graz, a cultural event supported by public funding. In 1988, the twenty-year anniversary of the festival coincided with the fiftieth anniversary of the »Anschluss,« the forcible uniting of Germany and Austria in 1938. For the steirischer herbst festival of 1988, artists were invited to produce temporary installations in public places that had played a significant role during the Nazi regime. One of the sites in the center of the city was the Mariensäule, a column crowned by a seventeenth-century gilded statue of the Virgin Mary, celebrating the Austrian victory over the Turks. When Hitler conferred the title Stadt der Volkserhebung (City of the People's Insurrection) on Graz in 1938, the ceremony on July 25 was held at the foot of the Mariensäule. For the occasion, it was hidden under a red obelisk, emblazoned with the Nazi insignia and the inscription »Und Ihr habt doch gesiegt« (And You Were Victorious After All). This claim referred to the failed Nazi putsch in Vienna on July 25, 1934. Graz had been an early Nazi stronghold in Austria.

The obelisk was reconstructed for the 1988 steirischer herbst festival as a memorial to Nazi victims with a tally: »The Vanquished of Styria: 300 Gypsies killed, 2,500 Jews killed, 8,000 political prisoners killed or died in detention, 9,000 civilians killed in the war, 12,000 missing, 27,900 soldiers killed.« During the night, a week before the closing of the exhibition, the memorial was firebombed. The bronze statue of the virgin was severely damaged. Within a week, the arsonist and the instigator of the firebombing, the latter a well-known sixty-seven-year-old Nazi, were arrested. They were convicted in a jury trial and sentenced to serve two-and-a-half and one-and-a-half-year prison terms respectively.

Hans Haacke, 2006

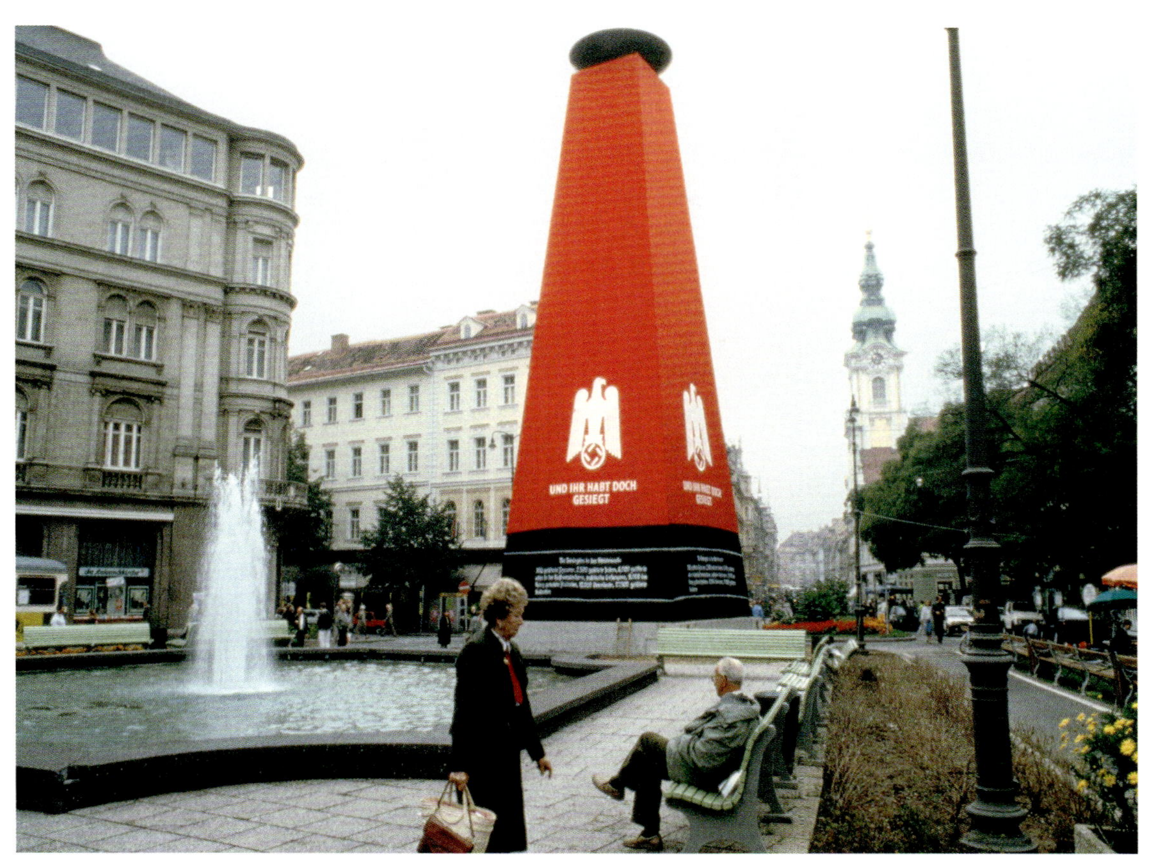

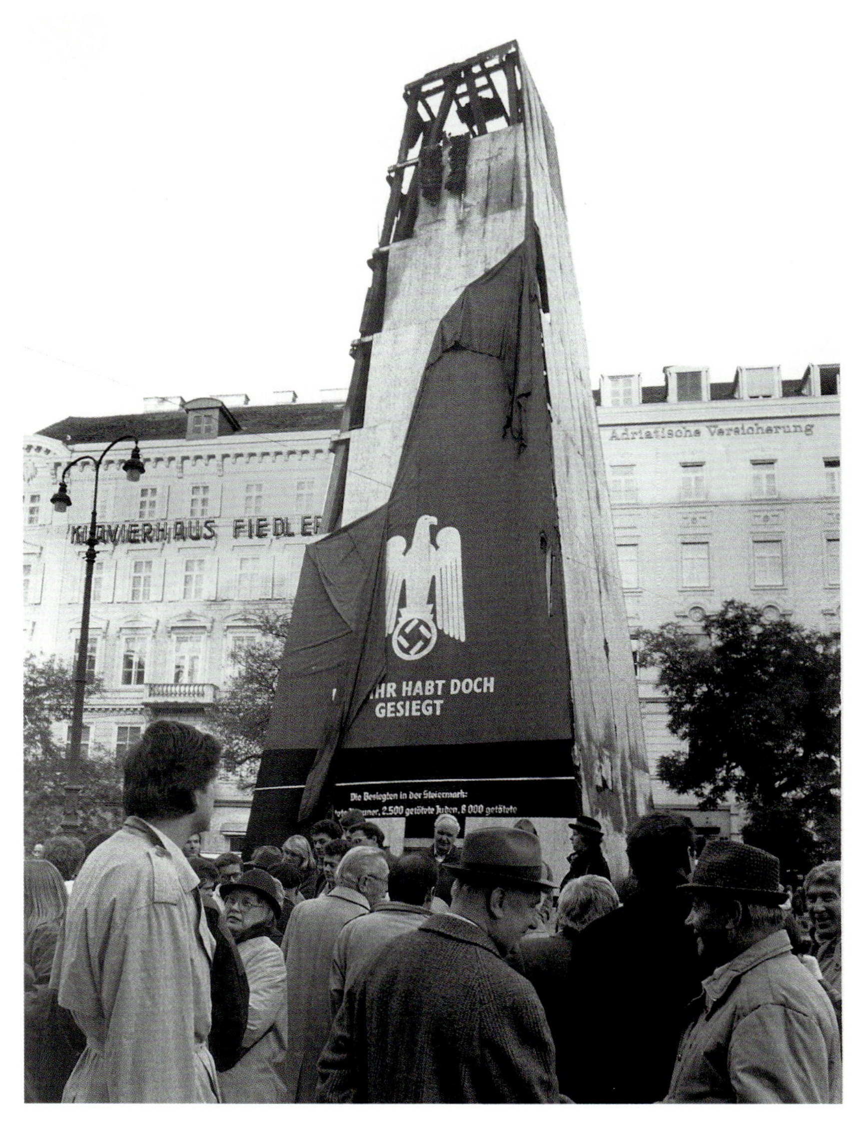

Und Ihr habt doch gesiegt
(And You Were Victorious After All), 1988

Calligraphie, 1989

The site of the proposal is the cour d'honneur of the Palais Bourbon, part of the French National Assembly's building complex in Paris. Members of the French Parliament were to contribute a rock from their respective election district. The rocks were fitted together and polished to form a perfect cone in the center of the upper part of the court. Raised, gold-leaf calligraphy on its surface spell, in Arabic, the motto of the French Republic: »Liberty, Equality, Fraternity.« A jet of water shoots up from the top of the cone. The water then flows down its surface and the sloping terrain toward the center of a balustrade. It rushes through a breach, which its force seems to have broken, onto the main court underneath, which is occupied by a large area in the shape of France. Common French crops are grown there in a four-year cycle: wheat, corn, rapeseed, cabbage, sunflowers, beans, peas, and potatoes. In the fourth year, the field lies fallow. The water is carried around the planted area in a shallow, graded trough toward the gate of the court, where it disappears into an opening in the ground. The entire volume of water is recycled.

Hans Haacke, 2004

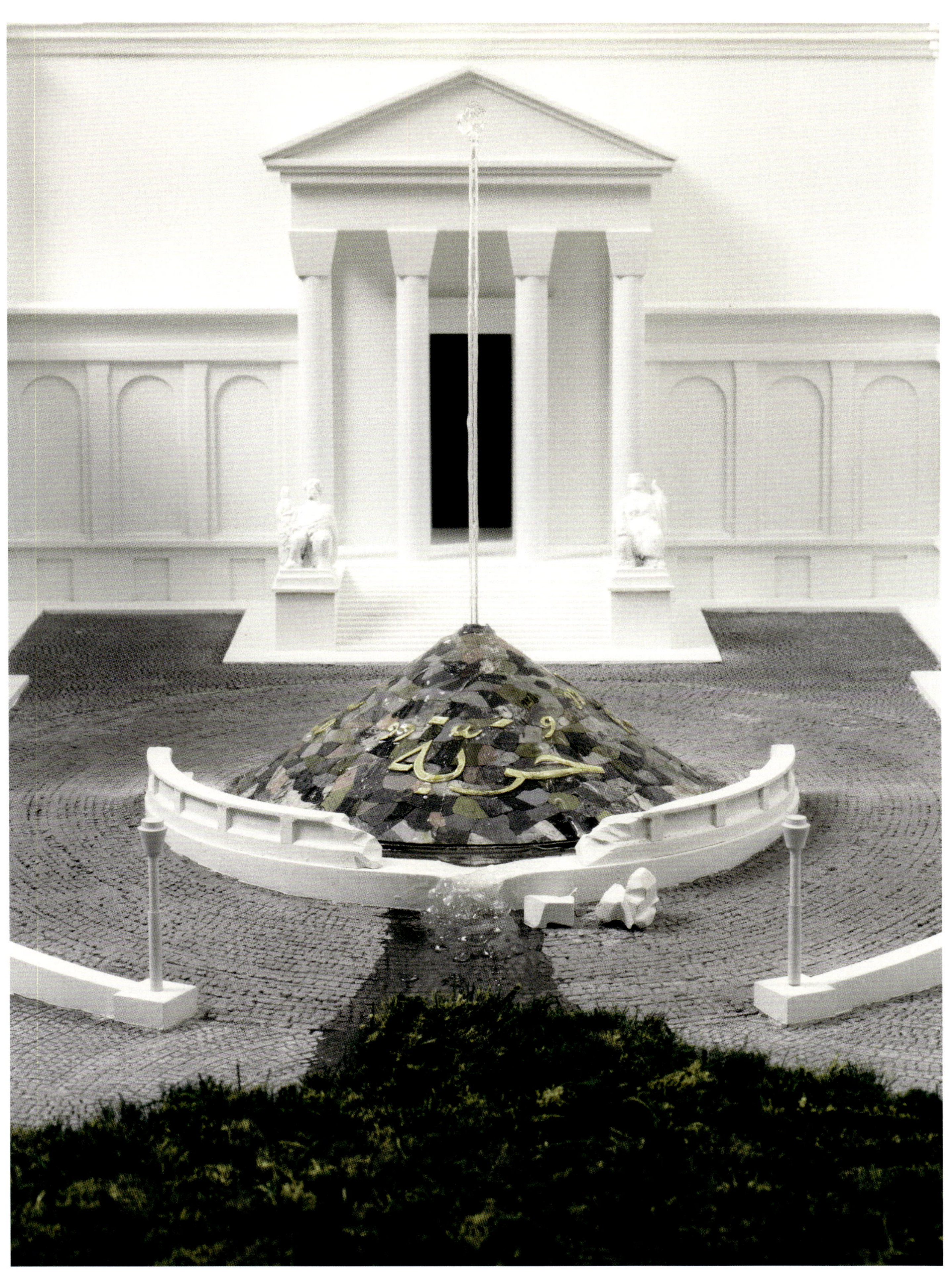

Calligraphie, 1989

Photo Opportunity (After the Storm / Walker Evans), 1992

During the Great Depression in the United States, Walker Evans, on assignment with the Farm Security Administration, photographed impoverished people in the South. His photographs are in the collection of The Museum of Modern Art, New York, and other institutions. On November 3, 1991, *The Washington Post* reported on a storm that had struck the East Coast of the United States the preceding day, describing how it had damaged President George H. W. Bush's vacation home in Kennebunkport, Maine. A photograph illustrated the article.

Hans Haacke, 2006

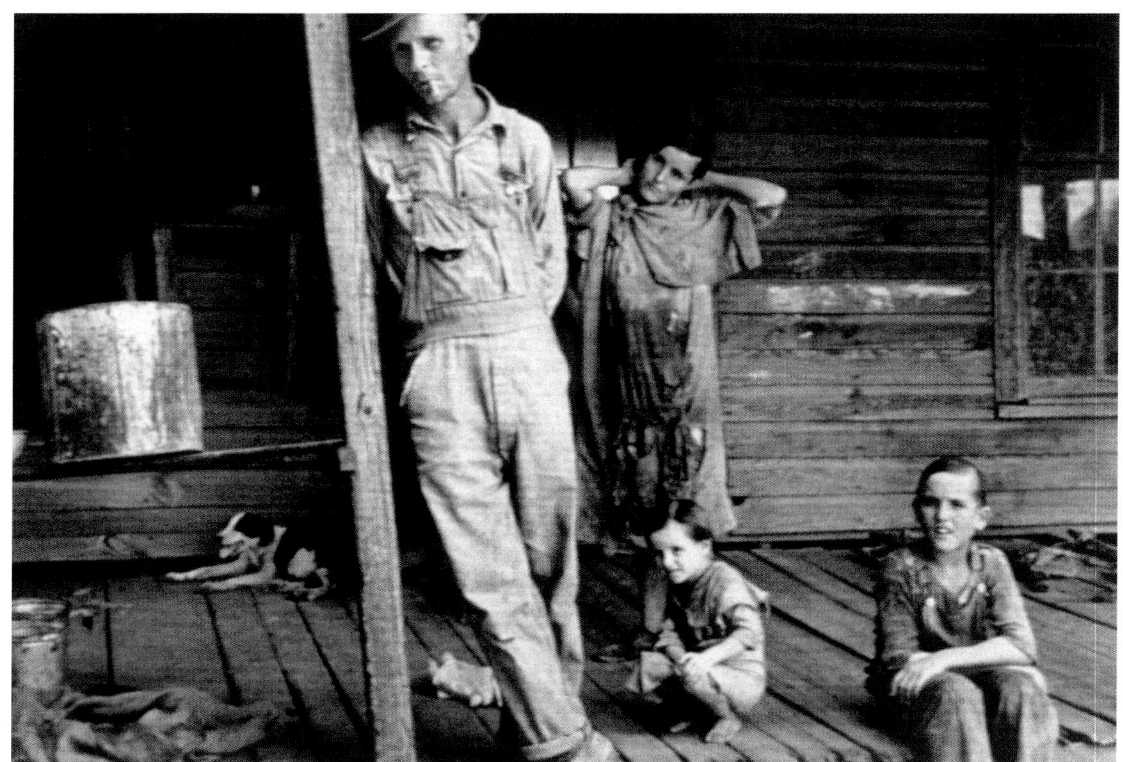

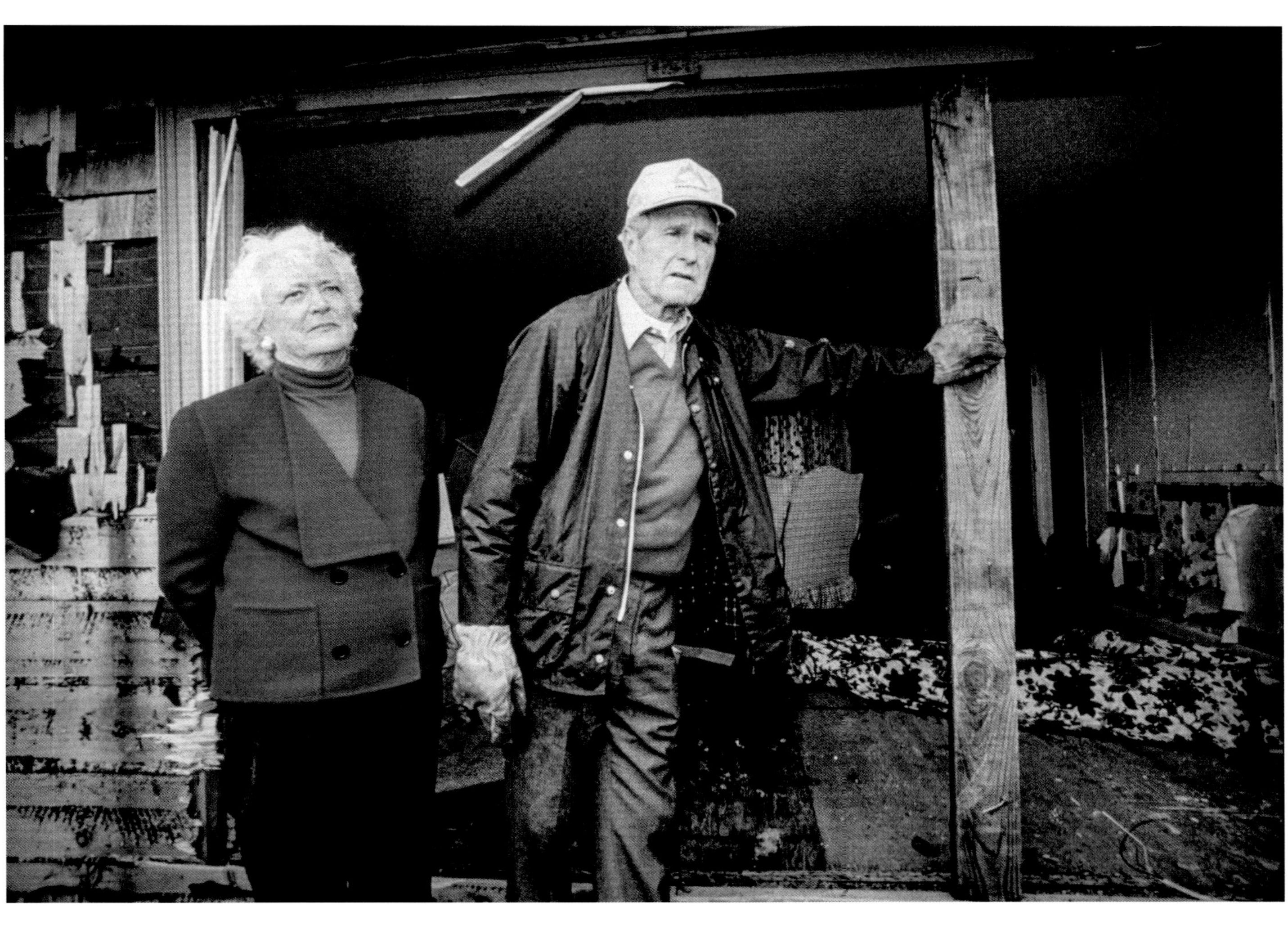

Photo Opportunity (After the Storm / Walker Evans), 1992

GERMANIA, 1993

After seizing power in 1933, Hitler's first trip abroad was to meet Benito Mussolini in Venice—and to visit the German Pavilion of the Biennale. He ordered a facelift of the building following the martial variant of neoclassicism that had been introduced by the new Haus der Deutschen Kunst in Munich. The parquet floor of the building was replaced by marble slabs. And on a hook above the entrance, the Nazi version of the German eagle was installed, with a wreath surrounding the swastika.

During the 1993 Biennale, the same hook held an enlarged replica of a 1 Deutsche Mark coin with a mint date of 1990, the year of the reunification of East and West Germany and the adoption of the West German currency as common legal tender. From the entrance, the view into the interior was blocked by a red wall with a black-and-white photograph of Hitler's visit to the pavilion in 1934. Once visitors had passed it to the left or right, they found the entire floor broken up. The word GERMANIA (Italian for Germany) on the pavilion's facade was quoted in the apse. GERMANIA had been the name Hitler had envisioned for Berlin after his expected victory in World War II and the imperial redesign of the German capital by Albert Speer.

Hans Haacke, 1993, updated in 2019

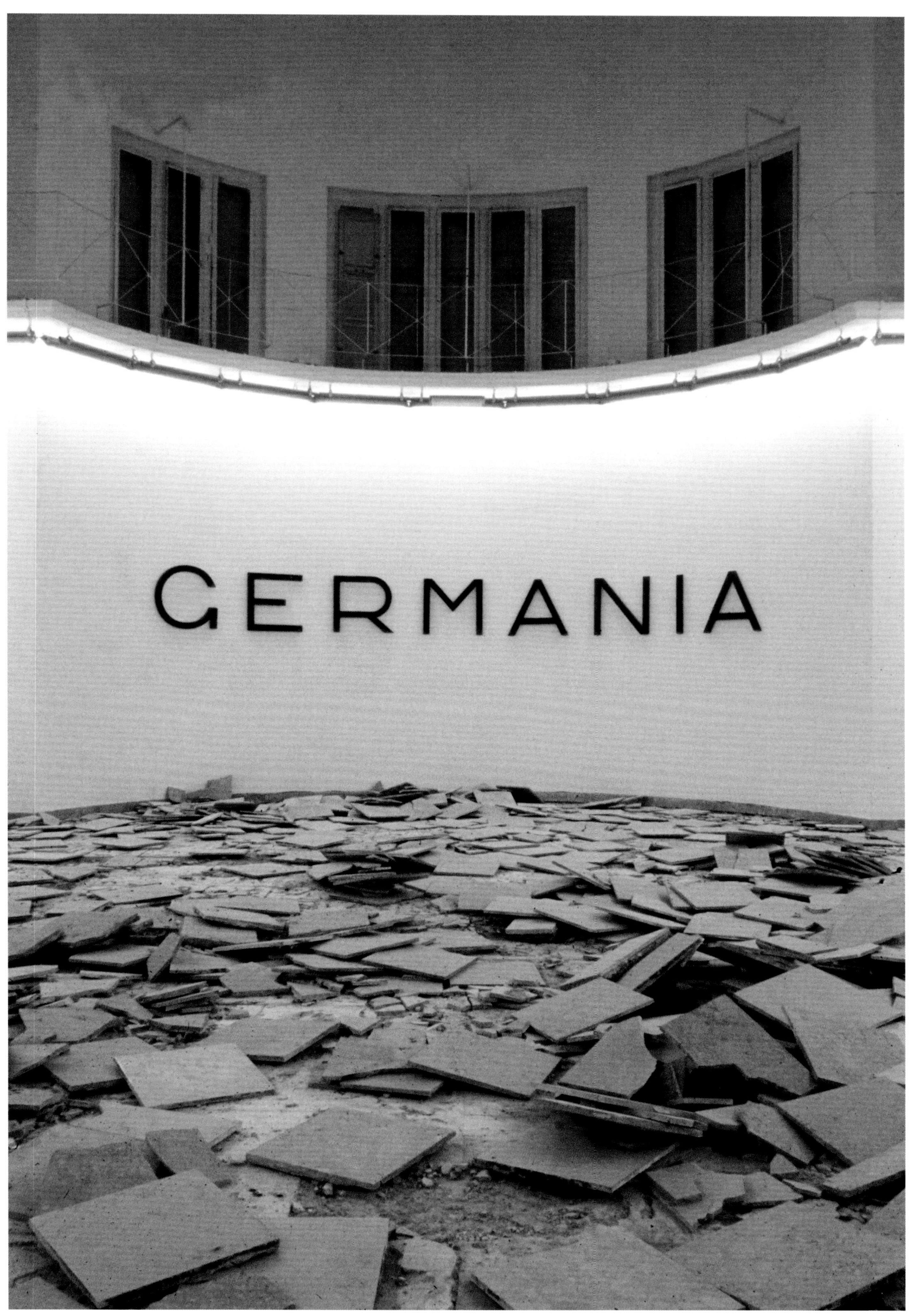

GERMANIA, 1993

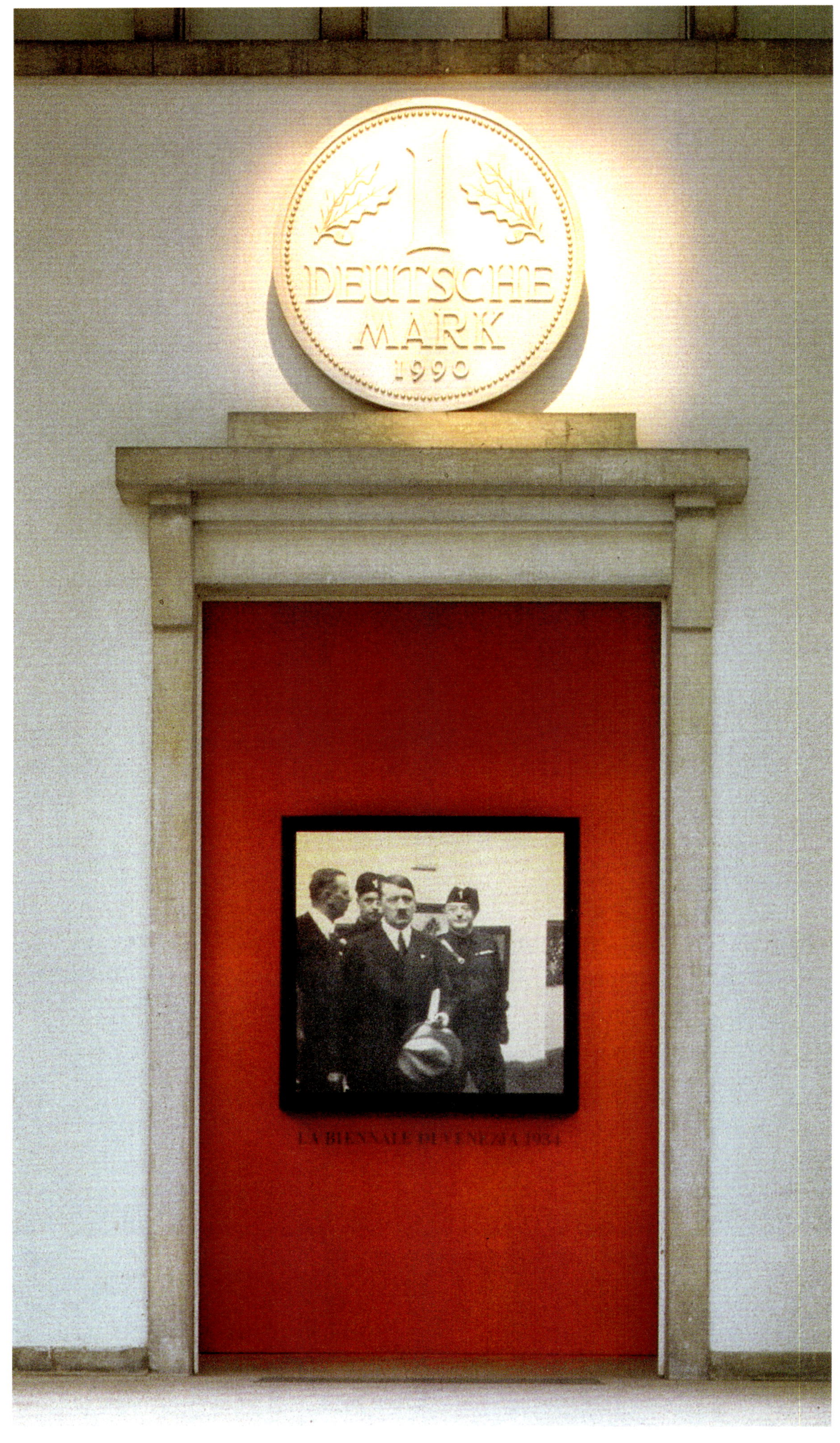
1
DEUTSCHE
MARK
1990

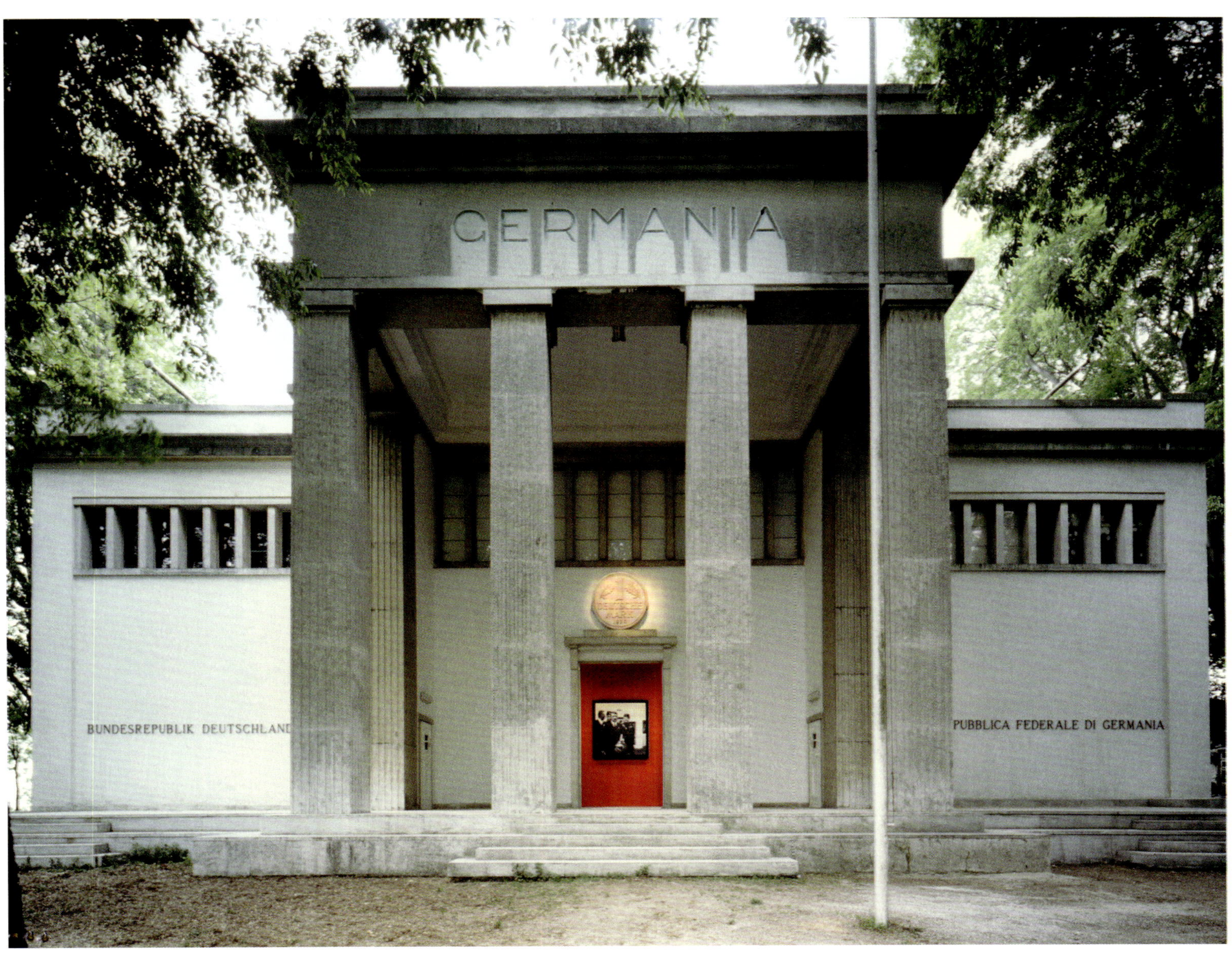

GERMANIA, 1993

Memorial to the Victims of National Socialism at the Military Target Practice Range »Feliferhof« in Graz, 1996

In the fall of 1995, an initiative led by the Styria Military Command and the Styrian Commission for Public Art prompted the office of Styria's municipal government to announce an open-call competition to design a memorial for the victims of National Socialism at the »Feliferhof« military firing range in Graz. Hans Haacke submitted a design that, as the artist writes, »conveys a sensory experience intended to grip visitors and sensitize them to the subject matter.« Between 1938 and 1945, the National Socialists had carried out executions at the Feliferhof military shooting range. In the last weeks of the war, a special Gestapo firing squad shot 142 people and buried them in a mass grave.

In his 1989 report »Execution and Killing by State Authorities in Styria, 1938 to 1945,« the historian Walter Brunner recorded the dimensions of the mass grave as 25 meters long, 2.5 meters wide, and 3 meters deep. Haacke used these dimensions for his design of the memorial and envisaged a trench beneath the site—still used as a military firing range—which could be accessed via an underground passageway.

Once there, visitors would stand in front of a concrete wall; dim daylight filters into the trench. Upon walking around the wall, the view opens up onto a 25 meter long shaft with 3 meter high walls of fresh earth rising vertically on all sides. As they look up, they see the sky and the top of a flagpole, which Haacke had placed on ground level at the narrow end of the trench on the right side. On the wall at this end of the shaft, they find a grainy black-and-white photograph etched into aluminum. The image was originally published in the *Neue Steirische Zeitung* on May 27, 1945, and shows the exhumation of the bodies from the mass grave at Feliferhof.

Another panel in the same material and dimensions provides information about the events: »A mass grave was uncovered at Feliferhof in May 1945. It contained 142 bodies, people who had been murdered by the National Socialists: 116 in civilian clothes, 10 in Hungarian uniform, 4 in German Wehrmacht uniform, 3 in French uniform, 3 in Russian uniform, 2 unclothed women, 2 unclothed men, 1 in American uniform, 1 in SS uniform.« Haacke hoped that the combination of the smell of fresh earth, the narrowness of the site, and the evocative panels would enable identification with those murdered by the National Socialists. The submitted design was not realized.

TDF

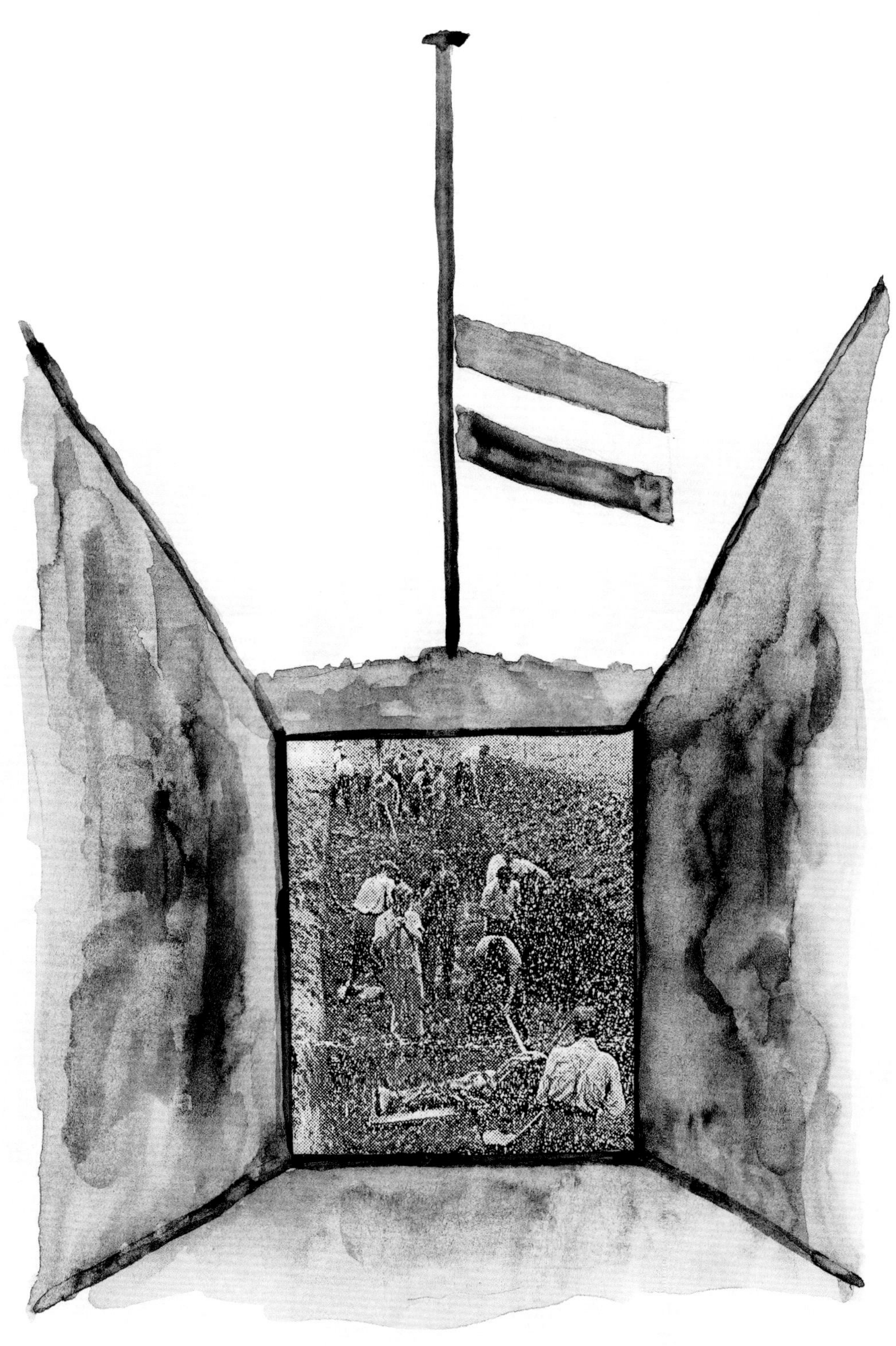

Memorial to the Victims of National Socialism at the Military Target Practice Range »Feliferhof« in Graz, 1996

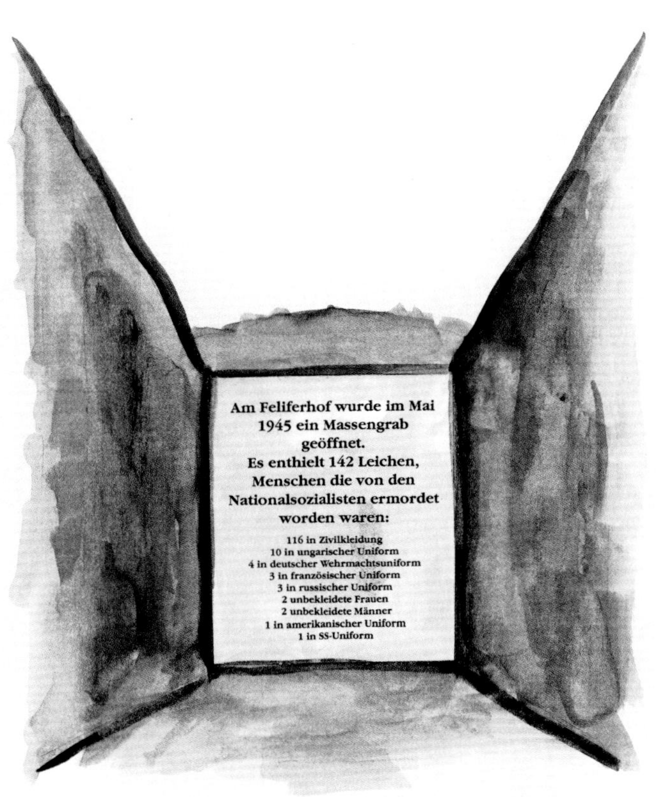
Am Feliferhof wurde im Mai
1945 ein Massengrab
geöffnet.
Es enthielt 142 Leichen,
Menschen die von den
Nationalsozialisten ermordet
worden waren:
116 in Zivilkleidung
10 in ungarischer Uniform
4 in deutscher Wehrmachtsuniform
3 in französischer Uniform
3 in russischer Uniform
2 unbekleidete Frauen
2 unbekleidete Männer
1 in amerikanischer Uniform
1 in SS-Uniform

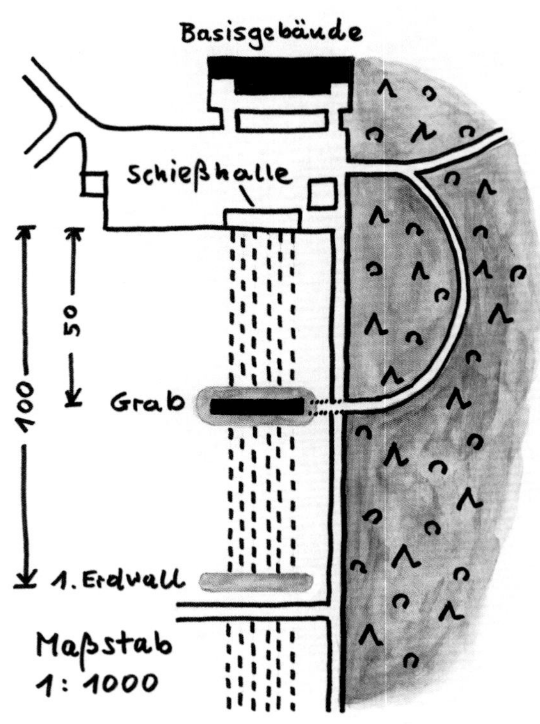
Basisgebäude
Schießhalle
50
100
Grab
1. Erdwall
Maßstab
1: 1000

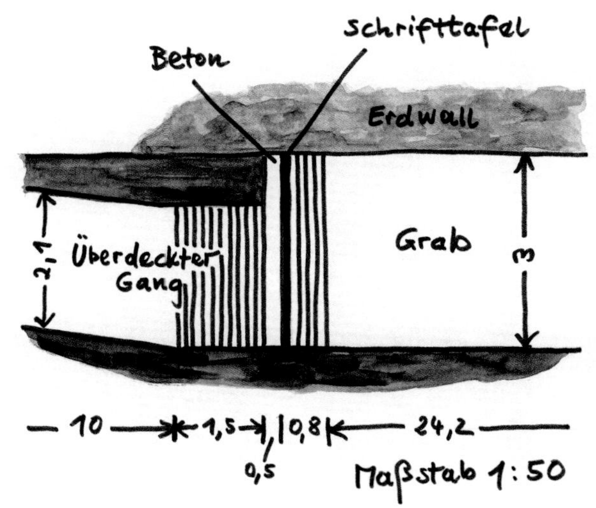

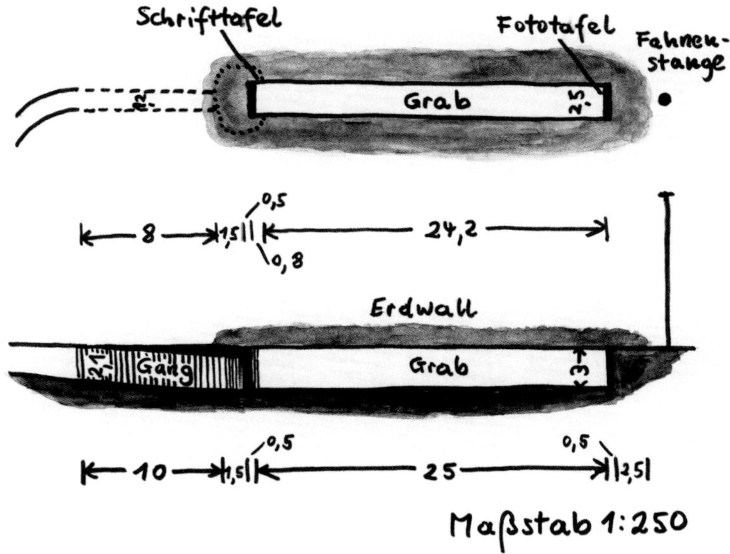

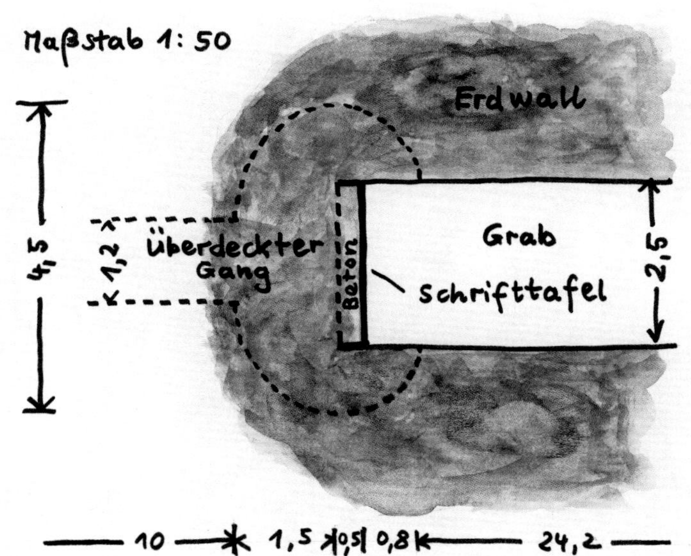

Memorial to the Victims of National Socialism at the Military Target Practice Range »Feliferhof« in Graz, 1996

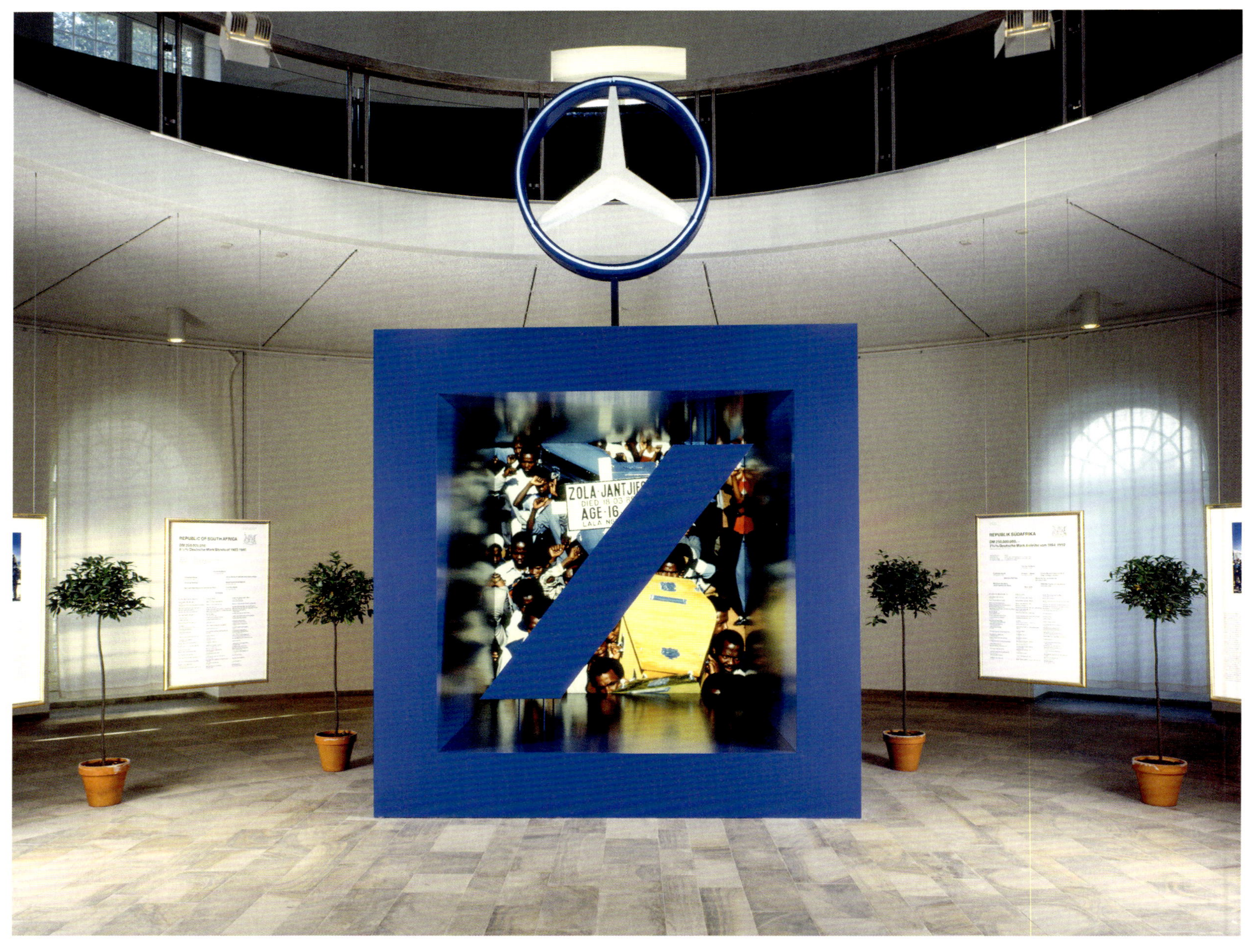

Fig. 1: Hans Haacke, *Continuity*, 1987, three-dimensional adaptation of the Deutsche Bank logo, rotating Mercedes star in neon, light box, color photography, neon lamp, 8 text and color photography panels, 6 laurel trees, installation at documenta 8, Kassel, 1987

Hans Haacke: Political Strategies and Timeless Critique

Vanessa Joan Müller

1
Hans Haacke: for real – Works 1959–2006, November 17, 2006, to February 4, 2007, Akademie der Künste, Berlin, and Deichtorhallen Hamburg.

2
This work title alludes to a *Volkslied* from 1840 called »Kein schöner Land in dieser Zeit« (No Country More Beautiful in This Time), which has long enjoyed popularity in German-speaking countries.

3
Haacke described *MoMA Poll* (1970) as his »first truly political work.« See Benjamin H. D. Buchloh, »Hans Haacke: Memory and Instrumental Reason,« *Art in America* (February 1988), p. 104.

On the occasion of his 2006 retrospective,[1] Hans Haacke covered the windows of the Academy of Arts in Berlin with digital prints bearing the names of forty-five migrants who had been murdered by neo-Nazis in reunified Germany between 1990 and 2006. Titled *Kein schöner Land – Weil sie nicht deutsch aussahen (No Country More Beautiful – Because They Didn't Look German),*[2] the work listed the age and country of birth of those killed, as well as the location, date, and manner of their murder: »beaten to death,« »stabbed,« »run over« (fig. 2). With its focus on facts, its solely textual argumentation, and its prominent positioning in public space, the work aimed not only at public commemoration, but also at debate and the political effects this can have in the public sphere.

Located at Pariser Platz, in the heart of Berlin's tourist district, the Academy of Arts became a resonant space for provoking reactions and triggering discussions in the contested field of the economy of attention. The institution's proximity to the Reichstag and its self-image as one of Europe's oldest cultural institutions provided an additional expanded context for driving home the facts of racism in Germany in its most brutal form, while at the same time prominently questioning the self-conception of the state and its population: Who and what counts as »German«? The last poster was only half as long as the others, thus conceptualizing the addition of potential future murders within the work.

Since 1970, Hans Haacke's political art practice has analyzed and exposed the relationships between art and ideology, as well as between political, institutional, and corporate power, especially when it comes to the economic and political foundation of institutions and social groups involved in the production and accumulation of cultural capital.[3] The fact-based aesthetics of his work—the effective collection and presentation of knowledge as ideological critique—has played a central role in the development of what we now call political art. For many activists, it became a model for visualizing their arguments. And yet, Haacke's art goes far beyond a committed foregrounding of the factual. By seizing on themes that seem predestined to provoke a strong public response, his works enter the sphere of political action: art becomes an amplifier

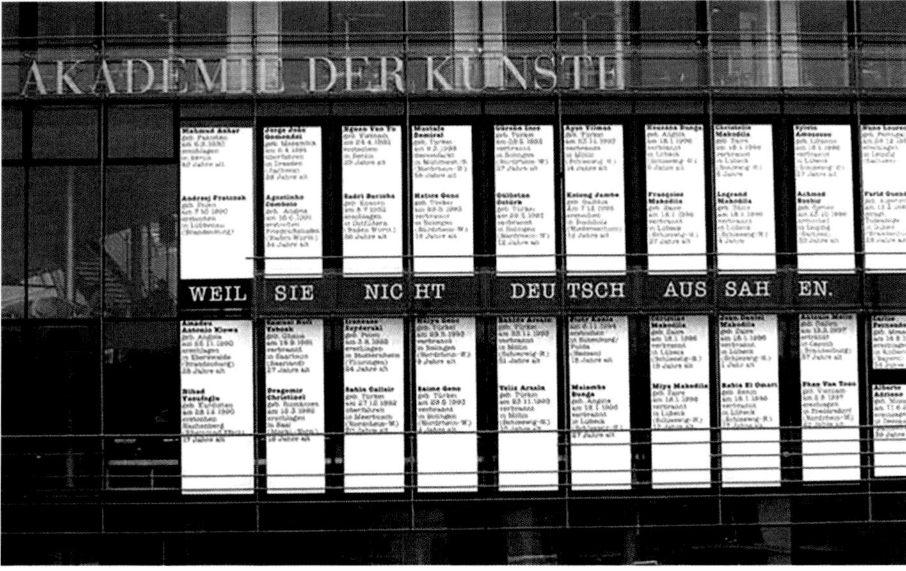

Fig. 2: Hans Haacke, *Kein schöner Land (No Country More Beautiful)*, 2006 (detail), courtesy the artist and Paula Cooper Gallery, New York

and resonating body for the artist's critical positioning in and toward the state-subsidized and/or corporate-sponsored art world, as well as a site for addressing political and social injustice, discrimination, and racism. Furthermore, Haacke's works examine the art world as an expansive social field with constantly shifting boundaries in terms of their potential to bring about social change.[4]

To this day, Haacke is concerned with demonstrating the »forms of domination that are exerted on the art world,«[5] as Pierre Bourdieu stated in his conversation with the artist, *Free Exchange* (1995), and the resulting feedback effects: art is not an isolated field, but responds to politics and society, just as these influence the production and reception of art. For Haacke, the artwork, along with its matter-of-fact, often textual form, functions within this constellation as a tool endowed with active agency; it is a communicator and a forcefully presented argument. It aims at public debate and the activation of the audience, at the enlightening visualization of relationships, and at a change in the viewer's consciousness.[6]

As work that manifests itself both materially and discursively, it is oriented to the context-specific situation in which it is viewed, absorbing the reactions it evokes, but is also dependent in its contingency on the viewing subject.[7] Its embedding in the larger ideological context—the ultimate goal of Haacke's analytical reflections on our present—takes place via nuanced references to the site and the exhibiting institution.

Particularly in his works for the various documentas, Haacke has used the sphere of international attention to make controversial statements. In his contribution to documenta 8 (1987), for example, he combatively criticized the sponsorship by certain German companies. In Kassel's Fridericianum, Germany's oldest public museum building, his installation *Continuity* merged the logos of Deutsche Bank and Daimler-

4
See Andrea Fraser, »From the Critique of Institutions to an Institution of Critique,« in *Hans Haacke: All Connected*, ed. Gary Carrion-Murayari and Massimiliano Gioni, exh. cat. New Museum, New York (New York: Phaidon, 2019), p. 157.

5
Pierre Bourdieu and Hans Haacke, *Free Exchange* (Cambridge: Polity Press, 1995), p. 1.

6
»Our social relations are structured and largely intelligible through verbal constructs.« Hans Haacke in conversation with Paul Taylor, *Flash Art* 126 (1986), https://flash---art.com/article/hans-haacke-2/.

7
See Rosalyn Deutsche, »Property Values: Hans Haacke, Real Estate, and the Museum,« in *Hans Haacke: Unfinished Business*, ed. Brian Wallis, exh. cat. New Museum, New York (Cambridge, MA, and London: The MIT Press, 1986), p. 23.

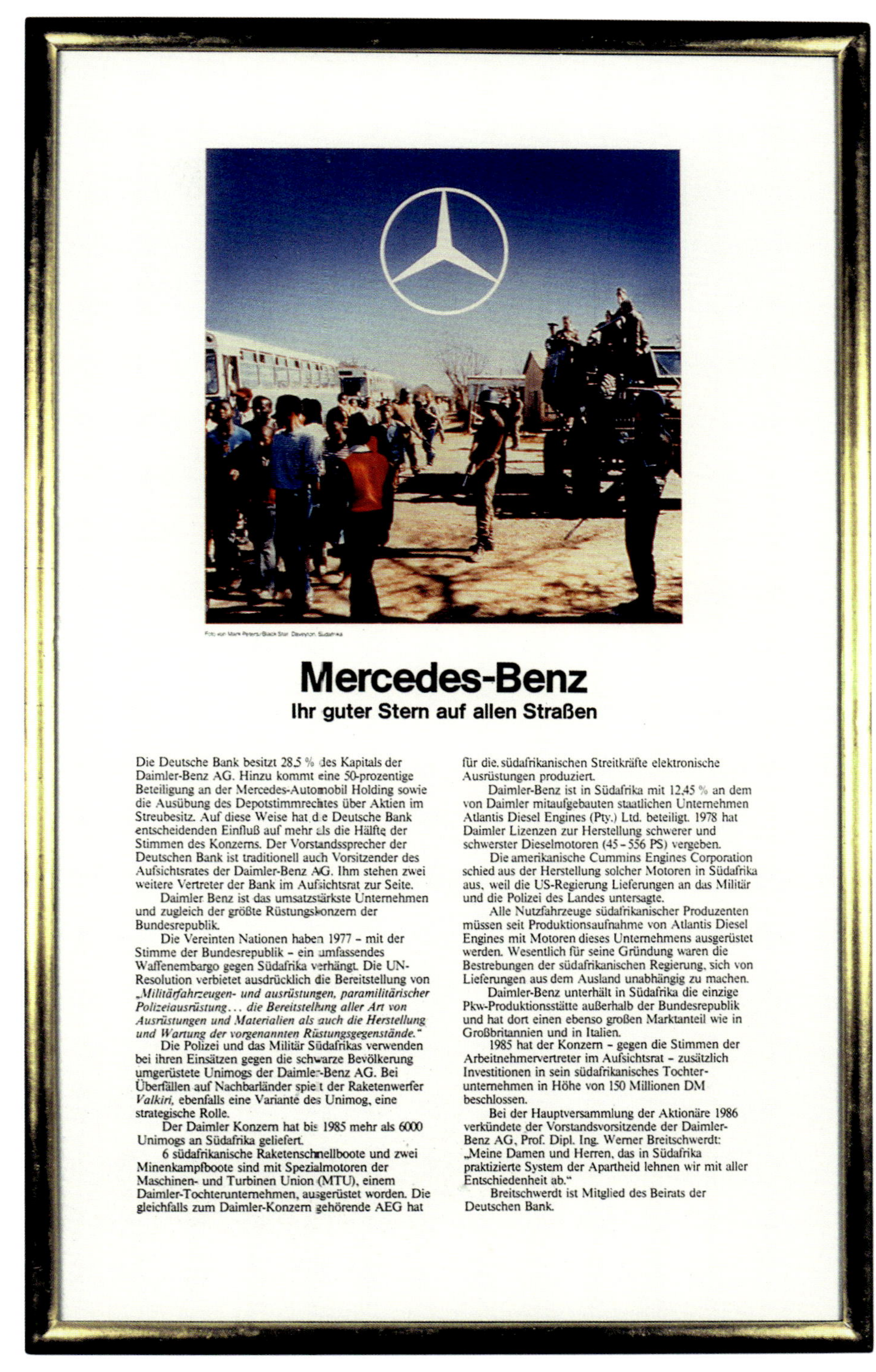

Mercedes-Benz

Ihr guter Stern auf allen Straßen

Die Deutsche Bank besitzt 28,5 % des Kapitals der Daimler-Benz AG. Hinzu kommt eine 50-prozentige Beteiligung an der Mercedes-Automobil Holding sowie die Ausübung des Depotstimmrechtes über Aktien im Streubesitz. Auf diese Weise hat die Deutsche Bank entscheidenden Einfluß auf mehr als die Hälfte der Stimmen des Konzerns. Der Vorstandssprecher der Deutschen Bank ist traditionell auch Vorsitzender des Aufsichtsrates der Daimler-Benz AG. Ihm stehen zwei weitere Vertreter der Bank im Aufsichtsrat zur Seite.

Daimler Benz ist das umsatzstärkste Unternehmen und zugleich der größte Rüstungskonzern der Bundesrepublik.

Die Vereinten Nationen haben 1977 – mit der Stimme der Bundesrepublik – ein umfassendes Waffenembargo gegen Südafrika verhängt. Die UN-Resolution verbietet ausdrücklich die Bereitstellung von *„Militärfahrzeugen- und ausrüstungen, paramilitärischer Polizeiausrüstung… die Bereitstellung aller Art von Ausrüstungen und Materialien als auch die Herstellung und Wartung der vorgenannten Rüstungsgegenstände."*

Die Polizei und das Militär Südafrikas verwenden bei ihren Einsätzen gegen die schwarze Bevölkerung umgerüstete Unimogs der Daimler-Benz AG. Bei Überfällen auf Nachbarländer spielt der Raketenwerfer *Valkiri,* ebenfalls eine Variante des Unimog, eine strategische Rolle.

Der Daimler Konzern hat bis 1985 mehr als 6000 Unimogs an Südafrika geliefert.

6 südafrikanische Raketenschnellboote und zwei Minenkampfboote sind mit Spezialmotoren der Maschinen- und Turbinen Union (MTU), einem Daimler-Tochterunternehmen, ausgerüstet worden. Die gleichfalls zum Daimler-Konzern gehörende AEG hat für die südafrikanischen Streitkräfte elektronische Ausrüstungen produziert.

Daimler-Benz ist in Südafrika mit 12,45 % an dem von Daimler mitaufgebauten staatlichen Unternehmen Atlantis Diesel Engines (Pty.) Ltd. beteiligt. 1978 hat Daimler Lizenzen zur Herstellung schwerer und schwerster Dieselmotoren (45 – 556 PS) vergeben.

Die amerikanische Cummins Engines Corporation schied aus der Herstellung solcher Motoren in Südafrika aus, weil die US-Regierung Lieferungen an das Militär und die Polizei des Landes untersagte.

Alle Nutzfahrzeuge südafrikanischer Produzenten müssen seit Produktionsaufnahme von Atlantis Diesel Engines mit Motoren dieses Unternehmens ausgerüstet werden. Wesentlich für seine Gründung waren die Bestrebungen der südafrikanischen Regierung, sich von Lieferungen aus dem Ausland unabhängig zu machen.

Daimler-Benz unterhält in Südafrika die einzige Pkw-Produktionsstätte außerhalb der Bundesrepublik und hat dort einen ebenso großen Marktanteil wie in Großbritannien und in Italien.

1985 hat der Konzern – gegen die Stimmen der Arbeitnehmervertreter im Aufsichtsrat – zusätzlich Investitionen in sein südafrikanisches Tochterunternehmen in Höhe von 150 Millionen DM beschlossen.

Bei der Hauptversammlung der Aktionäre 1986 verkündete der Vorstandsvorsitzende der Daimler-Benz AG, Prof. Dipl. Ing. Werner Breitschwerdt: „Meine Damen und Herren, das in Südafrika praktizierte System der Apartheid lehnen wir mit aller Entschiedenheit ab."

Breitschwerdt ist Mitglied des Beirats der Deutschen Bank.

Fig. 3: Hans Haacke, *Continuity*, 1987 (detail)

Benz—both prominently involved in art sponsorship during the 1980s—into a symbol of unscrupulous economic interests (fig. 1). The Mercedes star revolved above the bank's logo, which was underlain with a photo of a mass burial of victims of police violence in South Africa. Next to it, framed text and image panels listed both companies' political and economic ties to National Socialism as well as to the South African apartheid regime (figs. 3 and 4).

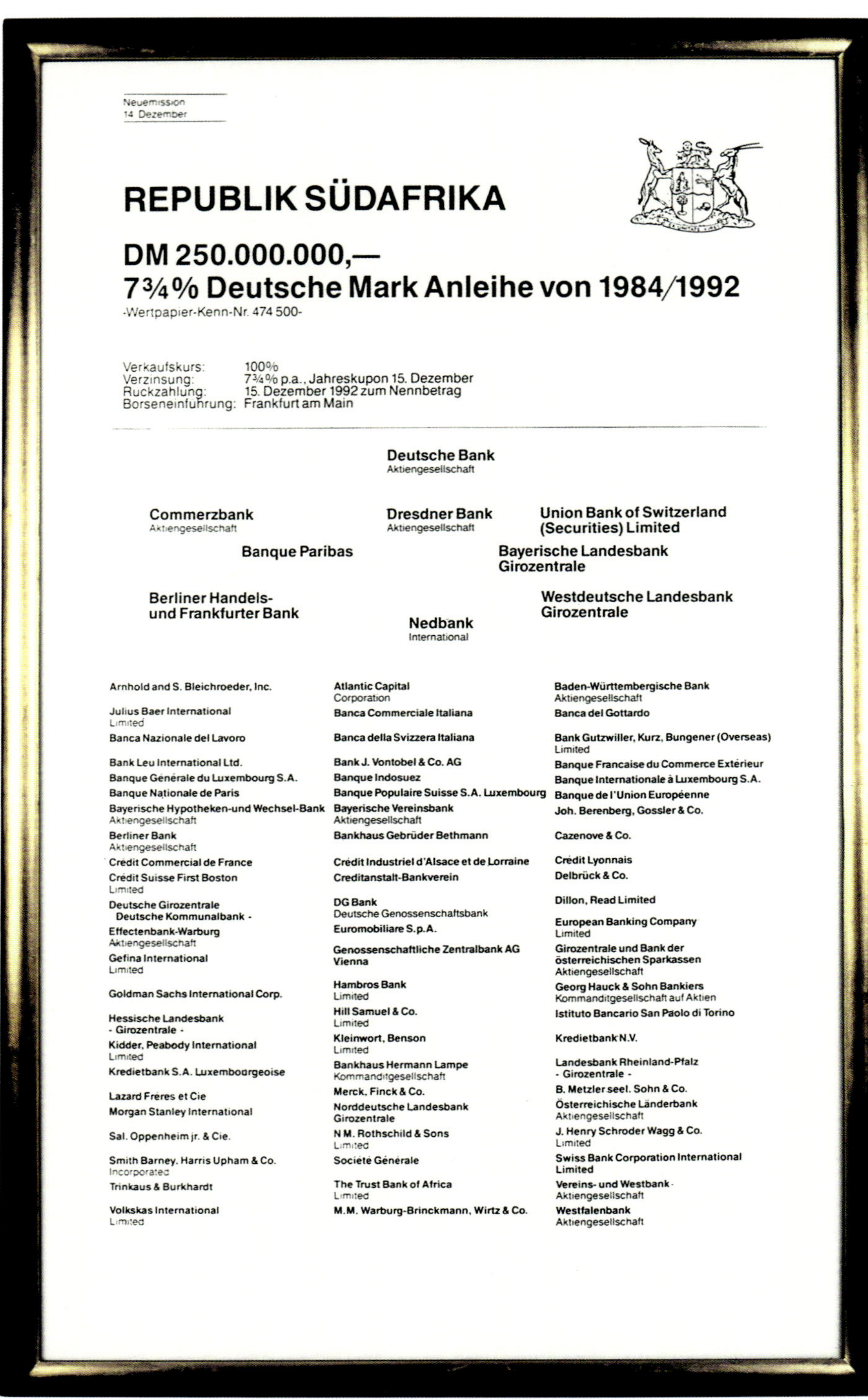

Neuemission
14 Dezember

REPUBLIK SÜDAFRIKA

DM 250.000.000,—
7¾% Deutsche Mark Anleihe von 1984/1992
-Wertpapier-Kenn-Nr. 474 500-

Verkaufskurs: 100%
Verzinsung: 7¾% p.a., Jahreskupon 15. Dezember
Ruckzahlung: 15. Dezember 1992 zum Nennbetrag
Borseneinfuhrung: Frankfurt am Main

Deutsche Bank
Aktiengesellschaft

Commerzbank
Aktiengesellschaft

Dresdner Bank
Aktiengesellschaft

Union Bank of Switzerland (Securities) Limited

Banque Paribas

Bayerische Landesbank Girozentrale

Berliner Handels- und Frankfurter Bank

Nedbank
International

Westdeutsche Landesbank Girozentrale

Arnhold and S. Bleichroeder, Inc.
Julius Baer International Limited
Banca Nazionale del Lavoro
Bank Leu International Ltd.
Banque Générale du Luxembourg S.A.
Banque Nationale de Paris
Bayerische Hypotheken-und Wechsel-Bank Aktiengesellschaft
Berliner Bank Aktiengesellschaft
Crédit Commercial de France
Crédit Suisse First Boston Limited
Deutsche Girozentrale - Deutsche Kommunalbank -
Effectenbank-Warburg Aktiengesellschaft
Gefina International Limited
Goldman Sachs International Corp.
Hessische Landesbank - Girozentrale -
Kidder, Peabody International Limited
Kredietbank S.A. Luxembourgeoise
Lazard Frères et Cie
Morgan Stanley International
Sal. Oppenheim jr. & Cie.
Smith Barney, Harris Upham & Co. Incorporated
Trinkaus & Burkhardt
Volkskas International Limited

Atlantic Capital Corporation
Banca Commerciale Italiana
Banca della Svizzera Italiana
Bank J. Vontobel & Co. AG
Banque Indosuez
Banque Populaire Suisse S.A. Luxembourg
Bayerische Vereinsbank Aktiengesellschaft
Bankhaus Gebrüder Bethmann
Crédit Industriel d'Alsace et de Lorraine
Creditanstalt-Bankverein
DG Bank Deutsche Genossenschaftsbank
Euromobiliare S.p.A.
Genossenschaftliche Zentralbank AG Vienna
Hambros Bank Limited
Hill Samuel & Co. Limited
Kleinwort, Benson Limited
Bankhaus Hermann Lampe Kommanditgesellschaft
Merck, Finck & Co.
Norddeutsche Landesbank Girozentrale
N M. Rothschild & Sons Limited
Société Générale
The Trust Bank of Africa Limited
M.M. Warburg-Brinckmann, Wirtz & Co.

Baden-Württembergische Bank Aktiengesellschaft
Banca del Gottardo
Bank Gutzwiller, Kurz, Bungener (Overseas) Limited
Banque Francaise du Commerce Extérieur
Banque Internationale à Luxembourg S.A.
Banque de l'Union Européenne
Joh. Berenberg, Gossler & Co.
Cazenove & Co.
Crédit Lyonnais
Delbrück & Co.
Dillon, Read Limited
European Banking Company Limited
Girozentrale und Bank der österreichischen Sparkassen Aktiengesellschaft
Georg Hauck & Sohn Bankiers Kommanditgesellschaft auf Aktien
Istituto Bancario San Paolo di Torino
Kredietbank N.V.
Landesbank Rheinland-Pfalz - Girozentrale -
B. Metzler seel. Sohn & Co.
Österreichische Länderbank Aktiengesellschaft
J. Henry Schroder Wagg & Co. Limited
Swiss Bank Corporation International Limited
Vereins- und Westbank Aktiengesellschaft
Westfalenbank Aktiengesellschaft

Fig. 4: Hans Haacke, *Continuity*, 1987 (detail)

As early as 1985, Haacke publicized Mobil's equipping of the South African police and military in his installation *MetroMobiltan* (fig. 5). At the time, Mobil was the sponsor of numerous exhibitions, including those at The Metropolitan Museum of Art in New York. Four years later, on Munich's Königsplatz, he had flags raised, listing the names of companies directly or indirectly involved in the Persian Gulf War (*Raise the Flag*, 1991). The respective formal languages that Haacke chooses—the aesthetics of advertising displays with large-format photographs or the flying of flags in public spaces—rely on an adaptation of the familiar, but also on a hard cut as to the realities evoked.

8 In 1998, the German Bundestag invited Haacke to propose a site-specific project for the Reichstag building. The Art Advisory Council's decision to accept his design triggered a heated discussion spanning all political parties, which led to the highly unusual procedure of having members of the Bundestag make the final decision on the art project. See »Der Bevölkerung: Ein Faxinterview von Astrid Wege mit Hans Haacke,« 2000, https://derbevoelkerung.de/faxinterview/.

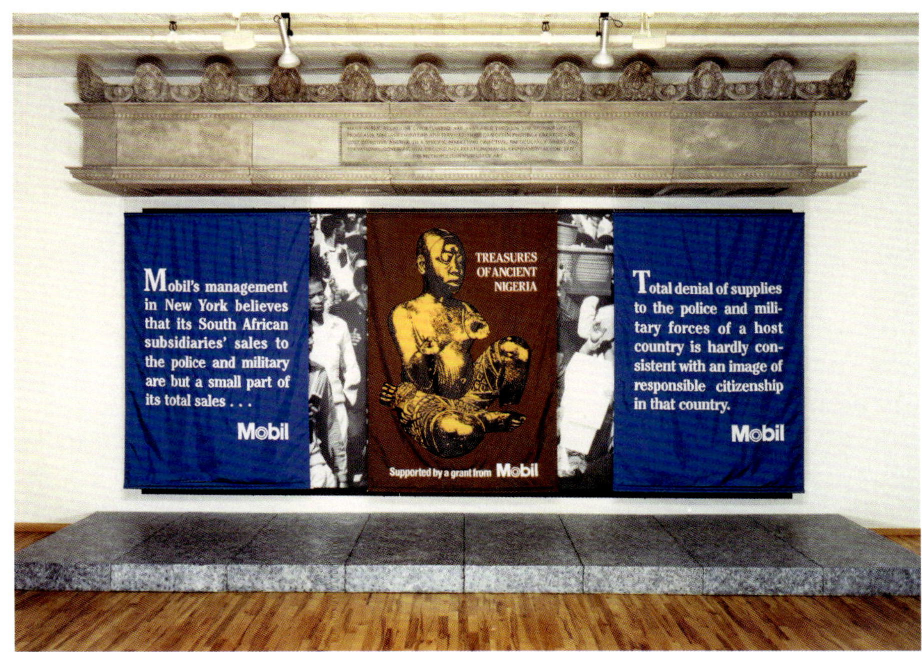

Fig. 5: Hans Haacke, *MetroMobiltan*, 1985, fiberglass construction, three fabric banners, photograph, 355.6 × 609.6 × 152.4 cm, MNAM Centre Georges Pompidou, Paris

It was at Pariser Platz that Haacke decisively presented his aforementioned reference to the growing racism and violence against migrants, where the National Socialists marched through the Brandenburg Gate in 1933 after Hitler seized power. In the entrance hall of the Academy of Arts, he confronted the audience with a monumentally enlarged photograph of a historical doll from London's Museum of Childhood (today, the Young V&A), a so-called interchangeable doll with two heads and two sets of limbs, one brown and one white, so that it can be assembled »flexibly.« This dialectical collage of inside and outside work deepened the connection between the recent victims of anti-migrant violence and historical racisms stemming from colonialism and National Socialism. At the same time, the juxtaposition pointed back to the vehement debate on citizenship and belonging that Haacke had initiated with his project for the Reichstag.

DER BEVÖLKERUNG

For the artist, *Kein schöner Land* was the final chapter of his work *DER BEVÖLKERUNG (TO THE POPULATION)* (2000) for the nearby Reichstag. *DER BEVÖLKERUNG* translates the essence of German democracy and the community it represents into a performative sculptural work that reflects the changing sense of identity in the German nation. It sets the inclusive phrasing »der Bevölkerung« (referencing the population) against the exclusionary semantics of the concept of »das Volk« (referencing the national ethnic group) that ties citizenship to the hereditary principle of jus sanguinis, that is, citizenship by blood.[8]

By inviting all members of parliament to bring 50 kilograms of soil from their constituency and place it in a large trough where the respective seeds and roots can grow freely without any horticultural intervention, Haacke correlated plant growth and legislative periods of the Bundestag and transferred the concept of entropy to the dynamics of parliamentary democracy. According to Gloria Sutton, the resulting biological diversity undermines the »dehumanization of ›foreign bodies‹ with biological contagions and underscores ideologies of disease and racialization that are bound up with both blood and soil.«[9] Some members of parliament brought soil from sites of xenophobic violence to Berlin; the then speaker of the Bundestag, Wolfgang Thierse, brought soil from the Jewish cemetery of the Berlin district he represented.

In the planted trough, Haacke placed the words »DER BEVÖLKERUNG,« which shine upward in white neon letters using the same font that Peter Behrens had designed for the inscription »DEM DEUTSCHEN VOLKE« (TO THE GERMAN PEOPLE) on the gable of the Reichstag building in 1916. Inspired by Bertolt Brecht's »Writing the Truth: Five Difficulties,« an essay he wrote while fleeing the Nazis in 1934 (»anyone who says population in place of people or race . . . is by that simple act withdrawing his support from a great many lies.«), Haacke argues for a historical contextualization of the term *Volk*. He points to the relationship and semantic differences between the two terms, with the once progressive, republican interpretation of »the people« overshadowed by nationalist appropriations: »The inscription on the Reichstag building does not inoculate itself against . . . an exclusively German nationalist interpretation.«[10]

Haacke's poster project *We (All) Are the People* (fig. p. 235) can also be read as a reaction to this rampant hostility toward migration in recent decades. Created for documenta 14 (2017) in Kassel and Athens, and having been shown many times since, it uses a text-based, easily accessible »information aesthetic« for the thousands of posters hung in public spaces. They repeat the slogan »We (all) are the people« in twelve different languages, from German and English to the languages of the major migrant groups in the respective country. While the posters' rainbow-colored background might suggest a celebration of cultural diversity, the text is an appropriation of the slogan »We are the people,« which was chanted during the mass protests of 1989 that finally led to the end of the East German regime of the German Democratic Republic (GDR).

In 2003, when Haacke was invited to submit a project proposal for the commemoration of the 1989 uprising that had begun at the Nikolaikirche in Leipzig, his idea was to project »We (all) are the people« onto the facade of the church, thus detaching the anniversary of the fall of the GDR regime from all national boundaries. After the right-wing, anti-migrant PEGIDA movement began chanting the slogan about ten years later, he used multilingualism to counter the slogan's contextual investment in nationalist ideas. In its inclusive address, the poster takes a clear stance: it not only reclaims public space, but unites us and all those not represented in a collective social »we.«

9
Gloria Sutton, »Hans Haacke: Works of Art, 1963–72,« in Carrion-Murayari and Gioni, *Hans Haacke: All Connected*, p. 15.

10
Quoted from Wege and Haacke, »Der Bevölkerung: Ein Faxinterview.«

11
See Sam Durant, »Hans Haacke and the Faces of Neoliberalism,« in Carrion-Murayari and Gioni, *Hans Haacke: All Connected*, p. 210.

12
See Susanne König, *Marcel Broodthaers: Musée d'Art Moderne, Département des Aigles* (Berlin: Dietrich Reimer Verlag, 2012).

Timeless Critique

Seen from the present, Haacke's older works that directly responded to current social and/or political upheavals may seem to have lost some of their immediate instigative power. However, as their once topical urgency fades, their principle of dialectical montage and their overall institution-critical approach, as well as the fundamental and thus timeless critique they articulate, come to the fore. Haacke analyzed the system of art not only on an institutional level, but also in its forms of representation, emphasizing the impossibility of separating rhetorical and aesthetic strategies from the ideological interests they are embedded in.

At documenta 7, the artist, who had long rejected any form of pictorial representation, showed *Oil Painting: Homage to Marcel Broodthaers* (1982, figs. pp. 165–67), a self-painted portrait of then US President Ronald Reagan inspired by Hans Holbein the Younger's Renaissance portraits.[11] Displayed in a golden frame with an engraved brass plaque and barrier cord, the work underscored its claim to stately representation. On the opposite side, however, a red carpet led to a black-and-white slide that was enlarged into photo wallpaper. It documented the massive anti-Reagan demonstration in Bonn that had taken place just a week before documenta opened.

The reason for the demonstration was Reagan's participation in a NATO summit conference in Bonn and his speech to the Bundestag, in which he advocated the stationing of cruise and Pershing II missiles in Germany. Haacke structured his commentary on the events as a strict dichotomy: on the one hand, the exaggerated rhetoric of realist painting, on the other, factual photography. Reminiscences of art history meet the documentation of contemporary history, and the original in oil meets the technologically reproducible photograph. By enlarging the photograph into a history painting, Haacke positions those themes that will be significant in the future within the museum context: the protesting masses and their resistance.

Haacke's commitment to documenting dissident reality was also conceived as a critique of the dominance of painterly positions within Rudi Fuchs's documenta curatorship and its affirmation of a capital-driven art business. The title of the work is another reference to the role of art in the service of state representation and authoritarian demonstrations of power. In his institution-critical museum fiction *Museum of Modern Art, Department of Eagles*, founded in Brussels in 1968, Marcel Broodthaers took up the titular bird of prey and the symbolism of domination associated with it. In an ever-changing sequence of »museum departments,« he deconstructed these in an excessively repetitive gesture of showing.[12]

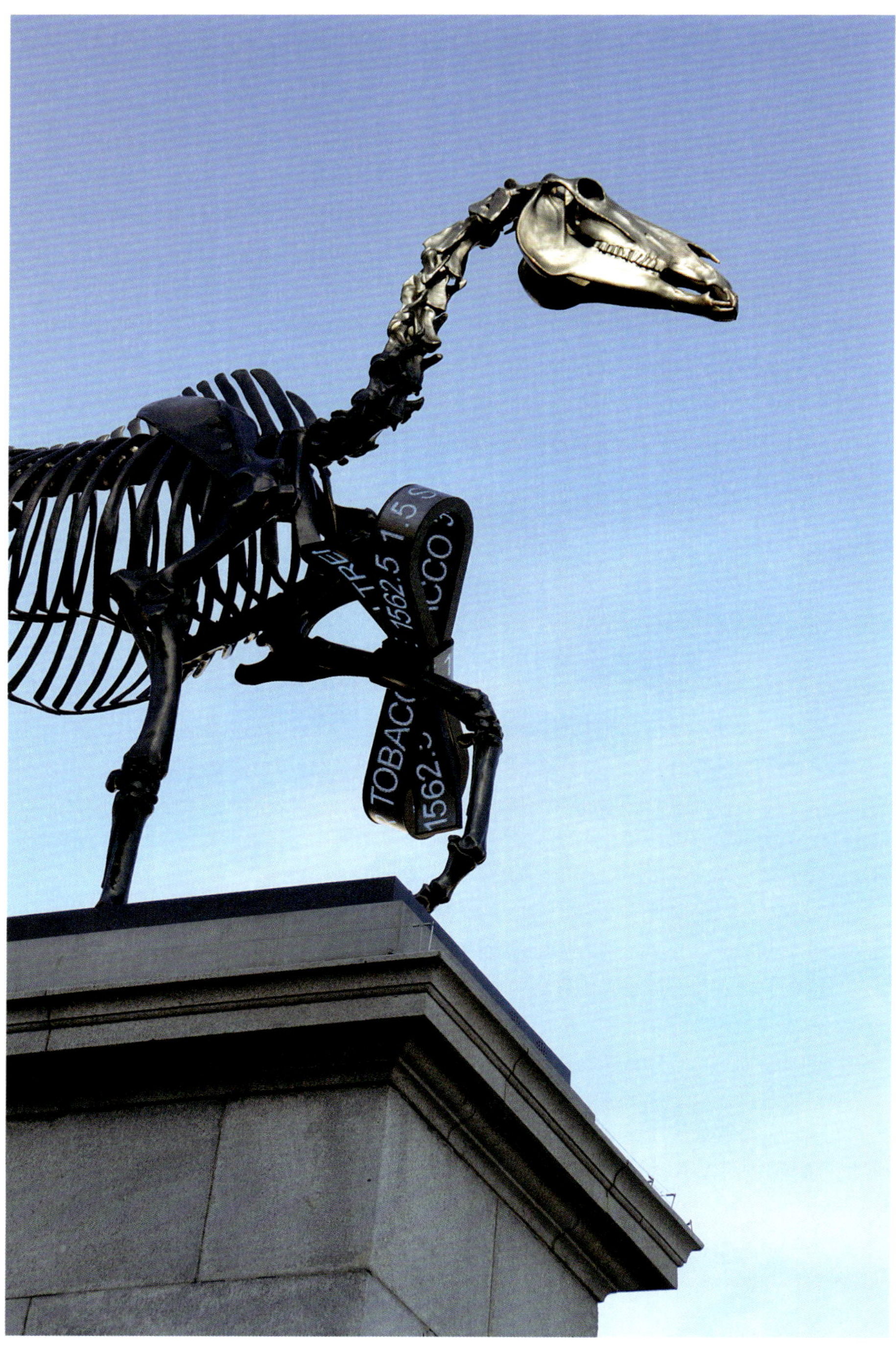

Fig. 6: Hans Haacke, *Gift Horse*, 2014, installation view Fourth Plinth, Trafalgar Square, London 2015–2016

Gift Horse

Haacke's continuity in pursuing his concerns while activating a wide variety of aesthetic processes becomes evident in *Gift Horse* (fig. 6, figs. pp. 231–33), created as recently as 2014, in its referencing of imperial forms of representation. Haacke presented a bronze horse skeleton on the fourth column in London's Trafalgar Square, still a symbolic site for both historical and contemporary power. The square's design around Admiral Nelson's victory column is dominated by three corner statues, yet the fourth plinth remained empty and has been used for a public arts program since 1999.

13
See Haus der Kunst, »Hans Haacke: Gift Horse,« https://www.hausderkunst.de/eintauchen/hans-haacke-gift-horse.

14
Ibid.

15
Taking Stock (unfinished) is an allusive allegory that also addresses the entanglements of Thatcher's election campaigns and the Saatchi & Saatchi advertising agency, known for its strategic collection of British contemporary art.

16
»Unveiling: Hans Haacke Gift Horse Replaces Blue Cockerel On Fourth Plinth,« *Artlyst*, March 2, 2015. Quoted from Onna Rageth, »Hans Haacke's GIFT HORSE: Zur Ausstellung, Konstruktion und Rezeption eines ›Gegen-Denkmals‹ des kapitalistischen Finanzsystems« (bachelor's thesis, University of Zurich, 2015).

17
When presented at other locations, the ticker shows the stock prices of the nearest stock exchange.

Haacke's horse skeleton is based on an etching by the English painter George Stubbs (1724–1806), but its foreleg is adorned with a bow-shaped ticker that displays the London Stock Exchange's stock prices in real time. *Gift Horse* refers in a multilayered way to the symbolic content and semantics of its surroundings, as well as to the historical and contemporary function of the square in creating identity and identification. It draws on an equestrian statue of King William IV that was originally intended for the plinth, but also forms a striking contrast to the existing equestrian statue of George IV.

In taking George Stubbs's anatomical drawing as a template, Haacke establishes a connection to his painting of a rearing Arabian stallion, which was commissioned by its enormously wealthy owner Charles Watson-Wentworth, second Marquess of Rockingham, Whig, and two-time Prime Minister.[13] The painting hangs in the National Gallery, also on Trafalgar Square. Described by Haacke as a »tribute to the City, the Wall Street of London,«[14] his »gift horse« decorated with a bow-shaped stock ticker is a symbol of a society that for centuries has been marked by class antagonisms and largely subjugated to the dictates of the market.

Haacke's criticism of the protagonists of state-enforced neoliberalism—Ronald Reagan and Margaret Thatcher—already articulated in *Oil Painting* and continued in its »counterpart,« the painting *Taking Stock (unfinished)* (1983–84, fig. p. 169),[15] resurfaces in the artist's allusion to Adam Smith (1723–1790). Smith's book *The Wealth of Nations* coined the idea of the »invisible hand of the market« as the source of general prosperity. »What happens if the invisible hand of the market ties the knot for us?,« asks Haacke, referring to social inequality fueled by capital gains.[16] *Gift Horse* materializes speculative, fluid financial market capital and, as a »counter-monument,« resists the pathos and symbolism of the other statues in Trafalgar Square, transforming them into the framework within which Haacke's work unfolds its subversive potential.

On the other hand, when the context-specific sculpture is presented elsewhere,[17] it is also removed from these layers of meaning—for Haacke, the artwork ultimately remains autonomous despite its resonance with the respective institutional framework. It then appears to have a hybrid temporality between a past laying claim to eternity and an accelerated present. Global capitalism pulsates in the ticker of stock prices, but *Gift Horse* is anchored in the here and now: a catalyst for our reactions, perhaps a Trojan horse.

Standortkultur (Corporate Culture), 1997

Hilmar Kopper, Deutsche Bank: »Whoever gives the money is in control.«

Hans J. Baumgart, Daimler-Benz: »Sponsoring is strategically used to build our image and public sympathy.«

Hagen Gmelin, Deutsche Telekom: »It serves to reach target groups who are otherwise reluctant to engage with traditional advertising.«

Peter Littmann, Hugo Boss: »We aren't philanthropists. We need to get something out of the money we're spending. And in the end we do.«

Raymond D'Argenio, Mobil Oil: »These programs build enough acceptance to allow us to get tough on substantive issues.«

The Metropolitan Museum, New York: »These can often provide a creative and cost effective answer to a specific marketing objective, particularly where international, governmental or consumer relations may be a fundamental concern.«

Alain-Dominique Perrin, Cartier: »It is a tool for the seduction of public opinion.«

PHILIPPE DE MONTEBELLO, METROPOLITAN MUSEUM: »IT'S AN INHERENT, INSIDIOUS, HIDDEN FORM OF CENSORSHIP.«

For the opening of documenta 10, posters were temporarily installed on advertising columns operated by Deutsche Städte Reklame GmBH in Berlin, Bonn, Bremen, Dresden, Düsseldorf, Frankfurt am Main, Hamburg, Hannover, Kassel, and Leipzig. In Kassel, they additionally appeared on surfaces operated by Deutsche Bahn. Posters also appeared in Vienna and Zurich.

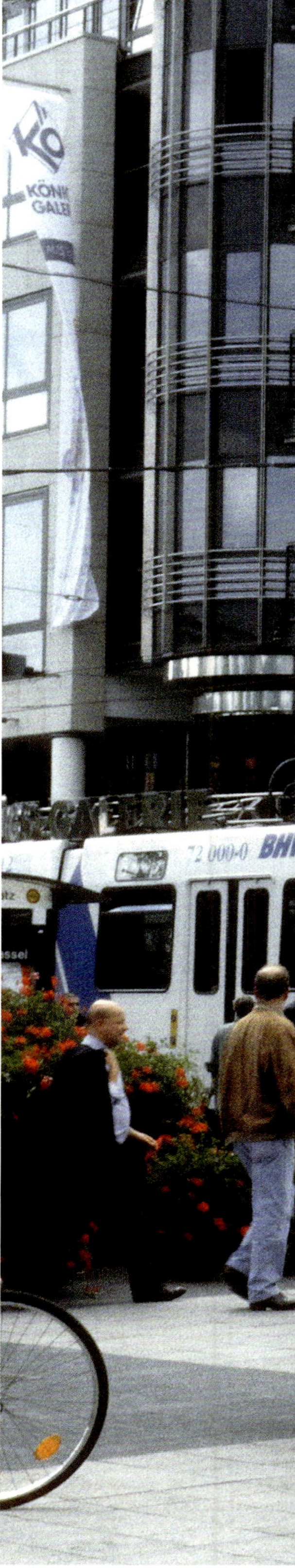

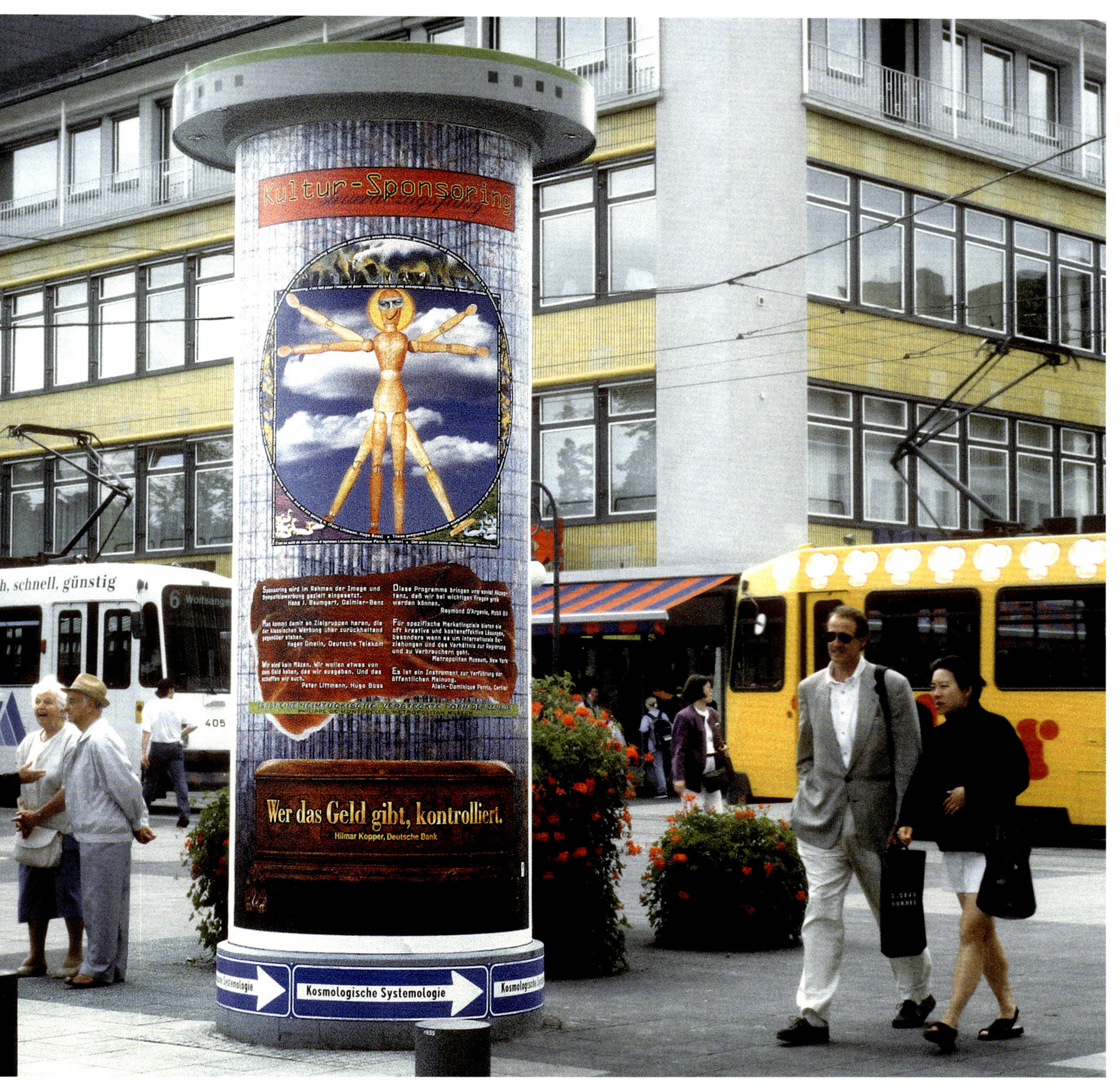

Standortkultur (Corporate Culture), 1997
Installation view documenta 10, Friedrichsplatz, Kassel, 1997

DER BEVÖLKERUNG (TO THE POPULATION), 2000

White neon letters beam the words »DER BEVÖLKERUNG« (TO THE POPULATION) upward toward the sky from the center of the northern courtyard of the Reichstag building. The letters, 47 inches (1.2 meters) high, lie on the ground along the courtyard's longitudinal axis. When viewed from the Assembly Hall, they are read from west to east. Visitors on the roof of the building can see the illuminated letters on the floor of the courtyard. The typeface is the same as that of the inscription »DEM DEUTSCHEN VOLKE« (TO THE GERMAN PEOPLE) above the west gate of the Reichstag building.

Members of the Bundestag are invited to bring approximately 100 pounds (50 kilograms) of soil from their election districts to the courtyard. The soil comes from 669 different regions of the Federal Republic (the current number of deputies) and is deposited into a wooden trough around the neon letters.

Seeds and roots are naturally embedded in the soil from their respective places of origin and left to sprout, as are airborne seeds from Berlin. They develop freely, without tending. When legislators leave parliament, a portion of soil commensurate with their contribution is removed. Newly elected members of the Bundestag, in turn, are invited to contribute to the soil in the courtyard and, in so doing, to the vegetation.

The process of plant growth and the ongoing addition and removal of soil, corresponding to the rhythm of the parliament terms, continue as long as democratically elected legislators meet in the Reichstag building.

Panels are installed at locations from which the words »DER BEVÖLKERUNG« can be seen: in the Assembly Hall, on the press floor, and in public areas on the roof. Listed on these panels are the names of all of the members of Parliament with their party affiliations and the districts and states they represent. The panels also provide concise information on the conceptual references of the lettering, the process of plant growth, and the dates on which members contributed soil. At the beginning of each legislative term, the panels are replaced so that they reflect the changed membership of the Bundestag.

In order to assure the highest possible public accessibility, this information, together with a current photograph of the courtyard, is posted on a website established for this purpose. A webcam overlooking the courtyard from a fixed position is programmed to take a photograph at 2 p.m. and 8 p.m., with the images saved on an ongoing basis. The site is updated daily. Thus, a databank develops with a constantly expanding picture archive, which allows the tracking of changes in the courtyard, compressed as if in a time-lapse recording.

A link on the website provides the legislators who have contributed soil to the courtyard an opportunity to present their own texts and images. Objects not intrinsic to the project are excluded from the courtyard.

Hans Haacke, October 1999

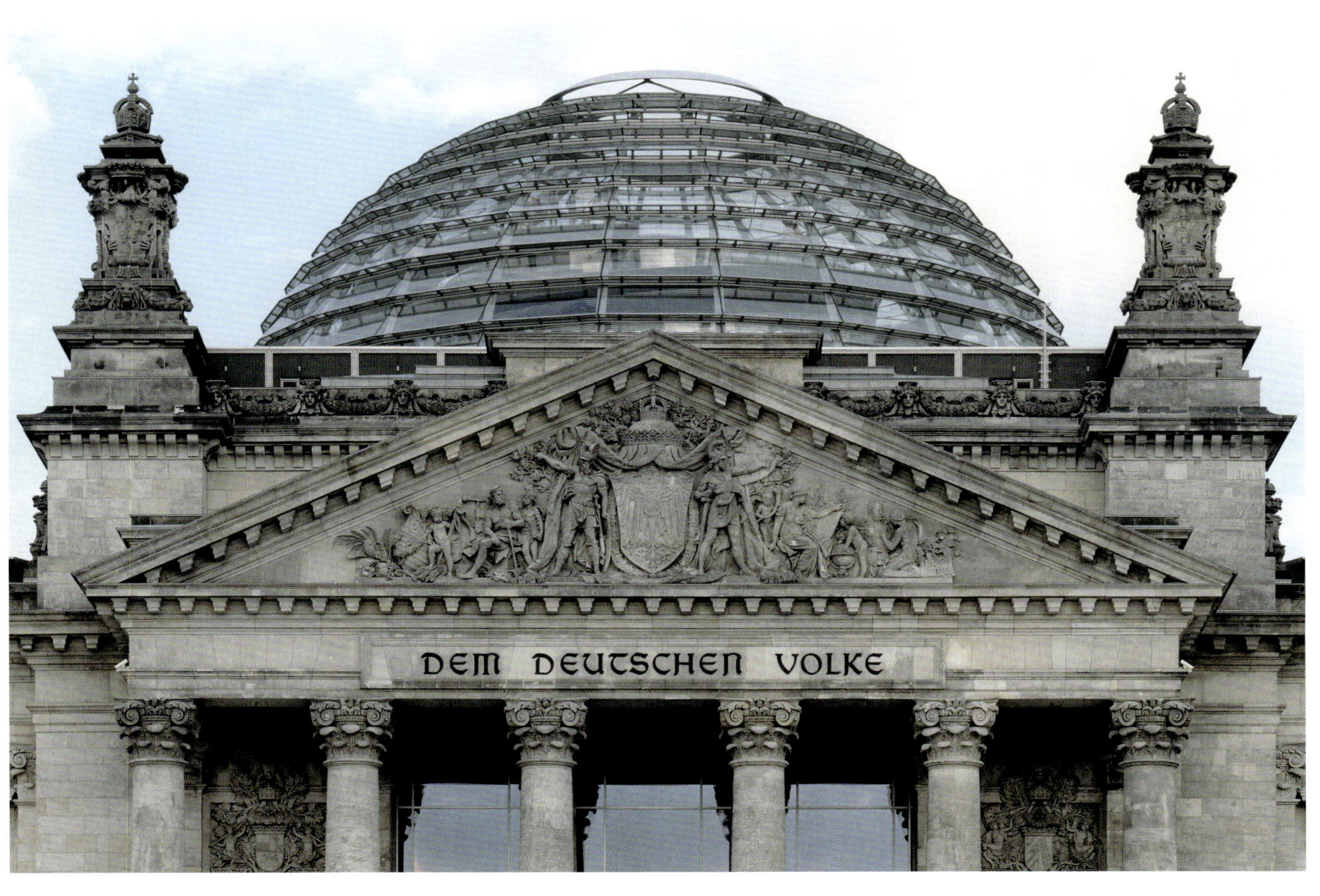

Reichstag building, Berlin

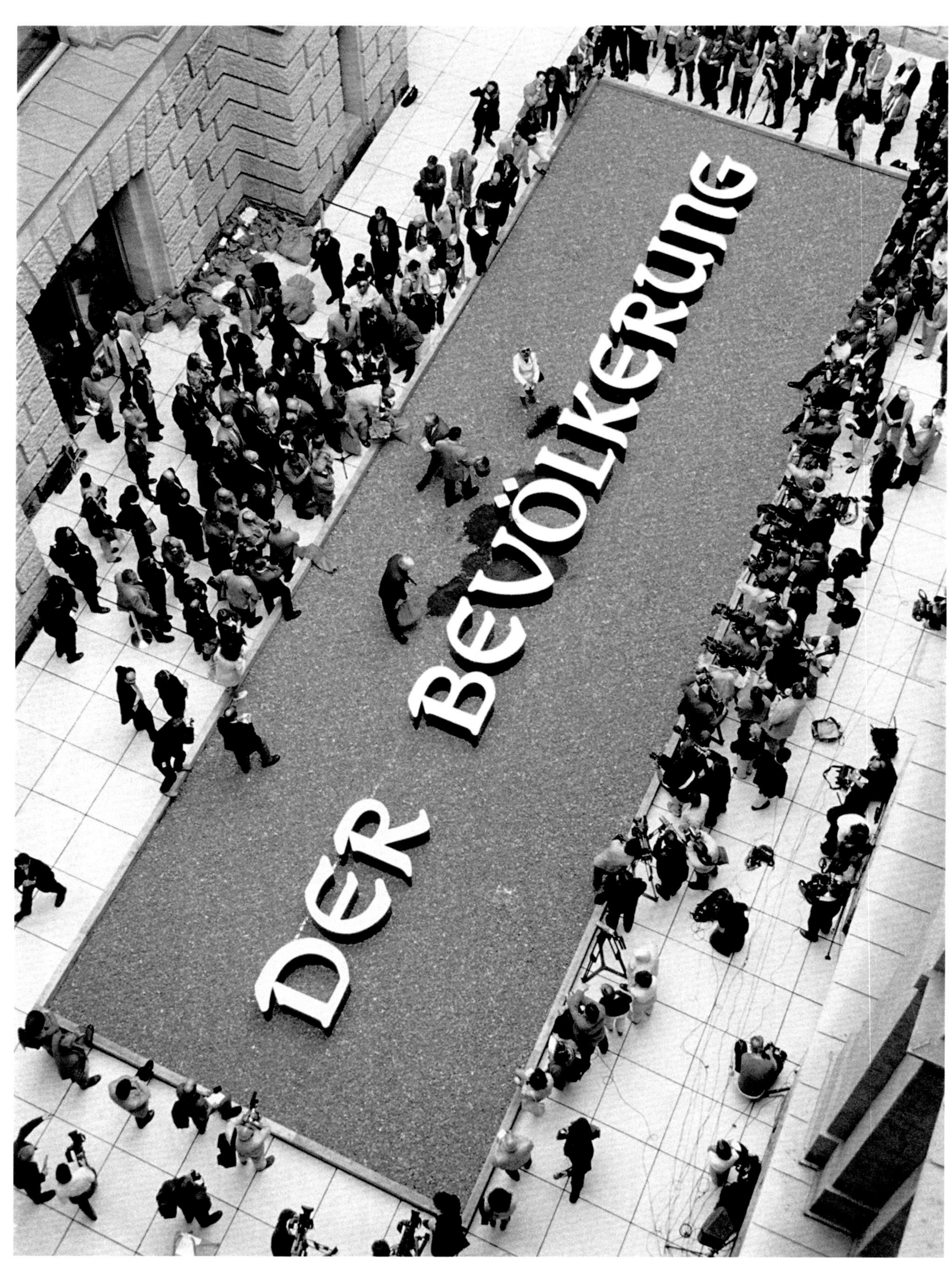

September 12, 2000: Inauguration of the art project
DER BEVÖLKERUNG (TO THE POPULATION) in the northern atrium of
the Reichstag building in Berlin

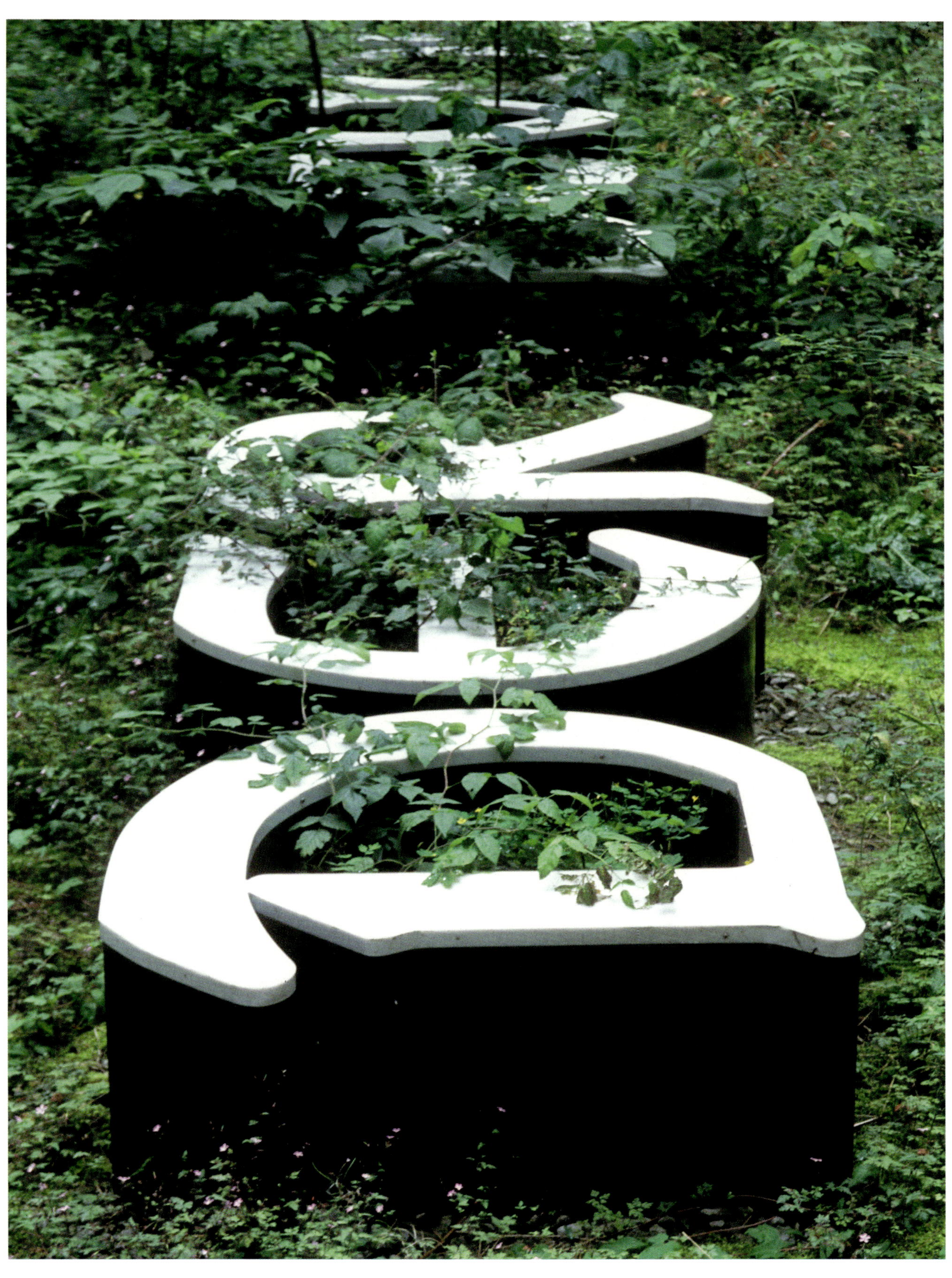

View of the installation *DER BEVÖLKERUNG (TO THE POPULATION)*
in the northern atrium of the Reichstag building in Berlin, 2008

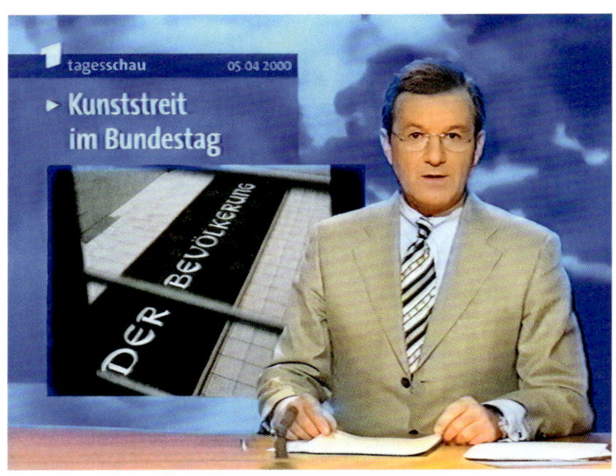

Report »Art Controversy in the Bundestag« on *tagesschau*, ARD, April 5, 2000

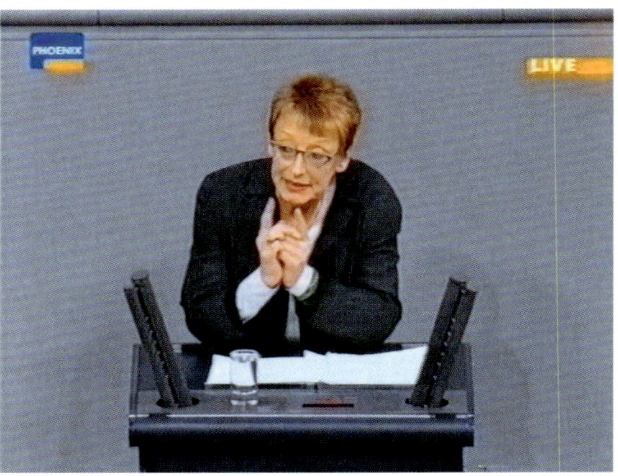

Franziska Eichstädt-Bohlig, Alliance 90/Greens

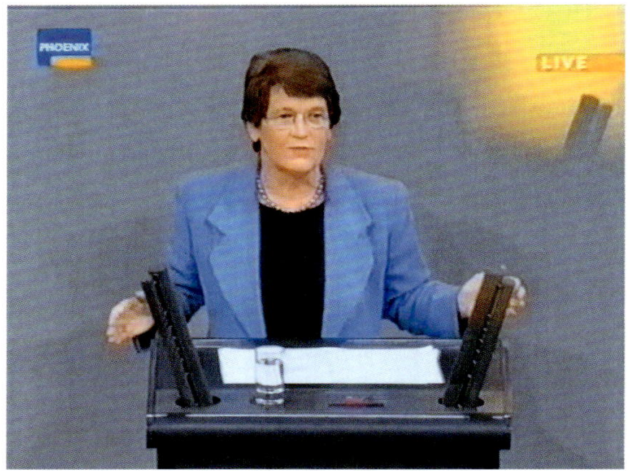

Rita Süssmuth, CDU/CSU

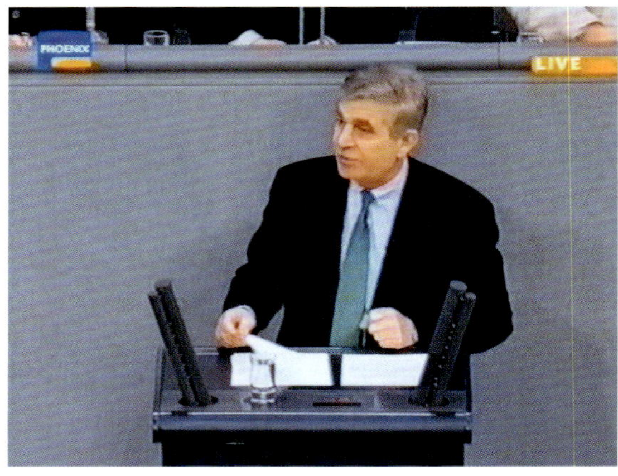

Ulrich Heinrich, FDP

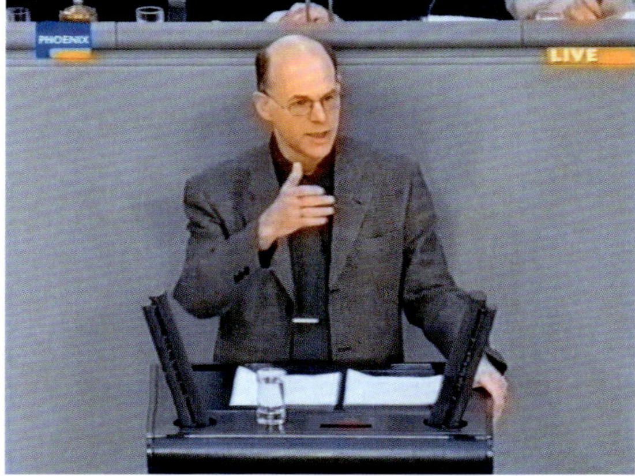

Norbert Lammert, CDU/CSU

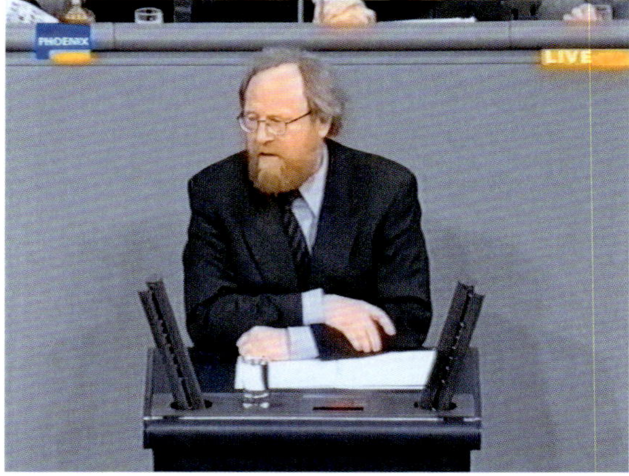

Wolfgang Thierse, SPD

Debate in the German Bundestag on April 5, 2000, before the roll-call vote on the art project *DER BEVÖLKERUNG* by Hans Haacke in the northern atrium of the Reichstag building

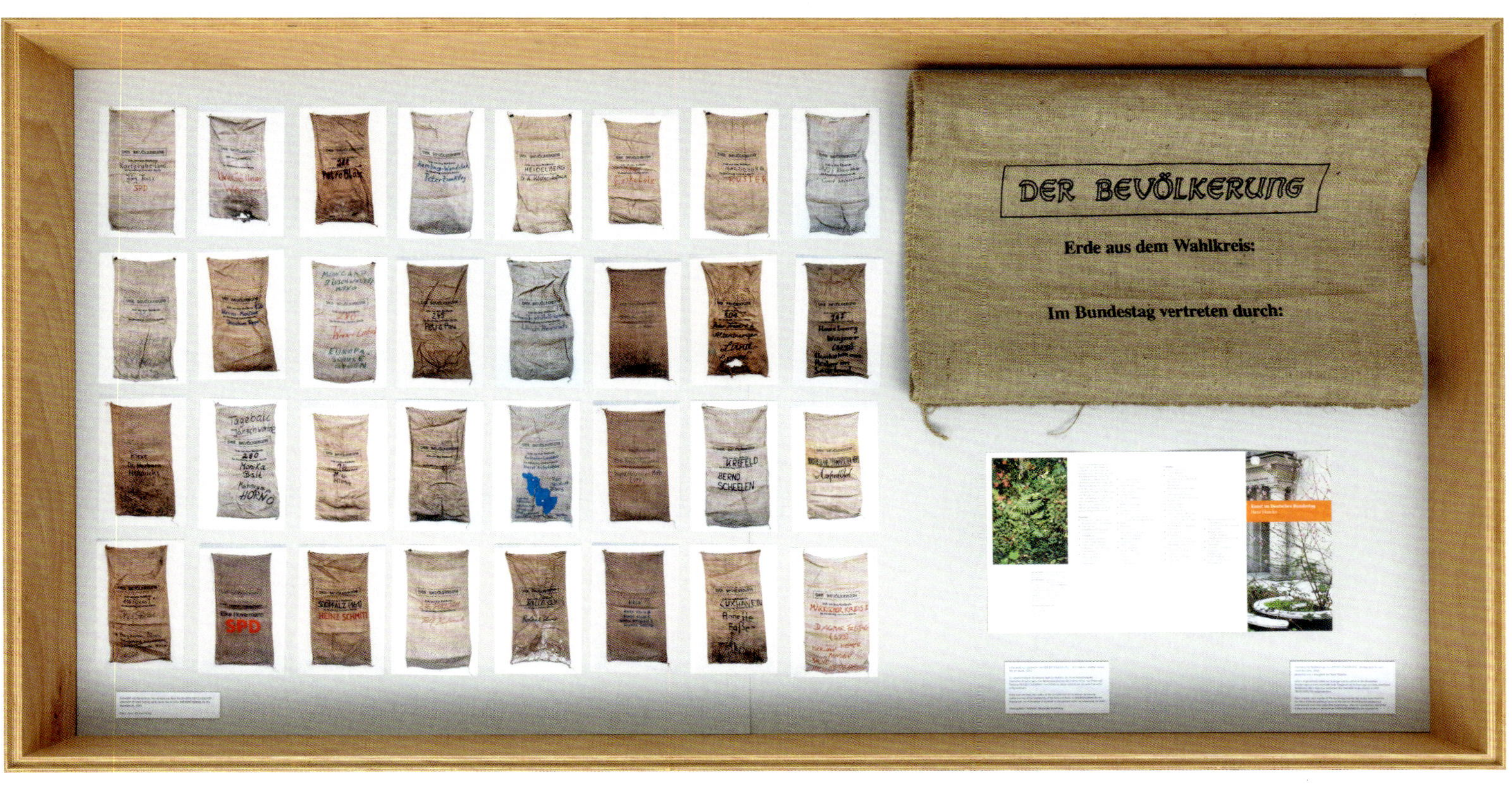

DER BEVÖLKERUNG (TO THE POPULATION), 2000
Photographs of a selection of used burlap sacks from the archive
DER BEVÖLKERUNG (TO THE POPULATION)

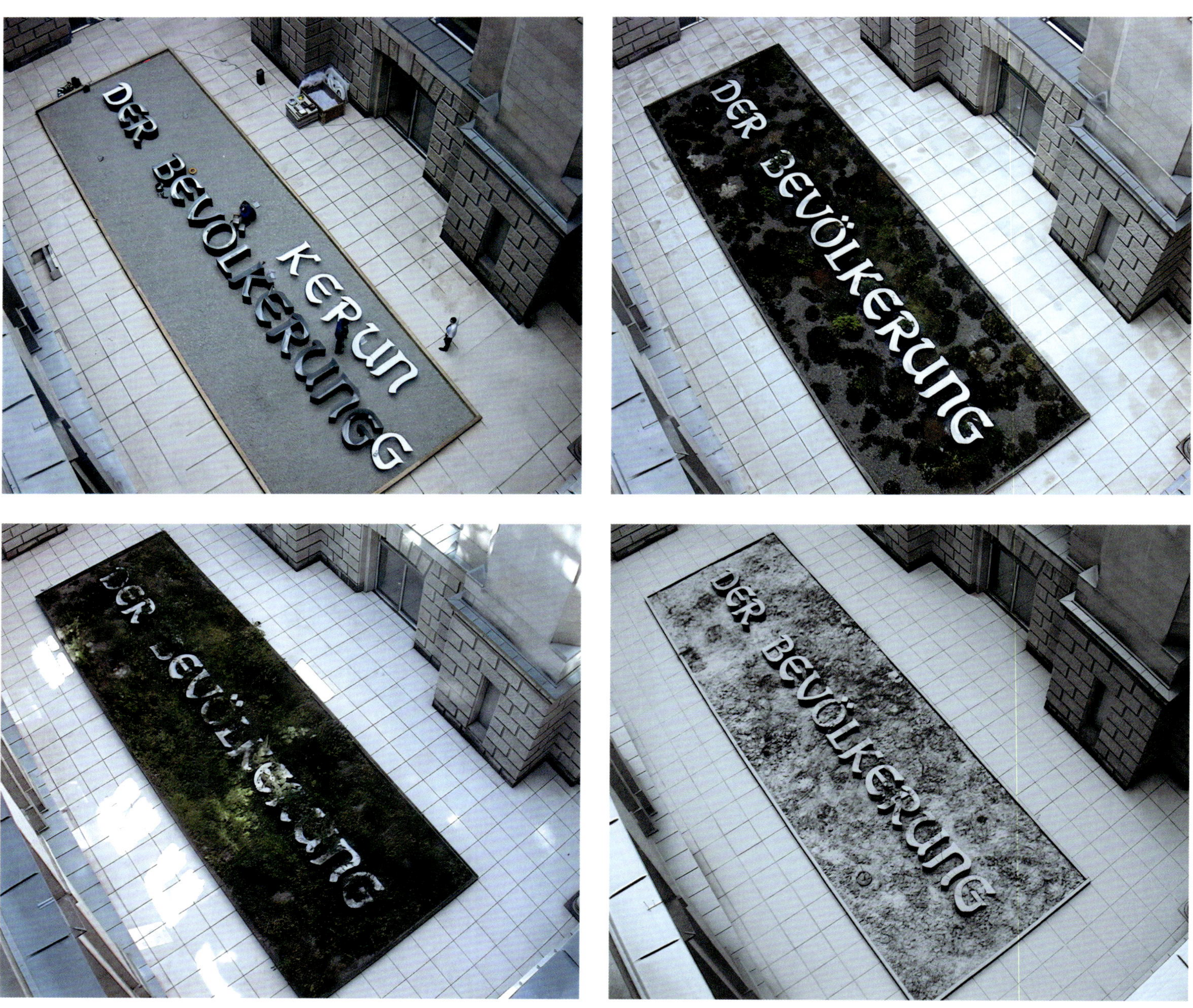
DER
BEVÖLKERUNGG
KERUN
DER
BEVÖLKERUNG
DER
BEVÖLKERUNG

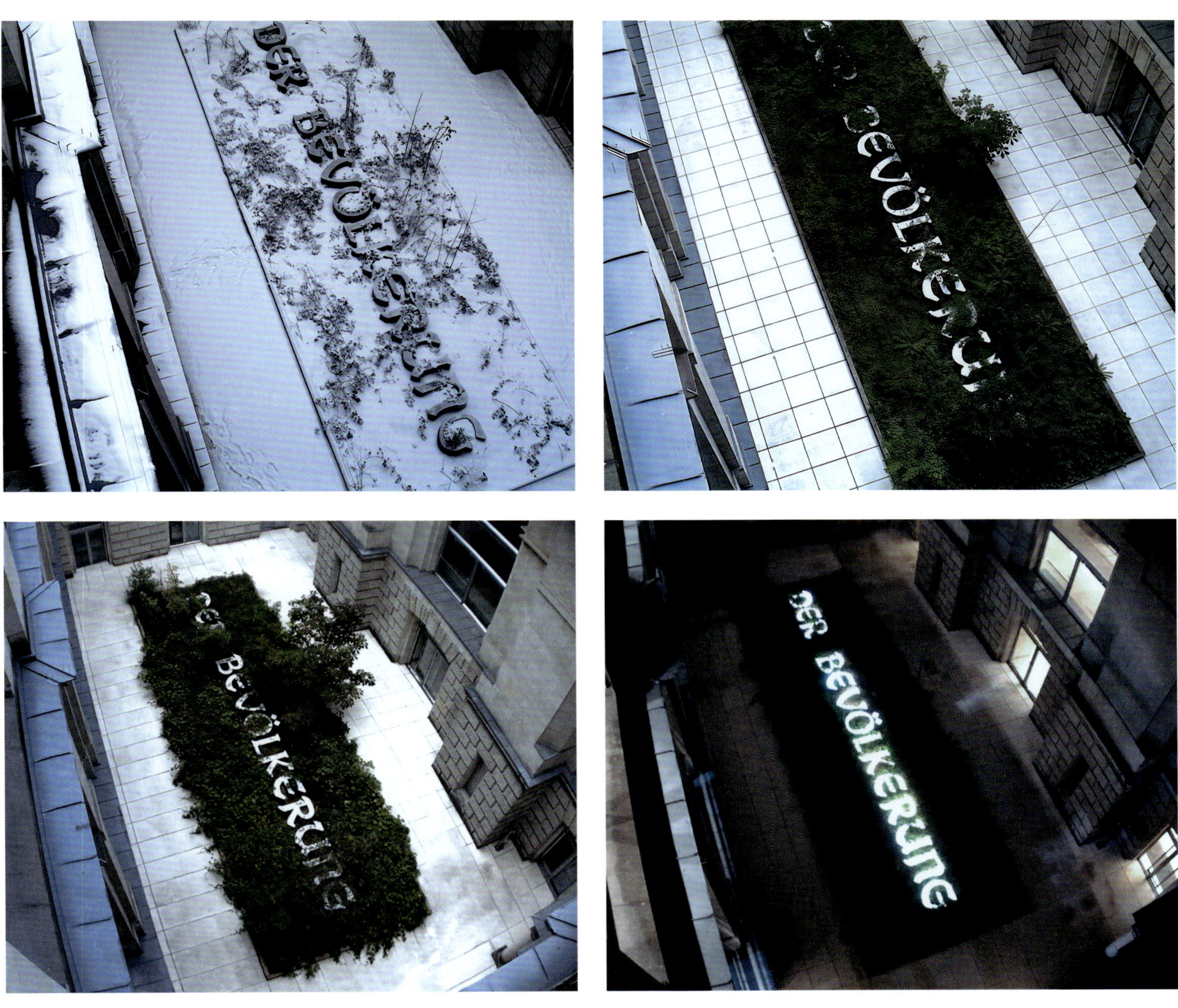

View of the installation *DER BEVÖLKERUNG (TO THE POPULATION)* in the northern atrium of the Reichstag building in Berlin, time-lapse webcam video from 2000 to 2024

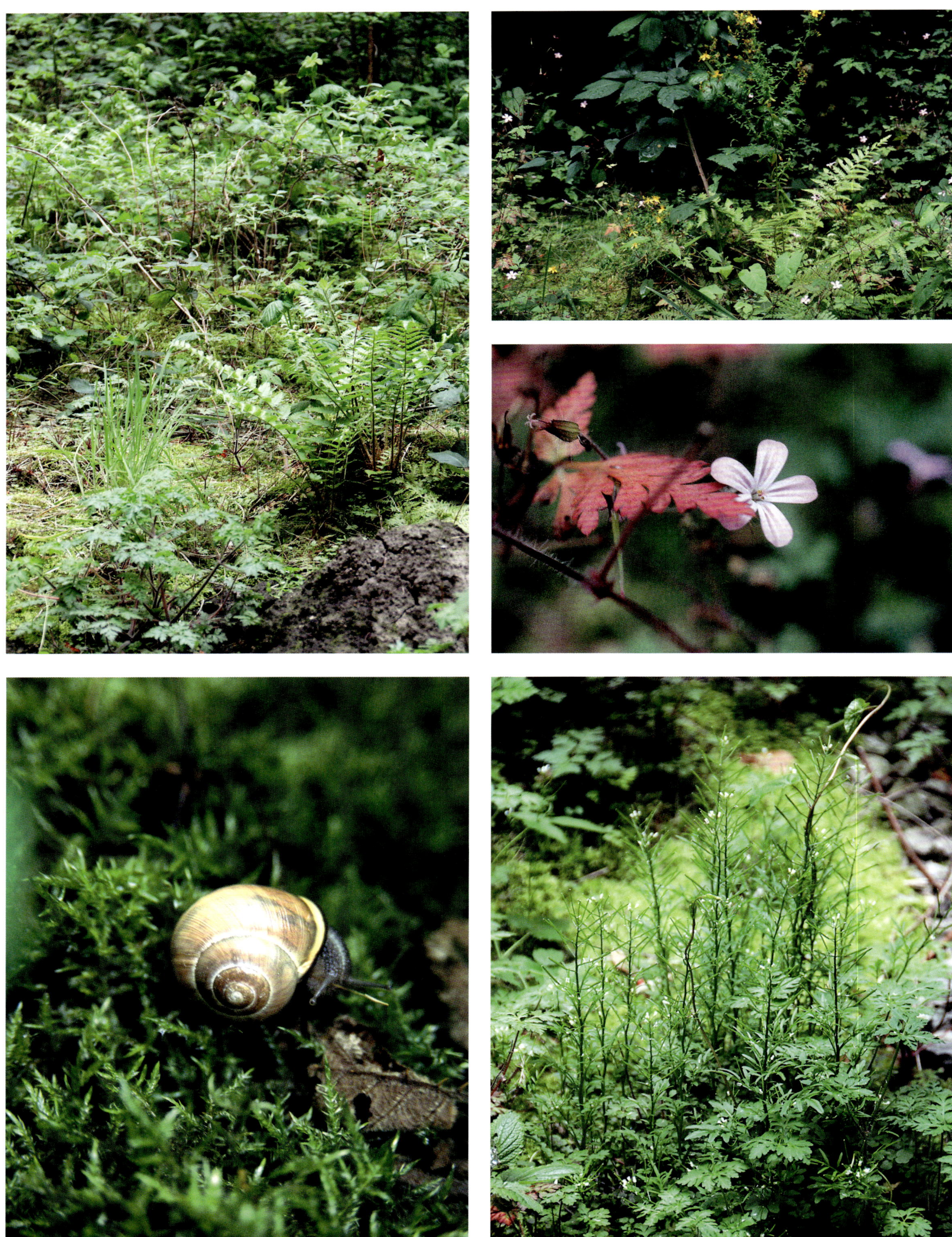

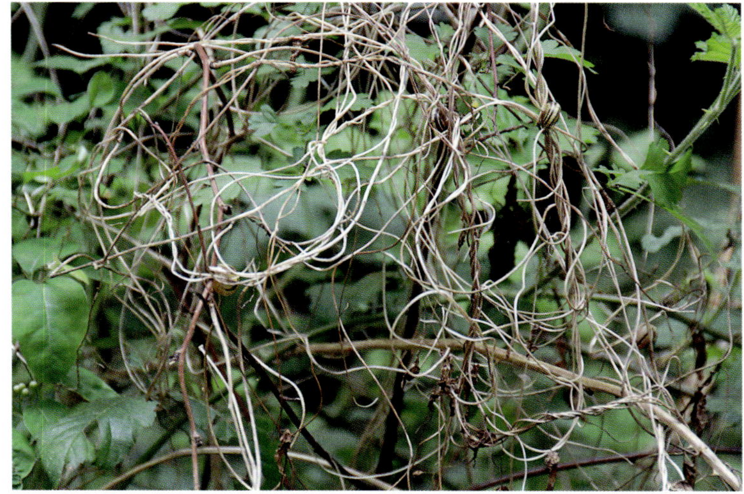

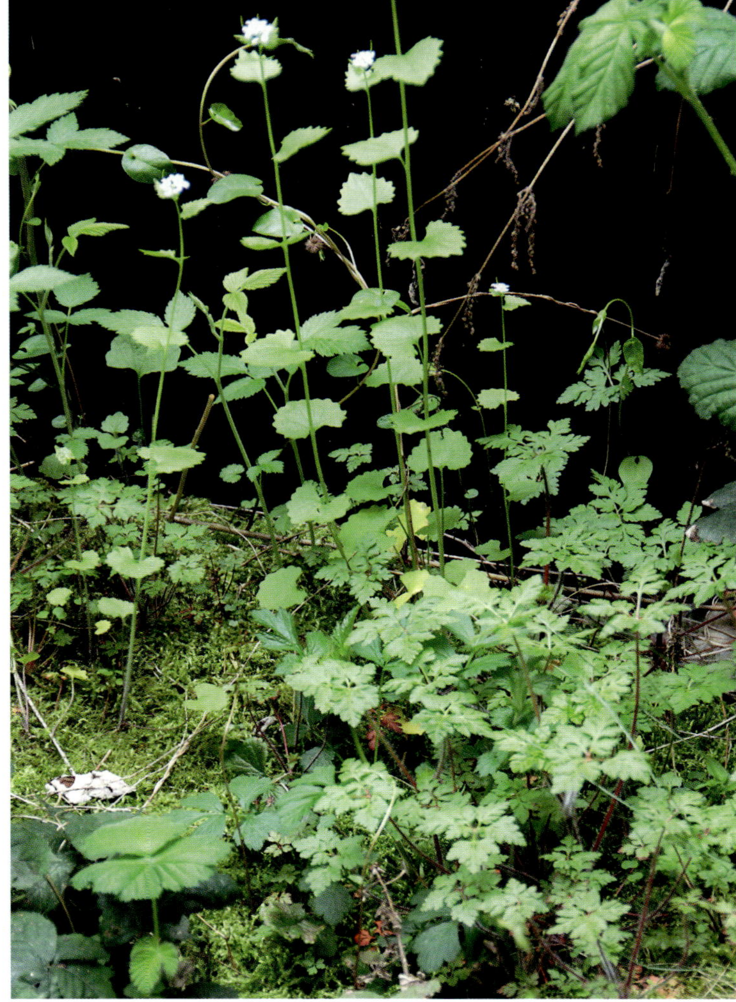

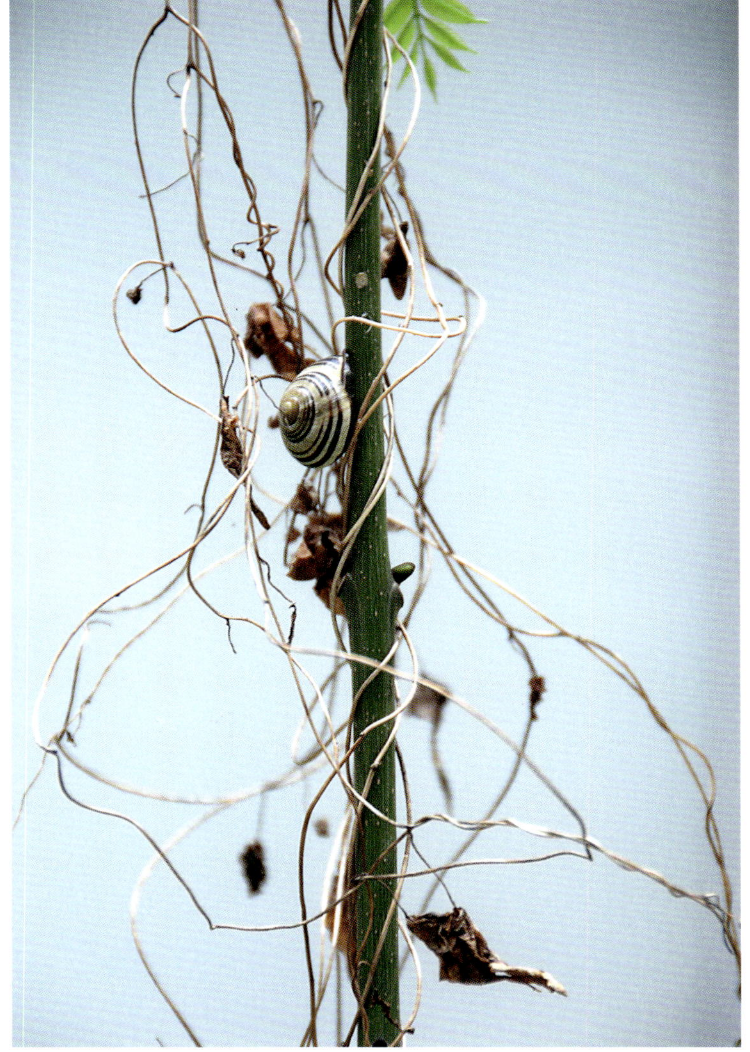

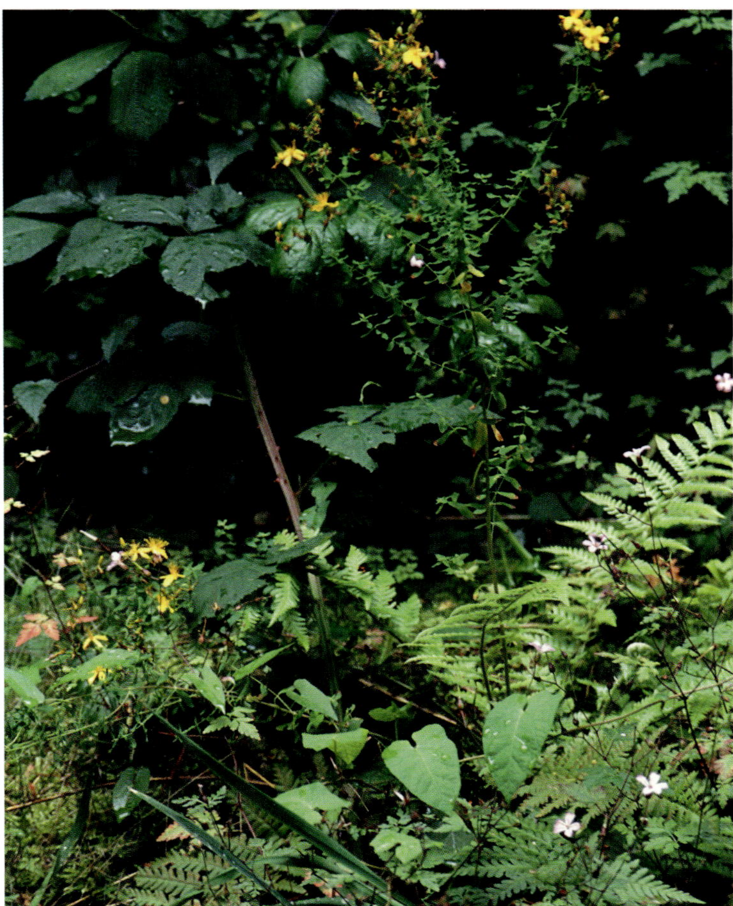

Federal Horticulture Show, close-ups of flora & fauna:
DER BEVÖLKERUNG (TO THE POPULATION), 2001–08

Gift Horse, 2014

The fourth plinth, on the northwest corner of Trafalgar Square in London, was meant to carry an equestrian statue of William IV (1765–1837). It is said that due to a lack of funds, he was never able to join his older brother, George IV (1762–1830), who is known for his »dissolute way of life« and whose horseback effigy occupies the plinth on the northeast corner of the square.

Both kings were younger contemporaries of George Stubbs (1724–1806), the English painter of horses and other animals whose paintings are held in the collections of the Tate and the National Gallery at Trafalgar Square.

In 1766, Stubbs published his study *The Anatomy of the Horse*: thirty etchings, all accompanied by very detailed explanations of the skeleton, the muscles, and other parts of a horse's anatomy.

A digitally altered version (orientation, limbs, neck, head adjusted) of the first skeleton plate of Stubbs's *The Anatomy of the Horse* serves to illustrate my proposal for the empty plinth.

A three-dimensional skeleton of a strutting horse occupies the plinth, facing the square, with the National Gallery in the back. Its size matches that of the horse carrying George IV.

A bow is tied around a frontal thighbone of the skeleton as around a gift. Both sides of the »ribbon« are capable of displaying electronic messages. They transmit, live, the FTLE 100 ticker of the London Stock Exchange (LSE). At times when no trading occurs—after hours and on weekends and holidays—the ticker of the most recent day of LSE activity is repeated.

The piece was later shown in Munich (2017) and Chicago (2018), where the ribbon displayed ticker information from the host country's leading stock exchange. In Munich, *Gift Horse* was exhibited at Haus der Kunst, formerly Haus der Deutschen Kunst (House of German Art), a neoclassical building inaugurated by Adolf Hitler in 1937.

Hans Haacke, 2012, updated in 2019

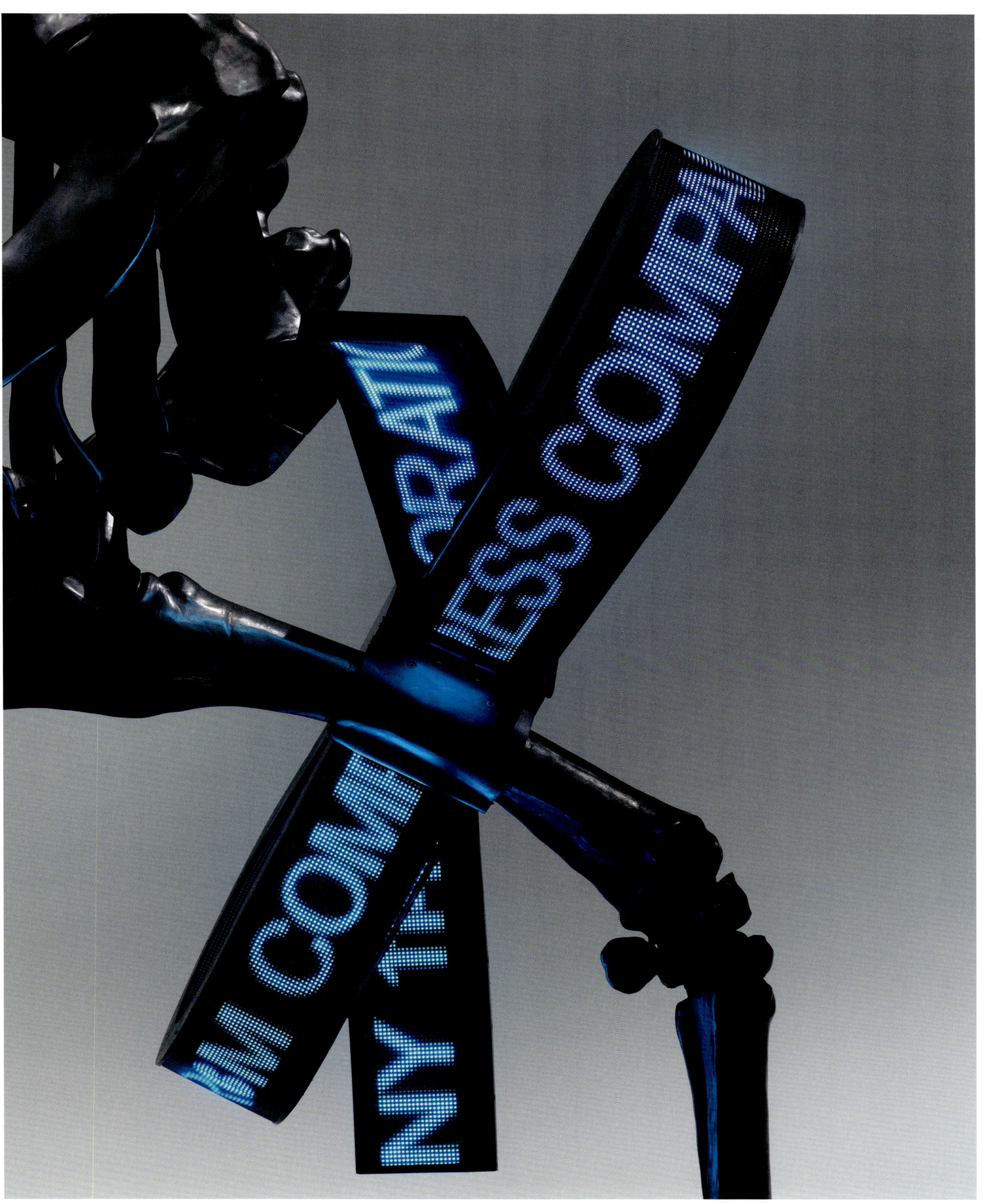

Gift Horse, 2014 (detail)

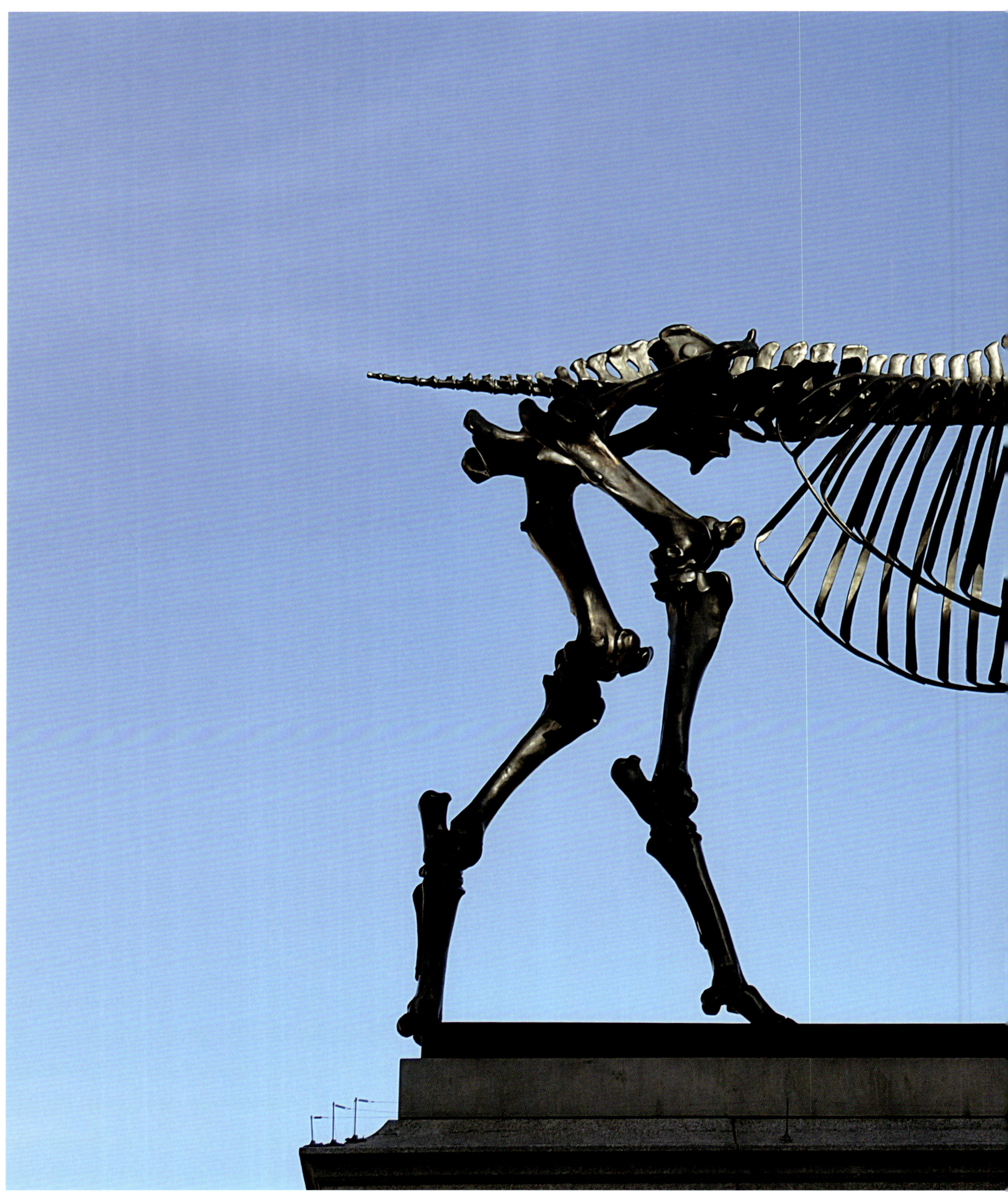

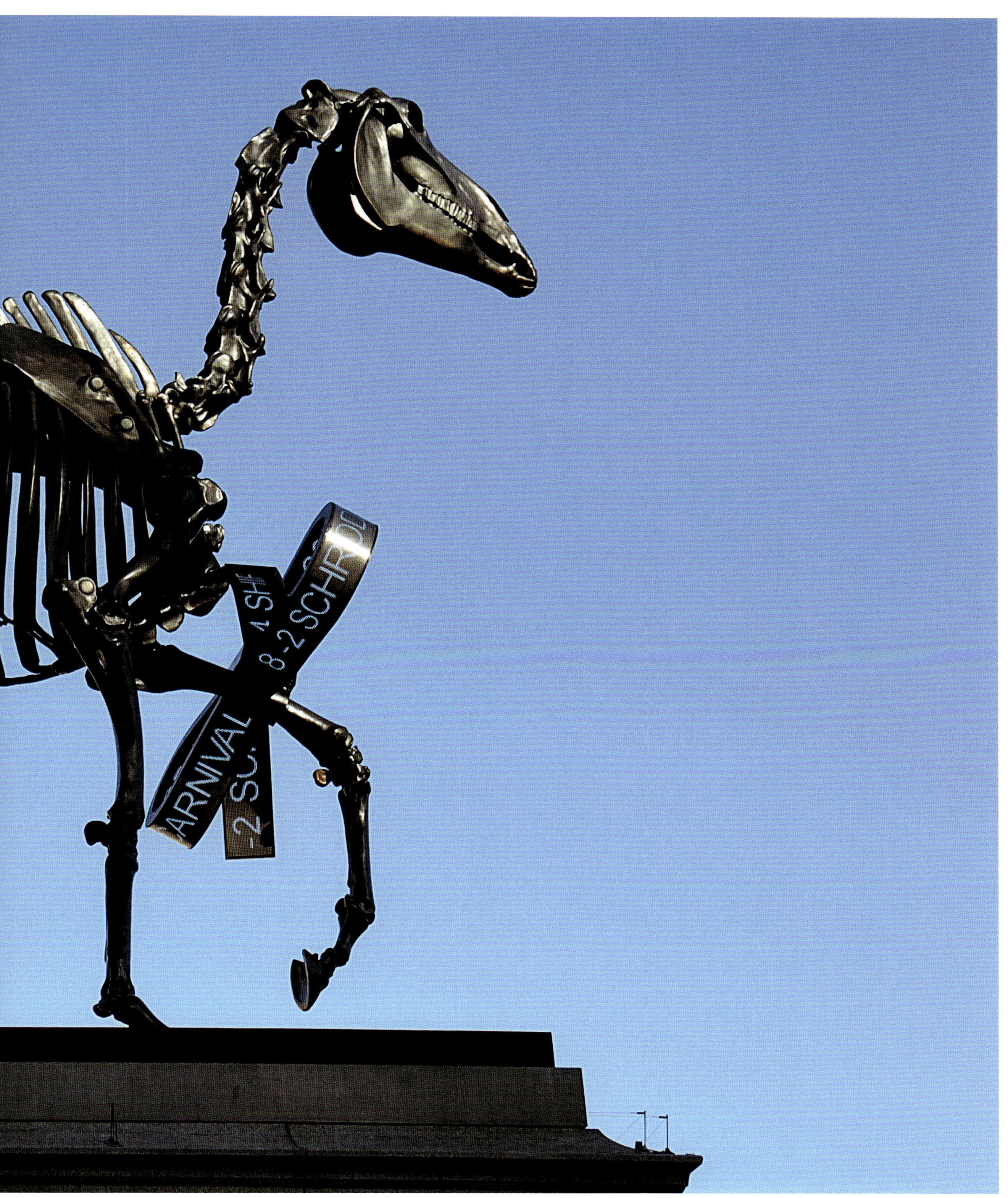

Gift Horse, 2014

We (All) Are the People, 2003/2017

In 1989, during protests in former East Germany, demonstrators shouted »Wir sind das Volk« (We are the people) at the *Volkspolizei* (People's police). This contributed to the downfall of the repressive regime and the unification of East and West Germany. By 2003, when I was invited to participate in a competition commemorating these events with a permanent installation in Leipzig, the originally liberating slogan »Wir sind das Volk« had been adopted by xenophobic groups in demonstrations against recent immigrants and refugees.

I therefore proposed to project an inclusive »Wir (Alle) sind das Volk« (We [all] are the people) onto the walls of the St. Nicholas Church in Leipzig, where the demonstrators had gathered in 1989. (The jury chose another artist's proposal.)

Three years earlier, the Bundestag had accepted a thematically related proposal of mine by a slim majority. Referring to the dedication »DEM DEUTSCHEN VOLKE« (TO THE GERMAN PEOPLE) on the portico of the Reichstag, Germany's parliament building, my dedication *DER BEVÖLKERUNG (TO THE POPULATION)* was realized as a permanent installation in one of the two open-air courtyards of the Reichstag.

At my invitation, more than three hundred members of the Bundestag have each brought 50 kilograms of soil from their constituencies to the dedication to all those who live in Germany. Seeds embedded in the soil have sprouted. Vibrant mixed vegetation has grown with and around *DER BEVÖLKERUNG*. The work *We (All) Are the People* emphatically expresses our communion with the desperate migrants and refugees currently exposed to virulent xenophobia, racism, and religious animosities in many countries around the world.

Hans Haacke, 2017

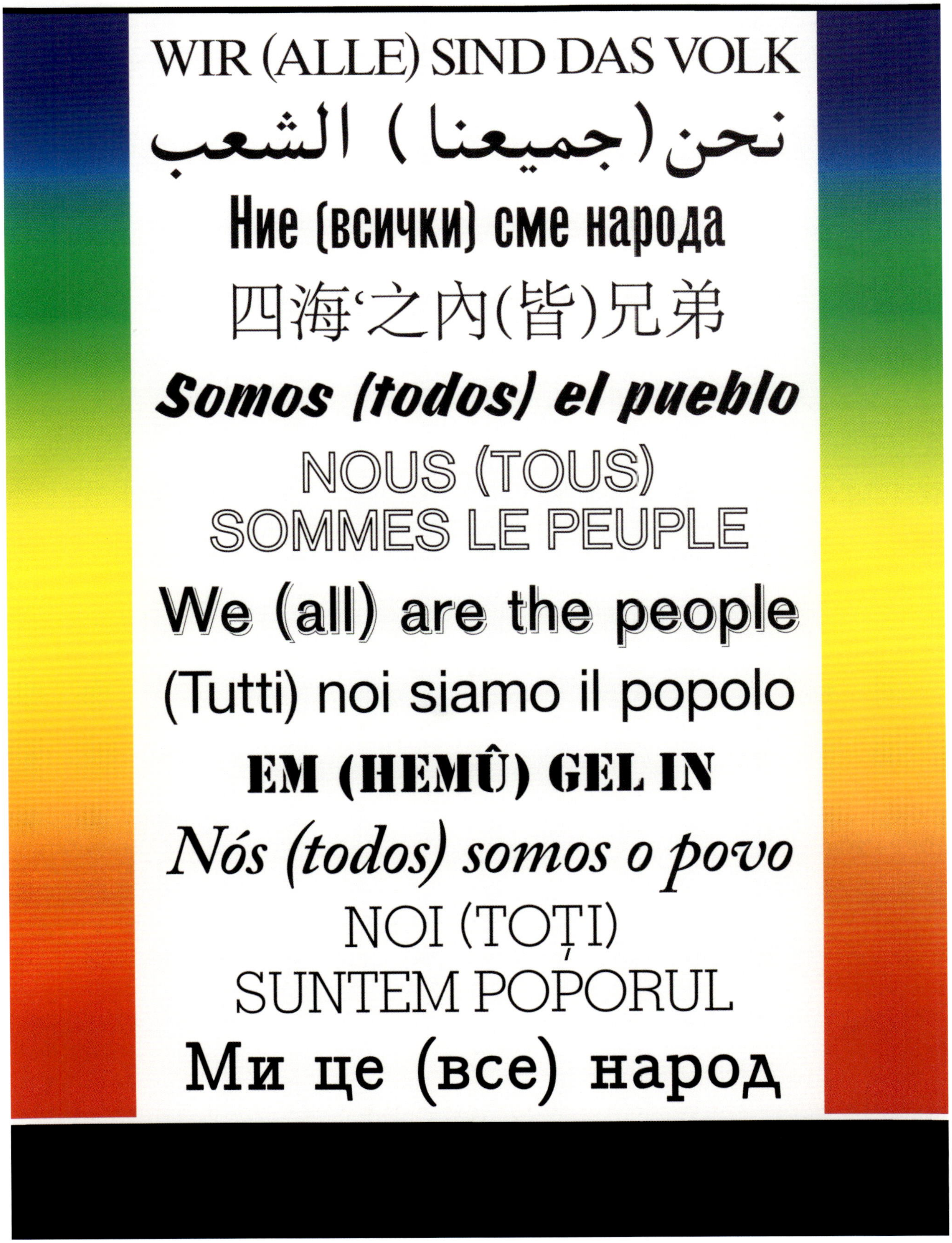

WIR (ALLE) SIND DAS VOLK

نحن (جميعنا) الشعب

Ние (всички) сме народа

四海之内(皆)兄弟

Somos (todos) el pueblo

NOUS (TOUS)
SOMMES LE PEUPLE

We (all) are the people

(Tutti) noi siamo il popolo

EM (HEMÛ) GEL IN

Nós (todos) somos o povo

NOI (TOȚI)
SUNTEM POPORUL

Ми це (все) народ

We (All) Are the People, 2003/2017

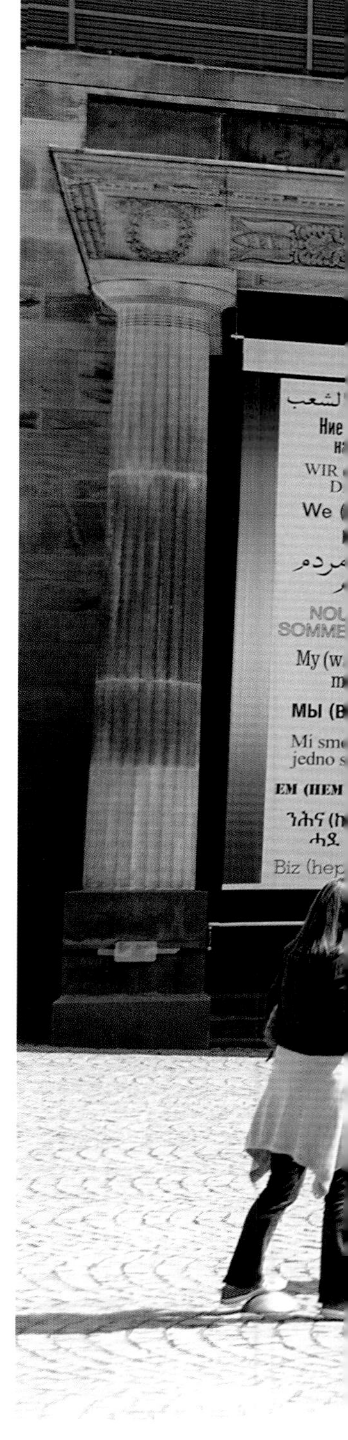
Ние
WIR
We
Biz

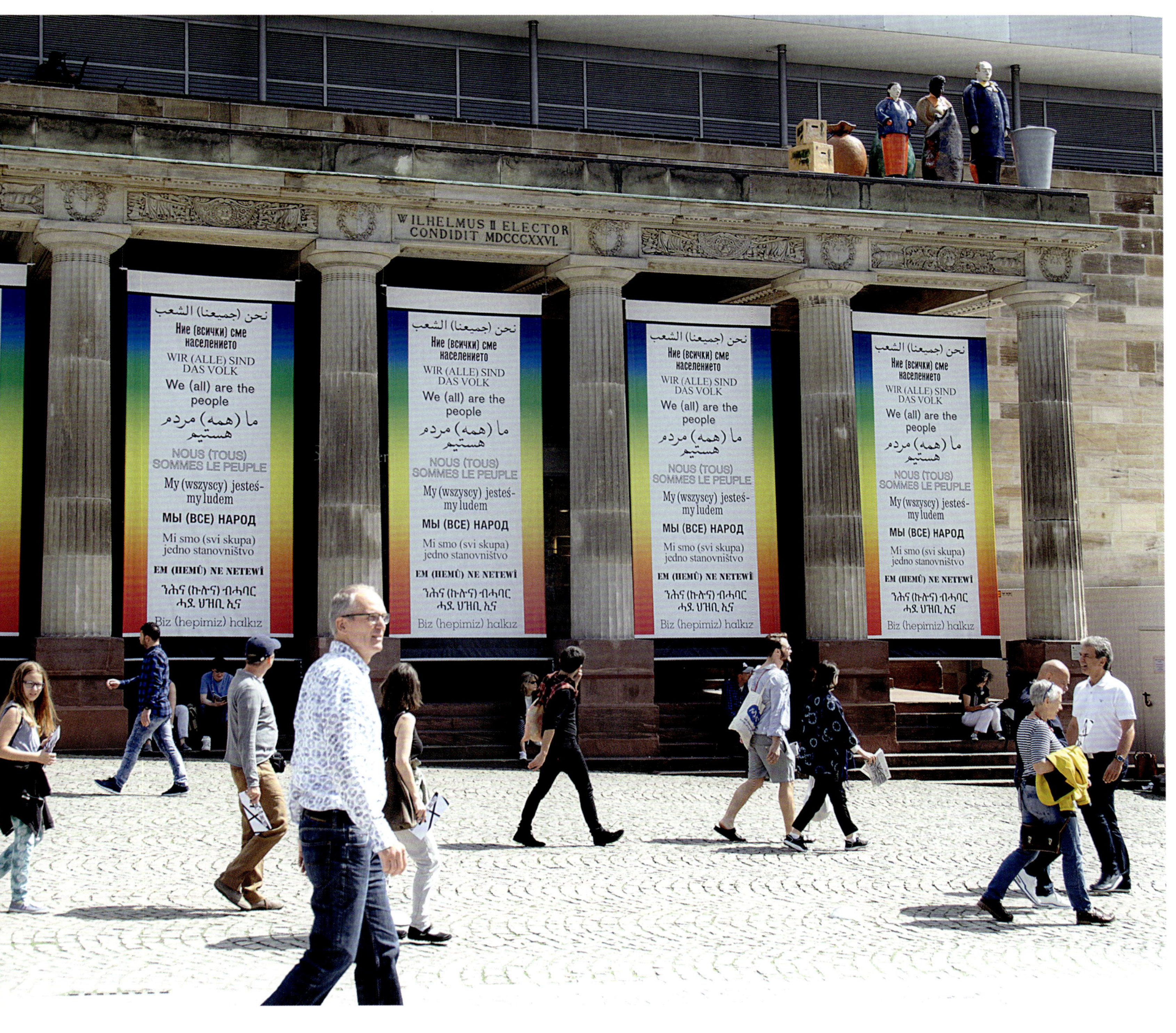

We (All) Are the People, installation view documenta 14, Kassel, 2017

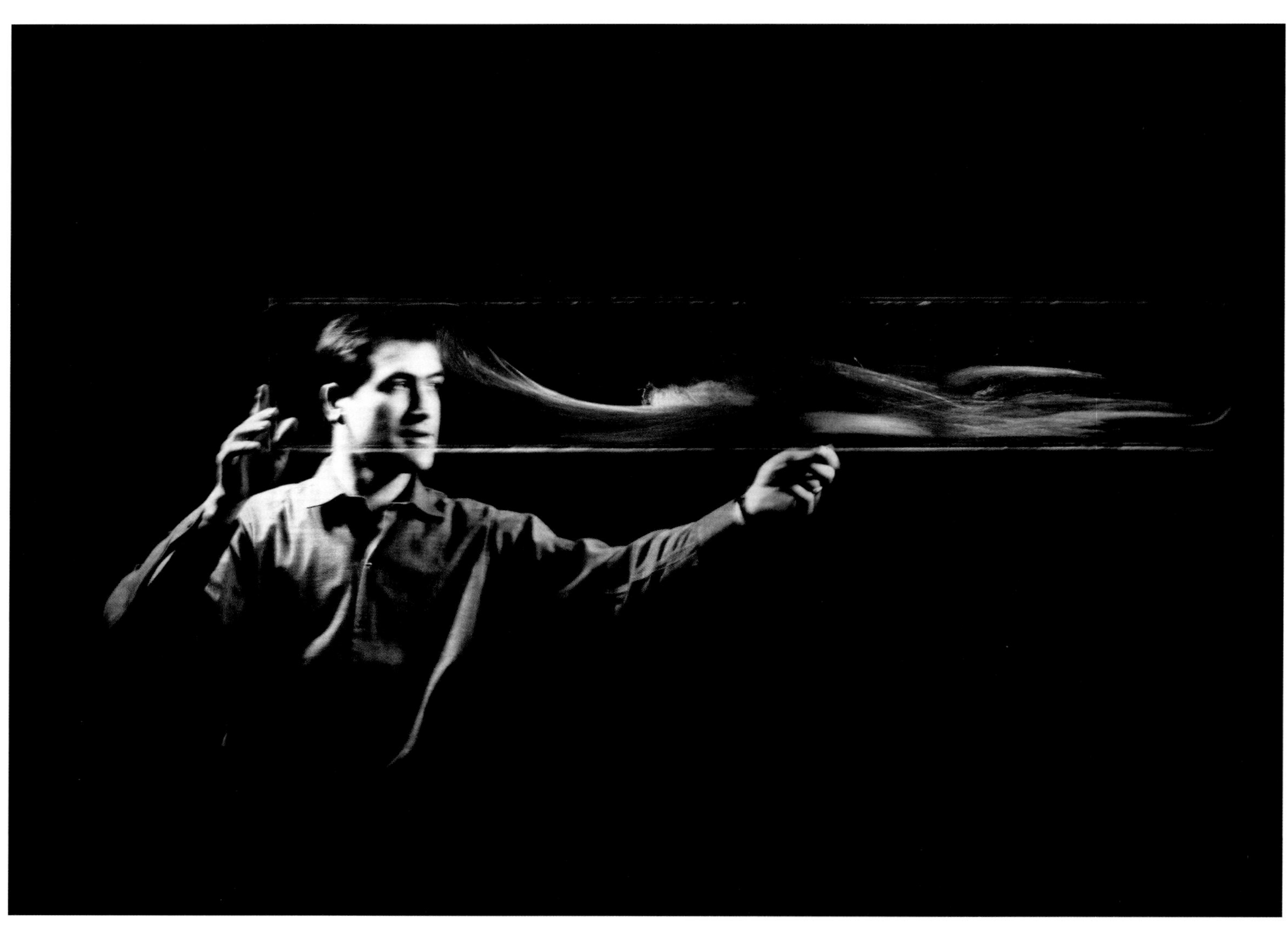

Hans Haacke with his *Wave* sculpture, 1965, Rudi Blesh papers, ca. 1980–83, Archives of American Art, Smithsonian Institution

Biography

Cornelia Eisendle

1936	Hans Haacke is born in Cologne on August 12 and grows up in Bad Godesberg.
1956–60	Studies at the Staatliche Werkakademie Kassel (State Art Academy), now the Kunsthochschule Kassel (Art Academy), under Stanley William Hayter, Marie-Louise von Rogister, and Fritz Winter, among others.
1959	Arnold Bode arranges a working student position for Haacke at documenta II, where he photographs the visitors in front of artworks (*Photographic Notes, documenta 2*, 1959). In the same year, he visits an exhibition by Otto Piene for the first time in Bonn and establishes contact with him.
1960	Graduates from the art academy, which has just been renamed the Staatliche Hochschule für bildende Künste Kassel (State University of Fine Arts), with the first state examination in art education. A scholarship from the German Academic Exchange Service (DAAD) enables Haacke to spend a year in Paris, where he attends and works at »Atelier 17«—an art school for experimental printmaking founded by Stanley William Hayter.
1961	Haacke attends the Tyler School of Art at Temple University in Philadelphia on a Fulbright Scholarship.
1962	During his one-year stay in Philadelphia, Haacke meets Jack Burnham, whose systems theory has a decisive impact on him. Haacke then moves to New York City for a year, where he exhibits at George Wittenborn's One-Wall Gallery on Madison Avenue. In this year, Haacke participates in an exhibition with the Düsseldorf-based ZERO group of artists for the first time—titled *NUL 1962* and presented at the Stedelijk Museum Amsterdam—where he showed plexiglass works and reliefs. By 1965, Haacke will have taken part in a total of ten exhibitions with the ZERO group in Italy, the Netherlands, Great Britain, the United States, and Germany.

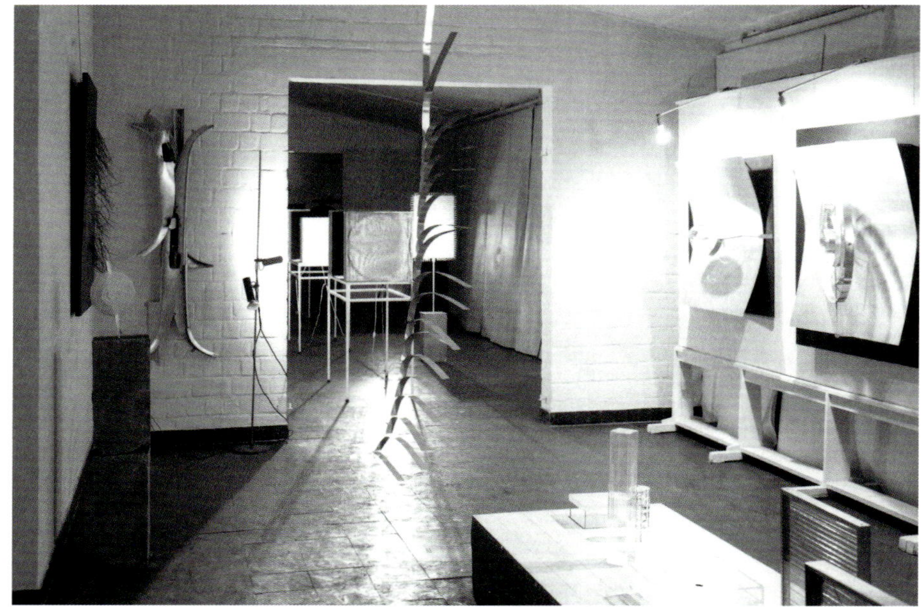

ZERO in Gelsenkirchen, 1963, exhibition view, Haftmannshof artists' residence, works by Oskar Holweck, Hans Haacke, and Adolf Luther

1963 In August, Haacke takes a bus to Washington, DC, to attend the civil rights movement's March on Washington where Martin Luther King made his most famous speech. In early September, Haacke returns to Cologne since his two-year student visa could not be extended. He then teaches at the Pädagogische Hochschule Kettwig (College of Education), the fashion school in Düsseldorf (as Otto Piene's successor), and at other institutions.

1963–67 Haacke develops the *Condensation Cube* in a smaller (1963–65) and a larger version (1963–67).

1965 His first solo exhibition in Germany, titled *Wind und Wasser*, is presented at Galerie Schmela in Düsseldorf. In November, Haacke returns to New York, where he resides permanently from then on.

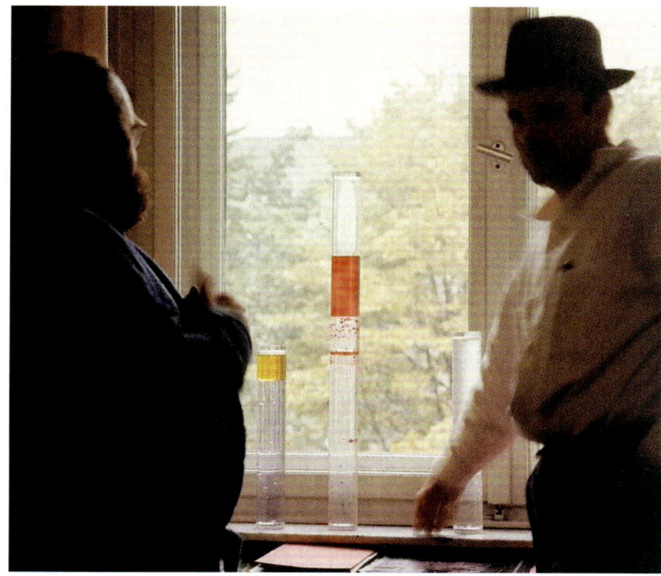

Alfred Schmela (left) with Joseph Beuys, 1965, and in the background several works by Haacke (*Column with Two Immiscible Liquids*, 1965)

1966–67 Haacke teaches at the University of Washington in Seattle, Douglas College at Rutgers University in New Jersey, and the Philadelphia College of Art, among others. In January 1966, his first solo exhibition at the Howard Wise Gallery in New York takes place under the title *Wind and Water*. In October 1967, he opens a solo exhibition at MIT's Hayden Gallery in Cambridge, Massachusetts, which was recreated in 2011 under the title *HANS HAACKE 1967*. From 1967 on, he first teaches as a lecturer, then becomes a professor of art at The Cooper Union for the Advancement of Science and Art in New York. His students include the artists Walter Dahn and Jiří Georg Dokoupil.

1968 Biologist Ludwig von Bertalanffy publishes his *General System Theory*, which has a lasting impact on Haacke's engagement with systems theories.

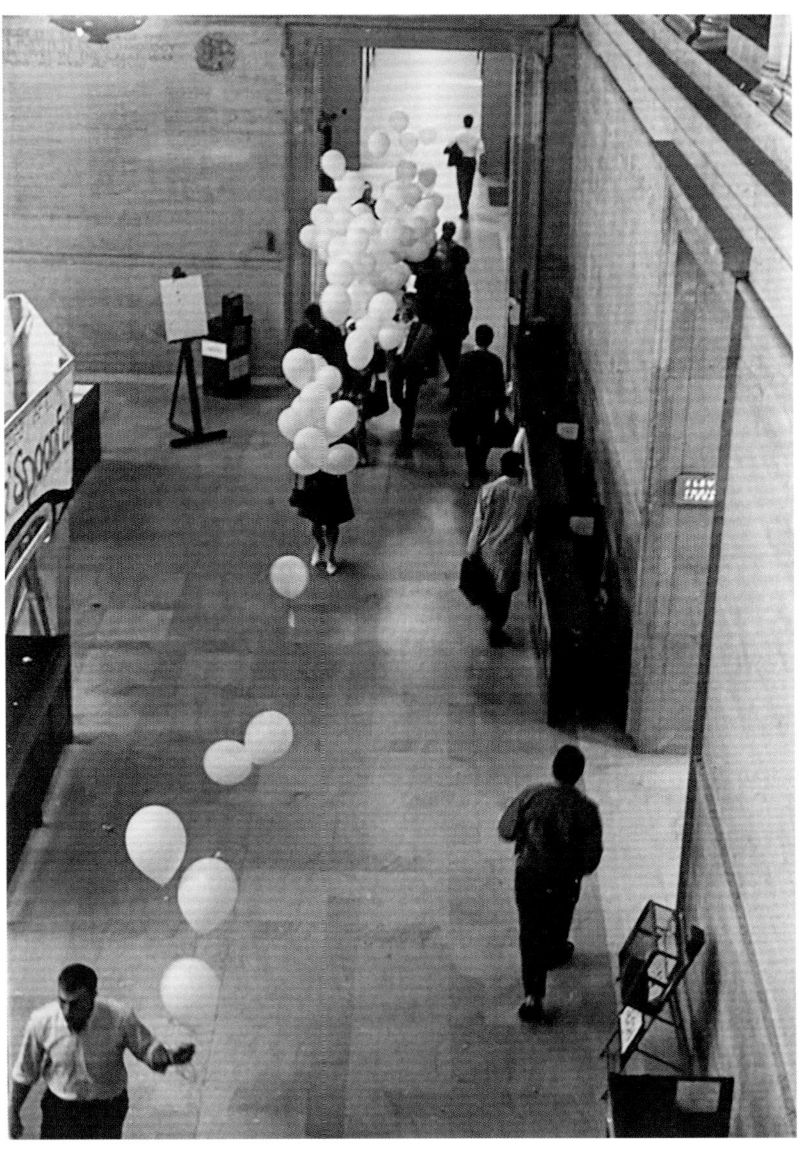

Hans Haacke, *Sky Line*, 1967, performance at Kilian Court, MIT Institute of Arts, Cambridge, Massachusetts

1969 On January 13, his eldest son Carl Samuel Selavy is born. Haacke documents this with the multiple *Newborn Identification (Collaboration Linda & Hans Haacke)*. In spring, he takes part in the group exhibition *Live in Your Head: When Attitudes Become Form (Works – Concepts – Processes – Situations – Information)* at Kunsthalle Bern, curated by Harald Szeemann. In the same year, Haacke refused to participate in the São Paulo Biennial due to the establishment of the military dictatorship in Brazil. He then became a cofounder and active member of the Art Workers' Coalition (AWC) in the fall of 1969. In light of the Vietnam War and the assassination of Martin Luther King, Haacke starts to feel a more urgent need to connect his work to society.

1970 For the group exhibition *Information* at The Museum of Modern Art in New York, Haacke develops a survey of museum visitors, his *MoMA Poll*, which actively integrates social issues for the first time. He also takes part in the exhibition *Software* at The Jewish Museum, New York.

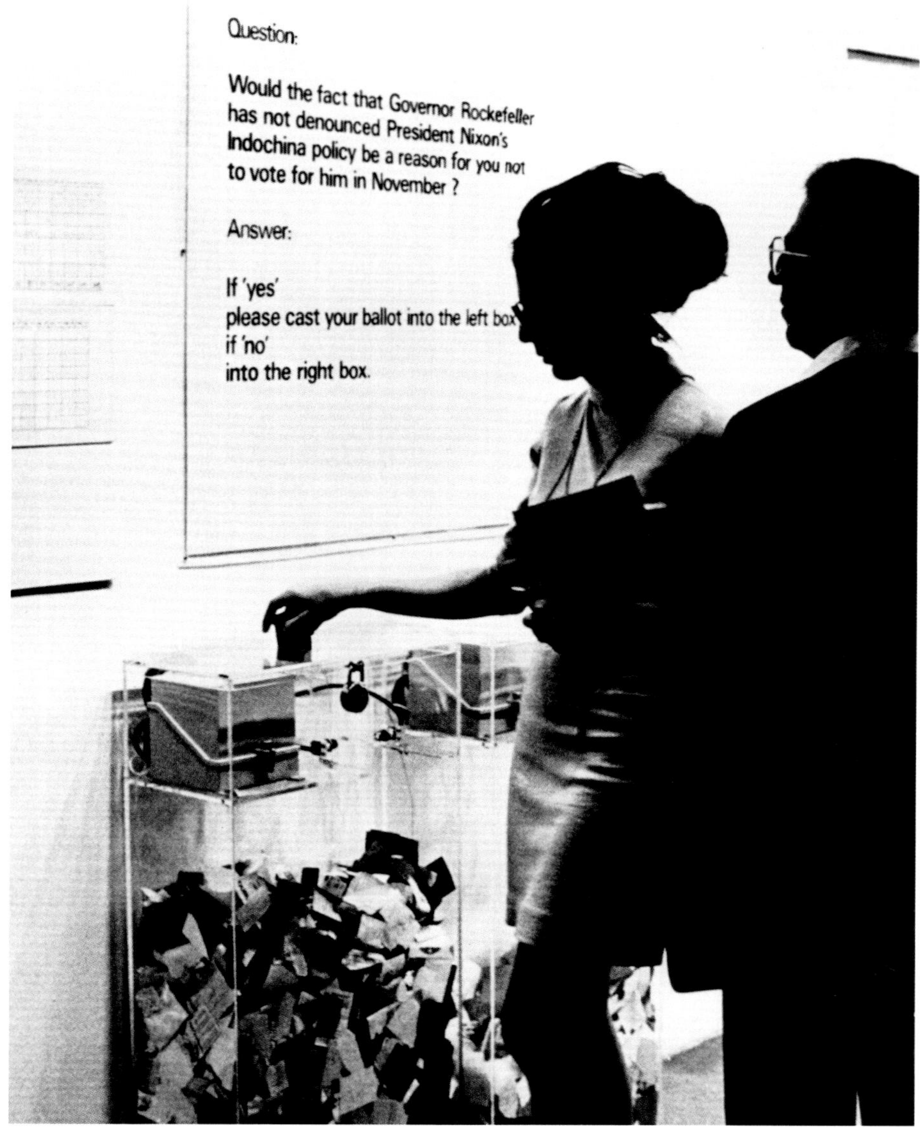

Hans Haacke, *MoMA Poll*, 1970, installation view at the exhibition *Information*, The Museum of Modern Art, New York, 1970

1971 Haacke is invited to do a solo exhibition at the Guggenheim Museum in New York. However, the work he realizes for it—*Shapolsky et al. Manhatten Real Estate Holdings, a Real-Time Social System, as of May 1, 1971*—leads the director Thomas Messer to cancel the exhibition shortly before it opens. It would take fifteen years for Haacke's works to be shown again in a US museum. In Cologne, Galerie Paul Maenz opens with a solo show by Hans Haacke. From this year on, the artist uses the contract drafted by Seth Siegelaub, the »Artist's Reserved Rights Transfer and Sale Agreement,« for the sale of his art. This contract form is the first to stipulate the artist's approval for the future use of the artwork, as well as the financial royalties on resale profits to be paid to the artist and their gallery.

1972 Haacke takes part in documenta 5 in October, followed by a solo exhibition at Museum Haus Lange in Krefeld in November. There he shows the installation *Rhine Water Purification Plant*.

1973 Haacke receives a scholarship from the John Simon Guggenheim Memorial Foundation. He presents his first solo exhibition at the John Weber Gallery in New York, which will represent him in the future. Haacke teaches as a visiting professor at the Hochschule für bildende Künste (University of Fine Arts) in Hamburg.

1974 The *Manet-PROJEKT '74* submitted for the anniversary exhibition of the Wallraf Richartz Museum in Cologne is rejected. On the day of the show's press opening, Haacke's work is presented at Galerie Paul Maenz instead, using a facsimile of Édouard Manet's *Bunch of Asparagus*. Following this censorship, the work's first institutional presentation is in the exhibition *Art Into Society – Society Into Art* at the Institute of Contemporary Arts (ICA) in London.

1976 Haacke participates in the Venice Biennale for the first time.

1978 Scholarship from the National Endowment for the Arts (NEA), the only federal funding organization for culture in the United States.

1979 Visiting professor at the Gesamthochschule Essen (Comprehensive University).

1981 For the large-scale exhibition *Westkunst* curated by Laszlo Glozer and Kasper König, Haacke conceives *Der Pralinenmeister (The Chocolate Master)*, a work about the influential Cologne collector Peter Ludwig. The curators decide not to present the work, which is then shown parallel to the exhibition at Galerie Paul Maenz in Cologne instead.

1982 Haacke participates in documenta 7 in Kassel.

1984 Exhibition *Nach allen Regeln der Kunst* at the Neuer Berliner Kunstverein nbK in Künstlerhaus Bethanien in Kreuzberg, Berlin, right next to the Berlin Wall.

1987 Haacke's works are exhibited at documenta 8.

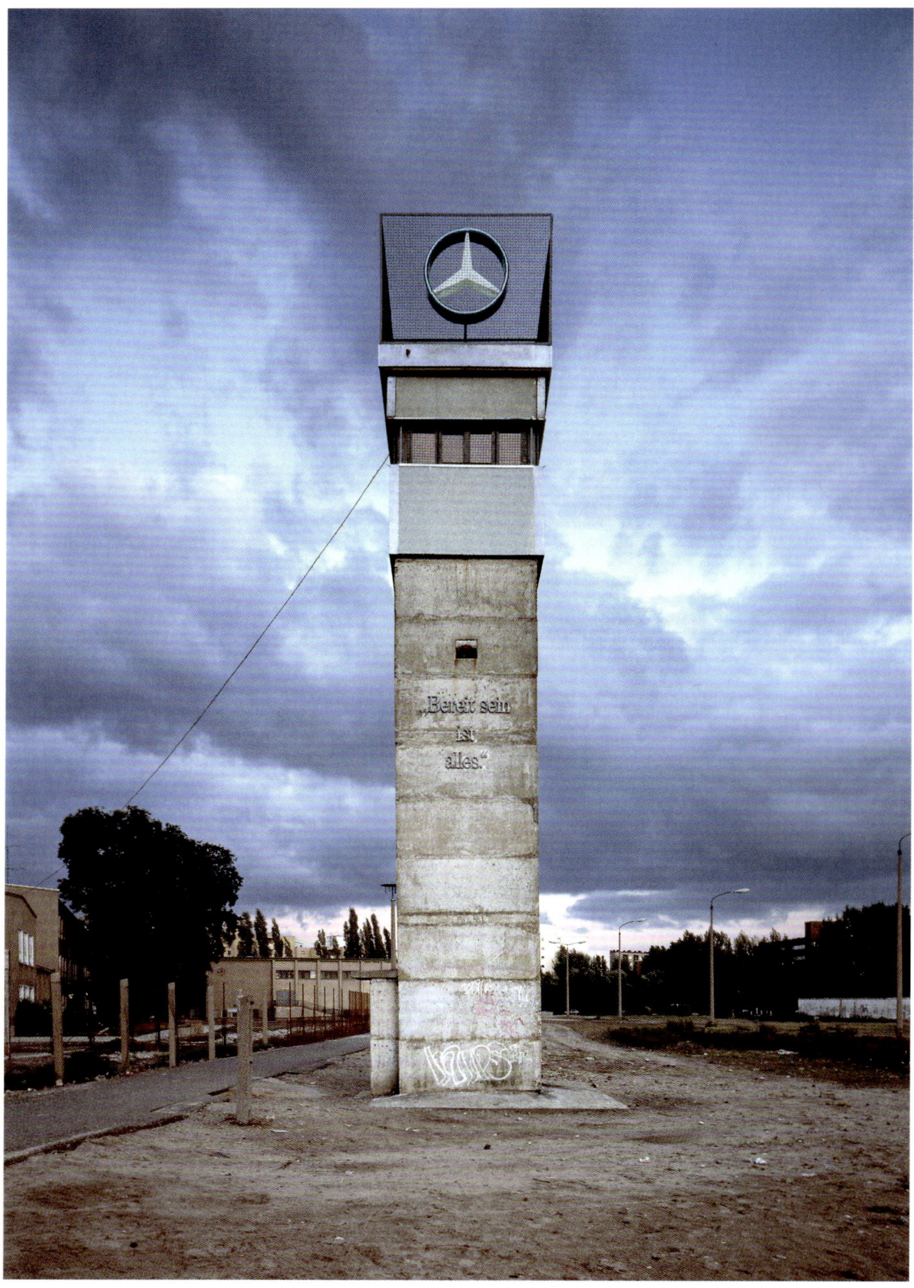

Hans Haacke, *Now Freedom Will Simply Be Sponsored—From Petty Cash*, 1990, documentation of the temporary exhibition in public space, line of the Berlin Wall

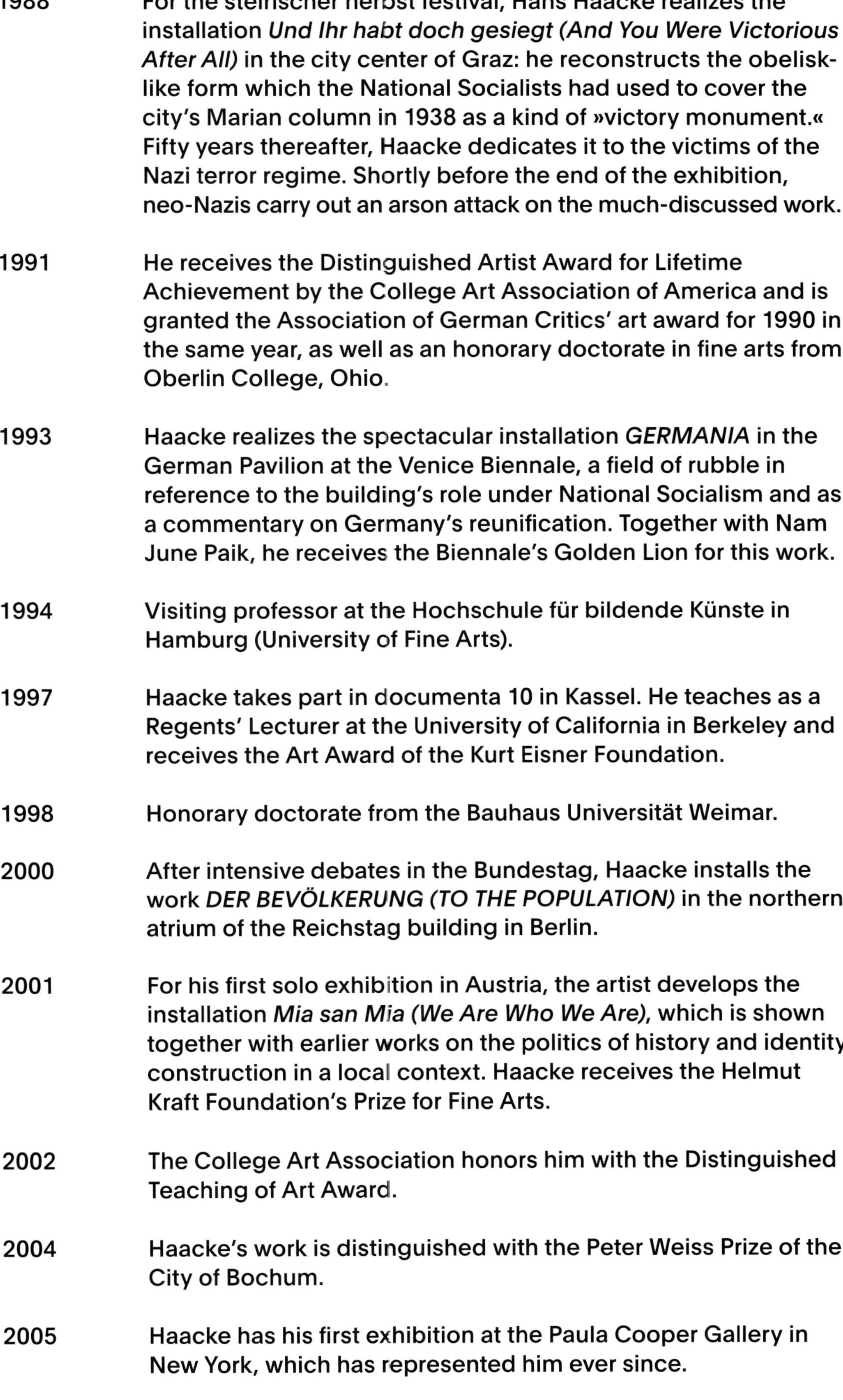

1988 For the steirischer herbst festival, Hans Haacke realizes the installation *Und Ihr habt doch gesiegt (And You Were Victorious After All)* in the city center of Graz: he reconstructs the obelisk-like form which the National Socialists had used to cover the city's Marian column in 1938 as a kind of »victory monument.« Fifty years thereafter, Haacke dedicates it to the victims of the Nazi terror regime. Shortly before the end of the exhibition, neo-Nazis carry out an arson attack on the much-discussed work.

1991 He receives the Distinguished Artist Award for Lifetime Achievement by the College Art Association of America and is granted the Association of German Critics' art award for 1990 in the same year, as well as an honorary doctorate in fine arts from Oberlin College, Ohio.

1993 Haacke realizes the spectacular installation *GERMANIA* in the German Pavilion at the Venice Biennale, a field of rubble in reference to the building's role under National Socialism and as a commentary on Germany's reunification. Together with Nam June Paik, he receives the Biennale's Golden Lion for this work.

1994 Visiting professor at the Hochschule für bildende Künste in Hamburg (University of Fine Arts).

1997 Haacke takes part in documenta 10 in Kassel. He teaches as a Regents' Lecturer at the University of California in Berkeley and receives the Art Award of the Kurt Eisner Foundation.

1998 Honorary doctorate from the Bauhaus Universität Weimar.

2000 After intensive debates in the Bundestag, Haacke installs the work *DER BEVÖLKERUNG (TO THE POPULATION)* in the northern atrium of the Reichstag building in Berlin.

2001 For his first solo exhibition in Austria, the artist develops the installation *Mia san Mia (We Are Who We Are)*, which is shown together with earlier works on the politics of history and identity construction in a local context. Haacke receives the Helmut Kraft Foundation's Prize for Fine Arts.

2002 The College Art Association honors him with the Distinguished Teaching of Art Award.

2004 Haacke's work is distinguished with the Peter Weiss Prize of the City of Bochum.

2005 Haacke has his first exhibition at the Paula Cooper Gallery in New York, which has represented him ever since.

2006 Haacke is honored at the Deichtorhallen in Hamburg and the Akademie der Künste in Berlin with the two-part retrospective *Hans Haacke: wirklich – Werke 1959–2006 / for real – Works 1959–2006*, and receives the Roland Prize for Art in Public Space that same year.

2008 Honorary doctorate from the San Francisco Art Institute.

2015 With the Fourth Plinth commission at Trafalgar Square in London, Haacke is awarded one of the world's most prestigious public art commissions and develops the *Gift Horse* for it.

2016 Honorary doctorate from the Maryland Institute College of Art.

2017 Haacke's oeuvre is recognized with the Roswitha Haftmann Foundation's Art Prize, the most highly endowed art prize in Europe.

2020 Haacke is awarded the prestigious Kaiserring art award by the City of Goslar.

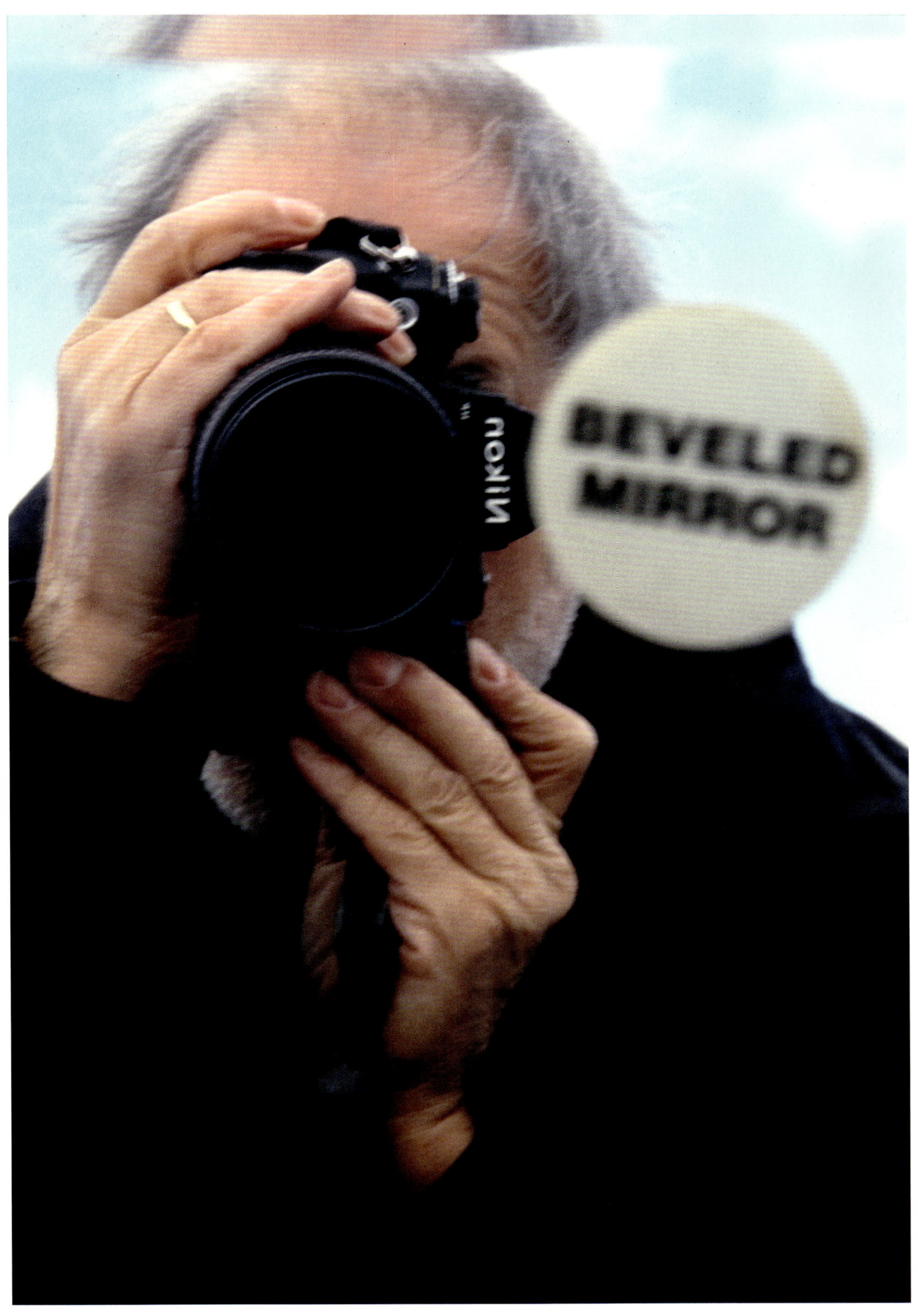

Hans Haacke, self-portrait

Following pages: *Water in Wind*, 1968

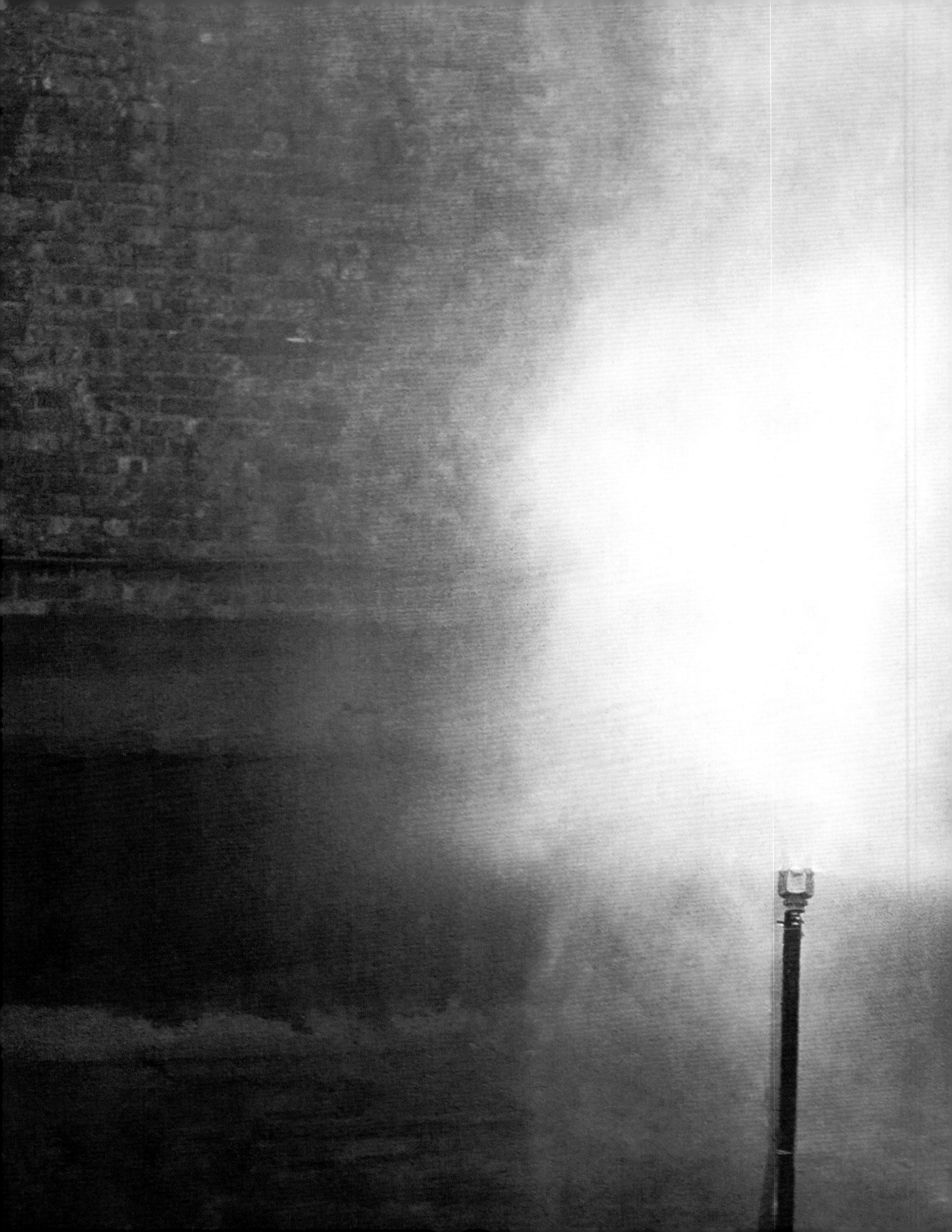

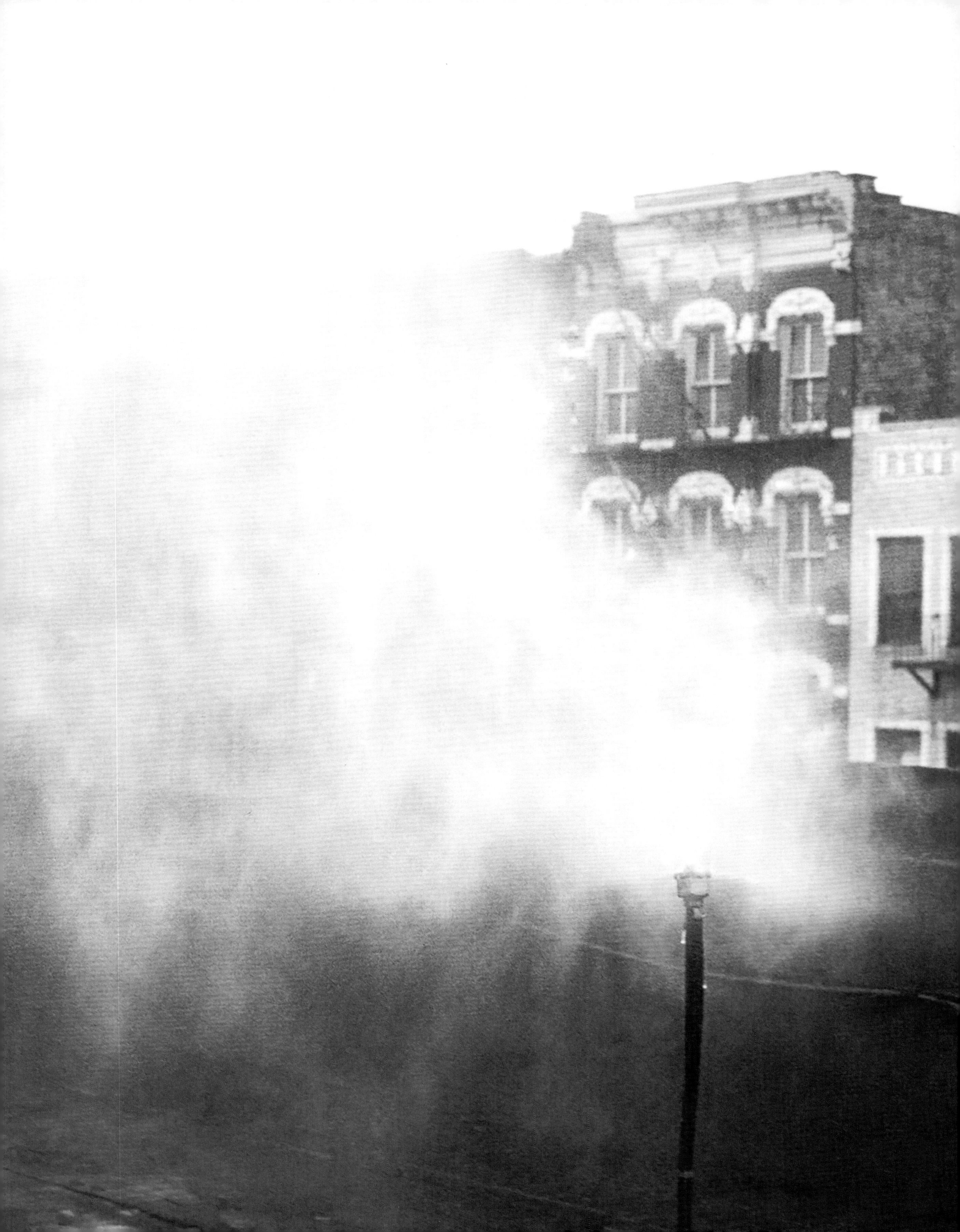

Photographic Notes, documenta 2, 1959
26 b/w photographs (selection)
16.8 × 25.1 cm each
Edition 2 of 3
Courtesy the artist and Paula Cooper Gallery, New York
pp. 15–19

Ce n'est pas la voie lactée (This Is Not the Milky Way), 1960
Oil on canvas
120 × 60 cm
Courtesy the artist and Paula Cooper Gallery, New York
p. 35

Untitled (Ohne Titel), 1960
Acrylic on canvas
95 × 50 cm
Courtesy the artist and Paula Cooper Gallery, New York
p. 34

A7-61, 1961
Reflective foil on hardboard
65.1 × 65.1 × 10.5 cm
Courtesy the artist and Paula Cooper Gallery, New York
pp. 37 (bottom)

B7-61, 1961
Reflective foil on hardboard
65 × 65 cm (rhombus)
Courtesy the artist and Paula Cooper Gallery, New York
p. 37 (top), 256 (detail)

Les Couloirs de Marienbad (The Corridors of Marienbad), 1962
Acrylic glass with perforated grid, metal mirror
30.7 × 30.7 × 9.5 cm
Staatliche Museen zu Berlin, Nationalgalerie, Marzona Collection
p. 46

Double Decker Rain, 1963
Acrylic glass, distilled water
12.7 × 35.6 × 35.6 cm
Edition of 3
Courtesy the artist and Paula Cooper Gallery, New York
p. 40

Large Condensation Cube, 1963–67
Acrylic glass, distilled water
76.2 × 76.2 × 76.2 cm
Edition of 5, exhibition copy
Courtesy the artist and Paula Cooper Gallery, New York
pp. 39, 264 (detail)

Blue Sail, 1964–65
Chiffon, oscillating fan, fishing weights, and thread
Ca. 272 × 272 cm
Edition of 3, exhibition copy 2
Courtesy the artist and Paula Cooper Gallery, New York
p. 51

Large Water Level, 1964–65/2011
Acrylic glass, distilled water, screws, nylon cord, and springs
152.4 × 7.6 cm (diameter)
Edition 2/3, 1 AP
Courtesy the artist and Paula Cooper Gallery, New York
pp. 42–43

Sphere in Oblique Air Jet, 1964/2011
Weather balloon, helium, fan with housing, electrical connection
Base: 58.4 × 27.9 × 38.7 cm
Exhibition copy
H.E. Sheikh Jassim bin Abdulaziz Al-Thani and H.E. Sheikha Al-Mayassa bint Hamad bin Khalifa Al-Thani
p. 49

Column with Two Immiscible Liquids, 1965
Acrylic glass, oil, and water
32 × 6 cm (diameter)
Replica
ETZOLD Collection, Museum Abteiberg Mönchengladbach
p. 41

Ice Stick, 1966
Stainless steel, copper, refrigeration unit
173.7 × 61.3 × 62.5 cm
Collection Art Gallery of Ontario, Toronto, purchased in 1969 (69/3)
p. 44

Sky Line, 1967
First performed as *Skyline* in *Kinetic Environment 1 and 2* in Central Park, New York, July and October 1967, executed for MIT as part of a one-person exhibition at the Hayden Gallery in Cambridge, Massachusetts
C-print on aluminum
152.4 × 99.7 cm
Edition 1/3
Courtesy the artist and Paula Cooper Gallery, New York
pp. 52–55

White Waving Line, 1967
Chiffon, fan, housing
Base: 25.4 × 45.7 × 45.7 cm, fabric: 4.4 × 175.8 cm
Edition 1/3, 1 AP
Courtesy the artist and Paula Cooper Gallery, New York
p. 47

Photoelectric Viewer-Controlled Coordinate System, 1968
14 infrared projectors, 14 photoelectric cells, 28 white light bulbs
Variable dimensions, ca. 305 × 345 × 345 cm
New production
Courtesy the artist and Paula Cooper Gallery, New York
p. 91

Water in Wind, 1968
C-print on sintra
40.6 × 60 cm
Edition exhibition print
Courtesy the artist and Paula Cooper Gallery, New York
pp. 248–49

Ant Co-op, 1969
C-print on sintra
39 × 60 cm
Edition exhibition print
Courtesy the artist and Paula Cooper Gallery, New York
p. 63

Chickens Hatching, 1969
Fertilized eggs, incubators, lamps, thermostat installed as part of the exhibition *New Alchemy: Elements, Systems, Forces*, Art Gallery of Ontario, Toronto
C-print on aluminum
51 × 76 cm
Edition exhibition print
Courtesy the artist and Paula Cooper Gallery, New York
p. 66

Chickens Hatching, 1969
Fertilized eggs, incubators, lamps, thermostat installed as part of the exhibition *New Alchemy: Elements, Systems, Forces*, Art Gallery of Ontario, Toronto
C-print on sintra
41 × 60 cm (close-up)
Edition exhibition print
Courtesy the artist and Paula Cooper Gallery, New York
p. 67

Circulation, 1969
Installation, plastic hoses (PVC), ø 8, 11, and 14 mm, Y-connectors, distilled water, circulation pump
Dimensions of the version with 32 branches, ca. 1,100 × 380 cm
Edition 1/3
Generali Foundation Collection – permanent loan to the Museum der Moderne Salzburg
pp. 57–59

Cycle, 1969
A plastic tube was perforated and arranged around the rooftop periphery, allowing water to trickle out, forming rivulets and flowing to the center of the roof (the lowest point), from where it was pumped back into the perforated tube; executed on the rooftop of the artist's studio at 95 East Houston Street, New York
C-print on sintra
40.3 × 60 cm
Courtesy the artist and Paula Cooper Gallery, New York
pp. 60–61

Gallery-Goers' Residence Profile, Parts 1 and 2, 1969–70 ***
737 b/w photographs, 189 typewritten cards, city map, pins
Photographs and cards: 12.5 × 18 cm each, city map: 177.8 × 236.2 × 15.2 cm
Courtesy the artist and Paula Cooper Gallery, New York
pp. 108–09

Grass Grows, 1969
Earth, grass
150 × 300 cm (diameter)
New production
H.E. Sheikh Jassim bin Abdulaziz Al-Thani and H.E. Sheikha Al-Mayassa bint Hamad bin Khalifa Al-Thani
p. 73

Hans Haacke: Self-Portrait of a German Artist in New York, 1969
Film, ca. 23 min.
WDR mediagroup
pp. 75–77

Live Airborne System, 1969
Executed at Coney Island, New York, by throwing breadcrumbs out to sea to attract seagulls on November 30, 1968
C-print on sintra
39.7 × 60 cm
Edition exhibition print
Courtesy the artist and Paula Cooper Gallery, New York
pp. 68–69

Newborn Identification (Collaboration Linda & Hans Haacke), 1969
Print
28 × 22 cm
Private collection
p. 33

News, 1969
Teletype machine, paper, wire service
Variable dimensions
Edition 2/3
Courtesy the artist and Paula Cooper Gallery, New York
pp. 10 (detail), 93–95

Bowery Seeds, 1970
Executed by placing a pile of soil on the rooftop of the artist's studio at 95 East Houston Street, New York, allowing airborne seeds to germinate
C-print on sintra
37.8 × 60 cm
Edition exhibition print
Courtesy the artist and Paula Cooper Gallery, New York
p. 72

Directed Growth, 1970–72
Beans trained to grow at an angle in the galleries of the Museum Haus Lange, Krefeld (then West Germany), as part of the solo exhibition *Hans Haacke: Demonstrationen der physikalischen Welt; biologische und gesellschaftliche Systeme*
Beans, earth, twine
Variable dimensions
New production
Courtesy the artist and Paula Cooper Gallery, New York
p. 71

Floating Ice Ring, 1970
Acrylic glass, refrigeration motor, methacrylate, and distilled water
20 × 120 × 200 cm
Replica
MACBA Collection. MACBA Foundation.
p. 45

MoMA Poll, 1970
Two transparent ballot boxes with automatic counters, color-coded ballots
Boxes: 101.6 × 50.6 × 25.4 cm, ballots: 7.6 × 6.4 cm each
Courtesy the artist and Paula Cooper Gallery, New York
pp. 96, 107

Monument to Beach Pollution, 1970
Slabs of construction material, plastic containers, and other detritus collected from a 200 × 50 cm stretch of beach and put in a pile, executed in Carboneras, Spain
C-print on aluminum
51 × 76 cm
Courtesy the artist and Paula Cooper Gallery, New York
pp. 78–79

Norbert: All Systems Go, 1970–71
An uncompleted project in which a mynah bird was trained to utter the phrase »all systems go« in the exhibition by Hans Haacke planned for the Solomon R. Guggenheim Museum, New York
C-print on sintra
39 × 60 cm
Edition exhibition print
Courtesy the artist and Paula Cooper Gallery, New York
pp. 64–65

Ten Turtles Set Free, 1970
Turtles from a pet store were set free, executed at Saint-Paul de Vence, France, as part of the exhibition *L'art vivant aux Etats-Unis*, Fondation Maeght, on July 20, 1970
C-print on sintra
40.6 × 60 cm
Edition exhibition print
Courtesy the artist and Paula Cooper Gallery, New York
p. 62

Shapolsky et al. Manhattan Real Estate Holdings, a Real-Time Social System, as of May 1, 1971, 1971
142 b/w photographs, 142 typewritten maps, 2 excerpts from a city map, 6 charts; gelatin silver print; printed; typed ink on paper
Photograph and map: 20.5 × 31 cm each diptych, excerpts from city map and charts: 61 × 51 cm each
Edition 2/2
MACBA Collection. MACBA Foundation. Purchased jointly by Fundació Museu d'Art Contemporani de Barcelona and the Whitney Museum of American Art, New York, with funds from the Director's Discretionary Fund and the Painting and Sculpture Committees. Gratitude: MACBA. Museu d'Art Contemporani de Barcelona
pp. 111–14, 119

Krefeld Sewage Triptych, 1972
C-print on aluminum (printed in 2023)
Three parts, 50.8 × 34.5 cm each
Edition exhibition print
Courtesy the artist and Paula Cooper Gallery, New York
pp. 84–85

Rhine Water Purification Plant, 1972
A system for harvesting polluted water discharged by the city sewage system into the Rhine, purifying it, and using it to sustain live fish; the overflow of clean water was carried to the museum garden, where it seeped into the ground; executed at Museum Haus Lange, Krefeld, as part of a solo exhibition
C-print on aluminum (printed in 2023)
51 × 76 cm
Edition exhibition print
Courtesy the artist and Paula Cooper Gallery, New York
p. 80

Manet-PROJEKT '74, 1974
10 panels, color photo reproduction of Édouard Manet, *La botte d'asperges (Bunch of Asparagus)*, 1880
Panels: 80 × 52 cm each, reproduction: 83 × 94 cm
Exhibition copy of unique work in the Museum Ludwig Collection, Cologne, ML/Dep. 7315/01–11
Courtesy the artist and Paula Cooper Gallery, New York
pp. 123–33

Thank You, Paine Webber, 1979
Two mounted color photographs in black anodized aluminum frames under glass
Diptych, 107.3 × 222.3 cm (overall)
Edition 1/2
Collection Lila and Gilbert Silverman, Detroit
p. 147

The Right to Life, 1979
Color photograph on tricolor silkscreen print, in brass frame under glass
127 × 101 cm
Edition 2/2
Collection Lila and Gilbert Silverman, Detroit
p. 145

Der Pralinenmeister (The Chocolate Master), 1981
7 diptychs, 14-piece, multicolor silkscreen prints, photographs, chocolates, and chocolate wrappers
100 × 70 cm each
Facsimile
Museum Ludwig, Cologne, ML/G 2018/040/01–14
Acquisition with the support of the Cultural Foundation of the German Federal States, the Peter and Irene Ludwig Foundation, the Ministry of Culture and Science of the State of North Rhine–Westphalia, and the initiative Perlensucher, Society for Modern Art e.V., 2018
pp. 150–63

Greetings from Aachen, 1981
Embossed silkscreened photograph
24.1 × 34.3 cm
Edition 2/5
Collection Lila and Gilbert Silverman, Detroit
p. 149

Oil Painting: Homage to Marcel Broodthaers, 1982
Oil on canvas, brass plaque, stanchions with velvet rope, red carpet, b/w photo mural, painting light
Oil painting: 90 × 74.9 cm, brass plaque: 11.4 × 30.4 cm, carpet: width 89 cm, length variable, photo mural: variable dimensions
Los Angeles County Museum of Art, Gift of The Broad Art Foundation
pp. 165–67

Taking Stock (unfinished), 1983–84
Oil on canvas, gilded frame
241.3 × 205.4 × 17.8 cm
Tate: Purchased by Tate with funds provided by the Art Fund, Tate Americas Foundation, International Council, the European Collection Circle, 2023
p. 169

Buhrlesque, 1985
Shoes, boxes, candles, fabric, color photograph under glass, wooden frame
Pedestal fabric: 243 × 143 cm, photograph: 60 × 47 cm, base: 94 × 194 × 94 cm
Collection FRAC Fonds regional d'art contemporain de Bourgogne
pp. 171–73

Broken R.M. …, 1986 ***
Enamel plaque, gilded snow shovel with broken plastic handle
Plaque: 31.1 × 20.6 × 0.3 cm, shovel: 45.7 × 34.3 × 5.1 cm, part of handle: 42.5 × 4.1 cm
Variable dimensions
Edition of 3
Courtesy the artist and Paula Cooper Gallery, New York
p. 174

Und Ihr habt doch gesiegt (And You Were Victorious After All), 1988/2001 ***
Two-part installation at the Platz am Eisernen Tor, Mariensäule, Graz
Bezugspunkte 38/88, steirischer herbst
Billboard with 16 posters, 119 × 84 cm each, black, white, red, with collages of facsimile excerpts from newspapers and documents, Graz, 1938, documentation
Posters: 119 × 84 cm each, facsimiles: 22 × 22 cm each, overall dimensions ca. 260 × 720 × 5 cm
Edition 1/3
Generali Foundation Collection – permanent loan to the Museum der Moderne Salzburg
p. 195

Calligraphie, 1989/2011
Competition entry for the French National Assembly on the occasion of the bicentennial of the French Revolution 1989 (not realized)
2 color photographs, 1 b/w photograph, text panel, architectural model
Color photo: 149.9 × 111.8 cm, color photo: 56.2 × 45.1 cm, b/w photo: 55.9 × 67.3 cm text: 42.5 × 86.4 cm, model: 41.9 × 148.5 × 97.7 cm
Courtesy the artist and Paula Cooper Gallery, New York
p. 197

Nothing to Declare, 1992
7 picture frames suspended from the ceiling, bottle drier
Variable dimensions
Courtesy the artist and Paula Cooper Gallery, New York
p. 175

Photo Opportunity (After the Storm / Walker Evans), 1992
B/w reproduction of Walker Evans photograph, framed; light box with press photograph and neon lamp
Photograph: 37 × 44.5 cm, light box: 96.2 × 185.4 × 7.6 cm
Courtesy the artist and Paula Cooper Gallery, New York
pp. 198–99

Memorial to the Victims of National Socialism at the Military Target Practice Range »Feliferhof« in Graz, 1996
Proposal for an art competition initiated by the Military High Command of Styria and the Styrian Art in Public Buildings Commission, administered by the Department of the Styrian Provincial Government in the autumn of 1995 (not realized)
7 sheets, 4 drawings, 1 photomontage, 1 collage, 6 photocopies of those
6 sheets with the desired graphic contrast, 5 pages of text by Hans Haacke
27 × 21.6 cm each
Generali Foundation Collection – permanent loan to the Museum der Moderne Salzburg
pp. 205–07

Standortkultur (Corporate Culture), 1997
Color poster
Variable dimensions
New production
Courtesy the artist and Paula Cooper Gallery, New York
pp. 218–19

Debate and vote on the art project *DER BEVÖLKERUNG* by Norbert Lammert, Franziska Eichstädt-Bohlig, Rita Süssmuth, Ulrich Heinrich, Wolfgang Thierse, and other members of the Bundestag in the debate on April 5, 2000
Video, various screens
TV archive of ARD & Phönix
Oliver Schwarz, Werkstatt DER BEVÖLKERUNG, Berlin
p. 224

DER BEVÖLKERUNG (TO THE POPULATION), 2000
Photographs of a selection of used burlap sacks from the archive *DER BEVÖLKERUNG (TO THE POPULATION)*, 2001; original burlap sack for soil contributions, designed by Hans Haacke, 2000; information leaflet, publisher: Deutscher Bundestag
Variable dimensions
Oliver Schwarz, Werkstatt DER BEVÖLKERUNG, Berlin
p. 225

DER BEVÖLKERUNG (TO THE POPULATION), 2000
Time-lapse webcam video from 2000 to 2024, loop, 3:20 min.
Oliver Schwarz, Werkstatt DER BEVÖLKERUNG, Berlin
pp. 226–27

DER BEVÖLKERUNG (TO THE POPULATION), 2000
Federal Horticulture Show, close-ups of flora & fauna: *DER BEVÖLKERUNG (TO THE POPULATION)*, 2001–08
60 photographs (of 224)
35 × 27.5 cm each
Courtesy the artist and Sfeir-Semler Gallery, Beirut/ Hamburg
pp. 228–29

DER BEVÖLKERUNG (TO THE POPULATION), 2000
View of installation *DER BEVÖLKERUNG (TO THE POPULATION)* in the northern atrium of the Reichstag building in Berlin, 2008
C-print on aluminum
232 × 178 cm
Courtesy the artist and Sfeir-Semler Gallery, Beirut/ Hamburg
pp. 9, 223

Gift Horse, 2014
Bronze with black patina and wax finish, stainless-steel fasteners and supports, and 5 mm flexible LED display with stainless-steel armature and polycarbonate face
464.8 × 429.3 × 165.1 cm
Commissioned by the Mayor of London's Fourth Plinth program
Courtesy the artist and Paula Cooper Gallery, New York
pp. 231–33

We (All) Are the People, 2003/2017
Banners and posters
Variable dimensions, selection of languages dependent on site of display
New production
Courtesy the artist and Paula Cooper Gallery, New York
pp. 235–37

*** Exhibited in Vienna only

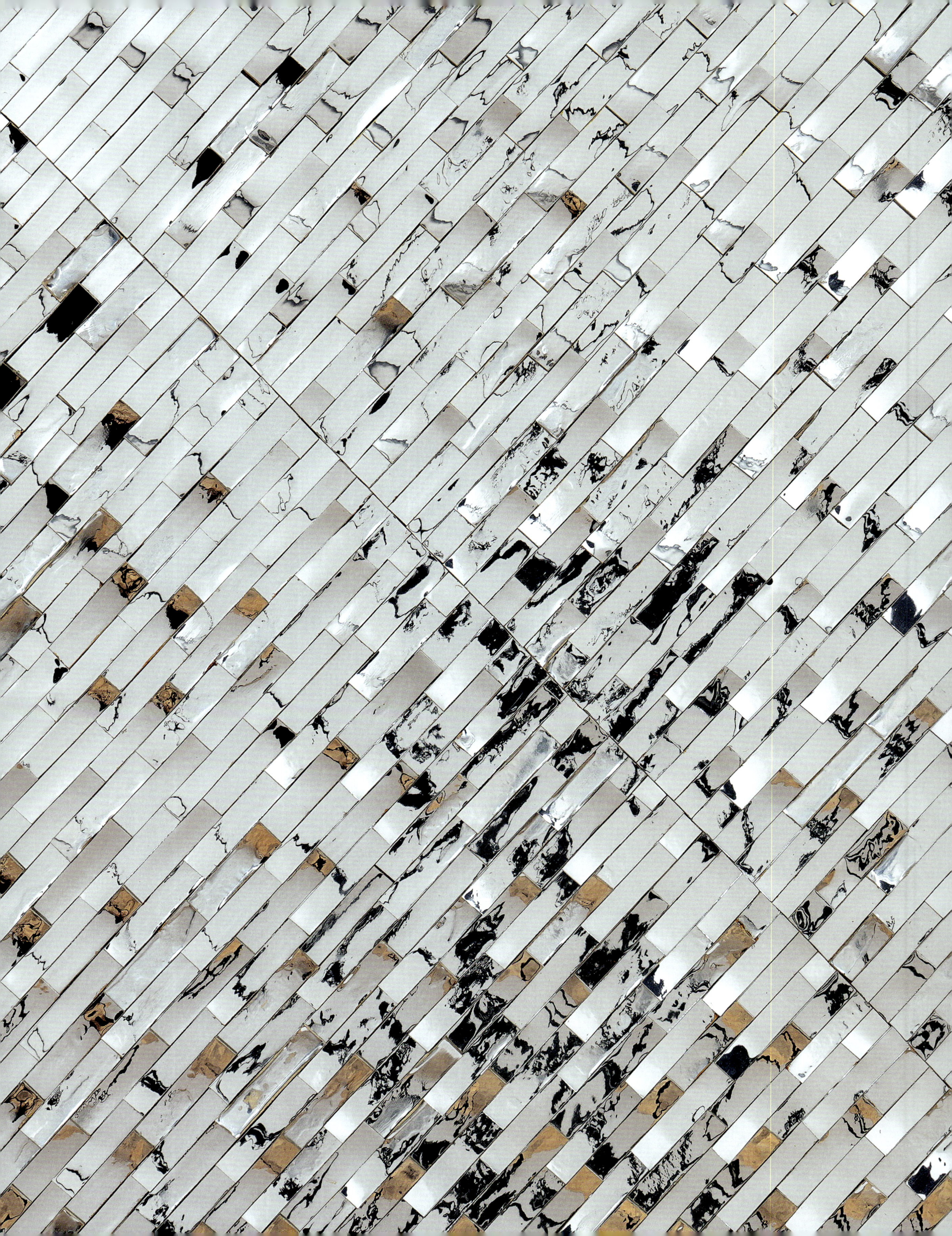

Sabeth Buchmann
(Berlin and Vienna) is an art historian and critic, and a professor of the history of modern and postmodern art at the Academy of Fine Arts Vienna. Buchmann is coeditor of PoLyPen—a series on art criticism and political theory (b_books, Berlin). She is also a board member of *Texte zur Kunst*, the European Kunsthalle, and the documenta Institut. Selection of her recent publications: *Kunst als Infrastruktur* (2022), *Broken Relations: Infrastructure, Aesthetics, and Critique* (2022, coedited), and *Putting Rehearsals to the Test: Practices of Rehearsal in Fine Arts, Film, Theater, Theory, and Politics* (2016, coedited). Buchmann was a member of the artist and author group minimal club (1984–99).

Hubertus Butin
studied art history in Bonn and Zurich and today lives in Berlin. In the 1990s, he worked as an art-historical assistant in Gerhard Richter's studio in Cologne. Since 1991, he has published numerous essays and books on contemporary art, art theory, and cultural policy. These volumes include a catalogue raisonné of Gerhard Richter's editions and the *Begriffslexikon zur zeitgenössischen Kunst*, both released in 2014. In 2020, Suhrkamp published his art-sociological book on art forgery. As an independent consultant, Butin works for museums, collectors, art dealers, auction houses, and investigative bodies all over the world. In 2021, he was a guest curator at the Kunstforum Wien and the Kunsthaus Zürich. He is also a freelance contributor to the *Frankfurter Allgemeine Zeitung*.

Theresa Dann-Freyenschlag
studied art history and market and public opinion research at the University of Vienna. Since 2023 she has been working as assistant curator for contemporary art and as assistant to the chief curator at the Belvedere, Vienna. From 2011 to 2023 she was assistant curator of the Verbund Collection Vienna, for which she realized international traveling exhibitions. She is the author of texts on contemporary feminist art.

Previous page: *B7-61*, 1961 (detail)

Cornelia Eisendle
studied Image Science (MA) at the Danube University Krems in Austria. Since January 2024, she has been working as an assistant curator at the Schirn Kunsthalle. Previously, she completed a curatorial internship at the ZKM | Center for Art and Media in Karlsruhe, a traineeship in concept design at Atelier Brückner in Stuttgart, and an internship at Kulturprojekte Berlin as part of the bauhauswoche berlin 2019.

Stephan Geene
is a member of the collective b_books and the author of various films and publications, including *SHAYNE* (2019) and *Freiheit 71: Ricky Shayne, Musik und die Materialität des Nachkriegs* (2023). He teaches at the Berlin University of Applied Science and Technology (BHT) on the theory and history of television. Among the books he has translated are *Countersexual Manifesto* and *Testo Junkie* by Paul B. Preciado, *Videophilosophy* and *The Making of the Indebted Man* by Maurizio Lazzarato, and *Die Filmfabel* by Jacques Rancière. Together with Sabeth Buchmann, he founded the theater and theory project minimal club in the 1980s. Geene is currently working on plastic, thingness, extractivism, and aesthetic theory and runs the website www.2222255.de in this context.

Vanessa Joan Müller
is a curator and author with a doctorate in art history. She lives and works in Vienna. She was head of dramaturgy at the Kunsthalle Wien (2013–20), director of the Kunstverein für die Rheinlande und Westfalen in Düsseldorf (2007–11), curator at the Frankfurter Kunstverein (2000–05), and has taught at Karlsruhe University of Arts and Design and the Vienna University of Technology. Numerous texts on contemporary art in exhibition catalogues, monographs, and magazines reflect both her interest in exhibitions and her analysis of contemporary artists.

Ingrid Pfeiffer
holds a doctorate in art history and is an author and curator. She studied art history and media studies in Marburg and has also worked as a journalist. From 1997 she worked as a curatorial assistant at the Museum Wiesbaden for four years, undertaking two research trips to New York in 1999 and 2000. She has been a curator at the Schirn Kunsthalle in Frankfurt since the beginning of 2001 and has curated numerous comprehensive exhibitions, including *Shopping* (2002), *Henri Matisse: Drawing with Scissors* (2003), *Yves Klein* (2004), *James Ensor* (2005–06), *Women Impressionists* (2008), *László Moholy-Nagy* (2009–10), *Barbara Kruger: Circus* (2010–11), *Surreal Objects* (2011), *Yoko Ono: Half-A-Wind Show; A Retrospective* (2013), *Philip Guston: Late Works* (2013–14), *Esprit Montmartre* (2014), *Storm Women: Women Artists of the Avantgarde in Berlin 1910–32* (2015–16), *Splendor and Misery in the Weimar Republic* (2017–18), *John M Armleder – Ca. Ca.* (2019), *Fantastic Women: Surreal Worlds*

from Meret Oppenheim to Frida Kahlo (2020), *Paula Modersohn-Becker* (2021–22), and *Lyonel Feininger: Retrospective* (2023–24). Alongside this role, she explores cultural, historical, and sociological themes in a wide variety of artistic media in her lectures and symposia.

Ursula Ströbele
is a professor of art history with a focus on contemporary art at Braunschweig University of Art. She was previously head of the Study Center for Modern and Contemporary Art at the Central Institute of Art History (ZI) in Munich and a research assistant at Berlin University of the Arts (UdK). She completed her doctorate at Heinrich Heine University (HHU) Düsseldorf on sculptors' reception pieces at the Royal Academy in Paris (1700–30). In 2020, she qualified as a professor with the thesis »Sculptural Aesthetics of the Living, Non-Human Living Sculptures, e.g. Hans Haacke and Pierre Huyghe.« In 2019–20, she curated the exhibition *Hans Haacke: Art Nature Politics* (ZI Munich and Städtisches Museum Abteiberg, Mönchengladbach). Ströbele's current research interests include digital, time-based sculptural phenomena, art and (queer) ecologies, (queer) intersecting histories of twentieth-century sculpture, and infrastructures of modernity.

Luisa Ziaja
is an art historian, curator, university lecturer, and writer. She has been chief curator at the Belvedere Museum Vienna since 2022, where she had previously been a curator of contemporary art since 2013. She is codirector of the postgraduate study program in exhibition theory and practice and »/ecm – educating, curating, making« at the University of Applied Arts Vienna (since 2006) and a member of the University Council of the Academy of Fine Arts Vienna since 2023. In her curatorial and discursive practice, she deals with the relationship between contemporary art, society, and politics (of history), as well as with the history and theory of exhibitions. Ziaja is the author and coeditor of numerous exhibition catalogues and anthologies on contemporary art, curatorial practice, and art and exhibition theory, including the series *curating: ausstellungstheorie & praxis* published by Edition Angewandte, most recently *Nicht einfach ausstellen. Kuratorische Formate und Strategien im Postnazismus*, Berlin/Boston 2024.

Selected Bibliography

Monographs

Burnham, Jack, ed. *Hans Haacke: Wind and Water Sculpture*. Evanston, IL: Northwestern University, 1967.

Fry, Edward F. *Hans Haacke: Werkmonographie*. Cologne: DuMont Schauberg, 1972.

König, Kasper, ed. *Hans Haacke: Framing and Being Framed; 7 Works 1970–75*. Halifax and New York: Press of the Nova Scotia Collage of Art and Design, 1975.

Bourdieu, Pierre, and Hans Haacke. *Free Exchange*. Cambridge: Polity Press, 1995.

König, Kasper, and Michael Diers, eds. *Hans Haacke – DER BEVÖLKERUNG: Aufsätze und Dokumente zur Debatte um das Reichstagsprojekt*. Cologne: König, 2000.

Grasskamp, Walter, Molly Nesbit, and Jon Bird, eds. *Hans Haacke*. London and New York: Phaidon Press, 2004.

Churner, Rachel, ed. *Hans Haacke*. With essays and interviews by Jack Burnham, Edward F. Fry, Walter Grasskamp, Yve-Alain Bois, Douglas Crimp, Rosalind Krauss, Leo Steinberg,Benjamin H. D. Buchloh, Rosalyn Deutsche, Luke Skrebowski, Sam Durant, and Jack McGrath. Vol. 18 of *October Files*. Cambridge, MA: The MIT Press, 2015.

Alberro, Alexander, ed. *Working Conditions: The Writings of Hans Haacke*. Cambridge, MA: The MIT Press, 2016.

Dissertations / Habilitation Theses

John, Philipp. *Verkörperte Allegorien: Fotografie und Skulptur im Werk Hans Haackes*. PhD diss., Freie Universität Berlin, 2014. Berlin: Logos Verlag, 2018.

Tyson, John. »Hans Haacke: Beyond Systems Aesthetics.« PhD diss., Emory University, Atlanta, 2015.

Ströbele, Ursula. *Hans Haacke und Pierre Huyghe: Non Human Living Sculptures seit den 1960er Jahren*. Habilitation thesis, Heinrich-Heine-Universität Düsseldorf, 2010. Berlin and Boston: De Gruyter, 2024.

Exhibition Catalogues

Hans Haacke, New York: Demonstrationen der physikalischen Welt; Biologische und gesellschaftliche Systeme. Exh. cat. Museum Haus Lange Krefeld, 1972.

Hans Haacke. Edited by Georg Bussmann. Exh. cat. Frankfurter Kunstverein, Frankfurt am Main, 1976.

Hans Haacke: Volume I. Exh. cat. The Museum of Modern Art, Oxford, and Van Abbemuseum Eindhoven, 1979.

Hans Haacke: Recent Work. Exh. cat. The Renaissance Society at the University of Chicago, 1979.

Hans Haacke: Nach allen Regeln der Kunst. Exh. cat. Neue Gesellschaft für Bildende Kunst, Berlin, 1984.

Hans Haacke: Volume II / Works 1978–1983. Exh. cat. Van Abbemuseum Eindhoven and The Tate Gallery, London, 1984.

Hans Haacke: Unfinished Business. Exh. cat. New Museum, New York, 1986.
Hans Haacke: Artfairismes. Exh. cat. Centre Georges Pompidou, Paris, 1993.
Hans Haacke: Bodenlos. German Pavilion at the Venice Biennale. Edited by Klaus Bußmann and Florian Matzner. Exh. cat. Venice Biennale. Stuttgart: Edition Cantz, 1993.
Hans Haacke: Obra Social. Exh. cat. Fundacio Antoni Tapiès, Barcelona, 1995.
Hans Haacke: Viewing Matters; Upstairs. Exh. cat. Museum Boijmans Van Beuningen, Rotterdam, 1996.
Hans Haacke: Standortkultur; Das Politische und die Kunst. Exh. cat. Bauhaus-Universität Weimar, 1998.
Mia san mia: Hans Haacke. Edited by Sabine Breitwieser. Exh. cat. Generali Foundation, Vienna, 2001.
Hans Haacke: for real – Works 1959–2006. Edited by Matthias Flügge and Robert Fleck. Exh. cat. Akademie der Künste, Berlin, and Deichtorhallen Hamburg. Düsseldorf: Richter, 2006.
Hans Haacke 1967. Exh. cat. MIT List Visual Arts Center, Cambridge, MA, 2011.
With Reference to Hans Haacke. Edited by Hans Dickel and Oliver Schwarz. Exh. cat. Staatliche Museen zu Berlin – Hamburger Bahnhof, Berlin, 2011.
Hans Haacke: Castles in the Air. Exh. cat. Museo Nacional Centro de Arte Reina Sofía, Madrid, 2012.
Hans Haacke: Once Upon a Time.... Exh. cat. Fondazione Antonio Ratti, Como, 2013.
Hans Haacke: All Connected. Edited by Gary Carrion-Murayari and Massimiliano Gioni. Exh. cat. New Museum, New York, 2019.
Hans Haacke: DER BEVÖLKERUNG; Wir (Alle) sind das Volk. Edited by Marius Babias, Oliver Schwarz, and Ursula Ströbele. Exh. cat. Neuer Berliner Kunstverein (nbk), Berlin, 2020–21.
Hans Haacke: Swiss Institute Visitors Poll. Edited by Simon Castets and Alison Coplan. Exh. cat. Swiss Institute, New York, 2023.
Hans Haacke Retrospective. Edited by Ingrid Pfeiffer and Luisa Ziaja. Exh. cat. Schirn Kunsthalle Frankfurt and Belvedere, Vienna. Munich: Hirmer Publishers, 2024.

Photo Credits

(c) Andrew Dickson White Museum of Art, Cornell University, Ithaca, NY, 1969, courtesy the artist and Paula Cooper Gallery, New York, photo: Hans Haacke, p. 73
(c) Archiv steirischer herbst, photo: Angelika Gradwohl, p. 189; photo: Peter Philipp, p. 176
(c) Archives of American Art, Smithsonian Institution, photo: Eric Pollitzer, p. 238
(c) Archivio Storico della Biennale di Venezia, ASAC, photo: Ferruzzi, p. 192
(c) Photo courtesy Art Gallery of Ontario, E-0651, photo: Hans Haacke, p. 31 (right); photo: AGO, p. 44; Edward P. Tylor Library and Archives, Art Gallery of Ontario, p. 31 (left)
(c) bpk / Hamburger Bahnhof – Nationalgalerie der Gegenwart, SMB, Sammlung Marzona, photo: Andres Kilger, p. 46
(c) Collection Anthing Vogel / Haags Gemeentearchief, Den Haag, courtesy 0-INSTITUTE, photo: Hans Haacke, p. 29
(c) Courtesy of the archives of the MIT Museum, MIT Committee for the Arts files, photo: Hans Haacke, pp. 52, 241
(c) Courtesy the artist and Paula Cooper Gallery, New York, photo: Manfred Grünwald, p. 89; photo: Hans Haacke, pp. 2, 15–19, 26, 27, 33, 40, 43, 53–55, 58–72, 78–80, 83–86, 91, 93–95, 102, 108–09, 137, 166–67, 178, 180–83, 199, 216, 218-19, 223, 232–33, 235–37, 247–49; photo: Walker Evans, p. 198; photo: Manfred Mayer, p. 210; photo: Roman Mensing, pp. 191, 201–03; photo: Stefan Müller, p. 221; photo: Wolfgang Neeb, p. 51; photo: PAC Werbeagentur, Kassel, pp. 208, 211–12; photo: Steven Probert, p. 37 (bottom), 39; photo: Udo Reuschling, p. 165; photo: Dirk Rose, pp. 34, 35, 37 (top), 256 (detail); photo: Fred Scruton, pp. 174–75, 197; photo: Ellen Wilson, p. 10; photo: Werner Zellien, p. 244
(c) Courtesy the artist & Sfeir-Semler Gallery Beirut/Hamburg, photo: Hans Haacke, pp. 223, 228, 229; photo: Stefan Müller, p. 9
(c) Courtesy the artist and Lila and Gilbert Silverman Collection, Detroit, photo: Steven Probert, pp. 145, 147, 149
(c) Courtesy the artist and 0-INSTITUTE, photo: Hans Haacke, p. 240 (top); photo: Philip Mechanicus, p. 24; photo: André Morain / Ad Petersen (Montage), p. 25; photo: Jon Naar, p. 240 (bottom)
(c) Hans Dickel and Oliver Schwarz / Hamburger Bahnhof Berlin, p. 105
(c) Collection ETZOLD im Museum Abteiberg Mönchengladbach, photo: Achim Kukulies, p. 41
(c) Collection FRAC Bourgogne, photo: André Morin, pp. 171–73
Sammlung Generali Foundation – Dauerleihgabe am Museum der Moderne Salzburg, (c) Generali Foundation, Hans Haacke, photo: Archiv Neue Galerie am Landesmuseum Joanneum, Graz, p. 195 (top); photo: Angelika Gradwohl, p. 195 (bottom); photo: Hans Haacke, pp. 57, 187, 205–07

Courtesy Generali Foundation (c) Hans Haacke, photo: Werner Kaligofsky, VG Bild-Kunst, Bonn 2024, pp. 57, 190
(c) Hans Haacke and Oliver Schwarz, pp. 224, 226–27, photo: Michael Arndt, p. 225
(c) Jens Liebchen, p. 222
(c) Fotofachlabor Rolf Lillig, p. 100
(c) MACBA Museu d'Art Contemporani de Barcelona, photo: Hans Haacke, pp. 20, 264 (detail)
Digital Image (c) MACBA Museu d'Art Contemporani de Barcelona / Whitney Museum of American Art, pp. 111–14, 119
(c) Paul Maenz, Cologne, pp. 138, 141, 143; photo: Benjamin Katz, p. 134
(c) MNAM Centre Georges Pompidou, Paris, photo: Fred Scruton, p. 213
(c) Museum of Modern Art, New York, photo: Ka Kwong Hui, p. 99
(c) New Museum, New York, exhibition view: Hans Haacke: All Connected, 2019, New Museum, New York, photo: Dario Lasagni, pp. 42, 45, 47, 49, 107, 231
(c) Eric Pollitzer, Archives of American Art, Smithsonian Institution, p. 238
(c) Rheinisches Bildarchiv Köln, rba_d048572_1-11, pp. 123–33, rba_d048571_1-14, pp. 150–63, photo: Sabrina Walz
(c) Robert Rauschenberg Foundation, RRF Registration# 70. D057, p. 87
(c) 2024 Photo Scala, Florence / Art Resource, Digital image, New York, The Museum of Modern Art, New York, Photographic Archive, photo: Hans Haacke, pp. 96, 242; Object no.: IN934.20., photo: James Mathews, p. 98
(c) The Estate of Sol LeWitt / VG Bild-Kunst, Bonn 2024, p. 101
(c) The Estate of Yves Klein / VG Bild-Kunst, Bonn 2024, photo: Hans Haacke, p. 23
(c) 2024 Tate, photo: Steven Probert, p. 169
(c) Universalmuseum Joanneum Graz / Multimediale Sammlungen, Inv.-Nr. RF086142, photo: Alfred Steffen, p. 186
(c) WDR mediagroup, pp. 75–77

Cover:
Front cover: Hans Haacke, *Sky Line*, 1967
Back cover: Hans Haacke, *We (All) Are the People*, 2003/2017

Following page: *Large Condensation Cube*, 1963–67 (detail)

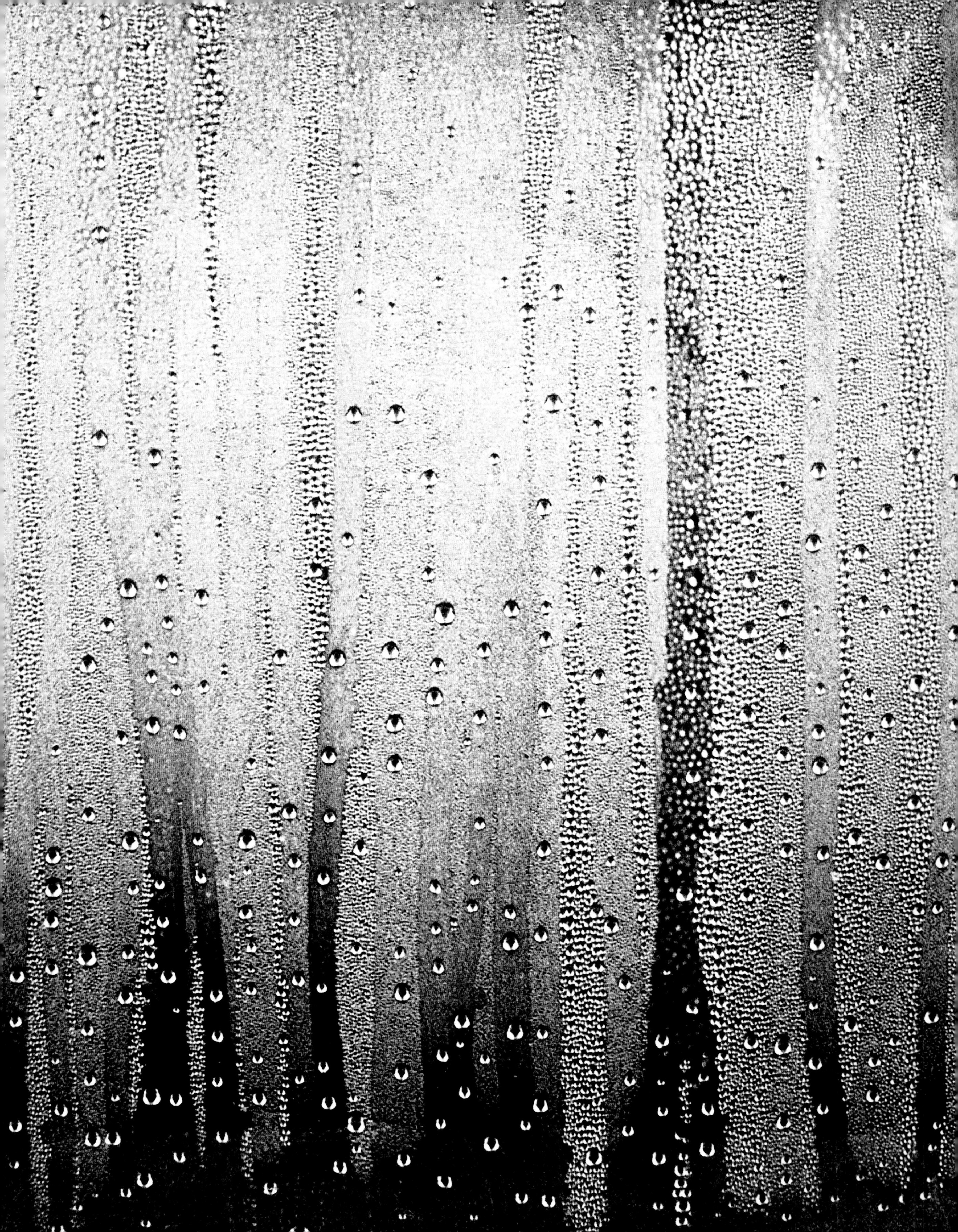